INTERMEDIATE
ENVIRONMENTAL
ECONOMICS

INTERMEDIATE
ENVIRONMENTAL
ECONOMICS

International Second Edition

CHARLES D. KOLSTAD

New York • Oxford

OXFORD UNIVERSITY PRESS

Oxford University Press, Inc., publishes works that further Oxford University's
objective of excellence in research, scholarship, and education.

Oxford   New York
Auckland   Cape Town   Dar es Salaam   Hong Kong   Karachi
Kuala Lumpur   Madrid   Melbourne   Mexico City   Nairobi
New Delhi   Shanghai   Taipei   Toronto

With offices in
Argentina   Austria   Brazi   Chile   Czech Republic   France   Greece
Guatemala   Hungary   Italy   Japan   Poland   Portugal   Singapore
South Korea   Switzerland   Thailand   Turkey   Ukraine   Vietnam

For titles covered by Section 112 of the US Higher Education
Opportunity Act, please visit www.oup.com/us/he for the latest
information about pricing and alternate formats.

Published by Oxford University Press, Inc.
198 Madison Avenue, New York, New York 10016
http://www.oup.com

ISBN 978-0-19-973265-4

Printing number: 9 8 7 6 5 4 3 2 1

Printed in the United States of America
on acid-free paper.

To Valerie, Jonathan, Kate, Katrina, Christine, Luis,
and the memory of George

elementary level but exhaustible resources are not. This is consistent with the course division at the University of California, Santa Barbara, where we have one ten-week course in environmental economics and one ten-week course in resource economics.

Although the book is targeted at undergraduates studying economics, it may also be useful for graduate students, particularly those pursuing a master's degree in economics or environmental management. Again, at the Bren School of Environmental Science & Management at the University of California, Santa Barbara, we use the text as a supplement for a master's level course entitled "Economics for Environmental Management."

I welcome comments from users of the book, both students and teachers. It is always gratifying to receive feedback, even when it involves an error in the text!

Finally, let me say that this book would not be possible without the support and encouragement of my extended family, to whom I dedicate this book.

1

ECONOMICS AND THE ENVIRONMENT

TELL SOMEONE YOU STUDY ENVIRONMENTAL ECONOMICS AND THE USUAL RESPONSE IS a look of puzzlement and the query "Just what is that?" A natural reaction, particularly considering the common belief in some circles that economics is the root of the "environmental problem."

Environmental economics is concerned with the impact of the economy on the environment, the significance of the environment to the economy, and the appropriate way of regulating economic activity so that balance is achieved among environmental, economic, and other social goals. What distinguishes a morally neutral chemical such as sulfur dioxide from the pollutant sulfur dioxide is the economy. The polluters who emit sulfur dioxide do so because it is a by-product of producing some good the public wants; consumers want the good associated with sulfur dioxide but at the same time obtain disutility (damage) from the sulfur dioxide pollution. The essence of the environmental problem is the economy—producer behavior and consumer desires. Without the economy, most environmental issues are simply research questions of concern to chemists or biologists with no policy significance.

There is no question that today environmental protection is recognized by societies and governments around the world, in both developed and developing nations, as being a top public policy and quality-of-life issue. Although people have been concerned about environmental quality for decades, or even centuries, the widespread societal recognition of the importance of environmental protection is a relatively recent phenomenon.

In this chapter we first consider the discipline of environmental economics, a subfield of economics. We then turn to a broad treatment of environmental problems and policy approaches that have been taken to provide society with higher levels of environmental quality.

I. ENVIRONMENTAL ECONOMICS AS A DISCIPLINE

For most goods and services in a modern economy, we rely on markets to match producer costs with consumer demands to yield the "right" amount of production (and thus consumption). The problem with pollution is that markets do not work to yield the socially desirable amount of pollution. This illustrates the breadth of problems that need answers: What are the incentives for the generation of pollution? What are the costs of cleaning up pollution? What are the societal gains from pollution control? What is the right balance between costs of control and gains from control? What regulatory mechanisms can be designed to ensure the right balance between costs and gains? Sometimes these issues are straightforward; othertimes they are exceedingly complex.

Although the field of environmental economics probably dates to the late 1950s and early 1960s with the important contributions emerging from the "think tank" Resources for the Future,[1] the field really took off in the 1970s and has been booming ever since. In the 1990s the payoff began to be seen in terms of influence on environmental policy. Marketable permits for pollution control are now widely embraced, valuation methods are an integral part of environmental prevention, environmental valuation is being used to make decisions concerning major public projects with environmental impacts, and environmental economics is playing a major role in the current climate change debate. Now, as the world works to develop regulatory means to control climate change, a very large proportion of proposed regulatory approaches involve markets for emission rights.

In the sections that follow we will more fully develop several of these dimensions of environmental economics. We first consider how environmental economics relates to environmental policy. Next, we examine how environmental economics meshes with the larger discipline of economics. We then discuss two related terms that have emerged in the academic and policy world—ecological economics and environmental economics. How do they differ? Environmental economics is also closely related to resource economics. What is the connection and what are the distinctions between them? Finally we consider several important issues, currently the subject of much research and debate, that confront the field of environmental economics.

A. Environmental Economics and Environmental Policy

Concern with the environment is not a passing fad but a deep-seated concern, brought on in large part by the coincidence of high incomes and high population density. If there were few people in the world, the earth's environment would be very forgiving and capable of absorbing most of what humans throw at it, cleansing itself automatically. The days of low population on the earth have passed; the total number of people on the planet and particularly the density of people in some parts of the planet magnify the size of environmental insults, overloading the capacity of the earth for self-cleansing. Income is also important, not only because rich people tend to consume more and thus generate more pollution, but also because the environment is often viewed as a luxury good. For the poor who struggle to keep food on the table, environmental issues often take a backseat to other more pressing needs related to survival. As people become wealthier, they turn their attention increasingly to the quality of their living environment, which ultimately is the planet. Thus if recent trends toward increasing wealth for the people of the world continue, we can expect concern for the environment to increase over time.

What are the typical issues facing most countries of the world with regard to environmental policy? In developed countries, pollution and the preservation of natural environments (e.g., wilderness areas) are major concerns. Pollution problems usually involve two major issues—what is the right amount of pollution and how can we get polluters to control their emissions?

Determining the right amount of pollution is not easy. Pollution is generated as a by-product of producing goods. To determine the costs of pollution control it is necessary to understand the structure of goods production and how costs will differ for different levels of pollution. Contrary to what most people might think, this is not an engineering question. Although it is easy to find out how much it would cost for a piece of equipment that is placed on a smokestack to reduce pollutants in the smoke (a "scrubber"), to an economist that is only the tip of the cost iceberg. Faced with the prospect of having to reduce pollution levels, the firm has many options. These include end-of-pipe treatment, modifying the production process, modifying the characteristics of the product, relocating the productive activity to reduce damage, and investing in research and development to find new ways of controlling pollution. If a pollution permit market exists, the firm has the additional choice of buying permits to emit, rather than reducing emissions. Consumers can also reduce consumption of the polluting good. Thus characterizing costs at a conceptual level, as well as measuring these costs empirically, is a complex question without easy answers. It is also the domain of environmental economics.

Determining the right amount of pollution also involves determining damages from pollution. The words "damages from pollution" deceptively suggest that this is a natural science question, such as counting the dead fish on a polluted lake or determining the level of pollution at which people begin to get sick. This is an oversimplification of the multitude of ways pollution affects people and the relative seriousness of these effects to people. Air pollution in an urban area can cause physical irritation (itchy eyes, running nose), reduced visibility, degraded visibility (a brown pale), soiled clothes, decreased lung capacity, worry about adverse effects, increased susceptibility to illness, and of course illness itself. Some of these effects are tangible, others are very intangible. Economics is accustomed to condensing this variety of effects into a single measure— the willingness to pay to reduce pollution. If pollution is bad, people are willing to devote some of their resources to eliminating the pollution. Leaving aside the fact that most people think the polluter should pay, one way of measuring the overall magnitude or importance of pollution reduction to a person is through his or her willingness to give up something valuable in exchange for improved personal environmental quality. Measuring this willingness to pay is not easy and is the subject of much research in environmental economics.

Having characterized the importance of pollution reduction to individuals (their willingness to pay), it is possible to sum up individual preferences to obtain a societal willingness to pay to reduce pollution. It is then easy to combine this with the cost of pollution control to determine the socially optimal amount of pollution reduction. But how to obtain this? The government could tell each polluter how much to emit, but this would be analogous to central planning in the old Soviet Union—we know it works up to a point but has severe problems, particularly when there are many firms and polluters involved. It is difficult to determine the best way for the government to intervene in the economy ("regulate") to yield the right amount of pollution control without excessive administrative costs or control costs while at the same time providing the right incentives to undertake research to reduce costs for the future.

So the "simple" job of fixing the problem of pollution is not so easy at the policy level and can involve hard-to-solve problems, many in the domain of environmental economics. The examples we have used are from developed economies but a very similar analysis could apply to a developing country. Air pollution is a big problem in many cities of the developing world. Water pollution is probably the most severe environmental problem in many developing countries: water contaminated by human waste kills millions of people annually. The same issues of costs, demand for clean-up, and how to regulate apply equally to this question.

Another important type of policy question is the preservation of natural environments, broadly defined. This could involve preserving wild and scenic areas from development or protecting animal and plant species from extinction. Here the primary issue is providing balance between the forces of development that threaten these environmental resources and the social value of preservation. How can both sides of this equation be quantified to help policymakers when they are confronted with very specific decisions (such as whether to allow logging in a virgin forest)?

These examples could go on and on. The point is that environmental protection usually involves the intervention of governments in the economy and it is often difficult to decide on the proper extent and nature of that intervention. Environmental economics as it is applied to real environmental problems can be invaluable in helping make those important decisions.

B. Positive versus Normative Perspectives

There are two fundamental uses of economics. One is to try to explain what we see in the economy around us. Another is to try to explain how we would wish the economy to allocate and distribute goods and services. The terms positive and normative are used to distinguish these two perspectives. Positive economics is more value free, aiming to explain economic behavior: why markets and institutions have evolved as they have and how they work. Examples are understanding why the price of gasoline increases when OPEC meets to restrict output and how the spatial distribution of pollution emissions changes when a marketable permit system is established to regulate sulfur emissions.

Normative economics, on the other hand, attempts to use economic tools to design government policies to intervene in the marketplace. Inevitably the question arises as to the "best" way of intervening in the marketplace. Clearly, this requires a way of defining what is best—a much more value-laden process than merely explaining why the economy works as it does. Normative and positive examples from climate change are explored in some detail in Chapter 2.

Unfortunately, when working with environmental problems it is not possible to restrict attention solely to positive economics. Fundamental to environmental economics is the notion of market failure. Repairing that market failure typically requires government intervention. What kind of government intervention? That is a normative question. And that is often the question that environmental economists are asked to help answer. In developing the normative theory of regulation to correct market failure or the public provision of nonmarket goods, we will try to make clear when value judgments enter the process of policy formulation. The practicing environmental economist should always be aware of the problems of venturing into the territory of normative analysis. This is one reason we turn in Chapter 3 to the question of social choice—the process of making societal decisions.

C. Environmental Economics and Economics

Economics is a well-developed discipline with an extensive body of theory, a paradigm associated with how the economic world works, strong empirical tools, and a number of branches, or fields of study, associated with pieces of the economy.

The fundamental building blocks of economics are contained in microeconomics—the theory of the consumer, the theory of the firm, and the theory of market interaction. This forms the basis for nearly all of economics. Related to microeconomics is the branch of statistics applied to economic phenomena—econometrics. Microeconomics permeates all of economics and econometrics permeates all of applied economics.

Branching out from basic microeconomic theory are the several fundamental fields of economics. These would include macroeconomics (the study of aggregate as opposed to individual phenomena), public finance (the study of goods not provided by the market and the study of taxation), industrial organization (the in-depth study of how firms interact with each other and with consumers and organize themselves into industries), and international trade (concerned with how distinct and independent economies interact). Each of these major fields is concerned with major portions of economic activity and each has unique contributions to make to the overall study of economics.

There are a number of applied fields of economics that draw on all of the basic fields as well as microeconomics. These would include labor economics, health economics, monetary economics, experimental economics, development economics, international finance, law and economics, and environmental economics. Each of these applied fields draws heavily on microeconomics and the basic fields of economics. For the most part, each of these fields has contributed in some way to understanding economics outside of its own narrow set of interests. For instance, labor economics has been the source for many innovations in econometrics that have found application across economics. The primary contribution of environmental economics has been in the area of nonmarket valuation, i.e., methods for measuring demand curves for goods when there is no market (or, equivalently, measuring the willingness to pay or willingness to accept compensation for nonmarginal changes in environmental quality). Other important components of environmental economics involve adapting tools developed in other parts of economics to questions regarding the environment.

The categorization above is by no means unequivocal. I would expect many economists in one or another of the fields mentioned above to dispute how their field has been categorized and placed in relation to other fields. To an extent they would be right: there are many different ways of summarizing the different fields of economics. The point that is being made is that environmental economics is an applied field, like many other applied fields in economics. Much of environmental economics involves adapting concepts developed in other branches of economics (particularly public finance and industrial organization) and applying them to environmental problems. Some aspects of environmental economics are unique to the field (such as valuation, mentioned above) and have potential use in economics outside of the environmental economics field.

D. Environmental Economics and Ecological Economics

This book is concerned with environmental economics. There is another field of study that largely has grown out of systems ecology called "ecological economics." These two fields take quite different perspectives, but are ultimately concerned with helping make social decisions about environmental problems. Unfortunately, in many non-English speaking countries the distinction between the two fields is lost in the translation because of the similarities between the words "environmental" and "ecological."

A simple distinction between the two fields arises from the fact that environmental economics tends to involve economists who have extended their discipline and paradigm to consider the environment, whereas ecological economics tends to involve ecologists who have extended their discipline and paradigm to consider humans and the economy. Another distinction between the fields is that ecological economics is very multidisciplinary. In contrast to environmental economics, which is a branch of economics, ecological economics welcomes and embraces practitioners from a wide variety of fields who wish to study the environment–society interface. But this is history; the appropriate question to ask is how do the two fields approach environmental problems and how do they differ?

Ecological economics (as well as conventional economics) is difficult to succinctly define. One of the leading ecological economists defines the subject as a "field of study that addresses the relationships between ecosystems and economic systems in the broadest sense."[2] The emphasis is on the very long-term health of the ecosystem, broadly defined (i.e., with humans as part of it). In a 2007 invited lecture to the European Society of Ecological Economics, Malte Faber argues that an interest in "nature, justice and time constitutes the defining characteristic of ecological economist."[3] He argues that the economy must be considered a part of nature, that doing what is just must be a central tenet of the field, and that the issue of time is oversimplified in conventional economics.

It follows that ecological economics tends to be normative, indicating what society *should* do, rather than positive, describing what society actually does (as discussed earlier). And one major distinction between the two fields is associated with value and thus the way in which social decisions are made that depend on measures of value of the environment. Conventional economists believe that value to society derives from the individual values held by human members of society. Ecological economists take a more biophysical view of value. For instance, some ecological economists measure value in terms of embodied energy content. Thus in comparing a typewriter to a computer, the appropriate question is which took more energy to create? Less energy is better. This is a direct extension of ecological theories that ecosystems operate to minimize the throughput of energy. To these researchers, minimizing the energy content of delivered goods and services should drive public policy. The criticism leveled at this "energy theory of value" by environmental economists is that there are many resources in short supply, including land and skilled people. Reducing the value of a good to the embodied content of any factor is an oversimplification. Environmental economists believe the value of a good stems from its embodied content of multiple scarce factors (including energy) as well as how much value individual people place on the final good. In other words, value cannot be reduced to a simple physical metric.

A recurring theme among some ecological economists (but not all) is the notion that economic growth is undesirable. Further, these practitioners argue that a central tenet of economics is that growth is desirable. To a large extent, this stems from a misunderstanding of growth. Technological progress and education, as well as population growth, have in fact led to economic growth. But it is not inevitable that this growth be at the expense of the environment. Consumption can be of material goods (such as steel or motor vehicles) or it can be of aesthetic goods (such as art or literature).

However, the greatest distinction between the fields emerges when considering environmental problems with very long-time horizons, such as global warming or disposal of nuclear wastes. As some environmental economists will readily admit, economics has a difficult time analyzing problems in which costs and benefits span long time horizons. For instance, storing nuclear wastes can involve potential risks that extend for a quarter of a million years. The benefits of the storage are reaped by the present consumers of nuclear power; the costs, if any, are borne by future generations that must live with the nuclear repositories. The conventional economic approach to this is to add up all of the costs and benefits, whenever they may occur, but to apply a discount factor to reduce the importance of future costs in the sum. Inevitably, this means that what happens a century from now has very little effect on the decisions that are made today. To many people, this is disquieting. Ecological economists have proposed other ways of dealing with the intertemporal decision problem, particularly the notion of sustainability. They argue that we should never undertake any action that is not sustainable in the long run. In the nuclear waste example, they would ask: Can we continue to bury waste forever and ever and be satisfied with the world that results? If the answer is no, then the action is not sustainable. It is not a matter of balancing costs and benefits. There is some intuitive appeal to such a philosophy.

Over the past decade, the lines between environmental economics and ecological economics have become more blurred, at least based on the content of the journal *Ecological Economics*, where environmental economists (as well as ecological economists) regularly publish. As a case in point, the first edition of this textbook cited no articles from the journal, whereas the current edition of this textbook cites several. The distinctions are clearly evolving.

E. Environmental Economics and Resource Economics

Nearly all textbooks combine the treatment of environmental and resource economics. In fact, most graduate programs that have a specialization in the area combine environmental and resource economics into one field. Undoubtedly this is because both concern the natural world. Environmental economics involves questions of excessive production of pollution by the market or insufficient protection of the natural world, due to market failure. Resource economics, on the other hand, is concerned with the production and use of natural resources, both renewable and exhaustible. Renewable resources would include fisheries and forests. Nonrenewables would include minerals and energy as well as natural assets such as the Alps and species of plants and animals.

So we see the distinction between the two areas but we also see the overlap. Typically, environmental economics is concerned with issues of market failure regarding the natural world—for a variety of reasons, markets do not function correctly, and as a consequence there is too much of some things (such as pollution) or too little of other things (such as wild and scenic areas). These problems may be essentially static, where time is not particularly important; in other cases, long time horizons are the essence of the problem. For instance, time is not really an issue in deciding on the right amount of air pollution in an urban area such as London.

Much of resource economics on the other hand is concerned with dynamics. Time is what makes renewable and exhaustible resource questions interesting. If we log a forest slowly enough, the forest can regenerate itself and we can continue logging indefinitely.

How fast we extract an exhaustible resource will determine its scarcity in the future, and thus its price in the future. It is time, rather than the failure of markets to operate properly, that is the essence of this logging example.

There are overlaps between environmental and resource economics. The management of a fishery to deal with overfishing is a good example in which the failure of markets is important (the fact that fishers may freely enter the market) as well as dynamics (growth and regeneration of the fishery is what makes it a renewable resource). Global warming is an example of a pollution problem with a very long time frame. There are other overlaps, primarily in the preservation of natural environments. These issues involve time so they could be relegated to resource economics. On the other hand, damage to natural environments is often the incidental result of economic activity with a different primary purpose. Species loss is usually the result of conversion of habitat to human use.

So we see that many environmental economics problems (but not all) are static, whereas many resource economics problems are dynamic.[4] Most environmental economics problems involve market failure, whereas many resource economics problems (but not all) do not. In other words, there is overlap between the fields. For the most part, in this book we are concerned with environmental problems involving market failure. As such, we cover pollution problems but also discuss the management of fisheries.[5]

II. THE QUALITY OF THE ENVIRONMENT

There are many comprehensive assessments of the state of the world's environment.[6] It is unnecessary to offer another review here. What we would like to do is provide some indication of the breadth of problems that are deemed environmental and to gain an appreciation for what problems are being solved and what problems remain difficult to solve and are likely to be a focus of attention in the coming decades.

Pollution problems are not new to mankind. There are records of the Romans complaining about the "stink of smokey chimneys."[7] Pollution control laws in other parts of Europe date from the Middle Ages. It has always been the case that urban areas have bad pollution problems, primarily because of the large concentrations of people. People are associated with emissions as well as being the reason pollution is damaging. But outside of cities, historically the earth's size has been vast enough to dissipate even the most serious environmental threat. What is new is the magnitude of the problem and the fact that the world is no longer infinite compared to the ability of people to pollute it. In the 1960s and 1970s many people around the world were galvanized into doing something to curb environmental degradation. In most countries, significant movements to protect the environment date from this period.[8] To a very large extent, the enormous size of our current world's population and the high standard of living of portions of the population are responsible for the pressures on the environment. A larger economy generates more pollution, all other things being equal; richer citizens usually demand higher levels of environmental quality. And as long as the world becomes more populated and wealthier, the pressures will only increase. This is not to say environmental problems cannot be solved, only that it will become increasingly difficult to protect the earth's environment.

We focus on four main categories of environmental problems: air pollution, water pollution, toxic emissions, and ecosystem health. This is not to suggest that this is a comprehensive list, just that these are four major categories that encompass many of the major environmental problems faced by man today.

A. Air Pollution

Air pollution is primarily a by-product of energy consumption. Impurities in fuels lead to emissions of sulfur dioxide and particulate matter. It is a basic fact of chemistry that burning carbon-based fuels leads to emissions of oxidized carbon—carbon dioxide, a major greenhouse gas. Because our atmosphere contains significant amounts of nitrogen in addition to oxygen, burning fuels inevitably leads to emissions of nitrogen oxides. Tropo-spheric ozone is not directly emitted from fuel combustion but results chemically from high concentrations of nitrogen oxides (from fuel combustion) and organic vapors (from paint drying and gasoline evaporating, among other things), in the presence of sunshine. It has proved to be very difficult to control ozone in many urban areas of the world.

To a large extent, air pollutants are at their worst in urban areas, due to concentrations of people, both as sources of the pollution (directly or indirectly) and as victims of the pollution. Air pollution can lead to health problems, including sickness as well as physical irritation and reduced human performance. The young and those weakened by other illnesses may be particularly susceptible to the effects of urban air pollutants. Urban air pollution also damages materials (such as buildings), increases the cost of maintenance (such as increased cleaning requirements), and degrades aesthetics (no one likes to live in a brown haze).

At a regional level, air pollutants may damage crops (though some sulfur and carbon pollution can help crops). Acid deposition is a regional problem in many parts of the world. Deposition of sulfur and nitrogen-based acids can harm forest and aquatic ecosystems. Regional haze from nitrogen and sulfur pollutants is also a problem in areas with less rainfall. Carbon dioxide is a global pollutant in that overall levels in the earth's atmosphere lead to increases in the heat-trapping capacity of the atmosphere, which leads to global warming. Controlling the precursors of climate change is the subject of intense current international debate.

Some urban air pollutants have been curbed with some success, though not without cost and not in all parts of the world. Sulfur dioxide emissions in Western Europe, North America, and the rest of the developed world have been the subject of significant control over the past two decades. Aggregate emissions appear to have peaked and are now declining. Table 1.1 shows a twenty-five-year time series for three pollutants for three countries, one in transition from poor to middle-income (China), one rich (Japan), and one in between (Iran). Note the dissimilarity among the three pollutants represented. Carbon dioxide emissions, which lead to global warming, have been increasing over the period and are higher in wealthier countries. Sulfur dioxide is almost the opposite. In fact, sulfur dioxide seems to be particularly troubling for the middle-income country, Iran. With money (income), the problem can be solved, as the Japan data demonstrate. Suspended particulates (soot) are worse in lower income countries and tend to be less of a problem as income levels rise. The story Table 1.1 tells is that not all air pollutants are the same; nor are the same pollutants always the most problematic across countries.

TABLE 1.1 Air Pollution Indicators for Selected Cities and Years

	1980	1990	2000	2005
China				
GDP per capita (2005 U.S.$)[a]	523	1,099	2,664	4,076
SO_2 concentration (Beijing)[b]	66	107	71	50
Particulate concentration (Beijing)[b]	475	413	106	89
Per capita CO_2 emissions (tonnes)	2	2	3	4
Iran				
GDP per capita (2005 U.S.$)[a]	7,087	6,254	7,667	9,314
SO_2 concentration (Tehran)[b]	130	165	209	NA
Particulate concentration (Tehran)[b]	226	261	71	58
Per capita CO_2 emissions (tonnes)	3	4	5	7
Japan				
GDP per capita (2005 U.S.$)[a]	18,652	25,953	28,613	30,310
SO_2 concentration (Tokyo)[b]	42	24	19	NA
Particulate concentration (Tokyo)[b]	61	NA	43	40
Per capita CO_2 emissions (tonnes)	8	9	9	10

[a]*GDP per capita from World Bank, computed using purchasing power parities, in constant 2005 International dollars.*
[b]*Mean annual concentrations in city center ($\mu g/m^3$). For reference, the U.S. primary ambient standards are 80 $\mu g/m^3$ for SO_2 and 50 $\mu g/m^3$ for particulates (PM_{10}), though in 1997 these were revised to distinguish between fine and coarser particulates.*
Source: World Bank, *World Development Report* (various issues); World Bank (1992); World Bank World Development Indicators online database (World Bank, 2009); United Nations Environment Program (2008); OECD (2006). In some cases, data unavailable for specific year; adjacent year used.

One of the major nonfuel air pollutants is chlorofluorocarbons (CFCs), substances that lead to depletion of the stratospheric ozone layer. These substances are now primarily used as refrigerants. CFCs have been controlled (in theory) by the 1987 Montreal Protocol, which has had some success. Worldwide production of these chemicals in 1995 was 20% of the level in 1986. Worldwide production of these chemicals peaked in 1988, dropped to 20% of that level by 1995, and had dropped to 3% of peak levels by 2005.[9] One problem is a growing black market in illicitly produced CFCs as well as rapid increases in CFC use and production in the developing world. Under the Protocol, the developing world faces significantly looser restrictions than the developed world, at least for the time being.

B. Water Pollution

Water pollution has traditionally been the result of organic material deposited in waterways or lakes. Organic waste is problematic since it needs oxygen to decompose. Thus one of the measures of the quantity of pollution is biologic oxygen demand (BOD). Oxygen is of course needed for fish to survive. So if pollution has such a high BOD that the water body becomes depleted of oxygen, the water body can no longer support much in the way of life. In addition, with oxygen depleted, decomposition is now from anaerobic bacteria, which do not require oxygen. Such decomposition tends to be very odiferous. A major type of organic waste is of course human waste, which usually also involves significant human pathogens.

TABLE 1.2 GDP per Capita, Mortality, and Access to Clean Water and Sanitation for Selected Countries, 2000

Country	GDP per capita[a]	Percentage of population with safe water[b]	Percentage of population with sanitation[c]	Child mortality rate[d]
Burkino Faso	896	56	9	190
Ghana	1,015	72	9	112
India	1,718	82	23	91
China	2,664	80	59	37
Brazil	7,921	89	74	32
Costa Rica	8,117	97	96	14
Mexico	12,071	93	76	38
Greece	20,574	99	98	6
United Kingdom	29,172	100	100	6
Denmark	31,721	100	100	6

[a]*2005 U.S.$ per capita, using purchasing power parities.*
[b]*Percentage of population with access to safe drinking water.*
[c]*Percentage of population with access to sanitation services.*
[d]*Annual mortality per 1,000 live births of children under age five.*
Source: World Bank Development Indicators Database (World Bank, 2009).

How serious is water pollution? The World Bank indicates that in 2005, 18% of the world's population did not have access to improved drinking water supplies. The World Bank also points out that life expectancy in cities in France went from about 35 years in 1850 to 45 years in 1900, with the timing of change closely corresponding to the introduction of modern water supply and waste water disposal. The importance of water supply and waste disposal is illustrated in Table 1.2. Note that for the ten countries shown, the child mortality rate is less correlated with income (GDP per capita) than with the population's access to safe drinking water and to proper sanitation services. Water contaminated by pathogens is probably the primary environmental threat in much of the world.

One particularly difficult water pollution problem is pollution of groundwater. Groundwater, water in underground aquifers, is the source of drinking water for many people. Because of the cleansing ability of the earth above the aquifer, groundwater has traditionally been relatively contaminant free. However, groundwater contamination does occur, primarily from leaking storage facilities on the surface, either waste storage or storage of bulk liquids such as gasoline. In the past, chemical wastes have been dumped on the surface, finding their way into the groundwater many years later. Another source of groundwater pollution is the leaching of pesticides and fertilizers into the groundwater.

As point sources (pollution sources with clear, identifiable, and practically measurable discharge pipes or smokestacks) of water pollution are brought under control (something that is occurring in much of the developed world), the remaining water pollution problems are tougher to solve. Remaining pollution problems are in large part from non-point sources of pollution (also called area sources)—urban runoff, agricultural runoff, as well as accidental spills.

Surface waters, such as lakes and rivers, are the ultimate repositories of much that is deposited on the land. And even the sulfur and nitrogen oxides that are emitted as air pollution are ultimately deposited on the land, either in dry form or as acidic precipitation. Lakes and rivers throughout the developed world suffer to varying degrees from excessive levels of nutrients (from agricultural runoff) and acidification. Nutrients can promote the growth of algae and phytoplankton, which increase the turbidity of the waters. Acidification has the potential of making lakes uninhabitable for most fish. Even the world's oceans are beginning to experience serious pollution, particularly smaller seas such as the Baltic and the Mediterranean.

C. Toxic Chemicals

Toxic chemicals in the environment have been a problem for decades. In fact, one of the books most important in coalescing the modern environmental movement was Rachel Carson's *Silent Spring,* a book about pesticides finding their way into the food chain and causing havoc with wild birds (among other species). The good news is that the most persistent pesticides (such as DDT) have been banned for decades in much of the world and that many threatened species are making a comeback. The bad news is that there are still significant discharges of heavy metals and other toxics into the aquatic environment, even in developed countries.

Another serious toxic problem from the perspective of human health is lead. During this century, the most significant source of lead poisoning has been through air pollution, due to lead in motor fuels. Lead has been blamed for very serious health effects (such as mental retardation), particularly in poor urban children. Lead has been a major air pollutant because of its use as a performance enhancer in automobile fuels. Most of the developed world now significantly restricts or bans the use of lead in automobile fuel. The result of such a ban can be dramatic. According to the U.S. EPA, the average annual lead concentration in a number of U.S. cities in the late 1970s was over 1 μg/m^3. In 1990, the concentration had dropped to 0.07 μg/m^3, and the ban on lead in gasoline had still not become complete.

Aside from intentional discharges of toxics into the environment, there are two other major sources of toxics—old toxic waste sites and accidental discharges. Toxic wastes do not rapidly decay and become harmless. Some abandoned industrial sites from the nineteenth century are still considered chemically hazardous. There are many sites of nuclear, mining, and chemical wastes from the post-World War II but pre-1970s period. These can be very expensive to clean up. Accidental spills, including oil spills, and chemical spills, will always be with us. And these can be very serious sources of environmental damage.

D. Ecosystems and Natural Environments

Most of the foregoing environmental problems (air, water, toxics) are sometimes referred to as "brown" issues—associated with pollution, often from industrial sources. Some environmental issues do not directly involve pollution in the conventional sense. These "green" issues concern the natural environment we all live in, depend on, and benefit from. As some brown issues are brought under control (though vexing brown issues remain), and population pressures continue to expand, increasingly the world is turning its attention to green issues.

TABLE 1.3. Forested Land Area, in Millions of Square Kilometers

	1990	2000	2005
Africa	6.99	6.55	6.35
Asia	7.44	7.31	7.34
Europe	9.89	9.98	10.01
Latin America	9.24	8.82	8.60
Near East	1.28	1.23	1.20
North America	6.78	6.78	6.77
WORLD	40.77	39.88	39.52

Source: FAO (2009).

Many green issues have to do with the health of specific species of animals or plants, or ecosystems, consisting of interconnected species of animals and plants. The rapid rise in the earth's population has inevitably placed great strain on wild ecosystems around the planet. Concern for the health of these ecosystems motivated the massive global Millennium Ecosystem Assessment, a United Nations project begun in 2000 to assess the consequences of ecosystem change around the world, and completed in 2005.[10]

It is difficult to quantify the severity of green issues with a few summary statistics. For one thing, many relevant data series do not go back very far in time. For instance, Table 1.3 shows the extent of forests in terms of millions of square kilometers around the world, from 1990 to 2005. What stands out is that with the exception of Latin America, the size of forested lands remains fairly stable. What is not shown is the extent of old-growth forests nor the massive deforestation that occurred many years ago in North America and Europe. Furthermore, forest extent is only one of the many dimensions of ecosystem health.

III. ENVIRONMENTAL REGULATION

There is a surprising amount of similarity in how countries around the world have responded to environmental problems. It is beyond the scope of this book to provide a comprehensive review of international environmental regulations.[11] We will content ourselves with a very superficial examination of environmental protection regulation in the European Union, Russia, and the United States.

These reviews will focus on two issues. First, we hope to convey a sense of how environmental protection is pursued in each of these countries. Second, we will try to indicate the extent to which economic incentives have been used in these countries, particularly emission charges, in which polluters pay a fee per unit of emissions, or marketable permit systems in which polluters may buy and sell the right to pollute a given amount, thus imputing a value to reducing pollution.

A. European Union

1. Regulatory Approach. The confederation of European states that started in the 1950s as an organization to promote trade in coal and steel has developed into a federal system of independent countries that is continually ceding more and more power to the central government. As an example, monetary policy has traditionally been made on a country-by-country basis by central banks. However, beginning in 1999, most member countries surrendered monetary policy to a single European Bank, in order to unify European currencies. The balance of power between the European Union (EU) and its member states appears to be continually evolving. In this sense, the EU is very much a work in progress.

There are several basic principles that seem to permeate EU environmental policy. One is the principle of subsidiarity.[12] The principle leaves all powers to individual member states unless there is an abiding reason to take action at the European level. Thus most pollution control, at least of pollution that stays within a member state, would appear to be totally the responsibility of the member state, not a problem to be addressed at the Union level. However, because differences in pollution control regulations from one state to another can influence comparative advantage within the Union, the division of power is not quite so straightforward.[13] Another principle is the "polluter pays." This means that polluters should be required to pay for environmental damage, environmental controls, and the administration of environmental agencies.[14]

European Union policy with regard to the environment is implemented through the issuing of what are known as *directives.* A directive is an EU "law" that is binding on the governments of member countries, requiring each government to pass its own legislation to implement the directive. One of the most widely noticed directives (at least outside of the EU) was the 1988 directive that set forth sulfur emission controls for large electricity-generating stations. The impetus for EU level action was the problem of acid rain and acid deposition, which are pollution problems that do not respect national borders. The directive is very specific as to how much emissions may come from new power plants; in fact, the directive specified the pollution control technology to be used on most new power plants. An interesting part of the directive was the establishment of country caps on emissions of nitrogen oxides and sulfur oxides from pre-1987 power plants (this was to address acid rain and acid deposition). But as with all directives, member countries are required to pass laws to implement the directive. In the case of the cap, each country must determine the best way of controlling existing plants to meet the cap.

Because pollution control legislation in most member states dates from the early 1970s (and before), when there was considerably less coordination at the Union level, the approach to pollution control tends to vary from country to country. Rather than review the regulations of each country individually, we will briefly mention some of the approaches to regulating pollution used in one member country, the United Kingdom.[15]

Pollution regulation has a fairly long history in the United Kingdom. In 1273, the city of London passed a measure to control smoke. Disputes regarding pollution were subject to nuisance law for centuries, and in the early nineteenth century, a parliamentary committee was convened to examine the problem of urban smoke. More problematic for many in the last century were the "noxious vapours" arising from chemical works, particularly the hydrochloric acid fumes given off in the manufacture of sodium carbonate. In 1863, the Alkali Act became law with the express purpose of controlling these emissions. The innovation of the Alkali Act was to set up the quaintly named Alkali Inspectorate, a set of experts with power to mandate emission control. The Alkali Inspectorate eventually metamorphosed into Her Majesty's Inspectorate of Pollution in the 1970s which was subsequently absorbed into the Environment Agency, part of the Department for Environment, Food and Rural Affairs (DEFRA). The Alkali Inspectorate was only permitted to regulate certain "difficult" pollution processes—"scheduled processes." The list of scheduled processes started with hydrochloric acid from sodium carbonate manufacture but was slowly expanded over time. Eventually, in large part due to the deadly London smogs of 1952, nearly all potential sources of air pollution, including generators of smoke, came under the authority of the Alkali Inspectorate (in the 1956 Clean Air Act). Despite this, "routine" pollution problems were specifically delegated to local authorities. The idea was that when abatement presented no particular technical difficulties, responsibility was to be transferred from the Inspectorate to local authorities.

The Alkali Act set the stage for how pollution would be regulated in the UK. One of the important clauses in the Act as amended was that scheduled sources shall use the "best practicable means" (BPM) of pollution control. Here practicable means not only technically feasible but economical, including justifiable on the basis of the damage from the pollution. This approach has long been favored over specifying particular emission limits. The thought is that not only is BPM more flexible but that it is more likely to encourage innovation than a fixed emission limit. Thus the regulatory approach is that polluters must be registered and a requirement for registration is the use of BPM. The government has prepared "Notes" on what constitutes BPM for various industrial facilities. These guidelines are used in the source-by-source negotiating process over the required registration and re-registration process.

Although the UK is not a federal system, there are different levels of government, ranging from local to national. In the environmental area, there are clear distinctions regarding which responsibilities reside at the local level and which at the national level. As the discussion of the Alkali Inspectorate indicates, certain scheduled sources of pollution are subject to control at the national level. These are typically the sources of pollution that are the toughest to control. Small scale sources of pollution, including municipal solid waste, are typically the responsibility of local authorities.

Water pollution regulation is the responsibility of the National Rivers Authority, though this body has been merged into the Environment Agency associated with the Department for Environment, Food and Rural Affairs (DEFRA). The regulatory approach is similar to that used for air pollution control in that polluters must register, and by doing so are subject to requirements regarding pollution control technology.

2. The Use of Economic Incentives. There is a longer history of the use of economic incentives in the EU than in most other parts of the world. Until the introduction of the European Trading System for carbon, emission fees had been the predominant type of economic incentive.[16]

One distinction frequently made in discussing European emission charges is between revenue-raising and incentive-oriented charges. There are a great number of charges in most countries of the EU related to pollution discharges. However, most of these charges appear to be at too low a level to provide any serious incentives to reduce pollution. Their primary purpose is to generate funds to operate the administrative agencies that oversee pollution regulation.

One of the clearest economic incentives in use in the EU is the German Water Pollution charge, instituted in 1976 and implemented in 1981. The charge is established (including the level of the fee) at the federal (national) level. It is left up to the states of Germany (Lander) to implement and enforce the fee. However, it is unclear how much pollution has been reduced as a result of the fee (OECD, 1989). Germany also has a form of a marketable permit system for cities with pollution exceeding allowed limits. New firms are allowed into these cities if they can show that pollution levels will drop. In other words, new firms must find polluters and pay them to reduce their emissions in order to offset the new emissions.

Another charge that appears to have some incentive effects is the Dutch charge on the discharge of organic material into sewer systems. The problem was how to pay for the water treatment facilities necessary to improve river water quality. Somewhat logically, the parties using the system were charged a fee, and the fee was based on the load the sources would place on the treatment facility. Thus the legislative motivation appears to be simply revenue raising. However, subsequent analyses of the program suggest that the fee had a very significant effect in reducing organic material discharges from industry.[17]

B. The Russian Federation

1. Regulatory Approach. Russia is a country in transition and that applies as much to environmental regulation[18] as to any other part of the economy. Thus elements of the current Russian approach to environmental protection will undoubtedly change as the country's institutions adjust to a new economic environment. Furthermore, simply having a regulation on the books does not necessarily mean that the regulation is fully implemented and enforced.[19]

Much of the Russian approach to environmental protection has its origins in the Soviet Union. The 1970s was the beginning of significant Soviet actions to protect the environment. Both water pollution and air pollution controls were instituted in this period, along with the establishment of the country's basic framework of pollution regulation. The then Soviet and now Russian regulatory approach relies on health-based ambient standards for a wide variety of pollutants.[20] These standards are developed at the national level for use throughout the country. The standards are not absolute but depend on the nature of the use of the ambient environment. For instance, ambient standards for air depend on whether the point of application is a residential or an industrial area. Ambient standards for water depend on whether the water is used for recreation, fishing, or drinking.

Ambient standards are generic federal standards that apply throughout the country. They are used to establish source-specific emission limits. These emission limits are embodied in the pollution permits each significant source of pollution must possess. The procedure is that new sources of pollution must submit an application for a pollution permit containing a technical analysis of the effect of emissions on ambient concentrations, at the boundary of a specified zone around the source. Background pollution concentration levels must be taken into account.[21] This application is the basis for establishing an emission limit for the source. Thus this is a source-by-source procedure that is driven by ambient standards, not by a consideration of best available technology or costs. Sources that existed prior to the regulations must follow a similar procedure to obtain an emission limit as well as a permit.

As might be expected, some pollution sources have difficulty meeting the permitted emission limits. In these cases, temporary emission limits are issued, with the idea that over time, the temporary limits will become increasingly tighter until they equal the (nontemporary) emission limit. The rate at which these temporary limits are tightened is apparently somewhat negotiable.

The regulatory authority responsible for implementing these laws at the national level has been the State Environmental Protection Committee.[22] In addition, there are nearly a hundred regional environmental protection committees, roughly one for every member of the Russian Federation. There are also local environmental protection committees in some of the major cities. These committees (primarily the regional committees) are responsible for implementing the environmental laws. Thus if a new source of pollution wishes a pollution permit, application is made to the regional environmental protection committee.[23]

One of the major differences between environmental regulation in Russia and the rest of the world is the use of the "environmental fund," though in recent years it has been absorbed into the general budget. The environmental fund is a major financial resource to be used to help clean up the environment and finance pollution control measures. Funds (pots of money) are associated with each level of environmental regulation—federal, regional, and local. The existence of such funds can probably be best understood in the context of the centrally planned Soviet Union. In the Soviet Union, the major stationary sources of pollution were state-owned enterprises. Resources were needed to pay for pollution control. Some of these resources were to come from the budgets of the enterprises but that was not considered to be sufficient. (For example, one might expect the Ministry of Steel to put environmental protection investments fairly low in its priorities for scarce investment funds.) Funds were also needed to clean up environmental accidents and other problems for which responsibility could not easily be assigned. The funds were also used to finance public environmental projects such as sewage and drinking water treatment. An interesting additional use of the funds was to pay compensation for environmental damage. In the post-Soviet era, the environmental funds have been a major source of funding for environmental protection. The funds are used for direct grants for pollution control as well as subsidized loans. An obvious question is why should a polluter pay to control pollution when a fund will pay for doing so? As might be expected, resources are limited in the funds. Polluters can make application to the fund for a direct grant or a loan or anything in between. The fund allocates resources on a case by case basis.

The focus in the above discussion is on air and water pollution from major sources. Automobile emissions are not regulated to any significant extent. Moscow bans leaded gasoline, but that is an exception. However, automobiles must undergo periodic checks on their emission rates for carbon monoxide. Nevertheless, it is not clear how strictly these limits are enforced.

2. The Use of Economic Incentives. Perhaps surprisingly, Russia makes extensive use of emission fees (as do many other countries of Eastern Europe and the former Soviet Union). In the late 1980s the Soviet Union was experimenting with emission fees and these were embraced by Russia in the early 1990s. The original intent of the emission fee was to finance the environmental funds. If the environmental funds were in turn to pay for environmental protection, it seemed logical that polluters should contribute to the fund based on their emission levels. Consequently, each source of pollution is required to pay a fee into the environmental funds per unit of emissions. Most of the payments go to local or regional funds. There are two levels of the fee, a base level, for emissions under the emission limit for the facility (described above), and a level five times greater for emissions over the limit. Although substantial revenues are collected with these fees (in 1993, nearly $100 million),[24] the individual fee levels are modest. In 1995 the sulfur dioxide base fee was 5610 Rubles (US$1.22) per ton.[25] This is significantly lower than the marginal cost of even modest pollution control, at least in the West. Several studies of the emission fee system report that the fee levels are too low to provide much of an incentive for pollution control.[26] Despite these findings, the fee system will be important to monitor as Russia's market economy evolves in the coming years.

C. United States of America

1. Regulatory Approach. The United States is a federal system with some powers vested and exercised at the national level and some powers residing at the level of the state. Although environmental protection legislation dates to the nineteenth century or before (as in many countries), substantive and major national environmental legislation was first passed in the 1960s. The post-World War II period saw rapid growth in the U.S. economy, along with increasing stress on the environment, increased per capita income, and thus increased demand for environmental quality. California took action in the early 1960s to establish emission standards for automobiles. This was quickly followed by national legislation requiring manufacturers to install certain antipollution devices on new cars and, eventually, to meet ever-tightening limits on emissions of particular pollutants per mile travelled.[27]

Several problems faced legislators in the 1960s in devising the appropriate way of controlling pollution emissions, primarily into the air and water. The problem was twofold: how to control the myriad of existing sources of pollution in a fair and equitable, but effective, manner and how to ensure that new sources of pollution (new factories, new cars) were constructed in an environmentally friendly manner. Because of the wide variety of local conditions involved in regulating existing sources of pollution, the approach taken was to let states decide how best to clean up sources of pollution that were in existence at the time environmental legislation was passed. The Federal government would promulgate goals for ambient environmental quality; states would construct "plans" to control polluters so that Federal goals could be met. These plans ("State Implementation Plans") were subject to approval by the Federal government. (Hazardous pollutants, such as chemical wastes and trace heavy metals, are regulated differently.) States are free to implement tighter standards than dictated by the Federal government.

New sources of pollution are regulated differently than old sources. One fear was that individual towns or states would relax environmental standards to attract business and jobs. To reduce this possibility, emission standards for new sources of pollution were set at the national level, without regard to location. The Environmental Protection Agency (EPA, established in 1970) would promulgate industry-by-industry emission control requirements for new sources. By doing this, concerns about environmental regulations would be eliminated from the factory location decision. The Water Quality Act of 1965 and the Clean Air Act Amendments of 1970 follow this approach to regulation. Over the years there have been some changes but the general pattern remains the same: ambient pollution goals are established at the national level, new sources of pollution are subject to nationally uniform emission standards, while local regulatory agencies oversee existing sources of pollution, with a significant amount of oversight from the national level.[28]

Land use is governed by local governments for some uses and by the Federal government for other uses. Agricultural use of land with problems of soil loss and pollution from runoff is governed by the Federal Agriculture Department. The Agriculture Department requires farmers who receive subsidies to file soil conservation plans. The conversion of wetlands to drylands is governed by a mix of Federal, state, and local laws. However, for the most part, local land use is controlled by local governments using local zoning laws, with little oversight from the Federal government, except for the Federal constitutional protection that private land may not be taken by the government without payment of compensation. For this reason, the extent to which environmental or aesthetic concerns enter into local land use decisions varies widely over the country. In recent years the Federal Endangered Species Act has occasionally had a major impact on some local land use. The Act protects species of animals and plants that the Federal government has declared endangered or threatened. In certain parts of the country this Act occasionally stands in the way of converting vacant land (habitat of endangered species) into housing tracts or commercial development. There is some debate over whether the Act's restrictions on private land constitute a "taking" that requires compensation.

Toxic wastes (also called hazardous wastes) might appear to include all pollutants; however the term is reserved for particularly hazardous pollutants that are dangerous in small doses. In the normal use of the term, pervasive pollutants such as sulfur dioxides, nitrogen dioxides, biological oxygen demand, fine airborne particulares, and tropospheric ozone are considered pollutants but not hazardous or toxic pollutants. Toxics are regulated at the Federal level in three different ways. Toxics in the workplace are regulated by the Occupational Safety and Health Administration. The generation, transportation, and disposal of toxic wastes are governed by the Environmental Protection Agency, the all-purpose Federal agency that promulgates and enforces environmental regulations. The applicable law is the Resource Conservation and Recovery Act (RCRA). A major component of the legislation is the requirement for tracking and accounting for wastes as they move through the economy, much as a registered letter would be tracked as it moves through the postal system. The Act also specifies technology standards to be used in disposing of toxic wastes. An omission from the legislation covering generation and disposal of toxic wastes is what to do when accidents occur or when old toxic waste sites are discovered. Yet another law, the Comprehensive Environmental Response, Compensation and Liability Act (CERCLA) of 1978, addressed these concerns. The law set forth liability rules apportioning responsibility for toxic waste leaks into the environment. The Act also set up a large fund (Superfund) to be used to clean up toxic waste sites immediately, without first having to seek out the responsible parties.

Pesticides are another major category of toxic substances, though strictly speaking they are not wastes but toxics that are intentionally introduced into the environment to control weeds, insects, rodents, fungus, or other pests. This does not include chemicals that are intentionally introduced into food (such as colorings), which are regulated separately by the Food and Drug Administration. Although there are several laws that regulate pesticides,[29] most pesticides (insecticides and herbicides) are controlled in a very simple and direct way by the EPA—the EPA simply certifies the label and instructions that are attached to the container before being sold. The label will be very specific— for instance, calling for use on strawberry plants at an application rate not to exceed x milliliters, diluted in y liters of water, per acre of crop. The label may also require application by certified personnel. Much of the EPA's oversight involves calculating how much of a pesticide residual will end up in the food supply, if the label directions are followed, and then how much a typical person will ingest, and whether that will consititute a health hazard.

A major gap in the previous discussion is who regulates the regulators. Specifically, when the Federal government takes actions that have environmental consequences, to whom are they accountable? In large part, it is the National Environmental Policy Act (NEPA) that applies in such cases. Whenever a project (such as building a dam) involves a Federal action, NEPA calls for the preparation of an Environmental Impact Statement (EIS), prior to the project being approved. An EIS reviews the environmental consequences of the project as well as the desirability of alternatives to the project or other steps that could ameliorate the environmental damage. Although strictly speaking this process is not a regulation, it tends to bring to public attention problems that may arise in pursuing a Federal action. If the consequences are severe enough, that is usually enough to stop the project, or cause it to be significantly modified.

2. Use of Economic Incentives. In 1990 a new market in sulfur emissions was established by legislation in an attempt to reduce sulfur emissions that lead to acid deposition (acid rain). At the time of the legislation, approximately 20 million tons of sulfur dioxide were emitted annually in the United States. The goal was to cut that in half. To accomplish that goal, a system of marketable emission permits was set up, phased in over a decade. This was the first major experiment in economic incentives in the United States. The experiment has been running for over a decade now and has generally been viewed as a tremendous success. The price of sulfur (which can be equated to the marginal cost of control) dropped from projected levels of over $500 per ton of sulfur dioxide prior to the market operating to as low as $65 per ton of sulfur dioxide after the market had been operating for a few years. Although there are many possible reasons for this price drop, it is a positive sign that control costs may be lower with the use of economic incentives. When there was talk of lowering the cap on emissions in 2004, the price of allowances shot up. In fact, the annual auction of allowances resulted in a market clearing price per ton of $172 in 2003, rising to $860 in 2006, dropping back to $380 in 2008.[30] Despite the price volatility, the sulfur allowance market has been considered a success and has led to other attempts to use market instruments for pollution control.

Although the sulfur permit market is the most significant experiment in economic incentives yet in the United States, there are other examples, most at the national level but some at the state or local level. One obvious type of economic incentive is the widespread adoption of volume-based pricing for municipal solid waste. It is now very common for households to pay by the "bag" for disposal services (see Fullerton and Kinnaman, 1996). This is in contrast to the widespread approach of a few decades ago of offering virtually unlimited household waste disposal for a fixed monthly fee. A very successful marketable permit system was that used to phase out lead in gasoline, starting in the early 1980s. The issue was how to apportion a shrinking overall cap on lead in motor fuel among different refiners. A system of tradable permits was used and appears to have worked quite well.[31] There have been a number of other emission trading schemes in the United States, most prominently the offset system whereby new polluters entering a heavily polluted area may pay existing polluters to reduce emissions. Robert Hahn (1989) has investigated many of these programs and has concluded that they have had negligible impact.

A program for trading emission in urban Los Angeles was started in 1994—the RECLAIM program.[32] This program was designed to reduce emissions from stationary sources of ozone precursors. It was working relatively well until California experienced an electricity crisis in 2001 which caused electricity prices to peak, which in turn resulted in RECLAIM permit prices rising by an order of magnitude. The market was temporarily suspended.[33]

D. International Agreements

Not all environmental problems are national in scope. When more than one country is involved, the typical solution is a treaty. The two major transboundary air pollution problems are stratospheric ozone depletion and global warming due to greenhouse gases. The first of these is the subject of a treaty; the second is currently being hotly debated around the world.

The Montreal Protocol on Ozone Depleting Substances is an international agreement to control the use of refrigerants and other chemicals that tend to deplete the stratospheric ozone layer. The Protocol limits the production of such chemicals (though they may be recycled) and provides penalties for countries that violate the agreement. It appears to have been successful, at least so far. Prices of banned chemicals have risen dramatically in resale markets, suggesting they are much scarcer than prior to the Protocol.[34]

In the early 1990s many countries of the world (including the United States) negotiated and ratified the Framework Convention on Climate Change, agreeing to "fix" the problem of greenhouse gas emissions leading to climate change. Absent from the Convention were specific actions to reduce emissions. In December 1997, most countries of the world met in Kyoto, Japan, to negotiate specific actions. What emerged is what has become the Kyoto Protocol. The agreement calls for reducing emissions in signatory countries by 2008–2012 to approximately 5% below levels in 1990. In 2005 the Protocol had been ratified by enough countries to go into effect. The United States is conspicuously absent from the list of signatories to the Protocol (even though it is a signatory to the Framework Convention). Discussions have since moved on to the next climate agreement, to cover the period after 2008–2012.

Another significant international treaty is the 1973 Convention on International Trade in Endangered Species (CITES), an agreement to limit international trade in rare animals as well as trade in animal parts such as elephant tusks or obscure parts of tigers or rhinos that are thought by some to have medicinal value.

There are truly a host of other treaties that can be classified as providing environmental protection.[35] These would include agreements to limit whaling, limit certain types of fishing practices, protect migrating birds, and protect the oceans from pollution. The list is very long. The list will undoubtedly get longer as more international environmental problems become the focus of international protection.

IV. THE COSTS OF ENVIRONMENTAL PROTECTION

As with most things that are worthwhile, environmental protection costs money. Although cost information with global coverage is scarce, we do have some country-specific information on the costs of protection, particularly for the United States. Total expenditures in the United States on pollution abatement and control by industry in the United States are approximately 2% of gross domestic product (GDP), up modestly as a fraction of GDP from expenditures in the early 1970s. These are direct costs to industry from pollution control regulations, as reported to the Census Bureau. Many components of cost are potentially omitted from such a measure, such as process changes that are induced by environmental regulations; the cost of operating the bureaucracy that administers environmental laws in the United States; indirect costs such as the costs of pollution control on automobiles or the costs associated with having to use products that are environmentally friendly but of inferior quality in other respects (e.g., bans on oil-based paints); and the cost to society of the residual damage from the pollutants that are emitted, even after controls have been put in place.[36] Nevertheless, the cost of a few percent of GDP puts a correct perspective on environmental protection: it is an important cost, ranging into the hundreds of billions of dollars per year to a country such as the United States, but still relatively modest compared with the costs of other socially desirable activities (health care is estimated to be one-sixth of GDP in the United States).

Specific industries are of course impacted harder than others. Table 1.4 indicates how pollution control costs impact specific industries in the United States. Total expenditures is not the correct measure of the impact of environmental regulations; a better measure is marginal costs or costs per unit of output. As can be seen from Table 1.4, as a percentage of the value of output, the petroleum and coal products industry is the hardest hit, but even in that case, gross abatement operating costs are less than 1% of the value of shipments from the industry. The chemical industry is the second hardest hit. Figures on capital expenditures tell a similar story. The petroleum and coal products industry devotes nearly 16% of its capital expenditures to pollution abatement. It is important to realize that it is not easy to measure expenditures on pollution control, and for that reason the figures in Table 1.4 are suspect. If a manufacturing process has been changed to reduce emissions, what costs are apportioned to pollution control? When a capital expenditure to remove pollutants reduces costs elsewhere in the production process, how much of the capital cost should be attributed to pollution control? The measurement problem is a difficult one in tracking the costs of environmental protection. Furthermore, the figures in Table 1.4 are for the United States; however, the figures undoubtedly are representative of the difficulty these industries have, wherever they may be located, in meeting local environmental regulations.

Having identified which industries are the most polluting, it becomes necessary to determine the total costs of control over all industries. Doing this is not particularly easy. Table 1.5 shows an estimate of pollution control expenditures for several European countries and the United States for the 1975–2000 period. Most importantly, the table indicates that pollution abatement is consistently between 1% and 2% of GDP in most developed economies. One issue in discussing figures such as these is determining just what is included in pollution control expenditures. Do we include the cost of pollution control devices on automobiles? Typically, yes. Do we include the cost of reduced performance in automobiles due to pollution control regulations? Typically, no, though we should. Of the several estimates of the cost of pollution control, most place the figure at less than 3% of GDP. But this of course excludes the damage to the environment—these are only costs of control.

TABLE 1.4 Pollution Abatement Expenditures for Selected U.S. Industries, 2005

Industry	Total capital expenditures	Pollution abatement capital expenditures (PACE)	PACE as a percentage of capital expenditures	Total value of shipments	Abatement gross annual operating costs (GAOC)	GAOC as a percentage of shipments
All Industries	128,325	5,908	4.60	4,735,384	20,678	0.44
Selected industries with high abatement costs						
Paper manufacturing	5,598	573	10.24	162,848	1,796	1.10
Chemical manufacturing	16,887	1,272	7.53	604,501	5,217	0.86
Petroleum and coal manufacturing	11,047	1,743	15.78	476,075	3,746	0.79
Primary metal manufacturing	4,475	512	11.44	201,836	2,291	1.14
Selected industries with moderate abatement costs						
Plastics and rubber products manufacturing	6,968	94	1.35	200,489	503	0.25
Fabricated metal product manufacturing	7,641	168	2.20	288,068	763	0.26
Computer and electronic product manufacturing	15,795	156	0.99	373,932	624	0.17
Selected industries with low abatement costs						
Printing and related support activities	4,343	68	1.56	97,095	239	0.25
Leather and allied products manufacturing	102	2	1.67	6,013	51	0.85
Furniture and related product manufacturing	1,410	31	2.18	84,291	133	0.16

Units: Millions of 2005 US $.
Source: U.S. Census Bureau (2008).

How are these costs distributed among types of environmental problems? Of the $5.9 billion U.S. industry spent on capital expenditures for pollution control in 2005 (Table 1.4), two-thirds was related to air pollution and 23% to water pollution control. Only 11% was spent on solid-waste disposal (U.S. Census, 2008). If we were to include public sector expenditures on water treatment, this picture would change somewhat.

It is important to realize that the reported costs of pollution control regulations reflect two things: the cost of pollution control and the unnecessary costs of inefficient regulations. Thus while pollution control regulations may cost a few percentage points of GDP, it may be that a much higher level of environmental quality could be achieved for that same cost. It is not really known to what extent accounting costs of pollution control regulations exceed the lowest possible cost of providing the same amount of environmental quality.

TABLE 1.5 Pollution Abatement Expenditures for Selected Countries, as a Percentage of GDP

	1975	1980	1985	1990	1995	2000
United States	1.6	1.6	1.4	1.4	1.6	NA
France		0.9	0.8	1.2	1.4	1.3
West Germany	1.4	1.5	1.5	1.6	1.3	1.6
Netherlands		1.1	1.5	1.6	1.8	2.1
United Kingdom		1.6	1.3	0.7		0.9

Sources: Jaffe et al. (1995); Pasurka (2008); OECD (2007). In cases where data for specific year was not available, data for adjacent year was substituted (if available).

V. REMAINING PROBLEMS

Though great progress has been made worldwide over the past few decades, solving environmental problems will be a challenge that will face the world for many decades to come.

Many of tomorrow's environmental problems will arise from a significantly larger global population and a significantly richer population (per capita) than today. More people tends to be unequivocally bad for the environment, though how bad is unclear. A richer population has mixed implications for the environment. On the one hand, people will desire more of the world's resources. On the other hand, people will also demand higher levels of environmental quality and be willing to divert their incomes into environmental protection.

Global warming is a problem we will be dealing with for many decades to come. Even if an international treaty is ratified to curtail emissions of greenhouse gases, the threat of climate change will remain with us for quite some time.

Congestion associated with the motor car has yet to be adequately addressed in the world. In most cities, drivers put up with a significant waste of time, resources, and clean air, all due to road congestion. Europe has tried using extremely high taxes on automobile fuel but that has not solved the congestion problem (though it would undoubtedly be worse without the high taxes). Experiments are beginning on using fees to regulate congestion in large cities (such as London), though the practice is not yet widespread.

One of the remarkable trends of the last century is the movement of more and more of the earth's natural resources from almost infinite abundance to scarcity. Vast stretches of formerly isolated forest ecosystems have been tamed by humans. Even the oceans, that almost limitless supply of water than could bounce back from any environmental insult, are being taxed by pollution and overfishing.

The cost of environmental regulation has yet to be faced seriously as a problem. Many view environmental protection as an absolute, to be provided at any cost. To the extent that such views dominate public policy, cost will take a back seat in debates over solving environmental problems. But the fact is that as environmental protection takes up more and more of a country's national income, the time will come when cost will matter. It will become necessary to ask if there are cheaper ways of providing the same level of environmental protection. If cost savings exist, they may be used to provide further environmental protection or to fund other worthy goals. When that day comes (and there is some evidence that it is here already), the efficiency of environmental regulation will be an important issue.

NOTES

1. Resources for the Future (RfF), a Washington, DC environmental and resource economics research organization, was set up in the early 1950s by the Ford Foundation to address problems of materials shortages. A number of very important works emerged from researchers at RfF in the 1950s and 1960s. One contribution was the development of methods for measuring recreation demand (Clawson and Knetsch, 1966). Another was the reinvigoration of the use of emission fees by Alan Kneese. This culminated in the still-impressive study of regulation of water pollution in the Delaware River system (Kneese and Bower, 1968). Another was the analysis of scarcity of natural resources by Barnett and Morse (1963). John Krutilla forged the basis for how we view natural environments by expanding the notion of value beyond simple use (Krutilla, 1967). Karl-Göran Mäler developed one of the first theoretical treatments of economics and the environment in his influential 1974 book (Mäler, 1974). RfF remains today at the forefront of environmental economics research.
2. Costanza (1991), p. 3.
3. Faber (2008), p. 2.
4. Cropper and Oates (1992) make the dynamic–static distinction in their excellent survey of the field.
5. In the first edition of this book, a sharper distinction was made between dynamics and statics, suggesting that environmental problems tend to be static and resource problems, dynamic. That distinction is probably not as good for distinguishing resource economics from environmental economics as the role of market failure.
6. World Resources Institute (2008) provides a good biennial review of the global environment. World Bank (1992) is a particularly good review of the environment in developing countries. The annual report of the U.S. Council on Environmental Quality (1997) provides a good picture of the environment in the United States. Information on the state of the environment in Europe is covered by Stanners and Bourdeau (1995). The information cited in this section is drawn in large part from these sources.
7. See Schoenbaum and Rosenberg (1991).
8. As always, there are exceptions. The Sierra Club, a major U.S. environmental advocacy group, was founded in California in 1892 to promote the protection of the Sierra Nevada mountains through the establishment of National parks, particularly Yosemite. In England, the National Smoke Abatement Institution was established in 1882 to lobby for pollution control in cities (Ashby and Anderson, 1981). There are undoubtedly other organizations in other parts of the world, established well before the current interest in environmental protection. Nevertheless, the bulk of environmental organizations in existence today date from recent times.
9. Data are from a survey of chemical firms conducted by AFEAS (part of the European Chemical Industry Council) and thus may not be complete.
10. There are a number of reports that emerged from the Millennium Ecosystem Assessment, many of which are downloadable from www.millenniumassessment.org.
11. To my knowledge, there is no one source providing an overview of environmental regulations worldwide. The Environmental Law portion of the International Encyclopaedia of Law (Kluwer Law International, Cambridge, MA) provides country-by-country assessments of environmental law for many countries, though it is written for lawyers rather than economists. Portney and Stavins (2000) provide a good review for the United States. The World Bank website on pollution regulation (www.worldbank.org/nipr) covers many developing countries.

12. Lenaerts (1995) defines and discusses subsidiarity in the context of environmental regulation. Angelini (1993) provides a useful glossary of terms relevant to EU environmental policy.

13. Ludwig Krämer, the former head of legal affairs within the Environmental part of the European Commission, has written a very good overview (current up to the 1990s) of the EU approach to environmental protection (Krämer, 1992).

14. The "polluter pays" principle is not always followed in the EU. As Krämer (1992) points out, there are many instances of government subsidies for pollution cleanup or financing pollution control investments.

15. Linklaters and Paines Solicitors (1992) provide a detailed review of U.K. environmental regulations. The section draws heavily on that source as well as the excellent history of air pollution in the United Kingdom by Ashby and Anderson (1981).

16. The Organization for Economic Cooperation and Development (OECD) has conducted several surveys of the use of economic incentives among member countries (most of the developed world). Refer to OECD (1989, 1994a,b, 1995). See also Margulis (1994).

17. Huppes and Kagan (1989) argue that the fee had real incentive effects in addition to raising revenue.

18. There is not a great deal of information on Russian environmental regulation that is available in English, although excellent references are Averchenkov et al. (1995) and Kozeltsev and Markandya (1997). The discussion draws in part on these sources.

19. Some fairly dismal pictures have been painted of environmental quality in the former Soviet Union. See Feshbach and Friendly (1992) for one perspective.

20. There are some 1,200 air pollutants for which there is an ambient standard—far wider coverage than in most if not all other countries.

21. Though there is always some latitude in conducting an analysis of the effect of emissions on ambient concentrations, the procedures for making such a calculation are indicated in some detail by federal authorities.

22. The State Environmental Protection Committee was abolished in 2000. The Federal environmental agency fluctuates from being a ministerial level organization (Ministry of the Environment) and a somewhat lower level organization (State Environmental Protection Committee).

23. This organizational structure was established in the late 1980s, though there were predecessor organizations.

24. Enforcement has been a major problem with the fee system. Kozeltsev and Markandya (1997) report that in 1995 the Ministry of the Environment collected only half of the 600 billion Rubles (US$130 million) it expected from the fees.

25. Other fees are higher. The fee for lead emissions was approximately US$200 per ton in 1995 for allowed emissions and the fee for allowed emissions of benzopyrene is over US$60,000 per ton (Kozeltsev and Markandya, 1997).

26. Kozeltsev and Markandya (1997) cite several studies on the incentive effects of Russian emission fees. In one, it was estimated that charges would need to be quadrupled to provide an incentive to reduce pollution. They also note that firms may refuse to pay the charges if they become significant; many companies are in tax arrears to the government and one more debt may not make much difference.

27. An excellent and readable review of U.S. environmental regulation is Portney and Stavins (2000).

28. The 1990 Clean Air Act Amendments established a new way of regulating sulfur emissions, using tradable emission permits (known as "allowances").

29. Historically, the two main laws covering toxic chemical substances introduced into the environment are the Toxic Substances Control Act of 1976 (TSCA) and the Federal Insecticide, Fungicide and Rotenticide Act of 1947 (FIFRA).

30. Data are from the EPA website: www.epa.gov/airmarkt/trading.
31. See Hahn (1989) and Hahn and Hester (1989) for information on the operation of this market.
32. Polesetsky (1995) provides an early description of how the program works.
33. Refer to Kolstad and Wolak (2008) for a discussion of this market and its interaction with the electricity market.
34. Murdoch and Sandler (1997) discuss the economics of the Montreal Protocol.
35. Barrett (2003) presents a detailed list of international environmental agreements.
36. Weitzman (1994) suggests that the total social costs may be two to three times these direct costs.

2

POSITIVE VS. NORMATIVE ANALYSIS

I. INTRODUCTION

There is a great divide, at least in the eyes of economists, between economic analysis that tells the public what should be done and economic analysis that merely describes the world around us. Economic analysis that is meant to identify what policy *should* be pursued is termed normative analysis. Economic analysis that objectively observes, quantifies, and characterizes behavior in the world around us is termed positive analysis.

Normative analysis can be very useful in public policy. Policy makers are often looking for guidance regarding which of several policies to pursue. A basic question is which policy will be best for society? Normative analysis is good for answering such questions, or at least providing the illusion of crisp answers to such questions. However, normative analysis suffers from one big shortcoming: it depends on a set of value judgments that most likely will not be embraced by everyone. It is not value neutral.

Positive analysis on the other hand is observational.[1] Though values may creep in from time to time, positive analysis typically confines itself to describing the world around us as it is, not as it should be. Nevertheless, positive analysis can be a very important input into public policy formation. For instance, a policy maker may wish to understand how polluters will respond to a tradable emission permit system. The policy maker can learn from a positive analysis how other polluters have behaved in the context of other, similar permit systems.

In the following sections of this chapter we examine two excellent examples of economic analysis of environmental problems, one normative and one positive. Both analyses relate to climate change, though there are many, many examples of normative and positive analysis in the context of other environmental problems.

II. CLIMATE CHANGE

Before delving into the positive and normative dimensions of climate change, it is important to define what we mean by climate, and to distinguish climate from weather.

Weather is what we experience in terms of temperature, precipitation, wind, or similar atmospheric processes. These experiences change on a minute-to-minute basis and certainly from day to day or month to month. Weather fluctuates wildly over the course of a year, and we expect there to be extremes. Climate, on the other hand, is average weather, roughly speaking: the average temperature over a year or the average annual rainfall. More precisely, climate is the distribution of weather. In fact, we do not actually observe climate. We observe weather and from that infer the climate. For instance, we observe 30 years of temperature in Bangkok and calculate the average. That average characterizes the climate in Bangkok, or at least one dimension of the climate. But we realize and understand that the actual temperature on a given day may be quite different from the 30-year average.

Climate change and global warming are two terms that are used synonymously, though technically there are some differences in the minds of some specialists—a higher average temperature is only one type of climate change.[2] The basic mechanism of climate change is that emissions of "greenhouse gases" (such as carbon dioxide) lead to an increased buildup in the atmosphere of those substances, which turns the atmosphere into more of a "greenhouse." The average temperature we all enjoy on earth is the result of a balance between the incoming sunshine, which warms the surface of the earth, and the outgoing infrared radiation given off by the warmed surface. If the balance is disturbed, the surface temperature of the earth changes. Greenhouse gases tend to make the atmosphere somewhat opaque to outgoing infrared radiation, and the more greenhouse gases in the atmosphere, the more opaque the atmosphere becomes to outgoing infrared. This tips the balance toward a warmer earth. Though this description is an oversimplification and there is some uncertainty regarding details, there is no dispute over the basic physics of this process.

The primary greenhouse gas, carbon dioxide (CO_2), is emitted in vast quantities in the world today, largely from the combustion of fossil fuels. In 2009, nearly 30 billion tons per year of CO_2 were injected into the world's atmosphere (this CO_2 contains roughly 8 billion tons of carbon). This is a continuation of what has been going on since the beginning of the industrial revolution, although obviously emission levels are higher today. CO_2 stays in the atmosphere for a long time. A ton emitted today will take decades to leave the atmosphere. The concentration of CO_2 in the atmosphere has increased from a natural background of approximately 280 parts per million (ppm) at the beginning of the industrial revolution (1750) to about 380 ppm today. The Intergovernmental Panel on Climate Change (IPCC, 2007) estimates that the global average temperature has already risen by ¾°C over that period and will most likely rise by an additional 1° to 3°C by the end of this century.

Rising temperatures can lead to all sorts of negative (and positive) consequences, including sea level rise, more frequent heat waves, increased insect-borne disease and changes in agricultural productivity. Abatement is straightforward for some pollutants. To control sulfur emissions from fuel combustion, polluters may switch to low sulfur fuel or utilize scrubbers to take the SO_2 out of the flue gas. However, it is difficult to burn (oxidize) fossil fuels (basically carbon) without emitting carbon dioxide, though some fossil fuels (natural gas) are better than others (coal). For the most part, actual reductions in fossil fuel use are necessary to achieve substantial cuts in carbon emissions. The bottom line is that abatement is costly.

As the IPCC has indicated, there is a good deal of consensus in the scientific community regarding the nature and scope of the climate change problem (though there is uncertainty regarding details). The climate is changing, and the emissions of greenhouse gases like carbon dioxide are generally accepted to be responsible for much of this. In the words of the IPCC, "warming of the climate system is unequivocal [and] very likely due to the observed increase in anthropogenic [man-made] GHG concentrations."[3] Nevertheless, there is uncertainty regarding details of the problem, including the magnitude of particular variables (such as climate sensitivity). Uncertainty is a fact of life for most complex environmental problems, and climate change is no exception.[4] It is perfectly normal to have scientific consensus over the basic process with some uncertainty regarding the details.

This is not to say there is no controversy over climate change. As a political, not natural science, question there is debate about where climate change stands in the list of major societal problems facing the world. In fact, that is where much of the controversy erupts. Some people feel this is a low- or medium-priority issue (at least compared to other social ills); others feel it is very high priority.

The positive analysis we examine next has value whatever one's position is on the political controversy over climate change. On the other hand, the normative analysis we subsequently examine will be viewed differently by different people, depending in part of their political take on the climate change problem.

III. A POSITIVE ANALYSIS OF CLIMATE CHANGE

One of the positive questions associated with climate change is how have different sectors of the economy responded to different climates and weather deviations in the past? More specifically, for agriculture, how have different climates resulted in different levels of agricultural profit within a geographic area such as the United States?

To help answer this, several economists at Yale University set out to measure the effect of climate change on agriculture in the United States (Mendelsohn et al., 1994). They noted that today there are many different climates in different parts of the United States; consequently, it should be possible to measure the effect of different climates on agricultural productivity and agricultural profit. It is then easy to estimate how a change in climate would affect agriculture (assuming nothing else changes). For instance, consider a plot of land in Minnesota and a nearly identical plot of land slightly to the south, in Iowa, with the only difference being that the average annual temperature of the Iowa plot is, on average, 2°C warmer than the Minnesota plot. We can infer that the difference in returns to agriculture in the two locations is attributable to the difference in climate. In fact, the difference in profitability between the two locations should be fully capitalized in the value of the land. If the Iowa plot is more profitable, the land there should be worth more. And the difference in land value between the two locations should fully capture the difference in the attainable stream of profits in the two locations.

The Mendelsohn et al. (1994) approach exploits this logic, comparing agricultural profitability in a number of different locations with different climates all over the United States. By statistically measuring the effect of climate on agricultural land values, the authors are able to infer the value of climate as capitalized in land values. This will allow them to estimate how land values, and thus agricultural profits, will change if the climate changes. Because of the focus on the fact that the price of land capitalizes a beneficial climate, and different climates result in different land values, this method has become known as the Ricardian approach, after David Ricardo.[5]

To see this approach, Figure 2.1 abstracts, for a particular parcel of land, how typical climate variables (such as average temperature or average rainfall) influence profits and the types of activities on that parcel. We see that each activity (such as growing corn) does well in some climate regimes and poorly in others. If the climate changes and the use of the land remains the same, then the consequences may be significant. If, on the other hand, the land use changes (adaptation), the consequences may be much less. For instance, if we start at point B with wheat, profits are very high. Suppose then the climate warms or drys out, moving us to point F. There would appear to be a significant drop in the value of wheat farming. If, on the other hand, the farmer switches to corn, profits will only drop to point D, which is only slightly less profitable than B. It is the upper envelope of curves in the figure that determine how climate affects the value of activity on the land, taking into account the adaptation that will inevitably occur if climate changes.

The approach of Mendelsohn et al. (1994) is to try to estimate the upper envelope of value in Figure 2.1 by observing different climates around the United States. In particular, they try to explain the value of agricultural land in each of the approximately 3,000 counties in the United States. They posit that land values depend on factors that determine agricultural productivity: climate (the long-run average weather), soil quality, altitude, slope (flat vs. hilly), latitude, and tendency to flood. A final factor that will contribute to land values but not agricultural productivity is proximity to urban areas. The equation to estimate is of the following form:

$$y = a_0 + a_c x_c + a_1 x_1 + a_u x_u + \varepsilon \tag{2.1}$$

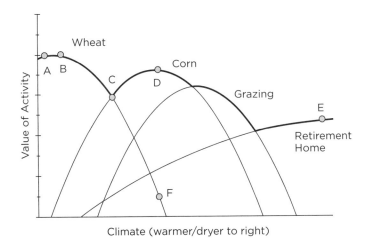

FIGURE 2.1 Value of activities versus climate. (Adapted from Mendelsohn et al., 1994.)

where y is the price per acre of agricultural land, x_c represents climate variables (e.g., average July temperature), x_l represents variables describing the quality of land from the point of view of agricultural productivity, and x_u represents variables relating to nonagricultural factors that might change the land price, such as proximity to urban areas. All variables are county averages, using readily available public data sources. The parameters a_0, a_c, a_u, and a_l are to be statistically estimated while ε is an error term. The authors statistically estimate Eq. (2.1) using 2,933 observations on counties around the United States for a single year.

The last step of their analysis is to use the estimated Eq. (2.1) to compute what the loss in land value might be from a nationwide increase in average temperature of nearly 3°C coupled with an 8% increase in annual precipitation. They calculate that the loss in land value (using 1982 prices) would be $141 billion.[6] Because this is a change in land values, this is a one-time, not an annual loss. We can interpret this as the willingness to pay by agriculture to avoid this level of climate change. To place this in context, the total valuation of agricultural land in the United States in 1982 was $730 billion; 1982 farm income was $164 billion, with the value of all crops produced approximately half of this, at $72 billion (United States Bureau of the Census, 1987).[7]

At one level, this analysis of the effect of climate on agricultural profits appears totally value free. And to a large extent it is. All the analysts are really doing is quantifying the relationship between climate and agricultural profits as embodied in land values. But, as illustrated in the previous paragraph, the major purpose of the analysis is to determine how agriculture might be affected by a change in the climate. And the reason for asking this question is to provide input into a normative decision of whether and what to do about climate change. Most of the criticisms of work such as this relate to its applicability in normative analyses of the climate problem.

IV. A NORMATIVE ANALYSIS OF CLIMATE CHANGE

There are a host of policy-relevant questions regarding climate change. What are the consequences of our current path of economic growth and associated carbon emissions? What actions can and should be taken to ameliorate the negative consequences of climate change? What abatement policies should be taken and when ("what, when"), based on the projected consequences of climate change? There are many other policy issues. This is where normative analysis of the problem can make a contribution.

There are a number of normative analyses of the climate change problem, providing answers to some of these policy questions. Two prominent recent analyses come to quite different conclusions: one by William Nordhaus (2008) suggests modest action is warranted; and one by the British Government and a team led by the former academic economist Sir Nicholas Stern of Her Majesty's Treasury (Stern, 2006) suggests vigorous action is warranted. Both of these analyses look at the potential damage from climate change and the costs of controlling greenhouse gas emissions and provide answers to the "what, when" question using intertemporal cost-benefit analysis. They come to dramatically different conclusions, underscoring the fact that normative analyses involve assumptions about which people may disagree.

Nordhaus has been examining the economics of climate change for longer than some readers of this book have been alive.[8] In the 1990s he undertook a careful sectoral analysis of the possible consequences of an increase in the global mean temperature, examining a variety of sectors, including agriculture, energy, water, recreation and coastal areas. Most of this work was in the United States, mainly for data reasons (that is where the data are more available). The result of this work was a damage function relating the increase in mean average temperature to economic damages, expressed in terms of percentage loss in GDP. He has periodically updated this work, and the latest (2008) figures are presented in Figure 2.2. For small changes in temperature, the losses are low. However, when the temperature change is 6°C, the annual loss is 10% of world GDP—a sizable number. The comparable figure from Stern (2006) is higher damage from similar temperature changes. The aggregate nature of the curve in Figure 2.2 obscures the detailed sector-level analysis of damages that form the basis for the graph. Despite the illusion of precision in the figure, it is important to realize that the damages from climate change are highly speculative and uncertain.

Figure 2.2 reflects the benefits of reducing emissions of greenhouse gases, and thus avoiding increases in global temperature. What about the costs? It might seem that estimating the cost of reducing greenhouse gas emissions is easier than estimating the damage from climate change, but such estimates are also fraught with imprecision and uncertainty. After all, the world has had virtually no experience in trying to reduce greenhouse gas emissions; most estimates are speculative. Stern (2006) in fact suggests that many of the options for reducing carbon emissions are actually free or even save us money. Nordhaus's approach to this problem is to assemble estimates of marginal cost-abatement levels in a number of different analyses of carbon control and then to conduct a statistical analysis of these estimates (a "meta-analysis") to generate an abatement cost function. What results is a relationship between the percentage reduction in carbon emissions (relative to no control) versus the marginal cost of control ($ per ton of carbon). Figure 2.3 shows the marginal abatement costs as a function of emission control levels (e.g., a 0.1 emission control level means that overall emissions are reduced by 10% over the uncontrolled level).[9]

Damage Cost of Temperature Increase

FIGURE 2.2 Annual damages from average global temperature increase. (Source: Nordhaus, 2008.)

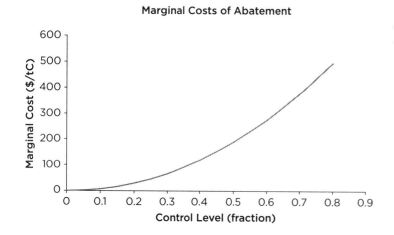

FIGURE 2.3 Marginal cost of emissions abatement.
(Source: Nordhaus, 2008.)[10]

Nordhaus then puts the assumptions embodied in Figures 2.2 and 2.3 together with a model of how emissions are translated into temperature changes as well as a number of other details necessary to "close" the analysis. Although his model is somewhat complex, conceptually it is simple. We are concerned with the utility of a representative consumer over time. The consumer derives utility from consumption of goods and services. Production of goods and services is determined by the capital stock (more capital yields more output) and by the global average temperature (higher temperatures yield less output). Consumption is what is left over after investment has been siphoned off from production. Investment, of course, is necessary to provide capital for tomorrow's production. Emission control (Fig. 2.3) costs money, which also has to come out of production. But emission control reduces the stock of greenhouse gases, which in turn keeps in check the increase in global average temperature. This completes the loop. Emissions control costs money in the short run but keeps the temperature increase in check, which expands output in the long run. The model is not difficult to understand; the interested reader is referred to Nordhaus (2008) for more detail.

Using this model, Nordhaus generates a plot of the "optimal" level of emissions control through time. "Optimal" in this case involves a balancing of the marginal cost of control and the marginal damage within the context of a model of efficient growth of the capital stock and output. Given the assumptions he makes, the path of "optimal" emissions control is in Figure 2.4.

This analysis, which results in the emission control trajectory in Figure 2.4, may seem totally logical and devoid of value judgments. That would not be the correct conclusion. First of all, basing social policy with regard to greenhouse gases on utility of a representative consumer is a gross simplification of societal preferences, as reflected in the political process. Furthermore, a number of key parameter values in the analysis are subject to considerable debate and controversy. For instance, it turns out that the way one discounts time is critical. Stern (2006), for instance, views costs and benefits that occur at different points in time as being roughly comparable and thus additive in generating aggregate costs and benefits. Nordhaus (2008), on the other hand, discounts time in such a way that costs and benefits that occur several decades from now are weighted considerably less than similar costs and benefits today.[11] This results in a different set of trade-offs

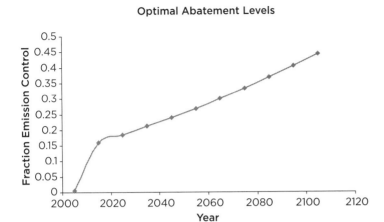

Optimal Abatement Levels

FIGURE 2.4 Optimal emission control. (Source: Nordhaus, 2008.)

between the present and the future. A consequence of this, for example, is that more modest expenditures for emissions control today are justified by the damages that may be incurred a century from now. The analysis of Stern (2006), on the other hand, concludes that much more aggressive action on emission control is warranted.[12] There are many other value-laden assumptions in normative analyses of the climate problem.[13]

The Nordhaus (2008) analysis of climate change is considered one of the best. Despite this (and like all normative analyses) it cannot and should not be used to infer unequivocally what we must do as societal policy with regard to greenhouse gases and climate change. The value of such a normative analysis is to provide key evidence in the societal debate over the right course of action. It is one of several inputs into the complex political calculus from which a societal decision emerges.

SUMMARY

1. Most empirical economic analyses can be categorized as positive or normative.

2. Positive economic analyses seek to describe the world as it is, necessitating few if any value judgments on the part of the analyst.

3. Normative economic analyses seek to contribute to public policy debate, addressing the question of what "should" be done, from an economic perspective. Often such analyses compare the costs and the benefits of taking particular public policy actions.

PROBLEMS

*1. A very simple version of the normative model described in the text involves a simple economic growth process converging to a steady-state, where values do not change over time.[14]

A simple model of the climate would involve a greenhouse gas accumulation equation and a temperature change equation: $dM/dt = \beta E(t) - \delta M(t)$ and $dT/dt = \alpha [\lambda M(t) - T(t)]$ where M is the stock of greenhouse gases (in billions of tons), $E(t)$ is the emission level (in billions of tons per year) and $T(t)$ is the global temperature increase (in °C over preindustrial levels), with values of β, δ, α, and λ of 0.50, 0.005, 0.02, and 0.003, respectively. Note that in 2005 world GDP was about $60 trillion and approximately 8 billion tons of carbon were emitted (in the form of carbon dioxide equivalent).

a. Using the simple climate model, what is the relationship between the steady-state emission level (E^*) and the steady-state temperature (T^*)? Recall that steady-state means that neither M nor T are changing.

b. Convert Figure 2.2 into a plot of the damage as a function of temperature change, assuming steady-state global GDP of US$100 trillion per year. Generate a plot of the marginal damage ($ per degree temperature increase) as a function of the temperature rise.

c. Use the results from parts (a) and (b) to generate a plot showing the marginal damage ($ per ton of carbon emissions) as a function of the fraction of emissions controlled (assume steady-state uncontrolled emissions of 12 billions tons of carbon).

d. What level of emission control balances the marginal cost of control with the marginal damage?

*2. Go to the library or the Internet and, for a particular year, put together a data set of profits in agriculture in different geographical units of your state or country (e.g., counties of a U.S. state; states of a federal government). Locate data on the average annual temperature at a typical location in each geographic unit. For each geographic unit you should have two numbers: agricultural profits and average annual temperature. Plot these data (profits on one axis, temperature on the other). Is there a relationship? Are there additional variables that might increase the explanatory power of your data? What can you conclude about the overall effect on profits of a 3°C increase in the annual temperature in each of the geographic units?

NOTES

1. A classic discussion of positive economics is by Milton Friedman (1953).
2. Other types of climate change include sea level rise, changes in storm frequency and intensity (e.g., hurricanes), changes in precipitation patterns, and even regional cooling.
3. Bracketed terms are inserted. Quoted sections are from IPCC (2007), pp. 2, 5.
4. Refer to IPCC (2007) for an exhaustive review of the current scientific consensus on climate change. Weart (1997) provides an excellent and readable history of thought on global warming over the past century.
5. David Ricardo was an English economist of the early nineteenth century who, among other things, is credited with exploring the subtleties of determinants of the rent for land, particularly the notion that differential qualities of land earn differential returns (rents).
6. The results presented by the authors are somewhat more ambiguous than this. They estimated two versions of Eq. (2.1), in one, placing more weight on the importance of the error for a county, depending on the agricultural significance of the county. When the weights were simply based on agricultural acreage in the county (more acres, more weight), the $141 billion loss resulted. When the weights were based on the value of agricultural output in the county, there was actually a gain associated with warming, on the order of $35 billion. The value-based weights tend to emphasize high-value crops such as vegetables grown in California or citrus in coastal areas, whereas the acreage-based weights tend to emphasize grains that have lower value but are planted widely in parts of the United States.

7. Over the years since the publication of the Mendelsohn et al. (1994) paper, there has been a good deal of controversy in the literature regarding how accurate the approach is in estimating the damage from climate change. For instance, Schlenker et al. (2005) criticized and corrected the treatment of irrigation. It has been correctly pointed out that the Ricardian approach measures the long-run effects of changes in the climate, which should be fully captured in the value of land. But it may take a very long time indeed for the long run to materialize. It may be that we are more interested in the short- or medium-term effects as the climate changes and farmers adjust. This cannot be determined from the Ricardian approach. Thus an alternative approach, first implemented by Kelly et al. (2005), is to look at how agricultural profits are influenced by weather and climate (rather than simply land values). Defining climate as the distribution of weather, Kelly et al. (2005) take the approach of econometrically estimating how climate *and* weather affect agricultural profits on a year-to-year basis and from these estimates, infer both short-run effects of climate change, as well as longer-run effects. Their work uses a pooled time-series cross-section of counties, though only in the Midwest United States. Deschenes and Greenstone (2007) extend the Kelly et al. (2005) approach to the entire United States, though they focus only on weather, not climate. There have been a number of studies examining the effects of climate on agricultural productivity in other parts of the world (particularly the series of books and articles by Robert Mendelsohn). The general conclusion of all of this research is similar: there are significant consequences to agriculture of climate change, though the effects are not enormous.

8. His first published paper on this topic is Nordhaus (1977).

9. The abatement costs and climate damage functions are specified in more precision in the lab notes accompanying the book and are available on the webpage of Prof. Nordhaus.

10. The detailed data for this graph are contained in the documentation lab notes for Nordhaus (2008), available at http://nordhaus.econ.yale.edu/Accom_Notes_100507.pdf.

11. As described in Nordhaus (2007), the annual discount rate on consumption used by Nordhaus is roughly 5% to 6%, whereas the comparable figure for Stern is 1% to 2%.

12. Stern (2006) uses a model similar to Nordhaus (2008), though parameterized differently, and concludes that stabilizing greenhouse gas levels at 550 ppm (recall from earlier that we are currently at 380 ppm) requires an emission control level of 60% by the year 2050, with further reductions after that point (more than twice the level in Fig. 2.3). Furthermore, Stern concludes that the costs of such action are around 1% of world GDP, whereas the damage associated with not taking action are 20% of world GDP. Drastically cutting emissions is a bargain, according to this analysis. This analysis is freely available from the U.K. government: www.hm-treasury.gov.uk/sternreview_index.htm.

13. Analyses such as those of Nordhaus (2008) and Stern (2006) must make assumptions about how the future will unfold and how policymakers "should" trade off costs and benefits. Time discounting, abatement costs, and damage from climate change are all important and highly uncertain dimensions of this, as mentioned in the text. Another important assumption is how technology develops over time, effectively reducing the costs of emissions control. Furthermore, the accuracy of economic models in representing the evolution of societies and economies is an issue.

14. See Nordhaus (1991) for a more sophisticated and realistic version of the model presented here.

3

MAKING SOCIETAL CHOICES

There are two basic questions in environmental policy: "What is the right balance between environmental protection and use?" and "How do we induce economic agents to use the environment in a fashion that we have determined is desirable?" The first of these questions is the concern of this and the next several chapters.

The normative question of how much environmental protection we should have is fundamentally a social and political question: How much land should be set aside to protect endangered species of plants and animals? Should a scenic canyon be dammed to provide electricity and irrigation water? What level of urban ozone is acceptable, given the costs of control? How safe is "safe enough" in drinking water supply? These are similar to other fundamental questions facing society such as how much income support should be provided to the less fortunate or how much of the tax burden should be borne by the wealthy? As with many social questions, there is no unanimity within society about the best course of action. Some argue that species extinction should be avoided at all costs. Others maintain that species should be protected but not all species are equally important. Some argue that the benefits of species preservation should be balanced against the costs in terms of land or lumber "losses." Still others could not care less about species preservation.

It is important to realize that when we make decisions about protecting the environment, we are making *societal* decisions. This is fundamentally different than an *individual* decision. Basically, a decision to exploit or protect the environment affects a large group of people. Within this large group of people there is a variety of opinion about the best course to take vis-à-vis environmental protection/exploitation. How can we decide what action is socially desirable? Whatever action we take, some will be pleased and others disappointed. Thus the first problem we have is to translate diverse individual preferences regarding the environment into a group or societal choice.

For individuals, there are a variety of philosophical positions on environmental protection, ranging from biocentrism to sustainability to anthropocentrism and beyond. We will discuss these later in this chapter. But it is very important to distinguish between philosophical views of the role of natural environments in human existence and methods for making actual societal decisions about regulations or projects that have environmental consequences (good or bad). It is one thing to believe that no action should be taken that is not "sustainable" in the long run. It is another to try to decide whether a particular open parcel of land should be set aside as an open space for species preservation or developed for housing.

To summarize, individuals in society have widely differing opinions and views regarding the answer to our question of what is the right amount of environmental protection. We assume that everyone is entitled to their opinion, no matter how perverse it may appear to be. Our main problem is not in understanding why people feel the way they do. Rather, we start from individual preferences and ask how social or group decisions can be made. Our focus is on developing methods for helping to make specific societal decisions, such as whether to develop a piece of open land.

One point should be made before delving into how we make decisions, and that is just what constitutes a choice about environmental protection. A choice about environmental protection not only includes the environmental consequences of an action but also the cost of providing the environmental protection. Simply couching a choice as being between good and bad is an oversimplification. Nobody is in favor of urban air pollution—it is the package of air quality improvements combined with the cost of achieving those improvements (and who bears those costs) that generates debate.

I. THREE EXAMPLES

It always helps to be concrete when discussing different ways of deciding about environmental protection. Consider three simple examples. Keep in mind that each of these examples involves a potential environmental improvement *and* a cost of the improvement. Without costs there is no issue—*everyone* is in favor of costless environmental improvement.

The first example concerns the control of air pollution in a large urban area such as Santiago, Chile. Santiago, like many urban areas around the world, suffers from severe air pollution.[1] This pollution originates from a variety of sources but particularly from diesel buses and automobiles. The pollution can be cleaned up but only at significant cost. If pollution from buses is to be reduced and bus owners are to pay for the clean-up, then the cost of transportation in the city will rise, affecting those who depend on public transportation. The wealthy are less likely to use the buses and may be particularly bothered by the pollution. On the other hand, the poor may be less concerned with pollution, having enough trouble getting food on the table. Furthermore, they are particularly likely to feel the impact of increased transportation costs. Thus, they may be less concerned with getting rid of the air pollution. So what should be done? If we vote, the poor are likely to have the majority and only modest pollution control will result. If we look at how much people would be willing to pay to reduce the pollution, the rich will count much more since they have more resources. In this case, the outcome may be quite different. Which is correct? Which approach should be used for making social decisions about pollution control?

Another example concerns the California gnatcatcher, a bird native to the coastal areas of Southern California and also an endangered species under U.S. law.[2] Coastal areas of Southern California are also favorite nesting places of people and the land is consequently highly valued. If the gnatcatcher's habitat is eliminated, the species may become extinct. To protect the bird, a significant amount of land resources will have to be devoted to habitat preservation. What should be done? How to decide? If we vote, who should vote? The country? The state of California? Residents of coastal southern California? The world? Clearly the outcome of the vote depends on how the cost of habitat preservation is distributed among the population. And what about future generations? Surely they have a stake in the extinction of a species. How can we make their vote count?

A third example is the Three Gorges dam in China (e.g., Yardley, 2007). This enormous dam is nearing completion. When completed, it will tame the Yangtze river, generating a reservoir over 500 km in length. On the positive side, the dam will generate a great deal of electricity and provide needed flood control. On the negative side, the dam will destroy ancient cities and inundate spectacular canyons; these are essentially irreversible consequences. Furthermore, there is always the possibility of spectacular failure of the dam. The social choice problem was whether to build the dam. Not surprisingly, opinions were (and still are) mixed. But only one decision could be made. This is not an easy social choice problem.[3]

These three examples illustrate three different types of tough environmental policy problems. The first case, pollution in Santiago, is in some ways the easiest to solve. All of the affected parties presently reside in Santiago, in contrast to the other two examples in which substantial intertemporal issues are involved. What makes the Santiago example tough are the distributional issues. One person–one vote results in one decision regarding pollution; a decision based on willingness to commit resources to clean up pollution will yield a different outcome, one in which the wealthy have a larger voice. This in fact characterizes the public policy dilemma at the core of many pollution control problems in cities worldwide.

The other two examples involve decisions with long-term implications. The basic problem is that many of the people who will be affected by these decisions have not yet been born and thus are unable to voice their opinions. The example of the gnatcatcher is tough because of the moral implications (to some) of destroying a species. This is clearly an irreversible action. A decision still needs to be made, however. The example of the Three Gorges dam has very long-term implications, though it is more an issue of trading gains to the present generation for losses to future generations, which will no longer be able to experience the undamed Yangtze.

II. INDIVIDUAL PREFERENCES REGARDING ENVIRONMENTAL PROTECTION

One of the sharpest criticisms leveled at economics, when it is applied to environmental problems, is that people do not like the conclusions of economic analysis. Economics is viewed more as a foe than a friend of the environment. For instance, when economists measure willingness-to-pay for protecting an endangered species and the answer is only a modest number, economics is often blamed. But the real culprit is the individual and his or her preferences. If society consists mostly of people who prefer a weekend in front of the TV to a weekend hiking in the wilderness, then it should come as no surprise that when an economist measures willingness-to-pay for wilderness protection, the number is not large. Conversely, if society consists of individuals who would much rather hike than vegetate, the answer will be different.

There are really two issues here: how do individuals view the environment and how do we collect or aggregate all those individual opinions to create an opinion for society as a whole? Before turning to the aggregation question, we examine several ways in which individuals perceive the environment. It turns out that differences in individual preferences are much more likely to be contentious than the manner in which we aggregate all those individual opinions.

Understanding individual preferences is somewhat unusual in economics. Our normal approach is to assume that any preferences are possible and not be too concerned about the nature of individual preferences. Although this is certainly just as true with regard to the environment, it is useful to understand the very different views individuals hold with regard to environmental protection.

The field of environmental ethics recognizes a variety of perspectives on what is "right" regarding environmental protection.[4] This is a complex subject and we make no pretense of adequately covering the subject here. We have chosen four very different philosophical perspectives, biocentrism, sustainability, the precautionary principle, and anthropocentrism, to illustrate different ethical perspectives. We do not claim to be complete in representing environmental ethics. In fact there are many other ways of viewing individual attitudes regarding the environment. Our goal is to make the reader aware that intelligent and thoughtful people can have *very different beliefs* about environmental protection. Keep in mind that we are referring to how individuals think. Combining individual beliefs into societal beliefs is a separate issue.

A. Biocentrism

Biocentrism encompasses a number of different philosophical views of humans and the environment (Nash, 1989). As the word suggests, biocentrism places the biologic world (primarily nonhumans) at the center of its value system.[5] An important distinction is made in biocentrism between instrumental value and intrinsic value. Instrumental value pertains to usefulness. Something has instrumental value if it can serve as an instrument in achieving some useful objective. In contrast, intrinsic value does not pertain to usefulness. Something can be totally useless and still have intrinsic value. Consider the smallpox virus. The instrumental value of that species is generally considered to be negative—it is not useful to any living creature and for humans it is very unuseful. Yet it can be argued from a moral perspective that life itself is intrinsically valuable and thus the smallpox virus has value for that reason. To bring the example into the human sphere, consider the case of a convicted mass murderer. Most would not dispute the fact that the instrumental value of that person's life is small or nonexistent. Yet many would argue that instrumental value is not the issue; human life has intrinsic value, regardless of the deeds or actions of any particular individual.

Biocentrism is the philosophy that all living things have intrinsic value, regardless of their instrumental value. The animal rights movement is an example of biocentrism, where the intrinsic value of an animal's life is recognized, just as most people recognize the intrinsic value of human life. Interestingly, biocentrism is in conflict with some ecologically oriented views of the environment. Aldo Leopold for instance (as we discuss in the next section) viewed ecosystems as intrinsically valuable but not individual members of the ecosystem. Thus, hunting would typically be anathema to a biocentrist but for Leopold it would be perfectly acceptable, and possibly desirable to reduce overpopulation.

B. Anthropocentrism

A second view of the environment is that it exists for only one purpose: to provide material gratification to humans.[6]

It is important to distinguish anthropocentrism from utilitarianism, at least as we use the terms here.[7] Although these terms are sometimes used synonymously, there is a distinction. Utilitarianism with regard to the environment emphasizes the well-being people attain from the environment, whether it be materialistic or spiritual, instrumental or intrinsic. The strictest definition of anthropocentrism places only instrumental value on the environment. If the California gnatcatcher is of no use to humans, then it has no value to a strict anthropocentrist. Utilitarianism on the other hand would admit individual value, no matter what the source of that value. If someone obtains a warm and fuzzy feeling from knowing the gnatcatcher is alive and well, that is a legitimate utilitarian value. Many of us have an image of the "untouched" rain forests of Africa, South America, or Southeast Asia. Despite the fact that few of us will ever visit those rain forests or benefit in a material way from them, we are enriched individually by knowing they exist, at least for the time being. Thus the standing forests may have utilitarian value even though that value is of an intrinsic nature with little instrumental value.

C. Precautionary Principle

One of the main issues in modern environmental thinking is that the future is uncertain, not so much in terms of environmental actions but more in the sense that no matter how careful we are, unexpected events seem to rule the day. Even though we may carefully screen a pesticide (or food additive) for safety, none of us is surprised if we eventually determine that it is hazardous. The gasoline additive MTBE is a good case in point. MTBE is a fuel oxygenate, added to gasoline to help improve urban air quality. Only some time after it came into wide use was it discovered that it is highly water soluble. Groundwater contamination by MTBE was becoming alarmingly common.[8]

A recognition that the future is unknown, and the fact that "stuff happens" led to the introduction of the concept of the safe minimum standard, more recently known as the precautionary principle.[9] The safe minimum standard at its extreme can be roughly characterized as minimizing regrets: take actions not based on maximizing the upside but rather based on minimizing the downside. If building a dam will flood a valley and eliminate an endangered species, look not to what the expected value is of the species (and build the dam) but rather look to the fact that you might just find that you want that species for some unspecified reason far into the future (and on that basis, decide not to build the dam).

Bishop (1978) argues that minimizing regrets, no matter how unlikely they are, may paralyze the decision-making process. He suggests a modified decision rule of adopting the safe minimum standard prescription for action "unless the social costs are unacceptably large." Although this may make intuitive sense, it will not be easy to implement for making actual decisions on public projects. In particular, where is the line between "unacceptably large" and "large but not unacceptably large"?

The precautionary principle has been articulated in a number of different forms. Principle 15 of the Rio Declaration of states:

"Where there are threats of serious or irreversible damage, lack of full scientific certainty shall not be used as a reason for postponing cost-effective measures to prevent environmental degradation."[10]

The "problem" with this definition is that it is completely consistent with an economic view of decision making under uncertainty: do not wait for certainty, rather, take action based on what is known and the probabilities involved. If it is the same as an economic prescription, why introduce the concept? However, as the principle has been interpreted in practice, there is much more of a focus on erring on the side of prevention when there is uncertainty and the potential for irreversible or very serious environmental or health damage. In fact there are many forms of the principle and a good deal of literature on the issued.[11]

To summarize, the safe minimum standard and the precautionary principle apply when there is uncertainty and irreversibility. The basic principle is to err on the side of precaution. Identifying how much to err or how to quantify how normal practices should be modified remains ambiguous; consequently, implementing the principle is difficult.

D. Sustainability

Sustainability, broadly defined, could be considered a recent manifestation of Aldo Leopold's "Land Ethic." Half a century ago Leopold (1949) argued that it is the health of ecosystems that is of paramount importance: an environmental policy is right if it preserves the integrity of an ecosystem and wrong if it does not. This philosophy is perfectly consistent with natural resource use, provided the use does not degrade the ecosystem. Thus fishing is acceptable but overfishing is not. Logging is acceptable, provided the long-term health of the forest ecosystem is not jeopardized. This view is the logical predecessor to what today is called sustainability—use the environment for human needs only to the extent that the long-term health of the environment is not jeopardized.

Sustainability has been an exceedingly popular word over the past few years when it comes to human interactions with the environment. Probably one reason for its popularity is that it sounds good but is difficult to define precisely. For this reason, traditional economists such as Robert Solow have embraced the notion as a concept that economists have been talking about for decades in the context of economic growth and the environment. At the same time, ecologists such as Robert Constanza and environmental activists have embraced the concept as a fresh alternative to blind economic growth (Costanza, 1991). If the term were defined more precisely, then undoubtedly more people would be taking positions on opposite sides of the issue.

One of the best known definitions of sustainability was generated by the "Brundtland Commisssion," the World Commission on Environment and Development, headed by the former Prime Minister of Norway. As quoted by Toman (1994), the commission defined sustainability as "development that meets the needs of the present without compromising the ability of future generations to meet their own needs." The debate over sustainability has focused on two key aspects: (1) the degree to which "natural capital" can be viably replaced by human capital and (2) the obligation the present generation owes to future generations.[12]

Nobel Laureate Robert Solow defines sustainability as making sure the next generation is as well off as the current generation and ensuring that this continues for all time (Solow, 1992). Key to this view is that man-made capital (machines, buildings) and knowledge are substitutes for natural capital, particularly natural resources. As we deplete the energy resources of the world, we invent ways of getting along with less energy and build machines that reduce energy use or extract energy from the sun.

There is significant justification in the historical record for this position. Barnett and Morse's classic study of a century of natural resource exploitation demonstrated that with the exception of timber, resources have been getting more plentiful (Barnett and Morse, 1963). This has occurred not because more oil has been produced by nature but because the technology of extraction and use has been advancing more rapidly than depletion.[13] Many proponents of rapid introduction of energy conservation and renewable energy sources have as their goal the substitution of man-made capital in the form of solar energy converters for natural energy resources such as oil, gas, and coal. We are also reminded of the bet between the late economist Julian Simon and the ecologist Paul Ehrlich. In the early 1980s Simon challenged Ehrlich to name several commodities he thought would be more scarce a decade hence (based on their price). When it came time to call the bet in, Simon had won hands down—all of the commodities were cheaper than they had been a decade earlier.[14] Although price is not the only measure of scarcity, it was the subject of the bet. It should be noted that Ehrlich may well have won if the bet were made in 2000.

The Solow view is that man-made and natural capital are substitutes. But an alternative view is that natural capital (natural resources, the oceans, wilderness areas, species of plants and animals) is only somewhat substitutable with man-made capital. Put simply, no amount of machinery or invention will make up for the loss of wilderness or key species. Which view is correct is not easily resolved. Certainly the historic record supports Solow's position on sustainability. The past, however, may or may not be a good predictor of the future. In fact, some critics of this view of sustainability point out that the one resource that Barnett and Morse found was getting scarcer (forests) was closest to what we now call natural environments.[15] The key difference between the views of Solow and others is the extent of substitutability between natural and man-made capital *in the future*. Because we are referring to the future, the extent of substitutability is an opinion, not a fact. To distinguish between these two views of substitutability, the terms weak sustainability and strong sustainability have been coined (see Neumayer, 2003). The term weak sustainability refers to a path of consumption over time that yields a nondeclining utility level, assuming substitutability between man-made capital and natural capital. The term strong sustainability means the same thing without allowing the substitution of man-made for natural capital. From a practical point of view, an action that depletes natural capital but enhances man-made capital may be weakly sustainable but could not be strongly sustainable. A consumption path that is strongly sustainable would necessarily also be weakly sustainable.

The economist Talbot Page of Brown University defines sustainability as managing depletion, pollution, and congestion (Page, 1991). For depletion, he calls for keeping broad aggregates of resources constant from one generation to the next, for example, energy, metals, wood, soils, and water. For pollution, he sees a need to balance pollution generation with the waste assimilation capacity of the environment. For congestion, he primarily means overpopulation, but the concept goes further than that.

An ecologist's views of sustainability may differ from Page's in detail but not in spirit. The idea is that we have a God-given endowment of resources, including species and natural resources, and that we have no right to squander that endowment for short-term gain, particularly when we do not really understand the implications of our actions. Don't fool with Mother Nature!

Often the term "resilience" will be used in conjunction with sustainability. Resilience and sustainability are related but different terms. Resilience refers to the ability of a consumption path or a policy to withstand unexpected shocks or events.[16] For instance, an environmental policy (that requires an energy input) may work very well with oil prices around $100 a barrel. However, if oil prices were to rise to $200 a barrel, the policy may fall apart. An alternative, more resilient policy (perhaps relying on non-oil energy) might be a bit more expensive with $100 oil but would continue to work if the price of oil were to rise to $200 or more a barrel. For example, the RECLAIM tradable permit market in Los Angeles fell apart when the price of electricity spiked during the 2000 California electricity crisis, driving the price of pollution permits to politically unacceptable levels.[17]

Resilience sounds good and it usually is in the context of the environment. But, as Levin et al. (1998) report, things like racial discrimination or high birth rates can also be resilient, which means resistant to change through public policy prescriptions and other attempts to perturb "the system." Like sustainability, resilience is a nice concept but difficult to implement in terms of specific projects or decisions about environmental protection.

III. SOCIAL CHOICE FROM INDIVIDUAL VALUES

In the previous section, we discussed many perspectives on the environment, ranging from biocentrism to anthropocentrism. Since our goal is to generate methods for making decisions about specific regulations or projects that have environmental impact, we move away from generality. In particular, we will construct different methods of making decisions based on values *individuals* place on environmental protection. These individuals may be biocentrists or selfish materialists. We make no restriction on their individual preferences.

A. The Utility Function

We start from a simple microeconomic view of the environment. Society consists of N individuals, each of whom consume a market good and an environmental good ("environmental quality"). The market good, x, can be considered a composite of all conventional market goods the individual consumes, and the individual consumption indicated by x_i. Different people may well consume different amounts of the composite market good. Environmental quality is also a composite, represented by e. In contrast to the market good, everyone must consume the same amount of environmental quality—it is a pure public good. This reflects the fact that we all consume the same amount of many environmental goods—for instance, we all face the same global climate. How an individual views the benefits provided by the market good and the environmental good are represented by a utility function, U_i. Typically, individual i will only care about his or her own consumption, in which case utility is $U_i(x_i, e)$.

The bundle of consumption in our society consists of what everyone consumes: individual levels of the market good and the quantity of the environmental good: $\mathbf{a} \equiv (x_1, \ldots, x_N, e)$. The bold-faced variable $\mathbf{a}$ is a *societal consumption bundle* and represents the N values of consumption of the market good for the N individuals plus the level of environmental quality, the same amount of which is consumed by each individual.[18]

This is a standard economic perspective on utility. Individuals have preferences that are represented by their utility function. When faced with decisions about trading-off x and e, they will attempt to maximize utility. Pure biocentrists have utility functions that permit no substitution of x for e. An extreme anthropocentrist may have a utility function that allows no substitution of e for x. Figure 3.1 shows a set of indifference curves for which the environment becomes more and more important as consumption of x increases. For low levels of x, environmental quality must increase substantially to offset a loss in material goods. For higher levels of x, a substantial increase in material goods is necessary to offset a small loss in environmental quality. Those who believe strongly in sustainability might have the utility of future generations as an explicit argument of their utility function.

In many cases of environmental protection, it is future generations who benefit from our actions today. For instance, in controlling carbon dioxide emissions to reduce global warming, the primary benefactors are citizens of the world in 2100 and beyond. Concern for others can take many forms, including a concern about the well-being of future generations (bequest) or simply a concern about others, in this generation or in future generations (altruism). In being concerned about others, we could only care about their well-being, in which case it is their utility that is of concern. Or we can be more "paternalistic," caring how they derive their utility. In other words, we may be more concerned about passing on an environmental legacy in the form of a high e than material goods, in the form of a high x, even though both contribute to utility.

Any of these perspectives is a perfectly acceptable individual view of the environment, and it is important to develop robust methods of analysis that can deal with a

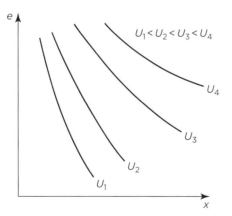

FIGURE 3.1 Possible set of indifference curves for an individual who values the environment more at higher levels of material consumption.

variety of preferences and ways of evaluating utility derived from environmental and material consumption.

B. Voting as a Social Choice Mechanism

Having specified how strongly individual people in society feel about the environment vs. material goods, we turn to the question of how to make social decisions. Suppose we have two "bundles" of material goods and environmental goods: $a' = ((x_1', \ldots, x_N', e')$ and $a'' = (x_1'', \ldots, x_N'', e'')$. For instance, a' may involve much more material goods and less environmental quality than a''. As is typical, material goods consumption may vary from person to person but everyone consumes the same amount of the environmental good. The question is, which should society choose—a' or a''?

This is the fundamental question of social choice. We know how an individual i feels about the preferability of a' and a''. But which does society prefer? What this amounts to is generating a set of societal preferences over different bundles, given individual preferences over those same bundles. A "social welfare function" analogous to a utility function for an individual might also be generated. The social welfare function would give the social utility—welfare—from a particular bundle. The desirability of two bundles could be compared by comparing the welfare each gives. The primary problem is not in constructing a social welfare function to represent group preferences, but in constructing social or group preferences out of individual preferences.

Most methods for making social choices from individual choices are forms of voting. Two choices are presented to individuals, each person ranks the alternatives, and a societal choice follows (depending on the way in which the votes are tallied). When society is choosing among more than two alternatives, voting methods are more complex but the basic concept of moving from individual rankings to a societal ranking is the same.

In the following sections we consider unanimity, unanimity with accompanying side-payments among individuals, majority rule, other types of voting between two alternatives, and voting among more than two alternatives. In all cases, we will be comparing two societal consumption bundles, $\mathbf{a}' = (x_1', \ldots, x_N', e')$ and $\mathbf{a}'' = (x_1'', \ldots, x_N'', e'')$. Each individual, i, has preferences in terms of $U_i(x_i', e')$ and $U_i(x_i'', e'')$ More complex preferences (e.g., altruism) are certainly admissible, though for clarity they are not included in the discussion.

1. Unanimity/Pareto Criterion. The starting point for evaluating the social preference for a' vs. a'' is to compare $U_i(x_i', e')$ with $U_i(x_i'', e'')$ for each individual i. If *all* individuals prefer one of these alternatives, we may conclude that society, too, should prefer that alternative. This is the Pareto criterion for social choice, named after the Italian economist Vilfredo Pareto (1848–1923). The Pareto criterion is a relatively noncontroversial way of concluding that one societal bundle is better than another, in the sense that if *everyone* prefers a' to a'', who could dispute that a' is not socially preferred to a''? We can summarize this in a definition:

DEFINITION *Start with two consumption bundles, $a' = (x', e')$ and $a'' = (x'', e'')$ and a group of people $i = 1, \ldots, N$ with utility functions, U_i, defined over the consumption bundles. Then for the group as a whole, a' is* Pareto preferred *to a'' if for every individual i, $U_i(a') \geq U_i(a'')$, and for at least one individual, $î$, $U_i(a') > U_i(a'')$.*

What this says is that for an allocation **a′** to be better than **a″**, everybody has to be at least as well-off with **a′** (compared to a″) and at least one person has to be better off with **a′**. Think of all members of society voting about whether they prefer **a′** to **a″**, casting a "yes," "no," or "I don't care" vote. All it takes is one "no" vote to conclude that **a′** is not Pareto preferred to **a″**. Thus leaving aside the individuals who are indifferent between **a′** and **a″** ("don't care"), the Pareto criterion is unanimity—everyone must prefer **a′** to **a″** for **a′** to be Pareto preferred to **a″**.

We can look at this graphically. Suppose we have a society consisting of two individuals, Anna and Brewster. Figure 3.2 shows possible utility combinations that are attainable for Anna and Brewster. Resources are limited, so only the shaded area is attainable. Think of an allocation as a bundle of goods for each of our two members of society. Each allocation will yield different utility levels, indicated by different points in Figure 3.2.

In Figure 3.2, compare points W and Z. Z is clearly Pareto preferred to W because the utilities of both Anna and Brewster are higher at Z than at W. The society of two will unanimously vote on Z being better than W. The same is true for allocations X and Y. Anna and Brewster will unanimously prefer Y to X; thus Y is Pareto preferred to X.

The strength of the Pareto criterion is that it is hard to fault. If Z is Pareto preferred to W, then *nobody* would rather have W than Z. In this case Z is unequivocally better socially than W, no matter what your social philosophy might be. The weakness of the Pareto criterion is that many allocations, in fact most allocations, cannot be compared. In comparing two arbitrary allocations, the most common situation is that some members of society will prefer one and some will prefer the other. In such a case, we can say nothing about which is Pareto preferred.[19]

This problem can be illustrated using Figure 3.2. Consider allocations X and Z. Although Z involves a little less utility for Anna and a lot more utility for Brewster, we cannot conclude which of these is better, on Pareto grounds. Similarly, we cannot compare B with Z. At allocation B, all of society's resources go to Brewster; poor Anna is left with nothing. Yet we cannot say that this is worse than Z, in which both have substantial utility.

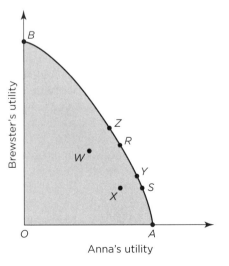

FIGURE 3.2 Utility possibilities for two-person society.

If the Pareto criterion is used to make societal decisions, then decisions may tend to be biased toward the status quo. If society is only willing to take steps that improve on the status quo for everyone, then implicitly, there is the assumption that the status quo is acceptable.[20]

2. Unanimity with Side Payments. One way around the problem of unanimity is to allow transfers of resources among individuals to increase the unanimity of opinion regarding alternatives. For instance, suppose 75% of the population prefers **a'** to **a"** and 25% of the population prefers **a"** to **a'**. Then according to the Pareto criterion, we cannot say anything about whether **a'** or **a"** is socially preferred. But suppose the 75% favoring **a** can pool enough resources (i.e., some of the market good) and transfer those resources to the 25% supporting **a"** to make **a'** more attractive to them. Presumably, if the resource transfer is large enough, unanimity can be reached on option **a'**.

The idea of transfers is a backdoor way of measuring the intensity of preferences, something that is missing in the unanimity criterion. Recall that with unanimity, individuals can only say which option they prefer, not how much more they prefer one option to another. On the other hand, if I prefer **a'** much more than **a"**, I would be willing to give up some of my market good if I were granted a' and still prefer it to **a"**. The market good I give up could be used to "encourage" individuals who prefer **a"** to switch their vote. That is the essence of this approach: **a'** is socially preferred to **a"** if the winners under **a'** can compensate the losers under **a'** so that everyone comes out ahead with **a'** (compared to **a"**).

The only missing variable from our previous definition of a societal consumption bundle is a set of transfers, $\mathbf{z} = (z_1,\ldots,z_N)$. Here a negative value of z_i means that individual i is giving up z_i units of the market good; similarly, a positive value indicates the individual is gaining. For z to be a valid set of transfers, the transfers must sum to zero: $\Sigma_i z_i = 0$. This simply means that what is given has to equal what is received, in aggregate.

We can now define what is known as a *potential Pareto improvement*:

DEFINITION *Assume an economy of* $i = 1,\ldots,N$ *individuals. Suppose we are comparing two bundles,* **a'** *and* **a"**. *If there exists a vector of transfers from individuals,* $\mathbf{z} = (z_1,\ldots,z_N)$, *which sum to zero, such that* $(\mathbf{a'},z) = (x_1' + z_1,\ldots,x_N' + z_N, e')$ *is Pareto preferred to* **a"**, *then* **a'** *is a* potential Pareto improvement *over* **a"**.

This definition is very similar to the Pareto criterion. The difference is that we are separating the tradable good from the other resources. When comparing **a'** and **a"**, we ask if there is some third allocation that shuffles around the x's that is clearly preferred to **a"**. If so, we forget about the amount of the shuffle and simply say that **a'** is a *potential* Pareto improvement over **a"**, potential because it is possible to find the right transfer to achieve a Pareto improvement.

This compensation is illustrated in Figure 3.3, which uses the same two-person society as Figure 3.2. Using the standard Pareto criterion, we cannot compare allocation X and Z. In moving from X to Z, Anna loses ΔA units of utility and Brewster gains ΔB units of utility. Although we cannot compare a unit of utility for Anna with a unit of utility for Brewster, the question is whether Brewster could transfer some resources that are not represented in this diagram to Anna to make up for any losses in Anna's utility. Brewster would not do quite as well having to transfer some resources to Anna. If we start at X,

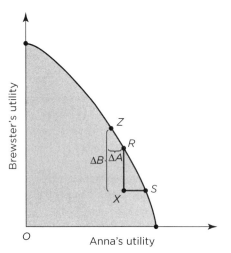

FIGURE 3.3 An illustration of potential Pareto improvement.

what utility levels would result if such "side-payments" could be made? Brewster would transfer only enough to keep Anna's utility from declining (enough to increase her utility by ΔA relative to Z, resulting in some sacrifice in Brewster's utility). If this is possible, then Z is a potential Pareto improvement on X. The point R in the figure is the utility pair that would most likely result if compensation occurs.

One problem with the potential Pareto improvement criterion is that it may not always be feasible or desirable to make such transfers. How can we identify exactly how much each individual would be willing to transfer or how much of a transfer it would take to make another individual switch from supporting **b** to supporting **a**? Furthermore, people may view such transfers as bad public policy—essentially buying support.

An alternative has been proposed, called the Kaldor–Hicks compensation principle or simply the *compensation principle*: If transfers could be made to achieve unanimity on a particular choice, then the choice is socially desirable, *even if the transfers are not actually made.* This principle is attributed to the two famous economists, Nicholas Kaldor (1939) and John Hicks (1940). As an example, when a dam is built, the government asks if those who gain from the building of the dam could compensate those who lose from the building of the dam. If the answer is yes, the dam is deemed a good idea, it is built, but no compensation is paid (except as required by law for those whose land is taken). The idea is that compensation is an issue of equity, a transfer of resources from some members of society to others, and that equity can be decoupled from determining whether the dam is or is not a good idea. This idea has met with a great deal of controversy.

3. Majority Rule. The basic problem with the Pareto criterion is the noncomparability of many bundles, which leads to incompleteness in the ordering of commodity bundles—it is not always possible to rank two social consumption bundles.[21] As mentioned above, the Pareto criterion is a form of unanimity: if no one opposes **a′** relative to **a″** then **a′** is Pareto preferred to **a″** (or perhaps there is indifference). Compensation solves some of this difficulty, but a bundle with compensation is really a different bundle than one without compensation.

Of course, a voting rule need not require unanimity. The typical voting mechanism is majority rule. In this case, if the majority prefers **a′** to **a″**, we would conclude that society prefers **a′** to **a″**, even though some individuals may strongly oppose **a′**, relative to **a″**. This suggests one of the problems of voting: it cannot take into account the intensity of preferences. If the majority is barely in favor of **a′** relative to **a″** but the minority is violently opposed to **a′**, it might be appropriate to question the social desirability of choosing **a′** over **a″** by simple majority rule.

4. Supermajorities. Voting can be a little more complex than simple majority voting on all issues.[22] It is common in many societies to have two tiers of rules or laws. There is the standard set of laws enacted by majority vote of the legislature (or some variant on that model). Then there is another set of rules or laws, often embodied in a constitution, that are much more difficult to change, requiring more than a 50% majority for a change. These rules or laws often are general statements of principles, such as the right of free speech, the right to legal due process related to criminal proceedings, or the rights of private property owners to be compensated for public taking of their property. These constitutional protections are often enacted based either on general principles of what is right and wrong or on a more pragmatic basis resulting from the expected outcomes of the protection over the very long term. Free speech may be considered morally correct. Protection of private property may have no moral basis but simply be seen as necessary for a well-functioning economy. Constitutional protection of private property is necessary to allow the government to credibly commit to providing property protection in the future—it must be difficult (though not impossible) to change the rules of the "game." Although these may be basic principles, they are decided by voting, although they often require more than majority rule.

The significance of these being constitutional protections is that they cannot be easily overridden, even if in particular cases they appear to generate bad outcomes. This is not to say that it is not possible to override these protections, only that it is difficult. In the environmental context, for example, it would be possible to prescribe a set of constitutional protections for endangered species that could be overridden but only with difficulty.

5. Voting with More Than Two Alternatives. Using voting to make choices becomes even more problematic when there are more than two choices. There is a large body of work describing the pitfalls, problems, and solutions to this problem—part of the field of Public Choice. Some of this work goes back to the 18th and 19th centuries. In fact, Charles Hodgson (the author of *Alice in Wonderland*, which was written under the pseudonym Lewis Carroll) has contributed to this scholarly literature.

One of the basic problems confronted by more than two alternatives is that voters no longer express their preference for one alternative or the other but have a more complex set of possible actions. Voters may rank alternatives, the process can involve multiple rounds of voting (such as in elections with runoffs), or voters divide alternatives into those of which they approve and those which they do not approve.

If each individual ranks the alternatives, according to his or her preferences, there are four common single-step ways of choosing a winner: (1) the choice ranked first by more than half the voters wins (termed majority rule); (2) the choice ranked first by the largest number of voters wins (termed plurality rule); (3) a more complex method in which the ranks associated with each social alternative as given by each individual are summed over the individuals and the winning alternative is the choice with the smallest sum (termed a Borda count);[23] and (4) a process whereby voters rank the alternatives, then the alternative ranked lowest by the most voters is eliminated, then rerank (a new vote is not necessary) and repeat until only one alternative remains, which is the winner (termed exhaustive voting).

A simple extension that involves multiple rounds of voting is to use majority voting on two alternatives at a time. The problem with this is that cycling may occur. If there are three choices, **a**, **b**, and **c**, then **a** may beat **b**, **b** may beat **c**, and **c** may beat **a**. So what is preferred? If there is an alternative that beats out all the others in pairwise majority voting, the alternative is termed the Condorcet winner, named after Condorcet first pointed out the problems with cycling in pairwise majority voting.[24]

C. Social Welfare Function

For individuals, we represent individual preference orderings with a utility function. By analogy, it is logical to represent social choices with a societal utility function. We call such a societal utility function a social welfare function:[25]

DEFINITION *Assume there are* $i = 1, \ldots, N$ *people in society, each with utility function* U_i, *defined over commodity bundles in the economy. Let* **a** *be a consumption bundle, indicating how much of each commodity is consumed by each individual; thus* $U_i(\mathbf{a})$ *is the utility individual i derives from* **a**. *Let W be a function that associates a single number with every distribution of utilities in society,* $W(U_1, U_2, \ldots, U_N)$. *If in comparing two consumption bundles,* **a′** *and* **a″**, $W[U_1(\mathbf{a'}), \ldots, U_N(\mathbf{a'})] > W[U_1(\mathbf{a''}), \ldots, U_N(\mathbf{a''})]$ *is equivalent to* **a′** *being socially preferred to* **a″** *then W is a Bergson-Samuelson social welfare function, or more simply a social welfare function.*

This way of writing social welfare is not the most general. We have implicitly assumed that it is the utility of different people that matters, not what is being consumed. This is not always the case. As a society, we might feel more concerned about members of society whose utility is low because of a lack of food rather than because of a lack of alcohol.

If a social welfare function exists to represent social preferences, we can draw social indifference curves, in much the same way as we draw individual indifference curves. Figure 3.4 shows a set of social indifference curves for the utility levels of Anna and Brewster. One line represents all of the utility combinations that yields social welfare W_0. The other line is the combination of utilities that yields social welfare $W_1 > W_0$. We see that point Y is Pareto preferred to point X and also yields a higher level of social welfare. Point Z is not Pareto preferred to point X but is nevertheless on a higher social indifference curve; thus Z is socially preferred to X.

There are a number of examples of social welfare functions:

$$\text{Benthamite } W(U_1, \ldots, U_N) = \Sigma_i \, \theta_i U_i, \, \theta_i \geq 0 \tag{3.1}$$

$$\text{Egalitarian } W(U_1, \ldots, U_N) = \Sigma_i U_i - \lambda \, \Sigma_i [U_i - \min_i (U_i)] \tag{3.2}$$

$$\text{Rawlsian } W(U_1, \ldots, U_N) = \min_i (U_i) \tag{3.3}$$

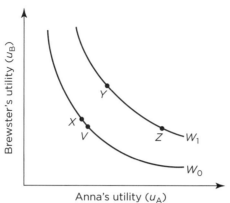

FIGURE 3.4 Social indifference curves.

The first of these, often called utilitarian, can be of different forms. All the weights (θ_j) may be equal or different people's utility can be weighted differently, most commonly on the basis of income.[26] With the Egalitarian representation, society cares about the total amount of utility as well as the distribution of utility. The second term in Eq. (3.2) is a measure of inequality, specifically the extent to which there is a divergence between the well-being of the worst-off member of society and the other members of society. And the λ parameter reflects the weight placed on this inequality term relative to individual utility. The Rawlsian welfare function, named after the Harvard philosopher, John Rawls, states that a society is only as strong as its weakest member. We see that these different welfare functions, all based on individual utility, can lead to very different views on what society considers desirable.

D. Impossibility of Perfect Choice Mechanism

Intuition suggests that there must be some best way of making social choices. It would seem logical that confronted with a set of different options, such as different levels of environmental protection, there must be a best way of making a societal choice—a best social choice mechanism (i.e., a way of turning individual values into a social choice).

Over a half century ago, Kenneth Arrow set out to find such a best choice mechanism. First, he defined the characteristics he thought a good social choice mechanism should have, assuming all we know is individual preferences (rankings) over social outcomes. Arrow came up with six basic requirements (axioms) for a social choice mechanism.[27]

A1: *Completeness.* We should be able to compare all social alternatives.
A2: *Unanimity.* If everyone in society prefers **a** to **b**, then society should prefer **a** to **b**.
A3: *Nondictatorship.* No one should always get their way, i.e., no one's preferences should be exactly the same as society's.
A4: *Universality.* Any possible individual rankings of alternatives is permissible.
A5: *Transitivity.* If **a** is socially preferred to **b** and **b** is socially preferred to **c** then **a** should be socially preferred to **c**.
A6: *Independence of Irrelevant Alternatives.* Society's choice between alternatives **a** and **b** should depend only on how individuals rank **a** and **b**, without regard to other alternatives.

The first four axioms are straightforward (at least upon reflection) and noncontroversial. For instance, the first axiom says that the mechanism should always work—we should always be able to compare two alternatives and say which is best (or that we are indifferent between them). Recall this was one of the problems with the Pareto criterion—often we could say nothing about two alternatives. The second axiom is probably the simplest and most obvious—if everyone likes one choice better than another, then society should too. The third axiom eliminates an obvious but unsatisfactory solution to Arrow's problem—declare somebody a dictator.

The fourth axiom, universality, is also straightforward. It simply says that individuals are free to have any sort of preferences that they want and we should still be able to come up with a way of generating a societal preference. But it turns out that some preferences are easier to aggregate than others. Restricting the possible preferences is one way of solving the problem of coming up with a way of making societal choices.[28]

The fifth axiom, transitivity, is intuitive and appealing. All it means is that if I like oranges better than bananas and bananas better than apples, I should like oranges better than apples. It is a basic requirement we assume about *individual* preferences when developing the theory of utility. But transitivity is violated by many common choice mechanisms, such as pairwise majority voting (these are explored in the problems at the end of the chapter).

The sixth axiom is quite a bit more subtle. Basically, it say that if society is choosing between A and B, then throwing in a clearly inferior choice (say C), should not affect the choice between A and B. For example, suppose we have a 10 candidates for mayor of a town. Everyone in town writes down in order their preferences: which candidate is their first choice, second choice, and so on. Then there is some social choice mechanism which chooses a winner. Now consider what happens if one of the candidates dies. Unless that candidate would have been the winner, the fact that the candidate dies should not change who wins, at least if the selection mechanism is reasonable.[29] That is an illustration of why independence of irrelevant alternatives may be a reasonable characteristic of a social choice mechanism.

But back to the real world. In the 2000 U.S. presidential election, the practical choice was between George W. Bush and Albert Gore. Polls suggested that Al Gore would win a two-way race. However, putting a third alternative on the ballot—Ralph Nader—caused the complex tiered way of electing a president in the United States to tilt to George Bush. This example suggests that the method of electing a president in the United States violates axiom A6. As another example, if you are choosing which you prefer, chocolate or strawberry ice cream, then your choice should not be influenced by the presence or nonpresence of chewing gum–flavored ice cream. But this is exactly the problem with some choice mechanisms, such as plurality voting or the Borda count.

Arrow (1951) proved the following:

Arrow's Impossibility Theorem. There is no rule satisfying A1–6 for converting individual preferences into a social preference ordering.

This is a very fundamental result. It is troubling in that it implies that we should forget about having a nice neat theory of social decision making, akin to what we have in economics for individual decision making. A great deal of effort has been expended over the last half century in trying to modify these axioms so that it becomes possible to generate a social choice mechanism. And there are some relaxations that yield specific choice mechanisms. For instance, if axiom A4 is weakened to include only a certain type of "well-behaved" preferences, then majority voting emerges as a choice mechanism satisfying the other axioms.[30]

The bottom line here is that there is no one clear unambiguous way of making social decisions. Yet social decisions must be made and are made every day. From a practical point of view, in making real social choices, the Pareto criterion or the compensation principle is often used. Arrow's impossibility theorem serves the purpose of alerting us to the fact that there may be other ways of making normative choices. But there is no holy grail lurking out there to resolve this issue of making social choices.

IV. CRITICISM OF THE UTILITARIAN PERSPECTIVE

Throughout the discussion in the previous section we assumed that basic individual values could be represented by utility functions and that we could then make social decisions using these utility functions along with assorted social choice mechanisms such as majority rule, supermajority voting, or the Pareto criterion. As might be expected, there are some vocal critics of this approach to making social decisions regarding the environment. This literature is quite large; we raise only a few points here.

One criticism is based on the assumption that we all have utility functions that represent our preferences and that these utility functions are immutable. Critics point out that people change their opinions over time; advertising has the express goal of doing just that. Consequently, if the environment is not highly valued by an individual, information and education programs can be used to increase the importance of the environment to that individual. However, if it is so easy to change someone's preferences, what utility function (if any) should be used to make public policy?[31]

Another criticism is that not all affected individuals are included in many voting processes. For instance, the as-yet unborn do not vote, but are affected by actions that impact long-term environmental quality. If a local matter is put to the vote, future citizens, who may move to the locale at a later date, will be excluded (rightly or wrongly) from voting.

A third criticism of the utilitarian approach is articulated by Sagoff (1994). He questions whether public policy should be based on individual preferences rather than a concept of what is right. He says our personal desires are often dominated by what we believe is morally right or feel is our obligation to others.

A related issue, also raised by Sagoff (1994), is that when voting we often think differently than when making private decisions. When voting we may consciously or subconsciously put ourselves in the role of a public policy maker, rather than of an individual expressing individual preferences.

V. THREE EXAMPLES REVISITED

Earlier in this chapter we presented three examples of environmental decision-making problems: air pollution in Santiago, protecting the California gnatcatcher, and the Three Gorges dam. Recall that a choice must not only include the environmental outcome, but also the means for paying for that outcome. We now return to each of these questions and examine how the outcome might differ depending on the social choice mechanism. We will also consider how the outcome might differ depending on the composition of society (e.g., if society is composed primarily of serious biocentrists).[32]

A. Air Pollution in Santiago

The issue is how much of a reduction in air pollution to pursue with polluters bearing the cost and possibly passing that cost on to customers (unless the polluters are individuals, perhaps polluting from driving cars). Other ways of bearing the cost are possible but will be ignored here.

Clearly on the basis of the Pareto criterion, the *status quo* will persist. It is unlikely that any amount of pollution control, however modest, will be supported by 100% of the population of Santiago. The poorest members of the population may be unwilling or unable to bear the increased transportation costs (due to pollution control) necessary to increase air quality. Thus under this criterion, no pollution control will be pursued.

With compensation, however, the outcome may be very different. If the wealthy feel strongly about cleaning up pollution, they can probably muster significant resources to make transfers to the rest of the population to make pollution control unanimously attractive. The compensation principle would indicate that pollution control should be pursued, even though decreased pollution levels and increased transportation costs may leave many worse off.

What about majority rule voting? The outcome depends on the composition of the population. A population with a large number of poor people may not support significant pollution reduction if they have to pay more for vital services such as transportation. In these circumstances, only modest pollution reduction is likely to be supported by a majority. If, on the other hand, the population is better off or feels deeply committed to a clean environment, more substantial controls will be supported.

If a supermajority is needed to make a social decision (such as a two-thirds majority), the pollution controls adopted will likely be more modest than under simple majority rule.

The point is that different outcomes will result from a different set of preferences on the part of the population as well as different social choice mechanisms. A corollary is that if analysis of an environmental problem concludes that only a modest level of pollution control is justified, "blame" can be placed either on the method of analysis (the social choice rule) or on the underlying preferences of the population. If many people would rather have a slightly larger TV than cleaner air, most social choice mechanisms will result in modest pollution control (and bigger TVs).

B. The California Gnatcatcher

The issue is protecting the habitat of the endangered California gnatcatcher (a bird), which nests in highly valued coastal land in Southern California. Suppose the proposal under consideration is for the government to buy all coastal land and set it aside for habitat protection. Consider two possibilities for covering this substantial cost:

- Option A: a percentage income tax surcharge on the wealthiest 10% of the population
- Option B: a uniform per-person-tax applied to all members of the population

Once again, the Pareto criterion is not much help. Neither option is likely to be supported by 100% of the population; thus the measure will fail. If, however, the population consists of committed biocentrists, even the richest 10% might agree that protection is a good idea. Thus option A would be favored. It is unlikely that option B would be unanimously favored because the poorest members of the population would likely find the head-tax onerous.

With compensation the two options become identical, since resources will move from those supporting habitat preservation to those opposing it. But what about the future generations of Southern California residents? They may be more than willing to compensate for setting aside habitat. However, their preferences are not known and methods are imperfect for transferring resources from the future to the present.

What about majority rule? Clearly option A would pass a majority rule test. For 90% of the population the proposal has no cost. Option B might or might not be supported by a majority, depending on how strongly the population feels about protecting the gnatcatcher. A population of biocentrists could undoubtedly muster a majority in support of option B.

But who should be voting on a proposal such as this? In the context of species preservation in Southern California, clearly the current population of Southern California is not the complete set of affected parties. Future residents of Southern California as well as people who do not currently reside in the area also have a stake in whether a species becomes extinct. Exactly who should vote is not an easy question to answer.

Consequently, we see that even a simple issue of protecting a species can be socially desirable or undesirable, depending on subtle changes in preferences as well as changes in the social choice mechanism. We cannot unequivocally conclude that such protection is socially worthwhile.

C. Three Gorges Dam

The issue is whether to flood a canyon, destroying it, for all practical purposes, for all time.[33] This is very much a problem of trading off net benefits in the present (electricity and flood control less dam costs) with costs in the future (environmental disamenities). The dam will generate electricity and provide flood control for the coming decades. To the extent this promotes Chinese economic development, future generations will be somewhat better off. However, eventually, the dam will fill with silt and from that point on provide little benefit. The loss of the river will be for all time.

Based on an intertemporal Pareto criterion, the dam should not be built. If the present generation as well as future generations are voting, unanimity will not be reached and unanimity is required to pass the Pareto test.

The compensation principle is a little more ambiguous. First, it is not possible for future generations to transfer resources to the present to compensate the present generation for not building the dam. Even if they could, it is not clear whether the benefits to the current generation would be greater or less than the compensation future generations would be willing to pay. It is likely that future generations of Chinese will be much more wealthy than the current generation and thus be able to pay considerable compensation to keep the Yangtze undammed.

What about majority rule? Clearly if we include all future generations in our list of eligible voters, the majority will vote against the dam.

Once again, we see that a complex environmental policy question will be resolved in different ways, depending on what type of social choice mechanism is adopted.

SUMMARY

1. General principles of the importance of the environment to human life should be distinguished from principles that can be used to make decisions about specific projects or environmental regulations. The former general principles are often difficult to use to make specific decisions.

2. Four basic philosophies are considered in this chapter: biocentrism, precautionary principle, sustainability, and anthropocentrism. Biocentrism views humans as just another species with no special claim on the world's resources. Anthropocentrism believes the environment exists only to serve people's material needs. The term sustainability suffers from ambiguity but generally prohibits actions that, if continued indefinitely, will lead to the eventual destruction of humans and the environment. The precautionary principle involves not letting uncertainty stand in the way of making a decision regarding environmental protection.

3. The basic question presented in this chapter is how to make group environmental decisions (i.e., decisions for society), starting from a disparate set of individual preferences regarding the environment. We summarize all the individual perspectives using individual utility functions, an approach that is quite general though not without detractors. We then consider several social choice mechanisms: the Pareto criterion, the compensation principle, majority-rule voting, and supermajority voting. Arrow's impossibility theorem suggests there is no perfect way of making social choices.

4. In choosing between two social alternatives, **a** and **b**, the Pareto criterion allows any member of society to veto a social choice. For **a** to be socially preferred to **b**, everyone must like **a** as well as **b** and at least one person must strictly prefer **a** to **b**. The main problem with the Pareto criterion is that it is an incomplete ordering—not all pairs of allocations can be compared using the Pareto criterion.

5. In choosing between two social alternatives, **a** and **b**, **a** is a potential Pareto improvement over **b** if resource transfers among members of society can make **a** Pareto preferred to **b**. In other words, **a** is a potential Pareto improvement over **b**, if the winners can compensate the losers.

6. The compensation principle says that if **a** is a potential Pareto improvement over **b**, then **a** is also socially preferred to **b**, even if no compensation occurs.

7. Voting is a common way of making social choices, particularly majority rule. In some cases principles or minorities are protected by more fundamental (constitutional) laws that require a supermajority to pass.

8. A social welfare function is a function that converts utility levels for all members of society into a number in such a way that the welfare function gives higher values for distributions of utility that are more socially desirable, and visa versa.

9. Arrow's impossibility theorem states that there is no perfect way of making social choices, given a set of "reasonable" assumptions. Some relaxation of these

assumptions is necessary for there to exist ways of making social choices, such as majority voting.

10. The utility function-based approach to social decision making is not without its detractors. Criticisms include the malleability of preferences and the incompleteness of decision making that involves long time frames, since future generations are not represented.

PROBLEMS

1. For each of the following social choice methods, which of Arrow's axioms (A1–6) are violated, and why:

   a. the Pareto criterion

   b. plurality-rule voting (of several choices, the one with the most votes wins)

   c. majority-rule voting

   d. pulling a choice out of a hat (random)

2. Assume a city of 1,000,000 people, 60% of whom are willing to pay $1 maximum (each) to clean up pollution. The rest of the population is wealthier and is willing to pay $100 each to clean up pollution. Pollution clean-up costs $2,000,000. It has been proposed that each person be taxed equally to pay for the pollution clean-up. Will that pass a majority-rule vote? Is it desirable from the point of view of the Pareto criterion? Is it a good idea, using the compensation principle? Which social choice mechanism do you think is best on intuitive grounds, and why?

3. Suppose there are three individuals, Boris, Maggie, and William. They are using majority rule to decide among themselves whether to go hiking in the wilderness this weekend (H), kayaking in the river (K), or birdwatching, looking for rare Dodos (D). Boris likes hiking best and Dodo watching worst; Maggie likes Dodos best and Kayaking worst; William likes kayaking best and hiking worst. Unfortunately, they must all do the same activity (for insurance reasons). They vote on alternatives pairwise (e.g., H vs. K; then the winner against D, etc.). Which choice will emerge as the group's choice? Can you help them with their choice?

4. In Figure 3.2, using the Pareto criterion, which of the labeled points are socially preferred to W?

5. Suppose we have a small inhabited island with three residents and a volcano that generates air pollution. Two people live upwind of the volcano and one person lives downwind. For $21,000 we can clean up the volcano with a patented "smoke guzzler." The two upwind people would pay $1000 each to get rid of the smoke whereas the downwind person would be willing to pay $15,000. Consider two plans to finance the "smoke guzzler." Plan A calls for a head-tax of $7000. Plan B calls for the affected party (the downwind person) to pay $21,000 and everyone else nothing. Compare each plan to the status quo and indicate society's choice using (a) the Pareto criterion; (b) majority rule; (c) potential Pareto improvement.

6. Suppose you have a society of n identical individuals and the environment. Each individual likes his or her material possessions as well as access to parks and wilderness areas. In fact, the utility function of each individual is $U(x,H) = x + H - 1/x - 1/H$,

where x is consumption goods and H is environmental health. H attains its highest level when it is pristine: $H = 100$. Consumption of goods degrades the environment but the environment has some ability to heal itself. In fact, the environment has health $H_t = H_{t-1} + g (100 - H_{t-1}) - n x$, where H_t is today's H and H_{t-1} is yesterday's H. The environment's ability to cleanse itself, g, is fixed.

a. Simply focusing on the utility function (ignoring the evolution of H), discuss the extent to which the utility function is consistent with (a) biocentrism or (b) anthropocentrism.

b. Suppose we start at $H = 100$. Assume $g = 0.1$ and $n = 1$. Plot how H would evolve for $x = 0.01, 0.1$ and 1.

c. Repeat part (a) except this time plot U instead of H. Feel free to try other values of x. Can you reach any conclusions about the level of consumption that maximizes utility?

*7. Society consists of two individuals, Tucker and Finch; there are two goods, food and water sport (recreation); and there are three social choices, A, B, and C, involving different amounts of the two goods for Tucker and Finch:[34]

Social Choices	Tucker		Finch	
	Food	Sport	Food	Sport
A	2.0	1.0	2.0	1.0
B	1.7	1.3	1.8	1.1
C	1.0	2.0	1.0	2.0

Tucker's preferences are a bit different than Finch's. Let (2.0, 1.0) represent an bundle of food (first argument) and sport (second argument). Tucker likes the following bundles, in order from best to worst: (2.1, 1.0) ▶ (1.0, 2.0) ▶ (2.4, 0.7) ▶ (1.7, 1.3) ▶ (2.0, 1.0). Furthermore, all bundles containing less than 0.9 units of sport are inferior to (1.0, 2.0). For Finch, the bundles, from best to worst, are (1.4, 1.4) ▶ (1.0, 2.0) ▶ (1.6, 1.3) ▶ (1.8, 1.1) ▶ (2.0, 1.0). For Finch, all bundles with less than 1.2 units of sport are inferior to (1.0, 2.0).

a. In a graph with food on the horizontal axis and sport on the vertical axis, draw an indifference curve for Finch and one for Tucker, through the point (1.0, 2.0). Apply the specific bundles for which we know rankings. Do individual preferences appear to be problematic?

b. Between social choices A and B, which does our two-person society prefer? Why?

c. Is there a way to shuffle around the total amount of food and sport in choice A (between Tucker and Finch) so that your answer to (b) is reversed?

d. Why does this result suggest the compensation principle is flawed? That is, to be meaningful, winners actually have to compensate losers for the social choice judgment to be valid.

8. The Borda Count is a common way of making a choice among more than two alternatives. As defined in the text, each member of society assigns a rank to the social

alternatives (1,2,…), with 1 corresponding to first choice, and so on. The ranks each alternative gets are summed over all the individuals. The alternative with the lowest sum wins; the second choice has the second-lowest sum, and so forth. Set up an example to show that the Borda Count violates the independence of irrelevant alternatives. *Hint:* Use a three-person society with three alternatives and rank them using a Borda Count. Then introduce a fourth alternative.

9. Consider the case of instant runoff voting when three or more social choices are involved. Each voter has one vote and votes for his or her favorite option. The option with the least votes is eliminated, and the process continues until there are two choices and the one with the majority wins. Suppose we have five voters and three societal alternatives (A, B, C). Two of the voters rank the alternatives, from first choice to last choice, (A,B,C); two of the voters rank them (C,B,A); one voter ranks them (B,A,C). Show that the instant runoff method violates the independence of irrelevant alternatives axiom (A6).

10. With three alternatives (A, B, C) in a society of three people (1,2,3), find a ranking of the alternatives for each person such that majority voting, two alternatives at a time, results in A beating B, B beating C, and C beating A. What does this show about pairwise majority voting?

NOTES

1. Refer to World Resources Institute (1998, 2008) and O'Ryan (1996).
2. See many articles in the popular press, such as Stevens (1996).
3. This is reminiscent of the controversies regarding dam development in the western United States (Reisner, 1986).
4. Des Jardins (1997) provides a particularly accessible survey of environmental ethics.
5. Albert Schweitzer and Paul Taylor have articulated the biocentrist philosophy (Des Jardins, 1997).
6. Nash (1989) utilizes a broader definition of anthropocentrism encompassing material and spiritual gratification from the environment. He distinguishes between biocentrism and anthropocentrism on the basis of the *rationale* for placing value on the environment. Biocentrics value the environment because that is what is morally right; anthropocentrics value the environment because it makes them feel good to protect the environment. Since these two perspectives are observationally equivalent in empirical analysis, we use the more restrictive definition of anthropocentrism to include only material gain from the environment.
7. Nash (1989) distinguishes utilitarianism from anthropocentrism by noting that early utilitarians such as Jeremy Bentham included the well-being of nonhuman animals in their calculations of the utilitarian well-being of society. Nonhumans obviously do not count to an anthropocentric except to the extent that animals give service or pleasure to humans.
8. For more on the MTBE issue, see Fernandez and Keller (2000).
9. The safe minimum standard is attributed to S. V. Ciracy-Wantrup (see Bishop, 1978).
10. Refer to UN document A/CONF.151/26 (Vol. I), available on the web. The Rio Declaration was a set of principles that emerged from the 1992 U.N. Conference on Environment and Development (UNCED), also known as the Earth Summit.
11. Refer to the book edited by O'Riordan and Cameron (1994). One of the few economic analyses of the precautionary principle is by Gollier et al. (2000).
12. Toman (1994) makes this point and goes on to provide a basis for understanding sustainability within the economic paradigm.

13. Slade (1982) argues that over the life cycle of exploitation of an exhaustible resource, technological change first dominates depletion, resulting in a price decline. But later in the life cycle, depletion dominates. Thus price eventually turns up. In an empirical analysis of many resources, she argues that the turnaround point has been reached for a number of resources.

14. See Tierney (1990) for a description of this bet. The root of Simon's optimistic view of the future was his belief in continued rapid technological advance, as has occurred in the past.

15. The term natural environment is used to encompass things such as natural parks, wilderness areas, and wetlands—regions that we value for being in their natural state. In the fifty years since the Barnett and Morse work, there have been a number of follow-up studies, two of which were published by Resources for the Future (Smith, 1979; Simpson et al., 2005).

16. Levin et al. (1998) discuss sustainability and resilience.

17. Refer to Kolstad and Wolak (2008) for more detail on this incident in the RECLAIM market.

18. Generally, we would expect individual i to care about x_i not the entire x. However, there is no loss in making U_i a function of x.

19. Mathematically, the problem with the Pareto criterion is that it is an incomplete ordering: many pairs of allocations cannot be ordered (one better than the other).

20. Starrett (1988) argues that the Pareto criterion is not as value free as many economists assume.

21. A complete ordering means that all pairs of bundles can be related to one another. In other words, for any two bundles, a and b, a complete ordering allows you to conclude that one of the following three alternatives is true: a is preferred to b, b is preferred to a, or a is equivalent to b. If there are any bundles for which you cannot reach one of these three conclusions, then it is an incomplete ordering.

22. Mueller (2003) lists at least eight voting alternatives to majority rule.

23. To be more precise about the Borda count, let there be M social alternatives and let r_{im} be the rank (an integer between 1 and M inclusive, with 1 corresponding to a top choice) given to alternative m by individual i. Then the alternative for which $\Sigma_i r_{im}$ is the lowest is the winner.

24. These approaches are described in more detail in Chapter 10 of Hindriks and Myles (2006) and in Mueller (2003).

25. The alert reader will remark that there is no one utility function that represents an individual's preferences, but a family of utility functions, any one of which works when examining individual choice. The problem is, if we are comparing members of society, we need more than just a family of utility functions; we need a single utility function to represent a consumer's preferences. This is the distinction between ordinal utility (the utility function is useful only for ordering different bundles) and cardinal utility (the magnitude of the utility function has meaning). In general, cardinal utility is needed to make a social welfare function meaningful. This is a more restrictive assumption that we do not usually have to make when examining only individual choice. The welfare function defined here is due to Bergson (1938) and Samuelson (1947).

26. In applications, we are usually concerned with changes in social welfare. If x is the amount of some good and we assume there is a social welfare function, then the change in welfare from a small change in x can be written as $dW/dx = \Sigma_i \beta_i (\partial u_i/\partial x)/(\partial u_i/\partial y_i)$ where y_i is income of individual i and $\beta_i = (\partial W/\partial u_i) (\partial u_i/\partial y_i)$. The β_i can be thought of as welfare weights, related to individual i's income. Thus in evaluating the change in welfare from a change in x, we first calculate the income equivalence of this change in x for each member of society and then sum these income changes over the population, weighting each element by β_i. If income differences are unimportant, then all β_i will be equal.

27. The Arrow impossibility theorem is presented in many advanced texts. See, for example, Luenberger (1995) and Mueller (2003). Geanakoplos (2005) provides a concise statement of the theorem and simple proofs. It is also possible to replace axioms A2 and A4 with a single axiom of Pareto optimality.

28. One restriction in the context of single-issue choices is that of "single-peaked" preferences. Each person has a first choice, and the further one is from the first choice, the less desirable it is. Think of restaurants, listed in order of increasing price. Assume I have a favorite. If my utility of a restaurant meal declines as I get further away from my first choice, I have single-peaked preferences. If, on the other hand, my first choice is an expensive restaurant (where the food is great, even thought I pay a lot) but my second choice is a cheap restaurant (that serves decent food at a very low price), then my preferences are not single-peaked. Refer to Mueller (2003).

29. This example is drawn from Arrow (1963).

30. There is a voluminous literature on these issues of "social choice." See Broadway and Wildasin (1984) for an accessible treatment of some of these issues.

31. Recently, researchers in behavioral economics have turned to the question of how one does cost–benefit analysis when preferences are changeable. See Bernheim and Rangel (2009) for a technical discussion of this issue.

32. Another example is provided by Kneese and Schulze (1985), who discuss the problem of nuclear waste disposal from several different ethical and economic perspectives. d'Arge et al. (1982) examine climate change policy from a utilitarian, egalitarian, elitist, and Paretian perspective, with and without the possibility of compensating the future.

33. A classic intertemporal analysis of the advisability of building a dam was done for the Hell's Canyon dam on the Snake River in Idaho in the United States (Krutilla and Fisher, 1985).

34. This problem is adapted from Arrow (1963).

4

WELFARE AND MARKETS

IN THE LAST CHAPTER WE TOOK A FUNDAMENTAL LOOK AT HOW WE MAKE SOCIAL DECISIONS based on individual preferences, though at a fairly abstract level. We now turn to a more detailed examination of this issue, within the context of the economics paradigm. One of the basic normative issues in economics is for specific goods: how much should be produced and who should produce and consume—the production and allocation decisions. This is also an important issue in environmental economics. How much pollution should be produced? Although it is counterintuitive to some, a certain amount of pollution is necessary, because the activities that accompany much pollution are socially beneficial. *Totally* eliminating all automobile pollution immediately would result in a loss for society greater than the gain obtained from cleaner air. Even more obvious is that too much pollution is undesirable. Having too much or too little pollution is viewed by economists as "inefficient."

Having determined how much pollution is desirable ("efficient"), we must determine how to achieve that desirable level of pollution. For instance, suppose we determine that ozone levels in a metropolitan area should be half what they currently are; we must then determine which polluters should reduce pollution and by how much. Each polluter could reduce emissions by 50%; this would probably achieve the overall pollution goal. Alternatively, those polluters for which pollution control is easy could reduce pollution more than those polluters for which pollution control is difficult. This would not affect the overall level of pollution but would reduce the costs of achieving it. Obtaining the right amount of pollution, but doing it in a way that costs more than necessary, is also viewed by economists as "inefficient."

These are two concepts of efficiency: efficiency in obtaining the right overall amount of pollution control and efficiency in allocating pollution control responsibility to specific polluters. In this chapter we will develop both of these concepts. We first define efficiency, using the concept of Pareto optimality defined in the previous chapter. We then show the relationship between efficiency and a market equilibrium: a competitive market equilibrium is generally efficient. We also show that market failures, including pollution, can result in inefficiencies in a market equilibrium that should be corrected by government intervention.[1] We note that much of the material in this chapter is covered in most intermediate microeconomics texts, though not in a pollution context. For that reason, the treatment here is concise.[2]

I. WHAT IS EFFICIENCY?

Many people in developed economies have heard the pronouncement that competition is desirable (at least up to a point) and that competition in an economy is somehow good for the country. There are really two reasons why competition may be desirable. One is that competition helps a market economy work smoothly. Competition usually makes an economy more agile and responsive in a changing world. Strong incentives are provided to firms and individuals as they make decisions.

The second reason competition may be desirable is somewhat more controversial. The issue is whether the outcome achieved by competition in a market economy (including the division of the "pie") is "best" for society. It is important to be somewhat cautious in jumping to such a conclusion, keeping separate the criteria for determining whether an economic allocation (production and distribution) is socially desirable from the conditions associated with a competitive market. Whether competitive markets result in the best social outcome depends on how social welfare is defined.

In the previous chapter we examined different ways of deciding what is socially "best." For our definition of best, we adopt the weakest criterion, that of Pareto. The Pareto criterion is an important one in economics. Despite the fact that it is not useful in comparing many social allocations, it is important for the notion of efficiency. To illustrate this, we return to the two-person economy developed in Chapter 3. Figure 4.1 shows attainable utility levels for the two members of our economy, Anna and Brewster. Note that for every allocation that is *inside* the feasible set *ABO,* it is possible to find a Pareto preferred allocation (a *Pareto improvement*). Basically, for any *interior* allocation, any allocation to the upper right (i.e., in the direction that improves both Anna's and Brewster's utility) is a Pareto improvement. Note in the figure that for *X,* all allocations in the shaded region are Pareto preferred to *X* (i.e., Pareto improvements over *X*). This is because all allocations in that region give both Anna and Brewster just as much utility as at *X,* and for at least one of them, more utility. What allocations cannot be improved?

FIGURE 4.1 Pareto frontier and efficiency.

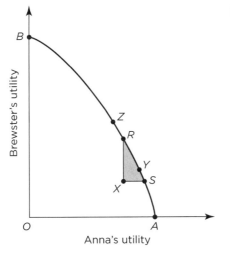

All allocations leading to utility on the curved line *AB* are as good as possible, in a Pareto sense. This leads to the notion of Pareto frontier.

DEFINITION *The* Pareto frontier *consists of all allocations for which there are no allocations that are Pareto preferred. Alternatively, the Pareto frontier consists of all allocations that cannot be improved in the Pareto sense.*

In other words, if *Z* is on the Pareto frontier, it is not possible to find another allocation that is preferred to *Z*. This is our notion of economic efficiency. It is also referred to as *Pareto optimality.*

DEFINITION *An allocation is* efficient, *or* Pareto optimal, *if it lies on the Pareto frontier; an allocation is* inefficient *if it is not on the Pareto frontier.*

This is an important concept that we will return to time and again. An allocation is inefficient if it is interior to the Pareto frontier. The obvious reason inefficiency is undesirable is that resources are "left on the table." In other words, it would be possible to move to an allocation where everybody does better and has more. Thus in Figure 4.1, *X* is inefficient because any allocation in the shaded region is a Pareto improvement over *X*. Nobody would choose *X* over these alternative allocations.

This seems like a straightforward concept. Where are the problems, then? The problem is that we cannot compare different allocations that lie along the Pareto frontier. In Figure 4.1, the curved line *AB* is the Pareto frontier. We cannot say anything about the relative desirability of any points along the frontier. Points *A* and *B* have all of the utility going to one of the two individuals (which is not too equitable). We cannot say whether *A* or *B* is more or less socially desirable than an allocation such as *Z*.

This is the basic source of controversy when economists call for actions that promote efficiency. Suppose society is at point *X* in Figure 4.1. Economists might promote a move to *S* because it is a Pareto improvement. However, some might view Anna as undeserving and might prefer *Y* or *R* or even *Z*, where the pie is divided a little more evenly. (Think of Anna as a successful entrepreneur making billions of euros a year.) A movement to *S* seems counterproductive. The bottom line is that efficiency may not be the only goal in dividing the social pie.

What would be real-world examples of inefficiency? An obvious one was mentioned in the introduction to this chapter. If polluters are being regulated in such a way that their marginal cost of pollution control (for a specific pollutant) vary widely, then there is an opportunity for a Pareto improvement: firms with high control costs pay firms with low control costs to undertake more responsibility for pollution reductions. The overall level of pollution remains the same but all firms spend less on pollution control—a Pareto improvement.

As another example, consider the problem of an automobile paint shop located next door to a coal-fired power plant. The paint shop needs a clean environment to obtain the best finish on its cars. The power plant is independent of the paint shop and sees no financial reason to control its pollution—it blames the paint shop for locating next door. A Pareto improvement could be for the paint shop to pay the power plant to clean up its emissions, increasing the profitability of the paint shop (even after paying the power plant) without decreasing the profitability of the power plant.

A final example involves carbon dioxide emissions leading to climate change. If the world would be a better place with significantly reduced emissions of greenhouse gases (a generally accepted conclusion of the economic and natural science communities), then there must be a way of controlling emissions (and paying for the control) so that everyone is better off—a Pareto improvement.

In all three of these examples, we were able to construct an alternative to the original situation that was a Pareto improvement—nobody is worse off and someone is better off. Because of this, the original situation is *inefficient*. This does not necessarily mean that the Pareto improvement always results in efficiency: that would be the case only if it is not possible to make a further Pareto improvement.

Note also that the distinction between a *Pareto improvement* and a *potential Pareto improvement* is blurred (as discussed in the previous chapter). When the resource transfer (money) is packaged together with the change in the physical quantity (pollution), then the two terms can be used interchangeably.

II. EFFICIENCY AND COMPETITIVE MARKETS

Efficiency is one of the most important words in the vocabulary of an economist. To an economist, efficiency means Pareto optimality; inefficiency means a lack of Pareto optimality. If an economy is operating on the Pareto frontier, it is efficient; if not, it is inefficient. Increasing the efficiency of an economy means moving closer to the Pareto frontier. Throughout this book we will use Pareto optimality and efficiency synonymously.

Typically, there are two types of inefficiencies that exist in an economy: inefficiencies in exchange and inefficiencies in production. Inefficiency in exchange means that resources could be moved around among individuals without making anyone worse off. For instance, take the case of municipal solid waste from a large city. Suppose a law prohibits the transport of wastes across state or regional boundaries.[3] This means that wastes must be disposed of locally, possibly in an area of high population density. There might be a rural region that would be willing to take the wastes for an appropriate fee (and at lower disposal costs), making everyone better off. Efficiency would be promoted by removing such a restriction on waste shipments.

The other type of inefficiency occurs in production. For instance, suppose an environmental regulation calls for the use of a "scrubber" on the smoke generated at a factory. The factory could achieve the same level of emissions reduction by changing its production process, but regulations do not allow using process changes to achieve emissions targets, only the scrubber. In this example, resources are wasted in production with no apparent gain. Everyone could be better off by using a method of pollution control that costs less. Providing too much or too little pollution overall would also be inefficient.

Two of the most important results in economics are (a) that competitive markets are efficient (i.e., on the Pareto frontier), and (b) that any Pareto optimum can be achieved with a competitive market by appropriately transferring income among individuals. The goal of this section is to demonstrate both of these results. What we will do is develop a simple model of an exchange economy (with two goods and two members of the economy), develop the Pareto frontier and the competitive equilibrium, and then show that these two are the same. We will confine ourselves to an exchange economy because it is simple and easy to grasp. We will briefly cover the extension to an economy with production but leave a full development of that to another course.[4]

A. Efficiency in Exchange

In the previous section we compared the attainable utility of two people, Anna and Brewster. We were not concerned with exactly how they achieved their levels of utility, nor how the utility of each depended on the actions of the other. Our goal was to develop the concept of Pareto optimality. We now expand this example somewhat and assume that Anna and Brewster have some resources and wish to enter into trade. We consider the example of two goods, rather than a good and a bad or two bads—just to keep the intuition simple. The two goods we consider are garbage disposal services and wine. Garbage disposal service is, of course, the good that corresponds to the bad, garbage.

Figure 4.2 shows indifference curves for garbage disposal services and wine, reflecting Anna's preferences. These are typical indifference curves. Note that they are concave upward by assumption. There are two ways of explaining the shape of these indifference curves. One explanation is that mixtures are better than extremes. Consider the dashed line, *CD*. Would we expect more utility from consuming one of the extremes (all wine, no garbage disposal or all garbage disposal, no wine) or a mixture of the two (point *X**)? Typically, we assume the mixture is better—thus the utility level is higher at *X** than at the points *C* or *D*. Another explanation of the curvature of the indifference curves is in terms of the marginal rate of substitution between garbage disposal services and wine. Recall that the marginal rate of substitution between garbage disposal services and wine at any point (like *X**) is the slope of the tangency to the indifference curve at that point. The marginal rate of substitution (MRS) of wine for garbage disposal services indicates how much wine consumption would need to increase to offset a one unit drop in garbage disposal consumption to keep utility constant. At a point such as *A* in Figure 4.2, where there is more garbage disposal services and less wine relative to point *X**, it is reasonable to think that more garbage disposal would be required to compensate for a one unit drop in wine—the MRS of food for garbage disposal increases as garbage disposal increases

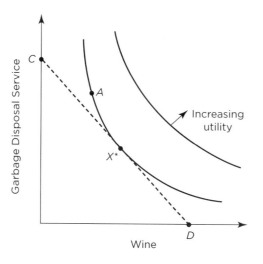

FIGURE 4.2 Utility maximizing choice of wine and garbage disposal services. *CD*, mixtures of the basket *C* (all garbage disposal) and the basket *D* (all wine); *X**, choice point.

and wine consumption decreases. (The more garbage disposal you use, the less valuable one more unit is and the less wine you have, the more valuable one more unit is.) If this is the case, then the indifference curves will have the shape shown in Figure 4.2.

Suppose Anna and Brewster are endowed with certain quantities of coupons for garbage disposal services and wine. We are interested in how these people might trade. We have no prices—this is pure barter. Assume Anna has coupons for a ton of garbage disposal (no wine) and Brewster has a bottle of wine (no garbage disposal). Both would prefer a little of each good.

The Edgeworth box is a useful graphic way of representing exchange of two commodities between two individuals. Figure 4.3 shows such an Edgeworth box for Anna and Brewster and their wine and garbage disposal services. Essentially what we do is take Anna's indifference curves (Figure 4.2) and superimpose them on a similar figure for Brewster, so that the origin of Brewster's set of indifference curves is in the upper right of Figure 4.3. The total amount of wine to trade is the length of the horizontal axis; the total amount of garbage disposal services to trade is the height of the vertical axis. Any *point* in Figure 4.3 represents a division of the two goods between the two people. In particular, point *A* in the upper left represents the initial endowment: Anna with all the garbage disposal services and Brewster with all the wine.

Any division of the two goods that lies between the lines *AB* and *AC* will result in increased utility for both individuals and thus will be a Pareto improvement. That is because all of these points (shaded in Figure 4.3) lie on higher indifference curves for both people. But this region is very large—many divisions are possible. Can we narrow the outcomes further? One way would be to focus on the Pareto frontier of the region *ABC*—the divisions of the "pie" for which one party cannot do better without making the other worse off. It turns out that any point in the *ABC* region at which the indifference curves of Anna and Brewster are tangent to one another lies on the Pareto frontier—also called the contract curve. To see this, consider a point at which tangency does not apply, such as point *A*. There are clearly allocations that are Pareto preferred to *A*—in fact, any allocation in the shaded lens *ACB*. Now consider those allocations on the dotted line *XY* corresponding to allocations where one of Brewster's indifference curves is tangent to one of Anna's. Along this contract curve (*XY*), one person can improve utility only by decreasing the other's utility. This is precisely the criterion necessary for the Pareto frontier. So whatever the initial endowment of the two individuals, we know the result of

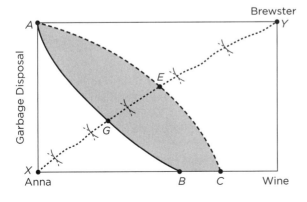

FIGURE 4.3 Edgeworth box characterization of wine-garbage disposal bargaining. *A*, initial endowment; *AGBCE*, points of Pareto impovement over *A*; *XGEY*, contract curve; *GE*, portion of contract curve that improves on *A*.

barter will be somewhere along the contract curve. In our case, starting at point *A*, the result of bargaining must lie on the segment of the contract curve, *EG*.

Tangency between the two indifference curves gives us a necessary condition for a Pareto optimum. What is the interpretation of this tangency? Basically, tangency is the same as the slopes of the indifference curves being simultaneously the same for the two people at a single point. The slope of the indifference curve gives us the rate at which each person can substitute wine for garbage disposal services while keeping utility constant. For instance in Figure 4.3, if Anna's slope at the point of tangency is 2, that means that if garbage disposal is decreased and wine increased small amounts in the ratio of 2:1, then utility will not change (or change only very slightly). This slope is, of course, the marginal rate of substitution between the two goods. Efficiency requires that the marginal rate of substitution of wine for garbage disposal services be the same for both Anna and Brewster. More generally, we have the following result: *at a Pareto optimum, the marginal rate of substitution between any two goods should be the same for all individuals.*

So how will the garbage disposal services and wine be divided? All we can say is that Anna and Brewster will end up somewhere along the *EG* portion of the contract curve, i.e., that portion of the contract curve that results in an improvement in utility (a higher indifference curve) for both individuals, in comparison to their initial position, *A*. Therefore, Anna will pay Brewster in coupons for garbage disposal for some of his wine. Furthermore, they will trade until the gains from trade are exhausted, ending up at a Pareto optimal division of the two goods.

We have seen how to represent exchange graphically. But more importantly, we have shown that in this simple model, free exchange leads to a Pareto optimal division of the goods. In other words, efficiency is achieved.

B. Markets and Exchange

Now suppose we move away from barter and introduce prices for the two commodities. We will allow trade to occur, but trade must be accompanied by payment. Thus the value of any bundle that Anna ends up with must have the same value as Anna's initial endowment. And the same for Brewster. Neither can generate income except through trade. To be more concrete, let G_0 and W_0 be Anna's initial endowment of garbage disposal services and wine respectively. Let G^* and W^* be the quantities of the two commodities Anna eventually ends up with. If we let prices of the two commodities be p_G and p_W, then Anna's budget balancing requires the following to hold for any (G,W) consumed:

$$p_G G_0 + p_W W_0 = p_G G + p_W W \tag{4.1}$$

Clearly if Anna has the same amount of money before and after trade, Brewster will too, since there is nowhere else for the money to go. Note that for a given set of prices, Eq. (4.1) basically describes a linear relationship between G and W with the left-hand side of the equation a constant. It may be easier to visualize Eq. (4.1) if we write it with G on the left-hand side and W on the right-hand side:

$$G = [G_0 + (p_W/p_G)W_0] - (p_W p_G) \, W \tag{4.2}$$

In Eq. (4.2), the portion in brackets is a constant. Equation (4.2) describes a straight line with slope $-(p_W/p_G)$. Equation (4.2) defines the budget constraint—combinations of G and W that are affordable. Obviously, the initial endowment is affordable, which can be checked by substituting (G_0, W_0) for (G, W) into Eq. (4.2).

This can be represented in an Edgeworth box. Figure 4.4 shows a simplified version of the Edgeworth box of Figure 4.3. In addition, Eq. (4.2), the budget constraint, has been drawn. As it should, the line passes through (G_0, W_0), the initial endowment, labeled point A. For an allocation X^* to be a market equilibrium, both consumers must be simultaneously satisfied with X^*, given the prices. In other words, both individuals, assumed to be price-takers, must have indifference curves tangent to the budget line at X^*.[5] This of course is the same condition for points along the contract curve—that indifference curves be tangent. Thus market equilibrium will occur where the budget line (the straight line from A in Figure 4.4) intersects the contract curve (X^* in Figure 4.4).

It is important to remember that the prices are unknown. In fact, the prices are what we are interested in determining. All we know is that whatever they are, they must satisfy two requirements:

1. The budget line (Eq. 4.2) must pass through the initial endowment.
2. There must be some allocation at which the indifference curves of both parties are tangent to the budget line.

If we are lucky only one line satisfies both of these conditions. It can be found by passing a straight line through the initial endowment (point A) and rotating the line (mentally) around A until the line intersects the contract curve in such a way as to be tangent to both indifference curves at the same time. This is the line AD in Figure 4.4.

As can be seen from Eq. (4.2), the slope of the budget line in Figure 4.4 is the negative of the price ratio $(-p_W/p_G)$. This is a negative number since the prices are positive. This price ratio is also equal to the marginal rate of substitution at X^* between garbage disposal services and wine for both Anna and Brewster.

So what? What we have shown, albeit in a somewhat simplified example, is that a market equilibrium results in a Pareto optimal allocation. Markets are efficient. Either Anna and Brewster can negotiate directly, leading to a set of possible efficient allocations along the contract curve or the market can operate, leading to one particular

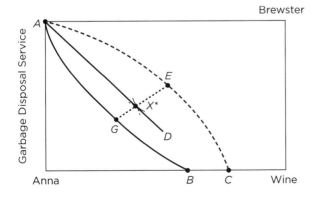

FIGURE 4.4 Market equilibrium in garbage disposal–wine bargain. *A*, initial endowment; *GE*, portion of contract curve that improves on *A*; *X**, market outcome with initial allocation at *A*; *AD*, budget constraint.

efficient allocation along the contract curve. Do not fail to notice that there are other allocations along the contract curve that are also Pareto optimal but will not result from the operation of a market as just described. Furthermore, if the initial endowment (point A in our example) is different, a different allocation may result. For instance, if Brewster possesses some garbage disposal services and not quite so much wine, he may buy less disposal services and agree to sell less wine.

In fact, note that by changing the initial distribution of cheese and wine, any point on the contract curve (Pareto frontier) can be obtained using the price system.

These two results are the fundamental results of this chapter (though derived here only for an exchange economy): a market equilibrium is Pareto optimal, and any Pareto optimum (any point on the contract curve) can be the result of a market equilibrium, simply by adjusting the initial endowment.

C. Efficiency in Production

In exchange, we are concerned with moving goods and bads around among individuals to improve everyone's welfare. Basically, we were looking at different ways of dividing pies. We now turn to the question of combining resources to produce new goods and bads. We are concerned with efficiency in production. Suppose we have a firm—Ivorytower Land Services (ILS)—that has land which can be used for producing wine or disposing of garbage.

We start with a few assumptions, continuing to focus on the production of wine and garbage disposal. Assume we have a fixed amount of resources to produce these two items—Anna's and Brewster's labor (L). If we put all of our resources into wine production, we will produce the maximum amount of wine, and dispose of no garbage. We can redirect some of our labor into garbage disposal, reducing the amount of wine produced. The question is how to split labor between these two activities. Alternatively, how much garbage disposal and wine is to be produced? Contrast this to the previous example, in which there was a fixed amount of garbage disposal and wine, and the question was how to divide it up between Anna and Brewster.

Figure 4.5 shows the possible production combinations of wine and garbage disposal (the shaded region). Note that to produce the maximum amount of wine, a minimum amount of garbage will be disposed. Analogously, more garbage means less wine. The points along the line AB are the efficient combinations of wine and garbage disposal—the Pareto frontier, also called the production possibilities frontier. Note that we could conceivably be in the interior of the figure ABC—the labor in wine production or in garbage disposal could be wasted. In such a case, we might obtain a point such as D in Figure 4.5. The point D is in the interior of the production possibilities set and is inefficient because it is possible to produce more wine and more garbage disposal (moving from point D to point E), which has to be desirable to everyone in the economy. So the first condition for efficiency is that the economy operates on the production possibilities frontier.

The inputs into production in our example (labor) are fixed resulting in costs C. But the producer does have a choice about how much wine and garbage disposal to produce. Profits for the producer are given by

$$\pi = p_{\mathrm{W}} W + p_{\mathrm{G}} G - C \tag{4.3}$$

Slope = MRT

E

Production possibilities

• *D*

Production
possibilities frontier

C *A* Wine

B (y-axis top)

Garbage Disposed (y-axis label)

FIGURE 4.5 Efficiency in production.

which can be rewritten with *G* on the left-hand side and *W* on the right-hand side:

$$G = (\pi + C)/p_G - p_W/p_G\, W \tag{4.4}$$

This is obviously a straight line with intercept $(\pi + C)/p_G$ and slope $-p_W/p_G$, which is negative because prices are positive. Profits are highest when the intercept is as high as possible, which means the line shifted as far to the right as possible, while still having a point in common with the production set. The profit-maximizing production combination is shown as point *E* in Figure 4.5.

The slope of the production possibilities frontier at any particular point is called the *marginal rate of transformation* (MRT) between the two goods. This MRT is shown in Figure 4.5 for the point *E* on the production possibilities frontier. In general, the MRT shows the rate at which output of one good has to be sacrificed to increase output of the other good. In our case, the MRT of wine for garbage disposal shows how much garbage disposal can be increased when wine production is decreased by one unit. For instance, if at *E*, 2 kg more of garbage can be disposed of by reducing wine output by 1 kg, then the marginal rate of transformation of wine for garbage would be 2 (kg garbage/bottles wine) at *E*. With a market, the marginal rate of transformation is equal to the price ratio.

One condition that is not obvious from Figure 4.5 is that if there are multiple producers of wine and garbage disposal, for efficiency to hold, the marginal rate of transformation between wine and garbage must be the same for all producers. Suppose there are two such producers (A and B). If producer A has a larger MRT between garbage and wine than producer B and if we reduce wine production from A by one unit and increase wine production from B by one unit, then wine production stays constant and overall garbage disposal increases (because it increases for A more than it declines for B). This is obviously a Pareto improvement. Consequently, a necessary condition for efficiency is that the marginal rate of transformation between any two outputs be the same for all producers in the economy.

This is an important point that in fact often fails to hold for most pollution regulations. If several firms generate pollution along with a useful good, what we have just shown is that the marginal rate of transformation between pollution and the good should be the same for all firms. In simple terms, the marginal cost of pollution control should be the same for all firms. This is what is known as the equimarginal principle and will receive significant attention in later chapters on regulation. Unfortunately, this principle rarely holds for actual environmental regulations. More often, firms will be told to reduce emissions by some percentage. For some firms this will be cheap and for other firms this will be expensive.

All that remains is to put production and exchange together. The basic necessary condition for efficiency is that the marginal rate of transformation (in production) between any two commodities be the same as the marginal rate of substitution between these two commodities for any individual consuming both commodities. Furthermore, the marginal rate of transformation should be the same for all firms producing the two goods.

One implication of this result pertains directly to pollution control. If more than one firm is generating emissions, then efficiency calls for the equality among those firms of the marginal rate of transformation between pollution emissions and goods output. In a more general context, this is equivalent to saying that for efficiency, the marginal cost of emissions control should be equal for all polluters emitting the same pollutant:

DEFINITION   Equimarginal Principle. *In controlling emissions from several polluters, all emitting the same pollutant, efficiency requires that the marginal cost of emission control be the same for all polluters.*

In this definition, the term "same pollutant" means not only that the pollutant coming from different sources is the same but also that the marginal damage from a unit of pollution is the same, regardless of which polluter it comes from. For example, spatial differences are not important.

The significance of this principle will become clearer when we turn to regulating pollution. The straightforward consequence of the equimarginal principle is that it is inefficient for different firms emitting the same pollutant to face different marginal costs of pollution control.

To see the intuition behind the equimarginal principle, suppose two firms are emitting SO_2 at different marginal costs of pollution control. We can reduce total costs without affecting the overall emissions of SO_2 simply by moving some of the responsibility for pollution control to the low-control cost firm, away from the high–control cost firm. This is a potential Pareto improvement and thus the original situation was not efficient.

D. Efficiency with and without Markets

In the previous sections we examined conditions that need to hold for economic efficiency. These conditions had nothing to do with prices; in fact, the conditions can be applied in an economy without prices. One basic requirement is that the marginal rate of substitution (in consumption) between any two commodities be equated to the marginal rate of transformation (in production) between those two commodities. Secondarily, we saw that for any two firms producing both commodities, the marginal rate of transformation between the two commodities must be the same for each firm. Similarly, any two consumers consuming both commodities must have the same marginal rate of substitution between the two commodities.

Equimarginal Principle and Kyoto Protocol

In December 1997, most of the countries of the world met in Kyoto, Japan to try to reach an agreement on controlling emissions of gases that lead to global warming. The Kyoto Protocol emerged from that meeting. The Protocol calls for countries to reduce emissions by a certain percentage below 1990 levels and to achieve this by the year 2012. The European Union (EU) would be expected to reduce emissions to 7% below 1990 levels, Japan 6%, Australia 8%, and the United States, 7%. Other countries have different targets. Overall, if all countries abide by the Protocol, global emissions should be 5% below 1990 levels (Anderson, 1998). One of the requirements the Europeans pushed for was the ability to pool European countries, reducing emissions more in some countries than others, simply requiring the 7% target be met for the EU as a whole.

Why would the EU want to pool emissions when determining compliance with the Protocol? Figure 4.6 shows one estimate of the marginal costs of controlling carbon dioxide emissions in various European countries. Although there is considerable debate regarding the true magnitude of these costs, Figure 4.6 illustrates the potential differences in control costs among different countries.[6] It is easy to see that a 7% reduction in emissions in each country of the EU would definitely not satisfy the equimarginal principle. Italy's marginal costs would be in the neighborhood of 300 ECU per ton of CO_2 while France and Germany's marginal costs would be significantly less than 50 ECU per ton. With an EU-wide emission reduction target, Figure 4.6 suggests that the reductions would most likely be concentrated in Germany, the United Kingdom, Denmark, France, and Belgium.

FIGURE 4.6 Marginal costs of emission reductions in 2010 relative to 1990 emissions. (Adapted from Hourcade et al., 1996, p. 318.)

We also saw in a simple exchange economy that a competitive market will generate prices so that the marginal rate of substitution is the same for all consumers and equal to the ratio of prices of the two commodities. We also showed that with a competitive market, the marginal rate of transformation will be equal to the price ratio.

These results can be generalized into two basic theorems, the first and second theorems of welfare economics.

> **First Theorem of Welfare Economics.** In a competitive economy, a market equilibrium is Pareto optimal.

This first theorem is a restatement of the results of this section. If we let a competitive market operate, a Pareto optimum will prevail.

The second theorem states that a market can be relied on to give *any* Pareto optimal allocation. As we saw earlier in the simple exchange economy between Anna and Brewster, the initial endowment of wine and garbage disposal services was important in determining the eventual split of garbage and wine between the two people. In fact, any point on the contract curve could be obtained using a market, simply by changing the initial endowment of wine and garbage disposal services. This can be extended to the case involving production:

> **Second Theorem of Welfare Economics.** In a competitive economy, any Pareto optimum can be achieved by market forces, provided the resources of the economy are appropriately distributed before the market is allowed to operate.

This all sounds very easy: let the market operate. Get out of the way and all problems will be solved. Then why is pollution a problem in a market economy? The reason is that the generation of most pollution violates one of the assumptions of a competitive market.

What are those assumptions? What conditions must prevail in a market before we deem it competitive and thus subject to these two theorems of welfare economics? Four conditions must hold before we declare a market competitive:[7]

1. *Complete property rights.* A well-defined, transferable, and secure set of property rights must exist for all goods and bads in the economy so that these commodities can be freely exchanged. All the benefits or costs must accrue to the agent holding the property right for the good or bad.
2. *Atomistic participants.* Producers and consumers are small relative to the market and thus cannot influence prices. Instead, they maximize profits or utility taking prices as given.
3. *Complete information.* Consumers and producers have full knowledge of current and future prices.
4. *No transaction costs.* It must be costless to attach prices to goods traded.

The first of these requirements is a fundamental one: if I am making a decision about consumption or production of a good or bad, then I must be able to capture all of the benefits and bear all of the costs associated with consumption or production; otherwise, my decision will not take into account the full implications of consumption or production. Pollution clearly violates this requirement. If I own a bottle of wine, I am the sole beneficiary. If I sell the bottle of wine, I transfer all of the benefits to the person who buys it, in exchange for a payment. On the other hand, if I have a factory belching smoke, I benefit from lower production costs by polluting but do not bear all of the costs of that pollution—the population living around my factory bears most of those costs. My decision about how much to emit will not be Pareto optimal.

The second requirement, that participants be atomistic, primarily pertains to the exercise of market power. If I am a dominant producer or consumer in a market, I may have the ability to strategically manipulate price, to my benefit but to the detriment of others in the market. This moves an equilibrium away from a Pareto optimum.

The third requirement is somewhat obvious—if consumers and producers in the market are differentially informed about prices, or even equally uninformed, decisions may or may not be Pareto optimal.

The fourth requirement requires that there be no hurdles to making Pareto-improving trades. If there is a fee for trading (a substantial commission on buying or selling a house is an example), then even though there are gains to trade, the transaction costs may prevent those from being realized, and thus prevent a Pareto optimum from being achieved.

In the next chapter we examine more closely just what it is about environmental goods that violates the assumptions of a competitive market. We will see that markets typically fail when pollution is present. We will also see how those market failures can be corrected through government intervention so that we may rely on the market to achieve a Pareto optimal outcome.

III. SUPPLY, DEMAND, AND EFFICIENCY

In the last section we took a fairly abstract look at the way markets operate. This was useful because it gives a fundamental understanding of exchange, production, and efficiency. We can also look at the question of efficiency and markets through a much more familiar lens, that of supply and demand. In doing so, we assume a market setting and ask if the market will give us efficiency (a Pareto optimum).

A. Demand and Willingness to Pay

A conventional demand curve shows quantity demanded as a function of price—for any price, how much will be demanded. Without a market there is, of course, no price. One might think that the concept of a demand curve is useless without market prices, but that assumption would be wrong. An individual demand curve results from utility maximization and represents how strongly a consumer desires a particular commodity when faced with alternatives. A demand curve is the answer to the question "If there were a price of $x for this good, how much would you want, taking into account your budget and the prices of other goods?"

Normally, we think of an individual demand curve as relating price to quantity demanded. An equally valid interpretation of a demand curve is as a relationship between quantity and the *marginal willingness to pay* (MWTP). To see this most clearly, consider an example. Start with Finch Ellsworth's individual demand curve for gasoline, relating price per liter to quantity demanded in a given period of time. Suppose that at a price of £1 per liter, Finch chooses to consume 50 liters per week. A second interpretation of these figures is that at 50 liters per week, Finch's marginal willingness to pay for one more liter is £1. If Finch's MWTP were more than £1, Finch would choose to buy more gasoline since the price is less than its value to him; if Finch's MWTP were less than £1, Finch would cut back on consumption since he is paying more than it is worth to him.

In other words, an individual demand curve can be viewed as either a price–quantity relationship or a MWTP–quantity relationship. Either interpretation is equally valid. When we turn to non market environmental goods, the MWTP–quantity relationship will be the most useful interpretation.

B. A Market Equilibrium Is Pareto Optimal

The first welfare theorem states that for a competitive market, a market equilibrium is Pareto optimal. We can also see this in a supply and demand context. If we take a commodity such as garbage disposal services, we know that we can represent a consumer's preferences regarding disposal services through a demand curve, an expression that gives the quantity of services demanded as a function of the price of garbage disposal relative to other goods. Alternatively, the demand curve may be viewed as indicating the marginal willingness to pay for one more unit of the good, as a function of the total quantity of the good being consumed.

Similarly, a supply curve represents the amount of garbage disposal services that will be supplied at various prices. Figure 4.7 shows such demand and supply curves for garbage disposal services. The market equilibrium is the point where the two curves cross at g^* quantity of garbage disposal services. To see that this is Pareto optimal, consider other quantities of garbage disposal services such as a little less, g_1, or a little more, g_2. At g_1 additional garbage disposal services could be supplied to our consumer at a cost less than the willingness-to-pay for the garbage disposal services. Clearly allowing such consumption would be a Pareto improvement. Similarly, at g_2, the last bit of wine (between g^* and g_2) is

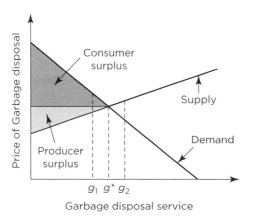

FIGURE 4.7 Supply, demand, and surplus measures in the market for garbage disposal services. g^*, market equilibrium quantity of garbage disposal; g_1, too little garbage disposal; g_2, too much garbage disposal.

worth less to the consumer than it costs to produce it. By reducing garbage disposal, we save the producer more than the consumer loses; transfers can make everyone better off. In this sense a market equilibrium is Pareto optimal.

C. Consumer and Producer Surplus

We know how to move from measures of utility (indifference curves) to a demand curve. This is the familiar maximization of utility subject to a budget constraint, which ultimately generates a demand curve. We can also move in the other direction. Starting with a demand curve, we can obtain a measure of the overall welfare gain associated with consuming some amount of good. The welfare gain is in monetary terms, since utility is not directly measurable. This is consumer surplus—the difference between what a consumer would be willing to pay for a bundle of goods and the amount the consumer actually has to pay. You have been walking through the desert all day without water and come upon a shop selling bottled water for 100 rupees (Rs 100) per bottle. You buy a bottle. What is the value of that purchase to you? Unless you are very poor, you would be willing to pay more than Rs 100 for the bottle, perhaps very much more. The surplus associated with that transaction is the difference between what you would have been willing to pay and what you did pay. Where do we obtain information on how much you would pay? From the demand curve.

This leads us to define several concepts, starting with the total (not marginal) willingness to pay for q^* units of a commodity, followed by consumer surplus, which is simply the willingness to pay minus whatever is paid for the commodity.

DEFINITION *The willingness to pay (WTP) for the quantity* q* *for a consumer with demand* Q(p) *is equal to the area bounded by the demand curve, the horizontal axis, the vertical axis and the vertical line* q = q*.

This is a natural extension of the MWTP–quantity interpretation of a demand curve. In the example of Finch Ellsworth's consumption of gasoline (50 liters per week at £1 per liter), the MWTP of the first liter may be £5, the second liter £4.90, and so forth until we get to the 50th liter, with an MWTP of £1. Summing all of these MWTPs results in the total WTP for 50 liters of gasoline for Finch.

DEFINITION *The consumer surplus associated with consuming* q* *units of a commodity for a consumer with demand* Q(p) *is equal to the WTP for* q* *less any payment the consumer makes for the commodity.*

Consumer surplus is almost exactly the same concept as WTP. The difference is that for consumer surplus, we are subtracting from WTP whatever is paid for the commodity. In the case of Finch, he pays £50 for his 50 liters of gasoline at £1 per liter.

It should be noted that although these definitions are for individuals, these concepts are generally applied to markets, using market or aggregate demand curves. The interpretation of WTP is the value consumers get for what is consumed, summed up over all consumers and over all quantitites consumed. The interpretation of consumer surplus is the extra value consumers get, over and above the price paid, for what is consumed, summed up over all consumers and over all quantitites consumed.

We can also carry this concept over to the producer. When supply curves are upward sloping, the interpretation is that the first units supplied are less expensive than subsequent units. This may simply be the result of using some scarce factor in production whose value is bid up as the industry expands. Whatever the reason, there may be a difference between revenue received and the cost of production—this is the producer surplus.

DEFINITION *Producer surplus is the difference between any revenue received for sale of* q* *units of a commodity and the cost of providing that commodity,* C(q*). *This difference is generally equal to the area bounded by the supply curve, a horizontal line through the price, and between the vertical lines* q = 0 *and* q = q*.

These definitions lead directly to the concept of total surplus, which is simply the sum of producer and consumer surplus. However, the market price cancels out when dealing with total surplus:

DEFINITION *Total surplus (consumer and producer surplus) associated with consuming* q* *units of a commodity with demand* Q(p) *and production costs* C(q) *is WTP less production costs.*

Generally, total surplus is the area bounded by the demand curve, the supply curve, and the vertical lines $q = 0$ and $q = q^*$.

These concepts are also shown in Figure 4.7, which is a representation of supply and demand curves for garbage disposal services. Shown in the figure are consumer surplus, producer surplus, and total surplus (the sum of producer and consumer surplus). Total surplus at q^* is the area under the demand curve less the area under the supply curve, measured between $q = 0$ and $q = q^*$. This is the shaded area.

Several qualifications are in order. One is that total surplus may not exist. If, for instance, the demand curve were asymptotic to the vertical axis, the area under it might be infinite. If this is the case, the best we can do is talk about the difference in surplus between consuming two different quantities, say four bags of garbage and two bags of garbage.

A second qualification is that the surplus measure depends on prices of other goods and, possibly, income. For instance if the price of packaging drops, we might expect the demand for garbage disposal services to shift. Or if incomes were to drop, demand for garbage disposal services might decline.

One important thing to infer from Figure 4.7 is that total surplus is maximized at the market equilibrium. It is easy to see that for any quantities of garbage disposal less that g^*, surplus (the shaded area) is less than at g^*. But for quantities of garbage disposal greater than g^*, note that the additional surplus from another bag of garbage disposal is negative. The area under the demand curve less the area under the supply curve is negative, to the right of g^*. Thus, at least graphically, we have shown the equivalence among a market equilibrium, a Pareto optimum, and a surplus maximum.

There is one semantic issue that should be mentioned, to avoid confusion for the case of pollution. Often, we speak of the damage from pollution or the benefit of having less pollution. But the marginal benefit of one less unit of pollution is the same as the marginal damage of one more unit of pollution—they are two sides of the same coin. The benefit of less pollution and the damage from more pollution are the same concepts, just opposite in sign. To muddy the waters further, the marginal benefit of having one less unit of pollution is the same as the marginal willingness-to-pay for one less unit of pollution. At the margin, these concepts are the same—it is just the sign that varies.

SUMMARY

1. The Pareto frontier consists of all allocations that cannot be improved on in the Pareto sense. In other words, all other allocations make at least one person worse off.

2. Efficiency to an economist means being on the Pareto frontier—no redistribution of resources can be undertaken without making someone worse off.

3. In a competitive exchange involving a good and a bad, the bad will be negatively priced and the good will be positively priced. Trade will generally take place.

4. In a two-good barter economy, exchange will take place where the marginal rate of substitution between the two goods is the same for all participants. Suppose consumption of one good is increased a small amount and consumption of the other good is decreased so that utility stays constant. The ratio of these two changes is the marginal rate of substitution.

5. In the context of trade and bargaining, the contract curve is another name for the Pareto frontier.

6. When prices are used for exchange in a two-good exchange economy, the equilibrium quantities of goods will generally be the point on the contract curve at which the slope of the budget line is equal to the marginal rate of substitution for each consumer and where the budget line passes through the initial endowment.

7. Efficiency in production requires that the marginal rate of transformation for a producer be equal to the price ratio. Suppose production of one good is increased a small amount and production of another good is decreased so that profit stays constant. The ratio of these two changes is the marginal rate of transformation.

8. Efficiency in a competitive economy with production and trade requires that the marginal rate of substitution between two goods be the same for all consumers consuming both goods, that the marginal rate of transformation between two goods be the same for all producers producing both goods, and that the marginal rate of substitution equal the marginal rate of transformation, which in turn equals the price ratio.

9. The first theorem of welfare economics states that a competitive market equilibrium is Pareto optimal.

10. The second theorem of welfare economics says that any Pareto optimum can be supported by a competitive market equilibrium simply by adjusting the initial distribution of resources in the economy.

11. Markets usually fail when pollution is present. Thus we cannot rely on markets to give us a Pareto optimum. It is usually necessary for the government to intervene to achieve efficiency. Benefit–cost analysis is a method for determining if such government actions are efficient.

12. Consumer surplus is a measure of the value of goods to consumers, over and above the amount paid for the goods.

13. Producer surplus is a measure of the gains from selling a good, after the cost of production has been taken into account.

14. Total surplus of increasing the quantity supplied from q^* to q^{**} is the area bounded above by the demand curve, below by the supply curve, to the left by the vertical line $q = q^*$, and to the right by the vertical line $q - q^{**}$.

15. In controlling emissions from several polluters, all emitting the same homogeneous pollutant, the *equimarginal principle* stipulates that for efficiency, the marginal cost of emission control must be the same for all polluters.

PROBLEMS

1. Suppose an environmental regulation requires all polluters to reduce emissions by 50%, even though the cost of pollution control differs widely from one polluter to another. Why might this be inefficient, using the definition of efficiency developed in this chapter?

2. Consider the market for electricity. Suppose demand (in megawatt hours) is given by $Q = 50 - P$ and that the marginal private cost of generating electricity is $10 per megawatt hour ($P$ is in the same units). Suppose further that smoke is generated in the production of electricity in direct proportion to the amount of electricity generated. The health damage from the smoke is $15 per megawatt hour generated.

   a. Suppose the electricity is produced by competitive producers. What price will be charged, and how much electricity will be produced?

   b. How would your answer in part a change if electricity were produced by an unregulated monopolist?

   c. In parts (a) and (b), what is the consumer surplus from the electricity generation? What is the net surplus, taking into account the pollution damage?

3. In Figure 4.5, the slope of the production possibility frontier (the MRT of wine for garbage disposal) is increasing (getting steeper) as garbage disposal decreases and wine increases. Does this make sense? Why?

4. Combine Figures 4.2 and 4.5 into a single figure showing how much garbage disposal and wine will be produced in an economy consisting of Ivorytower Land Services (ILS—the producer) and Brewster, our consumer. Show the relative price of wine and garbage disposal services in the figure. Assume Brewster's income is fixed.

5. In the context of Problem 4, suppose you know that CLS's MRT of wine for garbage disposal services is 2:1 (to obtain more bags of garbage disposal services requires a reduction of one bottle of wine (keeping inputs constant), and Brewster's MRS of wine for garbage disposal is 3:1 (he would be indifferent between being able to get rid of three bags of garbage or taking one bottle of wine). For this society, would you recommend more garbage disposal services or more wine production or the status quo? Explain your answer.

6. In a photocopy of Figure 4.1, find and label the following points:

   a. a point D such that Z and Y are Pareto preferred to D but S is not.

  b. a point E such that the arc BZ is the portion of the Pareto frontier, which are Pareto improvements on E.

*7. Suppose Humphrey and Matilda live together. Humphrey currently smokes 20 packs of cigarettes per month; Matilda hates the smoke. They currently have no agreement restricting smoking. Their only joint expense is monthly rent, which they split 50:50. Draw an Edgeworth box with two goods—smoke and rental payments. Make up some reasonable indifference curves. Show the initial endowment. What Pareto efficient points might result from bargaining to restrict smoke? How does the graph show what price per pack Matilda might pay to buy down Humphrey's smoking (i.e., show the relative prices on your figure)? How would your answers change if the status quo is that the two have an agreement for no smoking and Humphrey would *like to smoke* as much as 20 packs per month? He must seek Matilda's permission to do so. (Hint: For Matilda, redefine Humphrey's smoking as smoke reduction.)

NOTES

1. Government failure is also possible but not considered here. See Weimer and Vining (2005).
2. See also texts on applied welfare economics, such as Just et al. (1982) or texts on cost–benefit analysis, such as Gramlich (1990) or Boardman et al. (2006).
3. Although there are few prohibitions on the interstate transport of waste within the United States, there are differential regulations that discriminate against placing out-of-state waste in local waste disposal facilities. In the past, waste shipments from Germany to Eastern European countries have generated public criticism within Germany and elsewhere. There are international treaties prohibiting certain international waste shipments.
4. See Varian (2005) for a full development of a two-agent (Robinson Crusoe) economy with production and exchange.
5. The purist will correctly point out that this is not always the case—corner solutions can occur. We are ignoring those difficulties for the time being.
6. Hourcade et al. (1996) report a variety of cost figures for reductions in carbon emissions. What is clear is that there is a great deal of disagreement over the cost of abating carbon emissions.
7. These conditions for a market to operate are discussed by many authors, including Bator (1958). It is possible to relax some conditons (such as complete information) and still have a functioning market. An exploration of that issue would lead us too far astray.

PUBLIC GOODS AND EXTERNALITIES

IN THIS CHAPTER WE CONSIDER THE FUNDAMENTAL DIFFERENCE BETWEEN CONVENTIONAL goods (e.g., bread), which the market allocates and rations efficiently, and environmental commodities (e.g., pollution), which the market fails to allocate efficiently. It is the very nature of pollution that leads to this market failure. Economics has developed the concepts of public bads and externalities to describe the characteristics of these environmental commodities that lead to market failure. A bad is of course the opposite of a good. A good is individually beneficial and people want it; a bad does harm and people do not want it. Quite simple, really.

I. OPEN ACCESS

Why are many roads so annoyingly congested? Why are many fisheries threatened by overfishing? About a half century ago, a biologist at the University of California, Santa Barbara, warned of the "Tragedy of the Commons"[1] and popularized concern with open access resources. The tragedy, simply stated, is that when there are no owners of resources (such as the oceans or common grazing grounds) or if the owners are public entities which exert no control over use (such as open roads), then there is a real risk that the resources will be overused. Such resources are termed open access (anyone may access them), common property (everyone owns the property and has access), or common pool (everyone is drawing from a common pool).[2] We will use the three terms interchangeably.

A simple example of the problem of open access is the divided highway/road (freeway/motorway/autobahn), at least in cases where access is not regulated (i.e., when motorists can freely enter and leave the road). In many urban areas, these roads become highly congested, particularly at certain times of the day, and traffic may slow from a normal speed of 120 kph to much lower levels (e.g., 20 kph) or even come to a dead stop. Why does this occur? And what can be done about it?

Another example comes from urban air pollution, particularly in years prior to serious regulatory attention to the problem, which began in the mid-20th century. The airshed had been open access for polluters. Factories and automobiles alike treated the urban airshed as common property—everyone's property for waste disposal but nobody's property in terms of regulating use. The result was over use of the airshed—excessive pollution. What options are open to fix this?

The decimation of the American passenger pigeon is a sad example of an open access resource resulting in extinction of a species. The pigeon stock was open access and a tasty morsel for the settlers in 19th century America. The pigeon is now extinct due to overharvesting. Why did this occur and what could have been done to prevent it?

A final example is that of oil. Oil is of course found in underground reservoirs with boundaries that are usually at odds with surface delineation of property rights. If one person owns a small plot on the surface and drills down to the resource, then, potentially, that person can extract most of the oil in the reservoir, even though the reservoir extends far beyond his or her property. If multiple landowners try to drill down to the pool, they will engage in a race to extract the resource the fastest. Unfortunately, this results in higher extraction costs and lower ultimately recoverable resources.[3]

Although we will defer the question of what to do about these problems until later in the book, we are concerned here with the why and determining what should be the Pareto optimal level of use of a common property resource.

A fishery may be the simplest and most straightforward example to explore in detail to understand the problem of open access. Although at one time the oceans were viewed as having unlimited stocks, those days have passed. It is typical for a fishery to have too many fishers chasing too few fish, driving down profits of fishers and threatening species of fish with extinction or at least decimation.

As defined here, a fishery consists of a well-defined body of water containing fish. The fish are valuable (as food), but it takes effort to catch them. The fewer fish there are, the more effort it takes. The higher the total level of fishing effort in the fishery, the smaller the stock and the lower the yield per unit of effort. In this simple discussion, we will ignore the natural growth of fisheries (due to reproduction) and many other important details necessary to actually manage a fishery. We also assume all the fishers are equally talented and thus identical in all respects. There is a large pool of potential fishers who will enter into fishing if it is profitable.

Figure 5.1 graphically represents the details just described. The horizontal access shows the total output of the fishery (such as tons of fish). The vertical axis shows total value—either the total cost of the effort in extracting fish or the total gross revenue of the catch. The gross revenue is simply price of fish times quantity of fish and is thus a straight line. However, the cost of catching the fish is concave upward, reflecting the fact that as the catch gets larger, it costs more and more to get one more unit of output.

There are two basic questions: what will the fishers do absent regulation or intervention, and what should they do (i.e., what is efficient)? The answer to the first of these questions is that output will occur at Y_{OA}, where total revenue equals total cost. To understand this, assume for a minute that output is slightly lower than this, at Y'. At this level of output, the cost of the catch will be AB and the revenue will be AC. Fishing is profitable. Furthermore, and this is important, all of the fishers share in this profit. Unlike many markets, where some participants have an advantage (inframarginal producers) and some eek by (the marginal producers), all fishers have the same technology, share the same average cost (due to the difficulty in finding fish), and share the same average revenue

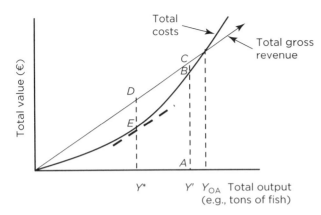

FIGURE 5.1 Illustration of an open access resource.

(based on the catch). As long as fishing is profitable, new fishers will enter the fishery and this process will only stop at the point Y_{OA}, where profits have been exhausted. At Y_{OA}, the total revenue in the fishery is exactly equal to the total cost. Although the fish will be sold for a substantial amount of money, the total gross sales revenue will exactly offset the cost of fishing. Thus the net value of the fishery is zero.

This is a rather discouraging result. We start with a tremendous natural resource, a viable fishery, with a large stock of valuable, tasty fish. But because of the open access nature of the fishery, there is no social value to the fishery—it costs as much to extract the fish as they are worth.

What is happening is that every time a fisher enters, he or she does not see the fact that entry makes it more difficult for all the other fishers to catch fish. If I am fishing, what determines my catch is a combination of my skill/equipment and the density of fish in the fishery—fewer fish makes my catch per unit effort go down. When a fisher enters a fishery, he or she makes the fish a bit more scarce, driving down the yield for everyone. The fisher entering sees only his or her costs of fishing and does not see the small increment of costs borne by all the incumbent fishers via entry.

This can be seen from Figure 5.1. Note that at Y_{OA}, the marginal cost of effort (the slope of the cost curve) is greater than the marginal revenue from effort (the slope of the revenue curve). At that point every extra unit of effort adds more costs than it returns in revenue.

What is the efficient amount of output? That is at Y^*, where the marginal cost of fishing exactly equals the marginal revenue (i.e., the slopes of the two lines in the figure are equal). At least as it is drawn in the figure, this occurs at significantly lower levels of output than Y_{OA} and, more importantly, generates real social value, in terms of DE. This value is the economic profit associated with the fishery (formally called the rent associated with the fishery). That profit or rent is dissipated with open access.

Note that this very same logic can be applied to most other open access problems. A congested road is congested because the last motorist entering did not take into account his or her slight effect on all the other motorists (in terms of reducing their speed slightly due to congestion). Thus too many motorists use the road during congested periods and dissipate the net value of the road (the gross value of the trips is equal to the cost of the trip, including waiting time).

II. EXTERNALITIES

An externality occurs when one person's or firm's actions affect another entity without permission.[4] If I like to play my stereo loudly, my neighbors must listen as well. If a laundry is located next to a steel mill, the act of making steel increases costs for the laundry because of all the dirt and smoke generated in making steel. A fisher entering an open access fishery makes it more difficult for all the existing fishers to catch fish. One more additional driver on a congested highway generates externalities for all the other drivers (as discussed in the previous section). Of course, there can also be positive externalities. In a classic example of externalities,[5] the owner of an apple orchard provides a positive externality for a neighboring apiary (in terms of the quantity and sweetness of the honey). And the apiary provides a positive externality to the orchard in terms of the bees pollinating the apple blossoms. The generation of knowledge also provides positive externalities in the sense that its benefits are rarely confined to those who generate the knowledge.

Suppose an individual's utility function is given by $U(x,e)$ where x and e are quantities of two goods (or bads) consumed. The individual chooses how much of x to consume but has no control over consumption of e. How much e will be consumed is chosen by others. This is an externality.

DEFINITION *An* externality *exists when the consumption or production choices of one person or firm enters the utility or production function of another entity without that entity's permission or compensation.*

It is important to exclude from this concept actions between two agents that are mutually agreed and for which payment occurs. When iron ore is sold to a steel mill, the mill's profits are improved, but that is hardly an externality; rather it is a simple transaction. It is unstated, but we also preclude from our definition of externality intentional harm to another (e.g., murder) or intentional good to another (altruism).

Figure 5.2 illustrates a production externality. Shown are production possibilities for steel and laundry—the maximum amounts of the two that can be produced. Note that with no externality, both can produce some maximum amount and the two firms are essentially independent of one another. With a modest externality involved (e.g., smoke), increased steel production will diminish laundry output (compare lines I and II in the figure). If the externality is strong enough (line III),[6] the possible output combinations can even be nonconvex, leading to potential pricing problems that will not be explored here.[7] What would influence the strength of the externality? Clearly location is important. As we move two firms away from each other, the strength of the pollution externality is bound to decline.

A production externality exists when one firm's profits are involuntarily affected by another's. More specifically, suppose the technology of producing laundry is given by

$$L = f_L(x_1, \ldots, x_n, e) \tag{5.1}$$

where L is output of laundry and $x_1, \ldots, x_n$ are n different inputs into laundry production. The variable e is smoke emissions from steel manufacturing, which is of course chosen

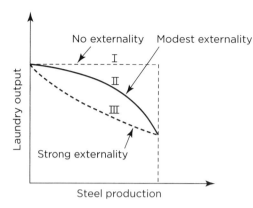

FIGURE 5.2 Production possibilites with an externality, steel and laundry.

by a steel mill. The steel mill produces steel (S) and smoke emissions (e) using inputs $z_1, \ldots, z_m$, according to

$$S = f_s(z_1, \ldots, z_m) \tag{5.2a}$$

$$e = f_e(z_1, \ldots, z_m) \tag{5.2b}$$

Note that e is chosen by the steel mill [Eq. (5.2b)] but e enters into the production function of the laundry [Eq. 5.1)]. The laundry has no say over what the level of e is nor how e enters its production function. Thus the smoke is an externality.

A consumption externality is very analogous. The difference is that we deal with utility functions instead of production functions [as in Eq. (5.1)]. Consider the utility function $U(x,e)$, where x is just a basket of goods chosen for consumption and e is levels of pollution, which enters the utility function through no choice of the consumer. This is a consumption externality.

Figure 5.3 shows an example of a consumption externality. The externality is generated by a paper mill that discharges pollution into a river that is used for swimming. For illustrative purposes, we will assume the water pollution is undesirable only to the extent that it degrades the swimming experience; for instance, the river may totally clean itself (naturally) within a few miles of the paper mill. Shown in Figure 5.3 is a set of indifference curves between pollution and other goods (for some typical consumer). Note the two distinct regions in Figure 5.3. To the left of $\hat{P}$ (low levels of pollution), swimming and pollution are inversely related. More pollution means the swimming experience is degraded. Thus additional quantities of other goods are needed to keep utility constant. At some point, however, swimming is just not fun anymore; the river has become so polluted that swimming ceases. This is the point of the kink in the indifference curves in Figure 5.3 (at $\hat{P}$). To the right of this point, increased pollution has no effect on utility. One problem with these indifference curves is that they are nonconvex.[8] As mentioned in the context of Figure 5.2, this can lead to serious problems with pricing, which will not be explored here.[9]

So why should we be worried about externalities? The basic problem is that the generator of the externality is deciding how much of the externality to produce but is not taking into account the effects of the externality on others. Figure 5.4 illustrates the case of the steel mill and the laundry with a modest externality in the form of smoke from the steel

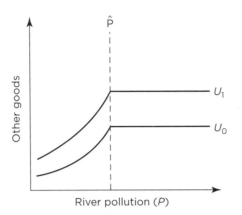

FIGURE 5.3 Indifference curves with consumption externality.

mill. Shown in Figure 5.4 are possible output combinations of laundry and steel given a fixed amount of inputs (production possibilities). The maximum amount of steel that can be produced with these resources is S_0. With no intervention, the steel mill will ignore the effects it might have on the laundry and produce S_0 of steel; the laundry will produce as much as it can, L_0. Assuming prices for steel and laundry (p_s and p_L, the total value of output can be read off the vertical axis as shown in Figure 5.4.[10] Now eliminate the externality by merging the laundry and steel mill into one firm. Steel production will adjust, taking into account the negative effects of the smoke, finding a point at which the total *value* of output (Y) is greatest, (S_1,L_1). Reading physical output off the vertical axis, we can see that indeed $Y_1 > Y_0$. Note that some smoke may still be generated, but the amount is chosen so as to balance the interests of the steel mill with those of the laundry. If there is a transfer from the laundry to the steel mill, this is a Pareto improvement (both the laundry and steel mill are made better off). If no transfer takes place, (S_1,L_1) is a potential Pareto improvement over (S_0,L_0). This is because the pie is bigger when the externality is corrected.

There is a question of semantics about whether we have eliminated the externality at (S_1,L_1). There is still smoke being produced so there is still an external effect. The convention is to distinguish between Pareto-relevant and Pareto-irrelevant externalities.[11] It is socially desirable to correct a Pareto relevant externality; after the correction, the externality becomes Pareto irrelevant. Thus smoke at (S_0,L_0) is Pareto relevant whereas smoke levels at (S_1,L_1) are Pareto irrelevant.

There is another type of externality that can best be illustrated by an example. Suppose you have been a swordfish eater for many years. Recently you have seen the price of swordfish rise dramatically due to the increasing popularity of fish in a healthy diet. The actions of others have driven up the price of fish so that now you have to pay more so you consume less swordfish. This is what is known as a pecuniary externality.[12] Basically, your prices change due to the actions of others. Your utility changes because your income remains fixed. While this is certainly an external effect, it is not something that we will be concerned about. The basic reason is that there is no inefficiency involved in introducing a pecuniary externality. Prices change, but we have efficiency before and after the price change. We have just moved from one point on the Pareto frontier to another. Although this may have distributional consequences, it does not have the efficiency effects of a conventional externality which involves the inappropriate physical amount of an externality.

FIGURE 5.4 Pareto relevance of externality. (S_0, L_0), steel and laundry production without coordination; (S_1, L_1), steel and laundry production with firms merged; Y_1, value of output of merged firm; Y_0 value of output without coordination; (p_s, p_L), prices of steel and laundry.

III. PUBLIC GOODS AND BADS

We have just examined two important reasons why markets may not always work to provide a Pareto optimal allocation of environmental goods: open access and externalities. We now turn to a more general treatment of the nature of goods and bads, with a particular focus on the market implications of different characteristics of goods and bads.

Economics has defined two fundamental characteristics of goods: excludability and rivalry. Excludability has to do with whether it is *possible* to use prices to ration individual use of the good. Rivalry has to do with whether it is *desirable* to ration individual use, through prices or any other means.[13]

A. Excludability

To be able to use prices to allocate a good, it is necessary to ensure that consumers do not consume a good unless an appropriate price has been paid. Thus it must be possible to keep the consumer from the good. This is excludability. Not all goods are excludable. For instance, a regular broadcast television signal can be received by anyone with a television set. It is not possible (or at least it is difficult) to selectively determine who will be able to receive the signal. Another example is the fishery on the high seas. Keeping consumers (in this case fishers) from using this resource is very difficult (i.e., costly). As an example of a bad, air pollution is also nonexcludable. Air, of whatever level of cleanliness, is all around us. We cannot exclude certain people from consuming air pollution.

DEFINITION *A good is excludable if it is feasible and practical to selectively allow consumers to consume the good. A bad is excludable if it is feasible and practical to selectively allow consumers to avoid consumption of the bad.*

Why is excludability important? Because to attach a price to the consumption of a good or bad, we have to be able to deny that consumption if the price is not paid. This is how market allocation works. For a good, this is a straightforward concept. If I produce hamburgers, I must be able to deny you the right to consume a hamburger unless you pay for it. Another example of a nonexcludable good would be a city park without a fence and entrance control. I cannot charge for admission because anyone can use the park, whether or not they have paid admission. Thus no one will pay admission. A fence and entrance control could be added, but this would be so expensive that its cost could outweigh any benefits associated with restricting entry to the park. Generally, we would expect to see exclusion only when the benefits of exclusion outweigh the costs of exclusion. Exclusion must be not only technologically possible but also not too costly, relative to the benefits of exclusion (if any). This is the reason the word "practical" is used in the definition of exclusion.

For a bad, the concept is a little more subtle. Suppose I have produced garbage and I want someone to take it off my hands—"consume" it. With excludability, I can pay someone to store it for me and I am rid of it. A price can be attached to the act of consumption. Without excludability, I can pay someone to consume the bad, but that person can give it right back to me—there is nothing to force that person to actually consume the bad. Thus prices do not work.

Household garbage is excludable with the right laws on littering and trespass; it is not excludable without those laws. Suppose I have generated some household trash and wish to pay someone to consume it (i.e., store it safely). Without laws on trash disposal, whomever I pay to dispose of my garbage could simply leave it by the side of the road or throw it back into my yard. With laws preventing such actions, when I pay someone to consume my trash, that person must retain control of the trash until someone else voluntarily (i.e., with pay) agrees to take it.

Urban air pollution is not excludable. It is not physically possible to selectively target who is to consume the air pollution (i.e., breathe it). Everyone consumes it to the same degree. If it were possible to exclude air pollution, only those people who agree to be compensated for the pollution would consume it. If someone is not compensated, they would not consume.

Two factors play a major role in excludability. One is the cost of exclusion and the other is the technology of exclusion and how it changes over time. Consider the Great Plains of the central United States. In the last century, it was an open access resource—open to everyone for grazing (for everyone's animals, that is), since the cost of fencing was prohibitively expensive compared to the gains from exclusion (prevention of overuse). Over time, the payoff to exclusion increased but, more importantly, the technology of exclusion changed (the invention of barbed wire), making fencing cheaper. A similar case applies to television, particularly those programs disseminated via satellite and cable. Historically, it has been too expensive to exclude consumers. However, with the development of low-cost signal scramblers and unscramblers, exclusion became economically feasible, particularly for high value programs such as recent films. A third example is local parks. A local park could be made excludable by building a fence around it and installing a gatekeeper to control access. However, compared to the value generated by the park, such costly measures are rarely warranted. Only when there are low cost ways of excluding, such as parking controls for parks that can be accessed only by car, will exclusion exist.

Thus exclusion must not only be physically possible but also must be a good idea, given the cost of exclusion compared to the benefits. In general, the benefits involve the additional social value of having limited as opposed to unlimited access to the resource. If the good is being provided privately, the benefit is the revenue that can be gained by charging admission.

Environmental goods have undergone some change in excludability over the past few decades, mostly through legal rather than technological changes. The simplest example is garbage (like the normal household type). Without institutions, garbage is not excludable. Without laws against littering, garbage will simply be dumped wherever convenient, much as it was in the Middle Ages in Europe when people would throw it out their window onto the street. This, however, has been defined as littering or creating a nuisance and is illegal in most locales. Consequently, garbage is now excludable. People can selectively choose to trade money and garbage. This is the economic transaction of the trash collector and the household. This legal aspect of excludability of course could also apply to ordinary goods. Without laws protecting property and outlawing stealing, all goods would be open access and exclusion would not be possible.

Space plays a particularly important and, in some ways, confusing role with regard to exclusion. Most nonexcludable goods and bads are provided locally—city parks, television, air pollution. A consumer can effectively be excluded through location. If a consumer can be prevented from living in a community then the consumer will live elsewhere and effectively be excluded from the community's locally nonexcludable goods. It will be too costly to travel to consume those goods. The basic point is that goods and bads may be locally nonexcludable though globally excludable.

Fisheries and Excludability

In an article in *Science* in 2006, a group of scientists projected that at the rate we are depleting fisheries in the ocean, all current fisheries will have collapsed by 2048 (Worm et al., 2006). In a column in the New York *Times*, John Tierney (2006) took issue with this conclusion, arguing that this result ignores the transition many fisheries have been making from nonexcludable to excludable. He points out that if researchers in the mid-19th century had plotted buffalo depletion, they could have reached a similar conclusion that overhunting doomed future inhabitants of the western United States to a life without fresh meat.

Tierney argues that to the early settlers the lack of wood for fencing and the vast expanses of the Great Plains of the United States made the Plains seem like the oceans today: exclusion was difficult and impractically costly. But innovation reduced the cost of exclusion: cowboys emerged, branding institutions were developed, and, in the 1870s, cheap barbed wire fencing was introduced. What had been nonexcludable became excludable, and overexploitation ceased.

He also argues that similar innovations are appearing in fisheries. Although nobody has figured out how to brand fish or fence the ocean, rights to fish are being defined and policed. And as a result, many fisheries that once were collapsing are now thriving. Though such solutions work better for some fisheries than others, the point is that if the incentives for exclusions are strong enough, technologies are more likely to emerge to facilitate moving resources from nonexludable to excludable.

In fact, Costello et al. (2008) have done just such an analysis, also in an article in *Science*. They collected data on a large number of fisheries from around the world, some managed with a property rights systems (transferable fishing quotas) and some not. They found that the use of property rights halted the collapse of fisheries.

Why is excludability important? For a price system to work it must be possible to take possession of the good or bad for which the price is being paid. Without excludability, a price system cannot work.

B. Rivalry

A second important characteristic of goods is rivalry. This is a slightly more subtle concept than excludability. Rivalry pertains to the manner in which a good is consumed. As an example, compare the consumption of a bratwurst with that of a flower garden. For the bratwurst, the act of consumption destroys the good and makes it unavailable for anyone else to consume. In contrast, the act of consumption of a flower garden involves light bouncing off flowers and being transmitted to the eyes of the consumer. This is fundamentally nondestructive to the flower garden and in no way diminishes the ability of someone else to "consume" the flower garden in precisely the same way.

These examples best illustrate the concept of rivalry. A good is rival in consumption if the act of consumption reduces the amount of the good that might be available for other consumers. A good is nonrival if consumption does not diminish what is available for others. Note that in contrast to exclusion, this is not a characteristic of a good that might change with technology or costs. A bratwurst will always be rival since the nature of consumption will not change. Thus rivalry is a more fundamental characteristic of a good or bad than is exclusion.

Garbage (the household variety) is an example of a rival bad. When I "consume" a bag of garbage, I am taking control of the bag, perhaps storing it in my backyard. When I consume that bag, it is unavailable for others to consume. Thus standard garbage is a rival bad.[14] Air pollution on the other hand is nonrival. When I take a deep breath in downtown London, I in no way diminish the ability of others to "enjoy" dirty London air.[15] My act of consumption does not diminish the quantity of the bad available to others. The global climate (threatened by greenhouse gases) is the purest example of a nonrival good. One person's enjoyment of the climate in no way impinges on the ability of others to enjoy the climate.

One way to view the idea of rivalry is through opportunity cost. When I consume a rival good such as a bratwurst, I am reducing the number of bratwurst available for others, or perhaps necessitating that another bratwurst be manufactured to return us to our starting point. In either case, there is an opportunity cost for others associated with my consumption. In contrast, when I consume a flower garden, there is no social opportunity cost (for others) of that consumption. The same amount of flower garden is available for others. No additional flowers need be planted. When I breathe the air in downtown Mexico City, I am not changing the amount of pollution available to others. Thus I am neither benefitting nor imposing additional costs on others. There is no opportunity cost (positive or negative) imposed on others from my breathing. If, on the other hand, my breathing reduced the amount of pollution, then there would be a negative social opportunity cost (an "opportunity benefit") associated with my breathing polluted air. This is the case for garbage consumption. When I consume a bag of garbage (i.e., store it in my back yard), I diminish the amount of garbage everyone else has to tolerate.

DEFINITION *A bad (good) is* rival *if one person's consumption of a unit of the bad (good) diminishes the amount of the bad (good) available for others to consume, i.e., there is a social opportunity benefit (cost) to others associated with consumption. A bad (good) is* nonrival *otherwise.*[16]

One complicating factor that applies to goods more than bads is congestion. A sparsely populated rural highway is nonrival in that there is no opportunity cost associated with one additional person using the road. We all know, however, that once congestion sets in, there is an opportunity cost of that extra driver and the road is no longer nonrival. A road is a congestible good—nonrival for low levels of consumption and rival for high levels of consumption. The typical reason for congestibility is an indivisibility in production that is closely related to economies of scale. We cannot produce a one-person road. Roads by their very nature can handle a certain amount of traffic without becoming congested. Alternatively, even if we could produce a one person road, it would be almost the same price as a many-person road. It would be less desirable to provide many one-person roads rather than a single multiperson road.

Why is rivalry an important issue? The key is efficiency. If there is no cost associated with incremental use, and if price equals marginal cost, the price should be zero. But with a price of zero, how can revenues balance costs so that the good or bad is efficiently provided? We return to this issue later.

C. Categories of Goods and Bads

We can now put these two concepts of excludability and rivalry together and classify goods on the basis of both criteria. Figure 5.5 shows these two criteria together. The degree of rivalry is shown horizontally and the degree of excludability is shown vertically.

We have already considered two of the types of goods presented in the figure: open access resources and (of course) private goods. These are the two types of rival goods, and excludability is what distinguishes them. On the right are two new categories of goods: club goods and pure public goods. Club goods are so named because excludability allows the formation of a "club" to provide the good—you only get it if you belong to the club and pay your dues. In practice, this might be a club as the English word is normally defined or it might be a local municipality that restricts access to local public goods either through parking restrictions or residency checks or simply by the fact of location—everyone within a reasonable distance of the good is a resident of the municipality and pays taxes to the municipality. The lower right corner of the table in Figure 5.5 is for goods that are both nonrival and nonexclusable. Nonexcludability creates problems for using a market (as we have already discussed), and nonrivalry suggests that a market would be undesirable. Figure 5.6 presents some examples of goods and bads in different categories to parallel Figure 5.5.

	Rival	Nonrival
Excludable	Private goods	Club goods
Nonexcludable	Open access resources	Pure public goods

FIGURE 5.5 A classification of goods.

	Rival	Nonrival
Excludable	Goods: Bratwurst Bads: Household garbage today	Goods: Local public beach with access control Bads: Water pollution in small lake
Nonexcludable	Goods: Fishery Bads: Household garbage in Middle Ages	Goods: National defense or global climate Bads: Greenhouse gases

FIGURE 5.6 Examples of goods and bads.

D. The Supply of Public Goods and Bads

The entire discussion in the previous several sections pertains to characteristics of good in consumption, not production. In general, goods characteristics in consumption are the most important from the point of view of market failure and efficiency of provision. On the production side, many public goods are no different than private goods. For instance, bridges, pollution control, and schools are goods that are produced in a normal fashion with the total supplied simply the sum of what is supplied by individual producers.

This can be made more precise by letting there be a set of $i = 1,\ldots,I$ different producers of a public good, each producer generating x_i of the public good. For most public goods or bads the total supplied, X, will simply be the sum of what individual producers produce:

$$X = \Sigma_i\, x_i \tag{5.3a}$$

This applies for goods (e.g., bridges) or bads (e.g., pollution). If each producer is represented by a supply curve, the aggregate supply will simply be the horizontal summation of the individual supply curves.

Although this is by far the most common way to look at the supply of a public good, it is not the only way.[17] The two other mains types of public goods, in terms of supply, are "weakest-link" goods and "best-shot" goods.

For a weakest-link good, the aggregate supply is the minimum of what is supplied by all producers:

$$X = \min_i \{x_i\} \tag{5.3b}$$

And for a best-shot good, it is the maximum:

$$X = \max_i \{x_i\} \tag{5.3c}$$

An example of a weakest-link good would be disease eradication, where the producers are individual countries investing in disease eradication. Clearly, as long as the disease exists somewhere it has not been eradicated. In the sense that a chain is as strong as its weakest link, the aggregate effort on eradication is equal to the lowest effort among different countries. Another example would be flood protection via a network of dikes or levees. If any one levee fails, flooding occurs.

The best environmental example of a best-shot public good is a race to develop a new cost-effective carbon-free energy source or other invention that has the power to transform an environmental problem. All that matters is the one who is successful. A variant on this is what is called a "better shot" public good.

In most cases, the production side of a public good looks like any other good: horizontal summation of individual supply curves yields the market supply. If no mention is made of the nature of aggregation (summation, best-shot, weakest-link), it is safe to assume the discussion concerns the case where aggregate supply is the sum of what is provided by individual suppliers.

IV. EFFICIENT PROVISION OF PUBLIC GOODS AND BADS

The problem now is to determine how much of a public good or bad should be provided, from a Pareto optimality perspective (efficiency). This is one of the basic questions in economics. Recall from the previous chapter that conditions for efficiency for a competitive economy (i.e., a private good economy) are that the marginal rates of substitution be equal among consumers and that the marginal rates of transformation be equal among producers and that MRS = MRT.

From a demand and supply perspective, efficient provision of private goods requires that goods be produced up to the point at which the marginal cost of production equals the price and where the quantity produced equals the quantity demanded at that price. Consumers and producers facing the same prices will automatically equate marginal rates of substitution and marginal rates of transformation. Quite simply, efficient provision of a private good requires production and consumption where the supply and demand curves intersect.

For a pure public good, these conditions must be modified (due to the nonrival nature of the good). Let MRS_i be the marginal rate of substitution between the public good and a numeraire good[18] for consumer i and let MRT be the marginal rate of transformation in production between the public good and the numeraire good. We can think of these MRSs and MRT as representations of the marginal value in consumption and marginal cost of production for the public good, in terms of the numeraire good. The claim is that for the Pareto optimal provision of the public good, G^*, it must be that

$$\Sigma_i \, MRS_i \, (G^*) = MRT \, (G^*) \tag{5.4}$$

Suppose otherwise. First suppose that the left-hand side of Eq. (5.4) is greater than the right hand side at the Pareto optimum G^*. In other words, the total value to consumers of G^* exceeds the cost of production—an expansion of G^* will bring the equation into balance. This is a Pareto improving move since another unit of the public good is worth more to consumers than it costs to produce, hence a contradiction. Similarly, if the left-hand side of Eq. (5.4) is smaller than the right-hand side, a reduction in G^* will be Pareto improving, and lead to another contradiction. This proves the validity of Eq. (5.4). Only when Eq. (5.4) holds will there be no possible improvement. In other words, at the Pareto optimum, G^*, the total marginal benefit to consumers [the left-hand side of Eq. (5.4)] should equal the marginal cost of production [the right-hand side of Eq. (5.4)]. Eq. (5.4) is known as the *Samuelson Condition* for efficient provision of a public good.[19]

If we are dealing with a public bad, such as pollution, the equation still holds and the interpretation is quite similar: the marginal rate of substitution between pollution and a numeraire good (i.e., the marginal damage to each individual consumer) should be summed over the population and equated to the marginal rate of transformation in production (i.e., the marginal cost of pollution abatement).

We can also look at the provision of pure private and pure public goods through the familiar lens of supply and demand curves. The conventional approach to demand for

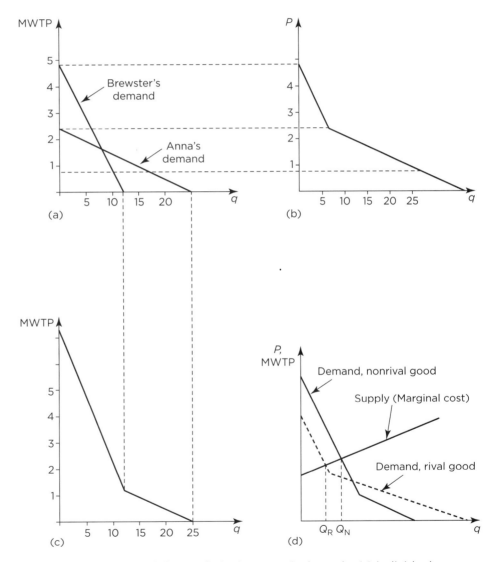

FIGURE 5.7 Supply and demand, rival vs. nonrival goods, (a) individual demands; (b) aggregate demand, rival good; (c) aggregate demand, nonrival good; (d) efficient provision. Q_R, quantity produced of rival good; Q_N, quantity produced of nonrival good.

goods is, for a given price, to sum individual quantity demanded to obtain market demands. At a given price, we see how many loaves of bread are demanded by each individual and sum these quantities to obtain the total number of loaves of bread demanded at that price. This is commonly referred to as horizontal summation of individual demands and is illustrated in Figure 5.7. Figure 5.7a shows the individual demands for some good by the two members of our society, Anna and Brewster. The horizontal axis shows the quantity and the vertical axis shows price or marginal willingness to pay (MWTP). The MWTP is how much one more unit of the good is worth to the person. In a market, the price is also equal to the value of one more unit of the good to the person. If the good is a rival good, then the aggregate demand is obtained by summing individual demands horizontally, as shown in Figure 5.7b. For any given price, we see the total amount of the good the consumers wish to consume.

If the good is nonrival then we proceed differently. We are interested in the total marginal willingness to pay for specific amounts of the nonrival good. In other words, for a particular price, how much of the good will consumers wish to consume? The difference here is that all consumers consume the same amount of the good. So the price paid to producers for the good is the sum of the prices paid by the individuals. For example, if Anna is willing to pay $1.90 for the fifth public park and Brewster is willing to pay $2.80 for the fifth public park then together they are willing to pay $4.70 for the fifth public park. To capture this, we sum demand vertically, as shown in Figure 5.7c.

The good is produced in the same way whether or not it is rival in consumption. Thus the same supply or marginal cost curve applies to its production. Supply is shown together with demand in Figure 5.7d. If the good is considered rival, consumption is Q_R, whereas if the good is considered nonrival, consumption is Q_N. Note that more of the good will be produced if it is nonrival, but this need not always be the case.

Also note that although we can infer the market price for a rival good from the intersection of supply and demand, we cannot do this for a nonrival good. At the price at which supply and demand intersect for the nonrival good, individual demand will be quite low, since aggregate demand is the *sum* of individual willingnesses to pay. It is not easy to induce the optimal provision of the nonrival good shown in Figure 5.7d.

It is worth emphasizing that supply and demand curves exist for any commodity, independent of whether there is a market for that commodity. Thus despite the fact that markets rarely exist for public goods or bads, demand curves still exist, though they may not be well known.

V. PRICING PUBLIC GOODS AND BADS

We have detailed how public goods and bads differ from private goods and bads and have intimated that markets will not work for public commodities. We have also examined how much of the public good or bad is desirable. In this section, we take this question further, examining what happens if markets are used. We will see that the basic problem is a mismatch between what is optimal for the producer and what is optimal for the consumer. We will assume excludability is possible; otherwise there is no hope of using prices as a rationing device.

The first question we examine is, what happens when markets are left alone to do their business? How far off from Pareto optimality will provision be? We then turn to the question of markets and what prices we would like to see for consumers and for producers. We would like consumers to face prices such that there are no opportunities for Pareto improvements among consumers. We would like producers to face prices such that the right amount of the public good is provided. And, finally, we would like those prices to be the same.

The last step in this section is to depart from the conventional assumption in economics—that there is one price. We turn to "personalized prices" as a way to obtain a Pareto optimum using the market. Personalized prices vary from one individual to another. Alas, we obtain Pareto optimality only by relying on government determination of the personalized prices (they do not emerge spontaneously in the market).

A. Market Provision of Public Goods

What happens if markets are used? We sort of know what the answer is but it is important to understand why: if we let the market operate without intervention, public goods generally will be underprovided.[20] To see this most simply, assume we have a society with N identical individuals. Each individual has income w and can consume two goods, a rival, excludable private good, x, and a nonrival, nonexcludable public good, G. To clarify things, the public good is nonexcludable in consumption (everyone gets to consume it) but it is of course excludable in production—it is produced like any other good at a cost and can be sold at a price to anyone. The price of the private good will be set to one and we will adjust the units with which we measure the public good, so that its price is also one. The utility of any of the identical people is given by

$$\text{Utility} = u(x,G) \tag{5.5}$$

We might think that G is out of the control of an individual, because it is a public good. However, individuals are free to purchase some of the public good, if that is in their own best interest (they are unlikely to take anyone else's interests into account). Let g be the amount of the good that one individual will purchase and let $\bar{G}$ be what is provided by everyone else: $G = \bar{G} + g$. This of course means that if our individual provides g of the public good, only $w - g$ of money is available for the private good. Thus we can rewrite the individual's utility as

$$\text{Utility} = u(w - g, g + \bar{G}) \tag{5.6}$$

Now our individual must decide how much g to choose to consume. The choice depends, of course, on how much of the public good is being provided by everyone else. Figure 5.8 shows indifference curves for our individual with the two goods being g and $\bar{G}$. Remember wealth or income (w) is fixed. For any utility level where it is desirable for our consumer to spend his money on both private goods and public goods, then indifference curves must be U-shaped. However, at high levels of public goods provision by others, $\bar{G}$, it is entirely plausible that our consumer will not want to purchase any more public goods. In this case, $\bar{G}$ needs to increase to keep utility constant as g rises from zero; indifference curves will be upward sloping in g.

Note that for a fixed $\bar{G}$ the best choice of g is the point at which one of the indifference curves just touches the horizontal line at the fixed $\bar{G}$. As $\bar{G}$ increases (other

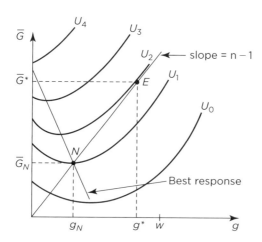

FIGURE 5.8 Market provision and efficient provision of a public good. n, number of identical people in society; g, individual's provision of the public good; $\bar{G}$, provision of the public good by everyone else; w, wealth of each individual; $N, g_N, \bar{G}_N$, market provision of public good; $E, g^*, \bar{G}^*$, efficient provision of public good; U_i, indifference curves.

people are providing more of the public good), the best choice g falls. If others are providing the public good, then we do not need to provide as much ourselves. The "best response" line in Figure 5.8 indicates the choice of g that will be made in response to the amount of the public good selected by others, $\bar{G}$. For a high enough $\bar{G}$, no g will be provided.

Now how much will be provided by our little society? Since everyone is the same, everyone will make the same choice about g. Thus $\bar{G} = (n - 1)g$. This is a straight line through the origin of slope $n - 1$, also drawn on Figure 5.8. The point at which it intersects the best response line (point N) indicates the amount of g and $\bar{G} = (n - 1)g$ that will be generated in this economy: $g_N, \bar{G}_N$. So some amount of the public good is provided privately.

How much should be generated in this society? In other words, what is the efficient level of g and $\bar{G}$? The reason we would expect the public good to be underprovided is that if consumers raise their g, they benefit individually but everyone else also benefits and they do not take that into account (there is an externality in consumption). Suppose they could be sure that when they raise their g, everyone else matches them by raising their gs? Then consumers see the full benefit of raising g. We can see this in Figure 5.8. If we assume that $\bar{G}$ stays at $(n - 1)g$ as consumers raise and lower g, then consumers see all of the advantage of raising and lowering g. In other words, if consumers know that g and $\bar{G}$ will lie along the upward sloping straight line in Figure 5.8, the best choice of g is the point at which an indifference curve is just tangent to the straight line, labeled E in Figure 5.8, resulting in public good provision g^* and $\bar{G}^*$.

Note that the noncooperative provision of the public good $(g_N, \bar{G}_N)$ is lower than the efficient provision $(g_N, \bar{G}_N)$, though still positive. The basic reason for this is that when each person chooses g noncooperatively, he or she sees some benefits from buying g (thus $g_N > 0$), but most of the benefits occur to others and are ignored in deciding how much to consume (thus $g_N < g^*$).[21]

We know that there is a great deal of private contribution to protect the environment—such contributions support international organizations such as Greenpeace, the Worldwide Fund for Animals/World Wildlife Fund (WWF), and many national organizations such as the Sierra Club. The Nature Conservancy is specifically set up to accept private donations and use these to purchase important natural areas and set them aside for prosperity—a very clear example of private provision of a public good.[22]

The public bad version of this involves a number of polluters. They are injured somewhat by polluting, but most of the damage accrues to someone else. Thus they will control pollution somewhat, reflecting the damage they incur, but they will not control pollution as much as is socially desirable.

The bottom line for both goods and bads is that the market may very well provide some public goods or public bads. However, left to its own devices, the market typically under-provides public goods and over-provides public bads.

B. Efficient Uniform Public Good Pricing: Consumers

Now suppose that somehow we could set prices for public goods and bads. Can we do this and obtain efficiency? We approach the case of generating an efficient price for the nonrival bad by first considering the nonrival good. Suppose we have a park with a fence around it and thus can control access. Suppose the park is large so that congestion is never a problem and suppose the cost of operating it is all fixed costs with no costs depending on visitation.

Finally, assume tastes for the park are widely distributed within the population, with some people valuing a visit highly, some people placing a very low value on a visit, and others (most) somewhere in between. What then should be the efficient admission price (one price for all consumers)? To answer this, we should determine first what is the efficient amount of use of the park. Since there is no cost associated with letting one more person use the park, efficient use clearly calls for everyone having access to the park. If we were to exclude anyone, then a Pareto improvement could be attained by allowing whomever has been excluded to use the park—costs would not change, current users would not have their utility reduced, and those newly admitted would have their utility increased.

What admission price would support this Pareto optimum? Clearly only a price of zero. Figure 5.9 shows a typical demand curve for park visits. At any price $p_1 > 0$, there will be a certain number of people (q_1) who will pay the admission price and visit the park. There will also be a number of people ($q_0 - q_1$) who will not visit the park because the price is too high. Observe that a lower price would be Pareto preferred. This is

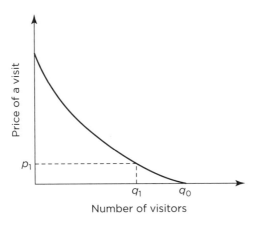

FIGURE 5.9 Demand for visits to nonrival, excludable parks. q_0, number of visitors with no admission charge; q_1, number of visitors when price is p_1.

because if the price is lowered, all previous attendees would be just as well off, some people for whom the price was previously too high would be able to enjoy the park at the lower price, and the cost of providing the park services is unchanged. This process continues until the price drops to zero. The consequence is that for a nonrival excludable good, the optimal price from the consumer's point of view is *zero*.

What is the analog for a nonrival bad? For the sake of simplicity, suppose we have a factory in the middle of nowhere generating smoke that fills a circular area around the factory 2 km in radius. There are no effects outside this circle. Furthermore, there is no good reason for anyone to live inside the circle—assume that workers at the plant are housed at a location 15 km away and are provided free transportation to the plant. The following question is before us: If people decide to live in the polluted area around the plant, what compensation should be paid for the damage they incur?

First it is necessary to determine the Pareto optimal location of consumers. Clearly it is Pareto optimal for nobody to live inside the polluted area. Anyone inside the polluted area can be made better off by moving outside the area, since we assumed there are no advantages to living close to the factory. What level of compensation to people living with the pollution would support this efficient location of consumers? The answer is zero compensation. Any positive level of compensation will attract those consumers for whom damage is less than the compensation offered. It is a Pareto improvement to lower the compensation, inducing those people to move outside the circle (or not move there to begin with). This is because the factory will be better off not paying compensation and the individual will be indifferent between living with pollution and compensation versus living without pollution (since the compensation exactly offsets the pollution damage). Consequently, the optimal compensation is zero since compensation induces people to inefficiently move to the pollution.[23]

This example is a bit stylized since there is no reason for people to live near the pollution. Consider a slightly more realistic example of an airport located within a city. Noise bothers people and the further they are from the airport, the less the noise and the annoyance. People live near the airport because they work near there so commuting is shorter. What compensation should the airport pay to consumers? The same argument applies. Without compensation, consumers optimally trade-off the noise with convenience in finding a place to live. The consumer lives where the marginal convenience cost of moving a little further away just equals the marginal gain to moving in reduced noise. Any positive compensation that is offered will diminish the net damage from the noise and cause the consumer to locate slightly closer to the airport.[24] This is not socially desirable. Key here is the nonrivalry. If the noise were rival (i.e., my consumption of it reduces the amount available to others), then my consumption provides a community service for which I could be paid. Because my consumption of the nonrival bad (noise) imposes no costs, positive or negative, on anyone else, there is no justification for my receiving payment for consumption. In fact, to the extent that such compensation distorts my decisions about where to locate, it is undesirable. However, if compensation does not distort decisions (e.g., lump-sum compensation to land owners is nondistortionary since land cannot be moved and thus the payment would not change locational decisions), compensation is neutral and perhaps desirable on equity grounds.

Another way of looking at this is that there are actions producers can take to reduce damage (e.g., emit less smoke or noise) and there are actions "victims" can take to reduce damage (e.g., change location or install household noise insulation). The pollution the victim suffers provides sufficient incentive to the victim to take action to reduce damage. Any compensation that distorts those incentives is undesirable. Nondistortionary compensation is fine for equity reasons but of no consequence to efficiency.

This point about the undesirability of compensation for consumption of nonrival bads is difficult to grasp intuitively.

C. Budgets and the Optimal Producer Price

Having discussed consumption we now examine production. We have seen that the optimal provision of nonrival goods involves a price to the consumers of zero. Production of nonrival commodities is similar to production of any other good or bad. There are costs associated with production that are positive for the case of goods and negative for the case of bads. Thus to efficiently supply a nonrival good, the private producer must have revenue sufficient to cover costs. Unfortunately, if the producer must price at zero, which we have just indicated is the efficient consumer price, then the producer cannot afford to provide the right amount of the nonrival good (in fact, he won't produce any). Budgets will not balance and a deficit will result. If the producer raises prices to generate revenue for provision, demand will be depressed. There will be too little of the public good provided.

For a nonrival bad, a similar thing happens. The cost of production of a bad such as smoke is negative, i.e., the producer saves money by producing the smoke. Since the price is zero (no compensation should be paid), the producer of smoke runs a budget surplus. In other words, the producer saves money by generating smoke and pays no compensation. Smoke is good for the producer; without intervention the smoke producer will ignore damage to the consumer. Now suppose we require a balanced budget, with the producer's savings paid out as compensation to consumers. This would be analogous to the private provision of a public good where the budget must balance. If people are compensated, they desire more smoke than if they were not compensated. Thus in this case there is an incentive to overprovide the public bad. Too much smoke will be generated.

This result occurs because even though it is costly to supply one more unit of a public good, it is costless to provide the public good to an additional consumer. Thus, relying on marginal cost pricing, the producer should receive a positive price (for a good) but the consumer should pay a price of zero. Obviously budgets are not going to balance. A similar thing happens for public bads.

D. Personalized Price

A theoretical but impractical solution is available for this problem using prices for public goods and bads. First decide how much of the public good is to be provided by determining where aggregate demand and supply intersect. Then charge each consumer his or her individual willingness to pay for that amount of the good. By construction, the total marginal cost of provision will be the sum of the individual willingnesses to pay, thus we should have budget balancing. If Anna loves to hike and really values public parks, she should pay her marginal willingness to pay for those parks. If Brewster couldn't care less, perhaps because he has an allergy attack when he goes outdoors, Brewster should pay little toward the public parks. If each pays according to his or her marginal willingness to pay, not only will the right amount of the public good be provided but the budget will balance—the amount collected will equal the amount necessary for provision.

The iterative process that extracts information from consumers on willingness to pay for the public good results in what is known as a Lindahl equilibrium, and the prices everyone pays are known as Lindahl prices. These are named after the Swedish economist Erik Lindahl.[25]

One of the main failings of the Lindahl equilibrium is that information is required on individual demand curves. Those demand curves must be provided voluntarily by individuals and they have every incentive to distort their articulated demand. Since the greater your demand, the more you will pay, you have an incentive to understate your demand. This is what is known as *free-riding*. Even if you have a large willingness to pay, you know that if you fib and indicate a low willingness to pay, you will still get the benefits from the good (assuming nonrivalry). You free-ride on everyone else's willingness to provide the public good. Everyone of course has this incentive so that all of the articulated individual demand curves can be assumed to understate demand, although by how much we cannot know.[26]

If we were to seek contributions from consumers to reduce pollution, we would expect some people to claim they were damaged only slightly since their contribution would be based on their announced damage. This is free-riding on the provision by others.

SUMMARY

1. Two basic characteristics of a good or bad are the degree of rivalry in consumption (termed rivalry) and the ability of producers to exclude consumers, preventing consumption (termed excludability).

2. Excludability is determined by the availability of a technology of exclusion. Furthermore, the costs of exclusion must be low enough that the benefits of exclusion exceed the costs.

3. Rivalry is a more fundamental characteristic of consumption of a good or bad. A good or bad is nonrival if its consumption involves no opportunity costs for others. In other words, one person's consumption does not change the amount of the good or bad available for others to consume.

4. A good or bad that is both rival and excludable is a *private* good or bad. A good or bad that is both nonrival and nonexcludable is a *public* good or bad. A good or bad that is excludable and nonrival is *club* good or bad. A good that is nonexcludable and rival is an *open access* resource.

5. Aggregate demand for rival goods is determined by summing individual demand curves horizontally; aggregate demand for nonrival goods is obtained by summing individual demand curves vertically.

6. Public goods may be privately provided by individuals in the market. In such a case, the market provision will be lower than is efficient. For public bads, market provision will be higher than is efficient.

7. Nonrival goods or bads should have a price of zero, which makes it difficult for revenues to equal costs. This also implies that no compensation be paid to victims of pollution, in general.

8. An externality exists when the consumption or production choices of one person or firm enter the utility or production function of another person or firm without permission or compensation.

9. A pecuniary externality occurs when one person's actions affect the prices paid by another person. Since prices do not enter into utility or production functions, this is not a conventional externality and in fact does not involve an inefficiency.

10. The fact that a public bad is nonrival means that everyone consumes the same quantity of the public bad. This is equivalent to the amount of consumption being chosen by someone else, the generator of the public bad. This is an externality. Thus there is an intimate connection, and in fact some redundancy, between the concepts of public bad and externality.

11. It is costly to supply one more unit of a public good, but it is costless to provide the public good to an additional consumer. Thus, relying on marginal cost pricing, the producer should receive a positive price (for a good) but the consumer should pay a price of zero. As a consequence, budgets do not balance. A similar thing occurs with public bads.

PROBLEMS

1. Consider an airport that produces noise that decays as the distance (d), in kilometers, from the airport increases: $N(d) = 1/d^2$. Fritz works at the airport. Fritz's damage from noise is \$1 per unit of noise and is associated with where Fritz lives. His costs of commuting are \$1 per kilometer (each way). The closest he can live to the airport is $d = 0.1$ km.

   a. Write an expression for Fritz's total costs (noise and transportation).

   b. What is the distance Fritz will live from the airport in the absence of compensation for the noise? What are his total costs?

   c. Suppose Fritz is compensated for his damage, wherever he may live. How close to the airport will he choose to live? How much will he be compensated?
   (*Hint:* Solve graphically or using calculus.)

2. Consider an air basin with only two consumers, Huck and Matilda. Suppose Huck's demand for air quality is given by $q_H - 1 - p$ where p is Huck's marginal willingness to pay for air quality. Similarly, Matilda's demand is given by $q_M = 2 - 2p$. Air quality can be supplied according to $q = p$ where p is the marginal cost of supply.

   a. Graph the aggregate demand for air quality along with individual demands.

   b. What is the efficient amount of air quality?

3. When sulfur dioxide is emitted into the air it is transported over long distances and is converted to sulfuric acid. This gradually falls to the ground, either as rain or snow or simply by settling out of the air. This is called acid deposition. In what way could acid deposition be consider a rival bad? [*Hint:* See the paper by Freeman, 1984.]

4. Two types of consumers (workers and retirees) share a community with a polluting cheese factory. The pollution is nonrival and nonexcludable. The total damage to

workers is p^2 where p is the amount of pollution and the total damage to retirees is $3p^2$. Thus marginal damage to workers is $2p$ and marginal damage to retirees is $6p$. According to an analysis by consulting engineers, the cheese factory saves $20p - p^2$ by polluting p, for a marginal savings of $20 - 2p$.

a. Find the aggregate (including both types of consumers) marginal damage for the public bad.

b. Graph the marginal savings and aggregate marginal damage curves with pollution on the horizontal axis.

c. How much will the cheese factory pollute in the absence of any regulation or bargaining? What is this society's optimal level of pollution?

d. Starting from the uncontrolled level of pollution calculated in part (c), find the marginal willingness to pay for pollution abatement, A, for each consumer class. (Abatement is reduction is pollution; zero abatement would be associated with the uncontrolled level of pollution.) Find the aggregate marginal willingness to pay for abatement.

e. Again starting from the uncontrolled level of pollution, what is the firm's marginal cost of pollution abatement? What is the optimal level of A?

f. Are the problems of optimal provision of the public bad (pollution) and the public good (abatement) equivalent? Explain why or why not.

5. Why is lump sum compensation for an externality nondistortionary?

6. In the manner of Figure 5.8, draw a set of indifference curves such that an individual's private provision of the public good increases as the number of people in the society increases. Explain your result. Are these indifference curves plausible?

7. Consider the problem of carbon dioxide emissions. We will abstract away from the problem slightly, assuming there are polluters and consumers in two regions, the OECD (O) and the rest of the world (R). Suppose the marginal cost of controlling CO_2 emissions is \$10 per ton of emissions. Let the marginal willingness to pay for pollution reduction be $13 - Q$ for region O and $12 - 2Q$ for region R, where Q is the amount of pollution reduction. The United Nations is considering two proposed methods for controlling CO_2 emissions, both involving polluters paying for the damage they cause. Proposal A involves the polluters paying damages to each region for the pollution generated. Proposal B involves the polluters in each region independently negotiating pollution reductions, assuming the other region is not undertaking pollution reduction.

a. Graph the marginal abatement cost and the total marginal willingness-to-pay schedules. What is the socially efficient level of emission reductions, Q?

b. How much total pollution reduction will occur under proposal A and what will be the total compensation received by regions O and R? If those payments were instead placed in the general coffers of the UN, would the outcome be any different from an efficiency point of view? Why or why not?

c. How much pollution would be generated under proposal B? Explain any differences between this answer and the answer to parts (a) and (b).

NOTES

1. Although Hardin (1968) made the problem of the tragedy of the commons widely known outside the economics community, the problem was well known to economists.

2. There is a subtle difference between open access and common property resources. Open access literally means anyone may have access. Common property resources belong to a group collectively and thus only members of the group have access. For example, fisheries on the open seas are open access, whereas fisheries in a country's coastal waters are common property, belonging to the country. From an operational point of view, both situations lead to inefficient use. Elinor Ostrom (1990) discusses many of the institutions that have emerged to solve the common property resource problem. In fact, she won the 2009 Nobel Memorial Prize in Economics for this work.

3. Libecap and Wiggins (1984) provide one of the classic discussions of solving the common property problem in the case of oil production.

4. There is a large and sometimes confusing literature on externalities. Some highlights are Heller and Starrett (1976), Baumol and Oates (1988), Freeman (1984), Buchanan and Stubblebine (1962), Mishan (1971), Plott (1983), Bator (1958), and Meade (1952, 1973).

5. See Meade (1952).

6. This example involving the "strength" of an externality is motivated by Baumol and Bradford (1972) and Baumol and Oates (1988).

7. A convex set is a set in which a straight line segment connecting any two points in the set lies entirely within the set. In Figure 5.2, a line connecting points A and C will not be entirely within the set of production possibilities for the case of the strong externality.

8. Nonconvexity for an indifference curve means a straight line segment connecting any two points on the curve does not lie entirely above the curve. A line connecting a point just to the right of the kink in any indifference curve in Figure 5.4 with a point just to the left of the kink will be entirely below the indifference curve, implying nonconvexity.

9. The problem with nonconvexities in either production or consumption is that a market equilibrium, supported by prices, generally cannot be relied on to exist when production sets (Figure 5.9) are nonconvex or when indifference curves (Figure 5.3) are nonconvex. The problem may be that for all possible prices, consumers will want one bundle of goods to consume and producers will want to produce some other bundle. Prices may never bring consumers and producers together, as is usually the case. See Starrett and Zeckhauser (1974). Cooter (1980) argues that this is a nonissue in practice.

10. If the total value of output (S_0, L_0) is $Y_0 = p_S S_0 + p_L L_0$, we want to solve for Y_0. If we plot $Y = p_S S + p_L L$, and pass it through (S_0, L_0), then that line will intersect the vertical axis at $L = Y_0 / p_L$.

11. See Buchanan and Stubblebine (1962).

12. See Viner (1931) and Baumol and Oates (1988).

13. This taxonomy is attributed to Head (1962). Randall (1983) provides an illuminating discussion of rivalry and excludability and related classifications. See also Musgrave (1959). See Laffont (1989) or Starrett (1988) for more advanced treatments. The economics community is not totally united in this classification of goods, however. Laffont (1989) provides a classification scheme that builds on rivalry and excludability, but adds the issue of jurisdiction (local vs. national) and the extent to which consumption is voluntary or not. Congestion also causes additional problems and has motivated the study of club goods (see Cornes and Sandler, 1996). These various distinctions are left to a more detailed examination of the theory of public goods.

14. When the garbage in the dump leaks into the groundwater it becomes both nonexcludable and nonrival.

15. Whenever I use this example in class, someone always points out that some of the pollution will stay in my lungs and diminish what is available for others. This is of course true but the effect is so minuscule that we ignore it.

16. See Starrett (1988) for further discussion of the notion of rivalry. Baumol and Oates (1988) use the term depletability to mean rivalry for the case of a bad.

17. Hirshleifer (1983) and Cornes and Sandler (1996), among others, have discussed the different kinds of supply for public goods.

18. Numeraire goods are common in simple theoretical economic models. What matters is relative prices rather than absolute prices. The fact that wine is twice as expensive as beef is more meaningful that the fact that wine is €5 a bottle. The numeraire good is the good that all other goods are compared to, in terms of price.

19. The Samuelson Condition for the efficient provision of public goods was first articulated by the MIT economist Paul Samuelson (1954).

20. There is a large literature on the private provision of public goods, with many important issues. For instance: How does the size of a society influence public good provision? How does government provision affect private provision? How close to efficient is the private provision? Bergstrom et al. (1986) is the seminal paper in this literature. Myles (1995) provides a good treatment of some of these issues.

21. The reason everyone provides a little of the public good is that everyone is identical. If one person provided none of the public good, everyone could be assumed to do the same and there would be no provision. If our society consisted of heterogeneous individuals then we would probably see some people providing some amount of the public good and other people providing nothing (see Bergstrom et al., 1986, or Myles, 1995).

22. One of the issues in private provision is the extent to which government provision will "crowd out" private provision. One empirical study of charitable giving in the United States estimated that every dollar of government support for charities crowded out (eliminated) private giving of almost $0.30 (Abrams and Schmitz, 1978). Theoretical studies indicate the effect could be even greater (Bergstrom et al., 1986). Experimental studies consistently show that individuals voluntarily contribute even more than this theoretical model predicts (see Isaac and Walker, 1988, and Burger and Kolstad, 2009).

23. Baumol and Oates (1988) discuss this issue of compensation in the case of public bads.

24. In law and economics, this is referred to as "coming to the nuisance" (see Cooter and Ulen, 2008).

25. I am grateful to Lars Mathiesen of the Norwegian School of Economics for correcting an error in the first edition of this book, in which I identified Lindahl as a Norwegian.

26. There is a fairly advanced literature on what are known as "demand-revealing mechanisms." These are complex ways of calculating payments for public goods based on articulated willingness to pay. It is possible to structure these so that people have an incentive to tell the truth about demand; unfortunately, for these mechanisms, we cannot always be assured that we will collect the right amount of money to pay for the public good. See Tideman and Tullock (1976).

6

DECISION MAKING AND ENVIRONMENTAL PROTECTION

THE PAST FEW CHAPTERS HAVE BEEN LEADING UP TO ANSWERING THE PRACTICAL QUESTION of how much environmental quality should be provided—a normative question. We now turn to how, from a practical point of view, one actually answers the question. Such questions are usually posed in two distinct situations—project evaluation and regulatory design. In the first case, a project (such as habitat restoration) is being proposed and the question is whether the project is a good idea. Related to this is the question of how large should the project be? The second type of question concerns regulations leading to pollution control. A regulation has been proposed and the question is whether it is a good idea and, if so, how strict should it be?

The two primary *practical* approaches to this problem are benefit–cost analysis and its simplified cousin, cost-effectiveness analysis. In benefit–cost analysis, measures of consumer and producer surplus (discussed in Chapter 4) are used as measures of social surplus, consistent with the potential Pareto improvement criterion—looking at the net gains from an action (project or regulation), aggregated over all individuals and firms. Although benefit–cost analysis is a large subject and the topic of entire courses of study, only some of the key aspects of the approach are highlighted here. There are also some shortcomings of benefit–cost analysis as a method for making social decisions about the environment, shortcomings that every practitioner or user should keep in mind.

Cost-effectiveness analysis is very similar except that the environmental goals are taken as given and the focus is on how best to achieve these goals from a cost point of view. Furthermore, there are several other variants of benefit–cost analysis for evaluating projects or regulations, including distributionally weighted benefit–cost analysis (taking into account the income of individuals who bear the costs and benefits) and multicriteria analysis (focusing on more than one social objective).

We will also consider an important complement to analysis of the benefits and costs of actions—the incidence of those actions. The incidence of an action refers to identifying which parties actually bear the costs or enjoy the benefits of a regulation or public project. A policy that tends to fall disproportionately on the shoulders of the working poor may be less politically attractive than a policy that distributes net benefits more evenly. The purpose of analyzing incidence is not to reach conclusions about what should be the distribution of benefits and costs but simply to provide additional input into the political process of policy making.

In fact, it is important to realize that for all of these methods, the conclusion of the analysis is only one input into the decisions policy makers must make regarding proceeding with either a project or regulation. A modern economy is full of distortions, regional considerations, and other real-world factors that cannot be fully taken into account in a quantitative analysis. Making public policy is a complex process involving criteria outside the scope of economics—for example, equity, administrative simplicity, or concentration of benefits and costs.[1]

I. BENEFIT-COST ANALYSIS

In the chapter 4, we saw how measures of surplus could be used as a welfare measure. For a competitive market, consumer plus producer surplus is maximized at a market equilibrium and at a Pareto optimum.

One of the primary tools for deciding on the appropriateness of a government intervention in the economy is benefit–cost analysis. The basic idea is simple: find the project that gives the largest surplus. As we saw in the chapter 4, total surplus (consumer plus producer surplus) is equivalent to total benefits less total costs. We know that in general a surplus maximum is equivalent to a Pareto optimum. The idea may be simple but implementing the idea is far from simple. The usual problem is difficulty in quantifying some of the benefits and/or some of the costs.

In the next few sections we will take a closer look at issues in benefit–cost analysis. In the next section we will consider the example of the control of particulate control. We will look at how to evaluate the net benefits (benefits less costs) of several governmental programs for regulating particulate emissions. We will then turn to issues of how to treat surplus in secondary markets, how to deal with market imperfectious, and how to treat benefits and costs that occur at different points in time. These are important issues in implementing benefit–cost analysis.[2]

A. Measuring the Effects of Government Programs

Consider an example of particulate pollution (fine dust). Particulates are emitted into the air by Riley's Renovation and Construction Company. The particulate emissions lead to concentrations of total suspended particulates (TSP) in the air, which cause problems for asthmatics (and others), such as Morgan Sandpiper, one of the local residents. We could of course generalize this to a group of polluters and a group of injured parties. (In this case, the individual supply curves would be summed horizontally to generate the aggregate supply and the individual MWTP curves would be summed vertically, as discussed in the previous chapter.) The government must step in to decide what the Pareto optimal amount of TSP might be. Or a less ambitious goal would be for the government to propose several levels of particulate abatement and determine which generates the most surplus. Alternatively, the government may propose a regulation (such as a tradable permit system for the generation of particulates or an emission fee) and wish to evaluate the surplus consequences of such a regulation.

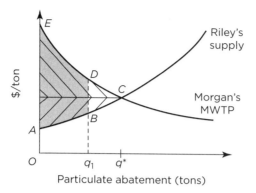

FIGURE 6.1 Total surplus from control of particulate emissions (particulate abatement). q^*, surplus maximizing amount of particulate abatement; *ABCDE*, resulting surplus; *ABDE*, surplus from quantity restriction to q_1.

Figure 6.1 shows the situation graphically. The horizontal axis shows the amount of pollution abatement (reduction in particulate emissions from the uncontrolled level). The vertical axis is in dollars per ton and represents either the marginal cost of pollution control (for Riley) or the marginal benefit (to Morgan) of pollution control (Morgan's marginal willingness to pay for pollution control—MWTP). Either would be measured in dollars per ton. The quantity q^* maximizes surplus (shown as the hatched area in the figure—*ABCDE*). This surplus is the area between the MWTP (demand) curve, supply curve, and the vertical lines $q = 0$ and $q = q^*$.

We now consider two regulations that the government is considering to control emissions of particulates. The two regulations we consider are as simple as possible—either a quantity control (the government tells Riley how much to emit) or a pollution tax (the government taxes Riley for the pollution his firm emits).

1. Quantity Control. Suppose the government decides that the amount of abatement should be q_1. The surplus associated with this level of service is the shaded area in Figure 6.1—*ABDE*.

This surplus is the area between the MWTP (demand) curve, supply curve, and the vertical lines $q = 0$ and $q = q_1$. The societal surplus loss associated with this level of particulate control (vs. q^*) is the difference between the two levels of surplus: *ABCDE—ABDE*: the region *BCD*.

2. Tax. Now let us evaluate the surplus consequences of a tax on the emissions of particulates—a unit tax (say $1 per ton) applied to every unit of particulates emitted and collected from each polluting firm. If Riley's Renovation is emitting 5 tons of particulates, it will have to pay $5 in tax. If it is emitting 10 tons, it will have to pay $10 in tax. For every additional ton of pollution it abates, Riley's pollution tax bill drop by $1.

This is shown in Figure 6.2. Riley's marginal cost of particulate reduction (abatement) is reduced by $1 per ton because of the tax savings associated with additional abatement. Thus the supply curve drops by $1/ton. Note that as the figure drawn, Riley will not abate at all, but with the tax, Riley will choose (of his own free will) to reduce emissions (abate) by q_1 units of particulates. This is because, for levels of abatement less than this, the marginal cost of abatement is actually negative—Riley saves money by

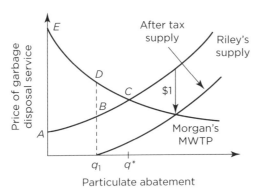

FIGURE 6.2 Effect of a tax on particulate abatement. q^*, efficient amount of abatement; q_1, amount of abatement with $1 unit tax.

abating up to q_1. In actuality, this just means that for low levels of abatement, Riley saves $1 of tax by abating a unit, but it actually costs less than $1 to abate a unit. On the other hand, for abatement levels greater than q_1, additional abatement is costly and thus will not be pursued by Riley's firm.

The main question is what is the surplus associated with the $1 tax on Riley's emissions? In calculating surplus, keep two things in mind: surplus is always calculated with respect to quantities, and surplus is calculated using the "true" supply and demand curves, not the distorted or post-tax/postregulation curves. To address the first part of the calculation, the question is really what is the surplus associated with the change in the quantity of abatement that result from the $1 tax. We know that the tax moves us from $q = 0$ to $q = q_1$. The second part of the calculation requires us to use Morgan's demand curve and the pretax Riley supply curve. This is in fact the same calculation we did in the previous section in the context of Figure 6.1. The surplus associated with applying the tax is $ABDE$ in Figure 6.2. Note that we are ignoring the amount of tax in the surplus calculation since that it really just a transfer from one part of society to another (from Riley to the government).

In sum, to evaluate the consequences of a tax or subsidy it is first necessary to determine what quantity of the good (or bad) will be supplied in response to the tax or subsidy. Having determined that, the undistorted supply and demand curves should be used to measure the surplus effects.

B. The Role of Secondary Markets

Often, a government action in one market will impact other markets. The obvious question is, how many markets do we have to examine in measuring the surplus associated with the government action? For example, suppose the government tightens regulations on sulfur dioxide emissions from industry. We would expect this to increase the demand for scrubbers (abatement equipment), which in turn might increase the demand for steel, which might increase the demand for iron. Where do we stop?

It turns out that secondary markets can be ignored so long as prices do not change in those markets.[3] Consider an example drawn from an actual empirical analysis of air pollution control. The case is that of a large American city, Baltimore. The question is how much particulate matter should be emitted into the air in the city—what should be the concentration limit on total suspended particulates (TSP)? This question was examined by several economists at the University of Maryland (Oates et al., 1989). The top panel of Figure 6.3 shows their estimate of the marginal cost to firms of different levels of the TSP standard (supply of pollution) and the marginal benefit of pollution (demand for pollution) in Baltimore.[4] Note that both are negative, consistent with pollution being a bad (whereas pollution abatement is a good). The demand for pollution is roughly horizontal—constant marginal benefits. The bottom panel of Figure 6.3 shows a hypothetical market for electrostatic precipitators, the primary means of controlling emissions of TSP.[5] The supply of precipitators is shown as a horizontal line, since it is assumed to be a constant cost industry. A constant cost industry is one in which the marginal cost of production does not change as the quantity provided changes. In our case, all we need is that prices in the precipitator industry (probably national or international) do not change with variations in quantity demanded in Baltimore. Also shown in Figure 6.3b are two demand curves for precipitators, one with no TSP control in Baltimore and one (further to the right) with significant TSP control. Note that there will be no price effect in the precipitator market. Thus we can ignore it.

Returning to the supply and demand for TSP concentrations (top panel, Figure 6.3a), note that 87 μg m^{-3} is the efficient level at which to set TSP limits. The benefits of moving from 120 μg m^{-3} to this efficient level is the shaded area in Figure 6.3a, equal to approximately \$45 million per year.

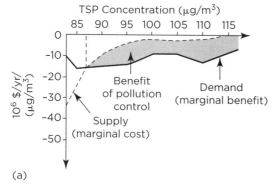

(a)

(b)

FIGURE 6.3 Benefit–Cost analysis of pollution (TSP) reduction in Baltimore. Supply and demand for (a) pollution (Adapted from Oates et al., 1989) and (b) pollution control (electrostatic precipitators).

C. Multiple Time Periods

Costs and benefits often occur at various points in time. For instance, we may spend money to reduce emissions of carbon dioxide today but see the benefits of this action only decades or centuries into the future. How do we evaluate such an intertemporal mixture of costs and benefits? The standard approach is to write a future cost (or benefit) as an equivalent current cost (or benefit), using a *discount factor*. The discount factor for time period t, β_t, is used to convert costs in time period t, C_t, into costs today, $\beta_t C_t$. For example, what would be the *current* equivalent of \$1 paid 2 years from now? Suppose the discount factor is $\beta = 0.9$. That would mean that we would be indifferent between receiving \$0.90 today and \$1 two years from now. In general, if we are faced with a stream of costs $\{C_0, C_1, C_2, \ldots, C_T\}$ and a stream of benefits $(B_0, B_1, B_2, \ldots, B_T)$, we can convert these streams into a net present value (NPV) of benefits less costs using the appropriate discount factors:

$$\text{NPV} = \sum_{t=0}^{T} \beta_t \{B_t - C_t\} \tag{6.1}$$

The next logical question is where do the values of β_t come from? There is some controversy over what the appropriate value of β_t is to use for environmental decision making—the social discount factor. The simplest answer is that the discount factors are market determined, based on how consumers and producers trade off the present with the future.

Figure 6.4 shows how the market might view decisions between consumption today (c_0) and consumption tomorrow (c_1). The line TXT' in Figure 6.4 is the production possibilities for our society between consumption today and tomorrow. If we consume less today and invest it (for example, plant trees to harvest tomorrow), we should have more to consume tomorrow. That is why the line segment OT is slightly smaller than the line segment OT'. The point T represents "consume everything today and nothing tomorrow." The point T' represents "consume nothing today and everything tomorrow." Points in between, on TXT', represent a mixture of consumption today and tomorrow. Which point along this production possibilities frontier will the market choose? We can represent demand by drawing indifference curves in Figure 6.4 based on a representative consumer. Consumers generally prefer consumption earlier, rather than later, reflecting impatience and risk (we are all mortal and may not see tomorrow). The indifference curve marked U_0

FIGURE 6.4 Market determination of discount factor.

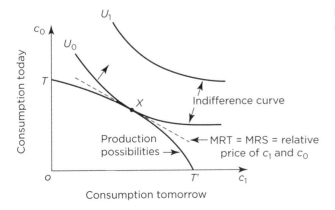

represents the highest level of utility attainable that is still feasible (intersects with TXT'). The point X is the equilibrium consumption point. This is the point at which the marginal rate of transformation of c_1 for c_0 is equal to the marginal rate of substitution of c_1 for c_0. The slope of the tangent to either curve at this point represents the price ratio between consumption today and consumption tomorrow. Suppose this slope is s. That means that if I increased consumption of c_1 by \$1 and reduced consumption of c_0 by s, my utility should stay the same. But this is the same definition we used for the discount factor.

Thus we see that the market discount factor is determined by two things: the consumer's rate of time preference (willingness to defer consumption) and how productive investments are (the marginal productivity of capital).[6] At equilibrium, these are both equal to each other and to the discount rate. The typical assumption regarding the discount factor is that discounting is exponential. In other words, β_t is defined by

$$\beta_t = (1 + r)^{-t} \tag{6.2}$$

where r is the market discount rate or market interest rate.[7] One characteristic of exponential discounting is that the future does not matter very much unless r is very close to zero. In Eq. (6.2), if r is 5% per year, then for $t = 100$, β_t would be 0.0076. This means that at this discount rate, you would not be willing to spend 1¢ today to avoid \$1 of damage in a century! This is somewhat troubling when trying to justify controlling carbon dioxide emissions today in order to avoid significant damage to the planet a century from now.

There are several ways out of this troubling conclusion. One is to recognize that while the market discount rate may be ideal for firms to use in evaluating investments, it may not be the correct discount rate to use for evaluating public projects or regulations. To make this distinction clear, we label the discount rate to use for public choices as the *social discount rate*. Unfortunately, the social discount rate is not easily observable; its true value is subject to some debate and to value judgments. We return to this later but there is a general consensus that the social rate of discount should be lower than the market rate. This has significant implications. As we saw in the previous paragraph, with a discount rate of 5%, we are only justified in spending less than 1¢ today to avoid \$1 of damage 100 years from now; with a discount rate of 1%, we could justify spending up to 36¢ today to avoid that \$1 of damage in a century—a very different picture.

One big reason the social discount rate is lower than the market rate is that risk is implicit in most observed market interest rates. But most environmental decisions are modest in the grand scheme of things for governments. If an individual or most companies lose a million dollars, it is a big deal; if a government makes a million dollar mistake, it is lost in the noise of government expenditures. The consequence of this is that societies should not typically include a risk premium in the social discount rate.[8] For this reason alone, the social discount rate will be lower than the market rate.

Another approach to understanding the difference between social discounting and market discounting is to question the exponential nature of market discounting—what results from the multiplicative nature of the right-hand side of Eq. (6.2), as was discussed in the context of that equation. One implication of exponential discounting is that the differential valuation we place on costs and benefits between this year and next has to be the same as between two adjacent years far in the future (such as year 50 and 51). In other words, $\beta_1/\beta_0 = \beta_{51}/\beta_{50} = 1/(1+r)$. But there is considerable evidence that people view the distant future differently than the near future, implying that the discount factor declines with time. In fact, biologists tell us that nonhuman animals also exhibit such behavior, rather than exponential discounting.[9] Hyperbolic discounting is a common alternative to exponential discounting that has just such a property, a gradual reduction over time in the discount rate.[10] There is a problem with hyperbolic discounting (or other nonexponential forms of discounting)—dynamic inconsistency. The problem is that if I make a decision today based on my assessment of the future, I may realize next year that I made the wrong choice. Dieting is a good example of a problem of dynamic inconsistency. We know full well that maintaining a svelte body is good for our health. But when faced with the tiramisu dessert, we tend to rationalize that we can correct the overeating tomorrow. But then tomorrow, the same situation repeats itself.[11]

Another way of viewing social discounting is to recognize that for intergenerational decisions (many environmental decisions affect more than one generation), the social discount rate emerges from an ethical judgment rather than a market process.[12] The idea is that there are two aspects to how we view a future generation relative to ours. One has to do with pure time preference—we do have a preference for today's generation relative to the next generation. Let δ be the rate at which we discount the future for this reason alone. Some have argued that δ should be small, if not zero—why should governments which will be around for a very long time favor the present over the future? A second fact is that future generations may be better off than we are—a dollar of gain or loss to a wealthy person should not count as much (to society) as a dollar of gain or loss to a poor person. Thus if we are getting richer at an annual rate of g (e.g., 2% per year), then we should take that into account when comparing one generation to another. Let η be the absolute value of the elasticity of the marginal utility of consumption, representing the curvature of the utility function. In words, η tells us if consumption goes up by 1%, how much marginal utility should go down, in percentage terms. If $\eta = 0$, then the marginal utility of a dollar of consumption does not change as incomes increase. If $\eta = 1$, then a 1% rise in income will reduce the marginal utility of consumption by 1%. The end result is a representation of an intergenerational social discount rate of

$$r = \eta\, g + \delta \tag{6.3}$$

The first part of the right hand side of Eq. (6.3) indicates how much more important we are than future generations, because of the fact that we are poorer. The second term represents our preference for the present over the future from a pure time point of view.[13] Although Eq. (6.3) helps understand the underpinnings of an intergenerational social discount rate, it does not solve the problem completely since now one must make judgments about η and δ (and even g), rather than r.[14]

A final word of caution is appropriate in choosing a social discount rate to evaluate an intertemporal environmental regulation or project. Many such environmental actions involve significant near-term costs and long-term benefits (often not materializing for decades). It is tempting to "choose" a discount rate that is low, which tends to justify near-term action. But there are many social investments in addition to environmental protection that may be considered worthy—education, poverty alleviation, or disease eradication, just to name a few. One should be consistent in the choice of a discount rate across the many actions that have intergenerational implications. If too many projects pass the benefit–cost test, there may be an inconsistency with how much the current population is willing to invest (instead of consume) for the benefit of future generations.

The Effect of Discounting on Climate Policy

In Chapter 2, we examined William Nordhaus's analysis of the normative question of how much action society should take to reduce greenhouse gases. His conclusion is that emission control levels should be ramped up over time. There have been other analyses, some of which reach very different conclusions. One such analysis, also mentioned in Chapter 2, is by Nicholas Stern and his colleagues at the U.K. Treasury. In a very readable analysis, Nordhaus examines the differences between the Stern Review (the analysis done by the Stern team) and his own (Nordhaus, 2007). He argues that to a large extent the differences between the two analyses are due to differences in discount rate, which is due to differences in Eq. (6.3).

The Stern Review views the problems from an ethical point of view, and argues for a specific ethical point of view. The Stern Review makes the case that the time discount rate (δ) must be close to zero, since it would be unethical for a government to place substantially different weights on different generations (they assume $\delta = 0.001$). They also assume a unitary utility elasticity $\eta = 1$) and a growth rate of 1.3% per year ($g = 0.013$). Applying Eq. (6.3) results in a discount rate of 1.4% per year that would be applied to dollars or euros of consumption. Nordhaus, on the other hand, adopts a time discount rate of 1.5% ($\delta = 0.015$), a consumption elasticity of 2 ($\eta = 1$), and other assumptions that yield a growth rate of 2% per year ($g = 0.02$). Together, this results in a discount rate of 5.5% per year. Nordhaus justifies his figures based on observing how people and markets *actually do* trade off time, whereas Stern justifies his figures on how he thinks governments and people *should* trade off time.

The implications of these differences are stark. Keeping all assumptions constant except the discount rate, Nordhaus calculates that under the Stern Review assumptions, the emission control rate in 2015 should be 53%, with a carbon tax of $360/ton. In contrast, using the Nordhaus assumptions on the discount rate, the emission control rate in 2015 should be 15% with a carbon tax of $35 per ton. This illustrates the dramatic differences discounting can make to policy on climate change (or other environmental problems that involve intergenerational trade-offs).

D. Using Benefit–Cost Analysis

What we have shown is that measures of demand and supply can be used to make normative decisions even if markets do not exist. In particular, demand and supply can give us monetary measures of the benefits of pursuing various governmental interventions on behalf of the environment. To be honest, we have painted a relatively rosy picture of benefit–cost analysis. Though potentially powerful, it is not easy to implement. Further, there are subtle assumptions built into the approach.

One assumption regards the distribution of income. As mentioned earlier, if incomes change, supply and demand curves will probably change, and thus so will measures of surplus associated with a government policy. Thus if one does not consider the income distribution "correct" or "just," then there may be reason to question the policy prescriptions arising from benefit–cost analysis.

Another assumption is that the compensation principle applies. Suppose cost–benefit analysis concludes that building a dam in a scenic canyon is a good idea because the benefits exceed the costs. This means that the gains to some from having the dam exceed the losses to others from having the dam. For there to be a Pareto improvement, the winners should compensate the losers so that everyone is better off with the dam. However, this compensation rarely occurs. This is the controversial Kaldor–Hicks compensation principle at work.

Another problem, not insurmountable, is that measuring the damage to the environment from pollution is no easy task. We will consider this in the next several chapters and show that great strides have been made. It would be foolish to pretend that it is easy to quantify the marginal willingness to pay for all environmental goods, since many are very intangible. This is not a fatal problem for benefit–cost analysis, only a factor that makes its application difficult in some cases. Furthermore, this can introduce a subtle bias into benefit–cost analysis. In practice, when benefit–cost analysis confronts thorny, difficult-to-quantify environmental benefits, the typical approach is to acknowledge these and specifically point out that they have not been monetized. The bias is that environmental benefits are more likely to be omitted from an analysis than the costs of the regulation or project.[15]

It is not just environmental damage that is hard to include in a benefit–cost analysis. Some other dimensions of a project that are socially, or at least politically, important may also be difficult to include. An obvious example is permanent jobs in an area with chronic unemployment.

Another implementation problem involves what economists call the theory of second best. If there are prior distortions in the economy, such as taxes or regulations, perhaps unrelated to the environmental problem at hand, supply and demand curves will be distorted. And distorted supply and demand may give distorted measures of surplus.

There are also philosophical objections to viewing all societal decisions through the lens of benefit–cost analysis, in the same sense that not all personal decisions are made through that lens (at least not for most of us). Several philosophers have been very critical of the reduction of all benefits and costs to a single metric, arguing that some values are nonmonetizable (moral duties) or that the act of valuation destroys value (such as trying to come up with the monetary value of a friend). Sometimes we place value on things not based on our personal benefits (often wealthy individuals will support progressive taxation even though it is not necessarily in their own personal best interest).[16]

This list of problems with benefit–cost analysis should not be taken as an indication of fatal flaws in the method. Benefit–cost analysis remains a vital part of quantifying and evaluating the desirability of government intervention in the economy on behalf of the environment. One should simply be aware of its shortcomings.

II. INCIDENCE

As we have seen, when a regulation is promulgated or a project is undertaken, there are benefits and costs. In standard benefit–cost analysis, we do not care who bears those costs and benefits. But often it matters a great deal to the public policy process who ultimately pays and who ultimately benefits. For instance, if particulate emissions regulations in a city are tightened up, some firms will pay more for pollution control. Perhaps they are able to pass these costs on to consumers, perhaps not. If they can pass them on, consumers bear the cost of the regulation. If they cannot pass them on, then either the labor force or the owners of the firm will bear the cost.

As should be clear from this example, when we speak of bearing the cost of a regulation, we are distinguishing between the direct costs to the firm or individual to whom a regulation legally applies (the statutory costs) and the ultimate bearer of the economic cost of the regulation. If a firm can pass the cost on to its customers, then it is the customer who pays the cost, from our point of view. The same applies to benefits.

Consider a firm producing cement; a regulation is imposed on air emissions that has the effect of raising the cost of production. This is shown in Figure 6.5. Prior to the institution of the regulation, the price of cement was p_0, and was equal to marginal costs. The regulation increases marginal costs by c_r. The net effect is that the price of cement rises to p_1 while the marginal cost of making the cement is $c_1 + c_r = p_1$. Note from the figure that price (to the consumer) has gone up by less than the marginal cost of the regulation. The net price the cement producers receive (not counting the cost of the regulation) has gone down. This can be most easily seen by examining producer and consumer surplus pre- and post-regulation. Prior to the regulation, consumer surplus (not counting the damage from the pollution) was the triangle GCE and producer surplus was GCA. After the regulation, consumer surplus (again, not counting the damage from the pollution) declines to FDE and the producer surplus declines to HBA. The cost of the regulation is $FDBH$ and is divided between the consumers and the producers in the sense that both consumers and producers have seen their surplus reduced by the regulation (again, not counting the benefit of reducing pollution).

With a little imagination, Figure 6.5 can be used to see what happens when the supply or demand curves are differently sloped. With a relatively inelastic demand curve (demand is steeply sloped), most of the cost of the regulation will be borne by consumers. With a relatively elastic demand curve (shallowly sloped), most of the cost will be borne by producers. This is intuitive. An elastic demand curve means consumers have alternatives; they will not tolerate much of a price increase. Consequently, producers cannot pass on much of the costs. An inelastic demand curve means the opposite—consumers have little alternative and will pay higher prices without balking. Consumers will bear much of the cost.

The extent to which a firm must absorb the costs of a regulation is termed *backwards incidence*. Similarly, the extent to which a firm can pass on these costs to consumers

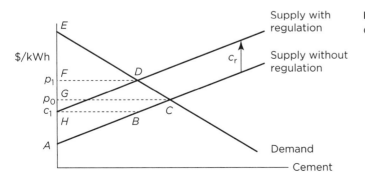

FIGURE 6.5 The effect of a regulation on the cement industry.

is termed *forward incidence*. Since firms are simply legal entities that combine capital (owned by humans), human labor, and land (owned by humans) to generate output, backwards incidence must fall in different proportion on these factors, and it is people of one sort or another who ultimately bear the costs. If labor has little alternative but to work in the firm, then the costs will be passed backwards to labor (wages will decline). If the regulated industry is small compared to the labor market, then the price of labor can be considered exogenous to the industry. In this case, the owners of capital will generally bear the burden of the regulation.

The most common reason why the cost of a regulation may be backwardly incident rather than forwardly incident is that the regulation pertains to a narrow slice of the market. If only some firms in the market for cement are targeted by the regulation, then consumers will have a choice of buying from an unregulated firm or a regulated firm and will not be interested in paying a higher price to a regulated firm. Or if a small country in Europe imposes a stricter regulation on its cement industry than applies to the cement industry in a neighboring country, free trade will allow consumers to choose the cheaper alternative. In essence, if consumers have choice, the demand curve will be relatively elastic.

Tracing who ultimately pays for an environmental regulation is an important part of the analysis of incidence. However, in the end, what is typically desired is an indication of how a regulation affects different groups of people (since consumers, labor, and capitalists are all people). These may be different income groups, different ethnic groups, or different geographic areas (and there are many other ways of categorizing a country's population).

We should also point out that the benefits of an environmental regulation, in terms of reduced pollution, also may fall disproportionately on different groups. A full analysis of incidence should take into account who ultimately benefits from the regulations, as well as who pays.

Incidence of Danish Carbon Taxes

In the 1990s, Denmark instituted some fairly high taxes on carbon emissions—initially on the order of €13 per ton of CO_2, rising to approximately €81 per ton by the late 1990s. By statute, consumers paid the most but businesses were also responsible for paying tax on their emissions. A group of Danish researchers (Wier et al., 2005) asked the question: what income classes bear the burden of this tax? They assumed that the tax was passed 100% onto consumers (full forward-incidence) and used the Danish input-output tables to calculate how much consumers pay. The input-output tables indicate for each industry, how much is purchased from other industries to make a unit of product.

The Danish researchers divided the population into ten deciles of income (poorest 10%, next poorest 10%, etc.). They find that CO_2 tax payments, as a percentage of expenditures, are remarkably constant over the different income groups. The highest burden is for the second-poorest decile, where CO_2 tax payments are roughly 0.51% of expenditures. The lowest is for the richest decile, where the tax payments are roughly 0.38% of expenditures.

III. OTHER EVALUATIVE APPROACHES

In some situations, a benefit–cost analysis may be difficult or unnecessary. For instance, if there is a legislative mandate to provide a specific amount of environmental protection, then the only job is to find the best way of providing that protection; one need not look at the monetized environmental benefits of that environmental protection. Cost-effectiveness analysis works well in these cases. In some situations, there may be several very important criteria for policy makers, criteria that resist monetization and synthesis in a single metric. In these cases, some analysts have used multicriteria analysis. In Europe in particular it is common to modify the compensation principle in an attempt to take into account the different marginal utilities of income for populations of different income. This results in distributionally weighted benefit–cost analysis, in which weights are used to give relatively more emphasis to net benefits that accrue to lower income individuals. We consider each of these approaches briefly.

A. Cost-Effectiveness Analysis

The biggest problem in conducting a benefit–cost analysis of an environmental action is correctly monetizing the environmental benefits. Frequently this is unnecessary. Often legislatures or other decision-making bodies have taken responsibility for defining the environmental objective, viewing it as too complex or politically charged to be defined by analysts or bureaucrats. The U.S. Clean Air Act specifically defines the manner in which ambient air pollution targets are to be defined and furthermore prohibits the use of compliance cost in setting those targets. The Kyoto Protocol for greenhouse gas abatement defines emission targets for participating countries.

Faced with environmental goals or targets that are exogenously specified, the problem reduces to the much simpler one of evaluating the costs of various approaches to achieving the goal or target. Whatever the lowest-cost alternative (all other things being equal) is the choice emerging from cost-effectiveness analysis.

For instance, suppose the goal is to reduce deaths from exposure to high peak levels of ozone in an urban area. More particularly, the goal is to reduce these deaths from 100 to 90 a year—a 10% reduction. Three policies are available—call them policies A, B, and C. For instance, policy A might involve heavy reliance on reducing the number of old cars on the road, policy B might focus more on stationary sources of ozone precursors, while policy C might involve encouraging the relocation of at-risk populations to areas less susceptible to high levels of ozone. The question is, which policy is most cost-effective? Table 6.1 shows the characteristics of these three policies emerging from a hypothetical cost-effectiveness analysis.

In examining Table 6.1, the two measures of relevance for each policy alternative are costs of the regulation (typically borne by industry) and the lives saved by the regulation. There is no need to compute the monetized benefits of the regulations. Given the stated goal of the regulation, to reduce deaths by 10 per year, alternative A accomplishes the goal at least cost.

An alternative way of using cost-effectiveness analysis is to compute the cost per unit of the objective (in this case lives saved). This would be the cost-effectiveness ratio. This might be of interest because different policies perform slightly differently in terms of

TABLE 6.1 Cost-Effectiveness and Effectiveness-Cost of Three Hypothetical Alternatives for Ozone Reduction

Cost and Effectiveness	Policy Alternatives		
	A	B	C
1. Cost of Regulation (millions of $)	100	108	150
2. Lives Saved per year	10	12	10
3. Cost-Effectiveness Ratio	10	9	15
4. Effectiveness-Cost Ratio	0.1	0.11	0.06

effectiveness. For instance, in Table 6.1, policy B saves a few more lives than "necessary," according to the policy objective. The table shows that policy B has the lowest (best) cost-effectiveness ratio: $9 million per life saved. Alternatively, it has the highest effectiveness-cost ratio, at 0.11.

Either of these approaches to cost-effectiveness analysis can be used—the lowest cost to achieve a stated objective or the cost-effectiveness ratio. The latter is sometimes used when the objectives are approximately met but not precisely—it allows the comparison of alternatives that do not quite yield the same results in terms of the objective.

B. Multicriteria Analysis

It is often difficult to monetize all important decision-making criteria, particularly with regard to the benefits of environmental improvement. Taking out a dam on a river can result in a small increase in the population of an endangered fish. Valuing that population increase can be extraordinarily difficult and definitely subject to error and uncertainty.

Given these difficulties, some authors have tried using multicriteria/multiple criteria/multiple goal analysis. Simply put, rather than reducing the outcomes of different programs to one metric, several metrics are used.

For instance, suppose several projects have been proposed to enhance the water flow in a river, at some cost. These projects will also result in enhanced habitat for steelhead trout, an endangered species. One way of evaluating the different projects is to reduce the project outcomes to two metrics: projected cost (C) and the estimated population of steelhead (S). Assuming that C and S can be accurately determined, with and without the project, let W(C,S) be the social welfare associated with outcomes (C,S). Alternatively, this might be the utility of the decision maker. The objective then is to take an action from the set of alternatives which maximizes W(C,S).

It may be that some alternatives are Pareto dominated by others and thus in a straightforward way, the number of alternative actions for consideration can be reduced. But ultimately, one is faced with determining the W function—how society trades off costs and the steelhead population. There are a number of ways of doing this[17] though often one resorts to a weighted linear function of the objectives. In other words, welfare would be a weighted sum of C and S with a good deal of effort expended in determining the weights. Leaving aside the problem of determining appropriate weights for aggregating C and S, a more fundamental problem is that not all welfare functions of two variables can be approximated by a linear function. For instance, suppose preferences are that costs are most important up to a point, after which the steelhead population becomes most important (lexicographic preferences). This way of looking at the problem is not amenable to an approach of the weighted sum of the two objectives.

The bottom line is that while multicriteria analysis may appear to reduce the problems of monetizing tough-to-monetize variables, the downside is in having to determine how various outcomes are traded off by society or the decision maker. In the end, this is likely to be no easier.

C. Distributionally Weighted Benefit–Cost Analysis

One of the criticisms of benefit–cost analysis is that it counts all benefits or costs as equal, no matter who benefits or pays. So if all the benefits accrue to the top 1% of the income distribution whereas all the costs are borne by the lowest 10%, all that matters is the sum of aggregate benefits and costs. Or if all the benefits accrue to firms in terms of producer surplus and all the costs are borne by consumers, again all that matters is aggregate benefits and costs.

Jean Dreze (1998) gives an example of Delhi, India, contrasting the relatively rich New Delhi and the poorer, but much more populated, Old Delhi. His example involves a decision of where to direct foreign aid to clean up pollution. If the criterion is reducing pollution for the greatest number of people, then the aid will be directed to projects for Old Delhi. But the residents of New Delhi will have a much greater willingness to pay for clean air (due to their wealth), and thus the net benefits will be greater for a project directed at New Delhi. He suggests weighting the benefits based on who in fact reaps the benefits, giving a greater weight to a rupee of benefit accruing to a poor person, relative to a rich person, reflecting the fact that the marginal utility of income is greater for the poor person as well as (possibly) societal desire to redress distributional inequities.

Other authors have argued that benefits accruing directly to individuals count more to politicians than benefits accruing to firms, if for no other reason than individuals vote and firms do not. This is despite the fact that benefits accruing to firms eventually end up in the pockets of individuals, as discussed in the previous section on incidence.[18]

SUMMARY

1. Total surplus of increasing the quantity supplied from q^* to q^{**} is the area bounded above by the demand curve (or MWTP curve), below by the supply curve, to the left by the vertical line $q = q^*$ and to the right by the line $q = q^{**}$.

2. Secondary markets can be ignored in a benefit–cost analysis provided the program or action being evaluated does not change prices in the secondary market.

3. The market discount rate is an equilibrium between consumer preference for earlier consumption and the productivity of capital, which produces a bigger pie over time.

4. The market discount rate, r, is defined as the number for which the market is indifferent between 1 dollar (or euro or rupee) today and $1 + r$ dollars (or euros or rupees) in a year's time.

5. The market discount factor between today and t years from now, β_t, is defined such that the market is indifferent between β_t dollars in t years and 1 dollar today. If the market discount rate is r then $\beta_t = (1 + r)^{-t}$.

6. The social discount rate, to be used for making public decisions about public projects or programs, is typically different than the social discount rate. One reason for this is less risk aversion in public decisions (due to the small size of most projects relative to the overall size of government).

7. Exponential discounting is the term applied to standard discounting whereby the discount rate, r, between any two years is constant and independent of the year and independent of whether the trade-off is near term or in the distant future. Hyperbolic discounting involves a discount rate that declines over time.

8. In using a social discount rate for intergenerational public decisions, there is some controversy regarding just what is the correct rate to use. One view is that the intergenerational social discount rate should be $\eta g + \delta$ where δ is the rate of pure time preference, η is the elasticity of the marginal utility of consumption, and g is the growth rate in income. This reflects the fact that as societies get richer, the marginal utility of income will decline—poorer people should count more.

9. Incidence of a regulation refers to a determination of who ultimately pays for the costs and who ultimately benefits from the regulation. Incidence can be important to public decisions about regulations or projects.

10. Forward incidence refers to the extent the costs of a regulation are borne by consumers. Backwards incidence indicates the extent to which the costs of a regulation are born by workers or owners of firms.

11. Other evaluative approaches to making decisions about environmental programs include cost-effectiveness analysis, multi-objective analysis and distributionally weighted benefit–cost analysis.

PROBLEMS

1. A dam is proposed on a stretch of wild river, a river that is currently used for recreation. The dam will generate electricity. The dam will have a useful life of 50 years, after which its reservoir will be full of sediment and the dam will need to be removed. The following are characteristics of the dam:

   Initial Cost: $100,000,000

   Electricity produced: 100,000 MWh per year, @ $100/Mwh.

   Cost of decommissioning dam: $10,000,000.

   Value of recreation lost: $5,000,000 per year

   a. If the social discount rate is 3% per year, is the dam a good idea?

   b. If the social discount rate is 10% per year, is the dam a good idea?

   c. Calculate the "cutoff" discount rate, c, such that the dam is a good idea for discount rates $< c$ and a bad idea for discount rates $> c$.

2. An investment of $100 today will avoid $1,000,000 of environmental damage in 100 years.

   a. At a discount rate of 10%, is this investment a good idea?

   b. At a discount rate of 1%, is this investment a good idea?

   c. At a discount rate of 2%, what is the maximum we would be willing to pay to avoid the million dollars of environmental damage in 100 years?

3. You are the mayor of the small town of Wasilla and a landowner has offered to sell you 1,000 hectares of woodland for $2,000,000. You are very tempted because of the wildlife which live there (such as moose) as well as the recreational value to your constituents. You look at the *Financial Times* and see that if you borrow money for this project, the interest rate will be 5% per annum, and so conclude the discount rate you should use is 5%. Your Parks department estimates that annual recreational and environmental benefits will be $100,000 a year.

   a. Looking only at the next 50 years, is buying the woodland a good idea?

   b. What is the maximum amount you would be willing to pay the landowner to lease the land for 50 years?

   c. How would your answers to (a) and (b) change if the recreational and environmental benefits increase by 3% per year, reflecting the fact that Wasilla is growing, not only in population but in income of the population?

4. You are a hyperbolic discounter. In fact your discount rate between year t and year $t + 1$ is given by $0.05/(1 + t)$ for $t = 0$(today), 1 (next year), 2, 3,.... This means the discount rate between today and a year from now is 0.05. The discount rate between a year from now and two years from now is 0.025. And so forth.

    You are considering an investment in energy conservation (better insulation for your house) that has a lifetime of 5 years. It will cost you $130 to install and will reap benefits in terms of energy saved of $10 in year 1, $20 in year 2, $30 in year 3, $40 in year 4, and $50 in year 5.

   a. Calculate your discount factors for each of the next 5 years.

   b. What is the net present value of the energy savings?

   c. Is the insulation a good investment for you?

   d. Would the insulation be a good investment if your discount rate were a constant 5% over the 5 years?

5. The housing market has been very slow in York. Millie has been trying to sell her house for a million pounds, but has no takers. The mortgage market involves 5% annual interest fixed over a 30-year term, with a 10% down payment (90% of value must be financed). Such a mortgage would involve the same annual payment each year until the mortgage is paid off at the end of 30 years. Millie decides to finance the mortgage herself, offering the house on the same terms as the mortgage market except interest free. From a buyer's perspective, this would be equivalent to offering the house for sale at what price, assuming the buyer would finance using the conventional mortgage market?

6. Consider the twin communities of Tuckerville and Matildastan. These are seaside resorts that neighbor each other and attract many tourists. Matildastan wants to raise some money to clean up the streams in town; their approach to this is to levy a "bed tax"—a per night tax on every visitor to a hotel. There are 3,500 hotel rooms

in Matildastan and 1,500 hotel rooms in Tuckerville. The rooms are identical and tourists do not really mind which town they stay in. There are no other nearby towns.

The variable cost of providing a hotel room (electricity, maid service, other labor costs, etc.) is $30 per room: $20 for labor (maids, clerks, etc.) and $10 for nonwage expenses like electricity. (Labor and electricity prices are set in a larger, regional market.) About the only cost for hotel managers is building construction and maintenance costs, including mortgage payments (costs that are independent of the number of rooms rented). The (linear) demand is such that at a price of $100 per room, demand is for 6,000 per day. If the price goes to $200, the demand would be cut in half. Assume the bed tax is $10 per room per night in Matildastan only.

a. Identify the groups of people who might be positively or negatively impacted directly by the tax (not by the cleanup). Include tourists, hotel owners, workers, others.

b. Identify the groups of people who might be positively or negatively impacted directly by the cleanup. Include tourists, hotel owners, workers, residents of Matildastan, and others. Discuss the nature of their impact.

c. Show graphically the effect of a $10 tax on beds covering both communities on prices of hotels. This involves showing the supply of hotel rooms as well as the demand. Be as accurate as possible, using as much of the preceeding information as you can.

d. Show graphically the effect of the $10 tax on beds in Matildastan (no tax elsewhere) on the price of hotels in Matildastan (compared to no tax).

e. In terms of the direct incidence of the tax (i.e., excluding the benefits of stream cleanup), identify who ultimately pays for the tax. Try to be as quantitative as possible and support your arguments.

NOTES

1. For more on the process of making public policy, refer to a good book on policy analysis (such as Weimer and Vining, 2005). More generally, this is the domain of political science and, to some extent, political economy.

2. There is much more to benefit–cost analysis than the short treatment here. For more, see a good book on the subject, such as Gramlich (1990) or Boardman et al (2006).

3. It is also important that the secondary market not be distorted by some other government program.

4. The marginal costs and marginal benefits are in 1980 US$. It is assumed that these are annual marginal costs and benefits, though that is not clear from Oates et al. (1989).

5. The precipitator market was not examined by Oates et al. (1989). It is used here for illustration purposes only.

6. When we observe discount rates in the marketplace, they usually have additional components added in, particularly uncertainty. Uncertainty about the future is risk that will inevitably cause one to discount further a promise of a dollar to be received in the future. Tax policy also drives a wedge in the market, making observations of the discount rate difficult. Nordhaus (1994), Arrow et al (1996), Lind et al (1982) and Stern (2006) provide good discussions of the use of the rate of time preference and the marginal productivity of capital to deduce a discount

rate. Weitzman (1994) discusses the role of uncertainty in determining discount rates and Newell and Pizer (2003) actually set out to measure long-term risk-free interest rates.

7. When time is discrete ($t = 1, 2, 3, \ldots$), the formula in Eqn. (6.2) applies. When time is continuous, the discount factor is written $\beta_t = e^{-rt}$. This is an exponential formula and the reason a constant discount rate is referred to as *exponential* discounting.

8. This result, that risk should be excluded from the social discount rate, is due to Arrow and Lind (1970).

9. See Green and Myerson (1996) and Cropper et al (1994). See also Ainslie (1992) for a review of the animal literature.

10. With hyperbolic discounting, the discount factor [b in (Eqn. 6.2)] drops over time and can be expressed as $\gamma/(1+\alpha t)$. Thus if $\alpha = 0$, the discount rate is constant. For $\alpha > 0$, the discount rate slowly falls over time. The discount *factor* [β_t in (Eqn. 6.2)] can be written as $(1+\alpha t)^{-\gamma/\alpha}$ which, for $\alpha \to 0$, reduces to $e^{-\gamma t}$. See Laibson (1997) and Harvey (1994) for more on this issue.

11. In a very interesting study of just such behavior, Burger and Lynham (2008) examine a peculiar bet people may place in betting parlors in the United Kingdom: betting on their own weight loss. The authors find that people generally lose such bets.

12. Appendix 2A of Stern (2006) provides a good, accessible discussion of these issues. See also Schelling (1995).

13. Eqn. (6.3) also emerges from a market-based representation of efficient economic growth. In fact this formula is known as the Ramsey equation and it emerges from a classic model of optimal growth. In this case the discount rate is also the real return on capital, consistent with Figure 6.4.

14. There is no "correct" number for the parameters in Eqn. (6.3). Some values can be inferred from observing private behavior on consumption and production. Pindyck (2009) suggests that the finance literature places η between 1.5 and 6.0, that the finance and macro literature places δ between 0.01 and 0.04, and that the growth rate can be inferred from history and is in the range of 0.020 and 0.025. This results in a wide range of discount rates, from 3% to over 10%.

15. For instance, the U.S. EPA is required to do a comprehensive analysis of the benefits and costs of the US Clean Air Act. They have done this (U.S. Environmental Protection Agency, 1997) and devoted significant manpower and resources to the task. Despite this, they were unable to quantify the value of ecological services and have thus omitted these from the analysis.

16. Critiques of benefit–cost analysis are too numerous to review here. See Sagoff (1994) and Kelman (1981) for two perspectives.

17. Keeney and Raiffa (1976) is a classic reference on multi-objective analysis. See Belton and Stewart (2002) for a more current treatment.

18. Mayeres and Proost (2001) provide a detailed example of using distributional weights to evaluate policies to reduce road congestion.

7

DEMAND FOR ENVIRONMENTAL GOODS

One of the cornerstones of economics is understanding consumer preferences for goods. The typical way those preferences are represented is through demand functions—relationships that indicate the amount of a good an individual at a given income level will desire, when facing a particular set of prices. A demand curve (another name for a demand function) is a way of summarizing how important a particular good is to an individual. Since every individual has a limited income, the demand curve tells us how much money the individual devotes to a specific good, out of the many choices available. The demand curve also tells us the marginal valuation a consumer places on a good at different consumption levels. Additional information is provided through an indication of how much of the good the individual chooses to forgo if the price increases. If a good is absolutely indispensable with no clear substitutes, demand will probably be insensitive to price (inelastic). If, on the other hand, the good is important, but there are ample substitutes, an increase in price will drive the consumer to substitutes, with a correspondingly sharp decrease in consumption of the good whose price rose.

All of this information is useful in understanding markets and the effects of changes in those markets. If we summarize an individual's preferences for a good by a demand curve, we can summarize the market's overall consumption of that good by an *aggregate demand curve*, the sum across all consumers of individual demand curves. We can then match that with a supply curve for that good to find out how much of the good is likely to be supplied in a competitive market and conduct positive and normative analyses of the effects of government interventions, such as taxes and regulations, in those markets.

In much the same way that demand curves are useful summaries of consumer preferences for use in analyzing markets for private goods, a demand curve can also be useful in summarizing preferences for environmental goods. The problem with demand curves for environmental goods is that there are typically no markets, so we have no observations on how much of an environmental good is consumed at different prices. Yet the idea of a demand curve as a representation of underlying preferences is just as valid for environmental goods as for tomatoes, bread, or gasoline. It is just harder to measure.

This chapter examines demand theory for environmental goods and bads. Much of this theory is the same as for conventional goods and services. There are some unique extensions however. In subsequent chapters we will delve more deeply into actually measuring the demand for environmental goods and services.[1]

I. WHAT IS SO SPECIAL ABOUT AN ENVIRONMENTAL GOOD?

There is a wide variety of goods that fall under the rubric of environmental goods. Included would be commodities such as air pollution and water pollution, or viewed as goods, air quality and water quality. Also included would be amenity values such as a beautiful vista over land or ocean or, negatively characterized, a smoggy vista over a city. Even more distant from the conventional notion of a good might be the existence of a species (which is important to many people) or the lives of particular members of a species (such as birds that might be killed in an oil spill). The challenge to economists is to be comprehensive, viewing all aspects of the environment, over which people have preferences, within the paradigm of consumer theory.

Why force the things we value in the environment into consumer theory? The most important reason is that all environmental problems really involve a trade-off between using resources (money) for conventional goods and services and using those same resources for environmental protection. Trade-offs are the essence of environmental protection. And that is precisely what a demand curve represents, at least from the consumer's point of view: How much is the consumer willing to give up (pay) for particular levels of an environmental good? No matter how esoteric or intangible the environmental good might be, its protection usually requires money. And it is usually appropriate to enquire how much people are willing to contribute to protect that environmental good. Eliciting true values is not easy; but that does not diminish the validity of the principle of demand for environmental goods and services.

One of the clearest distinctions between environmental goods and ordinary goods is the existence of a market. With an ordinary good, such as milk, the market allows us to observe a variety of prices (usually) and different purchases at different price levels. Thus it is "straightforward" (though not without difficulties) to deduce the relationship between price and quantity demanded (a market demand curve). A similar approach (with greater data demands) can be used to measure an individual's demand curve.

It is of course much more difficult to generate a demand curve for clean air in an urban area. Leaving aside how precisely we would define "clean air," we have no observations on different consumption levels at different prices. Yet clearly, individuals who value clean air would be willing to pay for it. At low levels of air quality, individuals would be willing to pay relatively more for additional units of air quality; when the air is fairly clean, individuals are willing to pay less for additional units of air quality. Alternatively, the more expensive clean air is to provide, the more people would be willing to tolerate some pollution; similarly, the cheaper clean air is, the more of it people would demand.

The absence of a market is the major factor that complicates finding the demand curve for environmental goods. But the absence of a market is the problem with nearly all public goods—including but not limited to environmental goods. For instance, schools are provided publicly in many parts of the world (education has elements of nonrivalry).

Finding the demand for public schooling is no easy task, basically because of the lack of markets.[2] But the big difference between environmental goods and ordinary public goods is the supply side. Ordinary public goods are produced at a cost. Thus citizens have a reference point of the cost of supply to take into account when determining how much of the good they want at particular prices. Although strictly speaking this should not impact the value to consumption, it can make the process of valuation easier. Furthermore, people may have experience with different points on their demand curve; perhaps they have lived in different communities with different amounts of the public good or are aware of the cost of private schools.

In contrast, environmental goods are often quite disconnected from the supply side. In determining how worthwhile the protection of a wilderness area might be, it is difficult to anchor that value, since the wilderness area is not produced. Air quality is in fact supplied, since there is a cost associated with cleaning up the air. However, this is a much more dispersed cost, much different than that associated with constructing a public school or park. This too makes the job of determining demand more difficult.

II. WILLINGNESS TO PAY

A conventional demand curve shows quantity demanded as a function of price. Without a market there is, of course, no price. As discussed in Chapter 4, this is not really a problem—the concept of demand works perfectly well and makes perfect sense without a market. Similarly, the consumer surplus associated with consuming a certain amount of a good is defined in terms of a market transaction. In this section we see how similar concepts are equally applicable to environmental goods in the absence of markets. The key concept corresponding to price and surplus is willingness to pay. Marginal willingness to pay is analogous to price and total willingness to pay is analogous to consumer surplus.

A. Prices and Marginal Willingness to Pay (MWTP)

In the next few chapters we will be taking a closer look at how the demand for environmental goods is measured. We start with an example. Leaving aside how it was obtained, Figure 7.1 shows the demand (at the household level) for nitrogen oxides (NO_x) air pollution in Boston, based on a study done in the 1970s. Figure 7.1 shows three different demand curves for NO_x, corresponding to three different levels of household income. For one more unit of NO_x, consumers are willing to pay a negative amount: they must be compensated to agree to consume more pollution. The demand curves are downward sloping but since NO_x is a bad, they are in the fourth quadrant (MWTP negative, NO_x positive). If the vertical axis were the marginal willingness to pay for pollution *reductions*, then the graph would be in the first quadrant, though it would be sloping upward to the right.

Although Figure 7.1 might seem a bit strange and certainly looks different than a demand curve for a market good, it is a totally appropriate representation of demand for NO_x pollution. It represents the strength of preferences for households of different

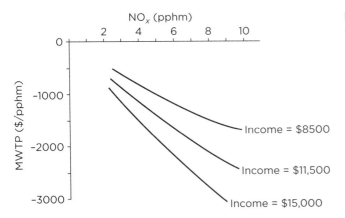

FIGURE 7.1 Marginal willingness to pay (MWTP) for nitrogen oxides (parts per hundred million, pphm) for Boston households at three different income levels. Figures for MWTP are annual, in 1970 US\$ per pphm. (Adapted from Harrison and Rubinfeld, 1978.)

income levels. The graph shows a negative willingness to pay for increases in pollution, or, equivalently, a positive willingness to pay for decreases in pollution. At a level of 6 pphm of NO_x pollution, lower income households have a marginal willingness to pay to reduce pollution to 5 pphm of approximately \$1000; higher income families would be willing to pay twice this amount.

There is a nuance that has to do with whether the consumer is acquiring one more unit of the good or giving up a unit. If the consumer is giving up a unit that is possessed (e.g., selling a liter of gas), the appropriate term is marginal willingness to accept compensation (MWTA). In most contexts, these two concepts are equivalent. We will have more to say about differences between these two terms later in this chapter.

There is one issue of terminology that arises in the case of pollution. Often, we speak of the damage from pollution or the benefit of having less pollution. The marginal benefit of one less unit of pollution is the same as the marginal damage of one more unit of pollution. Furthermore, the marginal willingness to pay for one more unit of pollution is negative and equal to the negative of the marginal benefit of one less unit of pollution or the negative of the marginal damage of one more unit of pollution. Confusing? Just keep in mind that benefits of less pollution are the other side of the coin of damages from more pollution. When expressed in monetary terms, these benefits and damages are simply willingnesses to pay, making sure that the sign (positive or negative) is correct.

B. Willingness to Pay versus Marginal Willingness to Pay

With pollution, we are often concerned with the total damage from pollution or total benefits from reducing pollution. For instance, Table 7.1 shows an estimate of the total benefits (1970–1990) from the cleaner air provided by the 1970 U.S. Clean Air Act Amendments. The table is taken from a U.S. Government study of benefits over the period 1970–1990 and compares the situation of pollution continuing to grow without the legislation with the levels of pollution that in fact resulted over the 20-year period. Thus Table 7.1 does not compare existing levels of pollution with pristine conditions but rather existing levels of pollution with much dirtier conditions that might have prevailed had there been no regulation of air pollutants (a level that is very hard to forecast). The point is

TABLE 7.1 Present Value of 1970 to 1990 Monetized Benefits[a] of Clean Air Act in Continental United States, by Endpoint (Billions of 1990 $, Discounted to 1990 at 5%)

Endpoint	Pollutant(s)	Present value ($)		
		5th %ile	Mean	95th %ile
Mortality	PM-10	1,991	13,542	30,968
Mortality	Pb	125	1,550	4,096
Chronic bronchitis	PM-10	2,143	7,156	12,613
IQ (lost IQ pts. + children with IQ < 70)	Pb	299	466	656
Hypertension	Pb	77	99	120
Hospital admissions	PM-10, O_3, Pb, and CO	18	24	33
Respiratory-related symptoms, restricted activity and decreased productivity	PM-10, O_3, NO_2, SO_2	31	76	149
Soiling damage	PM-10	7	76	196
Visibility	Particulates	55	72	91
Agriculture (net surplus)	O_3	11	23	35
Total		10,500	23,000	40,600

[a]*Benefits are with respect to a hypothetical baseline of no pollution control in 1970–1990, with resulting growth in pollution levels.*
Source: United States Environmental Protection Agency (1997), Table 20.

that Table 7.1 shows total benefits of the Clean Air Act, equivalent to the total willingness to pay for the attained levels of air quality, not marginal willingness to pay.[3]

This illustrates the connection among damage, willingness to pay, and benefits. Damage from pollution is equal to the negative of the benefits of eliminating the pollution, which is equal to the willingness to pay to eliminate the pollution. For example, suppose we are in an urban area with high levels of air pollution, such as Mexico City. We may think of the total willingness to pay for an individual citizen to eliminate all air pollution from the city. This would be the total willingness to pay to eliminate air pollution. It is the same as the damage (in monetary units) to the individual from all of the air pollution in Mexico City. Of course, we can also consider the willingness to pay to eliminate one unit of air pollution. This would be the marginal willingness to pay for air pollution reduction, which would be equal to the marginal damage from pollution.

Figure 7.2 shows hypothetical individual demand curves for two commodities: gasoline and air pollution. For gasoline, Figure 7.2a shows quantity demanded as a function of the price of gasoline. Remember "price" can be used interchangeably with "marginal willingness to pay." For air pollution, the lower part of Figure 7.2b shows the consumer marginal willingness to pay for pollution (MWTP) as a function of the quantity of pollution. The top part of Figure 7.2b shows the marginal damage from pollution, which is precisely the negative of consumer total MWTP.

Total willingness to pay to eliminate pollution involves adding up all of the marginal willingnesses to pay as pollution levels expand from zero to the current level. This is the area between the demand curve for pollution and the horizontal axis and is shown as the lighter shaded part of Figure 7.2b. Similarly, in Figure 7.2a, the shaded area shows the total willingness to pay for gasoline q^*. This shaded area consists of payments made (the rectangle) and consumer surplus (the triangle).

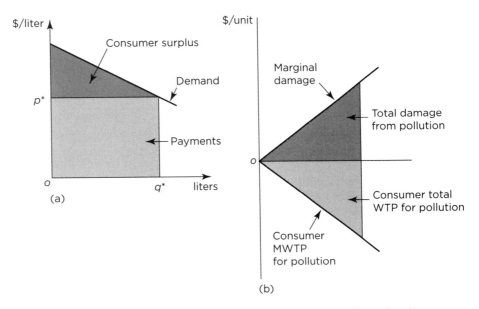

FIGURE 7.2 Demand curves and willingness to pay. (a) Gasoline; (b) air pollution. Note that in (b), total damage = −consumer total WTP.

Similarly, for an environmental commodity, the area under the demand curve between two different quantities of the commodity gives the willingness to pay for the environmental commodity. Since no payment is made for the pollution (as there was for gasoline), this is also consumer surplus (though note that it is negative). The lighter shaded area of Figure 7.2b is the consumer WTP for pollution. It is negative since pollution is bad and people must receive money to be willing to accept the pollution. The darker shaded area of Figure 7.2b is the total damage from pollution. WTP for pollution is the negative of total damage.

III. TYPES OF ENVIRONMENTAL GOODS

The environment is a very complex place. In understanding the value of the environment, it helps to use a classification scheme. We can classify goods based on the nature of the pollution: air quality is one good, water quality is another. Or we may classify goods based on the nature of the injured party: health effects of pollution, damage to agriculture, and damage to buildings and materials. Or we may categorize goods based on how people perceive the damages. This last categorization is a bit more subtle and has to do with whether consumers obtain utility from the environment by "using" the environment (e.g., hiking through the woods) or through more esoteric means (e.g., thinking about elephants roaming in Africa). Because this last dichotomy is somewhat unusual, we will examine it more carefully.

A. Use Value

Use value is the conventional notion of value associated with the consumption of a good. In the case of an environmental good, this could include current use ("I am currently visiting the park"), expected use ("I plan to visit the park later this year"), and possible use ("I might visit the park within the next 10 years"). Although this might be obvious, the point about possible use can be used to generate a positive value for a remote wilderness that few currently use, particularly if the very long term is taken into account.

There are several primary avenues whereby environmental goods impact humans.[4] One is through direct impact. This would include direct health effects of breathing polluted air (both mortality—death—and morbidity—sickness) as well as nonhealth effects such as bothersome odors, noise, or visual impacts. For instance, smoke from a power plant may result in a brown plume intercepting a vista you have come to enjoy. Although there may be no measurable physical impact on you from this plume, you find the view annoying and would be willing to pay some amount of money to be rid of it, should the opportunity arise. This is just as real an economic value as health effects. On the production side, pollution may enter directly into production functions, adversely affecting production processes. For instance, air pollution may make the manufacture of microchips (which require superclean conditions) more costly. Environmental goods may impact humans less directly, primarily through materials damage. Air pollution may damage or soil buildings, necessitating additional maintenance or cleaning.

A second avenue for environmental goods to impact humans is through damage to ecosystems. Agriculture, forests, and fisheries are ecosystems from which humans directly derive economic benefit. Clearly pollution that degrades the performance of these ecosystems is undesirable. More subtle ecosystem effects relate to recreational use of ecosystems. Urbanization or pollution that may disrupt the ecosystem in a national park will have negative consequences for recreational users of that national park. Ecosystems are also a source of economic benefit through mechanisms such as providing genetic material for new pharmaceuticals.

The value of ecosystems services has become an important and controversial area of valuation, in large part because of the difficulties in actually determining the tangible consequences of many disruptions of ecosystems (for instance, how do fewer species translate into impact on man?). In an effort to bring more structure to this important but often underemphasized area of environmental goods and services, the U.S. EPA's high-level Science Advisory Board recently developed guidelines for use in valuing ecosystem services (U.S. Environmental Protection Agency, 2009).

B. Nonuse Value

Nonuse value is a controversial aspect of value. Nonuse value is a gain in a person's utility without the person actually applying the good, applying the word "using" very broadly. We may value ecosystems in remote parts of the world for reasons other than intending to visit the ecosystem or potentially obtaining something useful from the ecosystem. I may value a blue whale being able to swim freely in the open ocean, despite the fact that I have no intention of ever seeing a blue whale swim in the open ocean.

The three basic types of nonuse value are existence value, altruistic value, and bequest value. Existence value is the value a consumer attaches to *knowing* something exists (e.g., the African elephant example mentioned earlier). This would be in addition to any value associated with actual or potential "use." Altruistic value derives not from my own consumption but from the fact that I derive benefit when someone else gains utility. So when my neighbor benefits from my cleaning my front yard, if I am altruistic, I obtain utility from the fact that my neighbor is better-off. Bequest value is similar, though associated with the well-being of descendants. If I value passing a wilderness area on to the next generation, that wilderness has a bequest value to me, even if I never use it or intend to use it.

The purpose of dissecting value and placing it into these various categories is to understand the complexity whereby environmental goods confer value on consumers. Simply looking at the use value of an environmental asset may obscure much of the value. In fact some environmental assets have little use value but very significant nonuse value. We should point out that empirically it is often impossible to separately measure the components of value, for instance, how much value is altruistic vs. bequest. This is a bit like dividing the value of an ice-cream cone into texture and flavor. The categorization simply provides an intellectual framework to help ensure completeness when valuing environmental goods.

IV. MEASURING DEMAND

Because of the absence of markets for environmental goods, measuring demand is not straightforward. There are two basic approaches to measuring demand: revealed preference and stated preference. In revealed preference, we observe a real choice[5] in some market and cleverly infer information on the trade-off between money and the environmental good. For instance, we may notice that two communities are identical except that one has high housing prices and clean air and the other has lower housing prices and dirty air. We may infer that the difference in housing prices reflects the value people place on clean air. The second approach, stated preferences, basically involves asking people how they would trade off money for the environmental good if they had the opportunity to do so. Opinion polls and surveys are used to derive this information. This approach is controversial because of the absence of real choices; only real choices involve actual trades between money and environmental goods. Hypothetical choices lack a realism that may be necessary to obtain accurate information. There is a good deal of division within the economics profession on this point. There is also a gray region between revealed preferences and stated preferences, for example, experimental markets in which subjects (usually students) are given some money and asked to make choices (perhaps somewhat unusual choices) using that money. The decisions are real; the context is contrived.

Within the category of revealed preference, there are two basic approaches to measuring demand, hedonics and household production. In the hedonic approach, the goal is to see how the price of a conventional good (e.g., a house) varies as the amount of a closely related environmental good changes (e.g., the air quality in the vicinity of the house). This relationship is then used to infer value. The household production approach starts with the assumption that consumers will combine private goods with the environmental good to "produce" another good, which is the real source of utility. For instance, soundproofing may be combined with noise that impinges on the outside of a house to obtain particular

> **Valuing Beach Recreation with Benefits Transfer**
>
> On Feb. 7, 1990, off of Southern California, an oil tanker named *The American Trader* spilled a significant amount of crude oil onto the beaches made famous in song by the Beach Boys, beaches which also happened to be a major source of recreation for the 15 million residents of the Los Angeles area. In the ensuing litigation to recover damage from the oil spill a major issue was the damage to environmental resources and recreation.
>
> In the case of beach recreation, the question faced by both sides of the litigation was twofold: what was the loss in beach use and what was the willingness to pay by recreators to avoid that loss of use? The loss in beach WTP is where benefits transfer enters, and both sides of the case used benefits transfer to estimate the damages. One of these benefits transfers is documented in Deacon and Kolstad (2000) and involves the use of studies of beach recreation in Florida, Massachusetts, Hawaii, Rhode Island, and several Southern California beaches. Although there is significant variation in the results of the studies and the applicability to Southern California, all studies placed the value of a lost person-day of beach recreation between $1 and $12 (in 1990$) with some narrowing of the range possible based on characteristics of the individual studies.
>
> Although an approach such as this does not give a definitive figure for the damage to the particular beaches in question, it is far cheaper than undertaking a new study; depending on what the policy need is, narrowing the range of damage may provide sufficient precision.

indoor noise levels. Indoor noise is what is assumed to matter. Or a national park may be combined with expenditures to visit the park to generate a park visit, which is what really gives utility. In either case, by observing expenditures on the complementary private good, we obtain a lower bound on the value of the environmental good or bad. The outside noise must cause at least as much damage as the expenditures on soundproofing. The national park visit must be worth at least the travel expenditures.

In the arena of stated preferences, the dominant approach is termed contingent valuation. Contingent valuation relies on direct revelation of demand from consumers. The name literally means "value contingent on there being a market"—if there were a market, how much would you pay for the environmental good? These values are obtained by directly questioning a sample of potential consumers of the environmental good.

Contingent valuation is a type of constructed market. In a constructed market, a researcher will take a situation in which no market exists and generate a market. Constructed markets can be hypothetical or real. For instance, in a study of duck hunting, Bishop et al. (1983), constructed a market for buying and selling duck hunting permits (the permits were normally distributed through a lottery). In this manner they were able to generate a demand curve for duck hunting permits. Laboratory experiments are also widely used to generate information on how people trade money for environmental goods. In a laboratory study of the value of risk reduction, Shogren et al. (1994) constructed an experiment (see box on pages 146–147 "Experiments with Food Safety" later in this chapter) in which students were given the option of eating food prepared subject to conventional safety standards (which entails some risk, though small) with food that had been prepared with even stricter standards. The researchers were interested in the behavior of demand for these risk reductions. Such laboratory experiments are useful because they enable the investigation of questions for which market data just are not available. These studies also involve real resource decisions ("real" money is on the line), which is an advantage over contingent valuation. Unfortunately, they are expensive to conduct, often involve non-randomly selected samples, typically students in economics or related fields, and are difficult to generalize. Another type of constructed market is the official referendum. Some environmental good is to be provided using a tax on residents of a community. The proposal is put to the voters of a community. Although this is a very real choice situation, its usefulness is obviously limited to the environmental goods offered to communities through referenda.

A somewhat different approach to valuation has come to be known as "benefits transfer."[6] In a sense this is a poor man's approach to benefits estimation. If you do not have the resources to conduct a new study for the particular issue in question, survey the literature and find similar analyses and "transfer" them to your application.

V. REVEALED PREFERENCE AND RESTRICTED DEMAND

Revealed preference measures are the gold standard for economic estimates of the demand for environmental goods and services. The concept is simple: based on actual choices people make, we infer how they must be making trade-offs between market goods and environmental goods. This allows us to derive a demand curve for environmental goods. For instance, we observe the demand for houses changes when air quality changes. People pay more for identical houses when the air is cleaner. That behavior in a market should allow us to infer how people are valuing air quality.

The standard approach to estimating demand for goods is to obtain a great deal of transaction data involving quantity demanded and price. Using statistical methods, we then tease out a relationship between price and quantity demanded. Demand for gasoline will depend on the price of gasoline (of course) as well as the price of public transportation, the price of alternative fuels, the price of housing close to work, the price of vehicles and a host of other prices (and income).

A major problem with using this approach with environmental goods is that there are no prices for environmental goods. It turns out that we can often get around this problem using the concept of *restricted demand*. We measure (statistically, using observations) how demand for a market good changes with the price of the market good and the quantity of the environmental good. We then use some sleight of hand to deduce the MWTP for the environmental good as a function of the quantity of the environmental good and the price of the market goods.

To see this, consider the simplest setup with one market good (x) and one environmental good (q). The price of the market good is p_x. For instance, houses (of a certain type) may be the market good and air quality the environmental good, in which case p_x is the price of a house and q is air quality. Using data on house sales and air quality in many different locations in an urban area, we are able to estimate the following relationship between the price of houses, air quality and the quantity of housing demanded (x):

$$x = h(p_x, q) \qquad (7.1)$$

Normally a demand curve has prices as arguments on the right-hand side; Eq. (7.1) has one price and one quantity on the right-hand side. We refer to this as a *restricted demand curve* in the sense that the arguments of the demand curve are both prices and quantities. For a conventional *demand curve*, the arguments on the right-hand side would all be prices (perhaps with other variables such as income).

A relationship such as Eq. (7.1) certainly helps us understand how housing markets work, but how could it help us understand the demand for the environmental good? The answer depends on finding the MWTP for q.

To find MWTP, we find the total WTP for the market good and observe how that changes when we change q a little. The ratio of the change in WTP to the change in q gives us the MWTP. This is illustrated in Figure 7.3. Shown in the figure is the restricted demand for the market good (housing in our example). In fact, two such demand curves are shown, one for q and one for $q + \Delta q$, with the assumption being that Δq is a small positive number. The figure is consistent with our intuition in our example—when air quality goes up in an area, demand for housing in the area also increases. The change in the willingness to pay is the change in consumer surplus for the two demand curves. This change is the shaded area between the two demand curves, as shown in Figure 7.3. If we know Δq and can compute ΔWTP, and then let the Δq become infinitesimally small, we can derive the MWTP:

$$\Delta\text{WTP} / \Delta q = \text{MWTP} = f(p_x, q) \qquad (7.2)$$

This is exactly what we are after—a demand curve for the environmental good, relating the marginal willingness to pay for the environmental good to the quantity of the environmental good.[7]

Although this seems to answer the question of how to obtain demand for an environmental good from demand for market goods, it turns out that this is really a lower bound. All of the value from the environmental good was expressed through demand for

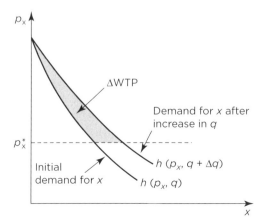

FIGURE 7.3 Marginal willingness to pay for an environmental good. p_x, price of x; h, demand for x; p^*_x, market price of x; Δq, change in environmental good, q.

the market good. If in fact the only purpose of the environmental good is to enhance the experience of consuming the market good, then the question has been resolved. However, that is rarely the case. Air pollution, for instance, certainly affects enjoyment of one's dwelling. But it also influences utility in ways unrelated to housing—in fact, whenever one is traveling, working, or recreating in a reduced air-quality environment—or even indirectly, through ecosystems that simultaneously provide services to people but are harmed by adverse environmental quality.

This is not to diminish the value of determining the demand for air quality through the demand for housing. It is only to caution that the demand so found may in fact be a lower bound on demand for the environmental good.

VI. DISCRETE CHOICE

Most empirical methods of measuring demand for environmental goods involve observing consumer choices. A consumer may consider many beaches for recreation but visit only one, or homeowners consider many houses but buy only one. Making real choices is a common form of revealed preference, and observing choices is a common way in which we infer demand for environmental goods. The important thing to keep in mind is that we learn from what consumers choose but we also learn from what consumers reject.

Because so many empirical approaches to estimating demand involve discrete choice, it is appropriate to consider the general approach to such problems. We will consider here what has been called the "random utility model," but the method can be used in a variety of contexts.

Consider Jose, who is buying a house. Jose observes many houses and chooses to buy one. A house has characteristics, z, and a price, p: (z,p). Let there be N different houses in Jose's town. Index all the houses by i so that the houses can be listed as $(z_1,p_1), \ldots (z_i,p_i), \ldots, (z_N,p_N)$. From these, Jose picks house k. That means he likes house k better than all the other houses in his town. Think of Jose spending his money on a composite consumption good, x, and his house. The units for the consumption good are defined so that its price is 1. Jose's income is y. The big question is, what can we learn from observing his choice of house?

One approach is to assume Jose has an indirect utility function, $V(z,p,y;\alpha)$ where α is a vector of parameters that we hope to estimate econometrically.[8] V says how much utility Jose gets when he chooses a house with characteristics z, spending p on the house, and the rest of his income, y, on consumption goods. But like many things in economics, V is an approximation of Jose's utility—Jose's true utility is V plus an error term, ε. This means that the actual utility Jose gets from choosing house i is $V(z_i,p_i,y;\alpha) + \varepsilon_i$.

Now consider Jose's choice between house k (which he chooses) and house m (which he rejects). This must mean house k gives higher utility than house m; that is,

$$\text{Choosing house } k \text{ over house } m \Leftrightarrow V(z_k,p_k,y;\alpha) + \varepsilon_k > V(z_m,p_m,y;\alpha) + \varepsilon_m. \quad (7.3)$$

But since ε is an error term, with noise and randomness in it, it is really more appropriate to view the choice probabilistically; i.e., Eq. (7.3) is equivalent to saying

$$\text{Probability [choosing } k \text{ over } m] = \text{Prob } [\varepsilon_k - \varepsilon_m > V(z_m,p_m,y;\alpha) - V(z_k,p_k,y;\alpha)] \quad (7.4)$$

Since Jose did in fact choose house k over m, we can find the value of the parameter vector α which maximizes this probability.

But if we stopped there, we have not used all the information at our disposal. Jose actually chose house k over *all* the other houses. Using Eq. (7.4), we can write the slightly more complicated expression for the probability of choosing house k over all the other houses in town. The econometric problem is to find a value of α which maximizes that probability since we know that Jose did, in fact, choose house k over all the others.[9]

This is a random utility model. We specify a functional form for indirect utility, complete with parameters to estimate, and append an error term. Rather than observe utility directly (which would make estimation very straightforward), we only observe choices. In this case, we find the parameter vector that makes the calculated choices most consistent with the choices we observe. The end product is an estimated indirect utility function.

Fresh Water Recreation in North Carolina

Dan Phaneuf (2002) asks a simple question: what would be the willingness of recreators to pay for improving water quality at a number water-based recreation sites in North Carolina (in the Southeastern United States)? The author has a database on the water quality in various recreation sites in the state (58 different watersheds in the state). He also has information on over 1,000 day trips to these recreation sites—where people come from, which site they choose, and their characteristics. This allows him to construct a cost for visiting any site, based on distance traveled—this is the "price" of visiting a site. Thus for each of the over 1,000 trips, he knows the "price" of visiting each possible site, the characteristics of each possible site, the characteristics of the individual recreator and the actual site the recreator chooses from among the 58 choices. The problem he develops and estimates is almost identical to the example in the text with a recreation site replacing a house.

The result of the estimation is an indirect utility function that indicates the utility a specific individual obtains from visting a site with a particular cost of visiting and site characteristics. He can then ask what would be the person's increased utility from and thus willingness to pay for an increase in site quality. He then examines several important recreation areas in the state and asks what the WTP would be for a 10% and a 25% improvement in a number of water-quality parameters. For a 10% improvement in water-quality indicators, he finds a willingness to pay ranging from $2.67 to $6.29 per recreation trip.

VII. WTP VERSUS WTA

An issue that has arisen for environmental goods and services is the distinction between what a person would pay for more of a particular environmental good versus what a person would accept as compensation for a little less of an environmental good. Both concepts could be used in making decisions on environmental programs, and if the answers are very different, we should understand why. Furthermore, which measure should we use in evaluating an environmental action?

Recall the example of Finch Ellsworth and his demand curve for gasoline—Finch demands 50 liters of gasoline when the price is £1 per liter. If Finch is voluntarily choosing to consume 50 liters at that price, what would he be willing to pay for an extra liter? Alternatively, what would he be willing to accept as compensation to reduce consumption to 49? Intuition, and economic reasoning, tells us that the answer in both cases is the same or very nearly the same and approximately equal to £1. Finch values a marginal unit of gasoline at £1 per liter, which means one more or one less liter is worth about the same—£1. Finch's marginal willingness to pay (MWTP) for one more liter of fuel is approximately equal to his marginal willingness to accept (MWTA) compensation for one less liter of fuel. In this example, the difference between these two concepts (MWTP and MTWA) is of little consequence.

But now think about the air pollution in the city or area in which you live. How much would you be willing to pay to clean up the pollution by one unit (MWTP)? Now suppose a manufacturing facility is expanding and will result in a decrease in air pollution of one unit. How much would the manufacturer need to pay you for you to agree to the one unit decrease in pollution (MWTA)? Many people would view MWTA >> MWTP.

Experimental evidence is consistent with this example, even for market goods (such as Finch's gasoline in the earlier paragraph).[10] For instance, Kahneman et al. (1990) set up an experimental situation where students buy and sell Cornell University coffee mugs. Some students are given the mugs and the opportunity to sell them to other students. All students are given cash to use in the transactions. The researchers find the sellers express a WTA for their newly endowed coffee mugs that exceeds the WTP for those students who are in a position to purchase one. Other experimenters have found similar results (see box below).

In the context of environmental goods and services, the question is often a non-marginal one. Is a person's willingness to pay to avoid the flooding of a scenic river (due to a dam) equal to the person's willingness to accept compensation for that flooding? Willingness to pay is limited by the income or wealth of an individual whereas willingness to accept is not. For this reason alone, it is easy to see that WTA and WTP may not be the same for many environmental goods.

The reason this is an important question is that in generating demand curves for environmental goods and services, we need to know whether we should be dealing with WTA or WTP (MWTA or MWTP). Which is correct?

To understand the problem more clearly, we can simplify to a problem with two goods—an environmental good (q) and a numeraire good representing all other consumption of market goods (x). We adjust the units of the numeraire good so its price (as is usual) is 1. Our starting point involves consumption of (x_0, q_0), yielding utility U_0. Consider an alternative with increased consumption of the environmental good: consumption of (x_0, q_1), yielding utility U_1 ($>U_0$). We are interested in two numbers: (1) starting at q_0, the WTP to move to q_1; and (2) starting at q_1, the WTA to move to q_0.[11]

Experiments with Food Safety

To test theories about the difference between willingness to pay and willingness to accept, Jay Shogren and colleagues at Iowa State University set up a series of laboratory experiments involving students at Iowa State (Shogren et al., 1994). Shogren was interested in whether there was a gap between WTP and WTA, and also whether there was a difference between market goods and nonmarket goods.

The experiment involved thirty students at a time, divided into two groups—buyers and sellers. In one experiment (involving a market good), the good in question was an easily purchased candy bar. In the second experiment, each student was given a sandwich purchased at the local grocery store—safe, but as with all commercial food, carrying some small chance of food poisoning. An alternative good in the second experiment was a sandwich that had been subjected to stringent tests to assure that it would have much lower health risks. This choice of a level of safety is not one normally faced in a market.

Students were divided into two groups, buyers and sellers. In the case of the candy bar, all students were given $3; the members of the seller group were also given a candy bar. A market price was determined by each student indicating: for sellers, what they would accept ($) to sell the candy bar (WTA); for buyers, what they would pay ($) for the candy bar (WTP). This bidding process was repeated five times. Interestingly, in the first trial, the average WTA was 50% higher than the average WTP, and statistically different. However, with repetition, the WTA declined (the WTP stayed relatively constant) so that by the third trial WTA and WTP were virtually identical.

The same sort of experiment was conducted for safe sandwiches except in this case each student was endowed with $15 and a sandwich. The buying students were endowed with the grocery-store-quality sandwich and were given an opportunity to exchange it for a super-safe sandwich. The selling students were endowed with a super-safe sandwich and were given an opportunity to exchange it for a grocery-store quality sandwich. Students were asked WTP and WTA questions as in the candy bar experiment. At the end, trades occurred and each student was required to eat his or her sandwich.

The results show that for these nonmarket goods (sandwich safety), the average WTA started much higher than the average WTP and that this difference did not disappear with repeated trials.

These results lend credence to the theory that substitutability with market goods reduces the difference between WTP and WTA. It also suggests that we may expect large differences between these measures for many environmental goods. But with any experiments it is important to keep in mind that results that are consistent with theory are not the same thing as a confirmation of theory. Experiments can disprove a theory, but in order to provide support for a theory, it would be important to test (and reject) other theories that have also been put forward as to why WTP and WTA may differ.

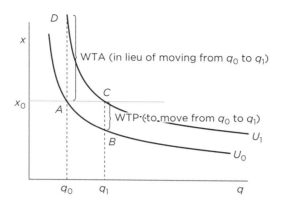

FIGURE 7.4 Willingness to accept vs. willingness to pay for a change in quantity of an environmental good (q).

This situation is illustrated in Figure 7.4. Shown in the figure are indifference curves between the environmental good and the numeraire good. WTP and WTA can be measured in units of x, since the price of x is 1. WTP is the distance BC, since going from q_0 to q_1 increases utility to U_1, our individual would be willing to give up as much of x as will keep him at the original level of utility, U_0. WTA, on the other hand, is the amount our individual would be willing to take in lieu of moving from q_0 to q_1. Since q_1 yields utility U_1, our individual would require enough x to keep utility at U_1, which is the distance AD.

Although Figure 7.4 has been drawn so that WTA > WTP, simply drawing a figure does not make it so. Suppose for instance that the indifference curves were close to linear (straight parallel lines). It is easy to see that in that case WTA = WTP. There are two situations that would result in such linearity. One is if q and x were perfect substitutes. If one more unit of q could be offset (keeping utility constant) by a fixed amount of x, then we would have perfect substitutes. In terms of the demand curve for q, if it is perfectly elastic (and the price of x is fixed), then this condition would hold. Another case that would result in nearly linear indifference curves is if the change in q from q_0 to q_1 is "very small." If the change in q and the corresponding change in U is small, then we are dealing with a much smaller region of the graph in Figure 7.4, where indifference curves are locally nearly linear. The easiest way to see that WTA and WTP are similar in this situation is to mentally move q_1 to q_0 in the figure, simultaneously (in your head) moving U_1 toward U_0. The difference between WTA and WTP shrinks to zero.

What conditions might lead to a significant divergence between WTA and WTP? One condition is if the change in the environmental good is large while x is not a perfect substitute for q. There are a number of conditions that yield this outcome. One necessary condition is that the indifference curves be curved (nonlinear), as drawn in Figure 7.4. This will occur with a downward sloping demand curve for q (which would be the normal situation). But it is also necessary that the change in q be substantial (nonmarginal). This would occur if the change in the environmental good is really big or, as is more likely the case, the environmental good is unique and losses in it are not easily compensated for by extra consumption of market goods.

SUMMARY

1. Environmental goods provide special challenges to demand theory because of an absence of markets and a frequent lack of a cost of provision.

2. Environmental goods can be classified by their effect or manner in which they enter utility or production. Effects would include direct impact (e.g., health or materials damage) and ecosystem impact. Use and nonuse value refer to the way an environmental good is perceived by the consumer. Nonuse value includes existence value, altruistic value, and bequest value.

3. There are three basic approaches to measuring demand for environmental goods. Hedonic prices and household production are two methods based on revealed preferences. Contingent valuation is the third method, and is based on stated preferences. There are several hybrid methods, including experimental and constructed markets.

4. Benefits transfer is a way of valuing an environmental good without actually conducting a valuation study of the particular good. Valuation studies of similar goods are collected and a reasonable value for the good in question is estimated. Hence the term "benefits transfer," for transferring the benefit estimates from one study to another.

5. A major dichotomy in the nature of value from environmental goods is "use value" versus "nonuse value." Use value is the value associated with actually experiencing and using the environmental good, such as breathing polluted air or viewing an elephant. Nonuse value accrues without actually experiencing the good. For instance, we value an endangered species, even though we will probably never encounter the species in the flesh.

6. Revealed preference methods of valuing environmental goods and services involve observing how people make real trade-offs in markets between money or other valuable resources and the environmental good or service in question.

7. Willingness to pay to acquire an environmental good may differ from the willingness to accept compensation to give up that good. Despite the fact that one might expect these to be similar for goods that are of low value relative to a consumer's income, the gap appears to be a real one. A number of explanations have been offered as to why there is the gap between WTP and WTA.

8. A restricted expenditure function involves one or more goods (usually environmental goods) specified in quantity terms instead of prices. In this case in which quantity changes, the expenditures necessary to achieve the same utility change. The ratio of the expenditure drop to the quantity increase is equal to the marginal value of the good [Eq. (7.2)].

PROBLEMS

1. Anna was interested in Felix's preferences regarding air quality in Santiago. She reasoned that since air pollution could be washed off with soap, Felix should view air quality (A) and soap (S) as substitutes. Air quality is measured by an index, with larger values corresponding to higher quality. Holding annual soap consumption

at five bars, she asked Felix to picture his utility with air quality at three different levels: 2, 4, and 5. Call these initial situations 1, 2, and 3, yielding utility U_1, U_2, and U_3. At each of these levels of air quality, she tried varying the amount of soap, asking how air quality should change to keep utility constant. During this mental experiment, she asked Felix to imagine his consumption of all other goods was fixed. She obtained the following data, showing values of A to keep utility constant at the three initial levels (U_1, U_2, U_3).

	Air quality (A) at		
S	U_1	U_2	U_3
1	10	20	25
2	5	10	12.5
3	3 1/3	6 2/3	8 1/3
4	2.5	5	6 1/4
5	2	4	5
6	1 2/3	3 1/3	4.17
7	1.43	2.86	3.57
8	1.25	2 1/2	3 1/8
9	1.11	2.22	2.78
10	1	2	2.5

Plot the three indifferences curves for soap and air quality implied by these data.

2. Using the data in Problem 1, suppose at air quality level 5, Felix chooses to buy four bars of soap when they are priced at $1 per bar. Now air quality rises to 10. How much money would we need to take from Felix to keep his utility constant? (*Hint:* ignore expenditures on all goods except soap.)

*3. We can generalize Problem 1 by stating that there are three commodities Felix consumes: air quality, soap, and a basket of other goods, denoted by x. Anna concludes from her research that Felix's utility function is $U(x,S,A) = x \, S \, A$. The price of x is always 1. Plot two restricted compensated demand functions for soap (price of soap on the vertical axis, quantity of soap on the horizontal axis). Recall that a compensated demand function depends on utility rather than income. One demand function should be for $A = 4$ and the other for $A = 5$. In both cases, assume the utility level is 100.

4. Suppose housing (H) and air quality (A) are the only two things entering into Jose's utility and Jose's utility function is $U(H,A) = A \cdot H$. Suppose Jose's income is $10 and the price of housing is $2.

    a. If air quality is $A = 2$, how much housing will Jose purchase? Plot Jose's indifference curve and budget constraint through this point, showing how much housing is consumed.

    b. Suppose air quality rises to $A = 4$. Plot Jose's new indifference curve and new consumption point.

    c. How much would Jose be willing to pay to increase air quality from 2 to 4?

5. In the Amoco Cadiz oil spill off of Northern France, fisheries, water fowl, and beaches were temporarily negatively impacted. List five types of consumers, identify the nature of goods these consumers demand that might be injured by the spill, and indicate the nature of demand for a contaminated environment (use or nonuse, bequest, altruistic, etc.).

NOTES

1. There are a number of books that are devoted entirely to this question, beginning with the classic by Rick Freeman (1979), expanded and updated in Freeman (1993). See also Braden and Kolstad (1991) and Champ et al. (2003), as well as a host of books on specific techniques of valuation.
2. See Bergstrom et al. (1982) for an analysis of the demand for public schooling.
3. Table 7.1 shows a mean benefit of $23 trillion dollars. The same report shows the present value of costs of reaching that level of benefits of $0.53 trillion dollars. Keep in mind that this says nothing about the marginal benefits and marginal costs.
4. Freeman (1993) discusses some of these categories.
5. A real choice means a choice that involves a commitment of resources. Your response when I ask you how much you would pay for a ticket to a concert involves no real choice; actually buying a ticket for £10 is a real indication that the value of a concert ticket to you is at least £10.
6. Kerry Smith and Bill Desvousges (1986) appear to be the first to use the term "benefits transfer." The general approach undoubtedly predates this used Rosenberger and Loomis (2003) provide a step-by-step guide to conducting benefits transfer.
7. For the purists, what has been described assumes compensated demand functions (see Braden and Kolstad, 1991).
8. The indirect utility function defines the utility that results from a utility maximization subject to a budget constraint. In our simple example, start with a utility function, $U(x,z)$ and a budget constraint, $x + p = y$. If the budget constraint is solved for x and substituted into the utility function, one obtains $U(y-p,z)$, which can be rewritten as $V(y,p,z)$.
9. This model is what is known as the conditional logit model (sometimes called the multinomial logit model) and was originally developed by Dan McFadden (1973). Details may be found in most econometrics books.
10. Horowitz and McConnell (2002) provide a survey of WTP and WTA studies.
11. Hanemann (1991) provides a clear exposition of this issue, building on the work of Randall and Stoll (1980) and Willig (1979). Kolstad and Guzman (1999) provide an alternative explanation for the divergence, arguing that if it is costly for individuals to determine how much a good is really worth to them, then there will be a gap between WTP and WTA. The "endowment effect" has also been invoked to explain this divergence—people value losing more than gaining (Kahneman et al., 1990). List (2004) provides experimental evidence that neoclassical economics adequately explains behavior for experienced consumers without resorting to the endowment effect.

8

REVEALED PREFERENCE: POLLUTION, LAND PRICES, AND WAGES

THIS IS THE FIRST OF TWO CHAPTERS THAT ARE CONCERNED WITH REVEALED PREFERENCE methods of inferring demand for environmental goods and services. Recall that revealed preference means that we infer preferences for environmental goods from observed behavior in actual market transactions. In this chapter we will focus on making the inference by observing markets that are closely related to the pollution or other environmental good. For instance, if air quality varies throughout a city, what can the variation in property values in the city tell us about how people value clean air? Or since some occupations are more risky than others (e.g., working on high voltage lines), what can the wage premium associated with risky jobs tell us about how people value risk differences?

The primary empirical approach to measuring these values is what has become known as hedonic price methods. The basic idea is best conveyed through examples: measure the price of houses for a variety of different air pollution levels and attempt to see how the price changes when the air pollution changes, keeping everything else constant. Or for risky occupations, measure how wage rates change with risk and then infer the change that would be induced in wages from a small change in risk. In either case, we start with an hedonic price function that gives the price of houses or the wage rate as a function of air pollution or risk as well as other variables. Once we have quantified this relationship, the next step would be to infer the marginal value of a change in the air pollution or risk variable.

In the next section we will look at the general problem of relating pollution levels to property values, ignoring whatever may be happening in the labor market. We will then generalize this to examine the effect of pollution on property values and wages when producers and labor are mobile. We then turn to a detailed examination of hedonic theory before examining a study of the demand for air pollution, based on property values. Another important and closely related literature concerns wage-occupational risk trade-offs and the value of statistical life. We also consider a recent methodological development termed equilibrium sorting, closely related to hedonic price methods applied to housing markets.

I. POLLUTION AND LAND RENTS

What determines the price of land? The price of a parcel of land is the value of the stream of services that the parcel can be *expected* to provide in the future, netted back to the present (the net present value). Note the word expected. There is some uncertainty in the value of land since it is unclear exactly how useful it will be in the future. This is one reason land prices fluctuate over time.

Because expectations are unobservable, we often distinguish between the rental price of land and the asset price of land. The rental price of land is the price of renting the land for a short period of time (for example, a year) and results from an equilibrium between short-term supply and demand. Expectations about the future play little or no role in the rental price. In contrast, the asset price of land is the price of taking title to the land in perpetuity. A farmer with agricultural land near a city may expect the land to be valuable for housing at some point in the future; this will increase the asset price of the land today. The rental price, however, will be totally related to the land's value during the rental period.

In a rural area, in which the land is used for agricultural purposes, the rental value of the land in any particular year is the expected value of output from the land, less the cost of labor, seed, and other nonland inputs necessary to obtain the output. If the land is poor (e.g., in terms of soil quality or access to water), the land will yield less, and thus its value will be lower. Or if air pollution is severe, the yield will also be less and thus the rental value of the land will be lower.

If the land is used for housing, it provides services to the occupants of the land, including a place to locate a house and pleasant surroundings. In contrast to agricultural land, location can be very important in determining the rental value of land used for housing. Land in the middle of the Amazon may support a house with a nice view, but if not many people want to live in the Amazon, housing demand will be low and most of the land will be used for agricultural purposes (or left undeveloped). In contrast, land in downtown Tokyo is expensive because there are more uses for the land than there is land available. The value of land in an urban area has little to do with the agricultural productivity of the land and everything to do with the balance between the demand for and the supply of land for building and land with buildings. The classic economic model of a city consists of a downtown in which everyone works, surrounded by concentric rings of housing. In each ring, the price of land is the same since the commuting time (to the city center) is constant. Rings that are further from the center have lower land prices since commuting times are longer. Far from the center, the price of land induced by housing drops so much that agriculture is a better use of the land than housing. This determines the extent of the city.[1]

A basic issue arises when air pollution varies from one location to another. Can we infer anything from the land value differences that might be induced by these variations in pollution levels? For instance, if land in a clean air area is priced higher than land in a dirty air area, can we assume that all of the difference is due to the difference in pollution levels? The problem is a bit more complex than it might at first appear. We will first consider the case in which the land is used for agricultural purposes and then turn to the slightly more complex case of land being used for housing.

To focus on the effects of pollution on land prices, we will assume that wages are unaffected by pollution. This might be the case if wages are set in a national or regional market and pollution varies over a smaller area. Thus wages will not vary from an area of high pollution to an area of low pollution. Later in this chapter we will explicitly introduce wages in addition to land rents and examine how both respond to differences in pollution levels. But for the time being, we assume wages are exogenous.

A. Agricultural Land

Suppose we have a valley devoted to agricultural production. Furthermore, the valley is divided into two regions, a clean region and a dirty region. This is illustrated in Figure 8.1. Crops do not grow as well on the land in the dirty region—productivity is lower than the clean region due to the pollution. This lower productivity will be reflected in lower rental prices for the land. We would expect the difference in value between the two regions to reflect the difference in productivity of the land in the two regions due to air pollution, since everything else is the same.[2]

Our primary question, however, is how much landowners in the dirty region would be willing to pay to clean up the pollution in the dirty region? Is it exactly the amount that land prices are depressed in the dirty region? If so, we just observe the land price differential and we have a measure of the willingness to pay for clean air. Whether this is true depends in large part on the nature of the agricultural markets for the produce grown on the land. If the market is purely local, the price of the agricultural output from the valley will be determined locally. Cleaning up the pollution will increase the supply of the crop and probably reduce the crop price, in both the dirty and the clean area. This results in a reduction in the land price in the clean area, in conjunction with an increase in the land price in the dirty area. Consumers have benefited from cleaner air (through lower-priced products) as well as producers (landowners). Thus the land value change will not fully capture the value of the cleaner air.

On the other hand, the market for many crops (e.g., wheat) is regional if not national or global. In such a case, the price of the product will be unaffected by the cleanup of the local air pollution. Thus the land price in the clean area will not change when pollution is eliminated in the dirty area. In this case, the land value change is a reasonable proxy for the value to agriculture of the environmental improvement.[3]

FIGURE 8.1 A valley divided into a clean region and a dirty region.

B. Urban Land

Now suppose we are dealing with land used for housing. In this case the value of the land does not reflect the value of the agricultural products produced from the land but rather the utility of the people residing on the land. Following the example above, suppose we have a city, part of which suffers from air pollution (the dirty part) and part of which is clean. Keep in mind that there are many factors that determine the desirability of a parcel of land, including proximity to jobs. We will assume that everything is the same between the clean and dirty regions (such as commuting time and neighborhood characteristics), except for air pollution. We can ask the same question as we did for the agricultural example: Does the lower value of property in the dirty region fully capture the damage from the air pollution? We also assume that everyone in the city is the same, both in terms of their preferences and in terms of their incomes.

We consider two types of cities, a "closed city" and an "open city." The closed city assumes in- or out-migration is not possible—the population is fixed. In contrast, the open city is assumed to be one of many cities among which the population is free to move, locate, and relocate. The closed city may seem contrived—there is no city in which the population is prohibited from leaving or arriving. However, the closed city is a metaphor for a region (perhaps a country) in which mobility is less than perfect.

If we have an open city, we can conclude that the utility level of the typical person is the same, no matter where they live. With an open city, mobility among cities is costless; thus if there is any city that yields higher utility, people will move there, bidding up prices and depressing attainable utility until the utility difference has been erased. The same applies for different locations within a city. This means that people who live in the dirty part of the city must have the same utility as people who live in the clean part; otherwise, they would not put up with the dirty air. To compensate for the pollution, living is cheaper. Now if we clean up the pollution, the value of land will increase. But only landowners will be any better off. Why? Because the utility level is the same over all of the cities and a clean up in one portion of one city will not significantly change the overall level of utility. Thus when the air becomes cleaner, the land value will rise to compensate exactly for the increased quality of life. Put differently, the increased value of the land is a perfect measure of the value of the air quality improvement. Of course if we relax our assumption of homogeneity, and in fact consider a heterogeneous population (different tastes, different labor skills, different incomes), this conclusion must be tempered.[4] We will consider the interplay between wages and property values in the next section.

Now we turn to the case of the closed city. Since there is no mobility among cities in this case, the utility level of the typical citizen of our closed city is determined by internal factors, not a multicity equilibrium driven by mobility. We do know that the utility level within our city is the same for all residents. Thus the difference in property values between the clean and dirty parts of the city reflects the damage from air pollution. Now suppose we eliminate the pollution. Will the rise in property values in the dirty area reflect the value of the cleaner air? Generally, the answer is no. Although property values will rise in the dirty areas, the overall well being of the typical resident will also increase—the city is a nicer place to live. The elimination of pollution has generated two effects, one observable (property value increases) and one unobservable (utility level increases).

What can we conclude from these various models of the effect of pollution on property values? The general conclusion is that in some but not all cases, the value of improving environmental quality will be reflected in increased property values. Situations in which this would not be the case involve secondary changes in utility or economic surplus brought about by the improved environmental quality, and not reflected in property values. This could be an increase in consumer surplus from lower agricultural prices or an increase in overall well-being brought about by the improvement and not bid away through higher land prices.[5]

C. The Effects of Climate on Agriculture

Recall that in Chapter 2 we considered the emissions of greenhouse gases and how they may lead to climate change. A major unknown in the climate change policy debate is just how much we should worry about raising global temperatures by a few degrees Celsius. To help answer this, a number of economists have examined how agricultural output and profits very with weather and climate. One of the earliest such analyses was by Mendelsohn et al. (1994) and is examined in detail in Chapter 2. Since that time, other researchers have refined this general approach, introducing water and irrigation,[6] the effect of weather,[7] and data from other parts of the world.[8] The key insight is that climates in different parts of the world or different parts of a country vary and by examining how those climate variations affect agricultural profits, we should be able to learn how climate change might affect agriculture. Their approach is very similar to the examples presented earlier in this chapter regarding different pollution levels over an agricultural valley. Here we have the entire United States and instead of pollution, we have different climates. Just as we can estimate the willingness to pay to reduce pollution by comparing land values in parts of the valley with different pollution levels, we should be able to infer the willingness to pay in agriculture to avoid a 3°C temperature rise (for example) by examining two agricultural areas that are the same in all respects except that one has a climate on average 3°C warmer than the other. Because of the focus on the fact that the price of land capitalizes a beneficial climate, and different climates result in different land values, this method has become known as the Ricardian approach, after David Ricardo.[9]

II. POLLUTION, LAND PRICES, AND WAGES

As we look at various communities around the world, we see that some are nicer to live in than others, for environmental as well as other reasons. In the previous section we examined the extent to which these differences are reflected in property values. But we all know that some of the worst places to live from the point of view of environmental quality have some of the highest property values (e.g., the center of many of the world's metropolises) and that many rural areas have high environmental quality and low property values. We also know that wages are often higher in cities than in rural areas. Do wages rise to compensate for deteriorating environmental quality? If this is the case, we must consider wage differences as well as property value differences in understanding the value of changes in environmental quality.

The basic question is, to what extent do higher levels of pollution depress property values but increase wages to compensate for the pollution? To understand the interplay among pollution levels, property values, and wages, we will construct a simple model involving multiple cities with competition among the cities for firms and residents. If pollution levels are different in the different cities, we expect to see differences in wages and/or property values.[10]

A. A Model of Wages, Land Prices, and Pollution

We start with a number of cities that differ in one respect: the level of pollution. Let the pollution level be denoted by p. In our example there is one composite produced good, call it X. Firms produce X using labor and land and may locate in any city. In a particular city, the wage rate is denoted by w and the land price or rent by r. These prices may of course vary from city to city. Firms seek to locate where X can be produced most cheaply. The price of the composite commodity is determined by the world market, outside of our analysis. We adjust the units for X so that the price of X is 1.

Consumers are identical in terms of preferences and use their wage income to purchase goods (X) and land for housing (L). Each consumer offers one unit of labor (such as a person-year) and receives a wage for that. If each consumer has the utility function $U(X,L,p)$, each consumer has the following utility maximization problem:

$$\max_{X,L} U(X,L,p) \tag{8.1a}$$

such that

$$w = X + rL \tag{8.1b}$$

This problem for the consumer results in some level of utility for each particular set of prices and pollution levels, w, r, and p. We can write the utility level that results from these prices and pollution as $V(w,r,p)$. Because we assume that people can move from one city to another easily and at no cost, it must be true that utility levels are the same for all cities. Call that constant utility level k. So $V(w,r,p) = k$, no matter what the prices or pollutin levels are.

Now consider the producer side of the market. With a constant cost industry,[11] the average cost of producing X must be equal to the product price, which is the same for all cities:

$$c(w,r,p) = 1 \tag{8.2}$$

Because each firm must sell its product for the same price, firms operating in different cities can use more of one input only if its price is less or there are cost savings in the use of the other input. If rents are higher in one city, wages must be lower to compensate, given the same level of pollution; otherwise, the firm would locate only in the lower cost city.[12]

Now how does pollution affect the firm? Obviously, if a clean environment is necessary for production, higher levels of pollution will make production more costly. In this case, we say pollution is "unproductive." Alternatively, high levels of pollution may be the result of lax pollution control regulations, in which case costs are lower for a polluting firm: pollution is "productive" in an indirect way. A third option is that pollution has no effect on the firm. Perhaps the firm is a law office that is unaffected by low or high levels of pollution. In this case we say that the pollution is "neutral."

Now let us consider two cities, both with firms producing X. One city has pollution level p_1, which is lower than the other city's pollution level, p_2. What can we say about land prices and wages? Remember that the utility level of a citizen of the first city must be the same as the utility level of a citizen of the second city. Because higher pollution is undesirable, some compensation is necessary to keep utility constant—in the high pollution city, either wages are higher or land prices lower or both. Figure 8.2 shows two lines of constant utility for the two cities, $V(w,r, p_1) = k$ and $V(w,r,p_2) = k$. Each line represents combinations of w and r that yield utility k for the particular level of pollution. Because pollution is undesirable to residents, the line associated with p_2 is lower than $V(w,r, p_1) = k$. Either lower land prices or higher wages are necessary to compensate for the increased level of pollution to keep utility constant at k.

Also shown in Figure 8.2 is Eq. (8.2) for the two different pollution levels. As shown, pollution is "productive" for the firm, meaning that higher pollution levels imply that the firm need spend less on pollution control. To keep costs constant as pollution increases, either land prices must rise or wages must rise to compensate the firm for the benefit of higher pollution levels, to ensure that Eq. (8.2) holds. Thus as pollution increases, the isocost line must shift to the upper right in the figure.

Now we can put these two perspectives together, comparing prices in the two cities. Point A is the level of wages and land prices with p_1 and point B is the level of wages and prices with p_2. It is clear from Figure 8.2 that when pollution is "productive," increased pollution levels raise wages while having an ambiguous effect on land prices. This is as expected. Higher levels of pollution drive away labor but attract firms. Higher wages in more polluted areas make up for the advantage to firms and tend to attract some people back. Higher land prices in the polluted area could also offset the cost advantage to firms, but higher land prices would not attract any workers. Thus wages must be higher in areas of higher pollution.

Pollution, of course, need not be "productive." If increased levels of pollution make it more expensive for a firm to operate, the two constant cost lines in Figure 8.2 would be reversed—the lower line will be associated with higher levels of pollution. In this case the equilibrium prices at low pollution levels will be point C while the prices for higher pollution levels will be point D. Pollution thus clearly depresses land prices but has an

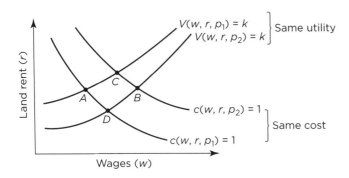

FIGURE 8.2 Effect of pollution on land rents and wages with productive pollution. A, wage/rent at pollution = p_1; B, wage/rent at pollution = p_2; $c(w,r,p)$ = 1, isocost lines; $V(w,r,p) = k$, isoutility lines. Note: $p_2 > p_1$.

ambiguous effect on wages. Basically, pollution is bad for firms and workers. For a high pollution city to have any firms or residents, firm costs must be lower (lower wages or lower land prices) and working conditions must be better (lower land prices and/or higher wages). This is why land prices clearly decline as pollution increases but the effect on wages is indeterminate.

The third possible situation is that pollution has absolutely no effect on a firm. In this case, the two lines of constant cost in Figure 8.2 will be coincident. We can then conclude that increased pollution will decrease land prices and increase wages. The relative magnitude of these changes depends on the slope of the isocost line in Figure 8.2. A steep line means that land prices are not very important to the firm, in which case elevated pollution will be manifest almost totally in lower land prices. If the isocost line is fairly flat, a small increase in land prices must be offset by large wage decreases to keep costs constant: this means that land is much more important to the firm than labor. In this case, an increase in pollution is almost completely reflected in higher wages.

The changes in wages and land rents as pollution changes can be summarized in a graph such as is in Figure 8.3. Assuming the pollution is productive (the normal state of affairs), wages increase as pollution increases. The figure also show land rents decreasing, though as we have seen, that need not be the case (they could increase). If you are a consumer at a particular level of pollution, contemplating a move to a slightly higher level of pollution, you will get a higher wage (good) and you may have a lower cost for housing (also good) but you will have to put up with more pollution (bad). In fact, at the margin, the increase in net discretionary income (i.e., after housing) is the compensation for more pollution (in order to keep utility constant). Discretionary pay (wages nets of housing costs) is also shown in the figure (where L is the amount of land purchased, which may change as the price of land changes).

What we have seen from this analysis is that it is not possible to clearly conclude that higher pollution levels are totally reflected in either land prices or wages. In actuality, the extent to which pollution changes influence wages vs. land prices depends on how pollution influences the productive sector of a city's economy. The model here is very stylized, which makes it difficult for us to conclude exactly how higher pollution levels in a particular city will actually be manifest. The main thing we learned here is that both wages and land prices may be affected by pollution.

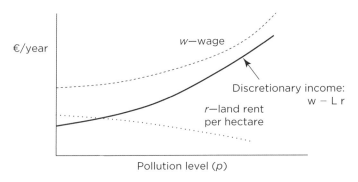

FIGURE 8.3 Wages, rent, and discretionary income, as a function of pollution levels.

> **An Application to Climate in Italy**
>
> As is described in the text, Jennifer Roback measured the effect of some climate variables (clear days and heating degree days) on wages and land rents, though these variables by no means completely characterize climate. Building on this structure, David Maddison and Andrea Bigano (2003) focus on Italy and a more detailed and complete representation of climate.[15]
>
> Rather than measure the wage line separately from the rent line, the authors measure the discretionary income line as shown in Figure 8.3. They do this for 95 Italian provinces, using annual data from the 1991–1995 period. The climate variables used by the authors to explain discretionary income are January and July temperature, precipitation and fraction of the month with clear skies (six variables).
>
> All of the climate variables are statistically significant in the most complete version of their model, with the exception of July precipitation. The theory tells us that we should look at the change in the discretionary income line to determine the marginal willingness to pay for particular climate attributes. The authors make this calculation and determine that an extra degree (C) of average July temperature causes a loss to an average household of approximately €350 per household per year. An increase in typical total January precipitation by 1 mm is equivalent to an income loss of approximately €15 per household per year.

B. Deriving Willingness to Pay

The framework developed in the previous section can be used to derive the marginal willingness to pay for local pollution reductions. As we discussed, if local pollution is reduced by one unit, a consumer will see two results: a wage change (up or down) and a rent change (up or down). The net effect (wage increase less rent increase) represents how much money the consumer will gain and can spend on other things; alternatively, it is how much a consumer would be willing to pay for the pollution reduction. If the pollution reduction is small, the result is the marginal willingness to pay. Keep in mind that utility for the consumer will not change because utility is equalized over all cities and the pollution change is only local; consequently, benefits of the pollution reduction have to be realized in either wages or rents.

In other words, we can write the individual marginal willingness to pay (MWTP) for a change in pollution, Δp, as

$$\text{MWTP} = \Delta w/\Delta p - L\ \Delta r/\Delta p, \tag{8.3}$$

where L is the amount of land consumed by the consumer.[13] When p increases, the wage increases according to the first term on the right-hand-side and the cost of land (price times quantity) increases (or decreases) according to the second term. So the right-hand-side of Eq. (8.3) is the amount of extra income necessary to keep utility constant with an increase in p. Our consumer would be willing to pay up to that amount to avoid the increase in p. Keep in mind that another interpretation of this is that the consumer would be willing to *pay* that amount for a *decrease* in pollution.

In the original application of this method, Jennifer Roback determined the statistical dependence of wages and rents on a variety of variables for 98 cities in the United States for the year 1973. The variables include the concentration of particulate pollution, the annual number of clear days and the number of heating degree days (a measure of how much heating is needed in the winter).[14] She applies these estimates to Eq. (8.3) and determines that for an average individual, an additional unit ($\mu g/m^3$) of particulate emissions is valued at –\$2.50; an additional clear day at \$69.55; and an additional heating degree at –\$0.20 (in 1973 US\$). Certainly the signs of these estimates are consistent with intuition.

III. EQUILIBRIUM SORTING

One of our assumptions in the wage–rent discussion of the previous section is that people are all the same. But, alas, the real world is not so simple. Just in terms of pollution, some people are more averse to pollution than others. More specifically, people differ in terms of their characteristics or "tastes." Perhaps we will observe these tastes, but more often than not, these tastes will not be observed (by the analyst anyway) and will be what economists refer to as "unobserved tastes"—characteristics of people that are important for behavior but that are unobserved by the analyst.

The problem of differences in tastes can be seen from Figure 8.4. We are comparing two communities (communities 1 and 2) with different levels of pollution—p_1 and p_2. Shown in the figure are representative wage–pollution indifference curves for two different individuals: a pollution-insensitive person (I) and a pollution-sensitive person (S). The figure shows how a person would trade off extra income with increased levels of pollution. (Each indifference curve is from a family of curves for each individual, with higher curves yielding higher utility.) The pollution-sensitive person would need a higher wage (relative to the pollution-insensitive person) to be willing to live in the higher pollution area (p_2)—compare point S and point S′. The pollution insensitive person would need less—that person is indifferent between I and I′. What would we expect to happen to wages in these two communities and, also, where would our two types of people choose to live? Suppose the same wage is offered in both communities. Then everyone is going to want to locate in the lower pollution area. To attract people to the higher pollution area, higher wages will need to be offered. As wages in the higher pollution area are raised, at some point pollution-insensitive people will decide they would rather work in the high pollution area for a higher wage. But too high a difference in wages will attract both types of workers. So the wage difference will be large enough to separate the two sets of workers but not large enough to attract all the workers to the high pollution area. We would expect the wage difference to be at least as high as the difference between I and I′ but not as great as the difference between S and S′. As a result, pollution-insensitive people will sort themselves into the higher pollution area; pollution-sensitive people would sort themselves into the lower pollution area.

This sorting and taste difference has several implications. One is that the difference in tastes must be taken into account in statistically estimating the wage–pollution relationship in order to avoid incorrect estimates. Second, if we are evaluating a nonmarginal

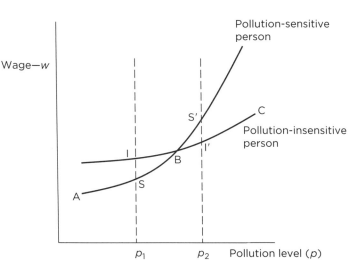

FIGURE 8.4 Representative wage-pollution indifference curves for two different individuals (higher utility associated with upward shifts in indifference curves).

change in pollution (i.e., a large change), we must take into account the fact that people may switch locations.

If we do observe the differences in tastes, then we would need to expand our model to account for the fact that people with different tastes will sort themselves into different communities. But if we do not observe how sensitive someone is to pollution (and that would be hard to observe), we will simply observe the lower envelope of the curves—the line ABC. In this case, alternative statistical methods are needed to generate accurate estimates of the wage–pollution line for individuals.[16]

A second problem associated with differences among people leading to different locational choices has to do with nonmarginal changes in pollution. With small changes in pollution, we can safely move from one point to another in Figure 8.4 without being concerned about people changing location. But if the change in pollution is large and covers all of the different cities, then overall utility may indeed change, violating one of the assumptions in our analysis of the previous section.

These problems can be addressed by explicitly representing the fact that individuals will choose where to live based on the wages, housing prices, and pollution levels in different communities. In fact, we would expect other factors to also play a role, such as the provision of schools and other public goods by different communities, as well as tax rates in those communities. We deal with these issues by developing a model of "equilibrium sorting" wherein consumers make a choice as to location, as well as the other choices described in the previous section.

In the previous section, we defined utility as depending on X (private goods), L (land or housing), and pollution (p). We now add a fourth variable, α, representing tastes. The higher is α, the more sensitive our individual is to pollution. Utility is now given by $U(X,L,p,\alpha)$. We do not observe α. If we don't observe α, how can we possibly figure out the correct relationship among pollution, wages, and rents?

The answer is that we do observe something related to α: community choice. For instance, in the context of Figure 8.4, we know people who choose the low-pollution community will have higher α than people choosing the high-pollution community, at least holding income constant. So by observing community choice, we are obtaining some information on α and, in turn, some information that allows us to correct our estimates of the MWTP for pollution reductions, based on unobserved tastes.

To be more specific, we can revise the utility maximization problem in Eq. (8.1) to reflect the addition of α:

$$\max_{X,L} U(X,L,p,\alpha) \tag{8.4a}$$

such that

$$w = X + rL \tag{8.4b}$$

We can write the utility level that results from these prices and pollution as $V(w,r,p,\alpha)$.

Now suppose we observe two individuals, A and B, located in two different communities (1 and 2). Assume A locates in community 1 and B in community 2. What can we infer? We can infer that their utility is higher where they are than in the other community:

$$V(w_1,r_1,p_1,\alpha_A) \geq V(w_2,r_2,p_2,\alpha_A) \tag{8.5a}$$

$$V(w_1,r_1,p_1,\alpha_B) \leq V(w_2,r_2,p_2,\alpha_B) \tag{8.5b}$$

In other words, A must be getting higher utility in community 1 than he would in community 2 and vice versa for B.

Climate and Brazil

Christopher Timmins of Duke University has applied the locational sorting method to the entire country of Brazil, examining the impacts of hypothesized climate change. Location choice for the entire country involves individuals choosing to migrate to a region of residence from their region of birth, a migration that involves some cost or barriers. Considering some 500 microregions of Brazil, ranging from the cool south to the warm north, he estimates an equilibrium sorting model for four different types of individuals, based on education level. Explanatory variables include local wages, rainfall in fall and spring, temperature, migration distance, proximity to transportation, population density and distance to both Sao Paulo and the state capital. (Source: Timmins, 2007.)

After estimating the coefficients of the statistical model, he uses an Intergovernmental Panel on Climate Change (IPCC) forecast of the change in climate across Brazil (a moderate change scenario). Under the scenario, rainfall decreases by as much as 20% in some regions, while increasing by nearly as much in other regions. Temperature increases everywhere, from 1.6° to 2.75°C. He applies this forecast to his statistical model and predicts where people may move to in 2050. This is then the basis for a calculation of the change in monetized utility associated with the change in climate. He computes that although the cool south actually does slightly better with climate change, the country as a whole suffers an annual loss of $1.6–5.9 billion (in 1991 US$) from the change in climate.

So our observation that A prefers community 1 and B prefers community 2 tells us that Eq. (8.5) applies, which in turn allows us to infer something about the distribution of tastes in the population.[17]

The situation of different communities with different pollution levels is very common. For instance, in a typical large city, there are many communities with different levels of pollution, different quality of schooling, and different tax rates. Households deliberately choose where to locate in the urban area based on the characteristics of the community, their own income, and their own tastes. People will make very different choices, depending on their preferences and income. In fact, most of the applications of this approach in the environmental arena have involved air pollution in large urban areas such as Los Angeles (Smith et al.,2004; and Sieg et al., 2004) and San Francisco (Kuminoff, 2007).

IV. HEDONIC PRICE THEORY

We now extend the issue of measuring the demand for pollution based on observations of how pollution influences prices and markets. In the previous sections we noted the circumstances under which changes in pollution influence land markets and labor markets. This is only the beginning of being able to measure the demand for pollution.

In the "real world," we are often confronted with bundles of goods with a single price for the whole bundle. Yet, we are in fact interested in the price of an element of the bundle. For instance, we observe the prices of houses that are bought and sold. But a house consists of a bundle of characteristics such as the number of rooms, the neighborhood quality, and the surrounding environmental quality. We note that houses with fewer rooms fetch lower prices, as do houses with lower air quality. By observing the prices of many houses with differing characteristics, is it possible to back out the implicit value that is being placed on air quality (for instance)? Similarly, different occupations (jobs) have different characteristics, including the level of health or mortality risk. Typically, jobs with greater risks pay higher wages. By observing the wages associated with many different occupations, can we infer anything about how much workers value small changes in risk?

These examples suggest the focus of hedonic price theory: inferring the value placed on specific characteristics of goods based on the observed price of a bundle of characteristics.[18] It is somewhat more complicated that these examples suggest, in part because of the interaction between the supply of characteristics (building more houses with more rooms) and the demand for characteristics.[19] In this section we will develop this theory, followed by some empirical examples in subsequent sections.

We will consider the simplest possible structure, that of a good with a single characteristic. It is probably easiest to think of this as houses with different levels of a characteristic (such as the number of rooms or pollution levels). Although we are considering a single characteristic, it is not difficult but it is tedious to extend this to the case of multiple characteristics. We will examine two basic questions. The first involves determining the price of the good in the market. The second involves inferring consumer willingness to pay for changes in the characteristic—a demand curve.

The basic setup is a single homogeneous area, such as a city or part of a city, which can be considered a single market from the point of view of our good (a house). Each house can be characterized by a single variable, z, which we will assume represents air quality levels. We are interested in how the price of a house varies with the pollution level. In other words, we are interested in $p(z)$, the house price as a function of air quality levels. This price function is an equilibrium concept, resulting from the interaction of supply and demand. In much the same way that conventional supply and demand interact to produce a single market price, forces of supply and demand interact to produce a price function—a single house price for every pollution level.

To understand the nature of $p(z)$, we need to look at both the consumer side and the producer side of the market. We will assume the market is competitive, which means that producers take $p(z)$ as given and consumers take $p(z)$ as given (just as in a conventional market, producers and consumers take p as given). The way in which producers and consumers react to $p(z)$ will give us insight into how $p(z)$ emerges in the market.

A. The Consumer

Suppose a typical consumer has utility function U and income y. The consumer buys exactly one house. The consumer must decide how to allocate income between the house (choosing the level of air quality z) and ordinary goods, denoted by x (nominally priced at 1). Thus utility depends on X and z: $U(X,z)$.

The standard way to approach this problem would be for the consumer to choose X and z to maximize utility subject to a budget constraint: $X + p(z) = y$. But in order to understand consumer behavior better, it is useful to ask an intermediate question: what would the consumer be willing to bid for a house of quality z in order to achieve some level of utility? To answer this question, look at consumer choice of X and z as a two-step process. Our consumer first decides how much he is willing to bid for his house, given the z and utility he desires. In other words, his bid will depend on his income, his desired z, and his desired utility. The second step will be for the consumer to match his bids with offers from suppliers in order to maximize utility.

Let $\hat{U}$ be the utility our consumer desires, let y be his income, and let θ be the maximum amount our consumer is willing to "bid" for the house to attain that utility. Thus we can write the consumer's problem of finding that maximum bid as

$$\max_{X,\theta} \theta \tag{8.6a}$$

such that

$$U(X,z) \geq \hat{U} \tag{8.6b}$$

$$X + \theta = y \tag{8.6c}$$

Eq. (8.6) states that the consumer should choose the maximum he can bid for the house, while assuring that he attains his desired utility and does not violate his budget constraint. Note that in Eq. (8.6), the variables X and θ are being chosen, whereas the variables y, z, and $\hat{U}$ are exogenous (and can thus be treated as parameters of the problem).

The end result is that, given values of z, y, and $\hat{U}$, we determine how much money is available for the house, $\theta\,(y,z,\hat{U})$. We call this a bid function because it represents the

FIGURE 8.5 Consumer choice. $\theta(y,z,U)$, amount of money avaiable to bid for house with air quality z, for a person with income y, obtaining utility U; $p(z)$, price of house with air quality level z.

amount of money the consumer is willing to bid for the house with characteristics z, to keep utility at the level $\hat{U}$, assuming income y.

Figure 8.5 shows, for a single consumer, two bid functions for two different levels of utility. Each function shows how much the consumer would be willing to bid for different levels of air quality (z). Note that the lower bid function is associated with higher levels of utility. Figure 8.5 also shows the hedonic price function, $p(z)$, determined by the market. The consumer's problem is to determine what level of z to choose to maximize utility. For this consumer, the point of choice is the point at which the bid function is just tangent to the price function, $p(z)$—the point at which the bid function just "kisses" the price line. This gives maximum utility with the requirement that the amount the consumer is willing to pay (θ) must be equal to the price, $p(z)$. If we were to do this same exercise for another consumer or even the same consumer with a different income, we would get a different set of bid functions and a different choice point for z.

B. The Producer

There are also producers of housing, and this side of the market is somewhat easier to characterize. Some producers are particularly good in building large up-market houses; other producers specialize in other segments of the housing market. Different producers will have different costs. Let us start with some particular producer with a given cost structure. We will assume there are constant returns to scale so that we may consider the costs of producing one house of characteristics z.[20] Suppose the producer faces input prices r; unit costs can be given by $c(r,z)$. If the producer offers a price of φ, then profits per house are given by

$$\Pi = \varphi - c(r,z) \tag{8.7}$$

We can rewrite this as the price necessary to obtain a certain level of profit, given the level of the characteristic, z: φ (r,z,Π). We call this the offer function. The offer function indicates the price at which the producer will offer the house to obtain a particular profit level, Π, given a particular value of input prices, r, and a particular value of z. If the producer wants to sell a house, this offer curve has to have at least a point in common with the price line. This is illustrated in Figure 8.6.

In Figure 8.6, the hedonic price function is shown, $p(z)$, as well as two offer functions for some particular firm, one function for each of two profit levels, Π_1 and Π_2 ($\Pi_2 > \Pi_1$).

FIGURE 8.6 Producer choice. $\varphi(r,z,\pi)$, house offer price when air quality level is z, input prices r, necessary to give profit π; $p(z)$, price of house with air quality level z.

Note that higher curves are associated with higher profits. Thus the correct choice of z is the one at which an offer curve just "kisses" the hedonic price line. As with the case of consumers, different producers will have different sets of offer curves and thus different choice points along the hedonic price function.

C. Market Equilibrium

We stated at the beginning of this section that we were working backward to see how the hedonic price function is constructed. We are now in a position to see that every point along the hedonic price function corresponds to a tangency between the bid function of some consumer and the offer function of some producer. This is shown in Figure 8.7. In Figure 8.7 we see three pairs of producers and consumers, each with a tangency between their offer and bid functions. This tangency determines a choice of z, along with a price, $p(z)$. In this manner, the entire price line is constructed. Thus at each point along the hedonic price function, we conclude that there is some consumer's bid function and some producer's offer function both tangent to the price line.

This tangency is important. It means that the slope of the offer function (with respect to z) is equal to the slope of the bid function, which is in turn equal to the slope of the price function. The slope of the price function indicates how much the price goes up if the level of z goes up by one unit. This is the marginal price and is analogous to a conventional price for z. To see this, suppose we have a shopping cart full of groceries, including three loaves of bread. We are unsure about the price of bread, but we do know that the value of the entire shopping cart is £40. We also know that if we add one more loaf of bread to the cart the value of the cart goes up to £41. What must the price of bread be? The marginal price of the shopping cart with respect to the number of loaves of bread is £1/loaf. Clearly, the price of bread is £1. If we were unable to buy loaves of bread individually, but only as part of bundles of groceries, we could use the same mental exercise to conclude the marginal price of a loaf of bread is effectively £1 per loaf.

The fact that the slopes of the bid, offer, and price lines are identical at each choice point means that the producer, the consumer, and the market all have the same marginal valuation on a unit of the characteristic. The slope of the offer function is the increased price necessary to compensate the producer for supplying one more unit of z. The slope of the bid function is the extra amount of money the consumer is willing to pay for one

FIGURE 8.7 Equilibrium in an hedonic market. φ_i, offer function for three producers, $i = 1,2,3$; θ_j, bid function for three consumers, $j = 1,2,3$; E_k, equilibrium between producer k and consumer k, $k = 1,2,3$; $p(z)$, price of house with air quality level z.

more unit of z. And in market equilibrium, these are equal and are also equal to the slope of the price function with respect to z.

D. Willingness to Pay

The previous sections described the origins of the hedonic price function. The hedonic price function on its own can be very useful for many applications. It shows how the price of a house varies with air-quality levels, or how the wage for an occupation varies with the probability of accidental death. The price line tells us how the market values the air pollution or risk (in the sense of how price varies with those characteristics).

But what is often of even greater interest is a demand function or marginal willingness-to-pay function for particular characteristics. For instance, suppose air quality surrounding a house is the characteristic of interest. We have measured the hedonic price function and calculated its slope at various points. Thus we know the marginal price of air quality at different levels of air quality (z). But this is not demand—all we know is what the market price is of air quality. What we really need to know, for a particular individual, is what that individual's marginal willingness to pay is for one more unit of air pollution. The problem is that each individual chooses only one consumption point along the hedonic price function, not several consumption points. One point does not a demand function make.

The distinction between the marginal price of z as a function of z and the marginal willingness to pay for z as a function of z is illustrated in Figure 8.8. Shown is the slope of a hedonic price line [p'(z)], not the hedonic price function [p(z)]. It generally trends downward in z. Also shown are two marginal willingness-to-pay (MWTP) functions for two different individuals. The point of intersection of these MWTP functions with the marginal price line gives us the choice of z for the individual. But how much each consumer is willing to pay for other quantities of z is obtained from the MWTP function, not the marginal price function. And these are different.

The solution to this is to assume the different individuals making choices along the hedonic price function are variants of the same person, simply with different incomes and observable characteristics (call these differences α). Thus we can translate the many observations on choice of z into a set of data on how marginal willingness to pay varies

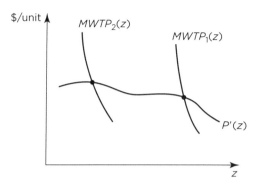

FIGURE 8.8 Marginal willingness to pay for z. $p'(z)$, slope of hedonic price line with respect to z (marginal value of z); $MWTP_i(z)$, marginal willingness to pay for one more unit of z, consumers $i = 1,2$.

with z, and thus statistically infer a marginal willingness-to-pay function. We can do the same with producers denoting their observable differences by β. We thus have the following equations for supply and demand:

$$p'(z)=f(z,\alpha) \tag{8.8a}$$

$$p'(z) = g(z,\beta) \tag{8.8b}$$

In Eq. (8.8), $p'(z)$ refers to the slope of the price function, $p(z)$, with respect to z.[21] The right-hand side of Eq. (8.8a) is a marginal willingness to pay function. Recalling that the slope of the hedonic price function is analogous to the price of the characteristic, or marginal willingness to pay for the characteristic, Eq. (8.8a) states that the marginal willingness to pay depends on the level of the characteristic and other variables such as income. This is precisely how we would specify an inverse demand function: price is some function of quantity, income, and perhaps some other variables reflecting tastes. Similarly, Eq. (8.8b) is analogous to an inverse supply function, with the price related to the quantity supplied (in this case quantity of the characteristic) and factors that reflect the costs of the industry, β.

Although there are some substantial statistical problems associated with implementing this methodology,[22] the basic idea is that we first observe the hedonic price function in a market. Then we measure the slope. Then, using this slope as a price of the characteristic, we measure the demand for the characteristic. So if the characteristic is air quality and the good is housing, we first note how the prices of houses vary with air quality. We then compute how much those prices change when air quality changes by one unit. This gives us a "price" of air quality. We then note how people of different incomes react to different prices of air quality in choosing how much to consume. In the next section we discuss an implementation of this approach.

E. Example: The Demand for Air Quality in Chicago

There have been a number of analyses of demand for environmental quality using the hedonic method.[23] One of the classic studies is by Harrison and Rubinfeld (1978) for Boston, Massachusetts. They faced a very real and also typical environmental policy problem: Are the benefits of a proposed air pollution regulation sufficient to justify the costs? Their problem was having to quantify the benefits from tightening the automobile emissions control regulation for nitrogen oxides in Boston. They first estimated a household-level marginal willingness-to-pay function for nitrogen oxides. Using a meteorological model, they were able to calculate the change in pollution concentrations at different locations in Boston as a result of the new regulations. Then using their marginal willingness-to-pay function for nitrogen oxides, they calculated the benefits of the cleanup for an average household. They compute a value per average household ranging from $59 to $118 per year, in 1970$.

Although the Harrison and Rubinfeld (1978) study appears to implement the hedonic theory correctly, it suffers from the econometric problems mentioned in the previous section; thus its empirical results are of questionable value. In a similar, though more recent, study of the Chicago housing market, Chattopadhyay (1999) has overcome many of the econometric problems found in earlier hedonic studies.[24]

The author uses data on actual house sales in the Chicago market for 1989 and 1990. This contrasts with the more conventional approach of using the average house price from the decennial U.S. census, at the smallest level of public spatial detail, the "census tract." Either data set not only has housing prices but also characteristics of houses, such as number of rooms, living area, age of the house, area of the lot, the number of bathrooms, and distance from roads and the downtown business area. Characteristics of the purchaser are also available. A different source indicates the ambient level of particulates (PM-10) and sulfur dioxide (SO_2). Characteristics of the house, including the pollution levels, would correspond to the z variable in the previous section. Characteristics of the individual would correspond to the α variable.

Rather that take a two-step approach as outlined above, the author simultaneously estimates the hedonic price function and the marginal willingness-to-pay function. Thus Eq. (8.8a) and p(z) are estimated in one fell swoop. The analysis is considered short run so that supply [Eq. (8.8b)] can be ignored.

To be more precise, let $p(z,\gamma)$ be the hedonic price function for housing in the Chicago market where γ is a set of parameters to be econometrically estimated. By differentiating this price function (before conducting the estimation), one obtains $p'(z,\gamma)$. The equation to be estimated is thus

$$p'(z,\gamma) = f(z,\alpha) \tag{8.9}$$

Although this looks remarkably like Eq. (8.8a), it is different in some important ways. The biggest difference is that p is not estimated first, then differentiated, and then the values used for a second stage estimation. Instead, Eq. (8.9) is estimated in one step. If the functions p and f are sufficiently different, then identification of γ and α is not a problem. To see why it could be a problem, suppose the functions are not very different; for example, assume p and f are both quadratic in z. In this case, z would enter linearly on both the right-hand and left-hand side of Eq. (8.9) and it would be impossible to separately identify the coefficients of z on the two sides. A second problem with Eqn. (8.9) is that z is not really exogenous to either side of the equation. Consumers choose z—characteristics of the house. The author uses econometric techniques to overcome this (instrumental variables).

The results of this analysis are willingnesses to pay for reductions in pollutant levels. The results for particulates (approximately $300 per $\mu g\text{-}m^{-3}$) are consistent with other studies; however, the authors could not compare their results for sulfur (approximately $1 per ppb) with other studies.

F. The Value of a Statistical Life

One of the major applications of hedonic price analysis is in studying how much more workers are paid for riskier jobs. Different occupations involve different risks, and it is reasonable to expect that employers need to pay a wage premium to induce workers to undertake jobs involving higher risk. If we could measure this premium, we could obtain an estimate of the market value of small changes in fatality risk. This is a particularly attractive application of hedonics because it is only the hedonic price function that gives us this information: generally, we do not have to proceed to the more tricky statistical estimation of the MWTP function.

A number of authors in several countries have tried to make just such a calculation.[25] The general approach is to estimate a function of the form

$$w = f(\pi, z) + \epsilon \qquad (8.10)$$

where w is the wage rate, π is the probability of death on the job, z is other characteristics of the job (such as required skill level of the job), and ε is an error term. As might be expected, there are problems in statistically estimating such an equation. One of the major problems is determining whose risk estimate should be used—the subjective risk as estimated by the worker or the objective risk as reflected in injury statistics. Another problem has to do with the age of the worker. Older workers have fewer remaining years left in their life; one would expect this to have some influence on their valuation of risk. Another problem is that there may be self-selection into high risk jobs. Workers who take such risks may place a very low value on their life, yet it is such workers who are setting the wage premium for riskier occupations. Nevertheless, a number of authors have estimated versions of Eq. (8.10). We will examine some of those estimates shortly.

Figure 8.9 shows a hypothetical relationship between on-the-job risk of death and wage. The scatter of points would be obtained from standard government statistical sources (for instance), which show not only the characteristics of jobs but the number of accidental deaths in particular years as well as the overall number of workers in those job categories. That is sufficient information to compute the objective probability of accidental death for a job category and thus plot a point on the graph in the figure. Having done that, the analyst can statistically estimate how wages depend on that risk (π) as well as other characteristics of the job (z). The result is the hedonic price line, $f(\pi, z)$, also shown in the figure.

The standard approach to using an hedonic price function, such as Eq. (8.10), is to examine how the wage rate changes with changes in risk—the slope of the hedonic price equation. In the case of Eq. (8.10),

$$VSL = \frac{\Delta w}{\Delta \pi} = \frac{\Delta f(\pi, z)}{\Delta \pi} = \frac{\partial f(\pi, z)}{\partial \pi} \qquad (8.11)$$

Equation (8.11) indicates, for instance, how much the equilibrium wage rate increases when the fatality risk increases by a small amount. This would be the slope of the

FIGURE 8.9 Wage–risk relationship.

hedonic price function in Figure 8.9. The slope of course varies if the hedonic price function is nonlinear. In the figure, the slope is shown for an approximate midpoint of the data.

The slope of the hedonic price function tells us how much extra wage is necessary to attract workers for a slight extra risk. Because the denominator of Eq. (8.11) is a probability (which runs from 0 to 1), the slope of the price line has become known as the *value of a statistical life* [VSL in Eq. (8.11)]. It is important to underscore the word statistical in the words VSL. This does not mean the value of a particular life. In fact the best way to think of it is in terms of a large population of people: for instance, if risk is decreased slightly for a large population (say 1,000,000 people), how many fewer anonymous (though real) deaths can we expect?

As an example, suppose we are at a risk level of 10^{-4} and we note that if the risk is increased to 2×10^{-4}, the annual wage goes up by $600. The slope of the hedonic wage function at this point would be $600/(2 \times 10^{-4} - 10^{-4}) = \$6,000,000$. One interpretation of this figure is that if we have 10,000 workers subject to an increased annual risk of 10^{-4}, we would expect, on average, one extra death to occur per year ($10^{-4} \times 10,000 = 1$). Workers would need to be paid $600 \times 10,000 = \$6,000,000$ in extra wages to willingly take this risk. If there are ways in which the employer can eliminate this increased risk for a sum less than $6,000,000, it would be in the employer's best interest to do so. Thus in a statistical sense, it is worth $6,000,000 to save a life.

This notion of placing a value on a statistical life sounds crass. But risks exist and it is not logical to spend enormous quantities of resources to reduce risks to the lowest possible level. In our everyday lives, we are constantly making trade-offs regarding risk, whether it involves using an old car with increased risk of mechanical failure but lower costs or the decision to take a plane trip (and risk a crash) to enjoy a vacation. In fact, the hedonic wage function indicates how workers willingly expose themselves to risk to have more of the resources income can buy.

Table 8.1 shows the results of selected hedonic wage studies involving risk-wage trade-offs, taken from a review of the literature by Kip Viscusi and Joe Aldy (2003). There are literally dozens of studies with results such as in Table 8.1; in fact, there is more variability in the results over all of the literature than in the table. Although the studies are from a number of different developed countries, the results do not differ dramatically. In fact, the authors of the survey find that most U.S. studies fall in the region of $6–9 million with a median of $7 million. Non–U.S. studies are consistent with these figures. The authors also conduct a "meta-analysis" of the dozens of studies.

TABLE 8.1 Selected Empirical Estimates of the Value of a Statistical Life, Based on Hedonic Wage Studies

Year	Country	Average per capita income[a] (2000 US$)	Implicit value of statistical life (2000 US$ million)
1985	Australia	23,397	4.2
1986	Japan	44,863	9.7
1982	United States	24,611	10.0
1986	Canada	25,387	2.2–6.8
1977	United States	31,092	9.7
1983	United Kingdom	12,810	9.4–11.5
1991	Hong Kong	11,668	1.7

[a]*Average income refers to study sample.*
Source: Viscusi and Aldy (2003).

A meta-analysis uses the results of different studies as data points in a statistical analysis. This approach has become a popular way of summarizing results of large literatures on the same issue. One of the results of their meta-analysis is that the income elasticity of VSL is in the range 0.5–0.6. This means that when income rises by 10%, the VSL estimates should rise by 5–6%.

We should point out that estimating Eq. (8.10) gives information only on how the market wage depends on risk. We have not taken the second step in hedonic analysis of estimating an individual's willingness to pay for risk reduction. For the most part, empirical research has been content with measuring the hedonic price equation and has not taken the second and more difficult step of estimating the marginal willingness to pay for risk.

SUMMARY

1. In an agricultural region, the value of a change in air pollution in an area that constitutes a small part of the agricultural market will be reflected in the change in the price of land.

2. If a change in air pollution affects a substantial amount of land so that the price of agricultural products changes, land price changes will not reflect the value of the change in air pollution.

3. In an urban housing market, the value of changes in air pollution in a part of the market will be reflected in changes in property values if the region is open with free mobility in and out of the region, and if producers are unaffected by the change in pollution and property values. If the market is closed in that in- and out-migration are restricted, the value of pollution changes will not be fully reflected in land value changes.

4. Over a region with different pollution levels in different locations, we would expect wages and housing prices to reflect in part the disutility and production effects of pollution. As pollution increases from one location to another, wages would be

expected to increase; whether land and housing increase in price depends on how pollution affects production.

5. With pollution varying over an urban area, we would expect people to sort themselves into communities with different pollution levels. How this sorting occurs will depend on both observed characteristics of people and communities as well as unobserved tastes of individuals.

6. If production is influenced by pollution or if property values are significant costs of production, a change in pollution will change both property values and wages. If pollution is "productive," in that more of it reduces costs for firms (perhaps because regulations are looser), an increase in pollution will raise wages and have an ambiguous effect on land prices. If pollution is "unproductive," in that more pollution increases production costs, an increase in pollution will depress land prices and have an ambiguous effect on wages. If pollution is "neutral" to the firm, an increase in pollution will decrease land prices and increase wages, although the amount of each depends on the relative importance of land and labor to production.

7. With hedonic price theory, we observe the price of a good as a function of certain characteristics of the good. For example, with housing we may observe that the price of a house varies with the air pollution level surrounding the house. From this we infer the marginal price of the characteristic as the slope of the price line with respect to the characteristic.

8. Hedonic price theory can further be used to estimate an individual demand curve. Having observed how the market values changes in the characteristic, we may estimate the demand or marginal willingness to pay for the characteristic using the marginal price of the characteristic, the level of the characteristic chosen by consumers, the income of consumers, and other factors that influence consumer preferences. There are serious econometric problems in estimating this demand.

9. In studies of wage–risk trade-offs, the marginal wage with respect to fatality risk has been called the value of a statistical life. The value of a statistical life is the ratio of the increase in the wage rate to the increase in the risk of fatality that induced the increase in wages. This is a market concept that is not the same as an average individual's marginal willingness to pay for risk reduction.

PROBLEMS

1. Oxana is conducting research on the demand for cleaner air in Novosibersk. She notices that the Ministry of Housing built many identical dwellings around the city approximately the same distance from the center. The only difference is the average level of air pollution. She notes the following rental prices and air pollution levels for these dwellings:

Pollution level ($\mu g/m^3$)	Rent (R/month)
30	497
50	492
70	485

Pollution level (µg/m³)	Rent (R/month)
90	475
120	455
150	430
200	375
250	305
300	219

Plot the relationship between pollution levels (on the horizontal axis) and rent (on the vertical axis). On a separate graph, plot the relationship between pollution levels (on the horizontal axis) and the marginal valuation of pollution implicit in the relationship between rents and pollution levels (on the vertical axis).

2. Suppose we have an agricultural valley 100 km by 50 km, with a polluting electricity power plant. The power plant causes pollution problems in a narrow strip of land downwind of the plant, and within this valley. 10 km in length and 500 m in width, but no problems outside of that area. The total effect of the pollution is to make crop land less productive. If we were to clean up the pollution, would we expect land prices to increase? Where? Would we expect wages to decline? Would the changes in land prices and/or wages fully reflect the benefits of cleaning up the pollution? Why or why not?

3. Pierre is a software engineer, working in a heavily polluted city in northern France. He does not like the pollution, but the pay is good and housing is relatively cheap. He is considering taking a job with a different software company in Cannes, a lovely seaside community in southern France with very low pollution levels. Unfortunately, he discovers that housing is very expensive in Cannes; many people wish to live there and this has bid up the price of housing. Pierre tells his potential employer in Cannes that he will need a higher wage to compensate for the higher cost of living. Is Pierre justified in making this request? Why or why not?

4. Figure 7.1 is drawn from Harrison and Rubinfeld's study of the demand for air pollution in Boston. Make a copy of Figure 7.1 and then estimate the total willingness to pay, for a household earning $15,000 per year, of reducing NO$_X$ levels from 6 to 4 parts per hundred million.

5. After conducting her analysis of housing prices in Novosibersk, Oxana notes that everyone in her study has exactly the same income, graduated from the same school, and listens to the same music; in fact, everyone in town appears to have exactly the same tastes and income. Does Oxana have enough information to construct a typical marginal willingness-to-pay function for pollution in Novosibersk? Why?

6. In the model described in section II, how would things change if land were not an input into production? In particular, how would the conclusions regarding how an increase in pollution would effect wages and land rents change?

7. An automobile maker is interested in the marginal willingness to pay by consumers for fuel economy in the cars the manufacturer produces. The automobile maker has asked you to conduct a hedonic analysis of automobile characterisitcs. Describe how you would carry out the analysis, being sure to discuss (a) which characteristics of cars you would measure, (b) how you would measure the hedonic price function, and (c) how you would translate this into a marginal willingness-to-pay function.

NOTES

1. This classic model is described more fully in Mills (1967).
2. As was mentioned earlier, it is really the rental price of land that should reflect the productivity differences. The asset (total) price of the land reflects future expectations, which are difficult to observe. For instance, people may expect air pollution regulations to be tightened in a few years, eliminating pollution problems. If so, the pollution will have only modest effect on the asset price of the land, even if it has substantial effect on the rental price of land.
3. This issue was the subject of much debate in the late 1960s and 1970s. See Freeman (1979) for a summary. The primary source papers are Lind (1973), Strotz (1968), and, Kanemoto (1988).
4. See Polinsky and Shavell (1976) for an analysis of a more general urban area.
5. There is a large empirical literature on using property values to infer the value of environmental improvement. The first such paper appears to be Ridker and Henning (1967).
6. Schlenker et al. (2005) is a good example of an extension of the Ricardian approach to include water and irrigation.
7. Kelly et al. (2005) move away from the cross-sectional approach of Mendelsohn et al. (1994) by examining how profits (rather than land rents) vary over time and space with both weather and climate. Using a similar approach, Deschenes and Greenstone (2007) conduct a very careful analysis of how time and space affect agricultural profits, focusing on weather excursions alone, not climate.
8. Mendelsohn and colleagues have been instrumental in extending the Ricardian method to the developing world. Refer to the 2007 special issue of the journal *Climatic Change* with an introduction by Mendelsohn (2007).
9. David Ricardo was an English economist of the early nineteenth century who, among other things, is credited with exploring the subtleties of determinants of the rent for land, particularly the notion that differential qualities of land earn differential returns (rents).
10. The model and results presented here are based on Roback (1982).
11. Recall that a constant cost industry has all firms operating at the bottom of their average cost curves. Further, there are no economies, diseconomies, or scarce factors that change industry prices or costs as the industry expands. Thus the long-run industry supply curve is horizontal, at a price equal to minimum average cost for any firm.
12. This assumption is debatable. One of the primary reasons suggested as to why cities exist is agglomeration economies—economies associated with different firms being located in close proximity. For instance, there are many law offices in central London because of the ease of interaction among firms, access to courts, the use of common services, and similar reasons. Agglomeration economies violate our assumption of a constant cost industry.
13. Mathematically, it turns out that we do not need to take into account small changes in L—they drop out (the envelope theorem).
14. Refer to Roback (1982). Coefficients on all of these variables are highly significant, with the exception of particulate levels, which are only modestly significant. In subsequent work, Roback (1988) determines that particulate concentrations are highly significant for individuals with more than a secondary school education.
15. Maddison and Bigano (2003) follow closely the approach of Nordhaus (1996), who conducted a similar study for the United States, using county-level data.
16. Unobserved tastes create a statistical problem in that the error term will be correlated with some of the supposedly exogenous explanatory variables, which leads to bias in estimating the parameters of the wage–pollution equation using ordinary least squares methods. Instrumental variables is the standard econometric approach for dealing with this problem.
17. The seminal paper in this literature is Epple and Sieg (1999). They not only define the problem theoretically, but they propose a method for estimating the V (indirect utility) and the distribution of tastes.

18. Although Court (1941) examined automobiles, Zvi Griliches reinvigorated hedonic analysis with his 1961 study of measuring quality change in automobiles (Griliches, 1971).

19. There is a substantial literature on this topic that dates back to Court (1941), as discussed in Goodman (1998). Tinbergen (1956) made important contibutions to modern theory, subsequently develeoed by Rosen (1974). The treatment here follows Rosen (1974), who is credited with originating modern hedonic theory, although it has been expanded by a number of authors (see Palmquist, 1991).

20. Recall that constant returns to scale simply means that the cost of two identical houses is exactly twice the cost of one house. Thus we can focus on the cost per house—the unit cost function.

21. The slope of $p(z)$ with respect to z is of course the derivative of $p(z)$ with respect to z; the derivative is often denoted $p'(z)$.

22. The statistical problems are quite difficult to overcome. There are two basic statistical problems—identification and endogeneity. Identification means being able to disentangle the hedonic price function from the marginal willingness-to-pay function. Because the same data that are used to generate the hedonic price function are used to generate the demand function, it may be difficult to sort out the effect of exogenous variables on hedonic prices from the effect on willingness to pay. The second problem, endogeneity, has to do with the fact that the consumer really chooses both the marginal price of the characteristic and the quantity of the characteristic at the same time. In Eq. (8.10), z is on the right-hand side of the equation as an explanatory variable and thus is correlated with the error term, particularly if there are unobserved tastes in the error term. For standard least-squares statistical methods to be unbiased, the right-hand side variables must be truly exogenous and uncorrelated with the error term. Palmquist (1991), Freeman (1993) and Taylor (2003) provide nice discussions of these problems. There are solutions to these problems in some cases, as discussed by Bartik (1987), Brown and Rosen (1982), Epple (1987) and McConnell and Phipps (1987). These problems with hedonics are reasons researchers have been attracted to equilibrium sorting models, as discussed earlier in this chapter. Recent research (Ekeland et al., 2004) suggests these concerns are overblown and that if set up properly, the hedonic model can always be correctly estimated.

23. For instance, Thaler and Rosen (1975) conducted one of the first analyses of the demand for risk reduction by examining how wages change with the riskiness of the job; Pommerehne (1988) conducts a hedonic analysis of property values in Basle, Switzerland to determine the demand for noise from airplanes and road vehicles; Quigley (1982) examines the effects of the presence of sanitation services on housing prices in El Salvador to determine the benefit of a public housing project. Bayless (1982) conducts a hedonic analysis of the salaries of university professors to infer the demand for air quality improvements. Clark and Nieves (1994) do a hedonic analysis of both wages and property values affected by noxious facilities, such as petroleum refineries. Smith and Huang (1993) survey hedonic air pollution studies, particularly those done in the United States. Boyle and Kiel (2001) survey the literature on studies of how environmental factors influence housing prices.

24. It is common to use data from multiple markets to deal with some of the econometric issues, as suggested by Bartik (1987). When using single-market data, as does Chattopadhyay (1999), complex functional forms are used to achieve identification of the appropriate parameters. See also Netusil et al. (2009) for an application of hedonics to estimating the demand for a tree canopy.

25. Viscusi and Aldy (2003) provide a very readable and relatively up-to-date review of studies of the value of risks to life based on hedonic wage studies and other methods.

9

REVEALED PREFERENCE: DEFENSIVE EXPENDITURES AND TRAVEL COST

We turn now to another form of revealed preference for environmental commodities. The approach we consider involves environmental commodities whose effect on a person can be modified using market goods. If we are speaking of an environmental good (e.g., a national park), the use of market goods allows the individual to enjoy the good fully. If we are speaking of an environmental bad (e.g., noise), market goods can be used to insulate the individual from the full damage from the bad.

Examples are instructive. First consider the case of a bad. If you are living in a house near a busy autobahn, the noise from traffic is a nuisance. However, what you may really be interested in is peace and quiet inside your house; at a cost you may insulate your house from noise and thus neutralize, at least partially, the damage from the noise. Although we as researchers cannot directly observe the damage to you from the noise, we can observe your efforts to neutralize the noise. These expenditures tell us something about how damaging the noise is to you. The more strongly you feel about the noise, the more you will spend on keeping the noise away. This is what is known as a defensive expenditure— money is spent to defend against the environmental bad. By observing defensive expenditures, we learn how individuals value the bad.

Now consider a good, such as a national park. To enjoy the national park fully, people must visit the park, and this costs money (for most people). The more utility a person gets from a visit to the park, the more money the person is willing to spend visiting the park. Without visitation, the park provides little utility. For instance, people travel thousands of kilometers and spend thousands of euros to visit the game parks of Kenya— evidence that these visitors value these parks highly. In this example, the expenditure to enjoy the park is observable and related to the benefit an individual obtains from the park. By observing travel costs, we learn how individuals value the park.

Both of the cases are examples of what is called "household production." A household (or individual) combines an environmental good or bad with market goods to produce an "experience" that directly provides utility. In the first case, the indoor noise level is the produced commodity; in the second case it is a park visit. Insight as to the value of the environmental good or bad comes from observing consumption of the associated market goods, even though such insight may tell only part of the story.

In the next section we consider the case of bads—defensive expenditures. In the subsequent section we consider the case of goods—travel costs.

I. DEFENSIVE EXPENDITURES

The problem of demand for environmental bads is our first concern. The example above of noise pollution is typical. What expenditures defend against highway noise? In a house, you can install extra windows, use thicker walls (in new construction), and construct a noise barrier or wall (this is common). The household suffering the noise pollution will continue to invest in defensive measures until the marginal cost of additional measures equals or exceeds the marginal benefit from the reduction in noise. It is easy to see in this case that defensive expenditures are a lower bound to the damage from the noise. It is likely that the noise has not been totally neutralized by the defensive expenditures and thus there is additional unaccounted for damage.

Air pollution is another example. What can be done to defend against air pollution? One damage from air pollution is soiling of property. An obvious defensive measure is to use better paint on a house or paint it more frequently. Another step related to the health effects of air pollution is to install air purifiers and/or air conditioners in your house. Furthermore, additional medical care may offset some of the deleterious health effects of air pollution. Although air pollution cannot be totally neutralized in its effects, it can be reduced by appropriate expenditures.

Water pollution is our last example. It is not necessarily polluted groundwater that is damaging but rather the water consumed by the individual. There are several ways of defending against such pollution, including using bottled water, purchasing water purifiers, and increasing the monitoring of the well that is the source of drinking water. Once again, by observing these defensive expenditures, we learn about the significance of the pollution to the individual.

In all of these cases an individual combines a quantity of a public bad with a quantity of a market good to produce what actually gives utility—noise in the immediate surroundings, air quality inside the home, or water quality, as ingested. These expenditures are sometimes called defensive expenditures (defending against pollution) or averting expenditures (expenditures to avert the damage from pollution). Whichever term is used, the meaning is the same. We will first consider a simple economic model of defensive expenditures and then examine an application to the demand for improved air quality.

A. A Simple Model[1]

Consider the case of an individual subject to noise pollution (P) from a nearby road (higher Ps are worse). The individual, however, is really only interested in the level of quiet within the house, Q (higher Qs are better). Fortunately, the homeowner may buy noise insulation and other equipment to reduce the level of noise within the house. We call these purchases *defensive expenditures* and denote by $D(Q,P)$ the expenditures necessary to achieve indoor noise quality levels Q when the outside noise is P. We assume that these defensive expenditures provide no additional services other than to produce indoor

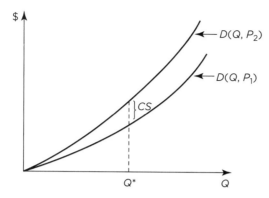

FIGURE 9.1 Defensive expenditures. Q, quality of personal environment; P_1, P_2, outdoor pollution; CS, surplus change from P_1 to P_2 at Q^*; Q^*, optimal choice of personal environmental quality at P_1; $D(Q,P)$, defensive expenditures

environmental quality. Noise insulation would fit into this framework but an air conditioning system that reduces noise levels while improving the indoor climate would not.

Figure 9.1 shows a typical shape for this defensive expenditure function. As the desired indoor level of quiet (Q) increases, for a given outside level of noise, the defensive expenditures necessarily increase. Furthermore, the marginal defensive expenditures increase as Q increases. This reflects the fact that it becomes more and more difficult (costly) to squeeze higher and higher levels of quiet from existing technology. Also shown in Figure 9.1 are two defensive expenditure functions, one for outdoor noise level P_1 and one for a slightly higher level of outdoor noise pollution, P_2. Note that as outdoor noise pollution levels increase, the quantity of defensive expenditures necessary to keep indoor levels of noise the same increases, and more so for higher levels of Q.

The individual is interested in consuming two commodities, quiet (Q) and other conventional goods (X). Only these two commodities enter into the individual's utility function. Outdoor noise does not enter explicitly, which is clearly a restrictive assumption in some cases. Assume the price of X is 1.[2] The consumer's problem is to choose X and Q to maximize utility, subject to a budget constraint that includes defensive expenditures:

$$\max_{X,Q} U(X,Q) \tag{9.1a}$$

such that

$$X + D(Q,P) = Y \tag{9.1b}$$

Equation (9.1a) indicates that it is necessary to adjust X and Q so as to maximize utility. Equation (9.1b) states that expenditures on X and on defensive measures must equal income (Y). In Eq. (9.1b), the variable P is outside of the control of the individual—the amount of road noise cannot be adjusted.

This consumer choice problem is represented graphically in Figure 9.2. (Remember that P is fixed.) Shown in Figure 9.2 is the budget constraint [Eq. (9.1b)]. In contrast to what we are used to for a budget constraint, in this case it is nonlinear. This is because of the presence of $D(Q,P)$ in Eq. (9.1b). Also shown in Figure 9.2 are two indifference curves involving X and Q. As is usual, higher curves represent higher levels of utility. The point

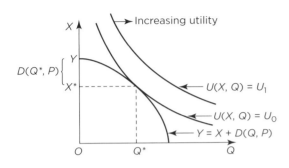

FIGURE 9.2 Consumer choice with defensive expenditures. $U(X,Q) = U_i$, indifference curves; X, numeraire consumption good; Q, quality of personal environment; $Y = X + D(Q,P)$, budget constraint; $D(Q^*,P)$, defensive expenditures; Y, income; X^*, Q^*, optimal choice of X and Q.

of tangency between the budget constraint and an indifference curve represents the optimal consumer choice of (X^*, Q^*). Also shown in Figure 9.2 is the corresponding defensive expenditure, $D(Q^*, P)$, assuming that when $Q = 0$, defensive expenditures are zero.

Now suppose we increase the level of noise pollution slightly, say from P_1 to P_2. How does the observed change in defensive expenditures compare to the willingness to pay to avoid the pollution increase? If they are the same, observations of defensive expenditures will tell us something about the demand for noise pollution. If defensive expenditures are predictably higher or lower than willingness to pay, defensive expenditures may provide an upper or lower bound on willingness to pay.

It is simple to see what the marginal willingness to pay is for a slight change in pollution. Focusing on Eq. (9.1b), if P is increased slightly, defensive expenditures necessary to maintain Q will increase slightly. Consumers given enough income to pay for that increase in defensive expenditures will maintain the same level of utility. Holding Q fixed, the amount D changes when P changes slightly is the marginal willingness to pay to compensate for the change in P. This is shown as CS in Figure 9.1 for Q^*.

But what is the total effect on observed defensive expenditures when P changes? Figure 9.3 shows how the budget constraint rotates downward when P increases. Furthermore, the increase in P results in a lower level of utility, shown as the indifference curve labeled U_2. The important thing to note is that the chosen Q drops as P increases. Q_1^* is chosen when $P = P_1$ and Q_2^* is chosen when $P = P_2$, with $Q_1^* > Q_2^*$. This is really quite intuitive. With an increase in outside noise, the cost of achieving a particular level of quiet indoors has increased. When something is more expensive, our normal response is to substitute other goods for that good. Thus with quiet a bit more expensive due to the increase in P, the consumer makes do with slightly less quiet in the house. This is what is shown in Figure 9.3. By cutting back on Q, the consumer is saving on defensive expenditures. This means that the observed defensive expenditures will be less than the marginal willingness to pay to avoid the pollution increase. This is important. This means that what we observe in the marketplace (changes in defensive expenditures) will understate the true marginal willingness to pay for pollution reductions.[3] Figure 9.3 is drawn so that the change in defensive expenditures is small. Recall from Figure 9.2 that the change in defensive expenditures is equal to the change in expenditures on X. In Figure 9.3 defensive expenditures could increase or decrease as pollution moves from P_1 to P_2.

This can also be seen algebraically. Let us start with indoor and outdoor noise levels Q and P. Suppose we change P slightly, by ΔP. Then let the consumer adjust the choice

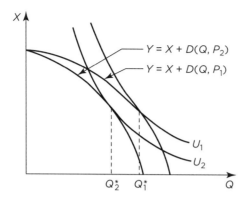

FIGURE 9.3 The effect of a change in pollution on defensive expenditures. U_1, U_2 indifference curves; X, numeraire consumption good; Q, quality of personal environment; $Y = X + D(Q,P)$, budget constraint; P_1, P_2, two levels of outdoor pollution, $P_2 > P_1$; Q_1^*, Q_2^*. optimal choice of Q for P_1 and P_2.

of Q and X. We would expect defensive expenditures to change by ΔD and indoor noise levels by ΔQ:

$$\Delta D = D(Q + \Delta Q, P + \Delta P) - D(Q,P) \tag{9.2a}$$

$$= D(Q + \Delta Q, P + \Delta P) - D(Q, P + \Delta P) + D(Q, P + \Delta P) - D(Q,P) \tag{9.2b}$$

$$= D_Q \, \Delta Q + D_P \, \Delta P \tag{9.2c}$$

where

$$D_Q = [D(Q + \Delta Q, P + \Delta P) - D(Q, P + \Delta P)]/\Delta Q \tag{9.2d}$$

and

$$D_P = [D(Q, P + \Delta P) - D(Q,P)]/\Delta P \tag{9.2e}$$

The interpretation of D_Q is the change in defensive expenditures associated with a slight change in indoor quiet levels, keeping outdoor noise levels constant. Similarly, the interpretation of D_P is the change in defensive expenditures from a slight change in P, keeping indoor noise levels constant.[4] As was argued earlier, D_P is precisely the marginal willingness to pay to avoid a change in P. Equation (9.2c) can be rewritten, dividing both sides by ΔP:

$$\Delta D/\Delta P = D_Q \, (\Delta Q/\Delta P) + D_P \tag{9.3}$$

This is the final result of our analysis. The last term on the right-hand side of Eq. (9.3) is the true marginal willingness to pay to avoid a small increase in P.[5] The left-hand side of Eq. (9.3) is the observed change in defensive expenditures from a small change in P. Generally, we can show that for small increases in P,

$$\Delta D/\Delta P < D_P \tag{9.4}$$

This means that observed changes in defensive expenditures will understate the true willingness to pay to reduce pollution. Equation (9.4) holds because the first term on the right-hand side of Eq. (9.3) is negative. This is because D_Q is positive (by assumption—see

Figure 9.1) and $\Delta Q/\Delta P$ is negative, as argued earlier (and as illustrated in Figure 9.3). An increase in P makes Q more expensive, which will result in less consumption of Q.

Calculus Derivation of Eq. 9.4

Calculus makes the derivation of Eq. (9.4) even more straightforward. If the indoor and outdoor noise levels, P and Q, are raised by infinitesimal amounts, dP and dQ, then the resulting change in defensive expenditures can be determined by totally differentiating $D(Q,P)$ to obtain the differential version of Eq. (9.2c):

$$dD = D_Q\, dQ + D_P\, dP \qquad (9.2c')$$

where D_Q and D_P are the partial derivatives of D with respect to Q and P respectively. Eq. (9.2c') can be rewritten to obtain

$$dD/dP = D_Q\, dQ/dP + D_P \qquad (9.3')$$

And by the logic described in the text, we obtain

$$dD/dP < D_P \qquad (9.4')$$

This result of course depends on the assumptions of our simple model. One significant extension of this model is to have the pollution level enter directly into the utility function. The most likely reason for this to occur is that it is not possible to defend against all of the deleterious effects of the pollution. For example, people live inside their house as well as outside, in their garden/yard.

B. An Example: Urban Ozone

There have been a number of empirical analyses of defensive expenditures, mostly in the health arena.[6] A study by Dickie and Gerking (1991) is a particularly interesting example of a defensive expenditures model being used to estimate the demand for ozone pollution in a major metropolitan area (Los Angeles, California). (Note that Bresnahan et al. 1997, provide a more recent analysis of the same data set used by Dickie and Gerking). Ozone pollution in many cities is one of the most difficult air pollution problems to control; very significant resources are expended in trying to manage the ozone problem. Thus information on the benefits of reducing ozone levels is critical.

The study by Dickie and Gerking (1991) concerned two cities in the Los Angeles air basin, Burbank and Glendora. The distribution of daily peak ozone concentrations in these two cities in 1985 is shown in Figure 9.4. Until 1997 the U.S. standard for maximum 1-hour ozone concentrations was 12 parts per hundred million (pphm); there had been discussions of revising it downward to 9 pphm (by 2010 it was significantly below this level). As can be seen from Figure 9.4, both these cities have a significant amount of air

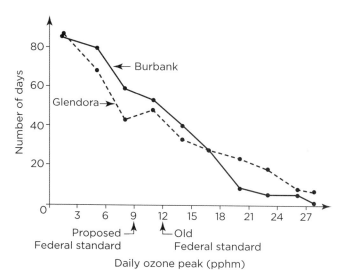

FIGURE 9.4 Distribution of peak ozone levels in 1985 in two cities in the Los Angeles air basin. (Adapted from Dickie and Gerking, 1991.) Ozone data are for intervals 3 pphm in width.

pollution, with many days during a year that exceed the Federal standards in effect at the time. Glendora is the more polluted of the two cities. The authors ask the following policy question: What is the willingness to pay for an average resident of each city to reduce the maximum ozone level during a year to either 12 or 9 pphm?

The basis of their analysis is the willingness of people to purchase health care to compensate for the health-related damage from ozone pollution. They posit that when ozone causes coughing or other breathing difficulties, people spend significant amounts of money on medical care to alleviate these symptoms. By observing these expenditures, the authors hope to estimate the willingness to pay for reductions in ozone concentrations. This is a classic application of the defensive expenditures model of the previous section.

Start with a typical person with a utility function. Three variables enter the individual's utility function: health (H), air pollution (A), and market goods (X). Health is produced by the individual by combining medical care in the current period with air pollution. Health is also influenced by the individual's predisposition to sickness and the individual's previous health record and care. We can now say that defensive expenditures on medical care (M) will depend on health (H), air pollution (A), and the individual's own health record and experience (R). However, instead of writing an expression that gives defensive expenditures as a function of (H,A,R), we can write a health production function as

$$H = h(M,R,A) \tag{9.5}$$

which tells us how much health will result if M is spent on medical care when air pollution is A and the individual's predisposition to illness is R. This is simply another way of writing defensive expenditures.

The budget constraint for our individual will be a little unusual. We will assume the individual has a certain amount of time available to earn income (T). If our individual becomes ill, time and thus income is lost by either being in bed ill or by spending time visiting the doctor's office. It is important to recognize that visiting the doctor's office involves more than just out-of-pocket expenses. Furthermore, sickness causes a loss of time that could be better utilized in some other activity.[7] The consumer's problem is to maximize utility:

$$\max_{X,M} U(X,H,A) \tag{9.6a}$$

subject to

$$H = h(M,R,A) \tag{9.6b}$$

$$wT = X + q_M M + w\, G(H) \tag{9.6c}$$

where w is the wage, T is the total time available, q_M is the price of M (including time costs), and $G(H)$ is the lost time due to poor health. Without loss of generality, the price of X may be normalized at 1. Thus the greater H (better health) is, the lower G will be. The consumer then maximizes Eq. (9.6a) in conjunction with Eq. (9.6b), subject to the budget constraint, Eq. (9.6c), yielding some maximum level of attainable utility that depends on prices, and the exogenous health record and air pollution, R and A:

$$v = V(w,q_M,R,A) \tag{9.7}$$

Eq. 9.7 is an important equation since it summarizes the decisions made by the individual and simply specifies the utility that the individual will obtain given the exogenous variables. This is what is know as an indirect utility function, since it depends on exogenous factors such as price and air pollution, rather than choice variables, which is the case with a regular utility function. If we could observe utility in the population, we could statistically estimate Eq. (9.7); it would then be a relatively easy task to estimate the demand for A.[8]

Dickie and Gerking (1991) are creative in compensating for not observing utility; they use what is known as a random utility model. Random utility models were discussed in Chapter 7 as a discrete choice method. These models exploit the fact that what we observe is whether people visit the doctor. If a person visits the doctor, that is evidence that there must be a utility gain from visiting, as opposed to sitting at home and not visiting the doctor.

To see this, fix (w,q_M,R,A), let V_0 be the maximum attainable utility without any medical care ($M = 0$) and V_1 the maximum attainable utility with medical care ($M > 0$). Both V_1 and V_0 depend on prices, R and A. Although we do not observe utility in the population, we can observe whether people visit the doctor. If they visit the doctor, we can conclude that the utility of visiting the doctor is greater than the utility of not visiting the doctor ($V_1 - V_0 > 0$). Similarly, if they do not visit the doctor, we must conclude that utility with $M = 0$ is no lower than utility for some positive value of M ($V_1 - V_0 = 0$).

Although this might seem like relatively skimpy information, this framework is amenable to statistical estimation using what is know as the Probit model.[9] Since $V_1 - V_0$ is measured with error, the probability of visiting a doctor is equal to the probability that $V_1 - V_0 > 0$. This is why the model is known as a random utility model (RUM)—there is a random element to utility.

The authors convert Eq. (9.7) to one involving both V_1 and V_0:

$$V_1 - V_0 = W(w, q_M, R, A) \tag{9.8}$$

The authors specify a functional form for the right-hand side of Eq. (9.8) and couple it with the binary choice problem:

$$M > 0 \quad \text{if } V_1 - V_0 > 0 \tag{9.9a}$$

$$M = 0 \quad \text{if } V_1 - V_0 = 0 \tag{9.9b}$$

Whether M is zero or not (whether a doctor's visit occurs) is observed, even though $V_1 - V_0$ is not observed. This is sufficient to estimate Eq. (9.8) using the Probit.

Although we do not need to go through the details here, the authors of the study are able to estimate W in Eq. (9.8) and from that, to compute the demand for changes in A (air pollution). The researchers deal with a sample of 256 residents of the two cities mentioned earlier. They conducted detailed interviews of the respondents who were drawn from a prior study of respiratory disease.

Air Pollution in Kanpur, India

An interesting application of defensive expenditures for measuring damage from air pollution was done in an urban area of India by Gupta (2008). Kanpur is a major industrial city approximately 500 km southeast of Delhi. The author reports that the average level of particulate pollution (PM_{10}) in the city is over 10 times the limit set by the World Health Organization. To assess the gains from reducing pollution in the city, the author estimated a model similar to that described in the text. Detailed data on a sample of Kanpur residents was collected, including information on health status and expenditures and activities intended to "defend" from or mitigate the effects of pollution. Data for 18 weeks of over 3,000 individuals was collected, resulting in a data set of weekly observations totaling nearly 60,000.

Rather than estimate the indirect utility function that emerges from the maximization problem Eq. (9.6), the author uses the demand for M that emerges from Eq. (9.6). Expenditures on health care, M, is a function of variables out of the control of the individual. In conjunction with the demand function, the author estimates Eq. (9.6b) directly, the health production function, where H is defined as the number of work days lost per week due to illness associated with pollution. Estimating both of these equations simultaneously, the author concludes that a 1 unit ($\mu g/m^{-3}$) reduction in pollution reduces the number of workdays lost for a representative consumer by 0.000072 days in a week. Using the estimated wage from the sample and extrapolating to the entire population of Kanpur, the author estimates that bringing particulate levels down to a safe level saves Rs. 112.5 million per annum (slightly more than US$2 million per year).

After estimating the model, they are able to calculate (for an average individual) the total willingness to pay for a reduction in the maximum ozone concentration on any given day to the legal limit, either 9 or 12 pphm. They conclude that such an average individual would be willing to pay $95–115 per year in Burbank to achieve the 12 pphm standard and $171–205 to achieve the 9 pphm standard. The average citizen of Glendora is willing to pay more (not surprisingly since Glendora is more polluted): $171–209 for the 12 pphm standard and $261–314 for the 9 pphm standard. These are substantial figures, particularly when compared to figures for annual damage presented in other studies. For comparison, Dickie and Gerking (1991) cite two other studies that report total individual willingness to pay of less that $4 per year per person.

The researchers also calculate the out-of-pocket medical expenses associated with elevated ozone in each of these two cities. Roughly speaking, the medical expenses are half the willingness-to-pay figures, suggesting that examining only the health costs of air pollution can significantly understate the damage.

II. TRAVEL COST

We now turn to the case of household production in which the consumer combines market goods with an environmental good (not a bad this time) to enhance enjoyment of the environmental good. In particular, we are referring to an environmental good that takes effort to enjoy, such as a national park. By observing the costly effort expended to enjoy the park, we can infer something about how the consumer values the park. When that effort consists of traveling to the park, what we are dealing with is the travel cost approach to valuing environmental goods. This method is most frequently applied to valuation of natural environments that people visit to appreciate. The most frequent application of travel cost to the demand for pollution is when pollution degrades a recreational experience, such as pollution affecting beach use. In this case, travel cost methods can be used to value the beach in its clean state and in its polluted state; the difference can be attributed to damage from the pollution.

The travel cost method is probably the oldest method of valuing environmental goods. Following World War II, the U.S. National Park Service solicited advice from a number of economists on methods for quantifying the value of specific park properties. Harold Hotelling responded in a two-page letter to the director of the Park Service, from which the following is excerpted:

> Let concentric zones be defined around each park so that the cost of travel to the park from all points in one of these zones is approximately constant. The persons entering the park in a year, or a suitable chosen sample of them, are to be listed according to the zone from which they come. The fact that they come means that the service of the park is at least worth the cost, and this cost can probably be estimated with fair accuracy.... The comparison of the cost of coming from a zone with the number of people who do come from it, together with a count of the population of the zone, enables us to plot one point for each zone on a demand curve for the service of the park. By a judicious process of fitting, it should be possible to get a good enough approximation to this demand curve

to provide, through integration, a measure of the consumers' surplus resulting from the availability of the park.[10]

This seemingly straightforward prescription has generated a half century of research and is widely used, though still not fully perfected.

There are three major dimensions to travel cost analysis of the demand for an environmental good. One concerns how demand depends on quality of the good (for instance, water quality at a beach). A second is associated with the number and duration of trips during a period of time such as a year. A third concerns the treatment of substitute sites, such as when a visitor to a national park faces the choice of several parks.

We will start with a simple model of travel cost, one in which there is a single environmental good of varying quality. We will then extend this to the case of multiple goods. Finally, we will turn to issues associated with implementing the travel cost method.

A. A Simple Model of a Single Site

We start with a single consumer and a single environmental good, say a park. Our consumer chooses two things—visits to the park (v) and a basket of market goods (x). We are interested in visits over the course of a fixed period of time, say a year. Assume that units in which x is measured are such that the price of x is unity. Let p_0 be the out-of-pocket expenses associated with a single trip to the park—automobile, train, or plane expenses, and food. Let f be any admission charges. Suppose our consumer works for L hours at a wage w to earn a certain income. We are now in a position to write the consumer's utility maximization problem:

$$\max_{x,v} U(x,v) \tag{9.10a}$$

such that

$$wL = x + (p_0+f)v \tag{9.10b}$$

The only problem here is that out-of-pocket expenses are not the only cost of visiting the park. Consumers must take time to travel to and to visit the park. And this time could be devoted to work in order to increase their income. They have chosen not to work, but to visit the park. But should we totally ignore their time commitments to the trip?

To answer this question, suppose our consumer has T hours of time available to devote to park visits and work. Whatever portion of T is devoted to work, the rest will be devoted to park visits, and vice versa. Denote by t_t and t_v, respectively, the travel time associated with a single round trip visit to the park and the on-site time associated with a single visit. The consumer then faces a time–budget constraint that must be appended to the utility maximization problem in Eqs. (9.10a) and (9.10b):

$$T = L + (t_t + t_v)v \tag{9.10c}$$

Equation (9.10c) can be substituted into Eq. (9.10b) to eliminate L and thus reduce the maximization problem to

$$\max_{x,v} U(x,v) \tag{9.11a}$$

such that

$$wT = x + [p_0 + w(t_t + t_v) + f]\, v$$
$$\equiv x + (p_t + f)\, v$$
$$= x + p_v v \tag{9.11b}$$

where

$$p_t = p_0 + w(t_t + t_v) \tag{9.11c}$$

and

$$p_v = p_t + f \tag{9.11d}$$

Note that Eq. (9.11) is a conventional utility maximization problem except that the price of a visit is composed of three terms—out-of-pocket travel expenses, the price of admission (if any) into the park, and the value of time devoted to the trip, with time valued at the wage rate. This is as expected. Since time spent traveling could alternatively be earning a wage, the opportunity cost of an hour of travel time is the wage, w.

As we will see later, this model is about as simple as possible. It is logical that consumers would rather be traveling than working on the assembly line. Thus they may not view leisure time as totally interchangeable with labor time. Further, they may not be able to earn additional money from wages, if their work hours per week are set by contract. How people value leisure time relative to their wage is an empirical question to which we will return later.

One can solve the maximization problem specified in Eq. (9.11) for a particular consumer. The result will be a demand function for visits to the park:

$$v = g(p_v, y) = g(p_t + f,\, y) \tag{9.12a}$$

where y is income (wT). Having determined an individual demand curve for park visits, the only remaining step is to sum these individual demand curves over the population to determine the market demand for park visits. In empirical implementation, the price of a visit is usually divided into the admission fee plus the travel cost portion of the trip, since from a policy point of view, one is usually interested in demand for the park as a function of the admission fee into the park. This will become clearer when we turn to implementing the travel cost method later in this section.

B. Including Site Quality

It is straightforward to include a term for the quality of the park into the development of the last section. In doing so, we end up with a demand curve, quite similar to Eq. (9.12a), except that the quality variable q will be included:

$$v = g(p_v, q, y) = g(p_t + f,\, q,\, y) \tag{9.12b}$$

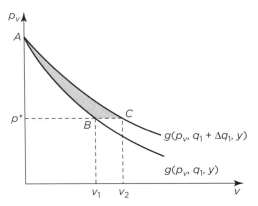

FIGURE 9.5 Surplus from a change in quality. v, number of visits to the park; q, quality of park visit; p_v, price of a visit; p^*, actual price of park visit; $g(p_v, q, y)$, inverse demand for park visits; y, income; ABC, surplus gain from quality increase from q_1 to $q_1 + \Delta q_1$.

With this expansion of the scope of the demand curve, we can ask the additional question: what is the willingness to pay for a small change in q? It turns out that this is exactly the problem we considered in Chapter 7 in the context of restricted demand.

Figure 9.5 shows typical demand curves for park visits: the vertical axis is the full price of a park visit and the horizontal axis is number of visits (per year). Shown in Figure 9.5 are two demand curves, one for quality level q_1 and one for a slightly higher level of quality, $q_1 + \Delta q$. Clearly consumers like this quality increase since they are interested in consuming more park visits for higher qs. At a price of a park visit of p^*, the consumer demands v_1 visits at the lower quality level and $v_2 > v_1$ visits at the higher quality level. The consumer's willingness to pay for this increase in q is the increase in surplus associated with the quality increase—the shaded area ABC in Figure 9.5. If Δq is very small, the shaded area will be small; the ratio of the area of the shaded region to the change in q, Δq, is the marginal willingness to pay for increases in q. If this exercise is repeated for a variety of quality levels, the marginal willingness-to-pay function for quality will be generated.[11]

C. Multiple Sites

Now we turn to the case in which the consumer is choosing among multiple sites. For example, suppose our consumer wants to take a vacation at one of the game parks in Africa, but can visit only one. The consumer will examine the cost of visiting all of the parks and make a choice. How can we represent this very real process in our travel cost model?

This problem of taking into account the choices a consumer may have has been a significant subject of research in the travel cost literature over the last three decades. At the simplest level, we can modify Eq. (9.12) to include the price of substitute sites. Thus if there are three sites, A, B, and C, the demand for any one site (e.g., site A) will be a function of the prices of visiting the other sites:

$$v_A = g_A(p_A, p_B, p_C, v) \tag{9.13}$$

Quality or other characteristics of individual sites could easily be included in Eq. (9.13). Conceptually, this representation of the role of substitutes is straightforward.

The problem is in empirically implementing a model such as Eq. (9.13): with many substitute sites the formulation becomes unwieldy. For this reason, there have been a number of approaches to simplify what amounts to the site choice problem for consumers. Freeman (1993) discusses a number of these approaches. We will focus on one, called the random utility model or RUM for short. The random utility model was discussed conceptually in Chapter 7 in the context of discrete choice methods for estimating demand for environmental goods and services. The ozone model discussed in the section on defensive expenditures was a random utility model as is the equilibrium sorting model of Chapter 8. A similar approach is even more common in travel cost analysis.

Suppose we have a consumer and a set of sites available for the consumer to visit, $i = 1,\ldots, I$. Each site has an access price, p_i—the travel cost. The consumer is also consuming unrelated market goods, x, which we assume have a price of 1. Visiting site i is hypothesized to give a certain amount of utility, which depends on the price of visiting i (not the price of substitute sites) and the quality of site i:

$$u_i = g(\beta, p_i, y) + \epsilon_i \tag{9.14}$$

where β is a set of parameters to be statistically estimated and ε_i is an error term that represents factors that are unknown to the observing economist. This is where the name of the approach comes from—the expression for utility in Eq. (9.14) has a random component, ϵ_i.

If we could observe utility, we could statistically determine the value of β in Eq. (9.14). But we do not observe utility; we never observe utility. What we do observe is consumer choice. And when the consumer chooses site i over site j, that must mean that the utility from i is higher than the utility from j:

$$\text{Site } i \text{ chosen} \Rightarrow u_i \geq u_j, \qquad \text{for all } j \tag{9.15}$$

Different values of β will yield different values of u_i and u_j. Since, in fact, u_i and u_j are random variables [from Eq. (9.14)], different values of β will yield different probabilities of the event ($u_i \geq u_j$, for all j). One value of β may make that event highly likely, whereas another value of β might make that event highly unlikely. Statistical methods can be used to choose a β that makes the observed consumer choices most likely.[12]

Having statistically estimated β in Eq. (9.14), we can compute the demand for trips to site i as a function of quality of the site and the price of a visit. We can then examine how this demand changes when the quality of the site changes. The details of this calculation need not concern us here.[13]

D. Implementation

Real problems always arise when we attempt to use theoretical models for empirical analysis. The travel cost model is no exception. There are two basic approaches to estimating the demand for a site based on travel costs, other than the random utility model discussed above. One method is essentially that suggested by Hotelling and is called the zonal travel cost model (ZTC), because of its use of geographic zones around the site as the basic units of observation. The second approach is more data intensive, and more recent, and is called the individual travel cost model (ITC), because of its reliance on observations of the behavior of individuals.

1. The Zonal Travel Cost Model. The zonal travel cost model follows directly from the original suggestion of Hotelling, quoted earlier in this chapter. However, the method was first applied and developed in detail by Marion Clawson and colleagues at Resources for the Future in the late 1950s and 1960s (Clawson and Knetsch, 1966). The only data that need be collected are a sample of visitors to the site in question, identifying the origin of those visitors' visits. Having identified the origin of visitors, it is possible to estimate the number of visitors per year from each origin "zone." Knowing the population of each origin zone gives a visitation rate for the zone (e.g., 1 person for every 1000 population). This visitation rate is explained by two things: the travel cost from the origin zone to the site (the "price" of visiting the site) and the demographic/ income characteristics of the population of the origin zone. The researcher thereby generates a set of data, one data point for each zone, indicating the visitation rate, travel cost, and characteristics of the zone.

The next step is to statistically determine how the visitation rate is affected by travel costs and zonal characteristics. Having done that it is possible to estimate how visitation will change if travel costs change, for instance, by applying an admission fee for the site. Choosing several admission fees and the resulting total attendance at the site generates points on a demand curve for the site.

To be more precise about this, we start with a given site, call it a park, and assume the distribution of people and alternative sites is fixed in the geographic region from which the park draws visitors. Divide the region around the park into Z zones, indexed by $z = 1,\ldots, Z$. These could be counties or postal codes (zip codes). A zone should be relatively small compared to the distance to the park and as demographically homogeneous as possible. Let the population of each zone be P_z and the average income in each zone, y_z. Let w_z be other demographic characteristics of the zone, such as the fraction of young people in the population (anything that might influence making a trip to the park). Compute the travel cost for visiting the park for each zone, excluding any admission fee to the park, and call that travel cost π_z. Let the admission fee be f (which is the same for all zones). Of course, f may be zero. The only "new" data that need be acquired are from a survey of park visitors during a year. Typically, this involves "intercepting" a sample of visitors to the park, often at the entrance gate to the park. At minimum, visitors are queried as to their residence location or the place where their journey began. This results in an estimate of the total number of visitors in a year, S, and the number of visitors from each zone, s_z. Define the visitation rate as $r_z = s_z/P_z$.

The next step is to statistically estimate a visitation equation:

$$r_z = g(\pi_z + f, y_z, w_z) \qquad (9.16)$$

This equation explains the visitation rate (akin to the probability that a randomly selected resident of the zone will visit the park) on the basis of the price of visiting the park $(\pi_z + f)$, income (y_z), and other characteristics of the typical zone resident (w_z). Demand for park visits (v) can then be written in terms of the function g:

$$v(f) = \Sigma_z P_z g(\pi_z + f, y_z, w_z) \qquad (9.17)$$

Although in statistically estimating g, the admission fee (f) was at its actual value, we can now vary f and see how $v(f)$ changes, using Eq. (9.17). This is the aggregate demand curve for the park.

The important thing to note from Eq. (9.17) is that there is only one variable—f. All of the other "variables" are actually data associated with each zone, such as the travel cost from a zone or the average income of a zone. Thus Eq. (9.17) gives the total number of visits to the park as a function of one variable alone—the price of admission to the park.

Damage from Oil Spill in Brittany

In 1978, the oil tanker Amoco Cadiz lost its steering entering the English Channel and crashed on rocks off the coast of Brittany, spilling over 200 thousand tonnes of crude oil. The damage from the oil spill in terms of lost recreation was the subject of a travel cost analysis (Brown et al., 1983; Brown, undated).

The basic idea behind their analysis is to estimate the demand for Brittany beaches for two different quality levels, one clean and one spoiled by oil. To accomplish this, visit rates (visits per 1000 population) were calculated for Brittany from 21 different regions of France in 1978 (the spill year) and 1979 (after cleanup). Two variables were posited to influence the visit rate: the travel cost to Brittany and the travel cost to the nearest alternate coastal area. The data on visitation rates were obtained from a survey of Brittany visitors (identifying visitor origin) in each of the 2 years, conducted by the French Institut National de la Statistique et des Études Économiques. The basic equation estimated in each of the 2 years was

$$r_i = \alpha_0 + \alpha_1 p_i + \alpha_2 a_i \qquad (9.18)$$

where r_i is the visitation rate for zone i, α_0, α_1, and α_2 are parameters to be statistically estimated, p_i is the travel cost from zone i, and a_i is the travel cost to the nearest substitute coastal area, for zone i. Equation (9.18) is then estimated for each of the two years using 21 data points, one for each zone. Applying this visitation rate to the population of all the zones generates a demand curve for Brittany beach visits.

Although the authors report some problems in interpreting the results of their estimated Eq. (9.18), they are able to calculate the change in consumer surplus between the 2 years (the shaded area in Figure 9.5). They compute a loss due to the oil spill of approximately 7 million francs, which is about 2% of the total surplus from beach visits in 1979.

---

2. The Individual Travel Cost Model. One of the strengths of the zonal travel cost model is that it is not data intensive. One of its shortcomings is assuming all residents of a zone are the same (since only average zonal characteristics are used). An alternative, is to collect more information on individual visitors (and nonvisitors) and use those data in estimating a model of demand instead of zonal averages. This is now a very common approach to implementing the travel cost method; however, there are two primary problems with this. One is that data are expensive to collect, and the more data that are collected from an individual, the more expensive it is.[14]

Another problem arises if the data used are generated by actual park visitors. The problem is bias introduced by the fact that the sample is self-selected, not a random sample of all possible visitors.[15] Although it is possible in principle to correct for this self-selection, the problem does not arise if the entire population of potential visitors is sampled. Unfortunately, it is generally too expensive to sample the entire population surrounding a park; a large sample size would be needed because most people will probably not visit the park.[16] Large samples are more expensive than small samples.

3. Computing Travel Costs. There are several problems associated with implementing the travel cost method. The most significant problem is in estimating the value of time. Although the simple model presented above suggests that the opportunity cost of travel time is the wage rate, that is generally not considered to be the case in actuality. Most people consider the opportunity cost of travel time to be substantially less than their wage rate. This may be because they like traveling more than working. Or it may be due to the fact that they receive a fixed wage and cannot adjust their hours worked, at the margin.

There have been many studies of the value of time spent in traveling. The primary use for such information is not for travel cost models of demand but rather for planning urban transportation systems. The typical approach to determining the value of travel time is to observe how individuals trade off their time with other expenses. For instance, if people willingly choose to save $1 by taking a bus rather than a train from point A to point B, thereby lengthening their journey by 15 minutes, we may conclude that they value their travel time at less than $4 per hour. The general consensus of the urban transportation economics literature appears to be that people value their travel time somewhere in the region of 20–50% of their gross wage rate (Bruzelius, 1979; Small, 1992).

Another problem with computing travel costs arises particularly in the case of automobiles. Is it appropriate to simply use the extra costs associated with the trip (which would typically exclude some depreciation, insurance, and taxes) or should average costs of operating the vehicle be used? How should one treat the fact that a person may have purchased an expensive four wheel drive vehicle or motor home specifically to visit a park or parks? Perhaps someone has chosen his or her home location so as to be closer to recreation areas, even though other costs, including the costs of commuting to work, may then be higher.[17] There are many other tough problems that confront the researcher when trying to implement the travel cost approach.

SUMMARY

1. The household production model involves a consumer combining a market good with a nonmarket good or bad to produce a third "synthetic" good that actually enters the consumer's utility function

2. In the case of combining market goods with nonmarket bads, the household production model is usually referred to as a defensive or averting expenditure model. The idea is that the consumer spends money to ameliorate the damaging effects of the bad. By observing defensive expenditures, we obtain information on the consumer's willingness to pay to reduce the level of the bad. In fact, observed defensive expenditures are a lower bound on the willingness to pay to avoid the bad.

3. The most common case of combining market goods with a nonmarket good is recreation in which travel costs are combined with a distant recreation location to produce

a visit to the recreation site. Although this method can be used to value the use of a recreation site, it can also be used to infer the value of improvements in the environmental quality in the vicinity of a recreation site.

4.   There are three basic versions of the travel cost model: the zonal travel cost model, the individual travel cost model, and the random utility model.

5.   Data requirements are modest for the zonal travel cost model. Based on a survey of visitors to a recreation area, visitation rates are determined for different zones around the area. These estimates are combined with the population distribution to generate a demand function for visits to the recreation area.

6.   The individual travel cost model takes an approach similar to the zonal travel cost model except that information on individual characteristics and behavior is used. This is more data intensive but can be more reliable.

7.   The random utility model is used most when individuals are making choices among competing recreation areas. It involves inferring the demand for a recreation area based on revealed choice of one area over another.

PROBLEMS

1.   In the travel cost analysis of the losses from beach use in Brittany due to the Amoco Cadiz oil spill (section II.D.l), can you think of any improvements that might improve the travel cost analysis? Avoid the necessity of collecting additional primary data.

2.   Consider Arturo, an individual with utility for a composite good (X) and indoor air quality (Q): $U = XQ$. Indoor air quality depends on pollution levels outside (P) and defensive expenditures (D): $D = PQ^2$. Let Arturo's income be Y.

   a.   Write Arturo's problem of utility maximization subject to a budget constraint, mathematically. Draw Arturo's budget constraint and several indifference curves.

   b.   Suppose $Y = 10$ and $P = 1$. What are the optimal amounts of X and Q for Arturo?

   c.   What happens to the optimal X and Q (show your work) when (i) P increases to 2 and (ii) Y increases to 20?

   d.   It is observed that low income individuals are exposed to more pollution. Is your answer to part (c) consistent with this?

3.   Consider a variant on the defensive expenditure model presented in this chapter. Suppose air pollution is the nonmarket bad and soap is the market good that can reduce the effects of air pollution—we bathe more frequently and wash our possessions more frequently. Our personal hygiene (H) is determined by the pollution level (P) and soap used (S). Suppose the price of soap is p_s. Set up the consumer's utility maximization problem for choosing the right amount of soap, other goods (x), and perhaps H and P. You do not need to solve the problem.

4.   We have discussed cases in which components of demand or willingness to pay for environmental goods and bads can be observed through their interaction with market goods. For each of the following public bads, identify possible related and observable market goods, and comment on aspects of demand that are not closely related

to any market behavior. For example, if an oil spill contaminates a coastal region for a period of time, lost beach visits are potentially measurable, whereas disutility from effects of the oil spill on marine life may not be inferable by observing consumption of any market good.

   a. Degradation of wild and scenic areas of Kakadu National Park due to mining activity.

   b. Global climate change.

   c. Urban air pollution.

   d. Stratospheric ozone depletion.

   e. Groundwater contamination.

5. Consider the demand for park visitation, Eq. (9.12b).

   a. We discussed (and illustrated in Figure 9.5) the effect of a change in q on demand for visits, v. How would you expect the other variables, p_v and y, to effect v?

   b. Given your answer to part (a), can we say what will happen to demand for park visits when the wage rate, w, increases? Keep in mind that y depends on w.

6. You have been commissioned to estimate the demand curve for admission to EuroLand, an amusement park in France. To do this, you spend a day surveying visitors to the park. Before doing this, you divide the area around the park into 10 zones, with the distance from the park approximately constant within a zone. You ask each person you interview where they come from. Based on that information, and figures on annual attendance at the park, you are able to calculate the annual number of visitors from each zone. Your data are shown below:

Zone	Distance from park (km)	Zonal population	Number of visitors
1	10	5,000	500
2	20	10,000	900
3	30	25,000	2,000
4	40	10,000	700
5	50	100,000	6,000
6	60	500,000	25,000
7	70	200,000	8,000
8	80	50,000	1,500
9	90	100,000	2,000
10	100	100,000	1,000

You note that admission to EuroLand is 150 euros per person. You also calculate that transportation costs, including time costs, are approximately 1/2 euro per person per kilometer in each direction. Ignore the value of time in the park.

Calculate the demand curve for visits to EuroLand, showing visits as a function of the entry price. How many fewer visitors would you expect there to be if the management raised the admission fee to 200 euros?

7. The text suggests that substitutability can affect demand for public goods and bads in the same way that it does for private goods and bads. To be more concrete, consider trying to estimate damages from an oil spill that caused the closure of several beaches along a coastal area. Why is it important to consider whether other local beaches were left uncontaminated and therefore did not close?

   Individuals may also have the opportunity to substitute across *time* as well as *space* in their consumption of environmental goods. What do we mean by substitution across time and why is it important in estimating the damage in a case such as this one?

NOTES

1. This model presented in this section is adapted from Bartik (1988) and Courant and Porter (1981). Some simplification has been necessary here; the interested reader is directed to either of these papers for a more rigorous development of the concept of defensive expenditures.

2. Since the units with which we measure X are arbitrary, there is no loss in generality in assuming the price is 1.

3. This result does not apply in all cases. Courant and Porter (1981), for instance, adopt very specific assumptions that reverse this conclusion. However, the result presented here generally applies.

4. Most readers will recognize that D_P and D_Q are simply partial derivatives of D with respect to P and Q, respectively. See box on p. 193. Clearly $D_Q(Q,P + \Delta P) = D_Q(Q,P)$ for ΔP infinitesimal.

5. Because utility is being held constant, D_P is actually termed the compensating surplus.

6. Gerking and Stanley (1986) examine damage from air pollution in St. Louis (United States) by studying health care expenditures. See also Harford (1984) and Shibata and Winrich (1983). The Bresnahan et al. (1997) study is an extension of the Dickie and Gerking (1991) study. Alberini and Krupnick (2000) take a similar (though distinct) approach to measuring damage from air pollution in Taiwan. Gupta (2008) examines the effect of air pollution on a city in India, using a household health production model. Um et al. (2002) estimate a defensive expenditure model of drinking water in Korea, where residents have various means for defending against perceived lower quality drinking water.

7. If the authors of this study explicitly included leisure in their model, the choice among work, leisure, illness, and doctor's visits could be made more explicit. That would be a much more complicated model, however.

8. Estimating demand for A from the indirect utility function [Eq. (9.7)] is beyond the scope of this book. See Kolstad and Braden (1991) for a detailed though somewhat advanced treatment of this issue.

9. The Probit model is described in any good econometrics book (e.g., Kmenta, 1986; Greene, 2007). The idea is that we are interested in the relationship between some unobserved variable, y, and a number of exogenous variables, x: $y = x \beta + \varepsilon$, where β is a vector of parameters and ε is an error term. We are interested in statistically estimating β. This is complicated by the fact that we do not observe y. But we do observe another variable, z, that takes on the value of 0 or 1, depending on the value of y. For instance, if $y > 0$, then $z = 1$; otherwise, $z = 0$. If we observe z, then the methods associated with the Probit allow us to estimate β.

10. Letter from Harold Hotelling to Director of National Park Service, dated June 18, 1947, reproduced in National Park Service (1949).

11. Figure 9.5 is comparable to Figure 7.4.

12. Hausman et al. (1995) discuss the implementation of this in the context of a travel cost model of recreation demand.

13. Refer to Bockstael et al. (1991) for an advanced treatment of this issue. Bockstael et al. (1987, 1989), Binkley and Hanemann (1978) apply this method to measuring the benefits of water quality improvement at beaches in Maryland and Massachusetts, respectively.

14. Some data are very difficult to collect on recreation surveys. Income is an example. Believe it or not, many people are unaware of their total income. Other people are part of a household; whose income should be used? Other people resent being asked about their income.

15. Bockstael et al. (1991) discuss this sample selection problem and some solutions in the context of travel cost models.

16. One prominent exception to this is the study done for the Exxon Corporation in support of their defense in the 1989 Exxon Valdez oil spill in Alaska (Hausman et al., 1995). In that study, a sample of the entire population of Alaska was used to estimate a travel cost model of recreation.

17. Randall (1994) discusses some of these problems and concludes that they present insurmountable obstacles to obtaining reliable information from the travel cost approach.

10

STATED PREFERENCES, EXPERIMENTS, AND REFERENDA

THE LAST TWO CHAPTERS WERE CONCERNED WITH INDIRECT, REVEALED PREFERENCE methods for determining the demand for environmental quality. As meritorious as these methods are, they can be used to value only a small fraction of environmental goods. The demand for many environmental goods cannot be completely estimated using revealed preference methods. Existence value (see Chapter 7) is one example of a value that is very difficult to estimate with revealed preference methods.[1] If one values something (e.g., an arctic wilderness or a rare species of animal) for its mere existence, unconnected with the possible use, the consumer's behavior with regard to market goods will be unaffected by whether that something is available. If behavior is unaffected, revealed preference methods are difficult to apply. Additionally, there are many goods for which there is no logical market through which value can be reflected. The value of a scenic vista or climate change is difficult to completely determine using revealed preference methods.

It is for this reason that constructed market valuation tools have been developed. Richard Carson of the University of California uses the word "constructed market" to refer to the broad classes of valuation techniques that involve the construction of a market, where one does not exist, to be used to generate the value or demand for an environmental good. There are two basic types of constructed markets—hypothetical and experimental. Valuation through hypothetical constructed markets goes by assorted names such as "stated preference," "hypothetical valuation," or most commonly, "contingent valuation." Consumers are directly asked what they would pay for an environmental good, *if there were a market* (hence the word "contingent"). The second type of constructed market is an experimental market. In an experimental market, the researcher constructs all of the characteristics of a market, including trading money for a good. The researcher then observes behavior. Experimental markets can be in the context of a laboratory, perhaps with students as the subjects, in which case we call them laboratory experimental markets. Alternatively, experiments can involve the general population in a realistic setting; we would call these field experiments. The only requirement for an experimental market is that real money change hands in exchange for a real good or bad. In other words, it is a real market, except that it has been contrived by the experimenter. The ultimate field experiment is an official referendum in which the "experiment" is officially constructed and voters are asked to commit public money to provide some sort of environmental good.

I. STATED PREFERENCES

Stated preference methods of valuation involve finding an individual's willingness to pay for a good by posing a set of questions regarding preferences directly to the individual. Other methods of valuation may also involve surveys (such as the travel-cost approach of asking people who visit a park where they started their trip), but such surveys simply ask for recall of factual information. In a contingent valuation (CV) question, the individual is asked to imagine some situation that is typically outside the individual's experience and speculate on how he or she would act in such a situation.

For example, in a classic study of the value of improving air quality in Los Angeles, Brookshire et al. (1982) were interested in how much people would be willing to pay to increase the air quality in their community. The researchers generated photographs depicting three different levels of air quality—poor, fair, and good, defined in terms of visibility. Furthermore, the researchers generated a sample of 290 people scattered over nine communities with varying air quality. People in a community with poor air quality were shown the photos and asked about their willingness to pay to move to fair air quality and people with fair air quality were asked their willingness to pay to move to good air quality. The results ranged from $5.55 to $28.18 per month, amounts respondents were willing to pay for an increase in air quality.

Stated preference methods appear to date back to the early 1960s when Davis (1963) conducted a study of the value to recreators of the Maine (United States) woods. However, it was not for another decade that researchers picked up on the idea and began applying it widely to environmental valuation.[2] Since that time there have been thousands of contingent valuation studies of environmental goods, though most remain unpublished.[3]

During the 1980s and 1990s contingent valuation became very popular for valuing environmental goods. This was due to a number of factors, including the early 1980s movement in the United States toward conducting cost–benefit analyses of most environmental regulations, and the rise of what is known in the United States as "natural resource damage assessment." Several laws in the United States permitted the government to sue for damage to the environment from events such as hazardous waste accidents or oil spills. Refer to Portney (1994) and Kopp and Smith (1989). To sue, it is necessary to compute the monetary equivalent of the damage. For many accidents, there is very little that can be done to place a value on damages, other than use contingent valuation.

CV has also found increased application in supporting government regulatory actions or provision of public goods. In Australia, the government debated whether to preserve or allow mining in an area known as the Kakadu Conservation Zone. In that debate, CV studies played a major role in steering public policy toward preservation (Carson et al., 1994).

Although it is quite easy to assemble a questionnaire, stand on a street corner, and administer the questionnaire to whomever walks by, it is quite another thing to conduct a careful, defensible CV study. There is a fairly well-developed protocol that is generally accepted by practitioners of CV. We will go through the details of the method, but first an example will serve to illustrate the approach.

A. An Application of Contingent Valuation: Drinking Water in Seoul

Korea has undergone dramatic economic development over the past few decades. But industrialization brings negative environmental side effects. In particular, several chemical spills into the Seoul water supply in 1991 caused great concern about the quality of the drinking water in that city of 10 million inhabitants. Any water supply can be made safer, including that of Seoul, by, for instance, increasing the monitoring of the water supply and increasing storage of water to be used when contamination occurs. Of course, these improvements cost money. To ascertain the value of reducing the risk of drinking water contamination, Kwak and Russell (1994) undertook a CV study of households in Seoul. They considered revealed preference methods, but rejected them. There is no water quality variation across neighborhoods, so an hedonic method seemed inappropriate. There are defensive activities such as traveling to the mountains to obtain spring water. They concluded that the trip to the mountains involved more than simply picking up water; thus a household production analysis would be inappropriate. That left contingent valuation.

The first problem they faced was defining the "good" they would seek to value. They decided that the good would be making the drinking water safe enough that future chemical contamination would be very unlikely—defined as "the probability that you will be the next President of Korea." The next problem was in determining whom to ask. Obviously, they could not ask all ten million residents of Seoul, so they decided to sample. In selecting a sample it is important that it be random.[4] To randomize their sample of approximately 300 households, they scattered their sample geographically over the city. They then had to decide whom to question within the household.

The researchers constructed a questionnaire to use in interviews (Table 10.1). The questionnaire was designed to give background information on the problem, describe the "good" in question, elicit willingness to pay, and collect background information on the respondent, such as age, income, and number of people in the household. Asking about the willingness to pay for reducing the risk in the water supply is never easy. The researchers chose to use what is called a "payment card," which is a card with a number of figures, spanning the range of responses that might be expected. Each card has payment amounts along with several reference expenditure amounts. Thus a different card is used for individuals with different incomes. Figure 10.1 shows a card used in the Seoul study.

Finalizing the questionnaire to use was a multistep process. After developing a first draft with the advice of survey experts, the researchers pretested it on two individuals. Then they tested the questionnaire further by setting up "focus groups," groups of citizens who were asked to take the survey and then discuss it. After each step, the questionnaire was revised and refined. Finally, the survey was ready to be administered; they used a professional survey firm to contact the several hundred individuals in their sample.

The next step is to analyze the data, developing a willingness-to-pay (WTP) function:

$$WTP(q_0, q_1) = f(P, q_0, q_1, Q, Y, T) \qquad (10.1)$$

TABLE 10.1 Excerpts from Seoul Questionnaire[a]

Section A — Introduction

Interviewer: Introduce yourself and explain the purpose of the survey. Indicate that the interview should take less than a half hour.

Section B — Background Attitudes and Information [6 questions]

1. What is your opinion about current tap water quality in Seoul?
   (a) very good; (b) good; (c) average; (d) bad; (e) very bad.
2. In the last five years, have you or your household taken any of the following actions to improve your drinking water?
   (a) installed water filter; (b) purchased bottled water; (c) boiled tap water regularly; (d) gone to a spring to obtain spring water.
3. What is the monthly combined income of your household after taxes, last year? [If refuses to answer, show card with ranges of income and ask to identify range of income]

Section C — Value of Water Quality Improvement

Interviewer: Two minute verbal description of major pollution accident in 1991 that contaminated the drinking water of Seoul. Because the consequences were not known immediately, many people drank contaminated water. [Visual props are used to describe the accident and its consequences.]

1. If the government takes no action, how many times do you think you might experience an accident similar to the NakDong phenol accident in the next five years?

Interviewer: Give one minute verbal description of continuous monitoring system that would prevent introduction of pollutants into the city water supply. Indicate that with the system, the chance of drinking polluted water will be similar to the chance "that you will be a president of Korea." Chart is presented showing how taxes are currently apportioned among various uses (such as education, roads, sanitary services, and defense). Payment card for household's income is presented.

2. What is the most your household would pay in increased monthly taxes to reach the goal attainable with the new monitoring system?
   [If response is zero, unusually high, or no response (refusal to answer), ask a follow-up question. If response is zero, ask reason for zero response. If refuses to answer, repeat question and try to get a response. If payment response is unusually high (higher than education expenditures), give respondent opportunity to revise his or her response.]

Section D — Background Information [7 questions]

1. What is your age?
2. What is the last grade of regular school that you and your spouse completed?
3. How many people live in your household? How many are under age 13?
4. What is your average monthly water and sewer bill?

---

[a]*Questionnaire follows an exact script that is paraphrased here.*
Source: Seung-Jun Kwak, personal communication, November 1997.

where q_0 is the initial risk in the water supply and q_1 is the risk after the water supply has been made "safe." P represents the prices of market goods, Q the quantity of other environmental goods, Y income, and T assorted characteristics of the individual, including tastes. In their analysis of their data, they asked respondents what they thought their current water quality was (see Table 10.1); the response was recorded as q_0. Variables representing individual characteristics included age, education level, number of children, and years resident in Seoul.

FIGURE 10.1 Payment card from Seoul water-quality study.

The average household's willingness to pay for cleaner water was 2560 Won ($3.28) per month, compared to the average water bill of 5000 Won per month. The researchers multiply the willingness to pay for the average household by the number of households to obtain an annual willingness to pay for Seoul of 83 billion Won ($106 million). The next logical step after constructing an individual willingness-to-pay equation is to use it to construct an aggregate, population-wide measure of willingness to pay.[5]

B. Designing a Contingent Valuation Study

The Seoul water quality contingent valuation example above serves as a good introduction to the steps that should be taken in conducting a high-quality stated preference study. Some of what is now considered "best practice" has evolved over the years through research and experience.[6] However, in 1992, the U.S. Government decided that CV had become so important (and controversial) to its management of environmental resources that a high-level review was needed of the validity of the CV method. The U.S. National Oceanic and Atmospheric Administration (NOAA), the agency charged with writing regulations under the 1990 Oil Pollution Act, convened a panel of six distinguished economists and survey researchers, including two Nobel laureates, to evaluate the CV method. The NOAA panel concluded that CV could be useful, but certain practices would seem to be necessary to generate reliable estimates of willingness to pay.[7] These recommendations had a significant influence on what is considered "best practice" in conducting a CV survey. We discuss these findings below.

The issue is how to construct a "best practice" CV study to value some environmental good. Perhaps you want to find the willingness to pay for some nonmarginal change in the good, such as avoiding the extinction of a species. Perhaps you want to generate a demand curve/marginal willingness-to-pay function for some continuously varying commodity such as the peak daily ozone concentration in a community. To accomplish this, you must design, administer, and interpret a survey. A survey will typically consist of three parts: background information on the study and the environmental good, a section eliciting value, and a section asking background information on the respondent.

Carson (1991) describes six main components to a successful CV study:

- Define market scenario.
- Choose elicitation method.
- Design market administration.
- Design sampling.
- Design of experiment.
- Estimate willingness-to-pay function.

We will consider each of these in turn below.

1. Define Market Scenario. The market scenario is the information to be conveyed to a respondent (i.e., one of the people who will be asked about willingness to pay), to place the respondent in the right frame of mind to give meaningful responses to questions.

One of the first decisions to make is how to define the good to be valued. If a beach has been harmed by an oil spill, what environmental good should be valued? A day at the beach? The view of the beach? A degraded beach? Water pollution? Describing the good to be valued is only the beginning. It is also important to describe the context within which the good is supplied. If it is a day at the beach, how would payment be made? An admission fee? A parking fee?

It is important that the description of the market be realistic to the respondent and at the same time true to the eventual economic model that will use the data collected. If the market scenario is not understandable and plausible to the respondent, the data will be of questionable usefulness. Plausibility is important. For instance, if you ask respondents how much they would be willing to pay to make nuclear power completely safe, they may not believe that the goal is possible. If respondents do not understand the scenario or think it implausible, they may substitute an alternative scenario or simply not take the valuation exercise seriously.

An additional issue that needs attention in constructing the market scenario is the payment mechanism. Simply asking the willingness to pay to avoid some event, such as a fouled beach, is too abstract. The market scenario must be rooted in real-world experience, including the payment vehicle. Thus if the good is avoiding an oil spill at a beach, then a believable payment vehicle might be a tax on gasoline to hire additional inspectors for oil tankers. Of course it is also important to avoid a scenario that grates on the respondent's notion of right and wrong. Some people may feel it is the responsibility of the oil companies to pay for inspectors and may bridle at being asked to pay a tax for the service. In this case, it might be more appropriate to ask if they would be willing to require inspectors on oil tankers even if it meant raising the price of gasoline. The point is, considerable care must be taken in defining the good and the payment mechanism.[8]

Another issue, which is not easy to address, is providing the right context for the survey. For instance, suppose we are attempting to value cleaner groundwater (water in underground acquifers). Most people know very little about groundwater—what it is used for, how serious contamination is, what risks are associated with contaminated groundwater. To obtain informed responses to questions on this topic, some information will probably need to be provided to respondents. Obviously, time and other constraints allow very little education of respondents in the course of administering a survey. This raises the question of bias introduced by incompletely or inaccurately "educating" the respondent.

The NOAA Panel makes several recommendations regarding the market scenario. One point they make is that respondents should be reminded that substitutes exist. For instance, in ascertaining the value of a beach contaminated by an oil spill, the respondents should be reminded that there are many uncontaminated beaches a short distance away (if that is the case). The Panel suggests that the survey should be designed to avoid generating spurious emotions, such as a dislike of "big business." The Panel also urges that there be checks within the questionnaire to be sure that the respondent understands and accepts the information in the survey.

2. Choosing Elicitation Method. Having properly defined the market scenario, the next step is to decide how best to obtain the valuation response. This is obviously a very important part of the survey, and one of the most difficult to administer effectively. There are four primary ways of eliciting value: direct question, bidding game, payment card, and referendum choice.

The direct question is probably the most obvious. After the good has been described, respondents are simply asked their willingness to pay for the good. As Carson (1991) points out, one problem with this is that this direct valuation of a good is unfamiliar to most people. There are few real markets in which we are asked to generate our reservation price (highest price we would be willing to pay). People may not spend much effort in determining their willingness to pay, which may result in extreme responses (zeros and very large numbers).

The bidding game approach, used in the first "modern" CV study of an environmental good (Randall et al., 1974), starts with a WTP number and seeks a yes–no response. If the respondent replies yes, the amount is gradually increased until a "no" is received. Similarly, if the respondent replies "no," the amount is gradually decreased until a "yes" is received. The primary problem with a bidding game is what is known as *starting point bias*. If the good is unfamiliar to the respondent, the cues given by the surveyor may influence the response. If the surveyor asks about willingness to pay for groundwater cleanup and starts the bidding at $500 per year, the results will probably be different than if the bidding were started at $1 per year.

A third method, the payment card, was described in the context of the example of water quality in Seoul, presented in the last section. One problem with payment cards is that they cannot be used for telephone surveys. There may also be cues built into the range of values that are included in the card.

A fourth method is what is called referendum or discrete choice. Essentially a willingness-to-pay figure is offered to the respondent who is asked if he or she would be willing to pay that amount, "yes" or "no." Different respondents are offered different WTP figures, chosen to span the plausible range of willingnesses to pay. This approach is recommended by the NOAA Panel, because they thought it minimizes possible bias and is also familiar, in that people often vote yes/no on public referenda. One problem with referenda is that more data are needed to obtain statistically significant results, and this raises the cost of the survey.

3. Design Market Administration. Having designed the survey, it must be administered, i.e., respondents must complete the survey and their responses collated. There are four basic approaches to survey administration: mail, Internet telephone, and in-person.

Mail surveys are the cheapest to administer, although they have problems. One problem is nonresponse. A mail survey is considered a success if only 30% of the surveys are not returned. But if there is some systematic reason for nonresponse, the results of the survey may be called into question. For instance, suppose people who feel less strongly about the environmental good tend not to respond. Another problem with mail surveys is that the respondent needs to understand the survey instrument. Therefore the survey must be relatively simple. Furthermore, there is no way to keep respondents from looking through the entire survey, which makes the control of the flow of the information in the survey difficult.

A variation on a mail survey is an Internet survey.[9] The Internet survey can be simply a mechanical way of administering a survey or can be an entirely new way of conducting a survey. One example is the Internet panel survey in which a group of survey respondents is recruited to be available to answer online surveys. Clearly, as the Internet becomes more and more ubiquitous, online surveys will become more and more important.

Telephone surveys are also relatively inexpensive to administer. However, telephones must be widely available within the population being surveyed. A telephone survey in Cairo (Egypt) would be most inappropriate because of the low penetration of telephones in the population. There may also be bias in terms of who answers the telephone. For instance, unemployed people may be more likely to be available. Another problem with telephone surveys is that visual cues cannot be used (e.g., photographs). This may lead to problems in eliciting values regarding changes in environmental quality, since photos are often used to convey the nature of the changed quality. In recent years, the rise of junk telephone solicitations have made it more difficult to reach potential subjects with the telephone. Many telephone subscribers will no longer engage with unfamiliar callers.

In-person surveys are the most expensive to administer but can be the most reliable. In fact, the NOAA Panel recommends in-person surveys whenever possible. One problem (other than costs) with an in-person survey is interviewer bias. It is difficult for an interviewer to always appear neutral when conducting an interview. Furthermore, since environmental goods are often perceived as desirable and socially "correct," respondents may be reluctant to reveal their unwillingness to pay if in fact they do not view the environment as very important (in the words of the NOAA panel, "social desirability bias"). Finally, if multiple interviewers are used, it is difficult to ensure that the results obtained by different interviewers are totally comparable.

Another issue in market administration is pretesting of the survey. The NOAA Panel emphasizes the importance of exhaustive pretesting of the survey instrument before the actual survey is conducted. This would include very careful analysis of the wording of each question and the organization of the survey. The survey can then be administered to test groups and adjusted based on feedback. The survey can also be administered to "focus groups" as was done in the case of the Seoul water quality survey. The NOAA Panel also urges that tests be done of interviewer and other biases.

4. Sample Design. There are two issues in choosing the people to answer the CV questionnaire. The first is to choose the group from which to draw the sample, and the second is to draw the random sample. The first issue is to determine the population of concern with regard to valuing the commodity in question. If we are dealing with visibility in

Switzerland, should we target residents or visitors? If residents, what geographical area is of interest? Another issue is whether to examine individuals or households. Should children be included? How will these people/households be identified? By voting records or geographically as in the example of Seoul water quality? The answers to these questions define the *sampling frame,* the precisely defined population from which the sample is drawn. The appropriate sample is then drawn and the survey administered.

5. Experimental Design. The typical goal of a CV survey is to develop statistically significant estimates of willingness to pay for a particular environmental good or to test a hypothesis about the willingness to pay for the hypothetical good. Considering the cost of data collection, it is important to construct a survey carefully so that the appropriate information is collected in an efficient manner without unintentional biases. This is the process of experimental design. For example, in many referendum format CV surveys, each respondent is asked to vote yes or no on a different possible value for the environmental good. How those values are selected for presentation to the respondent is important for the ultimate usefulness of survey results. For instance, if the value is generated by the interviewer on the basis of the respondent's income, a bias may unintentionally be introduced into the data being collected. On the other hand, if the values are simply randomly chosen from a very wide range of possible values, it may be necessary to administer a very large number of surveys to obtain statistically significant results. The point is that design of the CV instrument, its administration, and its ultimate statistical analysis are very important steps that should not be taken lightly. This is what is known as experimental design.

6. Estimation of WTP Function. The last step is to take the survey results and correctly estimate the WTP function. This is obviously an important step and must be kept in mind as the survey instrument is developed. Sometimes this step is neglected until after the survey has been conducted, only to find that some vital piece of information is needed but was not collected on the survey. This outcome would suggest a flawed experimental design.

C. Problems with Contingent Valuation

Contingent valuation is highly controversial. The problem is complicated by possible conflicts of interest within the economics community. As mentioned earlier, CV has found significant application in the United States in assessing damage from environmental accidents, such as oil spills. CV has been used to generate very high estimates of damage to natural resources, primarily by estimating nonuse values. Many firms, including oil companies, would gain from discrediting the approach. A good deal of the research identifying flaws in CV has been funded by the Exxon Corporation.[10] A conflict of interest, of course, does not mean that the "anti-CV" work is distorted, just that there is an appearance of that possibility existing.[11] On the other side of the issue, academic careers have been built on the validity of CV.

There are many problems that have been identified with CV. A primary criticism is that the values elicited in CV surveys are not based on real resource decisions—they are hypothetical. How many of us have gone to a store thinking we would buy a new product, only to have second thoughts when faced with the prospect of relinquishing real money in exchange for the product? Many argue that without real resources at stake, the response to a WTP question is meaningless. Another way of looking at this is that there is no budget constraint in a hypothetical survey and without a budget constraint, choices are meaningless. The counter to that position is that there may be more scatter (variance) in the response to a hypothetical question than if real resources were at stake, but the average response will be unaffected by the hypothetical nature of the exercise.

Another issue that has been raised concerns ambiguity in what people are valuing. When you are asked how much you would be willing to pay to avoid the extinction of the lemurs in Madagascar, does the amount you are offering truly reflect your concern for the lemurs or are you simply "purchasing moral satisfaction" by responding that you would contribute substantially to their defense.[12] You get a "warm-glow" by saying that you would be willing to pay to provide an environmental good. (The idea that public goods give a "warm glow" to the provider of the good is attributable to Andreoni, 1990). Seip and Strand (1992) conducted a CV study in Norway, asking respondents if they would be willing to contribute 200 Norwegian Kroner to the leading Norwegian environmental organization (NNV) to protect Norwegian environmental resources. Of their sample 63% answered yes to that question. These people were then targeted by the NNV with a mail solicitation, asking for a contribution, with no reference to the survey. Fewer than 10% contributed, suggesting that the CV results were unreliable.

Another problem with CV has been called embedding. A typical problem for a CV survey is to determine the value of a specific natural resource, such as a particular park.

The Value of Protecting an Urban Park in India

Most CV studies are performed in the developed world, in market economies.[13] There are unique issues to consider in applying the CV method to the developing world, as illustrated in a study (Hadker et al., 1997) of the value of a nearby national park to residents of Mumbai, India (a very large urban area in India). The 100 km² Borivli National Park (BNP) is located within the Mumbai metropolitan area, providing recreation to the residents of Mumbai as well as serving as a watershed for drinking water for the city and home for a number of endangered species. Thus the BNP is important for many residents of Mumbai, though it is a multifaceted environmental good (which complicates the problem of defining the good being valued).

The authors carefully constructed a CV questionnaire which they administered to over 500 individuals randomly distributed over the city. Thus the questionnaire was not simply administered to park visitors (as is often the case) but to the entire population of the city (though how the sample was generated is unclear). A number of innovative elements were included in the survey, including dealing with the problem of subsistence or unemployed respondents (a particularly acute issue in the developing world). Individuals were given the opportunity to contribute time rather than money to protect the BNP.

Although many details are omitted from the published account of the study, the end result is a determination that the mean individual WTP to protect the BNP was Rs 7.50 per month (approximately US$0.15). Extrapolated to the entire population of Mumbai, this results in an annual WTP of Rs 248 million (approximately US$5 million per year).

However, there are usually substitute parks outside of the domain of the survey and there appear to be inconsistencies in how people value individual parks versus groups of parks. People may place the same value on cleaning up one lake as on cleaning up 10 lakes.

A related issue concerns existence value. Recall that existence value is value over and above use value. People may value the preservation of a wild Amazon river, even if they have no intention of visiting the river. There is some question about whether this type of value is valid, since existence value is never connected to a real payment. For instance, Desvousges et al. (1993) conducted a CV study of a contaminated lake in which a number of migratory water birds were killed. The birds were not endangered; thus the existence of the species was not in question, only a number of individual birds. The lake was hypothetical and thus not used by any of the respondents. The question was how much people would be willing to pay to eliminate the contaminated lake and thus save the birds. The willingness to pay was the same whether the number of birds at risk was 2000, 20,000, or 200,000, suggesting an embedding problem and possibly a fundamental problem with the idea of existence value.[14]

II. EXPERIMENTAL MARKETS

Probably the single greatest criticism of contingent valuation is the hypothetical nature of the exercise—no money is at stake when people articulate their willingness to pay. One solution to this is to construct a market where none existed before. There are two ways of doing this—field experiments and laboratory experiments. (List, 2007, provides a nice review of the use of experimental techniques in environmental economics.)

A field experiment involves actually making a market in the "real world" where one has not previously existed. Typically, this is possible only where there is a governmental restriction or market imperfection that precludes market operation. An example would be markets in which goods are allocated with a lottery or on a first-come, first-served basis. An experimenter can obtain permission to substitute a market for such an allocation, and construct the experimental market in such a way as to learn about consumer behavior.

A laboratory experiment is much like the experiments psychologists have been conducting for decades. A group of volunteers is assembled (typically students), given real money to participate, and then faced with real decisions that involve giving up real money or receiving real money in exchange for the goods or bads the experimenter may present.

One characteristic of experiments is that their purpose is usually not to derive a value of a particular good for the general population but to test a theory in a controlled setting. This is in contrast to most other valuation methods in which the goal is to generate a marginal willingness-to-pay function that can be used for policy analysis or some other practical use. Experiments by their very nature apply in a very limited context. But because they are experiments, the conditions of the experiment are controllable by the experimenter. A major issue in valuation is the possible disparity between willingness to accept compensation (WTA) to give up a good vs. willingness to pay (WTP) to acquire a good. As discussed in Chapter 7, theory suggests that there should be little difference between these two measures,[15] yet there is considerable evidence that they are not the same.[16] This issue is perfect for exploration using experiments because it is possible to control for extraneous factors that may drive a wedge between WTA and WTP.

A. Laboratory Experiments

Laboratory experiments involve groups of subjects (typically university students) who are paid a fixed amount to participate in an experiment for perhaps a few hours. These experiments involve the participants exchanging real money for experimental commodities. Payment is set up so that two criteria are met: (1) participants make real decisions regarding real resources and (2) the participants leave the experiment richer than when they began. The second requirement induces people to voluntarily participate.

One of the major uses of experimental economics in the environmental arena is to explore the divergence between WTP and WTA as well as the validity of contingent valuation. Both of these issues were addressed in the goose hunting study discussed in the boxed example in the next section. There are two laboratory experiments that address these issues that are interesting and worth examining. One concerns the demand for consuming a foul-tasting liquid, important because of its connection to pollution. The other study concerns the existence value of an individual tree—also an issue of significant import in environmental economics.

1. Sucrose Octa-Acetate. In constructing an experiment in the demand for bads (as opposed to goods), the problem of not causing harm to an experimental subject is a significant constraint. It is most likely unethical, and in any event goes against most guidelines for experimenting on humans, to intentionally expose people to harm to determine their willingness to pay to avoid the harm. Psychologists have used a bitter and unpleasant tasting liquid, sucrose octa-acetate (SOA), for such purposes. SOA appears to be the only known laboratory substance that is very unpleasant and yet nontoxic. In an interesting use of SOA, Coursey et al. (1987) set out to answer several questions: How do hypothetical willingnesses to pay to avoid tasting SOA compare to "true" willingnesses to pay? And the same can be asked about willingnesses to accept payment to taste SOA. The second type of question is, how do WTA and WTP compare in an experimental market setting?

To answer these questions, they constructed two basic experiments, each consisting of several parts. One experiment concerned willingness to pay to avoid tasting SOA; the other experiment concerned willingness to accept payment to taste SOA. Each experiment involved eight economics students. Each experiment started by asking hypothetical valuation questions and by having subjects taste a few drops of SOA. Let us focus on the real experiments.

In the WTP experiment, each student was first asked about hypothetical values; after that the students participated in a series of auctions. Each student was asked to submit a bid as to how much he or she would pay to avoid tasting one ounce (approximately 30 ml) of SOA (tasting is defined as holding a one ounce cup of SOA in your mouth for 20 seconds). Bids were collected and ranked from highest to lowest. The fifth highest bid was announced to be the going price to avoid tasting SOA. The four individuals who bid highest would pay the going price (real money) to avoid the tasting; the other four individuals would have to taste the SOA. This procedure was repeated a number of times. The first four times it was done, no tasting occurred; these were considered practice runs. From that point on, however, real tasting did occur. The students were paid $10 to participate in each WTP auction. A similar procedure was adopted for WTA.

Two interesting things happened in these experiments. One result is that WTA starts very high when students have little experience with the SOA. After repeated trials, the WTA bids drop considerably. In contrast, WTP bids are much more stable, changing only slightly as auction trials are repeated. This suggests that WTP is a better measure of value than WTA, particularly when the goods are unfamiliar.

A second result concerns the validity of hypothetical values, in comparison to the "real" values that emerge from the experimental auctions. Hypothetical measures of WTA appear to be biased upward, whereas WTP measures are more consistent with experimental values.

2. Norfolk Pines. Another experiment that seeks to explain the divergence between WTA and WTP was done by Boyce et al. (1992). They explore the extent to which existence value may drive a wedge between the two measures. In particular, they suggest that if one "owns" an environmental good, ownership may be accompanied by a moral obligation of stewardship. This may not exist when the good is owned by someone else. Thus WTA will have to overcome a larger hurdle than WTP; we would expect WTA to be larger than WTP. Although this is a somewhat unusual theory that draws on unconventional arguments, the hypothesis can be tested with an experiment.

The experimenters utilized 115 staff members from the University of Colorado and conducted four basic experiments, two for WTA and two for WTP. Each person participated in only one of the four experiments and was paid $30–40 to participate. The commodity in question was a small potted plant, a Norfolk Island pine tree. These are commonly used as houseplants. In one of the four experiments, each subject was given a plant and was asked to submit a bid indicating the price at which they would sell their plant back to the experimenter (WTA). A price was then randomly generated and all offers below that price were accepted. A similar experiment was conducted in which the subjects were asked to submit a bid indicating how much they would pay to acquire such a tree (WTP). These bids are interpreted as representing the use-value of the Norfolk pines. The average WTA bid was 66% higher than the average WTP bid, a statistically significant difference.

So far, the experiment is quite standard. But the next step is to try to measure the existence value of the plant, over and above the use value. The experimenters do this by slightly modifying the experiment. They convince the subjects that if the plant remains with the experimenter (if the subject fails to purchase it or ends up selling it), the experimenter will kill the tree. The experimenters found that the death threat raised both WTP and WTA. WTP increased by 60% and WTA increased by 130%, and both of these increases are statistically significant. This suggests that the existence of the tree had value for the subjects, though that value may be a reflection of "duty" or moral obligation, which might not be the case in a more disconnected context. Furthermore, the fact that WTA was affected more significantly by the threat of tree death tends to reinforce the arguments about the importance of moral obligation, that it is higher when the subject has ownership of the tree.

This experiment does suggest the importance of existence value. But perhaps a more important contribution of the paper is to indicate the importance of experimental markets in exploring questions of valuation and even economic theory in the case of environmental goods where markets rarely exist.

B. Field Experiments

One criticism of laboratory experiments, particularly those involving students, is that the setting is too contrived. A major concern is that students (particularly economics students) are not good representatives of the general population. To address this issue, some experimenters have moved out of the classroom, into the "real" world. When this happens, the experiment becomes a "field" experiment.

Goose Hunting in Wisconsin

One of the classic papers in valuation involving constructing an artificial market as a field experiment was done in the context of goose hunting in Wisconsin.[17] The good in question was access to a 10,000-hectare region in Wisconsin for the purpose of hunting geese. The good is not really a goose (for eating or stuffing), but rather the experience of getting out in the "wilderness" for a few days to hike around, possibly shooting a goose. Although many readers will perceive an incongruity between a wilderness experience and hunting, the fact is that many people enjoy hunting for the outdoors experience.

The interesting thing about this particular setting is that hunting permits are required to use the area and those hunting permits are in short supply. However, rather than use a market to issue them, the state of Wisconsin uses a lottery. The researchers conducted three analyses of the willingness to pay for goose hunting in this area: travel cost, contingent valuation, and experimental markets. The CV experiment involved asking a sample of holders of the permit how much they would be willing to accept as compensation in exchange for their permit. A similar sample was drawn prior to the lottery to ascertain willingness to pay for a permit. Thus estimates of willingness to pay and willingness to accept compensation were computed. The most interesting part of the experiment was that the researchers also drew a sample of 237 permit holders and sent them checks for random amounts between $1 and $200 asking recipients to do one of two things: (1) cash the check and return their permit or (2) return the check and keep the permit. Only one person chose a third route (cash the check and keep the permit).

The researchers found that the CV results were subject to a great deal of variability. Depending on the elicitation method, the mean response for willingness to accept compensation from the CV survey ranged from $67 to $101. In contrast, the mean response for the willingness to pay was $11 to $21, depending on how the question was posed. The mean of the field experimental market was $63. A travel cost estimate of the value of a permit was $32. The significance of the experimental market result is that real money was involved in the decisions made by the respondents. Although the market was artificial, it was not hypothetical.

Field experiments come in a variety of shapes and sizes. In fact, Harrison and List (2004) classify field experiments as falling into three different categories:

- *Artefactual field experiments*—laboratory experiments using "real" people instead of university students;
- *Framed field experiments*—experiments using the general population as experimental subjects and a nonlaboratory setting, though still clearly experimental; and
- *Natural field experiments*—same as a framed field experiments except that the subjects naturally undertake the experimental activities and in fact do not even realize they are in an experiment.

Artefactual field experiments are probably the easiest to execute and involve the smallest change from a laboratory experiment. Rather than recruiting university students as subjects, subjects are drawn from other sources, such as community clubs or primary schools. In other respects, the experiments are the same.

Framed field experiments are the most common type of field experiment. The goose hunting experiment described in the box is an example of just such an experiment. A specific kind of framed field experiment is the social experiment, in which a government agency (typically) funds an experiment involving different policies applied differentially to different segments of the population. An example would be the RAND Health Insurance Experiment in which different health insurance schemes were tested on different parts of the population.[18] Such experiments are very costly but can yield invaluable information.

Natural field experiments are the most desirable, of course, but also rely on a serendipity of circumstances that will not usually exist.

III. REFERENDA

One type of constructed market is very official and not at all experimental—a voter referendum on the provision of some public good, often accompanied by a tax levy to pay for it. If we knew how individuals voted on such referenda, and the characteristics of the voters, we would be able statistically to estimate the demand for the particular public good. Unfortunately, balloting is usually secret. The best we can do is observe how groupings of voters vote, and utilize the characteristics of the grouping to explain the vote.

One of the earliest analyses of voting on environmental referenda is by Robert Deacon and Perry Shapiro (1975). They analyze two state-wide referenda in California, both related to the provision of a public good. One referendum concerned safeguarding the coastal area of the state from excessive development, providing an uncluttered coast as a public amenity. The authors examine a cross section of 334 California cities, comparing the percentage of the population voting in favor of the proposition with the characteristics of the city—income, education, political preference, and other variables. Although income did not turn out to be significant, other factors such as education, political orientation, and the fraction of the population in unskilled labor did turn out to be significant. Unfortunately, the data are not available to construct a demand curve for coastal protection, because information on the price is unavailable. Nevertheless, this approach gives important understanding of the demand for environmental goods.

The Deacon and Shapiro study was updated and expanded by Kahn and Matsusaka (1997). These authors also examine voting in California on environmentally oriented referenda, except that they are able to analyze 14 different such referenda. Furthermore, they use county-level voting data rather than city data. As with the Deacon and Shapiro analysis, they do not estimate a demand curve, since no prices are available for the environmental goods. They are able to measure how income affects demand and they reach some interesting conclusions. They find that most environmental goods are normal goods, meaning that demand increases as income increases. But some publicly provided environmental goods turn out to be inferior goods at higher income. It would seem that some goods, such as urban parks, are privately provided by high income people, which reduces their demand for public provision. The underlying goods of course may still be normal, even though when publicly provided they are inferior.

In summary, referenda can provide real insights on preferences for public good, though the approach is still not developed well enough to be able to generate demand curves for typical environmental goods.

SUMMARY

1. Stated preference methods of valuation are often termed contingent valuation. Contingent valuation is a method of valuing environmental goods that uses a survey of the population, with the survey directly asking willingess to pay for the environmental good. Thus the approach involves a hypothetical market with no real resource commitments behind the response.

2. Some consensus has developed regarding how to carefully conduct a contingent valuation study. The process of making a study more convincing and reliable almost always involves greater data collection expense.

3. The six basic steps in conducting a contingent valuation estimate of demand for an environmental good are define market scenario, choose elicitation method, design market administration, design sampling, design experiment, and estimate willingness-to-pay function.

4. The primary strength of contingent valuation is its applicability to virtually any good or bad. Criticism is usually based on either the lack of real resources being at stake or empirical evidence from existing studies showing logically inconsistent responses.

5. Experimental markets are another kind of constructed market. An experimental market involves defining a real market where none existed before. By real market we mean a situation in which real resources must be commited in association with decisions regarding the environmental good.

6. Experimental markets can involve artificial markets whereby a market is constructed in the population at large (field experiments) or they can involve laboratory markets in which a group of subjects is encouraged (usually by monetary payment) to participate, trading money for goods presented by the experimenter (laboratory experiments).

7. Field experiments can be further subdivided into artefactual field experiments (laboratory experiments with "real" people), framed field experiments (field experiments that are clearly artificial experiments), and natural field experiments in which the subjects do not even know they are the subject of an experiment.

8. Referendum statements of value involve official votes on proposals to provide an environmental good, usually financed by tax payments. Such methods can be reliable but are not common.

PROBLEMS

1. Consider being confronted with two possible scenarios while participating in a laboratory experiment:

   a. Someone offers to sell you a coffee mug. You have a reservation price for the mug (it is a nice one), and you bargain with the seller until you agree on a price that is less than or equal to your reservation price.

   b. Someone gives you a coffee mug, then begins to bargain with you to buy it back. You have a reservation selling price and you agree on a price greater than or equal to that reservation price.

   Is your reservation price in part (a) the same as your reservation selling price in (b)? Why or why not? Should such considerations matter in the design of experiments to elicit the value of public goods?

2. A truck carrying insecticide has crashed, spilling hazardous chemicals into a creek, killing fish. Eventually the creek recovers with no permanent damage. You are charged with assessing the environmental damage. Identify one commodity that has been harmed and describe a CV study to assess the willingness to pay to avoid the damage.

3. In the Exxon Valdez legal case, several contingent valuation studies were part of estimates of liability damages owed by the oil company, Exxon. Damages were argued to include the value for all U.S. residents of an unpolluted Prince William Sound (where the spill occurred), bringing the issue of nonuse value to the front of the debate. Describe why a resident of the United States far from Alaska might associate real value (be willing to devote real resources) to a place he or she will never see or experience, such as coastal Alaska or the Amazon basin.

4. In conducting telephone surveys, some households always refuse to participate, saying they "don't have time" or "can't be bothered." If researchers accept these inevitable nonresponses and base their study on the other households, those who patiently answer each question, what biases are likely to be built into the sample? Can you think of a way to deal with this type of problem, either practical or statistical?

NOTES

1. To my knowledge, the only possible revealed preference method of inferring the existence value of a commodity is by observing voluntary provision of public goods. This approach has not been widely utilized, however. Champ et al. (1997) is one of the few papers on this subject.
2. Refer to Bohm (1972), Randall et al. (1974), and Hammack and Brown (1974).
3. Carson (2010) provides a survey of some 7,500 studies from 130 countries.
4. The sample can be intentionally constructed to emphasize certain segments of the population, as long as the manner in which the sample deviates from random is known. Kwak and Russell (1994) use such a "stratified random sample."
5. Unfortunately, some of the explanatory variables are derived from the survey and unknown for the wider population (such as the subjective assessment of current water quality). This makes aggregation more difficult.

6. Carson and Hanemann (2005) provide a thorough treatment of the state of the art of Contingent Valuation. See also Boyle (2003), Carson (1991), and Mitchell and Carson (1989).

7. The conclusions of the NOAA Panel were reported in January 1993 in the *Federal Register,* a U.S. Government publication of official notices and regulations (National Oceanic and Atmospheric Administration, 1993).

8. The NOAA Panel recommends that willingness to pay be measured, rather than willingness to accept compensation. In the example just given, it would be preferable to ask what people would be willing to pay to avoid an oil spill rather than what they would be willing to accept from an oil company for the right to spill oil. The laboratory experiments described later in this chapter provide support for focusing on willingness to pay.

9. Refer to Champ et al. (2003) and Dillman et al. (2009) for further discussion of Internet surveys.

10. Much of this work is reported in Hausman (1993) and was done in support of Exxon in the Exxon Valdez oil spill litigation. Despite the source of the funding, the economists conducting the research are very well respected and the work is of generally high quality (though many have found fault with aspects of the work).

11. A very interesting set of papers on CV appeared in the Fall 1994 *Journal of Economic Perspectives.* In that issue, Paul Portney, a member of the NOAA Panel set the stage for two papers representing two sides of the CV issue (Portney, 1994). Michael Hanemann from the University of California presented a defense of CV (Hanemann, 1994) whereas Peter Diamond and Jerry Hausman from MIT presented a negative critique of CV (Diamond and Hausman, 1994). Not coincidentally, Hanemann (among others) was employed by the state of Alaska to conduct CV surveys in support of its claim of damage in the Exxon Valdez oil spill. Hausman was employed by the Exxon Corporation in support of its defense in that case, part of which rested on discrediting the CV work done by the opposition.

12. This point has been made in a widely cited article by Kahneman and Knetsch (1992).

13. Developing country applications may pertain to ecotourism by developed country nationals or may apply to environmental goods consumed by developing country residents. These are two quite different types of applications. An important mixture of the two, as well as a comparison of travel cost and CV, is the study of the recreational value of Lake Nakuru National Park in Kenya (Navrud and Mungatana, 1994). A representative CV study of a "brown" environmental issue is Whittington et al. (2002), which is an investigation of the willingness to pay for improved water services in Kathmandu, Nepal.

14. One possible alternative explanation is that respondents viewed the good being valued as "a world safe for these birds" rather than the size of the bird population. Carson and Mitchell (1993) suggest other problems in the Desvousges et al. (1993) study.

15. The main theoretical reason why WTP and WTA should differ is if the good is substantial relative to income. Thus there will be income effects depending on whether one is giving up the good or gaining the good. If the value of the good is small relative to income, these differences disappear. Hanemann (1991) and Kolstad and Guzman (1999) explore additional theoretical reasons for a divergence between WTP and WTA, even when there is no income effect.

16. Horowitz and McConnell (2002) review 30 years of studies of the difference between WTA and WTP and conclude that the more unfamiliar or nonordinary a good is, the greater the disparity between the two measures. Cummings et al. (1986), in an earlier review of the same issue, find a large disparity between the two measures.

17. Bishop et al. (1983).

18. The RAND experiment is described in Newhouse (1993). Refer to Ferber and Hirsch (1979) and Hausmann and Wise (1985) for reviews of social experiments.

BASIC ENVIRONMENTAL REGULATION

IN PREVIOUS CHAPTERS, WE DISCUSSED THE VIRTUES OF MARKETS FOR ALLOCATING GOODS and services but also the problems markets have in allocating environmental goods, particularly pollution.

In this chapter we introduce the government as an active player in solving the problems associated with pollution. In some cases, the government will play a modest role, simply laying down the ground rules for a quasimarket to operate to solve the pollution problem. In other cases, the government will play a much more visible role, directing specific polluters as to what emissions are allowed. Although governments can solve problems that decentralized markets cannot, governments can also fail. Government failure is not a focus here, but we should be aware that government intervention to cure market failure is not always successful.[1] Some ways of intervening to solve pollution problems are better than others.

I. RATIONALE FOR REGULATION

The theory of economic regulation goes far beyond the issues of concern in environmental regulation. In fact, environmental regulation is a special, and relatively recent, example of economic regulation. For that reason, it is appropriate to place it in a larger context.

Economic regulation involves the government intervening, in a variety of ways, in the private actions of firms and individuals. There are two basic theories of regulation, the public interest theory and the interest group theory.[2] The public interest theory of regulation views the purpose of regulation as the promotion of the public interest. In this context there are three general reasons why regulation might exist: imperfect competition, imperfect information, and externalities. The interest group theory of regulation views the purpose of regulation as promoting the narrow interests of particular groups in society, such as individual industries.[3] We consider these in turn.

To a certain extent, the public interest theory of regulation is a normative theory. Recall that normative theory seeks to explain what should happen in an ideal world. In contrast, the interest group theory is a positive theory, attempting to explain why the world works as it does.

Imperfect competition, particularly natural monopoly, is the traditional normative justification for government regulation.[4] In the case of natural monopoly (such as an electricity distribution company), economic efficiency calls for a single firm. It is not a good idea to have multiple sets of poles and wires traveling down streets, connecting residences to sources of power.[5] The role of government is to guarantee a monopoly to a particular firm (restrict the entry of new firms) and, in addition, to control prices in order to protect consumers from monopoly pricing.

A related role of government is to prevent undue concentration of power in markets in which multiple competing firms represent the best organizational structure. In this case, the government attempts to prevent collusion and restricts mergers that will create excessive market power. The array of U.S. antitrust laws, starting with the Sherman Act of 1890, is designed to preserve a competitive environment in the United States, outlawing practices that are deemed anticompetitive. The European Union also has strong antitrust laws. Many countries have a more laissez-faire attitude toward anticompetitive activities, since such activities often serve to bolster domestic industries in the international marketplace.

The second major rationale for government regulation is the case of imperfect information. Acquiring information is costly. As a consequence, when consumers are about to enter into a transaction, they may not always have complete information on items such as product quality. Furthermore, because of the cost of acquiring information, it may not even be desirable for consumers to acquire complete information—the costs may far exceed the benefits. Imagine that each time we entered a grocery store we had to conduct extensive tests on the safety of each food item. This is a justification for the government to step in to compensate for incomplete information.[6] The role may be a relatively "hands-off" type of intervention such as establishing a set of liability rules to encourage the provision of safety-related quality. If problems occur in consuming a product, a firm can be held liable. Properly designed, such liability rules can induce firms to provide an efficient level of safety-related quality. Of course, government can also more directly intervene in the market, specifying acceptable levels of quality, such as is generally the case with regulations on food additives and food crop pesticides.

A third rationale for government regulation is in the area of the provision of public goods and bads. Public bads and externalities are of course our focus. As we know from earlier chapters, when there are elements of "publicness" (nonrivalry or nonexcludability), private markets are inefficient. Government intervenes to try to correct the problem. Government may step in to directly provide these goods or bads at efficient levels, effectively eliminating the private market. This is frequently the case with public goods (e.g., national defense) and rarely the case with public bads. In the case of public bads, the usual approach is for government to define a set of institutions and regulations to govern the provision of these public bads, e.g., the government establishes a set of regulations to restrict the production of pollution.

The interest group theory of regulation maintains that rent seeking is the primary rationale for regulation.[7] As will become clear, rent seeking is less a justification for regulation than an explanation of why some regulations exist—a positive theory of regulation. What is meant by rent seeking? Rent seeking involves private individuals or firms using the government to guarantee extra profits (rents) through government-mandated restrictions on economic activity. For instance, U.S. requirements that a certain fraction of clean-fuel gasoline additives be from renewable sources is fundamentally a subsidy to producers of ethanol in the midwest United States (the requirement is largely unrelated to air quality). Groups that benefit from such regulation lobby government for regulations that provide them with rents (profits) that would not exist in a competitive market.

II. A POLITICAL ECONOMY MODEL OF REGULATION

The basic problem of environmental regulation involves the government trying to induce a polluter to take socially desirable actions, which ostensibly are not in the best interest of the polluter. But the government may not always be able to precisely control the polluter. To further complicate matters, the government faces a complex problem of determining exactly what level of pollution is best for society. In reality, the government faces pressures from consumers and polluters. Although a full development of this interaction is beyond the scope of this discussion, Figure 11.1 captures some of this complexity. Shown in Figure 11.1 is a highly stylized schematic of the interactions among government, polluting firms, and consumer citizens.

The government is shown in Figure 11.1 as consisting of three branches, the legislature, the judiciary, and the regulators. Although the nomenclature may vary from country to country, this is a reasonably general representation of basic government. In the United States, the legislature would be Congress, the regulators would be the EPA,

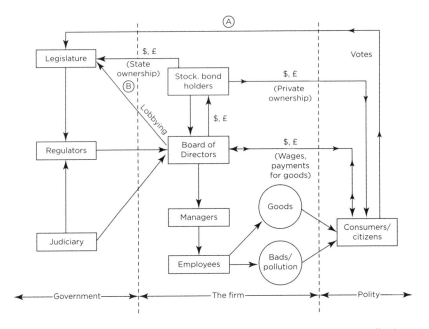

FIGURE 11.1 Schematic of interactions among government, polluting firms, and consumer citizens.

and the judiciary would be the Federal courts. In the United Kingdom, Parliament would be the legislature. The regulator would be the Department for Environment, Food and Rural Affairs (DEFRA), although other branches of national and local government also oversee pollution control (as in the United States). The courts, the House of Lords, and EU oversight would be the equivalent of the judiciary, though the regulatory process tends to be less litigious in the EU than in the United States. The legislature passes laws defining what the regulators are to do in controlling pollution. The regulators are charged with the detailed implementation of the legislature's laws. The regulator's actions are tempered by the judiciary. Note that the legislature may have difficulty achieving its goals since it does not directly influence the polluter but must act through another part of government. This other part of government—the regulator—may have different goals. For instance, regulators may be interested in job security or the size of the bureaucracy they control as well as in reducing pollution levels. Furthermore, the judiciary may temper the actions of the regulators.

The firm, as shown in Figure 11.1, consists of several pieces.[8] The Board of Directors is the core of the firm, although it is subject to oversight by the owners—the stock and bond holders. The Board issues directives to the managers; the managers issue directives to employees who produce the product of the firm as well as pollution. The key point is that regulators direct the Board to take certain actions, but the Board is removed, by several steps, from the employees who actually generate the pollution. Furthermore, the Board has other objectives in addition to pleasing the regulators (such as pleasing the stockholders). Generally, this is termed the principal-agent problem because of the inability of the EPA (the principal) to completely control the polluter (the agent). Note that the firm may not be a passive entity but may in fact influence legislation, through lobbying or financial incentives. These are shown as line B in Figure 11.1.

Finally, it is the consumers who consume the goods produced by the firm as well as the pollution generated by the firm. Consumers in turn are the citizenry whom the legislature is supposedly serving. Thus consumers direct votes and other influence to the legislature (line A), while at the same time sending money to the firm in exchange for the goods consumed.

There is obviously much detail missing from Figure 11.1. We could have employees or stockholders lobbying the legislature, for example, or firms lobbying the citizenry through advertising. Nevertheless, the essence of the process is represented in Figure 11.1.

There are really two important lessons that should be taken from Figure 11.1. The first is that there are many imperfect links between the legislature and the pollution-generating process. Since the legislature cannot physically control pollution directly, it must rely on indirect means to obtain its ends, and often these indirect means may be less than perfect. Regulation may be excessively costly, may result in considerable cheating, may result in excessive time delays, and may result in too much pollution.

The second point to take from Figure 11.1 is that the legislature does not necessarily act as an efficient benevolent maximizer of social well-being. Although we may think it is "best" if the legislature is influenced only by citizen welfare, as represented by line A in Figure 11.1, the legislature will likely be influenced by other interests, such as the well-being of the polluter, as reflected in line B. This is the distinction between normative theory, what *should* happen (perhaps maximizing citizen welfare with some concern for equity), and positive theory, what *will* happen (a balancing of interests, some "legitimate," some not). This distinction is important. Sometimes we are trying to design a best regulation, in which case we want to know what *should* happen. In other cases, we are trying to understand why a certain regulation is on the books, in which case we should be interested in what *will* happen or why something has happened. Often the inclusion of line B is termed regulation with *endogenous* politics; the omission of line B is termed regulation with *exogenous* politics. The representation of endogenous politics in Figure 11.1 reflects a political economy view of how politics works—economic interests influencing outcomes of the political system. It goes without saying that politics is more complicated than this representation, which is the reason for an entire discipline devoted to the topic—political science.

We can also view exogenous politics as coinciding with the public interest theory of regulation. Though it may be quite difficult to induce the firm to do the right thing, the fundamental objective of the regulatory agency is to maximize social welfare (however defined), subject to the regulatory constraints it faces. Typically, the objective of the regulator is viewed as maximizing the sum of producer and consumer surplus, perhaps with a slight bias toward consumer surplus.

The positive interest group theory mentioned earlier is consistent with the endogenous politics model of regulation. With endogenous politics, we are conscious of the ability of interest groups (boxes in Figure 11.1) to influence the regulators, legislators, and perhaps the judiciary. Environmental regulation is particularly susceptible to interest group influence. One interest group is clearly the firms potentially subject to environmental regulation—the polluters, or "browns." Another interest group, however, is the "greens," or environmental interest groups. Understanding how the browns and greens interact with the legislature and regulatory agencies can explain why we see the environmental regulations we do.

III. BASIC REGULATORY INSTRUMENTS

Having just discussed the prevalence of conflicting incentives and private information, this is an appropriate time to introduce the two major types of environmental regulation: economic incentives and prescriptive regulations. It should be noted that although most regulations fall into these two broad categories, there are other innovative approaches that have been developed, proposed or implemented. In particular, voluntary actions and measures have become popular in many countries (and are the subject of Chapter 14).

A. Prescriptive Regulations

Prescriptive regulation (often called command-and-control regulation) is the dominant form of environmental regulation in the world today. Although it can take many forms, the basic concept of prescriptive regulation is for the regulator to specify the steps individual polluters must take to solve a pollution problem. The essence of the approach is that the regulator collects the information necessary to decide the physical actions to control pollution; the regulator then commands the polluter to take specific physical steps to control the pollution. The regulator is generally quite specific as to what steps must be taken.

DEFINITION *Prescriptive regulations (also called command-and-control regulations) involve the environmental regulator stipulating the action that an individual firm or polluting facility should take with regard to pollution control or other environmental protection, though the firm may have some limited flexibility in how it meets the regulatory requirements.*

Prescriptive regulations can take many forms. One way of conveying the nature of prescriptive regulations is by example. For instance, the Clean Air Act in the United States requires the EPA to determine the minimum pollution control "performance" of new sources of pollution. The EPA is required to specify for each new category of source (e.g., new power plants or new tire factories) what pollution controls and emission rates are deemed acceptable. This means that the EPA must investigate the production process for literally every type of plant or factory in the United States, at least if significant pollution is involved. For instance, in tire manufacture, the EPA has hired engineers to examine the process of tire manufacture, generating a "Control Technology Guideline," which indicates what kinds of pollution control are appropriate for new tire manufacturing plants. In industries that apply surface coatings (e.g., furniture manufacture—see EPA, 1996), regulations may impose limits on the types of coatings that may be used or firms may be required to use a certain type of vent system to recapture vapors that are emitted during painting. Furthermore, products may be banned altogether as is the case with many oil-based paints in urban areas of the United States most severely affected by photochemical smog. Power plants (producing electricity) may be required to use certain technologies to reduce emissions of sulfur dioxide. At one time in the United States, flue-gas desulfurization was required on all new coal-fired power plants, regardless of the uncontrolled emission rate of the plant.

There are two basic types of prescriptive regulations: technology standards and performance standards. Technology standards typically specify a particular type of equipment that must be used. An example is the very first automobile pollution regulation (in California), requiring the use of a positive crankcase ventilation (PCV) valve on all engines. Technology standards have the virtue of being relatively easy to verify—an inspector simply needs to observe whether or not the equipment has been installed.

A second type of prescriptive regulation is the performance standard—typically the stipulation of the maximum emissions allowed per unit of economic activity. An example would be regulations on electricity facilities, limiting emissions of sulfur per unit fuel used or per unit electricity produced. A virtue of performance standards is that the regulation leaves some discretion in the hands of the polluter as to how best to meet the regulatory standard. This increased flexibility can help improve the cost-effectiveness of a performance standard, at least in comparison to a technology standard.

Often, performance standards are combined with technology standards. An example might be the U.S. standards for new automobiles: every new car may emit no more than x grams of carbon monoxide per mile driven.[9] Furthermore, all new cars are required to have a specifically defined system for capturing vapor that might escape from the gasoline tank during refueling. (In the case of automobiles, a major factor that bears on pollution is how much the car is used. There are virtually no regulations in the United States addressing distance driven except for modest taxes on gasoline.)

Prescriptive regulations may in fact be combined with significant fines and penalties associated with noncompliance. Such incentives to comply with a prescriptive regulation should not be confused with an economic incentive to abate pollution. Though they it may take many forms, there are two key features that distinguish prescriptive regulations from economic incentives: (1) restricted choice for the polluter as to what means will be used to achieve an appropriate environmental target; and (2) a lack of mechanisms for equalizing marginal control costs among several different polluters. For example, if a polluter is told by a regulator that it must use a particular type of equipment, the polluter has little choice in determining emissions. If there is a cheaper way to attain the same level of emissions, such cost savings cannot be pursued. Some prescriptive regulations may afford some discretion to the polluter. Polluters may, for instance, be told that they can emit up to a certain amount per unit of goods output (e.g., grams of SO_2 per kwh sold). This gives more discretion to the polluter, although the polluter is not free to adjust emissions among sources that have different pollution control costs. The one thing that characterizes all prescriptive regulation is a centralization of some of the pollution control decisions that could be made by the polluter.

The best analogy for prescriptive regulations is the system of central planning that existed in the former Soviet Union to manage its economy. Rather than let prices signal relative scarcity and thus direct goods around the economy, nearly all decisions on production, investment, and even interplant trade were made centrally, by central planners. In theory this can work as well as any system. The problem is that the informational requirements are enormous. In actuality, planners operate with very incomplete information, which leads to serious inefficiencies. Despite these problems, this is more or less how pollution generation is managed in most countries. Although this approach to running an economy proved too burdensome for the Soviet Union, environmental regulation in most market economies is unlikely to have such a dramatic effect since pollution control is only a modest part of modern economies. On the other hand, one might expect it to be possible to significantly improve on the current system.

What are the pros and cons of prescriptive regulations? Prescriptive regulations have one major advantage: more flexibility in regulating complex environmental processes and thus much greater certainty in how much pollution will result from regulations. In an urban area with factories at different locations contributing differently to overall levels of urban pollution, it can be difficult to fashion a workable set of emission taxes or other incentives to ensure a certain level of pollution. Furthermore, in an atmosphere of uncertainty, where it is unclear how a polluter might respond to an economic incentive, prescriptive regulations give greater certainty on how much pollution will actually be emitted.[10] Another advantage of prescriptive regulations is in simplifying monitoring of compliance with a regulation. If a regulation states that a particular piece of pollution control equipment must be used, monitoring simply involves seeing whether that equipment has been installed. This is easier than measuring pollution emissions.

There are of course disadvantages to prescriptive regulations. Because the informational costs are high, such a regulatory system can be very costly to administer. Each plant, or at least each industry, must be analyzed in detail to determine the appropriate level of emission control. This is very costly, not to mention fraught with errors. There is also the potential for fundamental information problems. The regulator often needs to rely on information from the polluter, either in terms of emissions or costs of control. Because of this, the polluter has an incentive to distort information provided to the regulator. (Though this problem often applies to other forms of regulation as well.)

A very significant problem with prescriptive regulations is reduced incentives to find better ways to control pollution. This may be purely a static issue, finding process changes or other means to reduce pollution. Or it might involve investing in research into better ways of controlling pollution. In either case, many types of prescriptive regulations provide weak incentives for innovation (see Jaffe and Stavins, 1995). Later in this chapter we examine the relative performance of different types of regulation in spurring innovation.

Perhaps one of the biggest problems with prescriptive regulations is difficulty in satisfying the equimarginal principle. It is almost impossible for prescriptive regulations to ensure that the marginal costs of pollution control are equalized among different polluters generating the same pollution. This could occur only if regulators are completely correct in their assessment of each firm's control costs. If the marginal costs of pollution are not equalized, costs of pollution control will be unnecessarily high.

This failure of the equimarginal principle is illustrated in Table 11.1, which shows the marginal cost of controlling biological oxygen demand (BOD), a measure of water pollution in rivers and lakes. Table 11.1 is drawn from an analysis of how the USEPA translates legislative mandates regarding water quality into regulations to apply to individual firms. Clearly, the equimarginal principle is violated. It would be much more cost effective, without hurting the environment, to relax regulations on some of the high cost industries and tighten regulations on some of the lower cost industries.[11]

As another example, Table 11.2 is a listing of a number of U.S. prescriptive regulations that are designed to protect health and save lives. Interpreting lives saved as the only goal of the regulation, the equimarginal principle also fails to hold. Some regulations save lives at very low cost, whereas some are extremely costly (e.g., formaldehyde in the workplace, at $72 billion per life saved).

A final problem is that with prescriptive regulations, the polluter pays only for pollution control, not residual damage from the pollution that is still emitted even after controls are in place. This effectively provides a subsidy to the polluter, which may create a variety of distortions. As an example of this consider paper manufacture with pulp (the raw material) either coming from recycled paper (assumed pollution free) or virgin wood (with associated pollution). Efficiently regulating the manufacture of virgin wood pulp involves seeing that the proper pollution control is achieved and that the damage from any remaining pollution is included in the price of pulp. This way the price of pulp reflects pollution control costs and residual damage. However, if regulations require only pollution control and not the payment of residual damage, the resulting price of virgin pulp will be lower. Why is this undesirable? It is easy to see that with a lower price of virgin pulp, paper manufacturers are more likely to choose virgin pulp over recycled pulp, because it is cheaper. As a result, there will be more pollution than is efficient.

B. Economic Incentives

Economic incentives, in contrast to prescriptive regulations, provide rewards for polluters to do what is perceived to be in the public interest. We are all familiar with incentives. Instead of closely monitoring a child's homework activity, a parent may provide a substantial reward for good grades (or a disincentive for bad grades). The idea is to align public and private incentives. In the context of pollution, there are three basic types of economic incentives: fees, marketable permits, and liability.

TABLE 11.1 Marginal Treatment Costs of BOD Removal, U.S. Regulations

Industry	Subcategory	Marginal cost[a]
Poultry	Duck—small plants	3.15
Meat packing	Simple slaughterhouse	2.19
	Low processing packinghouse	1.65
Cane sugar	Crystalline refining	1.40
Leather tanning	Hair previously removed/chromium	1.40
Poultry	Duck—large plants	1.04
Leather	Save hair/vegetable	1.02
	Hair previously removed	1.02
Meat packing	High processing packinghouse	0.92
	Complex slaughterhouse	0.90
Paper	Unbleached kraft	0.86
Leather tanning	Save hair/chromium	0.75
	Pulp hair/chromium	0.63
Poultry	Turkey	0.60
Cane sugar	Liquid refining	0.51
Paper	Paperboard	0.50
	Kraft—NSSC	0.42
Leather	Pulp or save hair/no finish	0.39
Poultry	Further processing only—large plants	0.35
	Chicken—small plants	0.25
Paper	NSSC—ammonia process	0.22
Raw sugar processing	Louisiana	0.21
Poultry	Fowl—small plants	0.20
	Chicken—medium plants	0.16
Raw sugar processing	Puerto Rico	0.16
Paper	NSSC—sodium process	0.12
Poultry	Fowl—large plants	0.10
	Chicken—large plants	0.10

[a] *Units: U.S. dollars per kilogram of BOD removed.*
Source: Magat et al. (1986), p. 136.

Pollution fees involve the payment of a charge per unit of pollution emitted. When a polluter must pay for every unit of pollution emitted, it becomes in the polluter's interest to reduce emissions.

A marketable permit allows polluters to buy and sell the right to pollute. Thus what starts as something akin to prescriptive regulations (a permit to pollute) turns into an economic incentive by allowing trading. Trading induces a price or value on a permit to pollute, thus causing firms to see polluting as an expensive activity; less pollution means fewer permits need be bought. There is an opportunity cost of emitting; by not emitting, the firm can sell more permits. A marketable permit system is often referred to as "cap and trade" in that the regulator sets a cap on overall emissions and allows trading among polluters to determine who emits what.

This is illustrated in Figure 11.2, which corresponds to the situation in which there are two polluters. We are interested in allowing 100 units of pollution in total. We start

TABLE 11.2 Average Cost of US Regulations to Reduce Risk of Death

Regulation	Initial annual risk	Expected annual lives saved	Cost per expected life saved (millions of 1984 $)
Unvented space heaters	2.7 in 10^5	63.000	0.10
Airplane cabin fire protection	6.5 in 10^8	15.000	0.20
Auto passive restraints/belts	9.1 in 10^5	1,850.000	0.30
Underground construction	1.6 in 10^3	8.100	0.30
Servicing wheel rims	1.4 in 10^5	2.300	0.50
Aircraft seat cushion flammability	1.6 in 10^7	37.000	0.60
Aircraft floor emergency lighting	2.2 in 10^8	5.000	0.70
Crane suspended personnel platform	1.8 in 10^3	5.000	1.20
Concrete and masonry construction	1.4 in 10^5	6.500	1.40
Benzene/fugitive emissions	2.1 in 10^5	0.310	2.80
Grain dust	2.1 in 10^4	4.000	5.30
Radionuclides/uranium mines	1.4 in 10^4	1.100	6.90
Benzene in workplace	8.8 in 10^4	3.800	17.10
Ethylene oxide in workplace	4.4 in 10^5	2.800	25.60
Arsenic/copper smelter	9.0 in 10^4	0.060	26.50
Uranium mill tailings, active	4.3 in 10^4	2.100	53.00
Asbestos in workplace	6.7 in 10^5	74.700	89.30
Arsenic/glass manufacturing	3.8 in 10^5	0.250	142.00
Radionuclides/DOE facilities	4.3 in 10^6	0.001	210.00
Benzene/ethylbenzenol styrene	2.0 in 10^6	0.006	483.00
Formaldehyde in workplace	6.8 in 10^7	0.010	72,000.00

Source: Viscusi (1996), pp. 124–125.

by giving each firm 50 permits. The marginal savings from polluting functions are shown in Figure 11.2 for the two firms. They have been drawn so that any point along the horizontal axis gives the number of permits each firm holds: read from the left for firm 1 and from the right for firm 2. Note that trading will occur until firm 1 holds e^* and firm 2 holds $100 - e^*$. The equilibrium price of a permit is p^*.

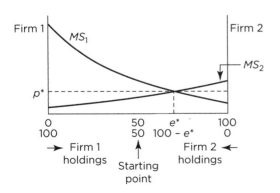

FIGURE 11.2 Illustration of permit trading for two firms. MS_1, marginal savings from emitting, firm 1; MS_2, marginal savings from emitting, firm 2; e^*, equilibrium holding of permits; p^*, equilibrium price of permits.

It is important to note that an emission fee of p^* would achieve exactly the same outcome. Suppose there is a little uncertainty. With an emission fee, we know precisely what the marginal cost of control will be; we are less sure about the quantity of pollution. With a marketable permit, we know exactly how much pollution there will be; we are less sure of the marginal cost of control.

Liability is a third type of economic incentive. The basic idea is that if you harm someone, you must compensate that person for damage. In theory, this means that when you undertake a risky activity (such as polluting or storing hazardous wastes), you will take all potential damage from your activity into account when deciding how carefully to perform your activity. The important issue is that the government is not telling you what to do, just that you will be responsible for any consequences. This creates an incentive to be careful when undertaking risky activity and, in fact, to take the socially desirable amount of precaution in undertaking such risky activity.

To illustrate liability, suppose we have a hazardous waste storage facility (a "dump"). The dump can do things to minimize the risk of hazardous wastes leaking into the environment. We can lump all of those risk-reducing activities into one term, "precaution." If the dump takes a great deal of precaution, the risk of a leak will be low. If the dump takes little precaution, the risk will be high. Precaution is of course expensive for the dump to undertake. All other things being equal, the dump would prefer to take little precaution. Damage to society also depends on the level of precaution. This is illustrated in Figure 11.3, which shows both costs to the dump and damage to society as functions of the level of precaution. There is some socially desirable level of precaution, x^*, at which the marginal costs of taking more precaution are just offset by the reduction in marginal damage from taking more precaution. Liability works by saying to the dump: "Do whatever you wish but should an accident occur, we will find the socially desirable level of precaution; if you were not taking that level of precaution, you will be responsible for all of the environmental damage from the accident." This is how negligence liability works, although other types of liability work in a similar fashion. This threat of being held responsible for accident damages is often a sufficient incentive for firms to take the socially desirable amount of precaution.

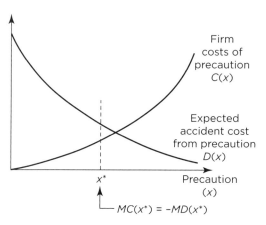

FIGURE 11.3 An illustration of precaution and liability.

One of the dominant questions in environmental economics and regulation over the past four decades is why prescriptive regulations dominate environmental regulation worldwide when most economists believe economic incentives are much better.

Clearly, economic incentives have a number of advantages over prescriptive regulations. First, informational requirements are less significant. It is not necessary to know what it going on within a firm to use an emission fee. Furthermore, economic incentives will provide an incentive for a polluter to innovate, finding cheaper ways of controlling pollution.[12] Also, in contrast to prescriptive regulations, economic incentives involve the polluter paying for control costs as well as pollution damage. Thus there is no implicit subsidy to the industry. As we will see, the fee payments approximate the damage associated with the pollution. Consequently the cost (and thus the price) of the product manufactured in association with pollution will reflect control costs as well as residual pollution damage. In the previous section, in the example of paper manufacture, we saw the importance of reflecting environmental damage in product price, something that prescriptive regulations fail to achieve.

Probably the biggest advantage of economic incentives is that the equimarginal principle will automatically hold for most types of economic incentives. For instance, with an emission fee, all firms set their marginal cost of pollution control equal to the fee. The equimarginal principle is trivially satisfied. When firms trade pollution permits, the price of the permit that will be determined by the permit market sends the same signal to all polluters regarding the opportunity cost of emitting. The equimarginal principle will hold. As we will see in Chapter 18, liability effectively has the polluter setting its marginal abatement cost equal to marginal damage. Thus the equimarginal principle will also hold. Why is meeting the equimarginal principle so important? Basically because the costs of regulation will be higher if the equimarginal principle does not hold, perhaps much higher. Thus economic incentives have this cost-saving advantage.

There are disadvantages to economic incentives. One problem is forging a set of economic incentives that can accommodate the complexities of environmental transformation without being excessively complex and impractical. Just think of urban air pollution in which the damage from a unit of emissions can vary considerably in both space and time. Developing an economic incentive that efficiently and perfectly takes these complexities into account can be very difficult.

A second problem with economic incentives is largely political. If there is a great deal of uncertainty associated with the environmental problem being controlled, it may be necessary to adjust the level of the incentive (level of the fee, number of marketable permits issued) over time, as information becomes available. This may be very difficult in many practical situations. For instance such an adjustment in the United States might require Congressional action. It took over 10 years of debate in Congress before the U.S. Clean Air Act was amended in 1990 to address the acid rain problem.

A third problem, also political, is that many economic incentives involve massive transfers from firms to the government. An emissions tax generates a tremendous amount of revenue for the government administering the tax. This may be good for the government, but instituting such a tax may be very difficult politically, precisely because of these wealth transfers. This explains in large part why substantial emission fees have gone nowhere in most market economies. In contrast, emission fees have been widely used in the former Soviet Union and Eastern Europe because of the traditional dedication of the fee revenue to investment in pollution control in state enterprises.[13] Marketable permit (cap and trade) programs have been popular, in part because the permits have generally been given away freely, at no cost to polluters. However, regulators are becoming more reluctant to freely allocate permits, moving toward auctioning, at least in part. It remains to be seen if significant revenue raising will create political problems for permit systems.

One problem with economic incentives is that some in society do not like the idea of turning the environment into a "commodity." For example, in an opinion article in the *New York Times*, Michael Sandel argued that turning the environment into a commodity removed the moral stigma associated with polluting, and that this was inappropriate (Sandel, 1997). Others have suggested that the sole goal should be to reduce pollution and that notions of morality should play little role. In the 1970s, many environmental groups shared Sandel's view of economic incentives. Now some (but not all) environmental groups have vigorously embraced the use of economic incentives as an effective way of advancing environmental agendas (the idea being that the best way to a polluter's heart is through its wallet).

IV. PUBLIC SOURCES OF POLLUTION

Much of our discussion of regulation applies to profit-maximizing firms. However, public sources of pollution are very significant, particularly for some media and in some countries. Sewage plants, for instance, are often owned and operated by local governments. In many countries, including the United States, large segments of the electric power sector are owned and operated by public or quasi-public enterprises. The prevalence of organizational forms (other than the for-profit firm) in the pollution-generating process suggests the importance of at least considering how regulation works in these contexts.

There are a number of theories about what drives and motivates managers of public organizations. A few authors examine these models of organizational behavior in the context of environmental regulation.[14] The primary driver of these models is the behavior of the head of the bureaucracy—the head of the polluting agency being examined.

Consider a public agency charged with producing a good (such as electricity or waste treatment). Let Q be the amount of the good produced and E the emissions. The agency hires workers, L, at a wage, w, to produce the good according to a production function:

$$Q = f(L, E) \tag{11.1}$$

More L yields more Q and less E yields less Q (it is harder to produce the Q without producing much pollution).

So far, our description of the agency is identical to how one would describe a profit-maximizing firm. The difference does not lie in the production technology but rather in how the agency management operates. The simplest model of bureaucratic behavior suggests the agency head cares about two things: the size of his or her kingdom (bigger Q is better) and the amount of discretionary funds ("perquisites") that can be used to make life more enjoyable for management. Let the amount of perquisites be indicated by P. Thus the goal of the agency head is to maximize utility:

$$\text{Max}_{Q,P,L,E} \ U(Q,P) \tag{11.2a}$$

Such that $$P = B - wL \qquad (11.2b)$$

$$Q = f(L, E) \qquad (11.2c)$$

where B is the agency's budget, which may be obtained from sales of Q or directly from the legislature. In either case, the assumption is that the agency has monopoly power, either over its consumers or over the legislature, able to extract all of the consumer surplus under the demand curve for Q, for whatever level of Q is provided. Thus B in Eq. (11.2b) can be written as a function of the demand for Q. Doing so explicitly makes the model more complex than necessary to capture the essence of the behavioral model.

In Eq. (11.2) there is no regulation or other restriction on the amount of emissions. This is our starting point. Two results emerge from this: the public agency produces pollution in an unconstrained way, up to the point where the marginal cost of pollution control is zero. This is the same behavior we would expect from an unregulated for-profit firm. The second result that emerges from the model in Eq. (11.2) is that the agency will act to minimize the labor cost of producing Q, just as a monopolist would do. What differs from a conventional for-profit monopolist is the amount of Q that will be produced. The objective for a monopolist is profits, whereas in this case it is utility of output and perquisites.

The intuition behind the result that the agency will be a cost-minimizer in using L is straightforward. Any choice of L that is not a cost-minimum way of producing L serves to reduce P (which gives utility) without any other payoff to the agency head.

Using this same logic, we can amend the model in Eq. (11.2) to include a regulation on emissions. If the regulation is prescriptive, specifying the abatement technology or the emissions level, then the agency will behave as a for-profit firm in terms of emissions control, since the regulation gives no choice. If the regulation is in terms of an economic incentive, then provided those incentives increase costs the same way wages increase costs, then the agency should behave as a cost-minimizer and act as a for-profit firm. However, as Lyon (1990) has suggested, it may be that pollution control expenditures directly enter into the utility function of the agency head (nobody likes to be known as a polluter), in which case the agency's behavior would differ from that of a for-profit firm.

We leave this topic, concluding only that a public agency may behave differently than a for-profit firm. However, how differently remains an unanswered question. It does appear that prescriptive regulations may work better and have less implementation uncertainty than economic incentives in this case.

V. SPATIAL AND TEMPORAL COMPLICATIONS

A. Space and Time

In contrast to most types of regulation, pollution regulation is complicated by the physical environment that interposes itself between polluters and consumers. This is illustrated in Figure 11.4. A polluter generates *emissions*. These emissions are transformed, possibly in a complex fashion, to *ambient concentrations* of pollution. Emissions cause no damage; it is ambient concentrations that cause damage. This is an important distinction. The word ambient refers to the world around us. That is its use here. Ambient concentrations are the concentrations of pollution in the air around us or in the water we drink. It is ambient

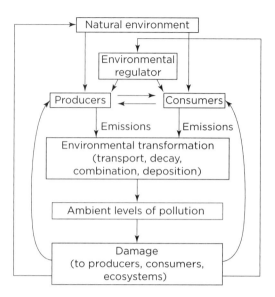

FIGURE 11.4 Environmental regulators face a complex task.

concentrations, not emissions, that should be of concern when we discuss environmental damage. The regulator, too, is interested in ambient concentrations because that is the source of damage. However, ambient concentrations are imperfectly connected to emissions and emissions are what firms emit and what need to be regulated. This creates a complexity that is not present in other forms of regulation, such as monopoly or occupational safety.

Space is a major player in environmental transformation. If we are interested in pollution levels in central Tokyo, sources nearby will generate more damage than sources located in distant suburbs. Or if we are interested in acid rain damage in the Black Forest, emissions from German power plants will be more damaging than emissions from more distant English power plants. We take this issue up in more detail in the next chapter.

Time is also a significant factor in environmental transformation, though probably less important than space. Urban photochemical smog (primarily ozone) involves sunlight and a mixture of nitrogen oxides and volatile organic compounds. Without sunlight, the problem is significantly less severe. Furthermore, the residence time in the atmosphere of some of these compounds is less than a day. Thus emissions in the evening or at night will be less damaging than emissions in the morning or mid-day. Seasonal variation is also important. In some areas, winter involves less heat and sunshine, which tends to reduce the problem of smog. Thus emissions in the winter may be less damaging than emissions in the summer. Designing regulations to reflect this hour-to-hour, day-to-day, and season-to-season variation is not easy.

B. Efficiency versus Cost Effectiveness

The complex and imperfectly understood relationship between emissions and ambient concentrations and, in turn, environmental damage, presents a conundrum for regulators. Ideally, regulations would target damage and ambient concentrations, but that is often too difficult. Often, regulations will have as a goal some overall level of emissions, with no clear connection to ambient concentrations. For instance, the 1990 U.S. acid rain legislation calls for a reduction in annual sulfur dioxide emissions of 10 million tons, without regard for where that reduction takes place. But emissions close to sensitive lakes and forests are much more damaging than emissions that, for instance, largely blow out to sea. However, it is too complicated to try to reduce acid deposition based on variable emission reductions at specific locations.

Efficiency calls for emissions that balance the costs of emissions control with the damage from ambient pollution, fully taking into account the complexities relating emissions to damage. When this is not practical (as is often the case), goals or targets will be established regarding desired levels of ambient concentrations or desired levels of emissions. These goals may be only imperfectly related to efficient levels of pollution, since efficient levels of pollution many vary through time and over space.

As another example, efficiency may call for the level of ozone in the Los Angeles basin to vary spatially (depending on population density, for example, and control costs) as well as temporally (depending on the time of day). But given the imperfect knowledge of ozone damage, formation, and transport, a second-best approach is to establish a target upper bound on concentration of ozone in the entire basin, averaged over an hour. But even such a simplified target may be impractically complex. Because of the imperfect knowledge of the ozone problem, regulations may establish targets for emissions that may be only imperfectly related to ambient concentrations. For instance, goals or targets are established for overall emissions of precursors of ozone (those pollutants that lead to ozone). Regulations apply to individual polluters and are designed to achieve approximately the emission targets for the basin.

This example illustrates the compromises that are often (though not always) necessary in actually regulating polluters. If regulators are unable to control emissions from individual polluters to balance costs and damage, a fall-back position may be to establish ambient pollution targets and regulate polluters in such a way as to achieve the ambient pollution target in the best way possible. But even this may not always be possible, in which case a target is established for emissions and this target may be only approximately related to the target for ambient concentrations. The goal of regulation then is to control individual polluters in such as way as to achieve the emission target in the best way possible.

Establishing emission targets or ambient targets is usually a compromise that sacrifices efficiency in pollution control. But even with an emission target, there are both good ways and less desirable ways of regulating emissions to achieve the target. Different polluters have different costs of pollution control. The least-costly way of achieving a given emission target involves controlling pollution from various sources in a way that reflects different costs of pollution control. If a set of environmental regulations achieves the emission target at least cost, we say the regulation is *cost effective*. If the regulation is cumbersome and poorly matches emission cutbacks with control costs, then it is likely the regulation will not be cost effective.

This is an important concept. Even though efficiency is not attainable for many regulations, cost effectiveness is attainable. Unfortunately many environmental regulations around the world are far from cost effective in achieving either emission targets or ambient targets. In some cases this lack of cost effectiveness is for very real and understandable reasons, particularly concerns about equity. Cost effectiveness may call for most of the damages or costs of emission control to fall on a few individuals or firms.[15] Society may deem this inequitable and consciously move away from cost effectiveness. However, it is just as common that regulations are poorly designed, leading to excessive costs for no particular reason.

C. Ambient-Differentiated versus Emission-Differentiated Regulation

We have already concluded that targets may be ambient targets or emission targets. Regulations, too, can apply to polluters based on their emissions or on their contribution to ambient concentrations. This is a bit subtle but actually relatively simple. Suppose we have an ambient target. Typically, a unit of pollution from one polluter will have a different effect on ambient concentrations than a unit of pollution from another polluter. An ambient-differentiated regulation will control these two polluters differently, based on their different contributions to ambient concentrations. An emissions-differentiated regulation will ignore the differences between the two polluters, though the overall level of emissions will still be controlled in such a way as to achieve the ambient target.

Using the example of ozone in Los Angeles again, regulation is driven by ambient targets on maximum concentrations of ozone at any point in the air basin. However, sources are regulated without much regard for their contribution to ambient concentrations. A source of a particular type (e.g., furniture manufacture) will be subject to the same emissions regulation regardless of its location in the basin. This is an example of emission-differentiated regulation. Contrast this with regulations applying to new sources of pollution in the Los Angeles basin. A new source seeking to locate in the basin must arrange for emission reductions from existing sources and demonstrate that the ambient concentrations resulting from the new source combined with the arranged reductions in existing sources will be better than the previous status quo. This is an example of an ambient-differentiated regulation.

This concept of ambient-differentiated regulations will be explored more fully in the next chapter.

VI. ISSUES IN ENVIRONMENTAL REGULATION

This chapter has served as an introduction to environmental regulation. Lest the reader be seduced into thinking that designing good environmental regulation involves a simple application of economic theory, it may be instructive to briefly mention some of the major issues in environmental regulation. In the succeeding chapters, we will examine many of these issues in more detail.

The debate over prescriptive regulations vs. economic incentives is still as lively as ever. Although there have been some major inroads of economic incentives into actual environmental regulation, the verdict is still out on how well these incentives work.[16] Furthermore, some of the more vexing environmental problems, such as urban air pollution, are so complex that no complete package of incentives has been suggested that might achieve efficient control of the problem. Furthermore, although prescriptive regulation is theoretically undesirable, empirical evidence is sparse on exactly how much money is being wasted in prescriptive regulation.

One important issue in environmental regulation concerns information, particularly private information polluters may have that regulators need. How best can regulations be structured to give polluters incentives to act efficiently and truthfully divulge information necessary for regulation? How can enforcement policies be designed to give polluters incentives to obey regulations? How can regulations be structured for the case in which we cannot observe emissions, such as soil erosion from multiple farms in a watershed?

Risk is becoming more important for many pollution problems. A hazardous waste dump may be well designed, but it still poses a risk to nearby residents, since failure of the dump is always possible. Toxins in the environment may not directly cause cancer but may increase the probability of getting cancer. How do we deal with these problems? What sort of regulations are appropriate?

Another issue concerns competition between jurisdictions vis-à-vis environmental regulations. With localities competing to attract industry, to what extent will environmental regulations be weakened as an incentive to attract a new employer? If pollution is coming from outside one's jurisdiction, can anything be done to try to reduce that pollution, such as countervailing tariffs? This issue applies to competition among states in a federation (e.g., states of the United States, countries of the EU, or republics of Russia) as well as competition among countries.

A related issue concerns the appropriate political level to institute environmental regulations. Also known as environmental federalism, the question is whether it is better to institute regulations at the Federal level or at the state level. In the case of the EU, should a regulation be promulgated from Brussels, applying to all member states, or should each state be allowed to develop its own regulations? Put differently, what kinds of pollution problems are best regulated at the Federal level and which problems should be left to member states?

Another issue concerns the incidence of regulations. When a regulation is instituted, who bears the burden (either in costs or pollution damage)? Who reaps the benefits? As discussed in Chapter 6, this is not as simple as it might seem. Consider a poor urban area with high levels of pollution. As is often the case, many people in the urban area rent their apartment or house, and the landlord/owner typically lives in a more desirable location, perhaps a different town. A regulation is proposed to reduce pollution in the poor urban area. Who benefits from this pollution reduction? It might seem at first that the poor residents benefit, but this is not correct. When pollution levels decline, property values rise. Thus the residents end up with cleaner air and higher rents. Property owners are the primary beneficiaries. Who pays for the regulation? If the polluters primarily serve the local market, they will most likely be able to pass the costs of pollution control on to local residents in increased product prices; if they serve a large market, the polluters will probably have to bear the costs. The question of who benefits and who pays for an environmental regulation is not easy to answer. And sometimes the answers are not what we expect.

For many environmental problems, innovation and new technology are considered very important to an ultimate solution. For instance, with regard to climate change, governments around the world are relying on yet-to-be-invented technology (e.g., high efficiency vehicles or cost-effective renewable sources of energy) over time to lower substantially the cost of reducing carbon emissions. One factor is vitally important in spurring innovation: there must be social pressure to reduce emissions of a pollutant, via some sort of regulation. For example, with the current modest level of regulation of carbon dioxide, the payoffs to carbon-reducing innovation are low.

Given that a pollutant is regulated, different regulatory approaches may well perform differently in terms of inducing innovation. Prescriptive regulations are of questionable effectiveness is spurring innovation. Technology standards per se provide little incentive for creating better ways of reducing emissions. Technology standards coupled with automatic ratcheting up of the standard (such as "best available technology" regulations) can provide some incentive for innovation. Performance standards provide more incentives for innovation. Economic incentives generally provide strong incentives for innovation.[17]

SUMMARY

1. There are two basic theories to explain the presence of economic regulation. One is the public interest theory, under which government regulates to correct a market failure and increase societal well-being. The other theory is the interest group theory. Under this theory, interest groups influence government to promote their own agenda. Since regulation tends to benefit some and hurt others, interest groups will lobby for those regulations that are in their self-interest.

2. Under the public interest theory of regulation, there are three primary reasons for regulation: imperfect competition, imperfect information, and externalities. The case of externalities is of most interest to us. Externalities generate market failure that government regulation seeks to correct.

3. Any market economy is a complex web of government agencies, firms with hierarchical structures, and consumers who wear multiple hats (consumers of goods, victims of pollution, stockholders in corporations, voters). Under the public interest theory of regulation, politics is exogenous to this complex structure. In such a case, the regulator designs regulations that maximize a weighted sum of consumer and producer surplus. However, the regulator may have incomplete control over the individuals who actually make the pollution cleanup decisions. This imperfect connection is termed the principal-agent problem.

4. There are two basic types of environmental regulations: prescriptive regulation and economic incentives. Prescriptive regulation involves the regulator making many of the pollution control decisions for the firm, reducing firm choice. Economic incentives give more choice to the firm, simply providing an incentive for the firm to find the best way to reduce pollution.

5. The advantage of prescriptive regulation is that there is more flexibility for the regulator in regulating complex pollution problems. It may also give greater certainty as to how much pollution will be emitted. On the negative side, prescriptive regulation typically is much more costly than efficient alternatives. One of the primary reasons it is more costly is that it is difficult for the equimarginal principle to hold.

6. Economic incentives fall into three main categories: emission fees, marketable emission permits, and liability. Emission fees involve the polluter paying a fee per unit of pollution to the government. Marketable emission permits involve the government issuing (selling or giving away) permits to pollute, which may be traded among polluting firms. This is also called cap and trade. Liability involves holding polluters

liable for any damage they may cause. Liability is particularly useful for regulating risky activities that lead to occasional accidents.

7. Economic incentives have the advantage of placing decision making for pollution control in the hands of those most familiar with pollution control options—the polluter. Economic incentives work to keep costs low and also to spur innovation. The equimarginal principle automatically holds with most economic incentives. A disadvantage of economic incentives is that it can be very difficult to design a set of economic incentives for complex pollution control problems, such as urban ozone.

8. One complication of environmental regulation is how to deal with space and time. We distinguish between emissions (which come directly from a polluter) and ambient pollution, the levels of pollution in the air or water around us. Ambient pollution causes damage, but emissions are what is regulated.

9. Regulations, too, may make a similar distinction. Emission-differentiated regulations treat all emissions as the same, no matter where they come from. Ambient-differentiated regulations treat emissions from different sources differently, based on their relative contribution to ambient pollution levels.

10. Because of the difficulty in designing regulations that achieve efficiency, regulations sometimes take the approach of specifying environmental targets (e.g., maximum pollutant concentration levels) and then ask what is the cheapest way of reaching these targets. This is termed cost effectiveness, as opposed to efficiency.

11. A public agency will likely behave differently than a for-profit firm in response to environmental regulations. Prescriptive regulations may work best is such situations.

PROBLEMS

1. A classic way of introducing pollution regulation into an urban area is the "rollback" method. First you determine the maximum tolerable level of a particular pollutant, x_s. Next you find the maximum current concentration of that pollutant in the urban area, x_m. Presumably $x_m > x_s$ (otherwise, there is no problem). Regulations then require all polluters in the city to reduce emissions from their current level of e_m to $e_s = e_m (x_s/x_m)$. Explain how this would work to bring pollution levels down to an acceptable point. What might be the efficiency problems with such an approach?

2. Explain how the public interest theory of regulation might come to a different conclusion regarding emission fees vs. marketable permits than the interest group theory.

3. Consider a simplified version of the model of a public agency captured in Eq. (11.2). Suppose inverse demand for Q is given by $D(Q) = 10 - Q$. Suppose the price of labor (w) is 1 and production of Q is in direct proportion to the amount of labor used: $Q = L$.

   a. Write an expression for the budget (consumer surplus) as a function of Q.

   b. In a plot of Q versus P, plot the budget constraint and sketch indifference curves for the agency head.

   c. On the same figure, sketch the objective function for a profit-maximizing monopolist.

    d.   How do the results differ in terms of choice of Q between the profit-maximizing monopolist and the public agency?

    e.   For a given Q, how would the choice of L differ between a profit-maximizing monopolist and the public agency?

4. The Kyoto Protocol, drafted in December 1997, calls for each developed country to cut its emissions of carbon dioxide by the year 2012 to approximately 8% below 1990 levels. Some countries are concerned about the cost of making such a cut in carbon emissions. Expectations are that the cost of pollution control will be $5–10 per ton of carbon emitted. However, there really is a great deal of uncertainty about what the costs might be; some say it will be easy to reduce carbon emissions, others say it will be very expensive. In one developed country, two proposals are being considered to achieve the reduction. Proposal A involves the issuance of permits for carbon emissions every year, with the number of permits equaling the targeted "8% less than 1990 emissions." Each permit will be good for emitting one ton of carbon. Proposal B is the same as Proposal A except that the government agrees to sell an unlimited number of additional permits for $10 each. Explain how each of these proposals works and what the price of permits might end up being under each proposal. Discuss the pros and cons of each proposal.

5. Suppose we have one hundred different firms emitting pollution. The Ministry of the Environment (MOE) currently regulates these firms by requiring specific pollution control equipment to be installed by each firm. The MOE is considering issuing tradable permits to each firm indicating how much pollution the firm may emit. Permits would be issued in such a way as to result in the same amount of pollution as the technology regulations. Discuss the implications of switching to tradable permits on the likelihood of seeing research and development to reduce the cost of pollution control.

NOTES

1. See any good policy analysis book for a discussion of government failure (e.g., Weimer and Vining, 2005).

2. See Laffont and Tirole (1993) for a good discussion of the basic theories of operation of regulatory agencies.

3. The interest group theory can be traced to Stigler (1971) and Peltzman (1976), though the ideas certainly predate these individuals.

4. This subject is treated in depth in the field of industrial organization and regulation. For example, see Carlton and Perloff (2004), Viscusi et al. (2005), or Spulber (1989).

5. The electricity industry is being deregulated worldwide. However, local retail distribution always (to my knowledge) remains a regulated monopoly or state-owned enterprise.

6. Although incomplete information is a problem, it need not always be solved by government intervention. In the case of food safety, private firms could test products and give their "seal of approval" to products meeting certain standards.

7. In general, rent is defined as a payment for a good in excess of the cost of provision. Not all rent is "bad." Scarcity rent is the payment for a scarce good (e.g., the premium that ocean-front property often obtains relative to more plentiful inland property). The problems with monopoly are due to the monopolist seeking monopoly rent. As we know, monopoly is usually undesirable because of the inefficiencies.

8. Milgrom and Roberts (1992) provide a thorough, though advanced, treatment of how firms and other organizations operate.

9. The 1990 Clean Air Act in the United States specifies the following "tailpipe" emission limits in grams per mile: nonmethane hydrocarbons, 0.25; carbon monoxide, 3.4; nitrogen oxides, 0.4. [Bresnahan and Yao (1985) estimate uncontrolled emission rates to be 8.7, 87, and 4.4, respectively.]

10. The view that prescriptive regulations give greater certainty as to pollution levels is sometimes misleading. Urban areas of the United States have been using prescriptive regulations for decades to try to bring ambient air pollution levels below statutory limits. In general, this effort has failed (though pollution levels have been reduced in many areas).

11. Assuming that the USEPA is rational, Magat et al. (1986) attempt to explain the failure of the equimarginal principle to apply in this case. They statistically analyze how industry-level BOD standards are affected by variables such as marginal contol costs (these are significant—higher costs lead to weaker standards), industry concentration, which is associated with greater economic power of the industry (this is significant—more concentrated indstries get weaker standards), quality of information on control costs (also significant—less uncertainty leads to tighter standards), and the volume of comments sent to the EPA by industry on the proposed regulations (this is insignificant).

12. It is widely accepted that providing an economic incentive to reduce pollution emissions will also provide an incentive to innovate and invent better and cheaper ways of controlling pollution. Laffont and Tirole (1996) suggested that economic incentives are not all equal when it comes to providing an incentive to innovate. In particular, they point out that if there are a fixed number of permits in a market, innovation may drive down the price and reduce the gains from innovation. They also suggest ways to avoid this potential problem.

13. Emission fees were used in the former Soviet Union. The fees were basically used to generate a pool of funds that could be used to purchase pollution control equipment for the state-owned polluting enterprises. Thus the fee was more of a way of raising an investment fund, charging firms in proportion to their emissions. There is no evidence that these fees provided any incentive to reduce pollution in order to reduce fee payments. In Europe, emission fees have been levied for many years, particularly on sources of water pollution. These fees were generally set at levels necessary to finance the operation of pollution control agencies rather than at levels associated with marginal damage (Bower, 1983). The general consensus is that such fees were set at too low a level to provide any meaningful incentive to reduce pollution (Howe, 1994). See Chapter 2.

14. Oates and Strassmann (1978) present one of the first such analyses, expanded in Oates and Strassmann (1984). Lyon (1990) further extends their bureaucratic model to explicitly include tradable permits.

15. For instance, in many urban areas, a good portion of auto emissions comes from older cars. Cost effectiveness usually requires substantial efforts to control these older cars Yet it is often the poor who own older vehicles. Thus cost effectiveness would impose a burden on the poor that may be considered unacceptable politically.

16. The U.S. marketable permit system for reducing sulfur emissions (authorized under the 1990 Clean Air Act Amendments) is generally considered to be a big success. The verdict is still out on the even more ambitious EU carbon emissions trading system (ETS), designed to help Europe meet its treaty obligations for 2008–2012 under the Kyoto Protocol (see Ellerman and Buchner, 2007). The RECLAIM trading system for regulating urban pollutants in Los Angeles is not considered a success.

17. Milliman and Prince (1989) compare the effectiveness of a number of different regulatory regimes. See also Denicolò (1999) and Laffont and Tirole (1996). Driesen (2007) provides a legal perspective on this issue. See also Jaffee et al (2003).

PRICING EMISSIONS

In Chapters 4 and 5, we saw that markets cannot be relied on to provide the right amount of pollution—markets fail when it comes to public bads. Normally, consumer preferences are communicated to producers through the price system. The basic problem in the case of pollution is that without a price system, polluters do not "see" the damage caused by the pollution they emit. The simplest way to correct this lack of a signal to polluters is to establish a price for pollution. Just as the price of labor signals to a firm to conserve labor inputs, a price on pollution will signal to the firm to cut back on pollution as much as is economically feasible. The theoretical idea of placing a price on pollution is from the English economist Arthur C. Pigou and dates to the early twentieth century.[1] The more practical idea of regulating pollution by charging polluters an emission fee per unit of pollution has its modern origins in the pathbreaking environmental economist, Alan Kneese, who spent virtually his entire professional career at Resources for the Future in Washington, DC.[2]

I. HOW DO POLLUTERS RESPOND TO EMISSION FEES?

Before turning to how one determines how large or small an emission fee should be, it is important to understand how polluters will respond when charged a specific fee for their emissions. We first define an emission fee:

DEFINITION *An emission fee is a price or fee paid by a polluter to a regulatory entity for every unit of emissions the polluter emits.*

Consider a firm producing some good (for example, electricity) along with pollution, x. If the emission fee is p and the polluter emits x units of pollution, the payment from the polluter to the regulator is px. To determine how much the polluter will emit, let $C(x)$ be the production costs associated with emitting x units of pollution, holding goods output fixed. One would expect C to decline as x increases—the polluter saves money by emitting pollution. Total costs for the firm (abatement costs and costs of the fee) are given by

$$TC(x) = C(x) + p\,x \qquad (12.1)$$

We know something is minimized when its marginal is zero; furthermore, the marginal of a sum is the sum of the marginals (the derivative of a sum is the sum of the derivatives). Therefore, total cost in Eq. (12.1) is minimized when x is chosen so that

$$p = -MC(x) = MS(x) \tag{12.2}$$

The interpretation of Eq. (12.2) is that the firm chooses to operate where the marginal savings from emitting one more unit of pollution (which happens to be equal to the marginal cost of reducing pollution by one unit) is equal to the price of pollution. Emitting a smaller amount of pollution would involve abatement costs that are higher than the pollution price—lowering emissions raises total costs. Emitting a larger amount of pollution than called for in Eq. (12.2) would mean that abatement costs are lower than the emission fee; thus increasing emissions increases fee payments more rapidly than abatement costs are lowered and is also a bad idea.

Equation (12.2) indicates that when faced with an emissions fee, firms will abate pollution up to the point where the marginal cost of abatement (or equivalently, the marginal savings from emitting) is equal to the emissions fee. This point is where the firm's total costs are lowest.

With multiple firms, each firm will abate to the point where the marginal cost of abatement is equal to the emissions fee. Thus the equimarginal principal will automatically hold—each firm sets the marginal cost of abatement equal to the same number (the fee), and thus the marginal cost is the same for all firms.

This is illustrated in Figure 12.1 for two firms—Riley Wreckers and Tucker Tools. In the left-hand panel of the figure, marginal savings to the firm are shown as a function of emissions: by emitting one more unit, there is a cost savings to each of the firms. The right panel shows exactly the same thing, except from the point of view of abatement and the marginal cost of abatement. With no pollution regulations, there will be no abatement and emissions will be at the point where marginal savings is zero: $\bar{E}_T$ for Tucker Tools and $\bar{E}_R$ for Riley Wreckers.

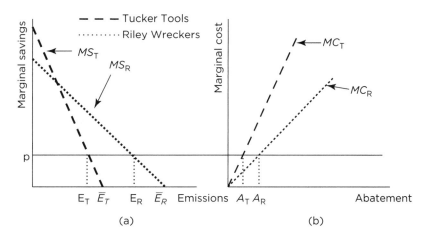

FIGURE 12.1 Firm choice of emissions/abatement when faced with emission fee, p.

With an emission fee equal to p, the two firms cut back on emissions (increase abatement) to the points E_T and E_R (respectively, A_T and A_R) for the two firms. Firms operate where the marginal cost of abatement/marginal savings from pollution is exactly equal to the emissions fee.

One of the bonuses of an emissions fee is that the equimarginal principle automatically holds. Because the two firms face the same emission fee, they will both set their marginal cost of abatement to the same number and thus marginal costs will be equalized between the two firms (or among any number of firms facing the same emissions fee).

The London Congestion Charge

One of the most successful applications of an environmental charge is the charge on automobiles in the centers of congested cities. And one of the most prominent of these is the charge in London, England. Although not a charge on emissions, the congestion charge is still a good example of the use of a tax or fee to correct an externality.

By the 1990s the speed of travel in central London was slower than it was in 1900, before the advent of the automobile. In 2002 the average daytime speed was less than 15 km/hr, compared to more than twice that speed in the less congested night time. In order to address this problem, in 2003 a charge of £5/day (raised to £8/day in 2005) was levied on all vehicles traveling or parking in central London during the day, excluding weekends and holidays. The charge is collected by voluntary payment of the charge by motorists, accompanied by enforcement using cameras and computers that read license plates. Enforcement is only 85% or so effective, yet the £100 penalty for scofflaws is sufficient for the system to work.

Although paying the charge is not popular (a similar system has been proposed for New York but has faced political opposition), a significant reduction in congestion has been achieved. Private car travel in central London is down by a third and daytime travel speeds have increased 20%.

(Source: Leape, 2006.)

II. PIGOVIAN FEES

As was mentioned at the beginning of the chapter, approximately a century ago the English economist Arthur C. Pigou argued for the imposition of taxes on generators of pollution. The Pigovian fee, as it has come to be called, is a special kind of emissions fee—an emission fee that is set at the marginal damage of pollution in an attempt to restore Pareto optimality to a situation of market failure:

DEFINITION *A Pigovian fee is an emission fee exactly equal to the aggregate marginal damage caused by the emissions when evaluated at the efficient level of pollution.*

We examine this definition in more detail, first for the case of a single polluter and then for the case of multiple polluters. In both cases, there are multiple victims of the pollution.

A. A Single Polluter

Suppose we have a factory generating pollution in the amount x at a cost $C(x)$, with marginal costs, $MC(x)$. Since costs decline as x is increased, marginal costs are actually negative. Another way of thinking about this is in terms of marginal savings—the savings from emitting one more unit of pollution. Of course the marginal savings is the negative of the marginal costs: $MS(x) = -MC(x)$. As in the case of an emission fee, this is exactly the same as the marginal cost of abatement.

Further assume there are N people surrounding the factory and that pollution causes damage. For the time being, assume that people cannot use locational choice to change the amount of pollution they face. Thus there is nothing a person can do to reduce his or her exposure, short of getting the factory to cut back. For person i, the damage from pollution is $D_i(x)$, which is positive and increases in x. There are several other ways of interpreting this damage. We could also say that person i benefits from the pollution in the amount $B_i(x)$ with benefits negative and decreasing in x. Or, we could say that $D_i(x)$ is the willingness to pay to eliminate the pollution. Total damages are given by

$$D(x) = \Sigma_i D_i(x) \tag{12.3}$$

The efficient amount of pollution is the amount that minimizes total costs and damages:

$$x^* \text{ minimizes } \{C(x) + D(x)\} \tag{12.4a}$$

We know that something is minimized when its marginal is zero. Further, the marginal of a sum is equal to the sum of the marginals. Thus we can set the marginal of the quantity in braces in Eq. (12.4a) to zero:

$$MC(x^*) + MD(x^*) = 0 \tag{12.4b}$$

Substituting the marginal version of Eq. (12.3) into Eq. (12.4b) and recognizing that marginal savings is the negative of marginal cost, we obtain

$$MS(x^*) = \Sigma_i MD_i(x^*) \tag{12.4c}$$

In other words, we seek a level of pollution such that the marginal savings to the firm from pollution $(-MC)$ is equal to the marginal damage from pollution over the entire population. Since pollution is a public bad, the aggregate marginal damage (MD) is the vertical sum of the individual marginal damages (MD_i).

This situation is illustrated in Figure 12.2 for the case of one polluter and two victims of the pollution. Shown in the lower half of the figure is the marginal cost of pollution. Note that this is negative since every extra unit of pollution the factory is allowed to emit lowers total costs for the factory (up to a limit of course). The marginal savings to the factory is the negative of this and is shown in the first (upper) quadrant. As the factory increases pollution from no emissions at all, savings are initially quite high. When emissions are relatively large, the savings from emitting a little more are much smaller. Thus $MS(x)$ is downward sloping.

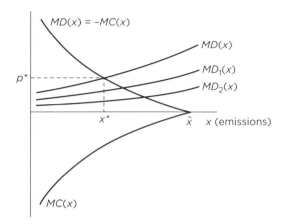

FIGURE 12.2 Pigovian fee on pollutant emissions with two victims of pollution. $MD_1(x)$, marginal damage to victim 1; $MD_2(x)$, marginal damage to victim 2; $MD(x)$, aggregate marginal damage; $MC(x)$, marginal cost of emitting for the polluter; $MS(x)$, marginal savings from emitting for the polluter; $\hat{X}$, pollution levels with no regulation; x^*, efficient amount of emissions; p^*, Pigovian fee.

Also shown in Figure 12.2 are the marginal damage functions for the two victims of the pollution: $MD_i(x)$. Marginal damage is the negative of the demand function for pollution for each of the individuals. Each of the marginal damage schedules is upward sloping. When pollution levels are small, one more unit of pollution causes little damage. When pollution levels are higher, that extra unit causes more damage. Since the pollution is a public bad, aggregate marginal damage, like aggregate demand, is the vertical sum of individual marginal damages. This is also shown in the figure [$MD(x)$]. The optimal amount of pollution is the x for which $MD(x) = MS(x)$, shown as x^* in Figure 12.2. Also shown in Figure 12.2 is the Pigovian fee, p^*. If the polluter is charged p^* per unit of pollution, the polluter basically sees pollution as priced at p^* and thus the polluter will pollute so that price equals marginal cost:

$$MC(x^*) = -p^* \text{ or } MS(x^*) = p^* \tag{12.5}$$

The total amount of money the firm pays for the pollution is p^*x^*.

Note that the Pigovian fee is defined as the marginal savings from pollution generation *at the optimal level of pollution*. If we are not at the optimum, the Pigovian fee will be neither the current marginal cost of pollution control nor the marginal damage from pollution. Thus the Pigovian fee is not any emission fee; it is the marginal savings from pollution at the optimal pollution level.

B. Multiple Polluters

We have seen how a Pigovian fee can generate the efficient amount of a public bad. The case we have looked at involves a single polluter. Suppose we have more than one polluter. For the time being, assume we have two polluters. Figure 12.3 illustrates the case for two polluters in which the marginal damage function *(MD)* is the aggregate damage to all consumers. Shown is the marginal savings to each of two firms from generating pollution. How much pollution should each firm generate and how should the Pigovian fee be set to support that level of pollution?

An aggregate marginal savings function for a group of polluters indicates what the marginal savings will be if the total amount of pollution increases by one unit. This

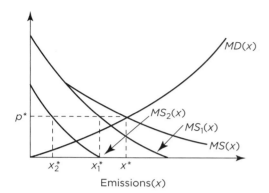

FIGURE 12.3 The case of two polluters. $MS_1(x)$, marginal savings from emitting firm 1; $MS_2(x)$, marginal savings from emitting firm 2; $MS(x)$, aggregate marginal savings from emitting; $MD(x)$, marginal damage from emitting; p^*, Pigovian fee; x^*, total amount of emissions with Pigovian fee; x_1^*, emissions from firm 1 with Pigovian fee; x_2^*, emissions from firm 2 with Pigovian fee.

depends, of course, on what assumptions are being made about how the total amount of pollution is distributed among the individual polluters. If one polluter is doing all of the pollution control and all other polluters are doing none, the marginal savings will be higher than if the pollution control were more "evenly" distributed among the polluters. One way of avoiding this ambiguity is to assume the polluters are sharing the obligation of pollution abatement in an efficient or least-cost manner. The logical (and cost-minimizing) way of apportioning the abatement responsibility is to equate marginal cost of abatement (marginal savings of emitting) among the firms. As we saw in Chapter 4, the equimarginal principle calls for the equalizing of marginal costs.

Numerical Example:
Suppose the two marginal savings functions in Figure 12.3 are given by:

$$MS_1(x_1) = 10 - 2x_1 \qquad (12.6a)$$
$$MS_2(x_2) = 5 - 3x_2 \qquad (12.6b)$$

To construct an aggregate marginal savings function, first solve each of these for emissions:

$$x_1 = (10 - MS_1)/2 \qquad (12.7a)$$
$$x_2 = (5 - MS_2)/3 \qquad (12.7b)$$

We now ask what is the total emissions ($X = x_1 + x_2$) for any given MS? By inserting MS into Eqs (12.7) and then summing the two equations one obtains:

$$X = (10 - MS)/2 + (5 - MS)/3 \qquad (12.8a)$$

Which, with a little manipulation, becomes

$$MS = 8 - 1.2X \qquad (12.8b)$$

The exact same approach would be taken in constructing an aggregate marginal abatement cost curve.

Returning to Figure 12.3, how do we aggregate the two marginal savings functions to obtain an aggregate? The aggregate marginal savings function is found by horizontally summing the marginal savings for the two firms.[3] The aggregate marginal savings curve is the curve that indicates for a particular pollution price, how much pollution each firm would generate. This is the standard way of generating an industry marginal cost function from firm-level marginal cost functions. Thus for any level of the fee, $MS(x)$ tells us how much x in total will be emitted and each $MS_i(x)$ tells us how much each firm will contribute to that total. We have constructed $MS(x)$ in such a way that the amount of pollution from each firm will sum to the total.

In Figure 12.3, to determine the efficient amount of pollution, we note where the marginal savings curve *(MS)* intersects the marginal damage curve *(MD)*. That determines the optimal amount of pollution (x^*) and the marginal savings to polluters at x^*: p^*. Thus p^* is the correct Pigovian fee. This is shown in Figure 12.3. At that fee level, firm 1 will generate x_1^* and firm 2 will generate x_2^*. Note that each firm operates so that marginal savings from polluting is set equal to the Pigovian fee:

$$MS_i(x_i^*) = p^* \tag{12.9}$$

Furthermore, by the way in which $MS(x)$ was constructed,

$$MS(x^*) = p^* \tag{12.10}$$

Equation (12.9) illustrates one of the primary virtues of the Pigovian fee: all firms will control pollution at the same level of marginal costs. Marginal costs of pollution control will be equated across all polluters. Firms with different pollution control costs receive the correct signals regarding how much pollution to generate. Those with high control costs will control relatively less than firms with lower control costs.

III. FEES VERSUS SUBSIDIES

The notion that the source or cause of a pollution problem should pay for cleaning up the problem rings true to most people. In many parts of the world, it is institutionalized in the *polluter pays principle*. But a logical question arises: is it possible to obtain the same outcome by subsidizing firms to reduce pollution? In the "real" world, is there any danger in providing tax breaks and other subsidies for pollution control, rather than making polluters pay for the pollution they generate? Is it possible to obtain efficiency using a subsidy instead of a fee? This is an important question since subsidies are usually much more politically popular than taxes or fees.

The answer to this is that these two approaches yield different outcomes.[4] The tax is efficient, whereas the subsidy can result in too many firms in the industry and thus an inefficient amount of both pollution and the good associated with the pollution. We will consider two cases. The first is for the short run—there is no time for new firms to enter the industry. The second is for the long run—there is time for entry and exit (although exit in the sense of shut-down is always possible, even in the short run).

A. The Short Run

Let us consider a competitive industry, producing some good in conjunction with pollution. Initially, assume all of the firms in the industry are identical. Under a pollution tax (t), the production costs of a typical firm would be

$$C_T(y,e) = V(y,e) + t\,e + FC \tag{12.11}$$

where y is the amount of the good being produced, e is emissions, $V(y,e)$ represents variable production costs for producing e and y, and FC is the fixed cost of production. To simplify things, suppose there is a fixed relation between output and emissions—the more you produce, the more you pollute. In particular, suppose emissions are related to output by $e = ay$ where a is a constant. We can rewrite Eq. (12.11) as

$$C_T(y,ay) = V(y,ay) + tay + FC \tag{12.12a}$$

Recognizing that V and C_T are now functions of y only, we let $TC(y) = C_T(y,ay)$ and $VC(y) = V(y,ay)$ and rewrite Eq. (12.12a) as

$$TC(y) = VC(y) + tay + FC \tag{12.12b}$$

This means that marginal production costs are

$$MC(y) = MVC(y) + at \tag{12.13}$$

So basically, marginal costs are increased by at.

Now consider what happens with a subsidy, s. With no attention to pollution control, a firm might pollute at the level $\hat{e}$. With a subsidy, the firm will be paid to reduce emissions. If the firm reduces emissions to e, the subsidy payment will be $s(\hat{e}-e)$. This means that costs will be

$$TC(y) = VC(y) + FC - s(\hat{e} - e) \tag{12.14}$$
$$= VC(y) + say + \{FC - s\hat{e}\}$$

Note that the term in braces is a fixed cost, consisting of the standard fixed cost plus a lump-sum transfer of $s\hat{e}$ that is independent of the firm's choice of y or e. Thus the variable costs in both cases [Eqs. (12.12b) and (12.12)] are exactly the same. Only the fixed costs are different. Consequently the short-run marginal costs of production will be identical in the two cases and the firm will produce exactly the same amount of pollution and the good. In fact, the marginal costs from Eq. (12.14) are

$$MC(y) = MVC(y) + as \tag{12.15}$$

which is exactly the same as Eq. (12.13) except we have an s here instead of a t.

Consequently, our first result is that in the case of identical firms in the short run, Pigovian fees and subsidies yield exactly the same outcome. We should note that this result applies even if there is a more complex relationship between output and emissions than the fixed ratio assumed here. Showing that is more cumbersome mathematically so we omit it here.

We now turn to an industry with heterogeneous firms. This may be because of different technologies used by different firms due, for instance, to their different ages. This case is best understood graphically. Suppose we have an industry composed of two classes of firms, old firms and new firms. Newer firms may have higher fixed costs but lower variable costs. We are concerned with industry behavior in the short run under Pigovian fees and subsidies. Since this is the short run, no new firms may enter. Any firm may, however, choose to produce nothing, shutting down. If a firm produces nothing, the subsidy disappears. In other words, we only pay firms to produce less pollution. We do not continue to pay firms if they decide to go out of business.

Figure 12.4 shows the marginal cost curves and average variable costs for these two types of firms. Since this is a short-run analysis, we are not concerned with total costs. The issue is whether prices cover average variable costs and, if they do, production will be at marginal cost equals price. As we saw above, the effect of a tax on marginal cost is identical to the effect of a subsidy on marginal cost—both raise marginal costs relative to the unregulated case. The U subscripts in the figure correspond to average variable cost *(AVC)* and marginal cost *(MC)* in the unregulated, pretax, or presubsidy case. The T and S subscripts refer to the case of a Pigovian tax or subsidy, respectively.

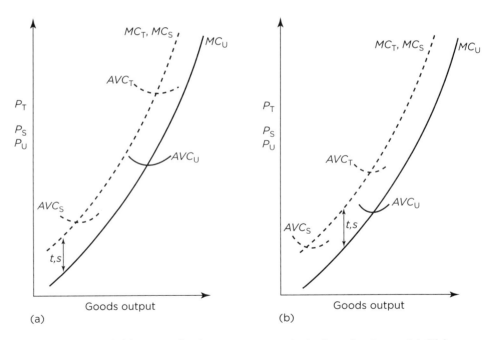

FIGURE 12.4 Variable costs for heterogeneous industry, short run. (a) Old firms; (b) newer firms, MC_U marginal cost unregulated case; MC_S, marginal cost, with emission control subsidy; MC_T, marginal cost, with emission fee; AVC_U, average variable cost, unregulated case; AVC_S, average variable cost, with emission control subsidy; AVC_T, average variable cost, with emission fee; p_U, goods price, unregulated case; p_S, goods price, with emission control subsidy; p_T, goods price, with emission fee.

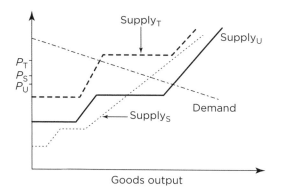

FIGURE 12.5 Short-run supply and demand, heterogeneous industry, with and without taxes and subsidies. Supply$_U$, goods supply, unregulated case; Supply$_S$, goods supply, with emission control subsidy; Supply$_T$, goods supply, with emission fee; demand, goods demand; p_U, goods price, unregulated case; p_S, goods price, with emission control subsidy; p_T, goods price, with emission fee.

Note in Figure 12.4 that although the tax and the subsidy raise the marginal costs by the same amount, the subsidy lowers average variable cost whereas the tax raises average variable cost. The reason is that we have assumed the subsidy applies only if the firm is operating. The lump sum $s\hat{e}$ in Eq. (12.14) goes away if the firm shuts down. Thus it counts as a variable cost. Fixed costs (FC) are incurred whether or not the firm shuts down (in the short run).

Now we turn to determining what the market price of the good might be under these three regimes. Figure 12.5 traces out the short-run supply functions for this industry for the three cases, unregulated, Pigovian taxes, and subsidies. Also shown is a typical demand function for the good. Recall that firms will operate on the portion of their marginal cost curve that lies above the average variable cost. We can see that with both the unregulated and subsidy cases, both types of firms are operating, yielding product prices of p_U and p_s, respectively. In the case of the Pigovian tax, only the newer firms operate, yielding product price p_X. These prices are shown on Figure 12.4. Note that all prices are above average variable costs for the newer firms, which is why they operate in all three cases. However, for the old firms, p_T is below AVC_T, the average variable cost for the Pigovian tax case. This is why the old firms shut down in this case.

Our conclusions are that taxes and subsidies have different effects in the short run. A subsidy may allow firms to continue operating that would not continue in the case of a tax. Which is efficient? The subsidy requires a lump-sum transfer, which has to be obtained from somewhere. Even more important, the subsidy involves the operation of firms that are really losing money (negative profits). This is not efficient.

B. The Long Run

We now turn to the case of the long-run effects of Pigovian taxes and subsidies. We saw in Eq. (12.12)–(12.15) that the effect of a tax or subsidy was to raise marginal costs, but that a subsidy lowered average costs while a tax raised average costs. This applies in the short run as well as in the long run. If we assume a constant-cost industry, all firms will operate at the bottom of their average total cost curve, in long-run equilibrium. Thus the supply schedules for the industry will be horizontal and as shown in Figure 12.6b. The result of this is that goods prices will be higher with a Pigovian tax than with a subsidy. Furthermore, there will be more firms in the industry with a subsidy than with a Pigovian tax.

Other than the fact that a subsidy has to come from somewhere, a subsidy is undesirable because it does not allow the market to communicate the true costs of the product

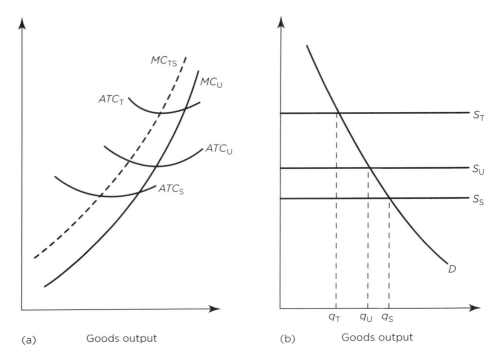

FIGURE 12.6 Long-run supply and demand, constant cost industry, with and without taxes and subsidies. MC_U, marginal cost, unregulated case; MC_T, marginal cost, with emission control subsidy or emission fee; ATC_U, average total cost, unregulated case; ATC_S, average total cost, with emission control subsidy; ATC_T, average total cost, with emision fee; D, goods demand; S_U, long-run supply of good, unregulated case; S_S, long-run supply of goods, with emission control subsidy; S_T, long-run supply of goods, with emission fee; q_U equilibrium goods output, unregulated case; q_S, equilibrium goods output, with emission control subsidy; $(q_T$, equilibrium goods output, with emission fee.

being consumed to the consumer. To be quite concrete, suppose we are dealing with paper mills producing paper from trees and polluting rivers at the same time (virgin mills). Other mills produce paper from recycled products and we will assume they are pollution free (which is not actually the case). A pollution subsidy to clean up the virgin mills will make virgin paper more attractive (compared to recycled paper) than if the virgin paper manufacturer had to pay a pollution tax. The result is that a subsidy results in the overuse of trees and underuse of recycled paper, compared to the case of a Pigovian tax. If a product generates pollution, we want consumers to see the full costs associated with producing that product when the consumers decide what to buy and how much to buy.

IV. IMPERFECT COMPETITION

When markets are not competitive, a host of efficiency problems generally arise, and controlling pollution is no exception. There are two cases we will consider. One concerns a monopolist in some goods market who is also a polluter. For instance, the monopolist may dominate the steel market while also generating smoke. The second case is more likely: a firm that is the only producer of smoke in some appropriate region. In this case we have a monopoly, but a monopoly in the provision of the bad.

The general conclusion that results from the analysis is that when there is market power, an emmisions fee can make matters worse. This is a result in what economists call the theory of "second best." When there is a distortion in an economy, such as monopoly, levels of output and prices will be distorted—not at their efficient levels. In such a case, the best way to correct inefficiencies such as pollution will not be to blindly use prescriptions from theory developed for efficiency. Other, "second best" methods must be used to correct the problems. This is a large area of study in economics. We will consider only the example of monopolists and monopsonists generating pollution.

A. Monopolist in the Goods Market

Assume the steel industry is a monopoly and it produces smoke.[5] There are many smoke producers but only one producer of steel. For simplicity we will assume, as in the previous section, that smoke and steel output are proportional. We know from intermediate microeconomics what the steel mill should do. This is illustrated in Figure 12.7. Shown in Figure 12.7 is a typical demand curve for steel and the associated marginal revenue function. Also shown is the marginal cost of producing steel, ignoring pollution, MC_U, and the marginal social cost of producing steel, including pollution, MC_T. The producer will produce where marginal costs equal marginal revenue, at S_U, and price on the demand curve. Conventional analysis would call for computing the inefficiency (the deadweight loss) as the sum of the hatched and solid portions of Figure 12.7. But pollution is being generated. Taking into account the social costs of steel production, the optimal amount of steel production would be S^*. So, in actual fact, the deadweight loss (inefficiency) associated with the unregulated output of steel is just the solid area in Figure 12.7. This is the area between the true marginal cost function (MC_T) and the demand curve, bounded by S_U and S^*. This is smaller than when we used MC_U instead of MC_T. The reason is that when an unregulated monopolist reduces output to increase profits, it also reduces pollution.

FIGURE 12.7 Imposing a Pigovian fee on a goods monopolist. MC_U, marginal private cost of producing steel; MC_T, marginal social cost of producing steel; D, demand for steel; MR, marginal revenue for steel; S_U, steel output level, unregulated; S_T, steel output level with Pigovian tax; S^*, socially optimal output of steel.

Suppose we impose an emissions fee on the smoke generation, raising the private marginal cost of producing steel to MC_T. The monopolist will not keep producing at S_U, but will produce where the new marginal cost function equals marginal revenue, at S_T. Now the inefficiency is the sum of the shaded and solid areas in Figure 12.7. The imposition of the emissions fee has made matters worse!

The intuition behind this is quite simple. Efficiency is not served if there is too much or too little pollution. Monopoly tends to reduce output and emissions, assuming there is no intervention. If an emissions fee is also imposed, output is restricted even further. Now we have much too little goods output and somewhat smaller smoke output than desirable. The emissions fee has overdone it.

B. Monopolist in Bads Production

The second case we consider is that of a firm that is competitive in its goods output market but is the sole supplier of pollution. This is a remarkably common situation. Consider the company town with one large producer of pollution. Since the pollution has relatively local effects, not spilling over to the next town, this firm is the monopolistic provider of pollution.

This situation is illustrated in Figure 12.8. We focus on the output of smoke since the goods market is competitive. Shown in Figure 12.8 is the marginal savings (MS) to the firm from producing smoke levels s. Also shown is the marginal damage to the populace (MD) from smoke. The enlightened population of the town where the polluter is decides to impose a pollution tax equal to marginal damage from the smoke. But rather than set the tax equal to marginal damage at s^*, they set the tax to $MD(s)$, at whatever level of s prevails. Because the polluter sees a slope to the marginal damage function, it knows it can lower its emission tax by reducing its emissions. True, this will cost the firm something in terms of increased abatement costs, but this is a trade-off the firm may be willing to take. This is very similar to a monopsonist consciously using less of an input (such as labor) in order to drive down the price of the input, even though production costs in other respects will be higher.

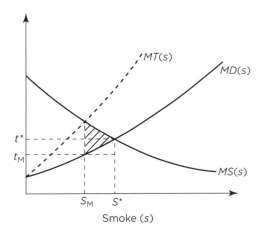

FIGURE 12.8 Monopolist in provision of pollution. *MS,* marginal savings from polluting; *MD,* marginal damage from polluting; *MT,* marginal emission fee payments; t^*, Pigovian fee; t_m, monopoly emission fee level; s^*, efficient amount of smoke; s_m, monopoly emissions of smoke.

To see how this works, note that the tax payment by the firm is

$$T(s) = s\, MD(s) \tag{12.16}$$

As is always the case, the firm wants to produce where marginal cost (i.e., marginal tax payments) equals marginal revenue (i.e., marginal savings from polluting). To compute marginal tax payments for some level of smoke, s, we start with total tax payments and purturb s a bit, by Δs. Total tax payments will also change:

$$T(s + \Delta s) = (s + \Delta s)\, MD(s + \Delta s) \tag{12.17}$$

The marginal tax payments will be the ratio of the change in taxes to the change in smoke levels:

$$
\begin{aligned}
MT(s) &= \frac{T(s + \Delta s) - T(s)}{\Delta s} = \frac{(s + \Delta s)\, MD\,(s + \Delta s) - s\, MD\,(s)}{\Delta s} \\
&= s\, \{[MD(s + \Delta s) - MD(s)]/\Delta s\} + MD(s + \Delta s) \\
&= s\, MMD(s) + MD\,(s + \Delta s) \\
&\approx s\, MMD(s) + MD(s)
\end{aligned}
\tag{12.18a}
$$

which can be more simply written using calculus:

$$MT(s) = dT(s)/ds = d[s\, MD(s)]/ds = s\, dMD(s)/ds + MD(s) \tag{12.18b}$$

The $MMD(s)$ in Eq. (12.8a) is the *marginal* marginal damage of smoke, i.e., how much marginal damage changes for a small change in smoke levels. Since $MD(s)$ is getting larger as s gets larger in Figure 12.8, $MMD(s)$ is positive. Also, the last approximate equality ($\approx$) in Eq. (12.18) applies if Δs is very small so that s and $s + \Delta s$ are virtually the same.

Note from Eq. (12.18) that the marginal tax payment is in excess of the marginal damage. If the firm generates one more unit of smoke, tax payments go up because the firm has to pay $MD(s)$ for that extra unit of smoke. But also, the tax rate goes up by a little, which means payments for all smoke, not just the last unit, go up a bit. Consequently the total tax bill goes up by more that just $MD(s)$. The discussion is exactly equivalent to why marginal revenue for a monopolist in a goods market is lower than price. As monopolists expand output by one unit, they gain the revenue for that unit (which is the price) but the price goes up a bit for all the units they are still selling. This is why marginal revenue is less than price.

Now the rational smoke monopolist will produce where the marginal tax payments equal the marginal savings from polluting, namely s_M in Figure 12.8. Efficiency would call for smoke levels of s^*. The firm is underpolluting. At s^* the emission fee would be t^*. However, the smoke monopolist has managed to drive the emission fee down to t_M. The deadweight loss associated with this is the shaded area in Figure 12.8.

To summarize, the monopolist provider of pollution can manipulate the emission tax by reducing pollution below the efficient level. It is tempting to say that this outcome is fine. We have less pollution than otherwise, which cannot be too bad. However, it is important to realize that too little pollution may mean too many resources are devoted to pollution control. Those resources are being diverted from other socially desirable purposes.

V. THE DOUBLE DIVIDEND

Governments must raise revenue. Unfortunately, most taxes tend to introduce inefficiencies and distortions into the economy. A labor tax (wage income tax) makes labor more expensive and thus discourages work. A capital tax makes capital more expensive and thus discourages investment. A number of authors have tried to measure the inefficiencies associated with taxation. Edgar Browning (1987) estimates that the last dollar collected through wage taxation in the United States has an additional welfare loss of approximately 40¢.[6] In other words, at the margin, the inefficiencies of such taxation run 40% of revenues collected—it costs $1.40 to raise $1 more of revenue.

In recent years, there have been a number of proposals to substitute pollution taxes for more traditional revenue raising taxes, such as income taxes. The general idea is that these "green taxes" would be revenue-neutral. Any income generated by the taxes would be offset by lost income from reductions in labor (income) taxes or other taxes. The idea is that such taxes would not only reduce pollution but would also reduce the distortions associated with existing taxes—a "double dividend." This policy suggestion has prompted an examination of the efficiencies of pollution taxes when there are preexisting distortions.[7] Consider the case of a competitive economy where distortionary taxes exist (such an income tax). Now suppose there is a polluting industry and the government levies an emission fee on that industry. What happens? Pollution goes down (this is a benefit); revenue comes in, which we use to offset distortionary labor income (this is a benefit); deadweight loss from the income tax increases from interactions between the emission fee and the income tax (this is a loss). This third interaction effect is not at all obvious, and we explore it further in the following paragraphs. So the double dividend has morphed a bit.

There are a number of implications of this result. One is that the net benefit of the emission tax (the sum of the three effects) may be smaller than just the gain from the reduction in environmental damage (i.e., the sum of terms two and three may be a cost, not a benefit). Another implication is that if an environmental regulation is used that does not generate any revenue (such as prescriptive regulations or freely distributed tradable permits), then only the first and third terms count—the net benefits will be lower than with a pollution tax.

These are classic results in what is known as the theory of second best. What is advisable in an economy without distortions is not necessarily a good idea when there are distortions, even in apparently unrelated parts of the economy.

To see this result, we start with a representative consumer who chooses how much labor, L, to provide (in exchange for a wage, w) and how much of a polluting good to consume, X. A polluting good means that pollution is generated when the good is produced. Suppose there is a tax on wages, t_L (which, for simplicity, assume the firm pays). With this tax on labor, a certain amount of labor *is* provided, L^*. With a lower tax, employers could pay more and thus more labor would be supplied; with a higher tax, less labor would be supplied. Figure 12.9a shows a supply curve for labor and a horizontal demand curve set at the value marginal product of labor (assumed constant). We see that the labor tax lowers the amount of labor supplied to L^*. We can also look at this in terms of demand for leisure, since workers divide their total time into labor and leisure. A tax on labor is the same as a subsidy to leisure. The higher the wage tax, the greater the subsidy to leisure and the more leisure will be provided (less labor). This is shown in Figure 12.9b,

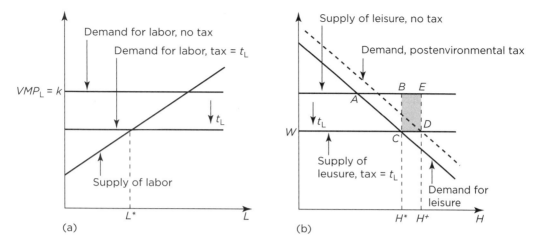

FIGURE 12.9 (a,b) Effect on leisure from environmental tax. VMP_L, value of marginal product of labor; t_L, tax on labor; w, wage rate; H^*,L^*, supply of leisure and labor with $t_x = 0$; t_x, tax on X; H^+, quantity of leisure with $t_x > 0$; $BCDE$, wage tax revenue loss from $t_x > 0$.

where H^* is the amount of leisure that will be consumed when the labor tax is t_L (ignore the broken line and the shaded area for the time being). Without the tax on labor, there would be more labor and less leisure. The deadweight loss from the labor tax is shown in Figure 12.9b as the triangle ABC. Thus to raise revenue $t_L L^*$, a deadweight loss of ABC is incurred.[8] Define V as the marginal deadweight loss, i.e., the deadweight loss that would be incurred to raise one more dollar of revenue when the tax rate is set at t_L.

Now consider demand for a polluting good, i.e., a good whose manufacture generates pollution. Figure 12.10 shows a typical demand curve for the good, as well as a marginal private cost curve and a marginal social cost curve that includes the damage from pollution. Without any intervention, the amount of the good produced is X^*. Now suppose we wish to reduce the amount of this good produced. This may be accomplished by taxing the production of the good (or the production of pollution) or simply by command and control, directing the firm to reduce pollution and thus incur additional production costs. In either case, assume marginal costs are increased by an amount t_x and the output is reduced from X^* to X^+. This is shown in Figure 12.10. If tax revenues result, then labor taxes will be reduced to keep the total government revenues constant.

The increased price of X has an effect on the demand for leisure. In general, we would expect X and leisure to be substitutes.[9] Thus an increase in the price of X will shift the demand for leisure outward, as shown by the broken line in Figure 12.9b. This results in an increase in the quantity of leisure to H^+. The amount of this shift can be computed from the cross-price elasticity of demand for leisure with respect to the price of good X:

$$\eta_{HX} \equiv (\Delta H/H)/(\Delta p_X/p_X) = [(H^+ - H^*)/ \Delta p_X] (p_X / H^*) \tag{12.19}$$

In Eq. (12.19), η_{hx} indicates how much the demand for leisure changes when the price of X changes. This is the cross-price elasticity of demand for leisure with respect to the price of X. For a substitute, this will be positive.

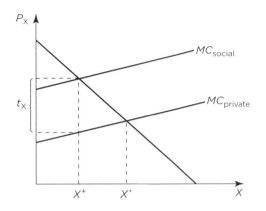

FIGURE 12.10 Supply and demand of polluting good. MC_{social}, marginal costs of producing X, including pollution damage; $MC_{private}$, marginal costs of producing X, excluding pollution damage; X^*, production without internalizing externality; t_X, product tax necessary to internalize externality; X^+, production with tax t_X.

We see from Figure 12.9b that the reduction in X has increased the quantity of leisure and thus decreased tax revenues by the shaded area in Figure 12.9b. The area of this shaded area is $(H^+ - H^*) t_L$. This loss must be made up and every dollar that is raised through labor taxation actually costs society $1 + V$. Thus [using Eq. 12.19] the indirect loss from the environmental controls on X is

$$IE = (1 + V)(H^+ - H^*) t_L = (1 + V) t_L \, \Delta p_X \, \eta_{HX} \, H^*/p_X \qquad (12.20)$$

This is termed the "tax interaction" effect *(IE)*. Though IE in Eq. (12.20) is positive, remember that it is a loss. The tax interaction effect is the extra inefficiency from a pollution regulation due to the fact that labor is already taxed. Note that if the labor tax rate is zero ($t_L = 0$), the tax interaction effect is zero. Furthermore, the greater the value of η_{HX}, the larger the effect. Basically, what is happening is that the pollution tax is generating a deadweight loss by marginally changing the very significant preexisting deadweight loss associated with labor taxation.

Although *IE* is unequivocally a welfare loss (provided the good is a substitute for leisure), there are two welfare gains that are possible from pollution regulation. The most obvious one is the reduction in damage associated with the pollution. Less pollution means less damage. Term this the Pigoevian effect *(PE)*. In the context of the double dividend debate, suppose any tax revenue raised by the pollution tax is offset by a reduction in labor tax. Call this the revenue recycling effect *(RE)*. In the context of Figure 12.10, clearly

$$RE = V \, t_X X^+ \qquad (12.21)$$

The revenue raised is $t_X X^+$, which is used to offset labor taxes that have a marginal deadweight loss to revenue ratio of V. It is clearly positive—a gain. Note, however, that if no revenues are raised through the environmental regulation, RE is zero. If the regulation is prescriptive, no revenue is raised. If the regulation is marketable permits for pollution, then revenue is raised if the permits are initially auctioned. If the permits are given away initially (as is often the case), then $RE = 0$.

To summarize, we conventionally think of the Pigoevian effect *(PE)* as the primary gain from a pollution control regulation. We have just seen that if pollution tax revenues can be used to reduce distortionary taxes, we have a bonus of the revenue recycling effect *(RE)*. But we have also seen that reducing pollution will generate a loss through the indirect effect on preexisting distortionary taxes *(IE)*. The big question is, how big a problem is this tax-interaction effect? That question is empirical. Using a very simple model and typical parameter values for the United States, Parry (1995) calculates that the optimal pollution tax should be 63% of marginal damage (not equal to marginal damage as suggested by conventional wisdom).

The lesson to be learned is that pollution regulation can result in significant indirect costs due to preexisting tax distortions in the economy. Much of this distortion can be eliminated if pollution taxation raises revenue, which is used to offset the preexisting distortion. Without revenue recycling, only much weaker environmental regulations are justified on efficiency grounds.

It might seem that it is "unfair" to have the environment bear the cost of the inefficiency introduced by the wage tax. But this is not really the correct interpretation of the result. In fact, in this sort of second-best environment, it is difficult to interpret what is happening with the emission tax without looking at the distortions throughout the economy introduced by the income tax. For instance, if the polluting good and leisure are substitutes as assumed, the subsidy to leisure may already have reduced consumption of the polluting good in the economy. Thus we do not need to reduce it as much with the emission tax. In fact, it has been shown that when there are no commodity taxes and an optimal income tax, it can be welfare improving to subsidize the consumption of goods that are substitutes for leisure.[10] Although we have made no assumption that the income tax is optimal, if it were and there were no tax or subsidy on the polluting good, the optimal action would be to simultaneously tax the polluting good at the full marginal damage but then add a subsidy to account for the distortions of the income tax. The net effect is that the tax on the polluting good is less than marginal damage.

SUMMARY

1. An emission fee or tax is a charge per unit of emissions levied by a regulator on a polluter.

2. A Pigovian fee is an emission fee set equal to the marginal damage of pollution, at the efficient level of pollution generation.

3. An emissions fee is levied by the government, which collects the fee revenue. The fee generally induces provision of an efficient amount of pollution.

4. With multiple polluters, efficiency in pollution control requires that the marginal cost of control be the same for all polluters, provided the emissions from each polluter contribute to damage in the same way. This is the equimarginal principle.

5. In comparing a subsidy for pollution control with a tax on pollutant emissions, both result in the same marginal conditions for pollution emissions. However, the subsidy results in excess production in the polluting industry, in both the short and long run.

6. If a monopolist is the sole producer of a good in a market and also pollutes as a by-product of goods production, an emission fee can make matters worse. An emission fee will raise costs of production and thus reduce output of the monopolized good even more, which increases the inefficiency associated with monopoly.

7. With a monopolist in pollution production, if an emission fee is set equal to marginal damage, the monopolist will drive the fee down below the level of a Pigovian fee and reduce emissions below the efficient level.

8. The "double dividend" refers to the possibility that imposing a revenue-neutral tax on pollution will have have two effects: (a) reduce pollution and thus pollution damage (the Pigouvian effect) and (b) reduce distortionary taxes on labor and thus the deadweight loss associated with those taxes (the revenue recycling effect). There is a third effect that acts in the opposite direction, the tax interaction effect.

9. When pollution is reduced, the demand curve for leisure is shifted outward (if the polluting good and leisure are substitutes). If labor is taxed, this shift will generate an additional deadweight loss that must be attributed to the reduction in pollution. This is the tax interaction effect.

10. A tax on pollution increases welfare through the Pigouvian effect and the revenue recycling effect but reduces welfare through the tax interaction effect.

11. The size of the tax interaction effect is an empirical question and will vary from one polluting industry to another. Ian Parry calculates that a pollution tax should be set at 63% of marginal damage to account for the tax interaction effect.

PROBLEMS

1. In Section IV,B does the problem of monopoly provision of a bad arise with a true Pigovian fee? Why?

2. Consider the case of a rival bad. Would efficiency require that a Pigovian fee be levied on the producer of the bad and the receipts given to the consumers as compensation? Does it matter if the bad is excludable or nonexcludable?

3. It is possible to show that the marginal welfare loss from a labor tax is $V = t_L \varepsilon / [w - t_L \varepsilon]$ where ε is the labor supply elasticity evaluated at the net of tax wage received by the consumer, w. Using this, show that the absolute value of the ratio of the tax interaction effect to the revenue recycling effect is given by $IE/RE = (X^*/X^+) (\eta_{hx}/ \varepsilon)$ where η_{hx} is the price elasticity of demand for good X with respect to the wage rate. Assume elasticities are compensated elasticities. If on average we expect $\eta_{hx} = \varepsilon$, what can you conclude about the size if IE relative to RE in this case? What is the significance of this result?

4. Assume an economy of two firms and two consumers. The two firms pollute. Firm one has a marginal savings function of $MS_1(e) = 5 - e$ where e is the quantity of emissions from the firm. Firm two has a marginal savings function of $MS_2(e) = 8 - 2e$. Each of the two consumers has marginal damage $MD(e) = e$, where e is this case is the total amount of emissions the consumer is exposed to.

   a. Graph the firm-level and aggregate marginal savings functions.

   b. Graph the aggregate marginal damage function.

   c. What is the optimal level of pollution, the appropriate Pigovian fee, and emissions from each firm?

5. In Figure 12.7, the unregulated monopolist produces less than the efficient amount of steel. Does this always have to be the case when external costs are present? Can you

redraw Figure 12.7 such that the profit-maximizing monopolist produces more than the socially efficient amount of steel? Could it ever be the case that the unregulated monopolist produces exactly the efficient amount?

6. The Fireyear and Goodstone Rubber Companies are two firms located in the rubber capital of the world. These factories produce finished rubber and sell that rubber into a highly competitive world market at the fixed price of £60 per ton. The process of producing a ton of rubber also results in a ton of air pollution that affects the rubber capital of the world. This 1:1 relationship between rubber output and pollution is fixed and immutable at both factories. Consider the following information regarding the costs (in £) of producing rubber at the two factories $(Q_F$ and Q_G):

| Fireyear | Costs: $300 + 2Q_F^2$ | Marginal costs: $4Q_F$ |
| Goodstone | Costs: $500 + Q_G^2$ | Marginal costs: $2Q_G$ |

Total pollution emissions generated are $E_F + E_G = Q_F + Q_G$. Marginal damage from pollution is equal to £12 per ton of pollution.

a. In the absence of regulation, how much rubber would be produced by each firm? What is the profit for each firm?

b. The local government decides to impose a Pigovian tax on pollution in the community. What is the proper amount of such a tax per unit of emissions? What are the postregulation levels of rubber output and profits for each firm?

c. Suppose instead of the emission tax, the government observes the outcome in part (a) and decides to offer a subsidy to each firm for each unit of pollution abated. What is the efficient per unit amount of such a subsidy? Again calculate the levels of output and profit for each firm.

d. Compare the output and profits for the two firms in parts (a) through (c). Comment on the differences, if any, and the possibility of one or both of the firms dropping out of the market.

7. The Rocky Mashed Potato Factory produces output at costs $C = Q^2$ (marginal costs $2Q$), where Q is the quantity of mashed potatoes produced, in tons. In addition, 2 units of emissions are produced for each ton of mashed potatoes $(E = 2Q)$. Pollution damage is $2 for each unit of emissions, which leads the government to charge $2 per unit of emissions as a Pigovian fee. The firm's output sells competitively for $10 per ton.

a. How many tons of mashed potatoes will the Rocky Mashed Potato Factory produce? How much does it pay in emission fees? What are its profits?

b. A device is invented that would reduce the firm's emissions to one unit for each ton of output $(E = Q)$. How much would the firm be willing to pay for such a device?

c. How would your answer to part (b) change if there were no government regulation of pollution emissions? What does this lead you to say about the relationship between government regulation and the market for pollution abatement equipment?

NOTES

1. See Pigou (1962). This rambling treatise covers many "imperfections" in a market economy and discusses how they can be repaired. The first edition was published in 1920. The

adjectival version of his name is attached to prices to correct these imperfections—Pigovian (Saffran, 1996).

2. To many, Alan Kneese is the father of environmental economics. He and other innovative thinkers at Resources for the Future developed in the 1950s and 1960s much of the field as we know it today. His first mention of emission fees appears to be in Kneese (1962).

3. Horizontal summation means adding up the pollution generated by the different firms for a given marginal savings. Mechanically, this means rewriting $MS_1(x_1)$ and $MS_2(x_2)$ as $x_1(MS_1)$ and $x_2(MS_2)$. We are then interested in $x(MS) = x_1(MS) + x_2(MS)$, which can be rewritten as $MS(x)$. This is illustrated in Problem 1.

4. Polinsky (1979) considers this in a manner similar to the approach here. See also Spulber (1985) and Carlton and Loury (1980).

5. This problem was first identified by Buchanan (1969). See also Barnett (1980) and Martin (1986).

6. There is considerable uncertainty over this figure for the marginal welfare cost of taxation. Browning (1987) suggests the figure is between 32¢ and 47¢ (compared to an *average* welfare cost of 16¢). Other authors (cited by Browning) suggest figures outside this range.

7. Sandmo (1975) first examined the issue of setting emissions taxes in conjunction with optimally designed, but distortionary, labor and commodity taxes. A readable survey of this literature can be found in Goulder (1995). See also Bovenberg (1999). Bovenberg and de Mooij (1994) and Parry (1995) are two of the earlier analyses of the double dividend. The Parry (1995) paper provides a graphic analysis from which the presentation here is drawn. Goulder et al. (1997) provide an advanced though accessible treatment of the theoretical results on the double dividend as well as an application to sulfur emission regulations in the United States.

8. To the extent that other prices in the economy change as a result of the wage tax, there may be other deadweight losses from the wage tax.

9. In general, goods are substitutes for one another. If the price of one item in a consumption bundle increases, we consume less of it and more of other things. There are of course exceptions.

10. This result is due to Christiansen (1984). It is somewhat intuitive. We have too much leisure so we have too little of goods that are substitutes for leisure. The problem can be partially ameliorated by a subsidy to those substitutes.

MARKETS AND PROPERTY RIGHTS

As the discussion of exclusion in Chapter 5 should have made clear, institutions play an important role in allowing markets to function to allocate resources. If stealing is not illegal, then nearly all goods are nonexcludable and thus cannot be rationed using prices. A simple institutional change, establishing enforceable property rights, makes goods excludable and thus allows a market system to operate. In the case of garbage, if no laws exist prohibiting littering, garbage is nonexcludable; with enforced prohibitions on littering, garbage becomes excludable and the price system works to ensure proper disposal of trash.

In fact, in the discussion of competitive markets in Chapter 4, one of the conditions for a market to be competitive was that there be "complete property rights" that are well defined, transferable, secure, and complete. Without such property rights, particularly for environmental goods and services, a market cannot be relied upon to efficiently manage those environmental assets. The basic point is that properly defined property rights can make a big difference in whether a market will allocate goods and bads efficiently.

In this chapter we consider the design of property rights for pollution and other environmental assets. We are concerned with institutions that can be implemented to effectively manage the environment. We first consider the somewhat esoteric (though important) issue of who should own property rights to the environment—the polluter or the victim—and whether it matters. We then turn to tradable permits, which are becoming a very important regulatory tool worldwide for controlling pollution and managing open access resources (like fisheries and global or regional air pollutants).

I. COASE AND THE ASSIGNMENT OF RIGHTS

The first question to ask is a simple one in the context of pollution: who should be granted rights, the polluter or the victim?

Should we all have the right to clean air, and if pollution occurs be entitled to elimination of the pollution or compensation for pollution damage? Or should polluters have the right to pollute? This seems like a simple question with an obvious answer.

The "polluter pays" principle is enshrined in public policy regarding pollution control in many parts of the world. On the other hand, most countries have implemented subsidies, particularly through the tax system, to encourage pollution control. This indicates at least some acknowledgment of polluter rights.

This is not quite as simple an issue as might first appear. Consider two people, a polluter and a victim. The conventional view of the problem is that the polluter is the source of the problem and that blame must fall on the polluter's shoulders. However, leaving aside any preconceptions of right and wrong, the victim could also be blamed for being next to the polluter. Without the victim, the pollution would not be a problem. Morally, it seems that responsibility for cleaning up the pollution should fall on the polluter. Can we use economic efficiency arguments to reach this same conclusion?

This subtle issue of who should have rights, the polluter or the victim, was raised in 1960 by Ronald Coase in an important paper that contributed to his winning the Nobel Memorial prize in economics. Coase (1960) asks whether it is logical to assign rights to one or the other of these parties—the victim or the polluter. One of Coase's conclusions is that under some conditions, it makes no difference to efficiency whether the polluter has a right to pollute or the victim has a right to clean air (although it will make a great deal of difference to each of the two parties). Since the right to pollute is a property right that has value, if trade is allowed in those rights, efficiency should prevail, no matter how they were initially allocated. If the right is worth more to the victim than the polluter, the victim will end up with the right, no matter how it was initially distributed. Of course, the initial distribution of rights does matter to questions of equity. Rights can be valuable. Vesting someone with a right is like giving them money and resources.

Coase's arguments regarding property rights are often dubbed the Coase Theorem, falsely suggesting precision.[1] There are two parts of the Coase Theorem, at least insofar as we consider it here. The first concerns the case in which there are no impediments to buying and selling pollution rights. In this case, the initial distribution of rights does not matter. The second case involves impediments to trading property rights. Not surprisingly, in this case the initial distribution of rights does matter.

A. An Example of a Car Factory and a Refinery

To most effectively present Coase's results, we rely on an example of a refinery and a car manufacturing facility, complete with paint shop. The car factory is the victim, since it needs clean air to put a perfect coat of paint on its new cars; the refinery is the polluter. These are the only two players involved, which implies that there would be no relevant pollution problem if either (a) the refinery were not there; or (b) the car factory were not there. This symmetry implies that it is not obvious where the pollution rights should be vested.

Figure 13.1 shows the possible levels of pollution abatement for the refinery, as well as the marginal cost of abatement and the marginal benefit to the car factory. Abatement can go from zero (no abatement) to one (full abatement and no pollution). Let the total profit for each of the two firms, not counting any monetary transfers between them, be given by $\Pi_R(A)$ and $\Pi_C(A)$, where the costs of pollution control are borne by the refinery.

To examine this question, we first determine what would be the efficient level of pollution. We then examine what happens if (a) the car factory has rights to a clean environment or, alternatively, (b) if the refinery has the right to pollute.

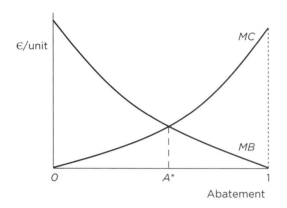

FIGURE 13.1 An illustration of the marginal conditions for an efficient level of abatement, trading off the marginal cost of abatement for the refinery (*MC*) with the marginal benefit to the car factory (*MB*).

1. Efficiency. In the marginal world, we know that efficiency calls for the marginal cost of pollution control (by the refinery) to be equated to the marginal damage of the pollution (to the car factory). This is shown as abatement level A^* in Figure 13.1 and results in total profits for the two enterprises of $\Pi_R(A^*) + \Pi_C(A^*)$.

But there are two other possible nonmarginal outcomes: the refinery ceases operation or the car factory ceases operation. For instance, if the refinery is a very marginally profitable operation without pollution control, it may well be socially more desirable to shut it down, thus eliminating the pollution, rather than investing in significant pollution control. Similarly, if the car factory shuts down, the refinery need not invest in pollution control since in our world, the only victim of the pollution is the car factory. In fact, society should examine three cases:

$$\text{Both facilities operate—total profit is } \Pi_R(A^*) + \Pi_C(A^*) \tag{13.1a}$$

$$\text{Car factory shuts down—total profit is } \Pi_R(0) \tag{13.1b}$$

$$\text{Refinery shuts down—total profit is } \Pi_C(1) \tag{13.1c}$$

Whichever profit level is the largest dictates the action that should be taken from an efficiency perspective.

2. Victim Has Rights. Now consider what happens if the car factory has the legal right to clean air—in other words, the legal right to abatement at $A = 1$. If the refinery wants to pollute, it will have to compensate the car factory for any damage. What this means for the car factory is that its profits are guaranteed to be at least $\Pi_C(1)$, since it is being compensated for any lost profits associated with pollution.

There are three possible outcomes here: (1) both the refinery and car factory operate and the refinery compensates the car factory for pollution; (2) the refinery shuts down; or (3) the refinery buys the car factory and shuts it down. The refinery is the decision maker (the car factory gets its profit no matter what), so what happens will be dictated by the level of profits for the refinery in the three cases.

If both the refinery and the car factory operate, our economic intuition tells us that for abatement levels between A^* and 1, the marginal benefit to the car factory of abatement is less than the marginal cost to the refinery, so presumably there are gains from negotiation. In fact, abatement will end up at A^*, where the marginal cost of abatement equals the marginal benefit.

To be able to emit at A^*, the refinery will have to bribe the car factory an amount $\Pi_C(1) - \Pi_C(A^*)$, in order to keep the car factory's profits constant at $\Pi_C(1)$. Thus profits for the refinery will be $\Pi_R(A^*) - \Pi_C(1) + \Pi_C(A^*)$.

If the refinery buys out the car factory and shuts it down, it will have to pay $\Pi_C(1)$ for the car factory and the resulting profit for the refinery will be $\Pi_R(0) - \Pi_C(1)$. Similarly, if the refinery simply goes out of business, its profits will drop to zero.

To summarize the refinery's decisions and profit:

$$\text{Both facilities operate—total refinery profit is } \Pi_R(A^*) + \Pi_C(A^*) - \Pi_C(1) \tag{13.2a}$$

$$\text{Car factory shuts down—total refinery profit is } \Pi_R(0) - \Pi_C(1) \tag{13.2b}$$

$$\text{Refinery shuts down—total refinery profit is } 0 \tag{13.2c}$$

Note that the conditions in Eq. (13.2) are identical to the conditions in Eq. (13.1) except that profit in each of the three cases in Eq. (13.2) is lower by the constant $\Pi_C(1)$. The refinery will take the action that results in the highest profit; the choice will be the same as in the case of efficiency in Eq. (13.1).

The reason these conditions are not quite the same is that in Eq. (13.1), we were looking at total profits for both enterprises. In Eq. (13.2) we are only looking at refinery profits. If car factory profits at full abatement, $\Pi_C(1)$, are added back into Eq. (13.2), it becomes identical to Eq. (13.1).

3. Polluter Has Rights. Now consider the case where the polluter has rights to pollute. If the car factory does not want the pollution, it will have to "bribe" the refinery to cut back.

As before, there are three possible outcomes here: (1) both the refinery and car factory operate, with the car factory bribing the refinery to reduce pollution; (2) the car factory shuts down; or (3) the car factory buys the refinery and shuts it down. The car factory is the decision maker (the refinery gets its profit no matter what), so what happens will be dictated by the level of profits for the car factory in the three cases.

As before, if both the refinery and the car factory operate, abatement will be at A^*, where marginal benefit equals marginal cost. The car factory will have to pay for the abatement, which is simply the reduction in refinery profits in moving to A^*: $\Pi_R(0) - \Pi_R(A^*)$. Thus its total profits will be $\Pi_C(A^*) - \Pi_R(0) + \Pi_R(A^*)$.

If the car factory buys out the refinery and shuts it down, it will have to pay $\Pi_R(0)$ for the refinery, and the resulting profit for the car factory will be $\Pi_C(1) - \Pi_R(0)$. Similarly, if the car factory simply goes out of business, its profits will drop to zero.

To summarize the car factory's decisions and profit:

$$\text{Both facilities operate—total car profit is } \Pi_R(A^*) + \Pi_C(A^*) - \Pi_R(0) \tag{13.3a}$$

$$\text{Car Factory shuts down—total car profit is } 0 \tag{13.3b}$$

$$\text{Refinery shuts down—total car profit is } \Pi_C(1) - \Pi_R(0) \tag{13.3c}$$

Note that the conditions in Eq. (13.3) are identical to the conditions in Eq. (13.1) except that profit in each of the three cases in Eq. (13.3) is lower by the constant $\Pi_R(0)$. The car factory will take the action that results in the highest profit; the choice will be the same as in the case of efficiency in Eq. (13.1). Furthermore, the outcome will be the same as when the car factory had rights to clean air: the outcome is independent of how property rights are assigned.

Town Buys Out Polluter

In Santa Maria, California, a cattle-fattening facility ("feedlot") had been in existence for many years, generating pungent smells but located well away from houses, and thus generating minimal atmospheric damage. But this changed as the town of Santa Maria grew. The city expanded and houses were built closer and closer to the feedlot, generating complaints from newly nearby residents. Rather than force the feedlot to control its pollution (the "polluter pays"), in the mid-1990s the City Council in Santa Maria voted to tax the residents around the feedlot and use the revenue to pay the feedlot owner to cease operations. Efficiency was attained even though the victims paid to attain it. (Source: Bedell, 1996.)

B. The Coase Theorem

The preceding discussion illustrates that bargaining between a polluter and a victim can solve pollution problems without worrying about the legal assignment of rights to a clean environment—you end up at the same spot in both cases. A key assumption in the discussion was that bargaining between the parties was easy. This of course is not always the case. If there had been 1,000 car factories and one refinery in our example, having all the car factories agree to pay the refinery to reduce pollution would be difficult. Or the next time you are in a restaurant and someone at the next table starts smoking a cigar (presumably to your consternation), try paying the person to stop smoking. Bargaining costs usually do exist. The results of the previous section assumed that bargaining was costless.

More generally, the previous section assumed *no transaction costs*. Just what do we mean by transaction costs? Transaction costs are the costs of entering into a transaction, over and above the exchange of money for a good. Transaction costs cover a multitude of different costs associated with agreeing to transact. At the simplest level, a transaction cost is an extra payment associated with consummating a transaction. For instance, in buying an automobile, there is the cost of the automobile itself but there are also a host of costs associated with the transaction: sales tax, registration, transfer tax, V.A.T., etc. In purchasing a house, the transaction costs can be even more significant.[2]

A more subtle kind of transaction cost is involved in bargaining. Paying smokers at neighboring tables in a restaurant not to smoke involves significant effort and perhaps some trauma. Many of us are shy about asking a stranger not to smoke. Even though there may be no monetary transaction costs, there are psychic costs associated with striking bargains with neighboring diners. The costs are just as real as monetary costs. That is why we also think of this impediment as a transaction cost, even though it is more subtle than a transfer tax paid when acquiring an automobile.

We are now in a position to state the Coase Theorem, one version of which was illustrated in the previous section with the car factory and the refinery. (It is called a theorem though its statement and its proof are considerably looser than most mathematical theorems.)[3]

> **Coase Theorem.** Assume a world in which some producers or consumers are subject to externalities generated by other producers or consumers. Further, assume (1) everyone has perfect information, (2) consumers and producers are price-takers, (3) there is a costless court system for enforcing agreements, (4) producers maximize profits and consumers maximize utility, (5) there are no income or wealth effects, and (6) there are no transaction costs. In this case, the initial assignment of property rights regarding the externalities does not matter for efficiency. If any of these conditions does not hold, the initial assignment of rights does matter.

What this theorem states is that if there are no barriers to reaching agreement (such as the car factory paying the refinery not to pollute), we get efficiency, regardless of how property rights are initially distributed.[4] In fact, the theorem goes beyond externalities broadly to all market failures. With a monopoly and no barriers to agreement, consumers can simply pay monopolists to produce at the efficient level, sharing the gains in efficiency. The most significant condition in the Coase Theorem is probably the zero transaction costs assumption. In most real-world situations, there are significant transactions costs, which limits the practical application of the Coase Theorem. In fact, Coase has stated that the case of zero transaction costs is of limited interest:

> We do not do well to devote ourselves to a detailed study of the world of zero transactions costs, like augurs divining the future by the minute inspection of the entrails of a goose.[5]

What the Coase Theorem does is direct our attention away from efficiency arguments to explain why property rights should be allocated in a particular way.

Cooter (1987) argues that even when there do not appear to be transaction costs, there are impediments to reaching bargains (such impediments are a form of transaction costs). He points out that in a bilateral negotiation with gains from consummating an agreement, the bargaining may break down because of an inability to decide on the precise division of the gains. Another instance in which there appears to be no transaction costs when in fact there are involves public bads in which many affected parties must bargain with the polluter. Because this example is important, we will consider it in more detail in the next section.

Another important clause in the Coase Theorem concerns wealth effects. If I am endowed with a right that has value, I am richer. If I do not have that right, I am poorer. We know that the demand for goods depends on our income; consequently, the existence of wealth effects would generate differences in the final bargain, depending on how rights were initially allocated. This is the reason for condition (5) in our statement of the Coase Theorem.

It is important to keep in mind that Coase is not saying property rights are not important. As we saw in Chapter 4, a complete set of property rights is necessary for a market to support a Pareto-optimal allocation. What Coase is saying is that for efficiency it may not matter how these rights are distributed. If the polluter has the right to use the air for smoke, that is a well-defined right, even though some of us might think it unfair.

If citizens have the right to clean air, that is also a well-defined right. Coase simply says that if trading in these rights is easy and costless, it does not matter how they are initially distributed; they will subsequently be traded so that they end up in the right hands.

Let us now focus on the second part of the Coase Theorem, when transaction costs exist. Consider the example of the previous section. If it costs $100,000 (in lawyer fees for example) for any payment between the car factory and the refinery, then unless the gains from negotiation exceed $100,000, no bargaining will take place. Thus the status quo will persist—either the refinery will be unable to emit any pollution or the car factory will be burdened with excessive pollution.

So we see that when transaction costs are present, it does matter where rights are initially vested. With transaction costs, the status quo tends to prevail. This means that when rights are initially established by the legal system, it is important to vest rights in those parties that have the greatest willingness to pay for those rights. One should not rely on trade to redistribute rights to pollute. Of course another conclusion may be that attention should be paid to reducing the transaction costs associated with trading rights to pollute.

C. Bargaining Problems

The problem of actually striking an agreement is fundamental to the Coasian view of property rights. There are two issues that are particularly relevant to the pollution problem that deserve additional attention. One concerns the public bad nature of most pollution and the fact that there are usually large numbers of victims and a small number of polluters. Furthermore, damage to victims is often private information, which creates incentives for free-riding. A second issue arises in actually striking a bargain when there are more than two individuals bargaining. We will see that sometimes this is not possible.

1. Free-riding. Let us modify our refinery/car factory example slightly to one polluting power plant surrounded by a number of people who suffer from the pollution. If the people own the right to pollute, the power plant will have to compensate people for damage. Although this can lead to problems as we saw in Chapter 5, some lump-sum compensation is possible. On the other hand, if the right to pollute is vested in the power plant, the people surrounding the plant will have to get together to pay the plant not to pollute. The problems of reaching agreement among the people surrounding the plant are significant. As we shall see, no matter whom the property right is vested with, the basic problem is free-riding and truthful revelation of demand.

Expanding our example, suppose there are 20 people surrounding the power plant, the cost of cleaning up the plant completely is $91, and the damage to each person from the pollution is $5. Thus the aggregate damage is $100 so it is socially desirable to undertake pollution control, for a net gain of $9. Although we have stated the damage is $5 per person, in reality, the damage is private information to the individuals. This is where the problems arise.

Suppose first that the right to pollute is vested with the power plant. The Coase Theorem suggests that efficiency (pollution control) can be attained via payments from the individuals to the plant. Indeed, one possibility is that all 20 people get together, each contributes $4.55 (for a total of $91), and the plant is paid to clean-up. However, it is entirely possible that one of the individuals pretends to not really mind the pollution, claiming he is not really willing to contribute anything. In this case the other 19 individuals can each contribute $4.79 (collecting a total of $91.01). One person free-rides but we are still able to obtain a Pareto-optimal outcome. However, if two people get the idea to free-ride, there is no way the other 18 people can pool money to raise $91 while individually paying no more than the $5 of damage. Consequently, the problems of free-riding combined with private information on damages make it very difficult to reach a Coasian solution when rights to pollute are vested in the power plant.[6]

Is it any better if the individuals have the right to clean air? The problem of not encouraging people to move to the plant should pollution continue can be solved by paying each person their damage, assuming they are behaving optimally. But the first question the plant must address is how much damage there is and whether it exceeds the cost of pollution control. Once again, the power plant must ask the citizens what their damage is; however there are incentives for individuals to overstate this damage, since compensation may be based on their response.[7] In this example, the result will be installation of pollution control equipment, the desired outcome. However, suppose damages are more modest and it is optimal to compensate. Then the tendency to overstate damage could lead to excessive compensation or overzealous pollution control measures.

Polluter Buys Out Town

The Gavin Power Plant burns 25,000 tons of coal a day and is located adjacent to the former town of Cheshire, Ohio. Cheshire was plagued by pollution from the power plant and the power plant was plagued by complaints and legal actions (threatened and actual), not only from townspeople but also from regulatory authorities. The owner of the plant had invested almost a billion dollars in pollution control equipment, but pollution levels remained problematic for the town. Rather than continue to battle the townspeople and face potential litigation from them for health damages (liability risk was apparently a real concern), plant operators chose instead to buy the town. They paid $13 million for the 90 or so homes in Cheshire. There were some holdouts initially (the free-rider problem?), but eventually everyone went along. The residents eventually moved away and the town no longer exists. (Google Maps gives an eerie perspective on the town—the streets show up on the satellite photo but the houses are gone.)

This is an example of a Coasian bargain. The power plant had an obligation to not cause harm to the townspeople and the existence of the townspeople increased the damage being caused by the plant. Faced with the choice of investing further in pollution control or eliminating the victims, it chose the later. It should be pointed out that eliminating Cheshire did not completely eliminate the requirement to install pollution control at Gavin, but it did reduce some of the pressure to install additional controls, such as switching to more expensive low-sulfur coal.

(Source: Seelye, 2002.)

The reason these problems arise is because of the nonrival aspect of the pollution. This leads to free-riding and difficulties in striking bargains. If the pollution were a rival good, such as garbage, the plant would offer the pollution at a price up to its marginal cost of control (as in the steel mill/laundry example earlier). If someone takes the pollution, there is that much less for others to consume. This is a characteristic of rivalry. In such a case, we do not have a problem.[8]

2. Bargaining within Groups.[9] The Coase Theorem is most applicable when two individual firms or people are bargaining. We do not have the problems of free-riding and negotiating costs we saw in the previous section. There is, however, a more fundamental problem when more than two people are bargaining: there may be no bargain that is agreeable to all three people simultaneously, even when transaction costs are not present. If this is the case, it presents additional problems for the Coase Theorem. We show this with an example.

We consider an example with two polluters and one victim. We will call the victim a laundry, which relies on clean air for low production costs. The two polluters are a steel mill (S) and a railroad (R). Furthermore, think of the physical nature of this example as being that the laundry is where the economic profits come from. Whenever a polluter gets together with the laundry, it is always best to shut down the polluter.

We are concerned with different bargains that may be struck among these three parties. Thinking of a bargain as several firms getting together into a "coalition"; we can indicate who is cooperating with whom by specifying the coalitions within the three-firm example. For instance, {(R,L),S} is a way of specifying a coalition (agreement) between the railroad and the laundry with the steel mill being on its own. The possible cooperative arrangements are $A_1 = \{(R),(S),(L)\}$, $A_2 = \{(R),(S,L)\}$, $A_3 = \{(R,S),(L)\}$, $A_4 = \{(R,L),(S)\}$, and $A_5 = \{(R,S,L)\}$. These are the five possible coalition structures. The first of these, $A_1 = \{(R),(S),(L)\}$, simply means that each of the three firms operates on its own. The second of these, $A_2 = \{(R),(S,L)\}$, means that the railroad operates by itself, but that the steel mill and laundry merge into a single firm and act for their joint good. The profits for individual coalitions are given in Table 13.1. Note that we have specified above what a coalition may get but not how that coalition would divide its profit among its members.

Now let us examine what will happen under two property rights regimes: the laundry has a right to clean air and the laundry has no rights to clean air. Suppose first that there is a right to clean air. The railroad and the steel mill will have to pay damages. Without the pollution, the laundry makes $40,000 and the railroad and steel mill make nothing [since the grand coalition of (R,S,L) involves stopping production of R and S]. If the laundry operates independently, it makes $24,000 for a loss of $16,000. In this case, the steel mill and railroad jointly make $11,000, so they cannot afford to pay the $16,000 damages and must shut down. All of the other coalitional structures result in a similar outcome. Consequently, in all cases the laundry and the steel mill shut down, which means the laundry earns $40,000 and there is no pollution.

TABLE 13.1 Payoffs to Coalitions: Example of Railroad, Steel Mill, and Laundry

Partition[a]	Payoff[b]	Description
A1{(R),(S),(L)}	{$3,$8,$24}	Each firm acts independently
A2{(R,S),(L)}	{$15,$24}	Railroad and steel mill merge
A3{(R,S,L)}	{$40}	All three firms merge
A4{(R),(S,L)}	{$3,$36}	Steel mill and laundry merge
A5{(R,L),(S)}	{$31,$8}	Railroad and laundry merge

[a] *A partition is a collection of coalitions; i.e., a particular way of dividing all of the firms into coalitions.*

[b] *Payoffs in thousands of dollars.*

Now suppose there is no right to clean air. Now the laundry must induce the polluters to stop polluting. There are two issues. First, will the laundry have enough money to induce the polluters to shut down? Second, will any arrangement the laundry sets up with the polluters be stable in the sense of there being no incentives for the participants to break the deal? The answers to these questions will become clearer as we delve into the problem.

The laundry stands to gain $16,000 by shutting down the polluters (compare A_3 to A_1 or A_2). The two polluters together can make $15,000 ($A_2$), so there should be enough extra money to induce them to shut down. This would leave the laundry with an extra $1000 from striking the deal. How will the railroad and steel mill divide the $15,000? The mill must get at least $8000 since that is what it makes on its own (A_1). That would leave the railroad with $7000. Thus the railroad makes $7000, the steel mill makes $8000, and the laundry makes $25,000. Call this the "grand bargain." Clearly, everyone prefers this arrangement to independent action (A_1). Would any smaller group of the three agents prefer to get together without the third? If the mill were to get together with the laundry (A_4), they stand to make $36,000, which is $3000 greater than the $33,000 the laundry and steel mill netted in the grand bargain. So the coalition (S,L) "blocks" the grand bargain. One could continue like this, selecting a coalition and a split of profits that looks better than an alternative, only to find some other coalition and split that dominates it. The point is, no matter what payments you propose from the laundry to the two polluters (to shut down), one of the other coalitions will be preferred by the alternative coalition's members. For this reason, there is no coalition and division of the pie that is not dominated by another. This means that no bargain will be struck. They will continue trying to strike a deal for all time.

The significance of this result is that striking a "deal" to eliminate externalities may not be as easy as suggested by the Coase Theorem. The outcome may indeed depend on who initially is allocated the rights to pollute. Another interpretation of this is that the problem of reaching an agreement over pollution is just another form of transactions cost. Consequently, the example we have given is not counter to the Coase Theorem. Although that is a valid interpretation, if difficulties in reaching agreement are excluded from the result, the Coase Theorem becomes weaker and even less applicable to real world problems.

D. The Policy Significance of the Coase Theorem

The Coase Theorem is remarkable because it is counterintuitive, at least when first encountered. But is it anything more than a curiosity of academic economics? Is the Coase Theorem relevant to environmental policy?

There are several clear policy implications of the Coase Theorem. One is that transaction costs matter to the efficient distribution of rights to a clean environment. This means that in designing a set of property rights for the environment, it is important both to distribute them approximately efficiently and/or work to reduce the costs associated with trading those rights.

As markets for rights to pollute become increasingly common, it is important to heed this advice. In the case of tradable emission rights in many urban areas in the United States, a great deal of paper work is associated with every trade in rights. As a result, the number of trades is often disappointing.[10] More attention to reducing transaction costs would help in such situations.

Another policy implication of the Coase Theorem is that victims of pollution should not be loathe to pay polluters to reduce pollution. Often the political power of polluters is such that it is impossible to force them to reduce pollution and get them to pay for it. This often results in a stalemate that can last for years. Rarely is the stalemate resolved by acknowledging reality with the victims paying for cleanup. The desirable outcome is the absence of pollution. Who pays is (to a certain extent) a secondary issue. This is a conclusion of the Coase Theorem that has yet to find wide acceptance in environmental policy.

Environmental NGO Brokers Fishery Solution

A persistent environmental problem off of the central coast of California has been destructive bottom trawling for fish and shellfish. Bottom trawling essentially involves scraping the bottom of the ocean and pulling up whatever is found. It is low cost but destructive to habitat. Environmental groups and the scientific community have been pressing the government to ban this practice. Not surprisingly, fishers have been vehemently resisting losing their livelihood.

The Nature Conservancy (TNC) and Environmental Defense Fund (EDF), two progressive environmental nongovernmental organizations (NGOs) saw an opportunity to redefine property rights to solve the problem. Tradable permits already are in place for fishing in this region; it is the fishing technique that is the issue. TNC and EDF negotiated with fishers to buy up fishing permits and harmful fishing equipment (neutralizing one of the complaints of fishers that they would be expected to absorb the cost of environmental progress). The two NGOs also agreed to lease the permits back to fishers, though with restrictions on the kinds of fishing practices that would be acceptable.

Rather than wrangling for years over who should bear the cost of environmental improvement, TNC and EDF stepped in and solved the problem by redefining who bears the cost of establishing the environmental property right.

(Source: Christensen, 2006.)

II. TRADABLE PERMITS

Perhaps the dominant economic incentive for pollution control in use in the world today is the tradable emission permit, becoming popularly known as a cap and trade system (and the related system for fisheries, the tradable fishing quota). Start with the familiar concept of an emission permit granted to a specific facility, authorizing specific emissions. Add to this the twist that the facility can transfer this permit to another polluter for a fee. In other words, the permit is tradable.

Like emission fees, the concept of a tradable emission permit dates to the 1960s.[11] The great virtue of tradable permits it that no matter how the permits are initially allocated, after trading the equimarginal principle automatically holds. Permits can be allocated on the basis of political expediency or concerns for distributional equity; trading then assures efficiency, or at least cost-effectiveness.

Nothing is perfect, however, including tradable permits. Some of the issues that will be addressed in this section are (1) how to initially distribute permits, including whether to sell them or give them away freely; (2) whether to allow banking permits for the future or borrowing permits from the future; (3) how to deal with dominant firms; (4) how to deal with a small number of firms (market thinness); and (5) the effect of transaction costs.

US Sulfur Allowance System

One of the major air pollution problems of the 1980s was acid rain, due in large part to large emissions of sulfur from power plants, which turned into sulfuric acid and resulted in acidic precipitation. This was a major issue in North America, Europe, and Asia. In the United States, annual sulfur emissions were on the order of 20 million tons. After a decade of political wrangling, the 1990 amended Clean Air Act was signed into law by George Bush the elder. The Act, called for a reduction of emissions to 10 million tons annually through the use of tradeable permits. Permits (called allowances) were issued annually to power plants based on their historic emissions so that the total sum of allowances issued equaled 10 million tons. Allowances could be traded among polluters. At the end of every year, an allowance had to be surrendered to the EPA for every ton of sulfur emissions. Allowances could be saved (banked) for the future, which occurred frequently. Borrowing was not permitted. Every March a small number of permits were withheld from the polluters and auctioned off; the revenue was then distributed to the polluters in lieu of the permits withheld. Prior to the start of the program, engineering estimates suggested allowances would sell for $300 or more, yet prices were well under $100 early in the program, suggesting the marginal cost of pollution control was less than anticipated. The figure below shows the price of allowances ($/ton of SO_2) over the first decade of the program:

The sulfur allowance system has been a tremendous success, particularly in terms of innovation and low administrative cost. Literally, an office of a few people in the EPA runs the entire program with virtually 100% compliance.

As an interesting addendum, in 2005 the EPA proposed dramatically reducing the number of allowances under what is known as the Clean Air Interstate Rule (CAIR). The mere *possibility* of the program sent allowance prices up to nearly $2000 in 2005; they had returned to less than $500 by the end of 2006.

(Source: Price data from U.S. Environmental Protection Agency, 2007; see Schmalensee et al. (1998) for more on the program.)

A. Permit Market Operation

To see how a tradable permit market might operate, we use the example from the last chapter that was used to illustrate an emission fee. Figure 12.1 shows the marginal costs of abatement for Riley Wreckers and Tucker Tools. The Figure shows the how the two firms will choose abatement and emission when faced with an emission fee of p. We see that emissions will be cut back to $E_T + E_R$.

Now instead of using an emission fee, suppose we issue a total of $E_T + E_R$ permits and let trading commence. Suppose the permits are initially divided equally between the two firms. What will happen when trading is allowed?

Figure 13.2 illustrates the outcome of trading. Shown in the figure are the marginal savings functions for the two firms, although drawn somewhat differently than in Figure 12.1a. The marginal savings curve for Tucker Tools is as before, however, a mirror image of the marginal savings from emissions for Riley Wreckers is drawn, with the origin on the far right and reading increased emissions to the left. We know that because the number of permits is fixed at $E_T + E_R$, then knowing how much Riley is emitting, we will automatically know what Tucker is emitting. Every point along the horizontal axis in Figure 13.2 shows the split between Riley and Tucker.

Even though the permits were initially allocated 50:50 between the two firms, trading will occur so that the marginal savings will be equalized between the two firms. Hence,

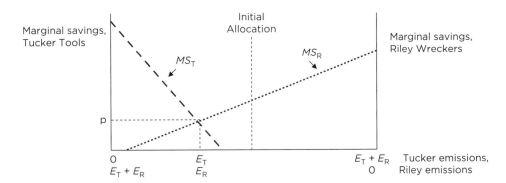

FIGURE 13.2 Illustration of trading of permits between two firms.

Tradable Sulfur Allowances and the Double Dividend

Larry Goulder and colleagues construct a model of the US economy and simulate the sulfur allowance market introduced under the 1990 Clean Air Act Amendments (Goulder et al., 1997). The authors are interested in generating real measures of the Pigovian effect, the revenue recycling effect and the tax interaction effect. Recall that the 1990 Clean Air Act calls for a 10 million ton per year reduction (from about 20) in emissions of sulfur dioxide from electric power plants. This is to be achieved using a marketable permit system with the permits distributed without charge based on historic levels of electricity generation. Thus this is a regulation without a revenue recycling effect. An alternative way of achieving the same effect but with revenue recycling would be to auction the permits. Goulder et al. (1997) calculate that the preexisting taxes on labor increase the total cost of the program by 71%. They further calculate that more than half of that increased cost is due to the fact that permits are given away rather than auctioned with the proceeds going to reduce taxes on labor. Another result is that the tax interaction effect *(IE)* is on the order of $100 per ton of pollution reduction (independent of how much pollution is reduced), about a third of their assumed private marginal cost of pollution abatement (on average $300 per ton of pollution). Thus if the damage from pollution does not exceed $100 per ton, no pollution control is justified unless there is revenue recycling.

permit holdings will result in exactly the same emissions for each firm as in Figure 12.1, with the emission fee. Furthermore, the price of the permits will be exactly what the emission fee was, *p*.

With multiple polluters, the logic is the same, though a graphical treatment is a little more difficult with more than two firms. The important point is that no matter how the permits are initially allocated, equilibrium in the market results in all firms holding permits and controlling emissions so that marginal savings (or marginal abatement costs) are equalized among firms.

B. Initial Permit Issuance

We just saw how the initial permit issuance makes no difference to efficiency. Literally, one could fly an airplane over the country dropping the right amount of permits out of the back of the plane and they would end up in the right place, so that marginal costs are equalized. This is one of the primary advantages of tradable permits. It is also why cap and trade is an apt description—all one needs to do is set the cap (overall number of permits) and allow trading.

Early permit programs, such as the U.S. sulfur allowance system and the EU carbon emission trading system, allocated permits to polluters at no cost to polluters. In essence, valuable permits are given to polluters as a way of buying off opposition to the pollution control regulations.

Many recent proposals for emission trading involve the auctioning of at least some of the permits, with the revenue going to the government. This of course reduces the attractiveness of the program to polluters, which may translate into political difficulties in implementing the regulatory program (an issue discussed by Buchanan and Tullock, 1975).

One of the reasons for auctioning permits, rather than giving them away, relates to the discussion of the double dividend in the last chapter. When a marketable permit system is imposed in conjunction with taxes on income (which is virtually always the case in most modern societies), then there are three effects of the permit system: (1) a Pigovian effect (society is better off because of less pollution), (2) a tax interaction effect (the permit system exacerbates the inefficiencies of the labor tax), and (3) a revenue recycling effect (the revenue from auctioning off the permits can be used to reduce inefficiencies due to the income tax). The first of these effects is always positive; the second is usually negative; the third is always positive. When permits are freely allocated, we do not get the third effect. Thus society is better off when permits are auctioned, bringing revenue into the treasury.

One way of allocating permits without the problem of a wealth transfer to the government is a zero-revenue auction, originally proposed by Hahn and Noll (1982). The idea is simple. In advance of the permit auction, the political process decides what fraction of the auction revenue should accrue to each existing polluter. This might be based on current emissions, historic emissions, or ability to pay. The permits are then auctioned but the revenues are distributed to existing polluters in an agreed-on manner. This system can also be used to ensure new entrants adequate opportunity to acquire permits. Anyone can bid for permits. The revenue from the auction is distributed to those parties who might resist (politically) a permit auction without revenue recycling. Such an auction is used in the United States annually for a small portion of the acid rain emission permits. It appears to have the added advantage of providing a clear signal about the current market price of the emission permits, information that facilitates market operation.

C. Dominant Firms

One potential problem with the initial distribution of permits may arise if there is market power in the permit market. In other words, if there is a single large firm (or potentially, several large firms), it can make a difference how permits are initially allocated.[12]

To see this, suppose there is one large firm in an area with many small firms which together make up a price-taking competitive fringe. Suppose the large firm has costs associated with emitting of $C(E)$ where E is emissions by the large firm. Assume that the competitive fringe has inverse demand for permits of $P(e)$. In other words, at a permit price of $P(e)$, the fringe will demand e permits. It is through manipulation of this inverse demand curve that the dominant firm can exercise market power. Suppose that L emission permits are issued initially, with L_B going to the big firm. There are no spatial considerations here; we are considering emission permits only.

The total cost of the big firm is given by

$$TC(E)=C(E) - P(L - E) [L_B - E] \qquad (13.4)$$

The last term is the revenue to the large firm from selling excess permits, (L_B-E). The price at which the large firm sells permits is determined by the inverse demand function and how many permits the fringe is buying, $e = L - E$. The large firm wishes to minimize costs by choosing the appropriate E. The problem is not unlike that of the monopolist choosing the right amount of output, driving price up by restricting output.

To solve this problem, we will see what happens to total costs as we change E by a small amount, ΔE. Costs will be minimized when a small change in E causes no change in TC. First increase E by $\Delta E = -\Delta e$:

$$TC(E + \Delta E) = C(E + \Delta E) - P(L - E - \Delta E)\,[L_B - E - \Delta E] \tag{13.5}$$
$$= C(E + \Delta E) - P(e + \Delta e)\,[L_B - E] + P(e + \Delta e)\,\Delta E$$

Now if we subtract Eq. (13.4) from this and divide by ΔE, we obtain

$$\Delta TC/\Delta E = \Delta C/\Delta E + \Delta P/\Delta e\,[L_B - E] + P(e + \Delta e)$$
$$\approx MC(E) + MP(e)\,[L_B - E] + P(e) \tag{13.6}$$

The right-hand-side of Eq. (13.6) is the sum of marginal costs (MC), a marginal price term (MP), and permit price (P). Cost minimization calls for Eq. (13.6) to be equated to zero:

$$MS(E) = MP(e)[L_B - E] + P(e) \tag{13.7}$$

Denote the emission level at which price equals marginal savings $[MC(E) + P(e) = 0]$ as E^*. Denote the solution to Eq. (13.7) as E^{**}. Referring to Eq. (13.7), efficiency basically calls for marginal savings from emissions $(-MC)$ to be equated to permit price. Unfortunately, the first term on the right-hand side of Eq. (13.7) drives a wedge between marginal savings and price. We know that marginal price is negative since demand is downward sloping (quantity increases when price declines).

So, what is the relationship between E^* and E^{**}? Inspection of Eq. (13.7) indicates that when $L_B = E^*$, we have $E^{**} = E^*$. So we will consider the two other cases, one in which $L_B < E^*$ and one in which $L_B > E^*$. In the first case, $L_B < E^*$, we ask if $E^{**} > E^*$ or $E^{**} < E^*$? Note that in this case of $L_B < E^*$,

$$E^{**} < E^* \Rightarrow MS(E^{**}) > P(e^{**}) \Rightarrow MP(e^{**})\,(L_B - E^{**}) > 0 \Rightarrow L_B < E^{**} \tag{13.8a}$$
$$E^{**} > E^* \Rightarrow MS(E^{**}) < P(e^{**}) \Rightarrow MP(e^{**})\,(L_B - E^{**}) < 0 \Rightarrow L_B > E^{**} \tag{13.8b}$$

But Eq. (13.8) implies $L_B > E^*$, which contradicts our original assumption. Thus it must be that $L_B < E^{**} < E^*$. A similar argument can be used to show that if $L_B > E^*$, then $E^* < E^{**} < L_B$. To sum up,

$$L_B > E^* \Rightarrow E^* < E^{**} < L_B \tag{13.9a}$$
$$L_B < E \Rightarrow L_B < E^{**} < E^* \tag{13.9b}$$
$$L_B = E^* \Rightarrow L_B = E^{**} = E^* \tag{13.9c}$$

This is illustrated in Figure 13.3, which shows both marginal savings $(-MC)$ and permit price (P), as functions of emissions from the large firm. These are the two solid lines and

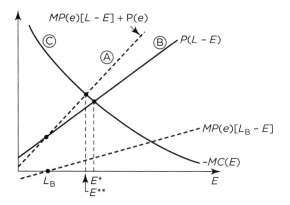

FIGURE 13.3 Illustration of how an inefficient initial distribution of permits can lead to a distortion when one firm has market power. $-MC$, marginal savings from emitting for large firm; $P(L - E)$, permit price; L_B, initial permit issuance to the large firm; E^*, efficient level of emissions; E^{**}, manipulated level of emissions.

they intersect at E^*. Note that the more the large firm emits, the fewer permits available to the fringe, which drives up the price. Also shown is the first term on the right-hand side of Eq. (13.7), for an initial permit issuance to the big firm of $L_B < E^*$ and the sum of this term and the price, $P(L - E)$—line A. Eq. (13.7) holds where lines A and C cross, yielding emissions E^{**}—lower emissions than the efficient E^*.

The intuition behind this result is that the large firm gains market power by selling or buying permits. So if the firm is initially allocated too few permits, it will buy, but not quite enough, in an effort to keep price down. Thus its emissions will be lower than is efficient. Similarly, if the large firm is given too many permits to start with, it will sell some, but not quite enough, in an effort to keep price high. The only way the large firm can be induced to emit at the proper level is to give it exactly the right amount of permits to start with.

It is important to realize that the total amount of pollution is unaffected by how the permits are initially allocated. The total amount of pollution will be L. But if the large firm is emitting too little or too much, the total costs of the large firm and the fringe firms will be too high. Thus the inefficiency is on the cost side.

Unfortunately, this is more than an exercise in marginals. Often in controlling pollution in a region, there will be dominant firms. This suggests that in such a case, some of the gain from using marketable permits may be lost. How much is lost is an empirical question.[13]

D. Market Thinness

A related problem with marketable permits arises if the market generally is thin. If there are only a few firms in the market, transactions may be infrequent or nonexistent. Thus the main rationale for marketable permits—equalizing marginal control costs among firms—will not be accomplished. Of course, the correct amount of pollution will result (equal to the permit issuance), but costs will be excessively high.

Often the firms in a permits market will compete with one another in a goods market. Withholding permits can then be used as an entry deterrent. Or permits can be used in other anticompetitive ways.

New Zealand Fishing Permits

As discussed in Chapter 5, open access resources suffer from nonexcludability. As illustrated in Figure 5.1, an open access fishery will be overused, depleting the value of the fishery.

As one might expect, fishing is important to New Zealand. In 1986, legislation was passed establishing "individual transferable quotas" (ITQs) for regulating fishing for what has grown to 70 different species of fish, covering a very large proportion of the entire commercial fishing industry in the country. The legislation defines an ITQ for a particular fishery in a particular geographical region as the right to catch a certain percentage of the annually defined total allowable catch (TAC) for that particular species and region. Every year the TAC is defined based on a biological assessment of the stock of the species in the region and a determination of the maximum sustainable yield.

Analysis of the market suggests that it is working well. ITQ prices have risen, particularly for economically important species, suggesting that the program is generating value for New Zealand fishers. Furthermore, in most cases there are enough participants and transactions to not be concerned about issues of market thinness or market power. (Source: Newell et al., 2005.)

E. Transaction Costs

A virtue of tradable permits is that any initial misallocation of the right to emit can be remedied by trading of permits; furthermore, the ability to trade makes the opportunity cost of emitting equal to the permit price. But if there are impediments to trade, these advantages disappear or are significantly diminished. Impediments to trade can be viewed as transaction costs associated with trade. These can be quite significant for tradable permit markets.

Robert Stavins (1995) identified three sources of transaction costs that might arise in permit markets, (1) search and information costs, (2) bargaining and decision-making costs, and (3) monitoring and enforcement costs. For a trade to take place, a potential buyer and a potential seller must identify each other (search and information costs), they must negotiate with each other and finally agree on a price for a trade (bargaining and decision-making costs), and the trade must be monitored and enforced. This last category of cost may be borne by the regulatory agency, but there are also costs that may be borne by firms. If a trade must be approved by a regulatory agency, that can add time and costs to consummating a trade.

Search and information costs become large the more heterogeneous a permit market may be. If emission permits involve a single pollutant with no spatial or temporal considerations, the market is homogeneous—there is only one "good," the emission permit. On the other hand, if we are dealing with an ambient permit market in which every permit must be viewed differently, in terms of its impact on ambient pollution, identifying likely buyers and sellers may be very difficult. Furthermore, if there are complex rules governing who may trade with whom, the problems of identifying trading partners becomes even more significant. Robert Hahn (1989) surveyed several attempts at establishing permit markets in the United States and Europe and identified transaction costs as a major reason for failure. In an examination of pollution trading in Los Angeles, Foster and

Hahn (1995) examine trading in small and large quantities of pollution. They argue that transaction costs are likely to be higher per unit of pollution for the small trades. They then show empirical evidence that trading is less likely for small quantities of pollution, in support of their hypothesis on transaction costs.

The main conclusion is that a nicely designed complex system of ambient pollution permits may look efficient on paper but transaction costs may make it fail. A simpler, though perhaps less efficient, permit system may perform better. Alternatively, when permit markets are designed, there should be a conscious effort to minimize transaction costs.

SUMMARY

1. Property rights are important to a well-functioning market. Without property rights, even the most ordinary market transactions are difficult.

2. Transaction costs are those costs associated with consummating a trade, over and above the trade itself (i.e., the money exchanged for the good). A simple example is the commission paid to an agent to sell a house. Transaction costs can also involve nonmonetary costs such as the difficulty in striking a bargain.

3. The Coase Theorem has two parts: one with transaction costs and one without. In achieving the efficient level of an externality (such as pollution), the initial assignment of property rights (right to pollute, right to clean air) is irrelevant if there are no transaction costs. With transaction costs, the initial assignment matters.

4. When transaction costs are present, it is important for the government to distribute property rights in an efficient way and to try to reduce transaction costs associated with trading rights.

5. With public bads, where there are a few generators of pollution and many consumers, bargaining implicitly involves costs. Thus the Coase Theorem states that the free trade of property rights cannot be relied on for efficiency.

6. Tradable environmental property rights, known as tradable emission permits in the case of pollution and individual transferable quotas in the case of fisheries, have become popular and important tools in regulating nonexcludable resources.

7. Tradable emission permits, also known as cap and trade, are in use today in a wide variety of markets, including carbon emissions in Europe and sulfur emissions in the United States.

PROBLEMS

1. Foster and Hahn (1995) have examined trading of air pollutant emission rights within the Los Angeles air basin in 1985–1991. They hypothesized that two factors would lead to high transaction costs: exchanges of thinly traded pollutants (few trades) and exchanges involving small quantities of pollution. Transaction costs for thinly traded pollutants would be high because of the difficulty in finding someone with whom to trade. The following is a table showing the number of trades for five pollutants during the period in question in Los Angeles. Shown are trades from one factory to another within the same company ("internal"), trades involving brokers or

other intermediaries ("brokered"), and trades between companies without assistance of intermediaries ("external").[17]

Pollutant	Internal	Brokered	External	Total
CO	3	3	1	7
NO_x	4	21	4	29
PM	6	4	1	11
VOC	32	55	61	148
SO_x	3	3	0	6

a. How would you expect the transaction costs to differ among the three categories of trade: internal, brokered or external?

b. Do the data in the table support the hypothesis that transaction costs might be higher for thinly traded pollutants? Why or why not?

c. What effect would you expect the size of a trade (number of tons of pollution) to have on transaction costs (per ton of pollution)? How would you expect the size of a trade to influence whether a pollutant is more likely to be internally traded, brokered, or externally traded?

2. Assume the marginal savings from emissions for an industry are given by $MS(e) = 30-e$ and that the marginal damage from emissions is given by $MD(e) = e$. Suppose that the tax interaction effect corresponds to a welfare loss of $10 per ton of emissions reduced. Suppose further that the cost of collecting revenue from labor taxes is $1.40 for every dollar collected ($1 for revenue plus 40¢ deadweight loss).

a. Plot marginal damage and marginal savings from emissions for this industry. What is the efficient level of an emissions tax, ignoring the revenue recycling and tax interaction effects? Derive this result graphically.

b. Now take into account the tax interaction affect. What is the efficient number of marketable permits, if the permits are initially distributed for free? Derive this result graphically.

c. If the permits in part (b) were initially auctioned, what would be the total surplus and what would be the magnitude of the tax interaction effect, the revenue recycling effect, and the Pigovian effect.

3. In the 1970s in U.S. cities, air emissions were governed almost completely by prescriptive regulations. One of the problems faced by regulators in large urban areas with air quality well below desirable levels was how to let new polluters into the city without reducing air pollution. Regulators came up with an innovative approach called the offset system. New sources of pollution had to "convince" existing sources of emissions to reduce emissions. The overall effect of all these reductions had to at least offset the pollution additions by the new source.

Explain why or why not this so-called "offset system" is equivalent to a marketable permit system.

4. In Section I.C.2 of this chapter, for each partition, propose a division of the profits that makes each firm at least as well off relative to independent action. Then

show how one or more firms can actually do better in a coalition in another partition.

5. Consider a pollution problem involving a paper mill located on a river and a commercial salmon fishery operating on the same river. The fishery can operate at one of two locations: upstream (above the mill) or downstream (in the polluted part of the river). Pollution lowers profits for the fishery: without pollution, profits are $300 upstream and $500 downstream; with pollution, profits are $200 upstream and $100 downstream. The mill earns $500 in profit, and the technology exists for it to build a treatment plant at the site that completely eliminates the pollution, but at a cost of $200. There are two possible assignments of property rights: (i) the fishery has the right to a clean river and (ii) the mill has the right to pollute the river.

    a. What is the efficient outcome (the maximum of total joint profit)?

    b. What are the outcomes under the two different property rights regimes, when there is no possibility of bargaining?

    c. How does your answer to (b) change when the two firms can bargain costlessly?

6. Consider a situation involving Finch's Footwear and Millie's Muffins. Finch's Footwear produces shoes (S) at a cost $C_S(S) = S^2 + 8$ and the Millie's Muffins produces baked goods (B) at a cost of $C_B(B,S) = B^2 + L\,S + 4$. There are fixed costs but no sunk costs. Note that costs for the Millie's Muffins depend on output of the shoe company, because of the pollution associated with making shoes (more money has to be spent by Millie to keep things clean). The price of baked goods, p_B, is fixed at 10.

    a. Calculate how much footwear and muffins will be produced if the two firms merge, assuming profit maximizing behavior. Do this for two different prices of shoes: $p_S = 8$ and $p_S = 14$.

    b. If Finch's Footwear has rights to pollute, how much baked goods and footwear will be produced at the same two prices for shoes ($p_S = 8$ and $p_S = 14$)?

    c. If Millie's Muffins has a right to clean air, how much baked goods and footwear will be produced, and what if anything will Millie receive for compensation? Use the same two prices for Finch's output ($p_S = 8$ and $p_S = 14$).

    d. Why is the foregoing consistent or inconsistent with the Coase Theorem?

7. Discuss the following statement: Most pollution problems can be traced to disputes over property rights, imperfectly defined property rights, or ambiguously defined property rights. Give examples to support your comments.

8. A beekeeper and a farmer with an apple orchard are neighbors. This is convenient for the orchard owner since the bees pollinate the apple trees: one beehive pollinates one acre of orchard. Unfortunately, there are not enough bees next door to pollinate the whole orchard and pollination costs are $10 per acre. The beekeeper has total costs of $TC = H^2 + 10H + 10$ and marginal costs $MC = 10 + 2H$ where H is the number of hives. Each hive yields $20 worth of honey.

    a. How many hives would the beekeeper maintain if operating independently of the farmer?

    b. What is the socially efficient number of hives?

    c. In the absence of transaction costs, what outcome do you expect to arise from bargaining between the beekeeper and the farmer?

    d. How high would total transaction costs have to be to erase all gains from bargaining?

9. Brussels has been considering two plans to control pollution caused by heavy trucks. Plan A calls for the institution and enforcement of tight emission standards on commercial trucks with fines for noncompliance. Plan B involves tax incentives for firms operating commercial trucks that achieve lower emission levels. You have analyzed these plans and conclude that each plan has identical effects on emissions from trucks and resulting pollution concentrations. What are the potential differences between these two plans, on the basis of efficiency or other criteria?

NOTES

1. There has been a large literature on the Coase Theorem. For a sampling, see Dahlman (1979), Hoffman and Spitzer (1982), Regan (1972), Schulze and d'Arge (1974), and Calabresi (1968). Cooter (1987) provides a nice summary.
2. High transaction costs have been blamed for the failure of several pollution trading systems. See Hahn (1989) and Stavins (1995).
3. The characterization of the Coase Theorem presented here is drawn from Hoffman and Spitzer (1982).
4. Baumol and Oates (1988) cite a Swedish example of a refinery damaging an auto manufacturing plant. Negotiation between these parties took place to eliminate the Pareto-relevant externality.
5. Coase (1981), p. 187.
6. Even if the damage figure were public knowledge so that everyone knew the individual damage was $5, the potential for holdout is still there. By this we mean that one or more of the people can refuse to pay, even though the payment would make them better off. Provided there is only one holdout, the mill can still be paid and Pareto optimality achieved.
7. Here the holdout problem (mentioned in note 6) does not exist. If the plant knows the damages of each, it simply offers compensation to everyone in the amount of $5 or, alternatively, installs pollution control equipment.
8. The potential for free-riding and holdout were described in the example of the Gavin Power Plant, earlier in this chapter. Another example of potential bargaining problems involves a single victim buying out multiple polluters: the Vittel water company in France paid farmers to change their practices to reduce the nitrate pollution in the groundwater and thus in the springs Vittel used for its bottled water. One of the problems that Vittel finessed was that key farmers realized they were very important to Vittel's being able to solve its pollution problem and thus held out for large payments (Depres et al., 2008).
9. This section is based in part on Aivazion and Callen (1981).
10. Hahn (1989) provides a very accessible treatment of this issue.
11. The idea of tradable permits is generally ascribed to Dales (1968) and Crocker (1966). As noted in the previous chapter, emission fees have their modern genesis in Kneese (1962).
12. Refer to Hahn (1984).
13. Hahn (1984) concludes that this may not be a serious issue, based on his calculation that a dominant firm in the Los Angeles area would not be able to manipulate the market much unless it received over half the permits issued in the region.

14

VOLUNTARY MEASURES

TOM TIETENBERG CHARACTERIZES THE LAST HALF CENTURY OF REGULATORY EFFORTS TO improve environmental protection in terms of three different waves of actions. The first wave corresponds to moving from very few restrictions on polluters to the use of extensive prescriptive regulations, primarily in the 1960s and 1970s, though such prescriptive regulations continue to this day to be developed for many environmental problems. The second wave, beginning approximately in the 1980s, corresponds to the widespread introduction of market-based incentives as a better means of providing environmental protection. Although we are still riding that wave, Tietenberg and others have suggested that a third wave has emerged, corresponding to the use of information disclosure so that consumers and other stakeholders can directly induce firms to be proactive environmentally as a way of doing business and growing their bottom line.[1]

Whether or not information disclosure is the driving force, one of the positive developments of the past few decades is the emergence of firms that appear to acknowledge corporate social responsibility—a responsibility to do good without being required to do so. To name but a few of many examples, DuPont voluntarily gave up the production of ozone-depleting chlorofluorocarbons, BP (formerly known as British Petroleum) has been marketing itself as "Beyond Petroleum," and Patagonia has long prided itself on its progressive environmental record, both in operations and product characteristics.[2]

Individuals, too, voluntary undertake socially responsible actions, such as buying offsets for carbon emissions and recycling when not required to do so. The behavior of individuals may be understandable or at least believable—after all, people can have just about any preferences they wish. And people certainly do make substantial charitable contributions that are purely voluntary.

But the actions of firms are a little more puzzling. Why would a firm voluntarily undertake something like pollution control, spending money without being required to do so and with no apparent benefit to the firm? Cynics, in fact, may suspect ulterior and less altruistic motives behind firms taking "voluntary" actions to protect the environment. Other observers are more positive, arguing that the new business paradigm for the postindustrial age is "doing well by doing good."[3]

Whatever the motivations, the use of "voluntary" approaches to environmental protection is becoming more common. Understanding these approaches is important to any comprehensive understanding of environmental regulation. From an economics point of view, do these approaches work? If they do, why?

The purpose of this chapter is to examine this issue more closely. We first define what we mean by voluntary actions and then explore the incentives profit-maximizing firms may have to undertake costly, but apparently voluntary, pro-environment actions. A related question is why governments would pursue voluntary measures when mandating behavior through direct regulation seems stronger and more certain.

Dupont's Decision to Stop Producing Chlorofluorocarbons[4]

Cholorfluorocarbons (CFCs—a family of chemicals marketed by Dupont under the brand name Freon) were invented in the 1920s by General Motors and developed jointly with E. I. du Pont de Nemours & Co. (DuPont). CFCs represented a seemingly safe alternative to the refrigerants in use at the time. Over the decades CFCs began to be used in a wide variety of applications, including as propellants in spray cans of consumer products. In the 1970s it was discovered that these CFCs were depleting the stratospheric ozone layer, which protects the earth from harmful ultraviolet radiation. As is often the case when a profitable product of a company is suspected of causing environmental harm, DuPont vigorously resisted government action to restrict CFCs, at least initially. In the 1980s DuPont softened its resistance and in 1988 announced it was phasing out CFC production entirely, confident that it could develop alternatives.

This seems like an example of corporate responsibility, and some of Dupont's actions certainly were in the public interest. Looking at the market for CFCs indicates that other reasons for DuPont's action may also be at work. The market for CFCs softened considerably in the 1970s as demand stopped growing and eventually contracted (primarily because of environmental concerns over CFCs), leading to excess production capacity. Furthermore, there were many producers for CFCs (the original patents had expired). Thus the product ceased being as profitable as it once was. One of DuPont's strengths was innovation in new products; DuPont was confident that its researchers could find substitutes for CFCs (patentable substitutes). Thus promoting a phaseout of CFCs could improve DuPont's bottom line by strengthening the market for CFC substitutes.[5]

I. A TAXONOMY OF VOLUNTARY MEASURES AND ACTIONS

Voluntary measures and actions encompass a very wide set of activities by firms, so it is natural to start with a definition.

DEFINITION A *voluntary environmental action* is an environmentally beneficial action by a firm or organization that is not induced by applicable laws or regulation, either through regulatory requirements or substantial positive or negative incentives.

For instance, if a firm cleans up its pollution in response to a law that stipulates substantial financial penalties for excess emissions, we would not deem the cleanup "voluntary." On the other hand, if the law provides for some modest official positive publicity for good environmental performance, we would probably call significant pro-environment actions "voluntary" due to the modest nature of the incentives relative to the costs. It is hard to draw a sharp line between purely voluntary and nonvoluntary environmental actions. One way of determining if an incentive is substantial or not is to observe whether all firms respond to the incentive. If virtually all firms take action in response to the incentive, we can consider the incentive substantial; if only some firms respond (and some do not), then that is a signal that the incentive may be modest, insufficient to motivate all firms.

What is most important for our purposes is to understand why firms would undertake voluntary actions, and if they do, how meaningful (in environmental terms) are the actions? As might be expected, we look at this problem through an economic lens (i.e., the profit motive for firms and utility maximization for individuals), asking what economic reasons there are for voluntary action. There may well be ethical or noneconomic motivations for firms doing good, but we will leave that issue to others. It is always useful to understand how well the profit motive explains what we see firms doing, without resorting to other explanations of behavior.

There are two broad divisions of voluntary actions. The first category is actions that are purely motivated by the market—consumers, employees, competitors, or investors. An associated regulatory structure is not necessary to explain these actions. Firms may be green because it helps sell products (consumers like green products). Or firms may be green because they can attract better employees. Firms may use environmental actions to enhance their competitive position in the industry. Or a firm may go green to signal to investors that the firm is a good financial investment (though why being green is a positive signal is not at all clear). If the capital market recognizes the firm as a good investment, this can lower the cost of capital to the firm.

A second category of voluntary actions requires the presence of a governmental regulator. The regulator may be actively engaged with the firm or simply hovering in the wings. In either case, a firm may take voluntary actions to improve its relationship with the regulator. At the simplest level, a firm may take voluntary actions to stave off an impending mandatory regulation. If a firm voluntarily does 80% of what a regulator might include in a mandatory regulation, the regulator may decide to move on to other, bigger challenges and abandon the pursuit of the mandatory regulation. Sometimes regulators offer regulatory programs that firms may voluntarily opt into. These programs usually have incentives (positive or negative) to induce firm participation. But consistent with our definition of "voluntary," these incentives are not strong enough to induce all (or even most) firms to participate. Furthermore, there are a number of examples of bilateral agreements between regulators and firms, aimed at solving specific environmental problems. Firms may also promote specific regulations as a way of disadvantaging competitors.

II. MARKET-DRIVEN VOLUNTARY ACTIONS

There is no question that some firms have taken being green to heart and are pursuing a pro-environment agenda in many arenas. In this section, we look at a few of the motives that have been suggested that might be driving such action without resorting to attributing it to regulators lurking in the shadows. In other words, we examine the pure market-driven reasons for firms being green, serving consumers employers or investors.

A. Green Consumers

There is considerable evidence that some consumers are willing to pay more for green goods. From our point of view, green goods are goods that are manufactured in a way that is environmentally friendly (e.g., wood products from certified sustainable forests or electricity produced from wind power) without direct impact on a consumer. These are sometimes referred to as impure public goods—a package of a private good and a public good.[6] In these cases, the green product is physically indistinguishable from the conventional product. Why consumers are willing to pay more for these goods is complex. The consumer may feel a duty to do no harm in consumption or may obtain utility from taking environmentally positive actions (a "warm glow"). Or, the consumer may view goods that are produced in an environmentally friendly way as being of better quality in terms of final consumption (e.g., shade-grown coffee).[7] Whatever the reason, it is clear some consumers are willing to pay for green actions that do not benefit them directly.

It is important to distinguish these types of goods from goods where the consumer derives direct personal benefit from the "greenness" (e.g., organic food).[8] Although for most goods it is somewhat ambiguous which of these rationales is operating, what we are primarily interested in are green goods where the green part is a public good.

It is not entirely clear why consumers are willing to pay more for green goods. The important thing is that what drives this demand is consumer preferences, and consumer preferences are considered sovereign. If consumers are willing to pay more for free trade coffee, that is their prerogative. We need not delve too deeply into why they prefer that coffee.

One example of green goods is "green electricity." In some communities, consumers are given a choice of conventional electricity or "green electricity." In fact, according to the U.S. Department of Energy, in 2008 approximately 25% of US electric utilities offered green power options to their customers.[9] Green power is simply electricity produced using renewable sources of energy. Of course, the electricity itself is completely indistinguishable from nongreen electricity. There are usually two ways in which a consumer may buy green electricity: either by buying green electricity directly or by contributing to the cost of building green electricity capacity. Consumers are clearly willing to spend more for green electricity.[10]

A prominent example of consumer preference for green production is the recent rise in popularity of retail carbon offsets. Offsets of emissions have long been used by firms to buy and sell the obligation to reduce emissions (see Chapter 15). For instance, decades ago in the United States, new emitters setting up business in an urban area had to "offset" their emission additions by finding (and paying) existing firms to reduce their emissions. In recent years, firms have used offsets to effectively reduce their emissions in order to provide a green image, particularly in the case of carbon emissions.

The purchase of offsets by consumers is different, however. When consumers buy offsets, they are making a purely voluntary contribution to the environment. Retail offsets (to distinguish them from offsets purchased by firms) are a way in which consumers can produce a green product from a "brown" product. For instance, if I am taking an airplane flight, and my share of the aircraft's emissions is 1 ton of carbon, I can make my part of the flight carbon neutral by paying someone else to reduce his or her carbon emissions by 1 ton. This is formalized in an offset market whereby sellers of offsets reduce emissions (hopefully in a certified, reliable way) and then sell these "reductions." The buyer of the offset gets "credit" for the reduction. If the offsets are legitimate (which is a big if), then from the environment's point of view the offsets have neutralized the buyer's emissions.[11] So in the example of the airplane flight, I can buy a 1-ton carbon offset in the market and make my part of the flight carbon neutral. Nobody is forcing me to do this; it is purely voluntary. Table 14.1 shows four such offset programs and the prices they were offering on October 13, 2008. For reference, in 2008 the per capita annual emissions in the United States were about 20 tons of CO_2.

Sustainable Forest Products Certification

Sustainable management of forests was one of the priorities to emerge from the 1992 Rio Earth Summit (the United Nations Conference on Environment and Development).[12] The concern was that forest products, particularly from old growth forests, be harvested in an environmentally sensitive and sustainable manner. One of the outcomes of the Earth Summit was the establishment of the Forest Stewardship Council (FSC). The FSC has established forestry management practices that are deemed sustainable, has an accreditation program for certifying well-managed forests, and offers a label that would producers may use to signal to wood consumers that the wood products come from sustainable forests. According to the FSC, roughly 7% of the world's productive forests participate in their program. Costs of producing sustainable wood may be higher, not only because of the forest practices involved but also because certification requires tracking the wood products as they make their way through the supply chain (the "chain of custody").

The idea behind the eco-labeling part of the FSC program is that consumers may be willing to pay more for sustainable wood products, and thus suppliers may be able to realize higher prices for these products. The enormous building supply retailers, Home Depot (North America) and B&Q (Europe), carry FSC-labeled wood products (though not all of their wood is so labeled). Although the FSC program appears to be working well, successes are mixed. As reported by Sedjo and Swallow (2002), in the 1990s Scott Paper introduced into Canada an eco-line of consumer paper products to compete against its regular line. The firm discontinued the eco-line after significant declines in sales.

One obvious question is, why would a retailer rely on third-party certifiers like the FSC instead of doing the job themselves and tailoring the definition of sustainability to their own needs? One answer to that is provided by Kotchen and van't Veld (2009), who argue that there are costs associated with providing credible certification and thus economies associated with working through a single certifier rather than having individual firms provide their own brand of sustainable wood products.[13]

TABLE 14.1 Price of Retail Carbon Offsets, October 13, 2008

Organization	Carbonfund.org	Greenlife.com	Terrapass.com	BeGreenNow.com
Price ($/metric ton of CO_2)	$10	$15	$13.18	$14

Source: Websites indicated in column heads.

One determinant of consumer preferences for green products is income. Wealthier consumers are willing to pay more for green than poorer consumers. This means that environmental protection is an avenue for price discrimination for firms that have some market power. When a firm (such as one of the big grocery chains) can offer several versions of a product, ranging from generic to branded to very green, the firm is effectively able to segment its market by income, practice price discrimination, and thus increase profits.[14] For instance, consider eggs. Free-range eggs are from chickens free to roam whereas regular eggs are from chickens raised in factorylike conditions (at a slightly lower cost). Assume richer customers tend to prefer the free-range eggs, whereas poorer customers are much less likely to pay for that luxury. Furthermore, demand from poorer customers may be more price sensitive (elastic). When a store offers both types of eggs, it is essentially asking customers to self-identify as rich or poor. This facilitates making more profit from the richer customers.[15]

B. Green as a Signal

In the previous section, we saw that there is real consumer demand for green products and for products from companies that are green. But most firms in the world are not retail firms—they sell to other firms who are presumably more hard-nosed than the typical consumer. The question then arises, *if we exclude green demand from consumers*, are there other reasons why a firm may choose to increase its environmental performance voluntarily?

There is a long-standing debate in the business management literature regarding two questions: (1) does improved environmental performance lead to improved financial performance for businesses? and (2) if so, why? This is a complex question that we can only touch on here.[16] If being green improves the way a company operates, the company will become more profitable (unless all the other companies in the industry also become green). Leaving aside the preferences of consumers, there are two main avenues through which green policies could increase the profitability of a company: stakeholder relations (particularly employee recruiting and retention)[17] and investor relations (lowering the cost of capital).

One way a company could improve its operations by being green is in employee recruiting. Dow Chemical Corporation has indicated that one of its motivations for greening the company was to help recruit better engineers to work in the company (Portney, 2005). If a company relies significantly on highly educated employees, the quality of employees it is able to attract may be affected by the company's reputation. A green company may be able to recruit better employees; this obviously helps the bottom line.

Rather than good environmental performance causing profitability, it is conceivable that the causality may actually operate in the opposite direction. The fact that a company is well run and profitable may induce it to become socially responsible, including environmentally responsible. In this case, being green signals to investors that the company is well run and attractive. This in turn makes capital more readily available (cheaper) to the firm which, to close the loop, lowers costs and increases profitability.

There have been a number of statistical studies that attempt to identify which of these various theories actually apply in the marketplace. In fact, Margolis et al. (2007) report 45 such studies of the relationship between environmental performance and the financial performance of companies, and far more studies (nearly 200) of the relationship between

---

Green Stock Portfolios

Traditionally, mutual funds have been assembled based on criteria that are related to economic characteristics—for instance, the largest 500 firms in the market. In fact, there are a number of indexes of market performance that are based on the performance of portfolios of stocks of companies screened on specific criteria, such as the New York–based Standard and Poors 500 large firms (S&P 500) or the London-based Financial Times Stock Exchange 100 biggest firms (FTSE 100). In recent years, indexes (and mutual funds) have also been constructed with *societal goals* in mind, including environmental concerns. One can buy mutual funds that purport to marry financial criteria with social responsibility or even specific criteria such as climate friendliness.

Meir Statman (2006) has analyzed[18] how such social responsibility stock indices perform relative to an index constructed without concern for societal goals (the S&P 500). The five indices he examined were the Domini 400 Social Index (DS 400), the Calvert Social Index (CSI), the Citizens Index (CI), and the U.S. portion of the Dow Jones Sustainability Index (DJSI). Using a common rating system for companies in the index (–10 to 10, with 10 being the most socially responsible), the author determined that the mean social responsibility score for the companies in the S&P 500 was –0.26 compared with mean values of 0.40 to 1.24 for the four socially responsible indices (with DS 400 scoring the highest). Focusing on environmental performance alone (a narrower criterion than social responsibility), the S&P 500 mean score was -0.26 compared to values for the four indices of –0.14 to 0.15, with the DS 400 being the best.

Financial performance was measured by the monthly return on the portfolio. For instance, for May 1990 to March 2004, the average monthly return on the S&P 500 was 1.0%, whereas the monthly return on the DS 400 (the only one of the indices in existence in 1990) was 1.10%. This might not sound like much of a difference, but small differences add up. Unfortunately, from a statistical point of view, the two returns are indistinguishable. This does not mean that there is no difference—just that there are not enough data to identify a difference, if in fact one exists. The bottom line of the analysis is that the author's evidence was not strong enough to show that socially responsible indexes performed any better than the market. Of course, the other side of that coin is that his evidence also suggests they performed no worse.[19]

company financial performance and social responsibility of firms, a broader category than environmental performance.

One way of learning from such a large number of sometimes conflicting studies is to conduct a "meta analysis." A meta-analysis is an analysis of analyses. Meta-analyses are most useful when there are many empirical papers addressing the same issue and reaching somewhat different conclusions. The goal of a meta-analysis is to reach a statistical conclusion regarding important hypotheses using the outputs of the various studies as inputs or data points for the meta-analysis. A meta-analysis is not a new analysis of new data but rather a potentially useful summary of an empirical literature. Several meta-analyses of this literature have been conducted over the years, with one of the most recent and comprehensive ones being that by Margolis et al. (2007). In their meta-analysis, they conclude that environmental performance and financial performance are positively correlated. Furthermore, they examine the broader issue of causality between social responsibility and financial performance: which causes which? They conclude that the evidence is weaker for social responsibility causing good financial performance (compared to the reverse causation).

III. REGULATORY GAMES

We now turn to a slightly different rationale for firms going green. In this case there is an environmental regulator or other government agency involved, either directly or "in the wings." There are three main categories of such voluntary actions. The most straightforward is when a regulator and a firm (or group of firms) negotiate an environmental agreement involving real actions and commitments on the part of the firm(s), though the firm enters the agreement voluntarily. An extension of this is what has become known as a voluntary program, whereby the regulator establishes an optional regulatory arrangement and asks firms to voluntarily agree to participate (or not). A third category is where a firm or industry association takes a pro-environment action unilaterally, to preempt threatened mandatory regulation or to shape mandatory regulation.

In all of these cases, firms are responding to regulatory carrots or regulatory sticks. Consistent with our earlier definition of "voluntary," these carrots or sticks should be modest. Regulatory carrots would be rewards for joining an agreement (e.g., good publicity, cost sharing, or flexible enforcement), or advantages from shaping a regulation for competitive advantage. Regulatory sticks would be threatened mandatory regulation. In the "real world," incentives can be more complex and the lines of demarcation among these three approaches can be blurry.[20]

A. Voluntary Agreements

A voluntary agreement (VA) is an agreement between a regulator and a firm or a group of firms (typically an industry association) to take some pro-environment action. It is voluntary in the sense that the regulator has no legal mandate to force the firms to do its bidding. Presumably, both parties see an advantage to reaching an agreement.

The goal of this section[21] is to formalize the description of the structure of a voluntary agreement, examining the strategic interaction between a regulator and a firm, an interaction that may or may not lead to an agreement. The stick that the regulator wields is a threat of possible mandatory regulation if the firm does not "volunteer." This also moderates the regulator in the sense that the regulator cannot be sure the legislature will follow through with a mandatory regulation. The carrot to the firm is reduced costs from a voluntary approach, which gives the firm more flexibility and thus the ability to provide a specific level of abatement at a lower cost than would be possible with a mandate to undertake that same level of abatement.

In our VA model, there are three actors, one passive (the legislature) and two active (the firm and the regulator). The legislature is passive in the sense that it only acts if a VA fails to materialize, in which case it adopts a mandatory regulation with probability p; it fails to act with probability $1 - p$. Thus the legislature is treated as a roll of the dice rather than as a strategic agent making decisions in its own interest.

Understanding this VA model is somewhat complicated. Not only do we need to understand the payoffs and incentives of the three actors but we also have to evaluate the strategic interaction among the three.

At issue is the level of abatement, a, that the firm pursues, either voluntarily or through a mandatory regulation. The costs to the firm of this abatement are given by $C_V(a)$ or $C_M(a)$, which we will assume involve constant marginal costs of abatement:

$$C_V(a) = c_V\, a \tag{14.1a}$$

$$C_M(a) = c_M\, a \tag{14.1b}$$

where c_V and c_M are constants with $c_V < c_M$. The reason $c_V < c_M$ is that we assume that it is cheaper for the firm to provide abatement if it is operating under a voluntary regime rather than a mandatory regime. The idea is that with a voluntary regime the firm will have more flexibility and thus be able to achieve any given level of abatement at lower cost than if operating under a mandatory regime. The firm is assumed to operate to minimize costs. The environmental benefits of abatement, $B(a)$, are independent of whether the regime is voluntary or not.

Having stipulated that the firm operates to minimize costs, we turn to the regulator. The regulator is idealistic and views its job as maximizing net social benefits, equal to the environmental benefits of abatement less the costs to the firm of abatement:

$$NSB_V(a) = B(a) - c_V\, a \tag{14.2a}$$

$$NSB_M(a) = B(a) - c_M\, a \tag{14.2b}$$

Figure 14.1 shows the levels of abatement that maximize surplus under the mandatory regime $(a_M{}^*)$ and surplus obtainable under an arbitrary voluntary regime (a_V). Shown in the figure is the net surplus between the marginal cost line and the marginal benefit line for $a_M{}^*$ and a_V. Surplus will be maximized for the voluntary regime at $a_V{}^*$, but that really only serves as an upper limit for the regulator, who has to worry about the firm accepting the offer of the voluntary regime. Note that by assumption, a voluntary regime may yield higher surplus than the surplus-maximizing mandatory regime. Of course, whether these

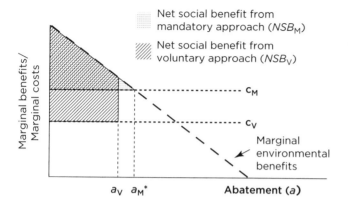

FIGURE 14.1 Net social benefits from optimal mandatory and arbitrary voluntary measures.

surpluses are obtained or not is uncertain. The legislature may fail to enact the mandatory regime and the firm may reject the voluntary regime.

Now consider the legislature, which only acts if the VA breaks down. The goal of the legislature is to choose a mandatory level of abatement which maximizes net benefits, given in Eq. (14.2b): $a_M{}^*$. But the catch is that nobody can be sure the legislature will actually take any action. There is a probability p that the legislature will enact a mandatory surplus-maximizing regulation $a_M{}^*$ and a probability $1 - p$ that it will enact nothing. Even if p is close to 1, the regulator may still prefer the voluntary agreement, as illustrated in Figure 14.1. An ideal voluntary agreement gives more social surplus than a mandatory agreement. Even a less-than-perfect voluntary agreement could generate greater net benefits than a mandatory regulation, due to the fact that c_V is lower than c_M. In Figure 14.1, it is easy to visualize a voluntary level of abatement lower than $a_M{}^*$ that yields a higher shaded area (net social benefit) than the mandatory regulation (that is in fact how the figure is drawn). This illustrates why the regulator would like to have a voluntary level of abatement. However, the regulator will not just take any voluntary level of abatement; it has to be sufficiently strong to generate higher expected net benefits than resorting to relying on (uncertain) mandatory regulations. Thus there is some smallest level of voluntary abatement that the regulator will prefer to mandatory regulation($a_V{}^{min}$).

We can now put these three actors (the firm, the regulator, and the legislature) together in a strategic interaction. Figure 14.2 encapsulates the interaction. The regulator first offers a voluntary agreement at a certain level of abatement. So, in actual fact, the regulator has two decisions: to offer a VA or not, and what level of abatement to include in the VA. The next move belongs to the firm and it is a simple one: accept or reject the offered VA. The final move belongs to the legislature. If the firm and the regulator have agreed on a VA, no further action is needed. If on the other hand, there is no VA, then the legislature will (with probability p) enact a mandatory regulation at a level of abatement $a_M{}^*$. On the other hand, with probability $1 - p$, the legislature will do nothing and the firm is off the hook and does not need to do any abatement. At the bottom of each branch of the tree in Figure 14.2 is the payoff that can be expected for the regulator and for the firm.

The regulator must choose a regulation that gives as much abatement as possible (up to a point—$a_V{}^*$), but it does not want to ask for too much for fear the firm will reject the

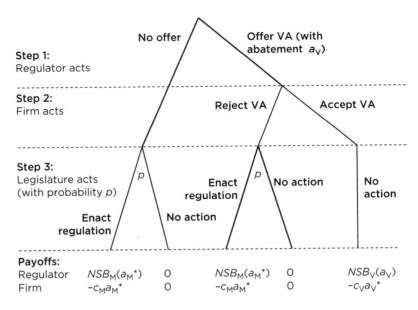

FIGURE 14.2 Structure of regulatory games for voluntary agreement.

offer. The firm, on the other hand, can either accept the regulator's offer or play dice with the legislature, risking getting an even worse deal from them.

As is the usual approach to this type of game, we start at the end and work backward. This is simple for the legislature. The expected payoff for the regulator if the VA falls though is $pNSB_M(a_M^*)$ and the expected cost to the firm is $pc_Ma_M^*$. Resorting to the legislature is the threat that forces the adoption of a VA, and these are the payoffs from that threat. For the VA to work, both the firm and the regulator must do better with the VA than with this threat.

Moving back one layer in Figure 14.2, we examine what the firm will do if it is offered a VA with abatement a_V. The firm will compare the payoff with a_V, which is $-c_Va_V$ with the payoff with the threat, and go with whichever gives the highest payoff:

$$c_V a_V \leq pc_M a_M^* \Rightarrow \text{accept } a_V \tag{14.3a}$$

$$c_V a_V > pc_M a_M^* \Rightarrow \text{reject } a_V \tag{14.3b}$$

Because of the simple structure of costs in Eq. (14.1), this can be reduced to a condition for accepting the VA:

Firm Decision: Accept $a_V \Leftrightarrow 0 \leq a_V \leq (p\, c_M\, a_M^*)/c_V \equiv a_V^{\max}$ (14.4)

In other words, a_V is a good deal for the firm if it is low enough, determined by Eq. (14.3). This determines a range of voluntary levels of abatement acceptable to the firm, ranging from $a_V = 0$ up to $a_V^{\max}$.

We now turn to the regulator's decision. It too has a lowest level of abatement it will offer in a voluntary agreement and a highest level of abatement. It always has to take into account the possibility that the firm will reject its offer and gamble with the legislature. The regulator, too, can decide not to offer a voluntary agreement and gamble with the legislature.

For the regulator, it will be willing to offer any a_V which gives at least the payoff associated with the legislative threat:

$$NSB_V(a_V) \geq pNSB_M(a_M^*) \tag{14.5}$$

Although we cannot write this out explicitly as in Eq. (14.4), we can see from Figure 14.1 that this implies a range of acceptable levels for abatement. The abatement level a_V can be low (though not as low as zero), so that the net social benefit associated with it is at least as great as that associated with a_M^*, diluted by the probability of getting mandatory regulations, p. As discussed in the context of Figure 14.1, we define a_V^{min} as the value of a_V for which Eq. (14.5) is an equality. Higher levels of a_V would automatically satisfy Eq. (14.5), up to a_V^*. The regulator would not want to go above a_V^*, which maximizes $NSB_V(a)$. We then have:

Regulator Decision: Offer $a_V \Leftrightarrow a_V^{min} \leq a_V \leq a_V^*$ $\qquad$ (14.6)

We have forgotten one thing for the regulator. If it offers a voluntary agreement in the range in Eq. (14.6), it hopes the firm accepts. The regulator must take this into account. The firm's decision is governed by Eq. (14.4). So the regulator really needs to combine the condition in Eq. (14.4) for firm actions with the conditions in Eq. (14.6) for its optimal decision. If there are levels of a_V that satisfy both conditions, we have a voluntary agreement. If there are no values of a_V which satisfy both, then the VA will not work.[22]

The important thing to take away from this model is that there are advantages to both the regulator and the firm from pursuing a voluntary agreement. Having said this, the firm and the regulator have goals that are in opposition—the regulator wants as much abatement as possible and the firm wants as little as possible. Critical to the negotiation is the threat looming in the background of mandatory regulations.

One thing we have not discussed is whether society is better off with a voluntary agreement than not. As we have set up the problem, with the legislature being unreliable, the answer is yes—the regulator looks out for net social benefits so anything that is okay with the regulator has to be okay with society. But part of the reason for the VA is that the legislature is unreliable and cannot be counted on to do anything about the problem. If it were more reliable, there would be less need for the VA. On the other hand, as we have set things up, the abatement costs are lower with voluntary actions; so even if $p = 1$, a VA can still be better off for society (as discussed in the context of Figure 14.1).

B. Voluntary Programs

Voluntary programs are an extension of voluntary agreements, and in fact the line between a voluntary agreement and a voluntary program is not bright. Instead of the regulator interacting with a single firm or industry association, the regulator allows some firms to join, others not. The structure of a voluntary program is that the regulatory agency designs the program, including what participants are expected to do, as well as any carrots that may be offered to participants.

It is useful to provide a generic structure to a voluntary program, keeping in mind that real programs come in many different shapes and sizes, probably differing significantly from this prototype. Most voluntary programs contain two features:

Was the EPA's 33–50 Program Effective?

In the early 1990s, the U.S. EPA instituted a voluntary toxics program known as the "33/50" program. The program had the goal of reducing the overall emissions of certain toxic chemicals by 33% in 1992 and 50% in 1995 (relative to 1988 levels). Firms were free to join the program, and there appears to be little tangible incentive that the EPA offered for participating the program. In that sense, the 33/50 program meets our criteria for being voluntary. Firms may, however, perceive a benefit to joining, perhaps by being able to more credibly market themselves to consumers as green.

Several researchers have examined this program to try to better understand why firms would participate.[23] A fundamental question is whether the program actually resulted in any additional emissions reductions over what might have occurred absent the program. It might be the case that firms that were more likely to reduce emissions happened to join, giving the false impression that it was the program that caused emissions to be reduced.

Khanna and Damon (1999) look at this question carefully. Their approach is to separate the participation decision from the emissions decision. Let the emissions decision be determined by

$$E_j = \alpha X_j + \beta D_j + \epsilon \tag{14.7}$$

where E_j is emissions for firm j; X_j is exogenous characteristics of firm j; D_j is the program participation decision (0 or 1) and ϵ is an error term. The variable D is not exogenous but is actually a decision variable of the firm, determined by the firm's assessment of the net benefits of program participation:

$$B_j = \gamma Z_j + \eta \tag{14.8}$$

In Eq. (14.8), Z_j are characteristics of firm j and B_j are the net benefits from program participation. Although the firm knows B_j, we do not—it is unobserved by the EPA and by the analyst. All we know is that if $D_j = 1$ (participate) then it must be that $B_j > 0$. The authors estimate Eq. (14.8) as a probit model, which allows the calculation of the probability of participation as a function of firm characteristics. This probability of participation is then used as data in place of D when estimating Eq. (14.7).

In estimating these two equations, the effectiveness of the 33/50 is bound up with the statistical significance of β. If β is significantly different than zero, then participation in the program changes emissions; if the variable is statistically indistinguishable from zero, then other factors are responsible for changes in emissions. The authors in fact find that β is not significantly different than zero. Emissions for firms in the program do decline, but it is not the program that caused the decline.

- **Environmental performance expectations from participants,** such as a 50% reduction in emissions of certain pollutants by a specific date relative to a baseline.
- **Rewards to participants,** such as prominent promotion of their participation in the program and associated positive publicity or relaxation of regulatory requirements in other contexts (relative to nonparticipants).

There may be other features as well, such as penalties for nonperformance or the stipulation that once a firm opts into the program, its choices are no longer voluntary.

A firm considering participating in such a program weighs the pros and cons—the advantages (from the rewards) and the disadvantages (additional pollution control). As has been stated, what makes this different from a standard regulatory system (where firms have environmental expectations and rewards for performing or punishments if they fail to perform) is that the rewards are modest. Otherwise we would not call this a voluntary program. As discussed earlier, modest rewards should induce only some firms to participate in the voluntary program.

A major concern with such voluntary programs is that the best-performing firms will join (environmental "good citizens" or those that may have intentions of reducing emissions for other reasons) and the laggards will not join. The net result will be that the firms in the program may appear to have lower emissions or better performance but in fact all that has happened is that the program has induced the best performers simply to identify themselves and no actual improvements in environmental performance have occurred. This of course is one possible outcome from a voluntary program. Another possible outcome is real environmental improvement. It is an empirical question which outcome has occurred.

Responsible Care and the Chemical Manufacturers Association

During the 1980s there were a number of tragic chemical accidents, most notably the accident at Bhopal (India) that killed thousands.[24] As a result, the public perception of the chemical industry became increasingly negative. The public increasingly believed that the industry (not just individual firms) was incapable of taking responsibility for its own products and processes. Clearly, further regulation was a threat to the industry. The industry association, the Chemical Manufacturers Association (CMA), was initially set up back in the nineteenth century to help protect member firms from injurious regulation.

In 1989 the CMA, along with its British counterpart (the Chemical Industries Association), set up the Responsible Care Program. According to the CMA, the two purposes of Responsible Care are to improve the environmental and safety performance of CMA members and as a result improve public perception of the industry. Responsible Care as originally designed consisted of a set of 10 general principles by which all CMA members had to agree to abide (such as agreeing to "develop and produce chemicals that can be transported, used and disposed of safely").

C. Preemptive Actions

The third class of voluntary environmental actions is the set of actions by firms that are partially motivated by a desire to preempt regulatory action. Typically, a new environmental threat will have emerged and governments may be considering taking regulatory action. If firms take aggressive "voluntary" action before governments act, the effect can be to defer or replace mandatory regulatory action.

A closely related class of actions occurs when firms take preemptive actions but with the intention of promoting the adoption of regulations that are advantageous and disadvantageous to competitors. One could view the DuPont action to forsake CFC production as an action that helped push a CFC ban to DuPont's competitive advantage.

SUMMARY

1. A voluntary environmental action is an environmentally beneficial action by a firm or organization that is not induced by applicable laws or regulation, either through regulatory requirements or substantial positive or negative incentives.

2. There are two broad sets of environmental actions. The first set is actions that are purely motivated by the market—by consumers, employees, competitors, investors, or other stakeholders. The second set involves a strategic game between the firm (or firms) and an environmental regulator.

3. In some markets, consumers are clearly willing to pay more for goods that are produced in an environmentally friendly way, and firms respond to that demand.

4. A firm being green can be attractive to employees and thus help attract and retain good employees.

5. A firm being green can be a signal that the company is well managed, attracting investors and potentially lowering the cost of capital for the firm.

6. In the category of strategic games between firms and regulators, there are three classes of voluntary actions: voluntary agreements, voluntary programs, and preemptive actions.

7. In a voluntary agreement, a regulator may settle for abatement levels that are less than might be mandated to avoid the uncertain process of obtaining legislative backing for mandatory regulations.

8. In a voluntary program, which firms are free to join (or not), environmental performance may appear to be above that of nonparticipants. In reaching this conclusion, it is important to take into account self-selection into the voluntary program.

9. Firms can take green actions in an effort to preempt regulatory action.

PROBLEMS

1. Consider the lucrative but highly competitive industry of dog toy manufacturers. The industry is dominated by Tucker's Toys, Finch's Frisbees, Morgan's Munchables, Riley's Rawhides, and Pecos' Pets. With five major firms, business is highly

competitive. If any of the firms tries to raise prices even by a little, customers flock to the lower-priced competitors. Demand for product from any one firm is virtually horizontal (perfectly elastic), and production costs are such that marginal costs are fairly constant over a wide range of output.

Finch, being a very shrewd business owner, decides that if he produces his goods in an environmentally friendly fashion, his customers will be pleased and as a result his dog toys will be seen as slightly different from those of the others. He can stand out a little from the rest of the pack. In other words, demand for his product will not be quite so elastic.

Before implementing the eco-policy, Finch's Frisbees are selling for $1 each, at which price he manages to sell 1 million a year and just breaks even. If the company implements an eco-policy, customers will become more loyal and the company will be able to charge $1.10 for its products, though at that price only sell 900,000 per year.

Assuming demand is linear, what is the maximum amount Finch's Frisbees would be willing to pay to green its company? Assume all of the other firms are sufficiently backward to not understand the advantages of becoming greener.

2. Consider the model of a voluntary environmental agreement discussed in section III.A of the chapter, in which there is a firm, a regulator, and a legislature. Benefits of abatement (in terms of reduced damage from pollution) are given by $B(a) = 100a - a^2/2$. The total costs of abatement under the mandatory regime are $c_m(a) = 20a$, and under the voluntary regime they are $c_v(a) = 10a$. In the event that no voluntary agreement is made, assume that the legislature acts with the optimal mandatory policy with probability $p = 0.5$. Your task is to determine whether $a_v = 80$ is an implementable voluntary agreement, and, if so, to determine its efficiency benefits to society in comparison to two different counterfactuals: (a) no-environmental protection, and (b) successful mandatory regulation.

NOTES

1. This characterization of three waves of environmental protection is due to Tietenberg (1998).
2. For a review of some of the issues related to "Corporate Social Responsibility," see the books by Hay et al (2005) and Heal (2008) and the review papers by Reinhardt et al. (2008), Portney (2008), and Lyon and Maxwell (2008) in the symposium on the topic in the *Review of Environmental Economics and Policy* (Summer 2008). For a specifically economic perspective, see the comprehensive, though somewhat technical, book by Lyon and Maxwell (2004). Vogel (2005) provides an excellent view of the issue from a political science perspective. Baron (2009) provides a positive theory of the subject. OECD (2003) provides a detailed discussion of voluntary approaches around the world, including a discussion of a number of case studies.
3. See Hawken et al. (1999), among many other books and articles on the subject.
4. Most of the information here on Dupont and CFCs is drawn from Maxwell and Briscoe (1997) and Lyon and Maxwell (2004).
5. A similar example of using environmental regulation to enhance competitive position has been alleged in the case of Atlantic Richfield's support of oxygenated gasoline standards in California, a technology in which the company had a comparative advantage vsi-à-vis its rivals. Denicoló (2008) discusses this example and develops a general theory of why firms might overcomply with regulations to promote competitive advantage.

6. Matthew Kotchen (2006) posits a consumer with three choices: consume a private good, donate to an environmental cause, or consume a green good, which is a bundle of a private good and public good (such as "green electricity"—manufactured in an environmentally sensitive manner). He shows that in some cases the availability of the green good crowds out donations to the same environmental cause that is being advanced by consuming the green good.

7. Wine is an interesting counterexample. A number of grape and wine producers pursue organic methods (e.g., Fetzer). However, many do not advertise that fact prominently. One possible explanation for this is that consumers do not necessarily associate organic wine with good-tasting wine (this speculation should be empirically validated).

8. Organic food is an example of a credence good; i.e., a good whose consumption gives utility to a consumer but for which the consumer does not know or perceive the extent of utility gain. Vitamin supplements would be another example of a credence good: we take them assuming they are good for us but we cannot verify that we are any healthier for taking them.

9. Refer to Bird et al. (2008) for a review of the status of green power marketing in the United States.

10. Kotchen and Moore (2007) examine in detail two green electricity programs in Michigan (U.S.) and quantify the motivation for participation by consumers.

11. The legitimacy of carbon offsets has been called into question by many. The main problem is the legitimacy of the offsets; are the sellers of offsets really undertaking additional emission reductions that they would not otherwise undertake (is there "additionality")? Critics of retail carbon offsets have called them nothing more than a modern version of medieval indulgences, which the Catholic Church used to sell as a way of atoning for sins (see Revkin, 2007).

12. The information presented here on wood products certification is derived from Sedjo (2002) and Sedjo and Swallow (2002).

13. Prakash and Potoski (2006) suggest that voluntary environmental protection is a club good and discuss the economies of having more firms participate in the club. Then the question arises of how institutions can be better designed to enhance the provision of these club goods.

14. This is a variant of using product quality to practice price discrimination ("vertical differentiation"). The classic example of quality differentiation is train travel in the mid-nineteenth century, where price discrimination explains why the third class section of the train used wooden benches, even though cushions would be cheap to provide—in order to force richer travelers to pay for first or second class (a similar example could easily be constructed for modern air travel). For more on these issues, see Tirole (1988).

15. Arora and Gangopadhyay (1995) develop a model of duopolists using compliance with environmental regulations as a means of quality differentiation.

16. Vogel (2005) provides a number of examples of firms being green either as a benefit for employees or to attract investors.

17. Stakeholders is a term used for a variety of groups that have an interest or are involved in the firm, ranging from employees to investors to the local community. There is some evidence that attitudes of the local community do influence environmental performance of firms (Pargal and Wheeler, 1996, find this in Indonesia). Vogel (2005) discusses reasons why employees may be attracted to a green firm.

18. There have been a number of other studies of relationship between stock prices and environmental performance, not necessarily reaching the same conclusion. For instance, Heal (2008) comprehensively examines this question. See also Orlitsky et al (2003).

19. Heal (2008) discusses the evidence that socially responsible investing pays off, discussing the often conflicting literature on this question.

20. The rewards of joining a voluntary agreement can be varied. Sam and Innes (2008) discuss this issue in the context of the EPA 33/50 program.

21. The model in this section is based on Segerson and Miceli (1998).
22. In fact, Segerson and Miceli (1998) prove that given the assumptions we have adopted here, there always is a VA in this case: $a_V^{min} \leq a_V^{max}$.
23. One of the first analyses of this program is Arora and Cason (1995), who examine characteristics of companies participating. Khanna and Damon (1999) examine emissions from the facilities covered by the program. Gamper-Rabindran (2006) uses a similar approach but more recent data.
24. Refer to King and Lenox (2000) for more information on this example; most of the information presented is drawn from that source. "Responsible Care" is a trademark of the Chemical Manufacturers Association.

SPATIAL AND TEMPORAL DIMENSIONS OF REGULATION

By now you should be relatively familiar with the concepts of emission fees and marketable emission permits as economic incentives for controlling pollution. Our goal in this chapter is to discuss this topic in more detail, looking at how these incentives might work and exploring some of the potential problems.

Several issues complicate using incentives to control pollution. One is space—pollution transport is often highly dependent on location. Another is time—primarily accumulation over time, such as the multidecade accumulation of greenhouse gases (but also including daily and seasonal variation). We consider these issues here. We also examine the practical problem of estimating the performance of different regulatory regimes and making quantitative estimates of the relative merits of prescriptive regulations versus economic incentives.

I. SPACE

A. Sources, Receptors, and Transfer Coefficients

The problem of dealing with spatial effects is very real for pollution control. At the simplest level, Figure 15.1 shows a river with two factories discharging organic waste (such as sewage) into the river and a municipal water supply taking water out of the river (yuk!). For the time being, ignore the fact that the river may be useful for many purposes (such as fishing, swimming, and ecosystem services) and focus on its use as a water source for the town.

The problem of course is that the two factories are upstream of the municipal water supply. Consequently, what these factories do is of importance to the municipality. Fortunately, the river is able to clean itself somewhat. As the river flows, bacteria will work on organic material that the factories have discharged into the river. So the further one goes downstream, the smaller the effects from the pollution. Although this is good for the environment, unfortunately it complicates our analysis. To correctly regulate the two factories, we must take into account their individual effects on the municipality.[1]

FIGURE 15.1 River with two factories discharging organic waste into it and a municipal water supply taking water out of it.

To take space into account, we will introduce two terms: *sources* and *receptors*. A source is a point of discharge of pollution. Each factory in our example is a source. A receptor is a point at which we care about the level of ambient pollution. (Recall that ambient pollution refers to the level of pollution in the surrounding environment.) In our example, a logical receptor is the intake point for the municipal water supply. If we are concerned about the health of the river at other points, we might have several receptors located at different points along the river. It might seem that we care about pollution everywhere, not just at a few receptors. While this may be true, in practice we usually identify a small set of receptors where pollution levels will be measured. Typically, these receptors are scattered over space and serve as good proxies for the overall level of pollution.

Generally speaking, there is some relationship between emissions at the various sources, $e_1, e_2, \dots, e_I$ (where I is the number of sources) and concentrations of pollution at any receptor j:

$$p_j = f_j(e_1, e_2, \dots, e_I) + B_j \tag{15.1}$$

where B_j is the background level of pollution at j (perhaps zero). Fortunately, in many environmental problems the physical environment is linear[2]; that is, Eq. (9.1) can be written as

$$p_j = \Sigma_i \, a_{ij} \, e_i + B_j \tag{15.2}$$

The coefficient a_{ij} is called the *transfer coefficient*. Often, we assume $B_j = 0$. Note that in Eq. (15.2), if we change emissions at some source i by a little (Δe_i), pollution will change by $a_{ij} \Delta e_i$. This brings us to a definition of the transfer coefficient:

DEFINITION *Suppose a change in emissions from source* i *(Δe_i) results in a change in pollution at receptor* j *(Δp_j). The transfer coefficient between the source* i *and the receptor* j *is defined as the ratio of the change in pollution at* j *to the change in emissions at* i:

$$a_{ij} = \Delta p_j / \Delta e_i \tag{15.3}$$

The concept of a transfer coefficient is really useful only when the relationship between emissions and pollution is linear, such as in Eq. (15.2). In general, for our analysis, we will make the linearity assumption. Eq. (15.3) in essence gives the conversion rate for emissions to ambient concentrations. For instance, if a_{ij} is equal to 2, then every unit of emissions at i yields two units of ambient pollution at j.

B. How Much Pollution Do We Want?

We first turn to the question of what is the efficient amount of pollution. As we know, efficiency involves equating marginal damage with the marginal savings to the firm from pollution generation. But marginal savings is in terms of emissions and marginal damage is in terms of ambient pollution. To link these, we must either convert a firm's marginal savings function to marginal savings *per unit of ambient pollution* or express marginal damages as marginal damage *per unit of emissions*. We take the second course. Let us term marginal damages per unit of emissions from source i as the function $MDE_i (e_i)$, which is in contrast to marginal damages per unit of ambient pollution, which, for clarity in the following discussion, we will denote $MDA(p)$. For now we will work with one receptor. We know that MDE_i is the ratio of the change in damages [$D(p)$] to the change in emissions at source i:

$$
\begin{aligned}
MDE_i &= \{D(p + Dp) - D(p)\} / \Delta e_i \\
&= MDA(p)\, \Delta p / \Delta e_i \\
&= a_i MDA(p)
\end{aligned}
\tag{15.4}
$$

This relationship between *MDE* and *MDA* is intuitive. If, as was mentioned in the previous paragraph, a_i is 2, one more unit of emissions yields two units of pollution and thus twice as much damage as one more unit of ambient pollution. Thus *MDE* is twice as big as *MDA*.

What is the efficient amount of pollution? As before, efficiency calls for equating the marginal savings from emissions with the marginal damage, and this must apply to all sources (from the equimarginal principle). So if there are $i = 1, \ldots, I$ sources, the following must hold:

$$-MC_i(e_i) = MDE_i = a_i MDA(p) \text{ for all } i = 1, \ldots, I \tag{15.5}$$

Eq. (15.5) is really a set of I equations, one for each source, setting that source's marginal savings from emissions equal to marginal damage. Dividing each of Eq. (15.5) by a_i implies that for any two sources, m and n,

$$MC_m(e_m) / a_m = MC_n(e_n) / a_n = -MDA(p) \tag{15.6}$$

The MC/a terms can be interpreted as the marginal cost per unit of ambient pollution. Thus Eq. (15.6) says that marginal cost in terms of ambient pollution must be equal to the negative of marginal damage. In other words, efficiency calls for all sources to have the same marginal costs of emissions, normalized by the source's transfer coefficient. Thus if a source has a larger impact on ambient pollution (a is larger), its marginal cost of pollution control (marginal cost of emissions) must be larger. This is the equimarginal principle, modified for ambient pollution.

To summarize, two conditions are necessary for efficiency. First, the marginal cost of emissions, normalized by the transfer coefficient, must be equalized for all sources. Second, that normalized marginal cost must equal the negative of marginal damage.

Numerical Example: Efficiency

Suppose that in our problem with the river and the municipality in Figure 15.1 the basic conditions are

$$a_1 = 2$$
$$a_2 = 3$$
$$MC_i (e_i) = -14 + 7e_i, \quad i = 1, 2 \tag{15.7}$$
$$MDA(p) = p$$

Also assume the background pollution level is zero. How much should each source efficiently emit?

Note that we have assumed that both sources share the same marginal cost function. This of course need not be the case. Note also that marginal costs of emissions are negative. Recall that firm costs decrease as emissions increase, yielding negative marginal costs. Marginal savings from emissions are, in contrast, positive.

Applying Eq. (15.6) to this example yields the following efficiency conditions:

$$MC_1 (e_1) / a_1 = (-14 + 7e_1)/2 = MC_2 (e_2)/a_2 = (-14 + 7e_2)/3 \tag{15.8a}$$
$$MC_1 (e_1) / a_1 = (-14 + 7e_1)/2 = -MDA(p) \tag{15.8b}$$
$$= -MDA(2e_1 + 3e_2) = -(2e_1 + 3e_2)$$

We have two equations in two unknowns that we know can be solved. First, simplify, rewriting Eq. (15.8) as

$$-42 + 21e_1 = -28 + 14e_2 \tag{15.9a}$$
$$-14 + 7e_1 = -4e_1 - 6e_2 \tag{15.9b}$$

which can be solved for $e_1 = 1$ and $e_2 = 0.5$. The marginal cost for firm 1 is -7 and the marginal cost for firm 2 is -10.5. The total ambient pollution is 3.5, which yields marginal damage of 3.5. Check that the marginal cost, normalized by the transfer coefficient, is equal to the marginal damage.

C. Emission Fees

Having set up the framework for dealing with space, it is relatively straightforward to see how emission fees should be structured to yield efficiency. We seek emission fees,

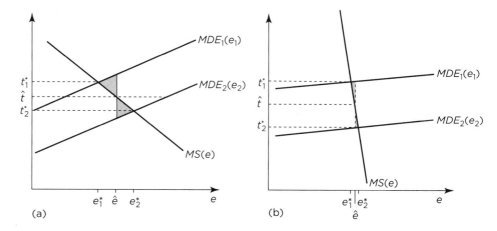

FIGURE 15.2 (a,b) Illustration of inefficiencies of uniform emission fee. MDE_1, marginal damage per unit emissions, firm 1; MDE_2, marginal damage per unit emissions, firm 2; MS, marginal savings from emitting, firm 1, firm 2, t_1^* efficient pigouvian fee, firm 1; t_2^*, efficient pigouvian fee, firm 2; efficient emissions firm 1; e_2^*, efficient emissions firm 2; $\hat{t}$, uniform emission fee; $\hat{e}$, emissions from firm 1 or 2, uniform emission fee. For $MDE_1(e_1)$, e_2 is assumed to be fixed at $\hat{e}$ and similarly for $MDE_2(e_2)$.

t_i one for each firm i, that yield efficiency, defined by Eq. (15.6). These will be ambient-differentiated emission fees. We know that whatever fee is used, the firms will respond by minimizing direct costs plus fee payments. This is equivalent to setting marginal cost equal to the negative of the fee:

$$MC_i\,(e_i) = -t_i, \text{ for all sources } i \tag{15.10}$$

This means we can rewrite the conditions for efficiency in Eq. (15.6) as

$$t_n\,/\,a_n = t_m\,/\,a_m, \text{ for all firms } n \text{ and } m \tag{15.11a}$$

and

$$t_n = a_n\,MDA(p), \text{ for any firm } n \tag{15.11b}$$

Thus the emission fees levied on the firms must be equal, after normalizing by the transfer coefficient. The second condition says that for any firm, marginal damage in emission units (MDE) must be equal to the emission fee. The first condition equalizes control costs across firms; the second condition equalizes marginal pollution damage and control costs. An alternative interpretation is that all firms face the same emission fee per unit of ambient pollution, but to convert it to emission units, it must be multiplied by the appropriate transfer coefficient.

Thus we see that ambient-differentiated emission fees can achieve efficiency. Sometimes, however, it is too complicated to let emission fees vary from location to location. For instance, there may be too much uncertainty about the level of the transfer coefficients; or it may be considered unfair to levy different fees on different firms. Most emission fees do not depend on location, even though damages do. How inefficient is applying a uniform emission fee when damages depend on location? Figure 15.2a is a graphic representation of Eq. (15.5). Shown is the marginal savings curve, assumed the same for each firm as well as marginal damages, normalized by the transfer coefficient. The figure is approximate since each *MDE* function really depends on both e_1 and e_2, though slight variations in emissions from the other source will not appreciably change the illustration. We know that efficient taxes are set so that Eq. (15.11a) holds. Thus for efficient taxes (t_1^*, t_2^*), emissions from the two firms will be as shown in Figure 15.2 (e_1^* and e_2^*). But suppose we use only one tax. If a uniform tax $(\hat{t})$ is used, both firms will emit the same $(\hat{e})$. The deadweight loss associated with this uniform emission fee is the shaded area in Figure 15.2. The "optimal" uniform tax is one that minimizes the total area of the two triangles.

The loss from a uniform fee depends on the nature of the marginal cost and damage functions. Figure 15.2b shows the same thing as 15.2a except with different slopes for marginal costs and benefits. Clearly, the deadweight loss is much lower. In fact, the steeper the marginal cost functions and the flatter the marginal damage, the smaller the deadweight loss.[3]

D. Marketable Ambient Permits

Marketable emission permits that take into account the effect of ambient pollution concentrations are somewhat more complicated, but in theory can work just as well as ambient-differentiated emission fees.

First we need to define what we mean by an ambient pollution permit.

DEFINITION *An ambient pollution permit for a receptor* j *gives the holder the right to emit at any location, provided the incremental pollution at receptor* j *does not exceed the permitted amount.*

An ambient pollution permit system is a set of permits, distributed to sources in a region, a well-defined way of computing the effects of emissions on ambient pollution at receptors, along with a right to buy and sell these permits.

1. Two Firms. First consider the case of two firms and one receptor (this is easiest). Suppose the EPA issues L_1 ambient permits to firm 1 and L_2 ambient permits to firm 2 for a total of $L = L_1 + L_2$ permits. Buying and selling of permits can then take place. Let l_1 and l_2 be the number of permits eventually held (after trade) by the two firms. Obviously,

$$L_1 + L_2 = l_1 + l_2 \tag{15.12}$$

We have several questions: (1) What will the price of permits be? (2) How much will each firm emit? Answering the second question first, a firm can emit whatever is allowed by its permit holdings. Remember permits are a right to degrade ambient pollution levels. Emissions and ambient pollution levels are connected by the transfer coefficient. Thus

$$a_1 e_1 = l_1 \tag{15.13a}$$

$$a_2 e_2 = l_2 \tag{15.13b}$$

provided all the permits are used. Now suppose the price of permits is π (an unknown). How much will be emitted? However many permits a firm may hold, if the price of permits is greater than the marginal savings from emitting, the firm will want to sell some permits and emit less. In contrast, if the permit price is lower than the firm's marginal savings from polluting, buying permits is easier than controlling emissions: the firm will buy permits and increase emissions. We seek a price for which the desired emission levels for each of the two firms corresponds to the number of permits issued.

Total costs (TC) for each firm are

$$
\begin{aligned}
TC_1(e_1) &= C_1(e_1) + \pi(l_1 - L_1) \\
&= C_1(e_1) + \pi(a_1 e_1 - L_1)
\end{aligned}
\tag{15.14a}
$$

and

$$
\begin{aligned}
TC_2(e_2) &= C_2(e_2) + \pi(l_2 - L_2) \\
&= C_2(e_2) + \pi(a_2 e_2 - L_2)
\end{aligned}
\tag{15.14b}
$$

where $C_i(e_i)$ is the direct cost to firm i, excluding permit costs. To minimize total costs, each firm sets the marginal total costs (MTC) to zero:

$$
MTC_1(e_1) = MC_1(e_1) + a_1\pi = 0
\tag{15.15a}
$$

$$
MTC_2(e_2) = MC_2(e_2) + a_2\pi = 0
\tag{15.15b}
$$

which implies

$$
\frac{MC_1(e_1)}{a_1} = \frac{MC_2(e_2)}{a_2} = -\pi
$$

$$
\frac{MS_1(e_1)}{a_1} = \frac{MS_2(e_2)}{a_2} = \pi
\tag{15.16}
$$

Equation (15.16) should look familiar. It says that marginal savings, normalized by the transfer coefficient, should equal the permit price. This is analogous to how an ambient emission fee works—marginal savings, normalized by the transfer coefficient, equals the same number for all firms.

There is one additional equation that gives us information. Combining Eqs. (15.12) and (15.13), we know

$$
a_1 e_1 + a_2 e_2 = L
\tag{15.17}
$$

Equations (15.16) and (15.17) constitute three separate equations in three unknowns (e_1, e_2, and π) and thus can be solved.

Numerical Example: Tradable Permits

Consider the previous example of the municipality and the river. We concluded that the right amount of pollution was 3.5. Suppose instead that permits for 5 tons of pollution were issued. What would be the resulting emissions? We know from Eqs. (15.16) and (9.17) that

$$\frac{MC_1(e_1)}{a_1} = \frac{(-14 + 7e_1)}{2} = -\pi \tag{15.18a}$$

$$\frac{MC_2(e_2)}{a_1} = \frac{(-14 + 7e_2)}{3} = -\pi \tag{15.18b}$$

$$a_1 e_1 + a_2 e_2 = 2e_1 + 3e_2 = 5 \tag{15.18c}$$

Eq. (15.18a) and (15.18b) indicate that whatever the price of permits might be, the two firms will emit so that marginal costs, adjusted by the transfer coefficient, are equal to the permit price. A high price will result in fewer emissions than a low price. Equation (15.18c) indicates that not just any emissions will do; additional pollution concentrations must be exactly 5 units. The price of permits, as well as emission levels, are unknowns in Eq. (15.18). These three equations can be solved for $(e_1, e_2, \pi) = (1.23, 0.85, 2.69)$.

2. Multiple Sources and Receptors. Suppose we have $e = 1, \ldots, I$ polluters and $j = 1, \ldots, J$ receptors. Suppose the government determines that the efficient pollution level is $\bar{s}$ at each receptor and thus distributes $L_j = \bar{s}$ ambient pollution permits for each receptor, j. How will firms buy and sell these permits? Let l_i^j be the number of permits held by source i for polluting receptor j. Because of buying and selling, l_i^j need not equal the number of permits it initially received. But because permits cannot be created (legally), we know that the "law of conservation of permits" applies:

$$\bar{s} = L_j \geq \Sigma_i \, l_i^j \tag{15.19}$$

If all permits are used and none is lost or destroyed, we would have equality in Eq. (15.19). Equation (15.19) simply states that after trading has occurred, the number of permits held by various firms for polluting each receptor j must be less than or equal to the number of permits initially issued for that receptor.

How much then can source i emit, assuming it has a portfolio of permits? Basically, the set of permits the firm has allows certain pollution levels at the various receptors. If the firm emits e_i, its pollution at receptor j will be $a_{ij} e_i$. The permit holdings require that

$$a_{ij} e_i \leq l_i^j \qquad \text{for all } j \tag{15.20a}$$

or

$$e_i \leq l_i^j / a_{ij} \qquad \text{for all } j \tag{15.20b}$$

This means that allowed emissions for source i are given by

$$e_i^* = \min_j \{l_i^j / a_{ij}\} \tag{15.21}$$

This probably seems more complicated than it really is. Consider Figure 15.1 again but suppose there is a swimming area between the city and polluter B. Call the swimming area receptor S and the city receptor C. Each polluter has permits to degrade river quality at C and permits to degrade quality at S. Emissions are governed by whichever receptor is most sensitive, taking into account permits held. This is Eq. (15.21).

With some receptors being more sensitive than others, it is entirely possible that some receptors will have less pollution than is allowed. For instance, if we are regulating a large region that contains an urban area, some receptors will be in the urban area and some in the surrounding countryside. It is entirely possible that pollution will be at the limit at the urban receptors and below the limit at the rural receptors. If the pollution is below the limit, it means not all of the initially issued permits are being used and thus the price of those permits must be zero.

This brings us to the question of what prices will result from trading. The permits are rights to trade the ambient environment. There will be a different price for this at each receptor, π_j. To a firm holding such a permit, the price per unit of ambient pollution is π_j and per unit of emissions is $a_{ij} \pi_j$.

To see this, assume a firm emits e_i. This results in ambient pollution at j of $a_{ij} e_i$, for which permit costs are $a_{ij} e_{ij} \pi_j$. Increase emissions by one unit and increase permit costs for receptor j by $a_{ij} \pi_j$. Total permit costs (over all receptors) change by $a_{ij} e_{ij} \pi_j$. The firm will emit so that

$$MC_i(e_i) = -\Sigma_j\, a_{ij}\, \pi_j \qquad (15.22)$$

There are three results that we will state but not prove:[4]

1. A market equilibrium exists in buying and selling ambient pollution permits for any initial issuance of permits.
2. Emissions from each source in a permit market equilibrium are efficient [i.e., are the least-cost way of attaining $\bar{s}$ in Eq. (9.19)], no matter how the permits are initially distributed.
3. If the price of permits in equilibrium equals the marginal damage from pollution, efficiency has been obtained.

These are important results. First, they indicate that a marketable ambient pollution permit system will work. Trade will occur and will eventually reach equilibrium. Second, trade in permits will yield efficiency in the sense of being the least cost way of attaining $\bar{s}$ at each receptor. For full efficiency, $\bar{s}$ must have been chosen initially so that marginal damage and marginal costs are equalized, in the sense of the discussion in the previous section on emission fees. If there is only one receptor, $\bar{s}$ must have been chosen so that

$$MC_i(e_i^*)/a_i = -MDA(\bar{s}), \text{ for all sources } i \qquad (15.23)$$

This condition is analogous to Eq. (15.6).

Although this system may seem complicated, a close analog has been used in the United States and Germany. In both countries, there are caps on pollution levels in most urban areas. For new economic activity to start up in a city, existing sources must be "convinced" (i.e., paid) to reduce emissions so that there is no net increase in pollution at any receptor in the urban area. This is the offset system and closely resembles the ambient marketable permit system described above.[5]

E. Zonal Instruments

We should mention that there is an intermediate territory between completely undifferentiated emission fees or permits (where space is ignored) and ambient fees or permits. Those are called zonal fees or permits. Consider first the case of a fee.

In the case of an undifferentiated emission fee, the same fee would apply to all polluters in a region, no matter what their effect on ambient pollution levels. An ambient fee is set at a different level at different locations. With a zonal system, a region or river basin is divided into zones—perhaps a few or perhaps many. Within each zone, the same emission fee applies. However, different zones have different fees. The advantage of a zonal system is that there is more flexibility with resulting gains in efficiency over the undifferentiated system, which is really a zonal system with one zone. The disadvantages are qualitatively the same as for ambient fees. In fact, as the zones become numerous and small, a zonal system becomes equivalent to an ambient system.

Zonal marketable permits are somewhat more complicated. Within a zone, permits are traded on a one-for-one basis, with none of the complexities of ambient permits discussed in the previous section. However if trades are made between firms that are in different zones, trade is as in an ambient permit system with different transfer coefficients for the different zones. Once again, there are efficiency gains from a zonal system as well as disadvantages due to complexity not encountered in an emission permit system.

We will not consider zonal systems further since they are a straightforward adaptation of the ambient permit or fee systems we have already discussed.

II. TIME

A. Stock Pollutants

So far, we have been concerned about emission fees and marketable permits in a purely static setting. Time has been of no concern. However, time does make a difference for many types of pollutants, particularly those that accumulate. When pollutants accumulate, the damage from emissions today is not just the damage today, but the damage in future time periods when today's emissions are still resident in the environment. Eventually virtually all pollutants are cleansed by the environment. But eventually may be a very long time.

Pollutants that accumulate over time are called *stock* pollutants.[6] We are concerned with the stock of pollutants rather than today's flow of pollutants.

DEFINITION *Assume a pollutant accumulates in the environment according to the process*

$$s(t) = \delta s(t-1) + e(t) \tag{15.24}$$

where s(t) *is the stock of the pollutant at any given time* t, e(t) *is emissions rate of the pollutant, and* δ *($0 \leq \delta \leq 1$) is the persistence rate of the pollutant. Further assume that pollution damage depends only on* s(t). *Then if* $\delta = 0$, *the pollutant is a pure flow pollutant (the stock* *completely disappears from one time period to the next); if δ >> 0, the pollutant is a stock pollutant; and if δ = 1, then the pollutant is persistent in the sense that once in the environment, it does not degrade.*

The idea is that when we put a pollutant into the air or water, the environment will dispose of the pollutant, perhaps quickly or perhaps slowly. For instance, when organic matter is discharged into a river, microbes work on the organic matter, decomposing it into harmless substances. Or when sulfur dioxide is emitted into the atmosphere, atmospheric processes eventually cleanse the air, removing the sulfur. The measure of the rate at which the environment is cleansed is δ. More specifically, δ indicates what fraction of the total stock of pollutants is still left in the air after one time period. Alternatively $(1 - δ)$ is the fraction of the stock that is cleansed out of the environment in one time period. Thus Eq. (15.24) describes the dynamic process of pollutant accumulation.

Basically, pollutants that accumulate over time are stock pollutants whereas pollutants that quickly fade away are flow pollutants. Greenhouse gases that have residence time in the atmosphere of decades are classic examples of stock pollutants, as are chlorofluorocarbons (CFCs) that deplete the stratospheric ozone layer. Particulates (e.g., soot) emitted into the atmosphere are flow pollutants since they settle out within a matter of hours or days.

The definition is not really quite as precise as it might seem. All pollutants accumulate over some period of time. If the time period is seconds, then even large particulates could be considered a stock pollutant. If the time period is centuries then greenhouse gases might look more like flow pollutants. The point is that there is no sharp line between flow and stock pollutants. Despite the potential ambiguity, the sense of the definition is clear. If pollutant accumulation is a dominant characteristic of the pollutant, it is not possible to have much effect on pollutant damage by adjusting emissions, at least in the short term.

Efficiency for a stock pollutant is somewhat more complex than for a flow pollutant. The marginal cost of emissions must be traded off with the marginal damage of the pollutant, where the marginal damage will occur over a period of time. This is more complex than the simple static analysis in which we trade off marginal savings from emitting with marginal damage. At a conceptual level it is the same, however; marginal damages must include damage over the time period when the pollutant is resident in the environment.

Suppose we are sitting in the present at time $t = 1$. The net costs of pollution emissions e_t, can be expressed as

$$\text{NetCosts} = NC = \Sigma_{t=1}^{\infty} \beta^{t-1} \{C_t(e_t) + D_t(s_t)\} \tag{15.25}$$

where β is used to discount the future [equal to $1/(1 + r)$ where r is the discount rate], indicating how we should trade off costs today with costs tomorrow. To determine the amount of emissions at any point in time, e_t, that minimizes net costs, we need to look at the marginal of Eq. (15.25) with respect to e_t. We can start by trying to determine the best current level of emissions, e_1:

$$\frac{\Delta NC}{\Delta e_1} = \Sigma_{t=1}^{\infty} \beta^{t-1} \{\Delta C_t(e_t)/\Delta e_1 + \Delta D_t(s_t)/\Delta e_1\} = 0$$

$$= \Sigma_{t=1}^{\infty} \beta^{t-1} \{\Delta C_t(e_t)/\Delta e_1 + [\Delta D_t(s_t)/\Delta s_t](\Delta s_t)/\Delta e_1\} = 0 \tag{15.26}$$

Focusing on the first term in braces in Eq. (15.26), note that we need to worry about marginal costs only when $t = 1$. All costs for $t \neq 1$ are constants with respect to e_1. Thus $\Delta C_t(e_t)/\Delta e_1 = 0$ for $t \neq 1$. Furthermore, inspection of Eq. (15.24) indicates that the stock of pollution at time t is simply the sum of previously emitted pollution, appropriately decayed:

$$s_t = e_t + \delta\, e_{t-1} + \delta^2\, e_{t-2} + \ldots + \delta^t\, e_{t-i} + \ldots + \delta^{t-1}\, e_1 + \delta^t s_0 \tag{15.27}$$

Thus

$$\Delta s_t / \Delta e_1 = \delta^{t-1} \tag{15.28}$$

Putting all of this together allows us to rewrite Eq. (15.26) as

$$\frac{\Delta NC}{\Delta e_1} = MC_1(e_1) + \Sigma_{t=1}^{\infty}\, \beta^{t-1}\, \delta^{t-1} MD_t(s_t) = 0$$

or

$$MS_1(e_1) = \Sigma_{t=1}^{\infty}\, \beta^{t-1}\, \delta^{t-1} MD_t(s_t) \tag{15.29}$$

What does Eq. (15.29) tell us? It indicates that for efficiency, we should set the marginal savings from emitting a unit of pollution today equal to the sum of all marginal damages that may occur in the future, with those marginal damages discounted by two factors: the discount factor (β) and the persistence rate of the pollutant (δ). Both act in a similar way. The discount factor diminishes future marginal damages. The persistence rate also diminishes future marginal damages because some of the pollution will have been cleansed from the environment. If the pollutant is a flow pollutant, $\beta = 0$, in which case Eq. (15.29) defaults to the familiar efficiency condition that marginal savings equals marginal damage.

B. Temporal Variability

Most people intuitively recognize that pollution levels vary over space. In an urban area, we expect pollution to be worse in some areas and better in others. But pollution also often varies through time, both because of temporally varying emission rates (the dead of night vs. mid-day), as well as temporally varying assimilative capacity (wind vs. still air). It should also be pointed out that this variation could be over the course of a day, a week, a season, or a year.

Because of temporal variability, emissions will cause different damages, depending on when they are emitted. Air emissions at night that quickly dissipate are less worrisome than emissions at mid-day. Air emissions in the winter may be less worrying than summer emissions in smog-prone areas.[7] This suggests that regulation could be time-varying to promote efficiency.

The analysis of time-varying regulation is very similar to the analysis of spatially varying emissions except that the transfer coefficient relates emissions at one point in time to pollution concentrations at another point in time. In essence, the previous section of this chapter can be viewed as a treatment of temporal variability by substituting the word "time" for "space." For this reason, we will not examine temporal variability in any more detail.[8]

III. MULTIPLE POLLUTANTS

Often several pollutants are responsible for an environmental problem. For instance, the generation of urban ozone requires both nitrogen oxides and volatile organic compounds to be present with sunshine. Acid deposition typically involves deposition of both nitric acid and sulfuric acid, derived from nitrogen and sulfur oxides. In either case, controlling the problem involves controlling both pollutants. Furthermore, each pollutant should be controlled taking into account the cost of controlling it as well as the contribution the pollutant makes to damage.

Multiple pollutants can be handled in much the same way as space or time. Think of there being $i = 1,\ldots, I$ types of compounds emitted into the environment (e_i) and $j = 1,\ldots, J$ types of pollutants that injure the ambient environment (p_j). The different compounds might be nitrogen oxides and sulfur oxides. The different pollutants might be acid deposition at different locations or different types of deposition at the same location.

So damage depends on pollution levels: $D(p_1,\ldots,p_J)$ and control costs depend on emissions of various compounds: $C_i(e_i)$, $i = 1,\ldots,I$. A transfer coefficient, a_{ij}, indicates the ratio of increased pollution of type j from increased emissions of compound i. Although a linear transfer coefficient worked well in discussing spatial issues, different pollutants often interact in a nonlinear way, making the concept of a single constant transfer coefficient inappropriate.

Efficient levels of pollution require the same two conditions as set forth in Eq. (15.5) and (15.6). Marginal savings from emitting the different compounds must be equated, taking into account the transfer coefficients. And these marginal costs must be equal to marginal damage, adjusted for the transfer coefficient.

An ambient permit system can function well in this environment. Permits would be issued to degrade the ambient environment. For instance, a permit might be issued for a certain amount of acid deposition. That permit could then be converted into emission rights based on different transfer coefficients. However, because of the similarity with the spatially differentiated permit system, we will not discuss this case further.

IV. COMPARATIVE REGULATORY ANALYSIS

In the real world of designing regulations to solve environmental problems, compromises are often necessary. Regulations that are less than perfect are often a first choice for non-economic reasons. For instance, prescriptive regulations may be much more acceptable to regulatory bureaucracies. Or spatially differentiated regulations may be deemed too complex for actual application. In these cases, the question arises as to the performance of less-than-perfect regulations, particularly in comparison with the theoretically ideal regulation. There have been a number of authors who have tried to answer these questions by conducting studies of actual environmental regulations, attempting to simulate the economic and environmental consequences of various regulatory regimes.[9] This sort of regulatory analysis can be very useful to regulators, legislatures, and other bodies contemplating environmental regulations or contemplating changes in a regulatory regime.

Most analyses focus on the spatial aspects of pollution generation, transport, and damage. Furthermore, most of the analyses share a common structure and solution technique—mathematical programming. Mathematical programming is a method of solving large maximization problems and has been implemented in many popular spreadsheet programs. Thus it is not necessary to be a master of complex algorithms to solve a typical mathematical program.

Perhaps the best way to explore how typical regulatory analyses are conducted is to consider an example. Scott Atkinson and Thomas Tietenberg conducted an analysis of the St. Louis metropolitan area in the United States.[10] Their goal was to examine current stationary sources of particulate pollution (soot and dust) as well as alternatives to the current regulatory regime. The alternatives the authors considered were marketable permits, both ambient permits and emission permits (undifferentiated with regard to space), as well as zonal permits.

One of the shortcomings of the analysis from a pedagogical point of view is that they do not consider pollution damage. Rather, they consider the U.S. standards for ambient levels of particulates to be the goal of regulation. The U.S. standard is a maximum highest concentration of particulates during the course of the year.[11] Thus theirs is a cost–effectiveness analysis.

The pollution problem can best be appreciated by considering a map of the St. Louis area with its sources and receptors. Such a map is shown in Figure 15.3. Note that there are 27 major stationary sources of particulate matter and nine receptors scattered around the

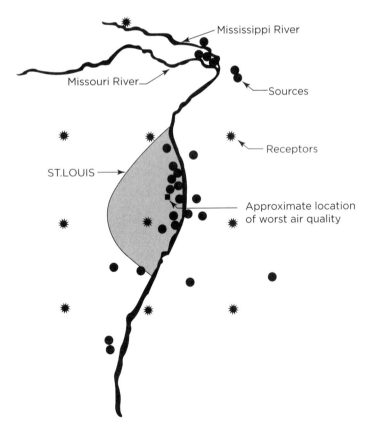

FIGURE 15.3 Map of receptors and sources for St. Louis region. (Adapted from Atkinson and Tietenberg, 1982, p. 111.)

metropolitan area. The authors' goal is to measure the short-run pollution control effects of different regulatory regimes. Thus they do not need to examine exit or entry. Further, they do not consider effects on the product markets of different emission control regulations, which of course could raise or lower product costs and thus sales and profits.

The authors obtain information on emission control costs, which is the basic driving force of the analysis. For each source, i, the control costs are quadratic in the amount pollution that is reduced:

$$C_i(e_i) = C_i(\bar{e}_i - e_i) + d_i(\bar{e}_i - e_i)^2 \tag{15.30}$$

where $\bar{e}_i$ is the amount of pollution the ith source will emit with no regulations and e_i is the amount of pollution the ith source will emit with regulation. The c_i, and d_i, terms are simply constants.

To find the least-cost way of controlling pollution, we must define the relationship between emissions and ambient concentrations. The following is a representation of the ambient standard:

$$\Sigma_i a_{ij} e_i + b_j \leq \bar{s} \tag{15.31}$$

where a_{ij} is the transfer coefficient between source i and source j, b_j is the background level of pollution, from other man-made sources and nature, and $\bar{s}$ is the standard—the maximum allowable concentration of particulates. Thus Eq. (15.31) must hold at all receptors.

The complete model can then be specified. We seek a set of e_i that satisfies the following:

$$\min_{e_i} \Sigma_i \{ c_i(\bar{e}_i - e_i) + d_i(\bar{e}_i - e_i)^2 \} \tag{15.32a}$$

such that

$$\Sigma_i a_{ij} e_i + b_j \leq \bar{s}, \text{ for all receptors } j \tag{15.32b}$$

$$0 \leq e_i \leq \bar{e}_i, \text{ for all sources } i \tag{15.32c}$$

This is what is known as a quadratic program (a special type of optimization problem) for whose solution there are numerous computer packages available. We will not concern ourself with how this is solved and move directly to results.

First, note that the solution of Eq. (15.32) defines an efficient level of emissions. That means that the solution to Eq. (15.32) corresponds to what happens with an ambient permit system. This is our lowest attainable cost of control; no other regulatory regime can do better.

To simulate an emission permit system, replace Eq. (15.32b) with

$$\Sigma_i e_i \leq E \tag{15.33}$$

where E is the cap on emissions in the region. To meet an ambient standard with this type of regulation, slowly reduce E from a large number (with consequent high levels of ambient pollution), thus slowly reducing ambient pollution levels at all the receptors.

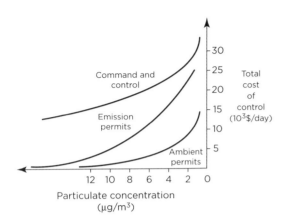

FIGURE 15.4 Total control costs for three regulatory systems, as a function of air quality (µg/m³).
(Adapted from Atkinson and Tietenberg, 1982, p. 114.)

When the ambient standard is just met at all the receptors, that is the correct amount of emission permits, E^*.

Finally, the current regulatory regime is simulated by replacing Eq. (15.32b) by

$$e_i \leq E_i, \text{ for all sources } i \tag{15.34}$$

where E_i is the source-by-source emission limit specified in the command-and-control regulations.

Figure 15.4 shows the results of this analysis for different values of the maximum particulate concentration at the nine receptors ($\bar{s}$). There is no question that the command-and-control regulations are very costly at accomplishing their objectives—as much as a factor of 10 in excess of what is necessary to achieve the objective. As expected, the undifferentiated emission permit does not do as well as the ambient-differentiated permit but is much better than command and control.

Note also from Figure 15.4 that as the desired maximum level of pollution becomes increasingly lower (the environmental regulations become increasingly tighter), the costs of control increase at an increasing rate. Thus in lowering the maximum concentration ($\bar{s}$) from 3 to 2 μg/m³, the cost increase is much greater (for all three regulatory approaches) than for lowering the maximum concentration from 9 to 8μg/m³. Costs really accelerate as one tries to tighten the standard.

It is this type of information that can guide a regulator in deciding what type of regulatory structure to govern emissions. Perhaps the regulator will decide that an emission permit system is relatively easy to implement and can save industry a considerable amount of money.

The point of going through this case is some detail is that the approach is very similar to what might be done in analyzing an urban area anywhere in the world. This type of analysis can be vitally important to decision makers contemplating changes in emission regulations.

SUMMARY

1. Sources of pollution emit; receptors are points at which we care about pollution concentrations. The transfer coefficient is the ratio of the increase in pollution at a receptor to the increase in emissions at a source.

2. Efficient emissions in a spatial environment with one receptor require that the ratio of marginal savings from emissions to the transfer coefficient be equated for all sources. That ratio would in turn be equal to the marginal damage from pollution.

3. Spatially differentiated emission fees for each source should be set equal to marginal damage at the efficient amount of pollution, multiplied by the transfer coefficient.

4. Ambient pollution permits (with one receptor) will be priced, in equilibrium, at any source's marginal savings from emissions, divided by the transfer coefficient.

5. Stock pollutants accumulate over time; thus simply controlling emissions does not directly control the damage from the stock. Flow pollutants do not accumulate significantly.

6. In a competitive permit market, the initial allocation of permits is not important. With market power on the part of any polluter, the initial distribution matters.

7. Empirical analyses of efficiency of different approaches to regulating pollution have shown very significant savings from moving to ambient pollution permits from command and control.

PROBLEMS

*1. An ambient differentiated emission permit gives the holder the right to emit anywhere provided emissions have no more impact on receptor j than one unit of emissions at source i. Let l_i^j be the quantity of such permits a firm holds.

    a. Suppose there is only one receptor and K sources. Write an equation showing allowed emissions for source k if it holds a portfolio of ambient differentiated emission permits $\{l_1^1, l_2^1, \ldots, l_K^1\}$.

    b. Generalize your answer to part (a) for the case of multiple receptors.

*2. Consider an abstraction of the Santiago, Chile air pollution problem. Assume all pollution damage is in downtown Santiago and is equal to $p^2/2$ where p is the pollution concentration in parts per million (ppm). Pollution comes from automobile emissions and a steel mill on the east side of town. Each unit of automobile emissions results in 2 units of pollution in downtown Santiago. Each unit of steel mill pollution results in one unit of pollution in downtown Santiago. Uncontrolled, there are 10 units of automobile emissions and 4 units of steel mill emissions. The cost of reducing emissions by q units is q^2 for the automobiles and also q^2 for the steel mill.

    a. What are the transfer coefficients for the automobiles and for the steel mill?

    b. What is the total control cost in terms of emissions for each source?

    c. What is the total control cost per unit of pollution (not emissions) contributed by each source?

    d. What is the marginal damage from pollution, in dollars per unit of pollution ($/ppm)?

    e. What is the marginal damage in dollars per unit of emissions from each of the two sources?

    f.   What are the efficiency conditions for the optimal amount of pollution?

    g.   What efficient level of emissions would come from each of the two sources?

3. Write the continuous time version of Eq. 15.24 and, using derivatives, derive the continuous time equivalents of Eqs. 15.25–15.29.

4. Two identical firms save money from polluting. A firm's marginal savings from emitting an amount e are given by $10-2e$. The two firms differ in their impact on ambient pollution concentrations. Two units of emissions from firm 1 result in one unit of ambient pollution. Firm 2 has twice the impact on the ambient environment from the same amount of emissions.

    a.   What are the transfer coefficients for each of the two firms?

    b.   If firm 1 is given two emission permits and firm 2 is given four emission permits and they are allowed to trade, how many permits will each firm end up with and what will be the price?

    c.   If instead each firm is given two ambient pollution permits and trading takes place, how much will each firm end up emitting and what will be the permit price?

5. Write the analog for Eq. (15.16) for the case of multiple receptors. Interpret your result.

*6. Carbon dioxide is well known as the most significant greenhouse gas, leading to climate change and global warming. But other gases are also greenhouse gases contributing to global warming and thus appropriate to regulate in controlling the problem. One of these is methane (uncombusted natural gas). Methane and CO_2 differ in how a kilogram in the atmosphere affects warming, and they also differ in how quickly the gases leave the atmosphere.

    Although we are oversimplifying the physical science, assume that after a kilogram of methane or CO_2 are emitted into the atmosphere, they decay exponentially, with half of the CO_2 disappearing in 100 years and half of the methane disappearing in 10 years. Although methane disappears quickly, while it is in the atmosphere it is more problematic for global warming in the sense that a kilogram of methane in the atmosphere causes approximately 25 times the warming as a kilogram of CO_2.

    For the questions below, assume a discount rate of 5% per year.

    a.   For each gas, graph the stock of gas remaining in the atmosphere following the injection of 1 ton into the atmosphere. You can put the two lines on the same graph. Take your graph out at least 100 years. [Hint: if $s = e^{at}$ and the stock declines from 1 to ½ when t goes from zero to the half-life, one can calculate a for each gas.] What is the persistence rate for each gas? [Hint: use the continuous time version of Eq. 15.24; see problem 3.]

    b.   You are advising the EPA on what emission tax to place on methane and CO_2. Assume first of all that the marginal damage from a ton of CO_2 in the atmosphere is $1 per year per ton and it is constant over time, and independent of the stock of greenhouse gases in the atmosphere. What would be the ratio of the tax on methane to the tax on CO_2, using efficiency as your guide in setting taxes?

c. How would your answer to (b) change if you only considered a horizon of 10 years? Of 50 years? Of 100 years? [One hundred years is the figure the Kyoto Protocol uses to consider trade-offs between methane and CO_2.]

d. How would your answer to (b) change if marginal damage from a ton of CO_2 increased at the rate of 1% per year?

e. Compare your answers to (c) and (d).

7. Acid rain is a problem in Scandinavia. Electricity-generating plants burn coal and emit sulfur dioxide. That sulfur dioxide is converted to sulfates, which travel long distances and are washed out of the air as acidic rain, particularly affecting Swedish lakes. Assume that power plants in England and Denmark are the primary culprits. Also assume that in a year one tonne of sulfur emitted in England generates deposition in Sweden of 1 gram of sulfate deposition and one tonne of sulfur from Denmark generates 3 grams of deposition in Sweden. Damage from acid rain is approximately 1 pence per gram of sulfates deposited. If q is the reduction in annual sulfur emissions (in tonnes) from uncontrolled levels, the marginal cost of controlling sulfur emissions is £q for Denmark and £$2q$ for England [1£ = 100p].

a. Write the damage function, giving damages as a function of total sulfates deposited.

b. Write the transfer coefficients for England and Denmark.

c. What is the efficient amount of emissions from England and Denmark and the resulting pollution in Sweden? What are the resulting control costs for the two polluting countries and the damage in Sweden?

d. First ignore the effects of pollution on Sweden and suppose we want simply to reduce emissions by 12 tonnes. How much of that reduction should come from Denmark, on the basis of cost efficiency? (*Hint:* Think of the marginal cost of emission control just like you think of the marginal savings for emissions.)

e. Now suppose we want to reduce emissions by 12 tonnes but we want to do it in a way that takes into account effects on pollution in Sweden. Although this might not be the right amount of pollution reduction, balancing the marginal cost of controlling pollution in Sweden from the two source countries would require how much of an emission reduction in Denmark?

8. Consider the case of carbon dioxide being emitted into the atmosphere. Assume that a ton of CO_2 emitted decays at a very slow rate; assume only 1% of the stock in the atmosphere decays in any given year. Also assume that the marginal damage in dollars per ton of CO_2 in the atmosphere is $1 per ton per year regardless of the amount of CO_2 in the atmosphere. Using a discount rate of 3% per year, calculate the marginal damage caused by emitting 1 ton of CO_2 into the atmosphere. What CO_2 emission fee would you recommend to control this greenhouse gas problem?

NOTES

1. For a detailed analysis (and one of the first) of river pollution, cleansing, and regulation, see Kneese and Bower (1968).
2. Often, linearity will apply up to some carrying capacity of the environment. For instance, in the case of the river, linearity is a good approximation up to the point at which the river

becomes so overloaded with organic material that oxygen (needed for aerobic bacteriological decomposition) is depleted. At that point the river's capacity to clean itself is greatly diminished. Many urban air pollutants follow linear chemistry and physics, but one major pollutant (urban ozone) does not. See Braden and Proost (1996) for a discussion of ozone and its control in the United States and in the European Union.

3. This problem of optimally designed uniform fees and their inefficiencies is explored further in Kolstad (1987).

4. These results are fully developed in Montgomery (1972).

5. Actually, the offset system as described is what is termed an ambient differentiated emission permit system. It turns out that an ambient differentiated permits system cannot be guaranteed to work. This was shown in a simple example in McGartland and Oates (1985). The distinction between the two systems is subtle and need not concern us here. See Montgomery (1972) for a discussion of ambient emission permit systems and ambient differentiated emission permit systems. See Foster and Hahn (1995) for a discussion of the U.S. offset system in practice.

6. Refer to Conrad (1999) for a more extensive discussion of stock pollutants.

7. In smog-prone areas, sunshine and heat facilitate ozone formation. Thus the summer is the worst time of year for this pollutant.

8. A fairly technical treatment of this issue can be found in Chapter 11 of Baumol and Oates (1988).

9. For example, see Kneese and Bower (1968), Atkinson and Lewis (1974), Atkinson and Tietenberg (1982), Atkinson (1983), McGartland and Oates (1985), Kolstad (1986, 1990), Oates et al. (1989), Seskin et al (1983), Klaassen (1995), and O'Ryan (1996).

10. These authors have several papers on this topic. The paper discussed here is Atkinson and Tietenberg (1982).

11. The standard is somewhat more complicated than this. There are both primary standards and secondary standards for many pollutants. Some of these standards excuse one violation per year. Further, there are different standards for different averaging times. For example, for some pollutants there is a 3-hour standard, a 24-hour standard, and an annual standard, where the time period refers to the length of time over which concentrations are averaged. We will ignore these details here.

16

REGULATION WITH ADVERSE SELECTION

WE NOW TURN TO A VERY REAL PROBLEM IN REGULATION NOT CONFINED SOLELY TO environmental regulation. That problem arises from differences in the amount of information possessed by the polluter and the regulator. Most frequently, this difference is that the polluter has private information that the regulator needs.[1]

Many of us are familiar with newspaper stories of the standoff between an old polluting factory and a regulator. The regulator tries to institute stricter regulations; the factory claims it cannot afford such costly regulations and will shut down if the regulations are imposed. The problem is that the regulator really does not have precise knowledge of the factory's pollution control costs, so the regulator doesn't know if the factory is bluffing or not. This is an example of regulations with unknown (or imperfectly known) pollution control costs.

Within the environmental economics literature, one of the earliest examples of this problem has to do with whether the uncertainty described in the previous paragraph tends to favor emission permits or emission fees. An extension of this problem allows for communication between the polluter and the regulator prior to regulations being promulgated. In this case, is there a type of regulation that can induce polluters to truthfully reveal that cost? These are the questions we will examine in this chapter.

I. A SIMPLE MODEL OF INCENTIVES IN ENVIRONMENTAL REGULATION

One of the key features of the schematic presented in Figure 11.1 is the disconnect between the organization seeking pollution control and the entity actually doing the pollution control. This is one of the central problems in regulation generally and environmental regulation in particular. The problem arises because of different objectives. The legislature may want least-cost pollution control. But the firm wants profits to be highest. Thus it may object to a regulation, saying that the regulation will drive the firm out of business because its control costs are so high. This clash of objectives between the polluter and the regulator would be less of a problem if there were full information. If the regulator knew the control costs of the firm, the firm could not falsely threaten to go out of business. This clash of objectives with incomplete information is the source of the regulatory problem we will examine.

To address this question, we will simplify Figure 11.1, reducing it to a two-agent model consisting of an environmental regulator (the "EPA") and a firm (the "polluter"). The EPA is not privy to the detailed information on the polluter's operations, particularly its precise pollution control costs. For some of this information, the EPA must rely on the firm's statements and reports. But the EPA will not know whether the firm is telling the truth. Our goal then is to design a regulation that makes the most of this imperfect state of affairs.[2]

A. Unknown Polluter Characteristics

The problem we consider is one in which the EPA is uncertain about particular characteristics of the polluter, typically pollution control costs. The polluter may be able to control pollution relatively cheaply or it may find pollution very costly to control. This is a classic issue in environmental regulation. Typically the EPA will claim pollution can be controlled at reasonable cost while the polluter claims that the environmental regulation will force it out of business. It is a credible threat because the polluter knows its own costs much better than the EPA. To simplify things, we will assume that the polluter is one of two types: either a high-cost polluter or a low-cost polluter. Suppose, to the EPA, there is a 50:50 chance of a firm being one type or the other.

The EPA's goal is to design a regulation that induces the firm to do the right thing, from the EPA's perspective. Although regulations can take many forms, let us suppose that the regulation takes the form of an emission fee (r), based on the amount of emission generated, e. Thus the emission fees collected will be re. The polluter's problem is to minimize total costs where costs include the emission fee:

$$\min_{e} TC(e) = C(e) + re \tag{16.1}$$

Of course the polluter will choose to emit where the marginal savings (negative of marginal costs) equal the emission fee:

$$-MC(e) = MS(e) = r \tag{16.2}$$

But the two types of polluters have different costs and thus will pollute at different levels. If the polluter is high cost, it will decide to generate e_H, whereas if it is low cost, it will generate e_L. We should think of these pollution levels as being dependent on the level of the fee. If r changes, both e_H and e_L will change.

The EPA's goal is to find a fee level that minimizes expected societal costs, assumed to be expected pollution control costs plus pollution damage. The problem is the EPA does not know whether the firm is high cost or low cost. This problem is illustrated in Figure 16.1, which shows marginal cost for the two types of polluters as well as marginal pollution damage. If the EPA chooses some emission fee level, say $\hat{r}$, emissions will be at the point at which marginal costs equal that fee: either $\hat{e}_L$ or $\hat{e}_H$. For the high-cost firm, we end up with too much pollution, with the shaded triangle A being the social loss. For the

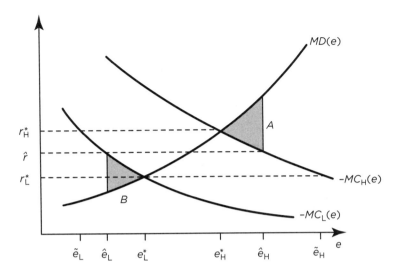

FIGURE 16.1 An illustration of regulating a firm with unknown pollution control costs, using an emission fee. $MC_H(e)$, marginal costs of emitting, high-cost firm; $MC_L(e)$, marginal costs of emitting, low-cost firm; $MD(e)$, marginal damage from pollution emissions; e_L^*, e_H^* efficient level of emissions, low-and high-cost firms; r_L, r_H, efficient emission fee, low- and high-cost firms; $\hat{r}$, best single emission fee; $\hat{e}_L, \hat{e}_H$, low and high-cost firms' response to $\hat{r}_L$; $\hat{e}_H$, emissions from high cost firm when it claims to be low cost; $\hat{e}_L$, emissions from low-cost firm when it claims to be high cost.

low-cost firm, we end up with too little pollution, with the social loss being the triangle B. Since there is a 50:50 chance of the firm being of one type or the other, the expected social cost of the fee $\hat{r}$ is the average area of the two triangles. The best level of the fee is the level that results in the smallest average loss (or area). One can see by inspecting Figure 16.1 that if $\hat{r}$ is raised, triangle A gets smaller while triangle B gets larger. There is clearly some best $\hat{r}$ that yields the smallest average of triangles A and B.

The problem is that no single emission fee can eliminate the triangles. Ideally, we would have two fees, one for the high-cost firm and one for the low-cost firm, thus eliminating the inefficiency triangles. In order to do this, we would need to know whether a firm is low cost or high cost. So why don't we just ask the polluter whether it is high or low cost? This is the obvious solution. However, it is easy to see that whatever the costs of the firm, it is in its best interests to claim to be a low-cost firm. This can be seen by looking at what a high-cost firm gains by claiming to be low cost. The emission fee will be set at r_L^*, in Figure 16.1, which will allow the polluter to emit much more than it otherwise would $(\tilde{e}_H)$, thus lowering its overall costs. A low-cost firm would never claim to be high cost since that would result in a high emission fee, higher total costs, and overcontrol of pollution.

Note that the opposite (though similar) outcome occurs if the form of the regulation is to tell the polluter how much to emit. In this case, the firm will want to be given a larger emission target. If the polluter knows the regulator will look at where marginal costs and benefits are equal in setting the pollution target, it will be in the firm's best interest to claim to be high cost, thus generating a target at e_H^* in Figure 16.1.

The ideal regulation in this case is one in which it is in the polluter's best interest to tell the truth. This is the incentive problem. Without knowledge of the important information the firm has, regulations will fail. To obtain the private information, the regulation must be designed so that it is in the polluter's best interest to help the regulator.

The simplest solution is to simply charge the firms the environmental damage of their emissions. It is easy to see that in this case, firms will balance their marginal abatement costs with marginal environmental damage to achieve a first-best outcome.

But suppose we are restricting ourselves to a simpler regulatory regime with a single price or quantity and a transfer payment. The solution is somehow to compensate the firm for admitting to something that goes against its interests but is in the social interest. In the case of an emission fee, the firm will need to be rewarded for admitting to being high cost, and rewarded in such a way that truth telling will be an optimal strategy for the firm. In the case of an emission target, the firm will need to be rewarded for admitting to being low cost.

To be more specific, consider the case of the firm being told what to emit. We first ask the firm whether it is high cost or low cost and then, based on the response, give the firm a monetary payment (that depends on whether the firm said it is high or low cost) and tell the firm how much to emit: (R_H, e_H) and (R_L, e_L). The question is, how might we design such a regulatory scheme so that firms tell the truth? First of all, we know a high-cost firm will tell us its costs without any reward, so we can set $R_H = 0$.

Clearly, one attribute of our regulation should be that if a firm is high cost, it should be cheaper for the firm tell the truth than to claim to be low cost:

$$C_H(e_H) < C_H(e_L) - R_L \tag{16.3a}$$

and similarly for a low cost firm,

$$C_L(e_L) - R_L < C_L(e_H) \tag{16.3b}$$

Putting these together, we obtain

$$C_L(e_L) - C_L(e_H) < R_L < C_H(e_L) - C_H(e_H) \tag{16.4}$$

This result can be appreciated from Figure 16.2. Shown in the figure are the marginal savings (−MC) for the two possible firms as well as marginal damages. The setup is similar to Figure 16.1.

In Figure 16.2, the gain from lying if one is low cost (leaving aside the rewards) is the area CDFE [the left-hand side of (Eq. 16.4)]; similarly, if a firm is high cost, the advantage of telling the truth is the area ABFE [the right-hand side of (Eq. 16.4)]. Any reward for admitting to being low cost that falls between these extremes will induce low-cost firms to tell the truth without providing a sufficient incentive for high-cost firms to lie.

This problem illustrates the potential difficulties in designing regulations. This class of problem is known as the case of unknown characteristics or unknown "types" (in this case, the characteristic or "type" is whether the polluter is low cost or high cost). It is also known as the adverse selection problem.[3]

The basic point is that it is often not easy to simply direct a polluter to generate the right amount of pollution. It is necessary to recognize the different levels of information

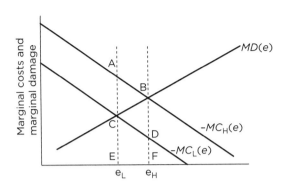

FIGURE 16.2 Finding the optimal reward for truth telling

that may exist between the regulator and the polluter. Futhermore, if the regulations are not structured with the correct incentives, the polluter's response may be socially detrimental.

B. An Example of Water Pollution Regulation

The example of the previous section is somewhat stylized but not far from real-world applications. In fact, Alban Thomas (1995) studied water pollution regulation in a part of France, noting that the regulator (the Water Agency) was lacking one key piece of information necessary to efficiently control polluters: pollution control costs. The Water Agency would obtain that information by offering a pollution control subsidy that varied depending on control costs. The subsidy is the reward of the previous section. By observing the operation of the regulator and the polluters, Thomas was able to infer information about the objectives of the regulator, the efficient Pigovian fee, and the costs of the polluters.

As with much of the "real world," the case examined by Thomas differs somewhat from the example of the previous section. In the case study, there is an emission fee, but it is set by political factors outside the control of the Water Agency. Typically, it is lower than the Pigovian fee. Thus the Water Agency supplements the emission fee by directly regulating the amount of pollution control equipment a polluter uses. However, to determine what the correct amount of pollution control equipment should be for a particular polluter, the Water Agency needs to know that polluter's marginal savings from polluting, information that is private to the polluter. To coax this information out of the polluter, the regulator offers to subsidize the purchase of pollution control equipment, with the level of the subsidy depending on the reported pollution control costs. If pollution control costs are reported to be high, the regulator is likely to require less abatement capital than when pollution control costs are reported to be low. Thus a straight question about costs would likely be met with all firms claiming to be high cost. A subsidy must be paid to those firms admitting to being low cost.

As in the model of the previous section, Thomas (1995) computes the smallest subsidy necessary to induce firms to truthfully reveal costs. Firms that admit their costs are directed to utilize the optimal amount of abatement capital and in return they receive a lump-sum subsidy for their cooperation.

Suppose the variable control costs for a firm are given by $C(Q, K, \theta)$ where Q is pollutant emissions, K is abatement capital, and θ is a parameter that shifts costs—a higher θ

means higher variable costs and higher marginal variable costs. But θ is private informa-tion to the firm and is not know by the Water Agency. The Water Agency's objective is to maximize weighted (by β) social surplus:

$$\text{Max}_{T,K} \quad \beta \{S(Q) + tQ - T\} - (1 - \beta) \{C(Q,K,\theta) + p_K K + t Q - T\} \tag{16.5}$$

where $S(Q)$ is the consumer surplus associated with pollution levels Q and p_K is the price of capital services. Note in Eq. (16.5) that the objective of the Water Agency consists of two parts. The first term in braces is the total surplus accruing to consumers, consisting of consumer surplus $[S(Q)]$ and pollution tax receipts $(t Q)$, less subsidies to the polluter (T). The second term in braces is the costs of the firm, consisting of direct costs $[C(Q,K,\theta) + P_K K]$, pollution tax payments $(t Q)$ less subsidies (T). The Water Agency may weight consumer benefits more heavily than polluter costs, which is the reason for the β, which may be any number between 0 and 1. As written, Eq. (16.5) assumes the firm reveals θ and calls for the Water Agency to choose T and K so that surplus is maximized. The pollution fee, t, is not a choice variable but set exogenously.

Note in Eq. (16.5) that the Water Agency is not choosing Q. That is chosen by the pol-luter. In fact there are two requirements that must also hold while maximizing Eq. (16.5). One is that the firm chooses Q to minimize costs (direct costs plus emission fees):

$$C_Q(Q,K,\theta) = -t \tag{16.6a}$$

where C_Q is the increase in variable costs associated with a unit increase in emissions. Variable costs would of course be expected to decrease with increases in Q. If there were no regulation of levels of K, the firm would choose K so that the price of capital equals the negative of marginal variable costs with respect to K.

$$C_K(Q,K,\theta) = -p_K \tag{16.6b}$$

Variable costs would be expected to decrease with increases in K. Let $[Q_0(\theta),K_0(\theta)]$ be the levels of pollution and abatement capital we would expect to see with the emission fee but with no directives on K. Let $Cq(B)$ be the total costs, including emission fee payments, associated with $[Q_0(\theta),K_0(\theta)]$.

Returning to Eq. (16.5), we need the value of Q. Q is determined by the firm accord-ing to Eq. (16.6a). But there are two other requirements. For the firm to be willing to divulge its costs, θ, it must be assured that its costs will be lower than if the firm remained silent, incurring costs $C_0(\theta)$:

$$C_0(\theta) > C(Q,K,\theta) + p_K K + tQ - T \tag{16.6c}$$

A second requirement is that telling the truth about θ must be more profitable than lying about θ. Let $H(\theta, \hat{\theta})$ be the firm's costs when its true type is θ but it tells the regulator it is really type $\hat{\theta}$. Telling the truth then requires that

$$H(\theta,\hat{\theta}) \geq H(\theta,\hat{\theta}), \qquad \text{for all } \hat{\theta} \tag{16.6d}$$

In other words, telling the truth results in lower costs than lying.

To sum up, the Water Agency tries to choose K and T to maximize social surplus [Eq. (16.5)]; given the constraints that the firm chooses Q [Eq. (16.6a)], the firm must be better-off reporting θ than not [Eq. (16.6c)], and lying must not be attractive [Eq. (16.6d)].

Of course it is entirely possible that the Water Agency will be better off remaining ignorant of the costs of some firms: the gain from learning θ may not offset the cost of obtaining the information (T). It turns out that there is some θ^* that separates the firms that admit their costs from the firms that refuse to participate. Firms with $(T) < \theta^*$ will tell the Water Agency their costs (θ) because the subsidy is sufficiently high. Firms with $\theta > \theta^*$ will choose to remain silent, leaving pollution and abatement capital at $[Q_0(\theta), K_0(\theta)]$.[4]

On the assumption that the Water Agency is acting optimally (which may be a big assumption), it is possible to infer both the variable costs as well as the weight β in Eq. (16.5) from a statistical analysis of actual pollution regulation. Thomas (1995) used a data set with information on subsidies, required abatement capital, emission fees, and emission levels for the Adour-Garonne Water Agency in southwest France. The data set contained 185 observations. Adopting a number of assumptions,[5] he was able to infer that the β in Eq. (16.5) was approximately 0.74 and that the existing emission fee was approximately half the Pigovian fee. The β greater than 0.5 means that the Water Agency weighted the consumer's welfare more than the producer's welfare. The results also show that the chemical industry has the lowest pollution control costs, whereas the iron and steel industry has the highest. Recall that subsidies tend to flow to those industries truthfully admitting to being low cost.

C. Implications

Although the example considered above may seem abstract, the lesson is very practical in the context of environmental regulation. The basic point is that it is often not easy simply to direct a polluter to generate the right amount of pollution. It is necessary to recognize the different levels of information that may exist between the regulator (the EPA) and the polluter. Furthermore, if regulations are not structured with the correct incentives, the polluter's response may be socially detrimental.

II. PERMITS OR FEES?

A. Pure Emission Fees or Pure Quantity Regulation?

One of the puzzles in the environmental economics literature of the past four or five decades is why economic incentives have not been used more when economists generally prefer them to direct regulation. A related issue concerns marketable permits and emission fees. Marketable permits are finding acceptance in parts of the world. Emission fees, in contrast, are rarely used as real incentives for pollution control. Most applications are in Europe and the former Soviet Union, where fees are usually used to finance regulatory activities rather than provide incentives for pollution control. Economic theory suggests that a marketable permit system and an emission fee system should work equally well in controlling pollution. It is from this debate that Abba Lerner and Martin Weitzman[6] suggested that if there were uncertainty and it was necessary to set a regulation and live with it, perhaps marketable permits and emission fees would not do an equally good job of controlling pollution. This in fact turns out to be the case.

The situation we consider involves a regulator and a firm. The regulator has two choices of regulation for controlling emissions: an emission fee and a quantity regulation. The emission fee means that the polluter pays the fee on every unit of pollution, and thus sets marginal savings from polluting equal to the emission fee. The quantity regulation means that the firm emits exactly the quantity of pollution specified by the regulation. Since there is only one firm, there is no issue of trading permits among firms.

To be a little more concrete, suppose we have a polluter with a marginal savings from emissions function that remains uncertain to the regulator. The marginal savings function is not, however, unknown to the polluter. We also have a marginal damage function that for the time being we assume is known with certainty. Our question is, which is better, an emission fee or a quantity control? Figure 16.3 illustrates this. Shown is the marginal damage function (MD) as a function of emissions. Also shown is the marginal savings function (MS), also a function of emissions. (Recall that the marginal savings from emitting is the same as the negative of the marginal cost of emitting, both of which are equal to the marginal cost of abatement.) However, to capture the regulator's uncertainty about marginal savings, low and high marginal savings curves have been plotted (MS_L and MS_H). The regulator knows the true marginal savings function must be one of these two but is unsure which. These low and high values average out at $\overline{MS}(e)$.

Note first that if there is no uncertainty or variability in marginal savings, then $MD(e)$ and $\overline{MS}(e)$ are the marginal damage and marginal savings functions. And in this case, there is no difference in terms of efficiency if the firm is told to produce e^* or told to pay p^* per unit of emissions (since in this latter case, the firm will emit where the fee equals marginal savings $-e^*$).

But with uncertainty, things change. If the regulator directs the firm to emit e^*, that is how much will be emitted, regardless of which marginal savings function is correct. If the regulator charges an emissions fee of p^*, the firm will emit e_H if the marginal savings function is high, and e_L otherwise. Although these *may* average out to e^*, we clearly do not have the perfect symmetry between price and quantity regulation that we had in the case of certainty.

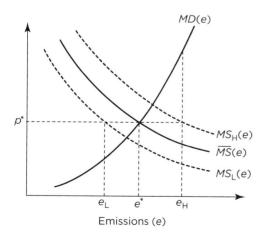

FIGURE 16.3 Fees vs. quantity regulations, unknown control costs. $MD(e)$, marginal damage from emitting; $MS_H(e)$, marginal savings from emitting if firm is high cost; $MS_L(e)$, marginal savings from emitting if firm is low cost; $\overline{MS}(e)$, average marginal savings from emitting; p^*, optimal emission fee; e^*, optimal quantity regulation; e_L, emissions from emission fee if firm is low cost; e_H, emissions from emission fee if firm is high cost.

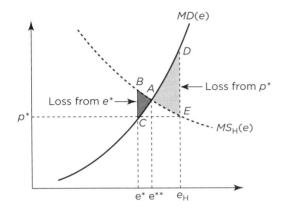

FIGURE 16.4 Losses if firm is high cost. $MD(e)$, marginal damage from emissions; $MS_H(e)$, marginal savings from emitting if firm is high cost; e^*, p^*, optimal quantity and price regulations; e^{**}, optimal emissions if firm is known to be high cost; e_H, emissions from fee p^*.

So which is better, prices or quantities? To answer this, we must determine the inefficiency of these two types of regulations. Figure 16.4 shows a portion of Figure 16.3: the marginal damage function and the high marginal savings function. Also shown are the price and quantity levels that would be optimal without full knowledge of firm costs, p^* and e^*. Note that if it turns out that the true marginal savings is $MS_H(e)$, the best level of emissions would be e^{**}, where marginal savings and marginal damage functions intersect. Clearly, both e^* and e_H are less that perfect. The inefficiency associated with e^* is the dark shaded triangle, ABC, and the inefficiency associated with e_H is the lighter area, ADE. In this particular example, it looks as if the price regulation results in more inefficiency than the quantity regulation (since ADE appears to be larger than ABC).

Of course, Figure 16.4 tells only half of the story since we do not know whether the true marginal savings function is MS_L or MS_H. Thus we must examine the area of the welfare loss triangles if marginal savings turns out to be MS_L. We then add up the areas of the two loss triangles for an emission fee (one for MS_L and one for MS_H), weighting the two areas in our sum by the likelihood that marginal savings are low vs. high. This gives the *expected* welfare loss from an emission fee. We then do a similar thing for the case of a quantity regulation. Comparing the two *expected* losses tells us which is better, the emission fee or the quantity regulation (smaller losses are of course better).[7] Figure 16.5 puts this all together. The light shaded areas are the losses associated with an emission fee, whereas the darker areas are the losses associated with a quantity regulation. Whatever the likelihood of high vs. low marginal savings, it is clear that in Figure 16.5a a quantity regulation results in smaller welfare losses and is thus to be preferred; in Figure 16.5b the regulatory preferences are reversed: the losses associated with an emission fee (light shaded area) are considerably smaller than the losses from a quantity regulation (dark shaded area). The only difference between Figure 16.5a and 16.5b is the slopes of the marginal damage and savings functions.

So we see that there are situations in which an emission fee might be best and other situations in which a quantity regulation might be best. The relative slope of the marginal damage and marginal savings functions are key to this. Focusing on Figure 16.5a, mentally rotate the marginal damage function clockwise around the (e^*,p^*) point. Visualize the changing size of the loss triangles, noting that the loss from a fee is reduced and the loss from a quantity regulation is increased. As the marginal damage function

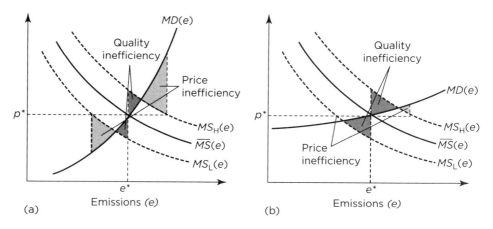

FIGURE 16.5 (a,b) Welfare losses from price and quantity control. $MD(e)$, marginal damage from emissions; $MS_H(e), MS_L(e)$, marginal savings from emitting for high (H)- and low (L)-cost firms; e^*, p^*, optimal quantity and price regulations; light shaded area, inefficiency from emission fee; dark shaded area, inefficiency from quantity control.

becomes more horizontal, the loss from a quantity regulation becomes larger than that of an emission fee (something like Figure 16.5b). So a small slope for marginal damage favors the emission fee; a large slope favors a quantity regulation. Analogously, try mentally rotating the marginal savings curves clockwise in Figure 16.5a. The same thing happens—as the marginal savings function becomes steeper, the loss from the emission fee is reduced and the loss from the quantity regulation is increased. So a shallow slope for marginal savings favors a quantity regulation; a steep slope favors an emission fee. Keep in mind that marginal savings have a negative slope. By more steeply sloped, we mean the absolute value of the slope is greater. These two results can be put together into the following[8]:

> **Proposition (Weitzman).** With uncertainty over marginal costs of emissions, quantity regulations are preferred if marginal damages are more steeply sloped than marginal savings from emissions; emission fees are preferred if marginal savings are more steeply sloped than marginal damages.[9]

This is an important result because it explains a good deal of the preponderance of quantity regulation in much of the world and also because of the policy implications for currently unregulated environmental problems, such as greenhouse gas accumulation.

For instance, much of health-based environmental regulations are based on the concept of a threshold of damage—no damage below a threshold and large damage above a threshold. In the vicinity of the threshold, the damage increases dramatically. This is roughly equivalent to very steep marginal damage in the vicinity of the threshold. This is illustrated in Figure 16.6, which shows three possible damage functions and the associated marginal damage functions. Linear damage (D_1) results in horizontal marginal

Permits vs. Fees for Controlling Haze

In the early 1980s, the U.S. Congress was considering ways to improve on the Clean Air Act, the primary law governing air pollution in the United States. As part of this effort, Congress established the National Commission on Air Quality to examine specific air pollution problems and recommend improved methods of regulation. One of the concerns of the Commission was air quality protection in the Southwest United States, an area with many national parks but also significant energy resources, the combustion of which would threaten regional air quality. There were two air quality goals in the region: protecting ambient air quality in national parks from combustion sources located nearby and preventing the buildup of regional haze due to region-wide emissions. The ambient air quality goal is specified in terms of a maximum concentration of pollutants within a park. The regional haze goal is simply to have as low a level of regional emissions as possible—there is no threshold. The uncertainty at work in this market relates to energy demand. If energy demand is high, marginal cost of emission control will be high; if demand is low, marginal control costs will be low.

Consistent with the theoretical analysis above, the first air pollution goal, the maximum ambient concentration, would appear to be best served with a quantity control on emissions. The second goal would appear to be best served by an emission fee, since there is no threshold effect. The issue is, what type of regulatory instrument might best suit these dual and conflicting goals? To answer this, a computer model of the relevant region of the United States was constructed and used to simulate the effects of different types of regulations, specifically a marketable emission permit system and a regional emission fee system for control of SO_2 emissions.[10] Further, the dual goals were assumed to imply a particular shape for marginal damage from emissions. The analysis concluded that a marketable permit system was approximately 20% lower in cost than an emission fee system except when marginal damages were close to linear. In this case, the fee systems resulted in 5–10% lower costs. Because damage was not thought to be linear, these results suggest that a marketable permits system is the best choice.

damage. Quadratic damage (D_2) results in linear marginal damage. Damage that is very low until it reaches the vicinity of a threshold, T^*, and then rises rapidly (D_3) yields a marginal damage function that is very similar (though not necessarily identical)—low below the threshold and steeply sloped in the vicinity of the threshold.

Unless marginal savings are even more steeply sloped, the above proposition suggests that a quantity regulation will be preferred in the situation in which damages exhibit a threshold effect. And in fact that is what we see around the world—limits on the quantity of pollution emitted are much more common than emission fees.

Another way of grasping this is to view a quantity regulation as yielding a sure quantity of pollution with an unsure marginal cost of control. An emission fee yields a sure

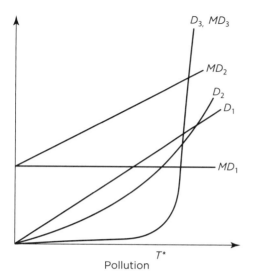

FIGURE 16.6 Three damage functions and their marginals. T^*, threshold; D_1, MD_1, linear damage, constant marginal damage; D_2, MD_2, quadratic damage, linear marginal damage; D_3, MD_3, highly curved damage (and thus marginal damage) in vicinity of threshold, T^*.

marginal cost of control but an unsure quantity of pollution. With steeply sloped marginal damage (e.g., thresholds in damage), a small error in the quantity of pollution can have very large effects on damage. (As an extreme example, a level of poison just over the lethal dose has much greater effects than an amount just under the lethal dose.) Erring on the control cost side has a relatively modest effect.[11]

On the other hand, if a pollutant is such that every unit has more or less the same marginal effect on the environment, marginal damage is constant and the proposition suggests that an emission fee is best. Over a broad range (though not necessarily a complete range), pollutants such as CO_2 may exhibit such constant marginal damage. This suggests that on efficiency grounds, an emission fee may be preferable to quantity regulation. There are of course many other issues that bear on the political desirability of one regulatory instrument over another, particularly in the context of global climate change.

B. Hybrid Price/Quantity Regulations

The problem with a pure emission fee or a pure quantity regulation is that if it turns out to be cheap to control pollution, we would like the firm to undertake more pollution control. On the other hand, if it turns out to be very expensive, perhaps we can be a little more lenient. And we would like that flexibility built into a regulation. Unfortunately, pure price or quantity regulations do not have that flexibility. It is a relatively straightforward step, however, to propose a quantity regulation coupled with a subsidy for emitting less than the firm is required and a penalty for emitting more.[12]

This situation is shown in Figure 16.7. As before, marginal savings can be high or low and the regulator does not know which (the regulator knows the mean value of the marginal savings–MS). The regulatory scheme is that the firm is told to emit e^* but if it emits less, it will receive s for each unit of pollution under the limit, for a total payment of $s(e^* - e)$. This of course is the same as the firm having to *pay* $s(e - e^*) =$

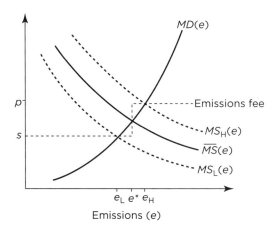

FIGURE 16.7 Permit system with penalty for over-emitting and subsidy for under-emitting. $MD(e)$, marginal damage from emissions; $MS_H(e)$, $MS(e)$, $MS_L(e)$, marginal savings from emitting: high-cost, average, low-cost assumptions; e^*, level of permit issuance; s, subsidy rate for underemitting; $e_L >$ emission rate if firm is low cost; p, penalty rate for overemitting; e_H, emission rate if firm is high cost.

$se - se^*$, which *is* a negative quantity if $e < e^*$. Similarly, if the firm emits more than e^*, it will pay a penalty—a total of $p(e - e^*) = pe - pe^*$. In the first case the marginal cost of emissions is s; in the second case, the marginal opportunity cost of emissions is p. This is the reason for drawing the emission fee in Figure 16.7, which has the jag at e^*. In Figure 16.7 $s < p$.

In Figure 16.7, if the marginal savings turn out to be low (MS_L), the firm will choose the subsidy. Why wouldn't the firm just emit e^* as told? At e^*, the marginal saving from emitting pollution is quite low—lower than s. Thus it is advantageous to receive a subsidy to cut back emissions, since that subsidy exceeds the marginal cost of cutting back emissions. Emissions are cut back to the point at which marginal savings equal the subsidy (e_L). Analagously, if marginal savings turn out to be high, at e^* the marginal savings from emitting a unit of pollution are high—higher than the penalty from overemitting. Thus it is cost effective to emit more than allowed and just pay the penalty. Emissions will occur when marginal savings equal the penalty (e_H).

What is the inefficiency of such a scheme? Remarkably, in the simple example of Figure 16.7, there is no inefficiency. No matter what the true marginal savings, the firm will emit exactly the right amount. Of course if marginal savings can take on more than two values, which is probably more common, we cannot achieve complete efficiency with this approach. Intuitively, since we have more flexibility with this approach than with pure fees or quantities, we must be able to do better than a pure emission fee or a pure quantity regulation. This is in fact the case.

One way to understand this result is to look at the complete solution to our problem. That is to present the marginal damage schedule to the firm and tell the firm to emit wherever the marginal damage schedule crosses the true marginal savings function (which is unknown to the regulator but known to the firm). A pure quantity regulation can be viewed as approximating this marginal damage function with a vertical line through e^*. A pure emission fee can be viewed as approximating this with a horizontal line through p^*. The hybrid system can be viewed as approximating the marginal damage with a step function (shown as a dashed line in Figure 16.7). Clearly we can get a better approximation with a step function.

Carbon Safety Valve[13]

One of the primary concerns of countries considering implementing greenhouse gas reduction programs is the cost of reducing emissions. In pulling the United States out of the Kyoto Protocol, George Bush cited costs to the U.S. economy as his main reason for abandoning the protocol. Other critics of aggressive climate policy point to the *possibility* that costs will be too high.

In response to these concerns, a number of policy experts have recommended incorporating a "safety valve" with any tradable permits system for managing carbon emissions. A tradable permit system would stipulate a cap on carbon emissions; trading would determine the price. Because of uncertainty in the costs of reducing carbon emissions, the permit price may end up high or may end up low. A safety valve would involve the government selling an unlimited number of additional permits to polluters at an agreed-upon price, typically higher than the permit price that is expected to prevail. This would cap the price of permits at the price specified by the safety valve.

Denmark implemented just such a safety valve for limited CO_2 emissions from power plants, although the price of additional permits was set quite low. The United States, as of 2009, had no nationwide limit on carbon emissions. However, the Bingaman-Specter "Low Carbon Economy Act," introduced into the U.S. Senate in 2007 (but not passed into law) used a cap and trade system to limit 2020 emissions to levels in 2006, and 2030 emissions to levels in 1990. In addition, the act stipulated a $12/ton safety valve for the year 2012, rising at 5% per year above inflation from that point (which would make it $30 a ton in 2030).[14] In other words, the cap and trade system would limit emissions but anyone could buy more permits from the government for the safety valve price, thus limiting the market price of permits and also limiting the overall emission reduction. Many people felt this proposed legislation was too weak to accomplish much reduction in greenhouse gas emissions.

III. OBTAINING PRIVATE CONTROL COST INFORMATION

In the last section, we assumed the regulator simply could not know the marginal cost or marginal savings to the firm from emitting. We now take the next logical step and assume the regulator can ask the firm what its marginal costs of emitting are. Now we have to be concerned about truthfulness.

The regulatory setup now consists of two steps. First the polluter reports to the regulator the marginal savings from emitting—$MS_R(e)$. Then the regulator issues a regulation, and the firm responds by choosing an amount to emit.

Let us look at the price and quantity instruments in this framework. Figure 16.8 shows the true marginal savings function (*MS*—unknown to the regulator) and the true marginal damage function (*MD*—known to the regulator). An emission fee will be set at the point at which marginal damage and marginal savings are equal. Clearly, if the

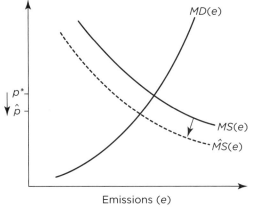

FIGURE 16.8 Emission fee encourages underreporting of marginal savings. *MD(e)*, marginal damage of emission; *MS(e)*, marginal savings from emissions; $\hat{MS}(e)$, reported marginal savings from emissions; p^*, efficient emission fee; $\hat{p}$, emission fee from misreported marginal savings.

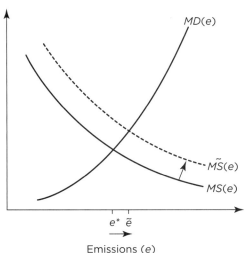

FIGURE 16.9 Emission permit encourages overreporting marginal savings. *MD(e)*, marginal damage from emissions; *MS(e)*, marginal savings from emissions; $\tilde{MS}(e)$, reported marginal savings from emissions; e^*, efficient level of emissions; $\tilde{e}$, emission from misreported marginal savings.

polluter reports a low marginal savings function (*MS*), the emission fee will be reduced, which is in the polluter's best interest. Thus with an emission fee, there is an incentive for the polluter to understate the marginal savings from emitting. This means that the cost of reducing emissions is understated—the firm says it can cheaply reduce emissions.

Figure 16.9 shows the other case, that of a quantity regulation. In this case, it is clear that it is in the polluter's best interest to exaggerate the marginal savings from emissions to increase the amount of pollution the firm is allowed to emit.[15]

So clearly neither a fee nor a quantity instrument will induce truthful revelation of costs. It turns out that a hybrid of the two works quite well, at least in this simple context.[16] To examine this hybrid, we must add more than one firm, so that we may have a market for emission permits with a known market price. The simplest way to do this is to assume we have many identical firms. After the regulator receives information on marginal savings functions, the regulator auctions off a certain number of marketable emission permits and announces a subsidy rate for firms emitting less than allowed by the permits they hold. Thus this is similar to the hybrid system in the previous section except that

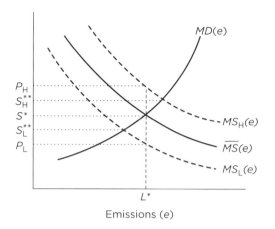

FIGURE 16.10 Hybrid permit-subsidy system. $\overline{MS}(e)$, reported aggregate marginal savings from emitting; $MS_H(e)$, true aggregate marginal savings if underreporting; $MS_L(e)$, true aggregate marginal savings if overreporting; L^*, number of permits issued; s^*, subsidy rate with reported $MS(e)$; s_L^{**}, subsidy rate with reported $\overline{MS}_L(e)$; s_H^{**}, subsidy rate with reported $MS_H(e)$; p_H, permit price when $\overline{MS}(e)$ is reported but $MS_H(e)$ is true; p_L, permit price with no subsidy when $\overline{MS}(e)$ is reported but $MS_L(e)$ is true.

overemitting is not allowed. It turns out that auctioning permits is not as simple as this suggests. If the permits are auctioned, then it is difficult to design an auction that works properly. If the permits are given away (as is often the case in tradeable permit schemes), firms have an incentive to mislead in order to obtain more permits (freely obtaining something of value).[17]

Figure 16.10 illustrates what the regulator will do. The regulator receives reports of marginal savings functions from each firm and then aggregates these to a marginal savings function for the entire industry. This is shown in Figure 16.10 as $\overline{MS}(e)$—the *reported* aggregate marginal savings function. This intersects the marginal damage function at (L^*, s^*). The regulator then auctions off L^* marketable permits to pollute and announces the subsidy rate s^*.

Suppose the polluters lied when telling the regulator their costs. Suppose they understated their marginal savings—their true marginal savings function is MS_H. With only L^* permits available, the various firms will compete for those permits, driving the market price up to p_H, the value of $MS_H(L^*)$. Since the subsidy is lower than this, none of the firms will choose to receive a subsidy to emit less than the number of permits held. If they had told the truth about the marginal savings functions, the subsidy rate would be higher (s_H^{**}), the number of permits would be larger, and thus the market price lower.

Now consider the other case, that the polluters' true marginal savings functions were lower—$MS_L(e)$. In this case, the market price might end up being p_L, using the same logic as before. But this is lower than s^*. Consequently, firms will choose to emit less than the number of permits held. Every permit held costs p_L but yields s^*. As long as $s^* > p_L$, there will be excess demand for permits. This will drive the price of permits to s^*. But if the firms had told the truth, the subsidy rate would be even lower, at s_L^{**}, which would result in a lower permit price. Thus by lying, the polluters have increased the price of permits in the market.[18]

In summary, not telling the truth about the marginal savings function has the effect of increasing the price of emission permits. The lowest permit price is obtained when the firms truthfully reveal their marginal cost functions.

SUMMARY

1. Regulation problems involving asymmetric information typically are associated with the regulator having less information than the polluter.

2. Adverse selection problems involve polluters having hidden characteristics (hidden from the regulator) such as their cost of pollution control. This makes efficient regulation difficult.

3. When a regulator must make a decision about the level of an emission fee or marketable permit system with uncertainty on the marginal cost of pollution control, the relative slopes for marginal savings and marginal damage functions determine which instrument is more desirable. If marginal damage is more steeply sloped than the marginal savings from pollution, marketable permits are preferred; otherwise, emission fees are preferred.

4. A marketable permit system with a subsidy for emitting less than permitted and a penalty for emitting more than permitted can perform better than either an emission fee alone or a marketable permit system alone, when marginal savings are uncertain to the regulator.

5. If a polluter has private costs about marginal savings from pollution, an emission fee will cause the polluter to understate marginal savings. A marketable permit system will cause polluters to overstate marginal savings. A marketable permit system coupled with a subsidy for emitting less than permitted will induce telling the truth about pollution control costs.

PROBLEMS

*1. Suppose we have two polluters that have a hidden characteristic, θ. The θ does not have to be the same for the two firms. Assume that θ can take on one of two values: 1 or 2. These two firms emit pollution, with marginal savings functions equal to $MS(e,\theta) = 1 - \theta e$. Total savings from polluting for each firm are $S(e, \theta) = 1 - \dfrac{(1-\theta e)^2}{2\theta}$.

Damage from pollution is $D(e_1 + e_2) = (e_1 + e_2)^2/2$ with a marginal damage of $(e_1 + e_2)$.

a. Suppose the regulator knew the value of θ for each of the firms, θ_1 and θ_2. For all possible combinations of θ_1 and θ_2, what would be the optimal amount of pollution for each firm: $e_1{}^*(\theta_1,\theta_2)$, $e_2{}^*(\theta_1,\theta_2)$?

b. Now assume the regulator does not know θ but asks each firm its true θ. After receiving those reports from each firm, each firm i will be charged an amount, $T_i(e_i,\theta_i)$, based on the reported θ_i, the report by the other firm, θ_j, and actual emissions, e_i:

$$T_i(e_i,\theta_i) = D[e_i + e_j{}^*(\theta_1,\theta_2)] - S_j[e_j{}^*(\theta_1,\theta_2),\theta_j]$$

where i and j are the two firms. The firms know this before they report their values of θ. Show that it is in the best interest of each firm to tell the truth about θ and also to emit the right amount of emissions, e^*. [*Hint:* Prove in general or enumerate for possible θ_i,θ_j].

*2. Consider a version of the problem discussed in section I.A. of the chapter, except that we will change the form of the regulation: an emission fee will be used instead of the firm being told how much to emit. A reward will still be paid to the firm for telling the truth.[19]

   a. Let the emission fee, based on announced firm cost, be r_L^* and r_H^*, respectively, depending on what the firm says its costs are. If the emission fees are based on an equating of marginal cost of abatement and marginal damage, what do we expect firms to tell us their costs are?

   b. Now develop the conditions for a reward for revealing a firm's costs. Write down the equivalent version of Eqs. 16.3 and 16.4.

   c. Draw a version of Figure 16.1, using linear (straight line) versions of marginal costs and marginal damage. Show (graphically or mathematically) that there is no simple reward (independent of emissions) that can induce truth telling every time.

3. In the hybrid fee-subsidy scheme described in Figure 16.7, suppose there are two additional marginal savings functions, one even higher than MS_H and one lower than MS_L. In this case, graphically show the inefficiencies associated with a fee-subsidy system.

4. Suppose the total cost of controlling the pollution in Bangkok is given by $TC = (3 + r)q^2$ where q is the amount of emissions controlled. Uncontrolled, there would be 2 units of emissions. Thus $q = 2-e$, where e is emissions. The variable r is unknown to the pollution control board. All they know is that it could take the value of either $r = 0$ or $r = 4$, and with equal likelihood. Marginal damage from emissions is given by $MD(e) = 4e$.

   a. Write the total cost of pollution control in terms of e. Graph this total cost as a function of e.

   b. Graph the marginal damages from emissions and the expected value (i.e., average over the two possible rs) of the marginal savings from emissions. Be as accurate as you can.

   c. What level of emission fee or emission permit should be chosen, not knowing what value r will take? Show your answer on the graph.

   d. Suppose after you have set the fee or permit in part (b). it turns out that $r = 4$. Show the deadweight loss from the permit and fee, assuming these instruments cannot be changed. Which instrument appears to be better?

5. Consider the case of a regulator and a single polluter. Suppose the regulator knows the marginal damage from pollution but is unsure about the firm's marginal savings from emitting. The regulator asks the firm to reveal its marginal savings from emitting schedule. Regulators know that if they use an emission fee, the firm has an incentive to lie about its marginal savings. Regulators also know that if they use a permit system, lying may still result. So the regulator announces that after being told the firm's marginal savings, the regulator will flip a coin to determine whether an emission fee or an emission permit will be used to control pollution. In this case, will the firm have an incentive to truthfully reveal its marginal savings from emissions? Why or why not? [*Hint:* Assume a firm is low cost; look at the possible costs or cost savings from telling the regulator it is high cost.]

NOTES

1. This issue is considered generally in an advanced review papers by Baron (1989) and Lewis (1996).
2. This is generally known as the problem of "mechanism design." Our goal is to design a way (a mechanism) to regulate polluters so that they behave in a socially desirable manner, given that we have imperfect control over the polluters.
3. One of the classic examples of adverse selection (and that illustrates the origin of the term) is the used car market. Typically, some used cars have hidden defects (we call these cars "lemons") and some do not ("peaches"), and both are offered for sale in the same market. Rational consumers would assume that the car they are considering buying may have hidden problems and thus shade the price they would pay downward. Thus the price of cars will be lower. This lower price will discourage owners of good quality cars from offering theirs for sale. This tends to result in the used car market having a high number of cars with hidden defects relative to the overall population of used cars. This is the "lemons problem" highlighted by Akerlof (1970). The problem of lemons can be so severe as to cause the market to fail to form to begin with, as often happens with insurance markets in which adverse selection is significant (e.g., private unemployment insurance).
4. For these firms that do not reveal θ, the Water Agency must calculate expected social surplus, based on the agency's assessment of the probability of different types occurring.
5. One of the major assumptions in his paper was that consumer surplus was linear in Q, which implied that the marginal damage from pollution is constant.
6. The definitive treatment of this issue is by Weitzman (1974), apparently motivated by a suggestion of Lerner (1971). Weitzman's work was criticized, and extended by Laffont (1977), among others. Weitzman generalized his results in a later paper (Weitzman, 1978).
7. We have glossed over the point that the optimal price or quantity regulation in the case of uncertainty may not be the same as for the case of certainty. In other words, if p^* and q^* are best with certainty, they may not be best in the case of uncertainty, even if average costs and benefits under uncertainty are the same as under certainty. The best price regulation would be the emission fee that makes the expected welfare loss (the weighted average of the two triangles) smallest. For this graphic exposition, this issue can be ignored.
8. This result is due to Weitzman (1974) and has application beyond environmental regulation (e.g., to import tariffs vs. quotas). For a specifically environmental version, apparently developed independently, see Adar and Griffin (1976).
9. Some qualifiers are necessary here, particularly the assumption that marginal savings and marginal damage are linear and that uncertainty is in the intercept of these linear functions.
10. The model and the results are described in several reports and papers, including Kolstad (1986, 1990).
11. Even when damages lack such a threshold, regulators that are unfamiliar with economics often prefer the sure quantity of pollution to the sure marginal cost of control (and unsure quantity of pollution).
12. Roberts and Spence (1976) first proposed this scheme.
13. Bulckaen (1997) points out that the incentive to distort reported marginal savings functions is greatly diminished if the regulator requries the firm to behave according to the marginal savings function reported. When the firm reports a marginal savings function, the regulator determines the optimal emission fee (t^*) as well as the emissions the firm should generate if the reported marginal savings are true (e^*). The regulator then not only charges the emission fee t^* but also requires the firm to emit e^*. This of course is more complex than the arrangement in which the reported costs are used only to set the fee level or the number of permits issued.
14. The result and model presented here are due to Kwerel (1977). It is one example of a much larger set of methods for achieving a similar end. Dasgupta et al. (1980) discuss a more general

approach to the same problem as does Spulbur (1988). Varian (1994) develops an iterative price mechanism in which all firms announce a complete set of pollution taxes. Duggan and Roberts (2002) develop a mechanism that relies on reporting into your own emissions (demand for emission permits), as well as those of a neighbor. You pay a penalty for the extent to which your estimate of your neighbor's demand differs from actuality. How well these mechanisms works depends on how much information each firm has about other firms. Montero (2008) provides a nice summary of this literature, including a discussion of the drawbacks.

15. Refer To Jacoby and Ellerman (2004) for a general discussion of the use of a safety valve in climate change policy.

16. The "Low Carbon Economy Act" is S. 1766 from the 1st session of the 110th Congress. See thomas.loc.gov/cgi-bin/bdquery/z?d110:S1766.

17. Montero (2008) solves the auction problem by rebating a portion of auction revenue to firms.

18. It should be pointed out that if other firms are not being truthful about their costs, then telling the truth is not necessarily the best strategy. This is a weaker notion of best: telling the truth is optimal for a firm if other firms are telling the truth. Telling the truth is a Nash equilibrium.

19. This problem emerges from an error in the first edition of this book, perceptively identified by Prof. Yoshinao Sahashi of Osaka Prefecture University.

REGULATION WITH MORAL HAZARD AND DYNAMICS

IN THE LAST CHAPTER WE WERE CONCERNED WITH A VERY SPECIFIC TYPE OF ASYMMETRIC information: when characteristics of the polluter (such as pollution control costs) are known to the polluter but unknown to the regulator. We now turn to a slightly different case of asymmetric information, one in which the polluter takes some action that is hidden from the regulator.

One example of this type of problem involves firms in which emissions are not directly observable by the regulator. Thus the unobserved action is emission levels. A case would be area sources of pollution (automobiles, agriculture), in which it is too costly to monitor individual polluters. Is there a form of regulation that can work when such an important variable is unobserved? Related to this, suppose firms self-report emissions. If it is costly to verify such reports, what kind of enforcement mechanisms, including spot audits, can most efficiently ensure truthful reporting of emissions? These are all examples of unobserved polluter actions. Our concern in this chapter is in developing regulations that can effectively deal with this sort of asymmetric information.

A related question that we will take up at the end of the chapter concerns dynamics. There are specific problems of asymmetric information that arise when dynamic regulation is concerned. For instance, if the reward to a firm from investing in cost-reducing research and development on pollution abatement is simply a tightening of the regulation, the incentive to undertake such research is diluted.

I. A SIMPLE MODEL OF INCENTIVES IN ENVIRONMENTAL REGULATION

As we did in the previous chapter, we will simplify Figure 11.1 reducing it to a two-agent model consisting of an environmental regulator (the "EPA") and a firm (the "polluter"). The EPA is not privy to detailed information on the polluter's operations, such as how much pollution the firm is generating. For some of this information, the EPA must rely on the firm's statements and reports. But the EPA will not know whether the firm is telling the truth.

In the last chapter we considered the case of adverse selection, in which the EPA is uncertain whether the polluter can control pollution cheaply. We now turn to the problem in which the polluter takes steps to control pollution but these steps are unobservable. For instance, the polluter must make efforts to maintain pollution control equipment, yet the EPA cannot know whether this is being done properly (without constant monitoring, which may be expensive). The problem we consider involves no uncertainty about costs or other characteristics of the firm but rather uncertainty about some action the firm is taking. The typical example is *effort* in controlling pollution. Effort by the polluter is costly and unobserved by the regulator, and often significantly affects pollution levels. For instance, if a regulation requires the installation of certain pollution control equipment it is very difficult to also require that it be maintained diligently. Maintenance, of course, is important to obtaining the intended amount of pollutant emissions, but good maintenance is hard to monitor, observe, and enforce.

The set-up will be similar to the adverse selection case except that this time pollution abatement (a) will be monitored by the EPA. The firm will combine abatement activities with maintenance and operation effort (f) to generate pollution levels. Higher levels of effort will be more costly to the polluter but will also reduce pollution levels. Effort cannot be infinitely large or small but rather must be drawn from a limited region—more simply, effort must be between a lower bound (f_L) and an upper bound (f_U). We will write the pollutant emissions as $e(a,f)$. The EPA does not observe e directly; rather it can see what abatement equipment is in place—a. But it is pollution (e) that causes damage.

The EPA will choose a regulation to control the polluter. In the last section, we considered an emissions fee. To diversify a bit, here we will assume the EPA uses an emissions standard. (We could carry out the analysis with any type of regulation.) Specifically, assume the EPA specifies a required level of abatement, $\bar{a}$.

From the point of view of the firm, both abatement and effort increase firm costs, $C(a,f)$. The polluter's problem then is to choose a level of effort, f, to minimize costs:

$$\min_{f} C(\bar{a},f), \qquad f_L \leq f \leq f_U \tag{17.1}$$

Note that abatement, $\bar{a}$, is specified by the EPA, so the polluter has no choice. The polluter chooses effort and it is obvious that the polluter will choose the lowest level of effort, f_L. This is because the costs of effort are lowest at this level and it will not affect the relationship with the EPA.

The way in which the EPA can compensate for this (at least in part) is to make the regulations even tighter, assuming the worst about firm effort levels. In particular, the EPA's problem is to choose a to minimize social costs:

$$\min_{a} C(a,f) + D[e(a,f)] \tag{17.2}$$

The problem is that f affects e, which affects D, but the EPA has little control over f. Suppose the EPA had full knowledge of f. In such a case there are optimal levels of abatement and effort, call them $a^\star$ and $f^\star$. We can examine behavior graphically. To do so, we simplify the costs to the firm, separating the cost of abatement from the cost of effort: $C(a,f) = C_1(a) + C_2(f)$. This implies that the marginal cost of abatement, $MC(a)$ is independent of effort. Fixing effort at $f^\star$, Figure 17.1 shows how the marginal cost of abatement curve and the negative marginal damage from abatement curve might look. Note that the abscissa is abatement and that the more abatement there is, the higher the marginal costs of abatement are. Furthermore, increasing abatement decreases pollution and thus damage. Marginal damage is negative and approaches zero as abatement becomes large. Shown in Figure 17.1 is the "first-best" outcome of a^*, assuming the polluter undertakes the desirable amount of effort, f^*. However, this will generally not be the case. The firm will take the minimum amount of effort, f_L, that will result in higher levels of pollution and thus higher marginal damages. This is shown in Figure 17.1. The optimal "second-best" level of abatement with minimal effort being exerted is a_L, which is clearly larger than a^*. Thus to compensate for low effort, the EPA must require extra abatement. Note from the figure that because abatement is higher, the costs of abatement are also higher. However, we are not able to see the total costs to the firm, since those also include the cost of effort. Nor are we able to compare total damages in the figure. We do know that total costs and damages will be higher with effort at f_L since (a^*,f^*) minimizes total costs and damages [Eq. (17.2)].

How can we circumvent this problem? There are a number of solutions, a few of which we will mention here. One is to identify a variable that is related to effort, perhaps imperfectly. This might be the number of staff employed in pollution control in the firm. Or it might be records (easily observable) of maintenance or inspection activities. Or it might be imperfect measurement of pollution, perhaps obtained by spot checks on emission levels.[1] Or the firm could be made to pay a fee related to pollution damage.

The bottom line is that if a polluter can take secret actions that impact pollution levels, it may be difficult to solve the pollution problem completely. Some way must be found to induce the firm to take the socially desirable level of effort. This is once again an incentives problem. Regulations must be designed to align with the incentives of the polluters. This particular problem of hidden actions is known more generally as the problem of moral hazard.[2]

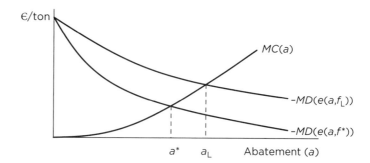

FIGURE 17.1 Illustration of unobserved effort. MD, $f = f_L$, marginal damage, effort at lowest level; MD, $f = f^*$, marginal damage, effort at optimal level; MC, $f = f_L$, marginal cost of abatement, effort at lowest level; MC, marginal cost of abatement, effort at optimal level; a^*, efficient level of abatement; a_L, second-best level of abatement, with effort at lowest level; f^*, efficient level of effort.

II. MONITORING EMISSIONS

As the world makes progress in solving some environmental problems, the problems that remain are typically the more difficult ones. Thus controlling large stationary sources of pollution is the first target of regulators. One of the most difficult types of sources to control is dispersed small polluters that individually contribute modestly to pollution but collectively have serious environmental repercussions. This would include individual farms that contribute to water pollution through agricultural runoff (pesticides, fertilizers, soil, animal wastes), automobile pollution in urban areas, and small generators of waste— households generating solid waste or small firms generating hazardous waste. In all of these cases, the problem is fundamentally one of monitoring emissions. It is either too costly or too difficult for the regulator to learn what individual emissions are. We will consider two variants of this problem. In the first, polluters have different impacts on ambient concentrations and we examine a method of regulating individual polluters based only on observed ambient concentration. In the second, we are interested in encouraging socially desirable behavior, such as disposing of waste in a safe repository. It is necessary to reward firms for safe disposal rather than penalizing them for unsafe disposal.

A. Regulation with Unobserved Emissions

The first case we consider involves a number of firms generating emissions that lead to ambient concentrations of pollution. We observe ambient pollution concentrations but do not observe emission from individual polluters. The point is that it is not impossible to monitor individual polluters, just too expensive. In other words, for practical purposes, the polluting actions of individual polluters are hidden to the regulator. This is basically a moral hazard problem in that firm actions are hidden. The question is whether there are regulatory mechanisms that can work in this situation.

There is a regulatory design (in fact, there are quite a few) that works in this case. We consider a simple one.[3] Since the problem can quickly become complex, we will consider the case of two polluters and a single environmental monitoring point. To add a little realism, suppose that we have two farmers, both bordering a river (Figure 17.2). One farmer (Bush) raises chickens and the other (Kerry) grows vegetables such as tomatoes and Belgian endive. Both contribute pollution through runoff to the river, although in different ways. We have one downstream monitoring point. Let p be the pollution level downstream and let e_i and a_i (for $i = K, B$) be the emission levels and transfer coefficients for Kerry (K) and Bush (B).

This is quite similar to the problem considered in Chapter 15. As in that chapter, the desirable amount of pollution is associated with emissions from each farm that equate marginal savings from emitting to marginal damage in emission terms:

$$-MC_i(e_i) = MDE_i(e_i) = a_i\, MD(p), \qquad \text{for } i = K, B \tag{17.3}$$

The compounding factor here is that the regulator cannot observe e_i, only p. Let p^* be the optimal amount of pollution, i.e., the amount of pollution that balances costs and damages as in Eq. (17.3). Consider the following tax scheme for $i = K$ or B:

$$\text{Tax}_i = t(p - p^*) \tag{17.4}$$

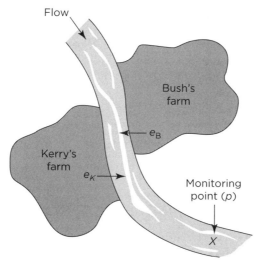

Flow

Bush's farm

e_B

Kerry's farm

e_K

Monitoring point (p)

X

FIGURE 17.2 Two farmers on a river.

Note that if the ambient pollution levels exceed p^*, each farmer pays a tax in proportion to the size of the exceedence. If the pollution levels are less than p^*, the farmers pay a negative tax—they are paid a subsidy. What will each farmer do?

The costs of each farmer i are given by

$$\text{Costs}_i\,(e_i) = C_i(e_i) + t(p - p^*) \qquad (17.5)$$
$$= C_i(e_i) + t(a_K e_K + a_B e_B - p^*)$$
$$= C_i(e_i) + ta_i e_i\, t(a_j e_j - p^*)$$

In Eq. (17.5), the j refers to the other farmer (i.e., if i = K, then i = B). Notice that the last term in Eq. (17.5) is independent of farmer i's emissions. It is just a constant. Thus farmer i does not take it into account in setting emission levels. In fact, from Eq. (17.5) we see that farmer i will minimize costs by choosing emissions such that

$$-MC_i(e_i) = a_i t \qquad (17.6)$$

Now we need to compare Eq. (17.3) and Eq. (17.6). Equation (17.3) is what is socially desirable. Eq. (17.6) is what the farmers will do. We can bring those together if we set t such that

$$t = MD(p^*) \qquad (17.7)$$

So we see that each farmer is charged the same amount per unit of pollution, an amount equal to marginal damage.

You might say that this looks the same as the situation we considered in Chapter 15. The environmental problem is the same. The difference (a subtle one) is that instead of an ambient-differentiated emission fee, we have a fee based purely on observed levels of ambient pollution. And without observing emissions, the two farmers will cut back emissions to the socially desirable level.

This may seem a little counterintuitive. How can a charge paid by a motorist in London, based only on observed air pollution levels in London, encourage that motorist to reduce emissions? The answer lies in Eq. (17.5). Clearly if we charged motorist i the amount $t \, a_i \, e_i$ we would expect pollution control as in Eq. (17.6). Under the system here we are charging that plus a fixed amount, $t(a_j e_j - p^*)$, which should not distort behavior. The total just happens to be $t(p - p^*)$.

The credibility of such a system breaks down when there are very many sources. In such a case, polluters may have to pay (or receive) huge sums of money, corresponding to the total incremental damages from all sources of pollution. Politically, this is unlikely to occur. It would seem that this system is most likely to work when there are only a small number of sources.

B. Midnight Dumping and Deposit-Refunds

The previous case concerned moral hazard—emissions were unobservable. We now consider a different though closely related problem of moral hazard. For simplicity, suppose a polluter can do two things with emissions—one socially desirable and easy to monitor and the other socially undesirable and difficult to monitor. The best example is the generation of solid waste. A generator has two options (more or less)—to dispose of the wastes "safely" in a regulated facility or to surreptitiously dispose of the wastes, e.g., dump the wastes illegally in the middle of the night. The first option is more costly to the firm, thus incentives are to "midnight dump." The second option, "midnight dumping," is more costly to society and also more difficult to monitor.[4]

A standard approach to discourage the generation of hazardous wastes would be to tax waste disposal at the marginal social cost of that disposal. In this case, that would have the unfortunate side effect of encouraging illegal dumping.

One solution is to reward proper disposal of wastes. Instead of taxing disposal, proper disposal (which is verifiable) is subsidized. Thus proper disposal becomes more attractive to the polluter than illegal disposal (which is not verifiable). But this raises two problems. It encourages excess waste generation and is a drain on the government budget.

The problem we are discussing is a problem of moral hazard. Taking care to dispose of wastes properly involves a hidden action. We cannot observe when wastes are improperly discarded. On the other hand, disposal of hazardous wastes in a properly constructed repository (also know as a dump) is verifiable—other, less desirable, ways of disposing of hazardous wastes are not verifiable.

In a world of perfect information, we would choose to tax the illicit disposal at a higher rate than the "safe" disposal, though both would be taxed at a positive level since both involve costs to society. The positive taxes on both would discourage the production of wastes. However, since we cannot tax illicit disposal, the best we can do is subsidize safe disposal, assuming it is possible to verify safe disposal. Safe disposal must be seen as more profitable to the polluter than illicit disposal.

Let us start by supposing that a firm generates wastes (w), and disposes of waste. Disposal is unobservable except in the case in which it is done safely (as in a landfill). Let $C(w)$ be the production costs of the firm as a function of its waste generation. This reflects the cost advantage of producing more waste: increases in w decrease costs. The marginal costs to the firm of safe disposal are c_s; for illegal (unsafe) disposal, the marginal costs are c_i. By assumption, the firm finds illegal disposal cheaper; thus $c_i < c_s$. From a societal point of view, illegal disposal creates more environmental damage. Let the marginal damage from illegal disposal be d_i and the marginal damage from safe disposal be d_s: $d_i > d_s$. One final condition is that from a societal point of view (taking into account disposal costs and damage), safe disposal is preferred: $(d_i - d_s) > (c_s - c_i)$.

The essence of the problem is that the regulator does not observe how the wastes are disposed (safely or illegally), though we can assume that the regulator observes the total quantity of wastes (w). This may be because wastes are a transformation of some input into production that is observable.

The regulator has two objectives: to assure that wastes are safely disposed of and to assure that the right amount of wastes are generated. A scheme to induce safe disposal and waste reduction is a deposit-refund. Let t be the tax per unit of waste generated (w) and s be the unit subsidy for safe disposal. The firm then sees total costs of

$$TC(w) = C(w) + c_s\, w + t\, w - s\, w \qquad \text{if wastes are safely discarded} \qquad (17.8)$$
$$ C(w) + c_i\, w + t\, w \qquad \text{otherwise}$$

1. A subsidy on safe disposal. In examining Eq. (17.8), it is easy to see that in order to encourage safe disposal, it is necessary to make safe disposal cheaper, which implies that the subsidy has to at least overcome the advantage of illegal disposal:

$$s > c_s - c_i \qquad (17.9)$$

Equation (17.9) assures us that the subsidy will be high enough that safe disposal will always be pursued.

2. A tax on waste generation. How much waste will the firm generate? To maximize profit, the firm with "take the marginal" of the top part of Eq. (17.8) and set it equal to zero, yielding

$$MC(w) + c_s + t - s = 0 \qquad (17.10)$$

This equation simply says that if wastes are being safely disposed, the firm will choose to generate wastes such that the marginal savings $(-MC(w) - c_s)$ are equal to the net tax $(t - s)$.

The only remaining question is what should be t? From a societal point of view, total costs (including environmental damage) of any w are given by (assuming safe disposal is pursued):

$$SC(w) = C(w) + c_s\, w + d_s\, w \qquad (17.11)$$

Minimization of costs implies

$$MC(w) + c_s + d_s = 0 \qquad (17.12)$$

If we compare the firm's choice criterion [Eq. (17.10)] with society's choice criterion [Eq. (17.12)], we see that they coincide when

$$t - s = d_s \qquad (17.13)$$

3. Policies to assure the right amount of safely disposed waste. To summarize, safe disposal is ensured by Eq. (17.9)—the subsidy must overcome the advantage of illegal disposal. And cutting back on wastes is assured by Eq. (17.13)—the net marginal cost of generating waste is equal to marginal social damage. This combined policy of a subsidy and a tax is equivalent to a deposit–refund—the deposit is akin to the tax on waste generation and the refund is the subsidy for safe disposal. Note that because t is greater than s, the regulator is assured of having a net positive inflow of resources. There is no issue of running a deficit with this deposit–refund system.

Three examples of this type of regulation come immediately to mind. Consider disposal of organic solvents used in metal fabrication. We may observe the amount of solvent used, since it is generally purchased from a manufacturer and leaves an "audit trail." But we do not necessarily observe what happens to the solvent after it is used—some evaporates, some is reused, some is safely disposed of and (perhaps) some is illegally dumped. Fortunately, we can monitor safe disposal. The results here suggest we should tax the use of solvents and subsidize the safe disposal of solvents.

Another example is household solid waste. A good portion of household waste in the developed world is product packaging. Although it is difficult to monitor the disposal of this waste, it is relatively easy to monitor the quantity of waste a household is generating, simply by monitoring the nature and quantity of product packaging purchased. The result suggests we should tax the use of packaging and subsidize proper disposal, either in a landfill or through recycling.

The clearest example of this type of regulation is the deposit–refund system for beverage containers. Simply taxing the use of these containers is insufficient to ensure their proper disposal. A payment is made when a beverage is purchased in a container; a refund is paid when the empty container is returned to the point of purchase or other suitable repository.[5]

Recycling Lead Batteries

Eighty percent of lead used in the United States is in storage batteries (such as car batteries). Though most of these batteries are recycled, they also constitute the largest source of lead in municipal solid waste streams. Lead is a notoriously harmful environmental toxin. Hillary Sigman (1995) examined several policies for reducing lead discharges into the environment: a tax on virgin lead used in manufacturing, a deposit–refund system for batteries, recycled content standards for batteries (minimum percentage recycled lead) and subsidies the recycling lead. The core of her analysis is an empirical estimate of supply and demand for virgin and recycled lead in the United States, including the importance of price for these two closely related commodities. She uses these estimates to conduct a cost-effectiveness analysis of these different policies for obtaining a given reduction in lead disposal. She concludes that a deposit–refund system behaves similarly to a virgin materials tax and that these two options are the lowest cost ways of achieving the objective. The worst policy is subsidies for recycling lead, in part because it lowers the price of lead and thus encourages its use.[6]

III. ENFORCEMENT

We turn now to the problem of enforcing environmental regulations.[7] Enforcement is really a special case of asymmetric information—the regulator does not know whether the polluter is doing what it says it has been doing. Primarily, enforcement involves identifying those polluters that are not doing as they should. Thus enforcement involves identifying private information on compliance with regulation, i.e., monitoring whether polluters are obeying the law.

In all of our discussion of regulation, we have either assumed that firms do as they are told and/or voluntarily provide private information to the regulator. We will relax that now and add the option that the regulator can audit a polluter, but *at a cost*. In other words, the polluter may have private information but the regulator may obtain it, at some cost to the regulator. Obviously, if the cost is very low, the regulator will usually obtain the information and we are back to the situation of perfect information. We are interested in the case in which the information is moderately costly so that the regulator will not seek perfect information from all polluters. The situation we have just outlined is the case of costly *audits* of polluters.[8]

This is very similar to the problem faced by a government taxation and revenue department. It is not cost effective to audit all taxpayers nor is it cost effective to audit no taxpayers (then many would cheat). The optimal amount of auditing is somewhere between these two extremes. Also, there is an interplay between the frequency of auditing and the penalities if caught cheating. If the penalties are low for cheating then no amount of auditing can induce taxpayers to behave appropriately. If the penalties are very high, quite infrequent auditing may be sufficient.

Thus enforcement of pollution control regulations has two components: finding out who is violating the regulations (auditing) and applying penalties to cheaters. The dual objectives of an efficient enforcement program are to induce polluters to pollute at the right level while keeping enforcement costs low.

Suppose we have a group of identical firms, each emitting pollution (e) at cost $C(e)$. As usual, C declines as e increases; thus polluting reduces firm costs and marginal costs with respect to e are negative. We are interested in what the typical firm will do when faced with an enforcement program as descibed above: the firm reports emissions to the regulator and has some probability, π, of being audited by the regulator. If cheating, the firm will pay a fine related to the size of the violation.[9]

A. Auditing an Emissions Standard

Consider the case of an emission standard. Suppose the regulator has decreed that each firm shall emit no more than $\bar{s}$ units of pollution. If a firm is audited and is found to be emitting more than allowed, the firm must pay a fine, f per unit of emissions in violation plus a fixed fine, $D,$ unrelated to the size of the violation. Thus the total costs to the firm, before it knows whether it will be audited, are

$$TC(e) = C(e) + F(e) \tag{17.14a}$$

where

$$F(e) = \begin{cases} \pi[f(e - \bar{s}) + D], & \text{if } e > \bar{s} \\ 0, & \text{if } e \leq \bar{s} \end{cases} \tag{17.14b}$$

The last term in Eq. (17.14a) is the *expected* fine from emitting at level e. By expected fine, we mean the amount of the fine times the probability (π) of having to pay it (i.e., the probability of being audited). And of course, it is in part proportional to the amount of the violation, $e - \bar{s}$. If there is no violation, there is no fine. A fixed fine (D) is also included in Eq. (17.14b). If the firm is found to be in violation, part of the fine is proportional to the violation and part is not.

This is shown graphically in Figure 17.3. In both Figure 17.3a and 17.3b, direct costs (C), expected fines (F), and total costs (TC) are shown as a function of emissions. The only difference between the two panels is the size of the fines—f and D. In the first panel, both are larger than they are in the second panel. And this changes behavior. Focus first on Figure 17.3a. Note that the rather peculiarly shaped total cost function (TC) has a minimum at $\bar{s}$. Thus under this system, the firm will choose to emit at the regulatory standard and not violate the regulation. It is a different situation in Figure 17.3b; here the optimal behavior for the firm is to emit at $e^* > \bar{s}$. The fine (f or D) and audit frequency are simply too low to induce compliance.

(a)

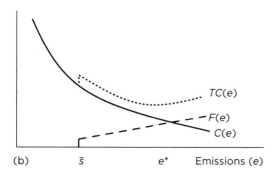

(b)

FIGURE 17.3 (a,b) Illustration of a fine with fixed and variable components. $C(e)$, direct costs of emissions; $F(e)$, expected fine for emission level e; $TC(e)$, total cost: direct costs plus expected fine; $\bar{s}$, environmental standard; e^*, cost-minimizing level of emissions.

In the case of Figure 17.3b, total costs can be written as

$$TC(e) = C(e) + \pi f(e - \bar{s}) + \pi D \qquad (17.15)$$
$$= C(e) + \pi f e - \pi f \bar{s} + \pi D$$

The firm will choose to operate at the minimum of total costs that occurs when marginal total costs are zero ($MTC = 0$). Note that costs are lower here than at $\bar{s}$. The marginal total costs can be separated into the marginal direct costs (MC) and the marginal fine (MF):

$$0 = MTC(e) = MC(e) + MF(e) \qquad (17.16a)$$
$$= MC(e) + \pi f$$

or, alternatively,

$$-MC(e) = MS(e) = \pi f \qquad (17.16b)$$

In other words, the firm will choose to pollute at the point at which the marginal savings from polluting are equal to the marginal expected fine. This is as expected. As long as the savings from emitting one more unit are less than the costs (in expected fines) from emitting one more unit, the firm will expand polluting. When the marginal savings are less than the marginal expected fines, the firm will cut back on pollution. When the two are the same, no further adjustments are necessary. In deciding whether to operate as in Figure 17.3a or 17.3b, the firm must compare total costs and choose the option that is least costly. Choosing between Figure 17.3a and 17.3b is not a marginal decision.

Note that what is important to the firm is the expected marginal fine, which is the product of π and f. Thus the specific values of π and f are not important, only their product. A small fine along with a large probability of audit will look exactly the same to the firm as a larger fine and a smaller probability of audit, as long as the product of the two remains the same. Alternatively, if D were large enough, we would return to the case in Figure 17.3a, in which marginal conditions are unimportant.[10]

Now that we have characterized the firm's behavior, we turn to the regulator, which must choose the level of the fine and the audit probability. For simplicity, focus on the unit fine, f, setting $D = 0$. Note first that because it is costly to audit and only the product of π and f matter to the firm, it is clearly best to audit infrequently and levy large fines. This makes the auditing costs very small. The only limit to the size of the fine would be the assets of the firm. A firm cannot be made to pay a fine that exceeds its assets or else it will simply declare bankruptcy. This would destroy the incentive properties of the fine. The next question is what should πf be set to? Clearly if the standard is $\bar{s}$, then πf should be set so that Eq. (17.16) is satisfied at s:

$$MS(\bar{s}) = \pi f \qquad (17.17)$$

If the firm chooses not to violate the standard all is well; if the firm considers violating the standard, it will see that it is not in its best interest to do so and will instead choose emissions equal to the standard, according to Eq. (17.17).

There are two main messages to carry away from the model developed here. One is that it is not necessary to closely monitor polluters. Provided the sanctions for violating the regulations are high enough, the same outcome can be achieved with infrequent auditing. The second message to carry away from this is that it is not sufficient to simply establish a regulation and some sort of enforcement program. An inappropriately set enforcement regime will not induce polluters to behave. The costs of cheating must be seen to be higher than the costs of adhering to the regulations.

B. Extensions

The model of enforcement presented in the previous section is very simple. It is possible to add significantly to the model's realism and at the same time to its complexity. The simplest extension is to consider the case of an emission fee in which the firm reports to the regulator the emission fees due. The firm might be inclined to underreport emissions to reduce fee payments. An appropriately designed auditing system can avoid this.

Another extension would be to make the auditing probability and the unit fine depend on the size of the violation. This is somewhat more realistic than purely random audits, since there would probably be some information that would direct the auditors to firms that are more likely to be in violation.[11]

One extension would be to allow firms to report their emissions. If their emissions are above the standard, they would pay a fine. The regulator would only need to audit firms who report emissions that are within limits. This can be shown to reduce the overall cost of an audit regime.[12]

The EPA has been encouraging firms to engage in what is called "self-audits." These are just as they sound—firms do the audit themselves and report results to the EPA. Although these sound like letting the fox in the henhouse, such self-audits seem to generate some admissions of violations, though generally only modest violations.[13]

Another extension can involve a more complex auditing program, involving dynamics and reputation. Firms can be assumed to belong to one of two (or more) groups. Firms in group A have never been found to be in violation—either they have never been audited or, if audited, were found to be in compliance. Firms in group B have been audited and found to be in violation. Firms in group B are audited more frequently. Such a two-state auditing program can significantly reduce auditing costs.[14] Another interesting characteristic of such a multicategory auditing system is that fines can be set quite low, at least for firms in group A.[15]

IV. DYNAMICS AND COMMITMENT

Most of what we have been discussing in this and the previous chapter ignores the dynamics of the regulatory process—the repeated interaction over time between the regulator and the regulatee. Our previous analyses have concerned one-time interactions between regulators and polluters. We have been concerned about structuring regulations so that the problems of asymmetric information are minimized. Reality is of course that regulators and polluters continue interacting. Furthermore, what each party does in one period may influence what happens in subsequent periods. There are two basic cases that we treat here, one concerning the cost of flexibility and the other concerning a combination of moral hazard and adverse selection.

First consider flexibility. Suppose the regulator promulgates a regulation today based on an assessment of costs and benefits of various levels of pollution control. There is a great deal of uncertainty about both costs and benefits. Regulators are uncertain about the right amount of control but promulgate a regulation anyway. The polluter sees a regulation but also perceives that the regulation could change, either becoming tighter or weaker in the future. Because of this, the polluter is reluctant to invest in expensive pollution control equipment, even though such an investment may be the cheapest way of controlling pollution in the long run. Instead, the polluter pursues a costly short-term strategy of pollution control and may lobby regulators to relax regulations in the future. Regulators in turn may observe costs and notice that they are higher than expected. Basically, it is more costly to be flexible. When regulators see that costs are higher, they may weaken the regulations. The desire on the part of the regulator to maintain flexibility has resulted in weaker pollution control. The regulator has legitimate reasons for retaining flexibility (in order to revise regulations when more becomes known). The down side is that when the regulator retains flexibility to revise the regulation, the polluter will in turn retain flexibility (at a cost) in anticipation of the regulation changing.

Why is flexibility always costly? Conceptually, flexibility is an additional condition imposed on the regulatory process, so it cannot decrease costs. Practically, the reason this makes any difference is that the cost of pollution control usually consists of a combination of short-run costs (such as using cleaner fuels) and longer-run costs (such as investing in pollution control equipment). It may be that the cheapest way to control pollution is to invest in pollution control equipment, perhaps with some use of clean fuel. However, if polluters think that the regulation is only temporary, they are unlikely to do any investing, instead relying exclusively on cleaner fuels. Although this is rational for the polluter, it makes pollution control more expensive than necessary. And if regulations are set to balance costs and damages, higher control costs will lead to weaker regulations and thus more pollution.

The other case draws from the adverse selection and moral hazard problems discussed earlier. Suppose the regulator is concerned with regulating a single firm. The pollution control costs are known to the firm but only imperfectly to the regulator. The firm reports its costs to the regulator. This is the adverse selection problem. We saw in the previous chapter that one solution to this problem is to reward low-cost firms for admitting that they are low cost, thus inducing them to tell the truth. But suppose we are dealing with multiple periods of time. If in the first period the firm admits to being a low-cost firm, in the second period, the regulator can change the rules and stop rewarding firms for admitting they are low cost (since the information is acquired in the first period). Because firms know this, how can we get them to cooperate in the first period?

As a concrete example of this, suppose the regulator is setting automobile emission standards for automobile manufacturers to follow. The regulator sets standards at some level in an initial period of time. Unfortunately, the regulator does not know how difficult it is for the automobile manufacturers to meet these standards. From the point of view of the automobile manufacturers, if they meet the standards easily, they are inviting even tighter regulations in the next period of time. If they complain about meeting the standard, they are more likely to get more lenient treatment in the next period.[16]

In both of these cases, the dynamic nature of the interaction between regulator and polluter leads to problems. In the first case, the polluter defers making long-run commitments to the cheapest form of pollution control because of the possibility that the regulation will change in the next period. This is the case of there being a cost of maintaining flexibility. In the second case, the firm realizes that the better it does in complying with regulations today, the more likely it will be that regulations will be tightened next period. This is called the "ratchet effect," from the tendency of the regulator to ratchet up the regulation if the firm behaves properly.[17]

The key factor generating these problems is the lack of commitment on the part of the regulator. Suppose the regulator could convince the polluter that the regulation will not change. In our first example, polluters would then be willing to invest in the pollution control equipment and achieve the lowest possible pollution control costs. In our second example, polluters would not worry about revealing their true costs. This is what is known as the problem of commitment. If the regulator cannot commit to a particular regulatory strategy, then polluters will not respond in the desired way. If on the other hand the regulator is able to commit, the polluter will have a different response. The downside for the regulator is that commitment is just that and precludes loosening controls later if the situation warrants.

The significant point is that commitment can be important to reduce costs and, as a result, pollution. Thus if a regulator does not need to maintain flexibility, it is in the regulator's best interest to pursue regulatory policies that involve commitment. Commitment is not easy, however. Even if a legislature were to promulgate a regulation and state that it will not be changed, in most countries it is not possible to prohibit the legislature from revisiting the issue and changing its mind at a later date.

What are examples of commitment or lack thereof in environmental regulation? One example is the case of marketable emission permits in the United States. In the sulfur allowance system governing emissions of sulfur dioxide in the United States, the legislation is quite specific that the tradable allowances being distributed to polluters are not property rights; in other words, they may be confiscated without compensation if the EPA changes its mind about relying on tradable permits. This sounds good for the EPA, but what is being sacrificed? The EPA is failing to commit to the allowance system and thus is discouraging (somewhat) long-term investments in pollution control, possibly raising the costs of pollution control.[18]

Interestingly, command-and-control regulation can have real advantages in the area of commitment. Often command and control specifies the control capital that must be used. This capital often becomes a sunk cost. By specifying that firms must make long-run investments, command and control is able to require firms to commit to a long-run strategy, an outcome that is difficult if the possibility is real that the emission fee can change next year.

A. Flexibility

We will consider an example that is overly simplified, but that illustrates the problem of retaining regulatory flexibility. Consider a power plant subject to sulfur emissions regulations. Think of the regulations as being either tight (T) or loose (L). The firm has two options for controlling emissions: buying scrubbers that remove nearly all the sulfur from the emissions and last a long time, or buying low-sulfur fuel. Once the scrubber is purchased, it is a sunk cost and cannot be uninstalled. Once installed, the scrubber costs $50 per year (this is the total cost annualized). Alternatively, the firm may buy cleaner fuel to reduce emissions. With tight regulations, clean fuel will cost $60 per year; with loose regulations, clean fuel costs only $30 per year. So if the firm knows regulations will always be tight, it is clearly cheapest to buy the abatement equipment. If the firm knows it will be subject to loose regulations, it pays not to buy the abatement equipment and buy cleaner fuel instead.

Suppose the regulator promulgates tight regulations but leaves open the possibility of loosening the regulations in subsequent years. What would we expect the firm to do? To answer this question, we will divide our example into two time periods: the present and the future. In the present, regulations are tight. But the EPA is conducting a study to decide whether regulations should be tight or loose in the future. We expect the results of that study before the second period begins. But our current assessment of what may emerge from that report can be summarized by saying that in the future, the regulations will be tight with probability π and loose with probability $(1 - \pi)$. Figure 17.4 is a representation of the decision that the power plant must make. Shown in the figure are the two first-period decisions by the power plant: to scrub (S) or not to scrub (NS). The first of these will cost (in the first period) $50, and the second, $60. Following the firm's choice of actions, the regulator "moves," deciding on whether the regulations should be tight (T) or loose (L) in the second period. The probability of T is π. Then in the last stage, the power plant moves again, deciding on whether to utilize a scrubber (S) or not (NS) as its pollution control choice. The last line is the total cost to the firm of pollution control in the two periods.

Remember that what we are really interested in is what first-period action the firm will take. Our goal is to calculate the expected firm payoffs under the two first-period actions: S and NS. To figure this out, we need to work backward from the last period, figuring out what the firm will do under all possible actions by the regulators. The best second period choices by the firm are circled in the figure.

This allows us to calculate the total cost to the firm from the two first-period actions:

$$TC = \begin{cases} 100 & \text{if S in first period} & (17.18\text{a}) \\ 110\,\pi + 90\,(1 - \pi) = 90 + 20\,\pi & \text{if NS in first period} & (17.18\text{b}) \end{cases}$$

Under what conditions would the firm choose S in the first period? Clearly if $\pi > \frac{1}{2}$, S in period 1 results in the lowest total cost in Eq. (17.18). In other words, if there is greater than an even chance that the regulator will loosen regulations in the second period, then it is optimal to avoid the capital investment in the scrubber and go with the more costly low-sulfur fuel.

The interesting thing is that an analysis of the cost of regulations without uncertainty indicates that tight regulations cost $50 per year whereas loose regulations cost $30 per year. However, introducing sufficient uncertainty over the two regulations has the effect of raising the cost to $60 per year as long as regulations remain tight and uncertain, not a figure somewhere between $50 and $30 as one might expect from uncertainty over whether the regulation should be loose or tight.

The bottom line is that flexibility costs money. If the regulator wants to retain flexability and is consequently unwilling to commit to tight regulations, firms respond by adopting more flexible control plans, though at higher cost. Although there may be a good reason for the regulator to want to retain some flexibility and ability to adjust

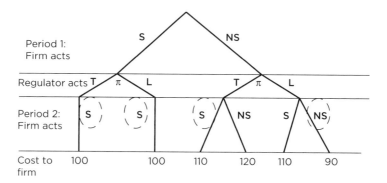

FIGURE 17.4 The decision to invest in abatement equipment. T, tight regulation; L, loose regulation. *Note:* Abatement equipment costs $50 per period. Clean fuel costs $60 per period with tight regulation and $30 per period with loose regulation. Circled actions in period 2 result in the lowest cost to the firm, for each different combination of firm and regulator action.

regulations in the future (which is in fact the case in our example), it is important for the regulator to be aware that there is a cost associated with this. In particular, a lack of commitment on the part of a regulator may cause an underinvestment in pollution abatement equipment and thus unnecessarily high pollution control costs.

B. The Ratchet Effect

The ratchet effect occurs when the regulator has incomplete knowledge of the firm's costs and the two must repeatedly interact. If the firm is capable of controlling pollution at low cost, and the regulator knows it, the firm will be subject to tight regulations. What makes the problem interesting is that the firm and the regulator interact repeatedly. Thus it is in the firm's best interest to disguise its true nature, or the regulator will ratchet up the intensity of the regulation in subsequent periods.

The mathematics of the ratchet effect is fairly complex, so we will content ourselves with a description of how a model of the effect might operate. We will draw on the model of automobile pollution regulation mentioned earlier and examined in detail by Yao (1988). (See box, p. 351.)[19]

We start with an automobile industry subject to regulation by the EPA. The goal is to set an emission limit for the industry that is tight but realistic. The industry will have to invest in R&D to meet the regulation. The EPA's job is to make sure the emission limit is attainable at acceptable cost (whatever that is).

To make the problem even simpler, suppose there are two time periods, today and tomorrow (which of course could mean this decade and next decade). The EPA sets a minimum level of abatement in each period equal to L_1 and L_2. How does the industry meet this limit? In contrast to the other models we have examined, the industry knows it can meet the limit; the only question is the cost. Furthermore, the industry can invest in research (R&D) to lower the cost of meeting the regulation. And the more industry invests, the more of a cost reduction will occur. To make things a little more interesting, the productivity of industrial R&D is not known to the EPA. In fact, we will keep the EPA in the dark about the amount of R&D as well as the productivity of R&D.

To be more specific, let the net costs for the industry be given by $C(a,r,\theta)$, where a is the amount of abatement, r is the investment in R&D, and θ is the productivity of R&D. These costs include both the abatement costs as well as the costs of R&D. More abatement (a) means higher costs; larger θ means higher payoff to R&D and thus lower costs; costs first decline as r is increased from zero, but then there comes a point of diminishing returns to R&D and C begins to decline from that point on. The EPA can observe C but cannot observe θ or r.

This is both a moral hazard problem (r is an unobserved action) and an adverse selection problem (θ is an unobserved characteristic of the industry). What would happen if the EPA could perfectly observe θ and r? In that case the EPA would balance the costs of pollution control, including R&D, with the benefits of pollution control.

But what happens when the EPA is unaware of θ or r? As we saw in the previous chapter when we were considering adverse selection, the EPA must reward the industry for admitting that it is productive and adjust the regulation, L, depending on the admitted productivity of the industry. But if the industry admits its R&D productivity, in the next period the EPA will dispense with the reward for providing truthful information and impose as tight a regulation as possible. In other words, if the industry admits it is low cost, it will pay dearly in the next time period.

So what should the industry do? First, it should be less willing to admit to being a productive industry. Second, when the EPA observes costs after the first period, it will have a better idea whether the industry is productive or not. If the costs of meeting the regulation are low, the EPA will be more likely to think the industry is productive. To avoid sending that signal to the EPA, the industry is likely to underinvest in R&D (r), artificially keeping the cost of meeting the regulation high.

This behavior becomes more meaningful if we return to the automobile industry example that motivated us. The EPA imposes regulations on new cars in terms of their allowed emissions. The automobile industry complains that it is difficult to meet the regulation. Furthermore, some years later, it turns out that the automobile industry was right, it was very costly to meet the regulation. Thus the industry gets gentler treatment in subsequent regulatory rounds.

What is missing is that the industry may have intentionally underinvested in R&D to send a signal (through high costs of meeting the regulation) that the industry has a

---

The US Auto Industry and Emissions Controls

Dennis Yao (1988) describes the game played between the U.S. auto industry and the U.S. government in the 1970s with regard to emission regulations.[20] The 1970 Clean Air Act Amendments mandated a 90% reduction in hydrocarbon emissions from cars to be achieved by 1975. In 1973, this was delayed by one year. Two further delays pushed the deadline to 1978. Then, following heavy lobbying by automakers, Congress modified the law making the deadline 1980. Throughout this period, the automobile industry claimed that the proposed standards would be very expensive to meet. Clearly the claim (true or not) that meeting the standards would be expensive was effective in staving off regulation. The government was hampered by not knowing how valid the industry's claims about costs were.

difficult time meeting automobile emission regulations. That signal can pay handsomely over years to come.

The solution to this problem is commitment. If the regulator can commit to a multi-year regulatory strategy, the gamesmanship the industry may play will not pay off. Such commitment is difficult, however, particularly for government regulators and legislators. If the legislature passes a law committing to a set of actions, all it takes is a new law by the next legislature to undo that commitment.[21]

C. Why Is Commitment Rare?

We have seen that for both of the examples we considered, commitment on the part of the regulator is generally desirable. In the case of flexibility, if the regulator can commit, the cost of emission control will be lower. We saw in the case of the ratchet effect that multiyear commitment can eliminate perverse incentives and thus decrease the costs of emission control.

The fact is that environmental regulators are rarely willing to commit. Why is this? One simple explanation is that they are unaware of the advantages of commitment; however, there may be other reasons (see Freixas et al., 1985). Commitment may not be possible. Even if the EPA were to say it will not change the regulation, we know that regulators change as do legislatures. Commitment typically requires a constitutional guarantee, which is rarely possible.

Another reason for a lack of commitment is that it is very difficult and costly to design regulations to apply many years into the future. One must carefully weigh different outcomes and contingencies. This is not easy and may be undesirable.

A third reason for a lack of commitment is learning and information acquisition. If the EPA expects to acquire new information, perhaps it should keep its options open. In the arena of environmental regulation, acquiring new information is a very real possibility. More is being learned every day, particularly about the damages associated with pollution.

In conclusion, commitment is generally (though not always) desirable and should be pursued if possible. However, we must recognize that commitment will not always accompany environmental regulations and, for that reason, such regulations are likely to be second best, with higher costs and fewer environmental benefits than would otherwise be the case.

SUMMARY

1. Moral hazard problems involve polluters taking important actions that cannot be observed by the regulator, such as diligently maintaining pollution control equipment. Consequently, moral hazard involves "hidden actions."

2. One problem with many area sources of pollution (e.g., automobile pollution or agricultural runoff) is that emissions are not directly observed. A properly constructed levy on observed ambient levels of pollution can induce the optimal amount of emissions, even when those emissions are unobserved.

3. For some pollutants, safe disposal is important while illegal disposal is cheaper for the firm. Subsidies to safe disposal accompanied by a charge on waste generation

can solve this problem. Such fee-subsidy systems are also known as deposit–refund systems.

4. In constructing an effective enforcement program, it is important to adjust both the fine for noncompliance as well as the probability of a firm being audited.

5. When a regulator retains flexibility by refraining from committing to a long-run regulatory strategy, polluters may fail to adequately invest in pollution control equipment, thus raising costs. Higher costs may result in pressures to relax the regulation in subsequent periods.

6. The ratchet effect involves repeated interaction between a regulator and a firm. If the firm is capable of controlling pollution at low cost and the regulator knows it, then the firm will be subject to tight regulation. Thus it is in the firm's best interest to disguise its true nature, or else the regulator will ratchet up the intensity of the regulation in subsequent periods.

7. Commitment can solve dynamic regulatory problems. However, it is difficult for governments and regulators to commit themselves not to take certain actions in the future.

PROBLEMS

1. Imagine that you are a manufacturer of inflatable rubber ducks. Unfortunately, the manufacture of ducks involves damaging water pollution. You have computed that your marginal savings in millions of dollars from emitting pollution is linear: $MS(e) = 10 - e$, where e is the amount of emissions in tons. The Ministry of the environment has decreed that your emissions should not exceed 2 tons.

   a. How much money does it cost you to obey the regulation rather than emit as much as you want?

   b. The Ministry has just instituted a program whereby it will audit you with a probability of 0.01. If you are found in violation, you must pay a fine of $10 million per ton of emissions in excess of the limit. How much is optimal for you to emit (optimal from your point of view)?

*2. Consider the problem of automobile pollution in a large city in Central Asia. There are a million cars in the city, each emitting 10 grams of carbon monoxide (CO) per kilometer (km) driven. On average, each car is driven 10,000 km per year. The average cost to each driver is approximately 1 Ruble/km whereas the marginal cost is lower and independent of km traveled, at about 0.3 Rubles/km (because of the large fixed cost of owning an automobile). A recent study of driver behavior determined that individual demand for kilometers driven was roughly linear; if a gas tax were instituted that raised the marginal cost of driving by 0.1 Rubles/km, the average car owner would reduce driving by about 1,000 km per year. Each kiloton (1,000 tons) of CO emitted in a year raises the average concentration of CO by 1 $\mu g/m^3$. A team of economists, biologists, and physicists determined that the marginal damage per unit of ambient concentration of CO is roughly constant, 10,000,000 Rubles per year per 1 $\mu g/m^3$.

   a. For an individual, what are the annual emissions when the "price" of emissions is zero? What about when the price rises to R10 per kg? R20 per kg? Draw an individual's supply curve for emissions—the relationship between price (R per kg) on the vertical axis and quantity of emissions (kg) on the horizontal axis.

b. Draw the aggregate supply for emissions over all individuals, showing the price (R per kg) on the vertical axis and the quantity of emissions (kilotons—millions of kg) on the horizontal axis. In another graph, draw the equivalent curve for the supply of pollution, showing the quantity of pollution on the horizontal axis ($\mu g/m^3$) and the price in millions of Rubles per $\mu g/m^3$ on the vertical axis. This is the marginal savings from polluting. Draw the marginal damage from pollution on the same graph. What is the efficient ambient concentration of CO? Call this value S.

c. What are the average emissions per car associated with this efficient concentration of CO? If you could observe emissions from each automobile, what emission charge would you levy per kg of emissions per car to obtain the efficient concentration?

d. You are advising the Local Environmental Protection Committee and point out that emissions from individual cars are very difficult to measure. You recommend an ambient fee to control this pollution. In other words, each driver would be assessed a charge, based on observed ambient conditions only (such a fee was described in this chapter). How much would each driver have to pay if ambient pollution levels exceeded S by 1 $\mu g/m^3$?

e. Discuss the answers to parts (c) and (d).

3. Some policy makers argue that it would be desirable to reward generators of hazardous wastes for appropriately disposing of their wastes. Describe a possible reward scheme. Why is it a good idea? What are its shortcomings?

4. Identify whether each of the following is an example of adverse selection or moral hazard and why:

a. A sawmill threatens to close down because of tight new environmental regulations.

b. Smog checks are required for automobiles in addition to emission requirements imposed on manufacturers.

c. There is difficulty in operating a program to buy the most polluting cars from consumers and retire the cars.

5. Describe how a tax scheme as detailed in Section II could be used to regulate automobile pollution in an urban area.

6. Contrast emission fees (fee per unit emissions) and marketable permits (permit to emit one unit in perpetuity) from the point of view of commitment in a society with well-defined private property rights (i.e., property cannot be confiscated without compensation).

*7. You are a polluter who is faced with the question of whether to comply with the regulations on emissions or to violate them. If you comply with the regulations, your costs are k. If you do not comply with the regulations, your costs are zero. The EPA has a new system whereby it audits your compliance with the regulation and gives you a black mark or gold star. If you have a gold star and are audited and found out of compliance, you pay a $50 fine and get a black mark. If you have a black mark and are audited and found in compliance, the EPA flips a coin and gives you a gold star with probability 0.5. If you have a black mark, are audited, and found out of compliance, you are fined $100. The probability of audit depends on whether you have a gold star (probability 0.1) or a black mark (probability 0.5). These probabilities and costs are annual.

Based on your costs, four strategies are available to you: never comply, always comply, comply only if you have a gold star, comply only if you have a black star. Call these strategies, nn, cc, en, and nc. One is always best for you, and it depends on your costs of compliance, β. Suppose you repeatedly interact with the regulator year after year. Your discount factor is k (you are indifferent between $1 tomorrow and β today) and is equal to 0.9. Define your expected costs from all future interactions as $C_{ij}(m)$ where ij is nn, cc, en, or nc and m is gold star or black mark.

Calculate the value of $C_{ij}(m)$ for both ms and all four ijs. [*Hint:* write an equation for a particular $C_{ij}(m)$ in terms of this year's costs and next year's $C_{ij}(m)$, which must be the same as this year's.]

What is the highest value of k for which you always comply with the regulations? What is the lowest value of k for which you never comply with the regulations?

NOTES

1. Cremer and Gahvari (2001) and Schmutzler and Goulder (1997) consider the problem of pollution generation in which taxing the output of emissions is difficult, generally because of monitoring costs. Eskeland (1994) examines the practicality of a tax on gasoline as a substitute for a tax on emissions associated with gasoline. McAusland and Costello (2004), in an innovative application, examine the problem of controlling the introduction of invasive species viewed as a by-product of international trade. They examine a combined tax on goods trade with monitoring (inspection).

2. This is a rather peculiar term with its genesis in the insurance literature. If you are a smoker with your own house, you will be careful about smoking in bed, because of the risk of fire. But if your house is fully insured against fire, you lose some or all of the incentive to be morally upright, taking care to prevent fire. Furthermore, the insurance company cannot know how careful you are. Your care is the analog to effort in our example. The insurance has created a "moral hazard."

3. The model presented here is due to Segerson (1988). Cabe and Herriges (1992) extended Segerson's work. The problem we are considering is more generally known as the problem of moral hazard in teams. A team is a group (such as a football team) in which the actions of individuals are unobservable but clearly contribute to the sucess of the team. How do you reward individuals based solely on the performance of the team? Holmstrom (1982) provided the first definitive treatment of this question. Xepapadeas (1991) considers a slightly different system of random fines, which can be tied to partial information on emissions.

4. Three empirical analyses of illegal disposal are worthy of note. One is by Hillary Sigman (1995) and concerns the disposal of lead acid batteries (see box later in section). In another analysis, Hilary Sigman (1998) examines the illegal disposal of waste motor oil in the United States. She shows that the higher cost of legal disposal, the greater the rate of illegal dumping. Fullerton and Kinnaman (1996) examine the extent to which illegal dumping of municipal trash is affected by the cost of legal disposal. They conclude that higher legal disposal prices increase illegal dumping, though their data source for this conclusion is questionable.

5. Porter (1983) conducts a detailed benefit–cost analysis of a beverage container deposit–refund program.

6. Sigman (1998) examines a similar problem for the case of disposal of used oil.

7. Russell et al. (1986) provide a good overview of the literature through the mid-1980s. There is a growing literature on the effect of enforcement on compliance. Gray and Deily (1996) provide a good empirical analysis of enforcement and compliance in the U.S. steel industry. Magat and Viscusi (1990), Eckert (2004), and Keohane et al. (2009) also provide empirical analyses of the interplay between enforcement and compliance: does a record of compliance result in relaxed enforcement, and does more stringent enforcement result in better compliance?

8. The problem of when to conduct costly audits goes beyond the environmental economics literature. See, for example, Baron and Besanko (1984).

9. Harford (1978) provided one of the earliest analyses of this problem in the context of environmental regulation. See also Downing and Watson (1974).

10. Although the theory suggests that a larger fine should decrease violations, Stafford (2002) examines a significant increase in fines associated with hazardous wastes in the United States and finds that the increased fines induce little decrease in the number of violations. The empirical literature on the probability of inspection does suggest that higher probabilities of inspection decrease violations. See, for example, the study by Telle (2009) of Norwegian industries.

11. Malik (1990) considers this for a permit market.

12. Kaplow and Shavell (1994) consider just such an arrangement.

13. Pfaff and Sanchirico (2000, 2004) examine such self-audits from both an empirical and theoretical point of view.

14. See Harrington (1988), Harford (1987), and Harford and Harrington (1991) for more on models of this type. Also refer to problem 7 at the end of this chapter.

15. The apparent motivation for Harrington's (1988) development of the multicategory auditing system was his observation for the United States that (1) there was a low frequency of monitoring, (2) fines are relatively low and infrequent, and (3) most firms were not in violation of the law. He showed that the multicategory auditing system can have just such characteristics. The threat of being audited more frequently leverages relatively low fine levels. Heyes (1996) offers a different explanation for low fines, suggesting that high fines would discourage cleaning up environmental accidents. However, Heyes and Rickman (1999) provide empirical evidence to support the Harrington explanation. Helland (1998) provides a nuanced empirical analysis of targeting enforcement activities, concluding that self-reporting of violations is a common firm response.

16. This is precisely the problem considered by Yao (1988).

17. See Freixas et al. (1985) for a discussion of the ratchet effect in the context of central planning. See Laffont and Tirole (1993) for a broader though advanced treatment of this issue.

18. Hahn (1989) cites the lack of permanence as a major factor in the failure of some experiments with marketable permits.

19. Gersbach and Glazer (1999) provide a number of other examples and also derive a theoretical model, suggesting that a tradable permit system solves part or all of the problem.

20. See also Gerard and Lave (2005).

21. Puller (2006) describes a different outcome for the dynamic interaction between regulator and firm when firms have market power. He describes several cases where firms have accelerated innovation and pushed regulators to adopt rules that favored the innovator while raising the costs for competitors.

18

RISK AND UNCERTAINTY

As a government makes its first moves to provide environmental protection, it initially focuses on environmental problems for which the relationship between pollution sources and damage is clear and certain. Attention is first directed to the large industrial plants that spew smoke or effluent that causes people to sicken, crops to die or wilt, or buildings to decay. These sources, with a clear connection between pollution and damage, are usually the easiest to bring under control.

As time goes by, and these large sources of pollution are cleaned up, attention inevitably turns to the more difficult sources of pollution. Frequently these more difficult sources of environmental damage are in the realm of risk, often characterized by accidental discharges of pollution. A landfill is built to contain the material it is storing, but accidents do happen and occasionally the groundwater under a landfill becomes contaminated. Oil tankers are designed to carry, not to spill, oil. Yet large amounts oil are, on occasion, unintentionally spilled. These are both examples of risk. Because accidents do happen, these activities for which environmental degradation is not an intentional by-product are risky and need to be regulated as much as large smokestack industries spewing smoke over the city and countryside. The goal is not to eliminate risk; that would be futile. The goal is to manage risk.

The environmental risks described above are harmful. A conceptually similar uncertainty relates to the benefits that the environment may provide; these benefits may be threatened by pollution and development. Certain ecosystems or natural areas may not appear to be particularly valuable, yet there is a possibility that significant benefits (such as new drugs or improved crops) may emerge from such ecosystems. Pollution and land development may threaten these environmental resources that have uncertain benefits. How can economic activities that threaten these uncertain benefits be managed?

In this chapter we will seek to understand risk from a conceptual perspective as well as understand the various means for reaching socially acceptable levels of risk. This may involve the private market, as with insurance; it may involve decentralized regulation, such as liability; it may involve public provision of risk-reducing technologies; or it may involve conventional direct regulation of activities that are risky or lead to exposure to risk.

I. WHAT IS RISK?

Risk is more complicated to manage than "simple" deterministic pollution problems. The cause and effect links are fuzzy and exposure to pollution does not ensure an adverse effect on people, property, or ecosystems, only an elevated *probability* of an effect. In addition, the effects may be so subtle that science is unable to evaluate the seriousness of the risk. It is not difficult to see a chemical cause adverse effects in Petri dishes or in laboratory animals; it is quite another thing to demonstrate the effect in a human population.[1] Of course this uncertainty about whether a risk exists is just part of the risk itself—we are unsure about whether an action may lead to any adverse effects in any given individual.

A. Environmental Risks Are Complex

Think of the chain of causality associated with environmental risks. Consider two examples, first the case of disposing of benzene in a well-constructed landfill. If all goes well, the benzene stays in the landfill (or evaporates). But there is a chance that the landfill will leak. Even if it leaks, the benzene may not leave (the leak may be in a portion of the landfill that contains no benzene). But the benzene may leak from the landfill and if it does, it may or may not make its way into the groundwater. If it makes it into the groundwater, it may find its way into a drinking water well. But it is possible that it will be detected before it makes it into the drinking water supply. Finally, if drinking water is contaminated, it may or may not cause an adverse effect in the individual drinking the contaminated water.

Pesticide residue poisoning starts with the application of pesticides to an agricultural field. The pesticides may be unevenly distributed, perhaps resulting in parts of the field having particularly high concentrations. The pesticides may or may not be present in the food that is harvested and may or may not be present after the food is washed by the processor or consumer. The pesticide may then be ingested by the consumer. The likelihood that an adverse reaction occurs (such as cancer) depends on a variety of factors, including other synergistic pesticides that may have been ingested and the age and other characteristics of the consumer.

In both of these examples, we see a long and tortuous chain of events between introduction of the hazard into the environment (spraying the pesticide or depositing the benzene in the landfill) and the possible deleterious health effects. Parts of the process are uncertain but potentially knowable, such as the amount of pesticide residue in the food supply. Other parts may involve a much greater element of randomness, such as whether an individual may develop cancer from ingesting a specific amount of pesticide residue.

B. Causation

Given that an adverse health effect occurs, it is not easy to work backward, to ascribe the effect to a particular cause. There is uncertainty about the cause of the effect. For instance, if a large quantity of oil washes up on a beach, it is likely that someone has spilled the oil; what is uncertain is who spilled it. Or if a solvent shows up in groundwater, it is clear that the solvent has leaked from a containment area or been deliberately dumped; what is uncertain is who is responsible for the contamination. More complicated is the case where damage has occurred (such as ground water being contaminated or someone contracting cancer) and several parties are potentially responsible. Perhaps several firms accidently dumped solvents on the ground. Which accident caused the adverse effect? Perhaps an individual was exposed to contaminated drinking water and also air pollution. Which caused the cancer?

It is particularly difficult to establish causation in the case of environmental hazards, in part because of the long time delays that are often involved. In may take years or even decades for a hazard to turn into a risk. Establish a landfill and it may take some time to leak. After leaking, it may take a long time for the contaminants to penetrate into the groundwater aquifer. After reaching the aquifer, it may take some time before it migrates to a drinking water well. After drinking contaminated water, cancer (or other effects) may take decades to develop.

C. Subjective versus Objective Risk

A question that has become central in public policy is whose assessment of risk is most appropriate? Nuclear power is the classic example. The risks of nuclear power have consistently been perceived to be greater by the general public than they have been by experts.[2] In setting public policy, whose assessment of risks do we use?

Although there can be some debate over the probability of a nuclear accident (because they happen so infrequently), there can be little debate over the frequency of death from tornadoes, botulism, or heart disease. These happen frequently enough that we have objective statistics that indicate the probability that a randomly selected individual will succumb to one of these. Table 18.1 shows a number of risks, all of which are estimated to involve a risk of loss of life of one in a million in a particular year. These are risks in the sense described earlier—the probability is clearly measurable based on past events. But that does not mean people understand these risks in the same way, for instance, that we understand the risks from a coin toss. When presented with data, most of us are surprised at the magnitude of many of these risks; although the activities described are relatively familiar, we have a difficult time assessing the risks. Psychologists have shown that individuals have a difficult time assessing probabilities or risks. Individuals consistently overestimate the likelihood of low probability events and underestimate the likelihood of high probability events.[3] This anomaly leads to the term *objective risk* to refer to the statistical relationship between exposure and adverse effects and the term *subjective risk* to refer to an individual's *perception* of his or her objective risk. Figure 18.1 is a classic example of the difference between objective risk (the horizontal axis) and subjective risk (vertical axis) as articulated by a large number of lay people.

D. Risk versus Uncertainty

To many of us, risk and uncertainty are synonymous. This is an oversimplification, as is illustrated by the following quote from a prominent "thinker":

> There are known known's. There are things we know that we know. There are known unknowns. That is to say, there are things that we now know we don't know. But there are also unknown unknowns. There are things we do not know we don't know.[4]

TABLE 18.1 Equivalent Risks

Risks that increase the chance of death by one in a million per year	Causes of death
Smoking 1.4 cigarettes	Cancer, heart disease
Drinking 1/2 liter of wine	Cirrhosis of the liver
Spending 1 hour in a coal mine	Black lung disease
Spending 3 hours in a coal mine	Accident
Living 2 days in New York or London	Air pollution
Traveling 6 minutes by canoe	Accident
Traveling 10 miles by bicycle	Accident
Traveling 500 km by car	Accident
Flying 1,000 miles by jet	Accident
Flying 10,000 km by jet	Cancer caused by cosmic radiation
Living 2 months in an average stone or brick building	Cancer caused by natural radioactivity
One chest X-ray taken in a good hospital	Cancer caused by radiation
Living 2 months with a cigarette smoker	Cancer, heart disease
Eating 40 tablespoons of peanut butter	Liver cancer caused by aflatoxin B
Drinking Paris drinking water for 1 year	Cancer caused by chloroform
Living 5 years at site boundary of a typical nuclear power plant in the open	Cancer caused by radiation
Living 20 years near a polyvinylchloride (PVC) plant	Cancer caused by vinyl chloride
Living 150 years within 30 km of a nuclear power plant	Cancer caused by radiation
Eating 100 charcoal broiled steaks	Cancer from benzopyrene
Risk of accident by living within 8 km of a nuclear reactor for 50 years	Cancer caused by radiation

Source: Adapted from Wilson (1979).

Although this quote suggests more nuances that we care to treat here, there are two main distinctions that are important to matters environmental. One is that there are well-defined events, such as the risk of my house burning to the ground, to which we can attach probabilities. Generally, such events or very similar events have happened many times in the past and will undoubtedly happen in the future.

There are other events that are much vaguer, such as a new species of influenza sweeping the world next year (killing many), or the West Antarctic ice sheet breaking up within the next year (leading to sea level rise), or the world oil price rising to $250 a barrel within five years. In fact, although we know all three of these example events may or may not occur, we also know that it is very difficult to assign a probability to these events. Often such events happen infrequently or may not even have happened before.

Nearly a century ago, Frank Knight, a famous English economist, distinguished risk from uncertainty in a way that parallels these examples. Risk is measurable, or at least potentially measurable, as in the first examples mentioned in the paragraph following quotation. Probabilities can be determined and assigned for the risky events. Even though

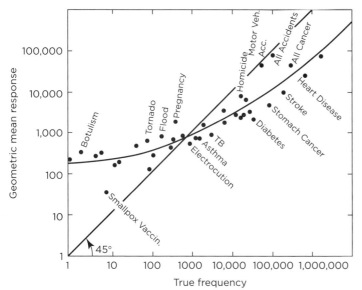

FIGURE 18.1 Subjective estimates of risk versus true risk for group of 40 subjects. *Note:* Data points are geometric means of estimates of risk from a group of 40 subjects told that there are 50,000 motor vehicle accidents per year in the United States. Frequencies are deaths per year in the United States. (From Slovic, et al., 1979.)

we might debate its exact value, it is possible to assign a probability to the event that my house will burn down within the coming year. Houses have burned down before; we can use that experience to determine a probability. On the other hand, it is very difficult to assign a probability to some events (such as the second set of examples, in the preceding paragraph). Knight calls this "uncertainty". Uncertainty involves not only a probabilistic event (one that may or may not occur) but a difficulty in assigning a measurable probability to that event.[5]

The risk analysis literature makes a somewhat different though consistent distinction between risk and uncertainty. Lichtenberg and Zilberman (1988) define risk as the probability that a randomly selected individual will contract an adverse health effect from some environmental hazard, such as the storage of wastes in a landfill. However, this probability may not be known with certainty. There may be some uncertainty over exactly what the magnitude of the risk may be. This is termed uncertainty. For example, we may say that the risk of death in a given year from smoking 1.4 cigarettes is one in a million. We may also say that there is uncertainty in this risk, making the confidence interval from one in 500,000 to one in 1,500,000. The connection to the economic definition is that the one in 1,000,000 figure may come from scientific measurements. However, we may know that these measurements are subject to errors, so that we posit a range of possible risk figures.

In any event, we should not be too concerned with the semantic difference between the terms risk and uncertainty. The main point is that risk and uncertainty can be evaluated subjectively and objectively. When objective and subjective assessments of the same risk are different, it is not easy to decide which estimate should be used for public policy purposes. For example, a policymaker may know the public overstates the risks from nuclear power. In making decisions regarding nuclear power, on behalf of the public, should the decision maker use subjective or objective risks?

E. Voluntary versus Involuntary Risk

Leaving aside disagreements over the probability of an unpleasant event happening, it appears that our determination of how important a risk is depends on whether our exposure is voluntary or involuntary.[6] Studies of the wage differential necessary to induce people to undertake risky jobs suggest that the extra compensation is much less than what people demand for a similar involuntarily imposed risk, such as the risk from a nearby hazardous waste landfill. We are quite willing to take significant risks for often very marginal benefit when we drive in a car. If we are exposed to risks involuntarily, we demand a much higher level of safety.

II. MAKING CHOICES ABOUT RISK

Making choices that involve risks is not easy. Should we buy the inexpensive airline ticket on the carrier that has a spotty safety record? How frequently should we test our well water for contamination? Should we drive home from a party after one drink or take a taxi? Should we install a dam and flood a pristine canyon and lose uncertain future environmental services from the canyon but gain hydroelectric power? Should we install a safe municipal water system to replace wells in an area with many hazardous waste dumps that may leak into the groundwater? Should we protect a biologically diverse ecosystem from commercial development on the off-chance that some obscure species in the ecosystem may be the source of a wonder drug?

These are all choices that involve risk and uncertainty. In some cases, the risk is that something nasty may occur, such as a hazardous waste landfill contaminating the drinking water supply. In other cases, the risk is that something good will occur, such as the discovery of a useful species in the environment. There are several questions that arise in either case. How do individuals value risky outcomes? Can we extend utility theory to cover risks? Another issue concerns the value of investments that reduce or eliminate risk. This would include a public water supply to ensure drinking water is safe, even if a landfill leaks. (Such a water supply would have positive value as a reducer of risk.) Or it might include development that destroys an ecosystem, eliminating the possibility of discovering a wonder drug from the members of that ecosystem. (Such development would have negative value in terms of risk reduction.)

We consider these issues in turn.

A. Expected Utility

We start with a simple risk. Suppose we have a single good, *x,* but are unsure how much we will have to consume. That is the risk. Two things can happen and we do not know which. With probability π_A, event A will occur. With probability π_B, event B will occur. If event A occurs, the quantity of *x* we receive is x_A and if event B occurs, we receive x_B. We call A and B "states of the world" and we call x_A and x_B payoffs under these different states of the world. Furthermore, these states of the world will occur with known probabilities. We might think that these states of the world are exhaustive and mutually exclusive (one or the other but not both will occur). In that case, $\pi_B = 1 - \pi_A$.

One can think of this risk as a lottery: several events can happen (A or B) and there are probabilities attached to them. Furthermore, there are payoffs associated with these events (x_A and x_B). At some point, the dice are rolled and the uncertainty is resolved. The question is, what is the utility or value of such a lottery? We know what the value is of event A happening for sure: $u(x_A)$. Similarly for event B: $u(x_B)$. But a lottery is a more complex commodity. In order to understand risk, it would be very useful to be able to value the lottery in the same way we value certain events.

If we start with a conventionally defined utility function, $u(x)$, which is defined for payoffs that are sure (known with certainty), is there an easy way of extending this utility function to risks? The answer is yes. If we make some assumptions about individual behavior under uncertainty, we can define the utility of a lottery as the expected utility[7] from the individual payoffs in different states of the world:

$$U(x_A, x_B, \pi_A, \pi_B) = \pi_A\, u(x_A) + \pi_B\, u(x_B) \tag{18.1}$$

When utility of a lottery can be evaluated in this fashion, we say that this utility function defined over lotteries (U) is a von Neumann–Morgenstern utility function, named after John von Neumann and Oscar Morgenstern, who first developed the concept. What we have done is start with an ordinary utility function, u, and developed another utility function, U. U is identical to u when goods are not risky (π_A and π_B are 0 or 1). However, u is not defined over lotteries or risks, whereas U is.

How much this lottery is worth can be seen in Figure 18.2. Shown is a utility function, which depends on only one commodity, measured in monetary terms. The utility function increases at a slower rate as the amount of the good increases. In other words, when you are poor, you receive more utility from an extra dollar than when you are rich. Payoffs from for-sure events A and B are shown on the horizontal axis. Each event yields utility as indicated on the graph: event A yields x_A with utility $u(x_A)$ and event B yields x_B with utility $u(x_B)$. The expected quantity of the good that results from this risk is shown as EP (the expected payoff), which is $\pi_A x_A + (1 - \pi_A)x_B$.

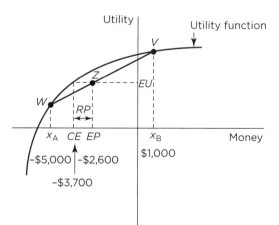

FIGURE 18.2 Expected utility. x_A, payoff with probability π_A; x_B, payoff with probability $1 - \pi_A$; *EP*, expected payoff $= \pi_A\, x_A + (1 - \pi_A)\, x_B$; *EU*, expected utility from risk; *CE*, certainty equivalent of risk; *RP*, risk premium $=$ *EP* $-$ *CE*.

The *utility* of this lottery is similarly, $\pi_A u(x_A) + (1 - \pi_A)u(x_B)$, which is shown as *EU* (expected utility) in Figure 18.2. Basically, the point *Z* in Figure 18.2 is located between points *W* and *V* in proportion to π_A and $(1 - \pi_A)$. *Z* is a weighted average of *W* and *V* with the weights being π_A and $(1 - \pi_A)$. The horizontal coordinate of *Z* is *EP* whereas the vertical component of *Z* is *EU*.

Note that because of the curvature of the utility function, there is some certain amount of money (less that *EP*) that would yield the same amount of utility as the risk. Calling that amount of money the *certainty equivalent of the risk, CE*, it is defined by $U(CE) = EU$. In Figure 18.2 *CE* < *EP*. The person is indifferent between having *CE* for sure as opposed to *EP* on average as a risk. The difference between these two quantities, *EP*—*CE*, can be called the risk premium (*RP*). This is the extra amount of money needed to induce our consumer to take a risk as opposed to a sure thing.

Numerical Example:

Assume that the events A and B are mutually exclusive and exhaustive: one or the other will happen. The probability of A (π_A) is 0.6, which means the probability of B (π_B) is 0.4. If event A happens, there is a loss of $5,000 ($x_A$ = –$5,000), and if event B happens, there is a gain of $1,000 ($x_B$ = $1,000). Note that if this lottery is repeated over and over, the expected value of the lottery (in dollars) is 0.6 *x* (–$5,000) + 0.4 *x* $1,000 = –$2,600. So a lottery in which you might lose $5,000 or might win $1,000, on average will yield a loss of $2,600. This is the expected payoff (*EP*) and is shown in Figure 18.2. Also shown in the figure is the certainty equivalence (CE), at –$3,700. (This cannot be computed precisely without knowing the utility function exactly.)

Our consumer is indifferent between losing $3,700 for sure versus taking this risk, even though on average only $2,600 will be lost. This is because of the risk involved, the risk of possibly losing $5,000. The difference between the two figures, $1,100, is the risk premium, the amount of money our consumer would be willing to pay to convert the risk to a sure average value of *EP*.

The utility function, as drawn in Figure 18.2, is for someone who is risk averse. It is easy to visualize the utility function drawn in Figure 18.2 being more linear. As the utility function becomes closer to a straight line, the risk premium would decline. If the utility function were a straight line, there would be no risk premium—the consumer would be risk neutral. It is also possible to draw utility functions for consumers who are risk loving. This is not the common assumption however; risk aversion is most commonly observed and most consistent with intuition.

B. The Value of Risk Reduction

The next question concerns actions that reduce risk. If, at a cost, we can reduce a risk, how much is it worth to reduce that risk? In the previous section, we saw that the certainty equivalent was one way of converting a risk into a sure thing. We now look at that question a little more carefully and from several different perspectives.

To be concrete, think of two examples of risk reduction. In the first, we have a small community with a number of hazardous waste landfills in the surrounding area. The people in the community have private water wells that are risky because they may become contaminated if a landfill leaks. The risk reduction policy could take many forms, but let us assume that a municipal water supply, with frequent testing for water quality, is being proposed.[8] It will cost money but it will reduce risk. How much is it worth to the community to reduce (perhaps eliminate) the risk?

Our second example is a small but unique ecosystem located in a highly desirable coastal area, near a large and growing city. We know from past experience that many of our most valuable drugs have come from obscure plant and animal species. Although we do not know how valuable our coastal ecosystem is, we know there is some chance that one of the species may become very valuable. The risk, then, is that we may find something valuable in the ecosystem or we may not.[9] We usually think of environmental risks as being harmful, but this is a risk that is beneficial, in contrast to the previous example of the hazardous waste landfill. The risk reduction policy that is being considered is housing development, which will reduce the risk by destroying the ecosystem. The housing development has value (for housing). How does that compare to the lost value from reducing the risk?

Focusing on the example of the hazardous waste landfill, there are two possible states of the world that may materialize: the landfill leaks (L) or it remains sound and secure (S). The probability of L is π_L, which means that the probability of S is $1 - \pi_L$. We are interested in how an individual views risk reduction, though ultimately we will need to aggregate the views of individuals to determine if the risk-reducing municipal water supply (W) is a good idea. For our individual, let utility depend on three things: income, the state of the world (L or S), and whether the municipal water supply is available (W = 0 or W = 1): $U_L(Y, W)$ if L occurs, $U_S(Y, W)$ if S occurs. We will assume our individual has income Y available. This is slightly different from the previous section where the payoff was state-dependent. Now we make the utility itself state-dependent. This is basically the same thing: if the landfill leaks, the consumer will have less utility holding everything else constant than if the landfill does not leak.

We now turn to valuing the water supply in terms of risk reduction. We are interested in a measure of the risk-reducing benefit of the water supply so that we may compare that to its cost. Conceptually, there are two ways of thinking about the benefit. One would be to look at how beneficial the water supply is if the landfill leaks (state L) and how beneficial it is if the landfill remains sound (state S). The expected value of these benefits (taking into account the probability of the two states occurring) would be one measure of benefit. We call this the expected surplus.

Another way to look at the benefits would be to ask what quantity of money would our consumer be willing to pay up-front in order to assure the presence of the water supply, no matter which state of the world turns up. We call this the option price. The intuition is that this would be the price of having the option of the water supply, no matter which state turns up (S or L).

Are these two measures the same? It turns out that risk aversion (as well as income effects) makes the two measures different. Which is a better measure of benefits? That is difficult to say although if money needs to be generated in advance to pay for the water supply, the option price may be the best measure. In any event, it is useful to examine these two measures in more detail.

First consider the expected surplus measure. To compute this, we need to know the value of the municipal water supply in each state of the world and then look at the expected value of this based on the probability of the different states of the world occurring. We would compute the economic surplus of the water supply if the landfill were to leak, V_L, and the economic surplus from the water supply if the landfill does not leak, V_S. The *expected surplus* would be defined as

$$ES = \pi_L\, V_L + (1 - \pi_L)\, V_S \tag{18.2}$$

This is one measure of the value of the municipal water supply and, in fact, is very commonly used to value public projects under uncertainty. Where can we obtain V_L and V_S? They can be derived from the underlying utility functions:

$$U_L(Y - V_L, 1) = U_L(Y, 0) \tag{18.3a}$$

$$U_S(Y - V_S, 1) = U_S(Y, 0) \tag{18.3b}$$

Equation (18.3) states that we should compare utility with the water supply ($W = 1$) with utility without the water supply ($W = 0$). The value of the water supply under state of the world L is the amount income must be reduced to make utility with the water supply (and with lower income) equal to utility without the water supply (but with no income reduction). Equation (18.3) can in theory be solved for the unknowns, V_L and V_S.

The second measure of the value of the municipal water supply is how much money our individual would be willing to pay for the water supply, up front, before uncertainty is resolved, the *option price*. Option price can also be defined using our state-dependent utility functions:

$$\pi_L U_L(Y - OP, 1) + (1 - \pi_L)\, U_S(Y - OP, 1) = \pi_L U_L(Y, 0) + (1 - \pi_L)\, U_S(Y, 0) \tag{18.4}$$

What Eq. (18.4) indicates is that option price is the amount of money taken from income regardless of which state of the world is realized, so that the expected utility with the water supply but with the reduced income is equal to the expected utility without the water supply but with full income. Our consumer would be indifferent between the two sides of Eq. (18.4). Equation (18.4) can be solved for the unknown *OP*.

An obvious question is, are there any differences between option price and expected surplus? To answer that question, we define yet a third way of measuring how the consumer feels about the municipal water supply. But before doing so, we need to introduce the idea of a pair of *state-dependent payments* for the water supply (P_L, P_S). The idea is that you sign an agreement, in advance, to pay P_L if in fact the L state develops and P_S if in fact the S state develops. We ask, what are all the possible pairs of state-dependent payments (P_L, P_S) that will equate expected utility with the water supply with expected utility without the water supply (and without the payments):

$$\pi_L U_L(Y - P_L, 1) + (1 - \pi_L)\, U_S(Y - P_S, 1) = \pi_L U_L(Y, 0) + (1 - \pi_L)U_S(Y, 0) \tag{18.5}$$

You will note that Eq. (18.5) is a slight variation on Eq. (18.4). In Eq. (18.4), the same value (*OP*) is used for both states of the world: $P_L = P_S = OP$. In Eq. (18.5), we allow the payments to be different in the two states of the world, but in such a way that expected utility with the water supply and with the payments is the same as expected utility without the water supply and without the payments.

All of the possible (P_L, P_S) pairs that satisfy Eq. (18.5) have been plotted in Figure 18.3. The locus of points is concave downward primarily because of risk aversion on the part

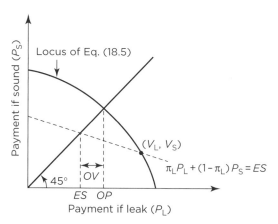

FIGURE 18.3 Willingness-to-pay locus for risk reducing investment. *OP*, option price; *ES*, expected surplus; *OV*, option value; (V_L, V_S), state-contingent surplus from risk reducing investment.

of our consumer. If the consumer were risk neutral and there were no income-effects, the locus would be a straight line. One point we know is on the locus: (*OP,OP*). Since Eqs. (18.4) and (18.5) are so similar it is easy to see that (*OP,OP*) satisfies Eq. (18.5) and is thus the point on the locus in Figure 18.2 that intersects the 45° line.

Another fact to notice is that V_L and V_S as defined by Eq. (18.3) satisfy[10] Eq. (18.5); thus this pair is on the locus in Figure 18.3. But what is *ES* on the graph? If we plot a variant of Eq. (18.2), namely the line

$$\pi_L P_L + (1 - \pi_L) P_S = ES \tag{18.6}$$

on the graph, it must pass through the point (V_L, V_S). since that point satisfies Eq. (18.6). This line has a slope of $-\pi_L/(1 - \pi_L)$ and is shown in Figure 18.3, passing through (V_L, V_S). But note that (*ES,ES*) also satisfies Eq.(18.6). This means that the point at which Eq. (18.6) intersects the 45° line defines expected surplus. This is shown on Figure 18.3.

Note that these two values (*ES* and *OP*) are different, at least they appear different in Figure 18.3. This is because of risk aversion. If our consumer were risk neutral, the locus shown in Figure 18.3 would be essentially a straight line. And it is easy to see that if the locus is a straight line, *ES* = *OP*. But with risk aversion, the two quantities are different. The difference is called the *option value: OV = OP–ES*. Recall that option price is the amount of money that can be paid up front to guarantee the option of having the water supply, no matter which state of the world materializes. The option value is the extra amount of money, over and above expected surplus, that the consumer would be willing to pay to be sure of having the municipal water supply in place under either state of the world.

Option value is analogous to the risk premium we developed in the previous section. There is a difference however. Option value depends on attitudes toward risk as well as income in different states of the world and is thus a little more complex than the risk premium. In fact, option value can be negative (see Schmalensee, 1972), as is alluded to in one of the problems at the end of this chapter.

Which measure, option price or expected surplus, is the most appropriate measure of the value of the municipal water supply? Since money is needed ahead of time to build the municipal water supply, it is logical that the quantity of money our individual is willing to pay in advance is the best measure—the option price.[11]

We return briefly to our other example of the unique ecosystem that will be destroyed by development. The two states of the world in this case might be discovery of a useful species or nondiscovery of a useful species. The expected surplus would involve the probability of these two states of the world occurring as well as the economic surpluses associated with discovering a useful species and not discovering a useful species. The option price would be the amount of money an individual would be willing to pay, up front, to preserve the option of finding a valuable species. The option value would be the amount that would need to be added to expected surplus to account for keeping the option of discovery open.

C. The Value of Information

In the previous section we implicitly assumed that the municipal water supply had to be installed before the hazardous waste landfill leaked. This was because it takes time to build a water supply and it also may be difficult to know when the landfill leaks. But suppose we had better information on whether the landfill was intact or not. If we know that the landfill has leaked, we will have plenty of time to build a municipal water supply to counteract the damage to the water supply. What would be the value of such advance information on the condition of the landfill? This is not idle speculation because it may be possible, at a cost, to reduce or eliminate the uncertainty about whether the landfill has leaked (for instance, using monitoring wells). This may save resources because we may need to take action, such as building a water supply, only *if the leak occurs*. If the leak does not occur, we need do nothing.

The important question here is, how much would we be willing to pay to eliminate (or reduce) uncertainty? This does not mean the elimination of the possibility of the landfill leaking. It just means we will know about the leak in time to build the water supply to ameliorate the adverse effects. It turns out that we do not need risk aversion for the information about the leaky landfill to have value. To see this, we will assume our consumer is risk neutral and that there are no income effects between the two states of the world (thus option price equals expected surplus).

The situation is that the municipal water supply costs C_W. If we do not know whether the landfill will leak, we will assume municipal water is a good idea (i.e., $ES = OP > C_W$). But if we could wait and see if the landfill leaks before constructing the water supply, we would build it only if a leak occurred, and not otherwise. In other words, $C_W > V_S$. Recall that V_S is the value of the water supply if the landfill remains sound.

We consider two cases, one in which the water supply has to be built before uncertainty is resolved (U) and the other case in which the water supply will be built only if it turns out that the landfill leaks; the case of perfect information (P). If we build monitoring wells, we have the case of perfect information, P. If we choose not to build monitoring wells, we have case U where we must build the water supply before knowing the state of the world. We are interested in the net benefits (expected surplus less expected cost) for both uncertainty (B_U) and perfect information (B_P):

$$B_U = ES - C_W = \pi_L \, (V_L - C_W) + (1 - \pi_L) \, (V_S - C_W) \tag{18.7a}$$

$$B_P = \pi_L \, (V_L - C_W) \tag{18.7b}$$

In Eq. (18.7a), we have used the definition of expected surplus found in Eq. (18.2). In Eq. (18.7b), the water supply is built only if a leak occurs. If a leak does not occur (event S), the water supply is not built so the net benefits are zero; thus the form of Eq. (18.7b). The expected value of perfect information (*EVPI*) is simply $B_P - B_U$:

$$EVPI = B_P - B_U = (1 - \pi_L)(C_W - V_S) \tag{18.8}$$

Note that Eq. (18.8) is positive because, by assumption, the water supply is a bad idea if the landfill does not leak (which is the same as $C_W > V_S$). As might be expected, having more information is valuable because it gives more flexibility. The water supply need be installed only under certain conditions. If a set of monitoring wells around the landfills will provide perfect information, those monitoring wells will be a good idea provided they cost less than *EVPI*.

D. Irreversibilities

A variant on the discussion of the previous section applies when information arrives over time. Our example of the unique ecosystem threatened by development is particularly appropriate here. We illustrate this problem with an example of a dam being proposed in an isolated area.[12] The dam will flood a pristine valley. Suppose the dam costs $800 million to build and is expected to generate $150 million of annual electricity production (forever). With an annual discount rate of 10%, the net present value of the dam (in millions of dollars) is

$$NPV = -800 + \sum_{t=0}^{\infty} \frac{150}{1.1^t} = 850 \tag{18.9}$$

In this equation, the first term is the cost of the dam (incurred today). The second term is the benefits of electricity generation from the dam ($150 million a year) summed to the present using a discount rate of 10% per year.[13]

But (and there is usually a but!), in our example there is the possibility of environmental damages from flooding the valley. In fact, there is a 50% probability that the valley will prove to be very valuable for future recreators and lovers of the outdoors (valuable to the tune of $100 million per year). In this case the net present value of the dam is a *loss* of $250 million (check the arithmetic). If you know the environmental damage will be high, you will choose to not build the dam.

But there is an equal chance that there will be no lost environmental value. In other words, there is a 50% chance the environmental damages from building the dam will be $100 million per year and a 50% chance there will be no damages from building the dam, for an average (expected) damage of $50 million per year. And for simplicity, we assume that next year we will know which of these outcomes is correct.

Taking into account the expected environmental damage, the net present value becomes

$$NPV = -800 + \sum_{t=0}^{\infty} \frac{(150 - 50)}{1.1^t} = 300 \tag{18.10}$$

The annual electricity benefits ($150 million) have been reduced by the expected annual environmental damages ($50 million). The project is still a good idea. This would be the standard result of a simplistic benefit–cost analysis of the dam, and presumably the project would go forward.

But this is the wrong conclusion! Forgotten (as is often the case) is the third option, to wait a year without building the dam and reconsider the decision next year. If we wait until next year and then only build the dam if environmental damages turn out to be zero, the calculation of benefits is different:

$$NPV = 1/1.1 \times \left[0.5 \times \left\{ -800 + \sum_{t=0}^{\infty} \frac{150}{1.1^t} \right\} + 0.5 \times 0 \right] = 1/1.1(\$425) = \$386 \tag{18.11}$$

In Eq. (18.11), the 0.5 reflects the 50% probability that the environmental damages will be zero, and thus the dam is built and the net benefits of the dam realized (the quantity in braces). There is also a 50% probability that environmental values will be high and thus that the dam will not be built, hence the second term in brackets. Expected benefits next year are represented by the entire expression in brackets. This in turn is divided by 1.1 to bring it to the present, reflecting the fact that we will have to wait a year before having the benefit stream.

What we see from the example is that by waiting, the net present value of the dam project has increased by $86 million. This is the value of retaining flexibility, of avoiding taking an irreversible action. Alternatively, it can be interpreted as the value of the information about whether environmental damages are high or low. If we had not received the information, the value would be $300 million. By building the dam prematurely, we would have made the information about environmental damages useless (since we would not be able to use it).

This is an illustration of an *irreversibility*. Development is irreversible, at least as far as the environment is concerned. There is a certain asymmetry here. If we preserve a piece of land and tomorrow decide to build houses on the land, preservation has not hindered our ability to use the land for development. On the other hand, if we destroy an ecosystem and then realize next year that we really need that ecosystem, we cannot reconstruct it. Often (but not always) environmental damage is irreversible, whereas the economic activity associated with that damage is deferrable.

In the first of our two time periods, we are uncertain about the value of our ecosystem (and perhaps also uncertain about the value of development, but that is less important). Between the first and the second time period, we acquire information. In the extreme, we could assume we acquire perfect information. Thus in the second period we know exactly how valuable the ecosystem is and how valuable development is. In the second period we can take action under conditions of certainty.

What might a rational policymaker do? One alternative would be to measure the expected surplus in the first period and decide if development is a good idea, ignoring the fact that information will be acquired between the two periods. If development looks good, then the decision maker will develop. Now information arrives. If it turns out that the ecosystem is quite valuable, decision makers may want to undo their previous decision to develop. But they cannot; destruction of the ecosystem is irreversible. If decision makers hold off in the first period to see how valuable the ecosystem really is, all that is lost is the value of the development in the first period. Development can always be pursued in the second period.

If we hold off on development in the first period, the information that arrives will have value because it allows us to condition our actions on the information. We call the value of that information, provided development does not occur first, the *quasioption value*.[14]

Quantifying Quasioption Value from Genetic Discovery

Fisher and Hanemann (1986) provide a nice numerical example of quasioption value,[15] though the example is based only partially on real data. They are concerned with availability of genetic material for maize (corn), which they indicate is the Western Hemisphere's most important food crop. They point out that current high-yield varieties are very homogeneous and thus highly susceptible to disease and other stresses. In the 1970s, a perennial maize plant that grows wild in a very small part of Mexico was discovered. Such a plant has great potential for strengthening the varieties used in commercial food production. Yet agricultural and other development could have destroyed this promising addition to our genetic toolbox. They use this discovery to motivate protecting ecosystems for the potential benefit of future agricultural crops.

The setup[16] is a two-period model with an area of land that contains an ecosystem that has potential benefits to commercial maize production. The land has potential development benefits of $3 billion. The value of preserving the land is harder to quantify. They assume that there is a 25% probability that new genetic material will be discovered that will benefit commercial maize production. Figure 18.4 shows demand and supply curves for maize in the United States, based on empirical estimates of the market in the United States (ignore the fact that the United States is only a portion of the world maize market). The upper supply curve is the current supply curve for maize, resulting in a price of approximately $2 per bushel. If new genetic material is discovered in the threatened ecosystem, a more productive maize plant will result, costs will be lowered and the supply curve will drop as shown, resulting in a price of approximately $1.30 per bushel. The benefit (surplus) of this discovery is the shaded portion of Figure 18.4. The shaded portion has a value of approximately $3 billion (similar to the development benefits), but because there is only a 25% chance of it occurring, the expected benefit is only about $0.75 billion.

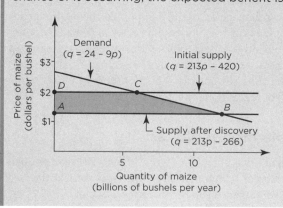

FIGURE 18.4 Demand and supply for maize, with surplus from genetic discovery. *ABCD,* surplus gain from lowered supply curve.

Price of maize (dollars per bushel)

Demand ($q = 24 - 9p$)

Initial supply ($q = 213p - 420$)

Supply after discovery ($q = 213p - 266$)

Quantity of maize (billions of bushels per year)

> So what can we conclude from this? The expected surplus from avoiding development is less than a billion dollars, whereas the benefits of development are $3 billion. So development looks like a good idea. But if we wait, we get to see whether the ecosystem has any genetic material that is of benefit to agriculture. It turns out that the quasioption value is $0.3 billion, nearly half the expected value of the ecosystem benefits. This means that if the cost of waiting, the cost of deferring development until next period, is less that $0.3 billion, it is worth deferring development.
>
> We see that what looks like a case for development may in fact be a case for deferring such development until the future. This is why the quasioption value is such an important concept when actions result in irreversible damage to the environment. In fairness, the quasioption value is not always significant; this example could have been constructed to result in a very small quasioption value.

III. REGULATING RISK WITH LIABILITY

Risk is of course not new to our society. Driving a car, or in earlier days riding a horse, can lead to accidents. We clearly do not want to eliminate risky activities from society, only reduce risks to acceptable levels. How can we be assured that people will take appropriate care when driving, riding, or otherwise engaging in risky activities? We can develop laws that indicate how people should behave in undertaking risky activities—for instance the vast body of law in most countries regarding driving motor vehicles. However, there is an element of moral hazard (hidden actions) that cannot be proscribed (in the case of driving, one must be alert and drive cautiously, behavior that is not easily observed). It is also difficult, or at least burdensome, to develop a set of laws for all possible risky activities.

Around the world, a body of law has developed over the centuries that deals with risky activities—liability. Although such laws may differ somewhat from country to country, the English common law approach of liability is illustrative.[17] The basic idea is that anyone engaging in an activity that involves risks to other people may have to compensate any victim of an accident. When a victim is injured in an accident, the victim may sue the injurer to recover damages. Contrary to popular belief, the primary purpose of liability law is not to compensate the injured but rather to provide incentives to potential injurers to behave responsibly and take precautions when engaging in risky activities. Liability effectively internalizes the accident damage into the cost–benefit calculation of the person undertaking the risky activity. This should ensure the "right amount" of risk or the "right amount" of precautionary behavior.

A. A Simple Model of Liability

The action of liability is shown in Figure 18.5 for a simple example of risky behavior. We will call the person or firm undertaking the risky activity the "potential injurer" and the individual who is damaged should an accident occur, the "victim." The potential injurer can take steps to either reduce the severity of the accident or reduce the probability of an

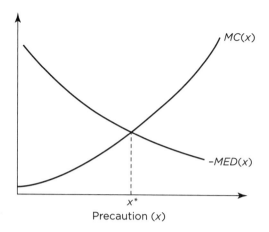

FIGURE 18.5 The socially optimal amount of precaution. *MED(x),* marginal expected damage; *MC(x),* marginal cost of precaution; *x*,* efficient amount of precaution.

accident occurring or both. We will bundle all of these steps together and call them "precaution." So the potential injurer can take precaution to reduce the effects on the victim.

With no precaution, the effects on the victim may be large. If we multiply the probability of an accident by the damage to the victim should an accident occur, we obtain the expected damage. For instance, if there is a 10% probability of an accident that causes £10,000 of damage, we say the expected damage is £1000. This allows us to reduce the uncertain event to something certain. So with little precaution, the expected damage will be quite high. The more precaution taken, the lower the expected damage. We can speak of the marginal expected damage as a function of the level of precaution. Since expected damage decreases as precaution increases, the marginal expected damage is negative. Furthermore, we would expect that at low levels of precaution, the marginal expected damage would be quite large (in absolute terms)—a little precaution goes a long way in reducing expected damage. As levels of precaution increase, the marginal expected damage will be smaller (again, in absolute terms). This is shown in Figure 18.5. The negative of the marginal expected damage function (–*MED*) is shown. It exhibits the behavior just described.

Also shown in Figure 18.5 are the marginal costs of taking precaution. These costs of course fall on the potential injurer. Intuitively, when levels of precaution are low, the marginal cost of precaution should also be low. The first precautionary steps will be the cheapest. Similarly, as precaution levels rise, and fewer and fewer opportunities for precaution remain, the marginal cost of providing it should rise. This is shown in Figure 18.5.

Now what will the potential injurer do? Without liability or any other form of intervention, no precaution will be taken. Precaution is costly and the benefits do not accrue to the potential injurer. But if the law says that the costs of any accident must be borne by the potential injurer, then total costs are the sum of the costs of precaution and expected damages. The potential injurer will now seek to minimize this total, which occurs at the point at which the marginal costs of precaution equal the (negative) marginal expected damages, *x**. Note that for any level of precaution less than *x**, the potential injurer can increase precaution at a cost that is less than the money saved in lowered expected damages. Thus it is in the potential injurer's best interest to increase precaution. In an analogous manner, if precaution is in excess of *x**, it is in the potential injurer's best interest to reduce precaution. The optimal level of precaution will be x^*. This is optimal from the perspective of both the potential injurer and society.

B. Strict Liability versus Negligence

Two basic types of liability exist in most countries—fault-based liability (negligence) and no-fault (strict) liability. Strict liability is what was described in the previous section. If an accident occurs, the potential injurer compensates the victim. No matter how careful the potential injurer is, he or she must pay compensation in the event of an accident.[18]

Negligence, on the other hand, is somewhat more lenient toward the potential injurer. Only if the potential injurer has taken less than the right amount of precaution will he or she be liable for damages to the victim from an accident.[19] The idea is that risky activities are an integral part of society. Particularly in the past, risk was all around. The primary goal of negligence is to ensure that all potential injurers are being good citizens and taking the right amount of precaution without being told directly to do so. We all have a *duty* to exercise a certain amount of precaution. How does negligence work? We present a simplified economic perspective on liability, not a legal perspective. If an accident occurs, the victim takes the injurer to court. The court then determines the two curves in Figure 18.5 and "computes" x^*. This x^*, the socially desirable level of precaution, is termed the *legal standard of care*. If the potential injurer is found to have been taking precaution at least equal to the legal standard of care, no damages need be paid. If, on the other hand, the injurer is taking an insufficient amount of precaution, the injurer is liable for all damages.

This is shown in Figure 18.6. In contrast to Figure 18.5, here we see the total costs and damages, not the marginals, though still as a function of the level of precaution. $C(x)$ is the direct cost of precaution to the potential injurer and $ED(x)$ is the expected damage to the victim. The broken line is the sum of these two costs and it reaches a minimum at x^*, the legal standard of care. The total costs to the potential injurer are shown by the heavy line. At levels of precaution below x^*, the potential injurer's costs include the damage to the victim. For levels of precaution in excess of x^*, the potential injurer's costs are simply direct precautionary costs, since he or she will not be held liable for damages. Note that costs for the potential injurer are still a minimum at x^*. So if potential injurers are acting

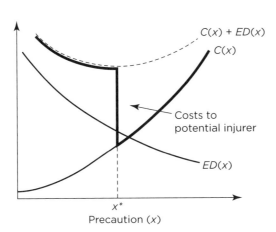

FIGURE 18.6 Total costs under a negligence rule. $C(x)$, costs of precaution; $ED(x)$, expected damage to victim; x^*, socially optimal level of precaution.

in their best interest, they will choose x^* as their level of precaution. This is a socially efficient outcome.

So are these two approaches basically the same, since they both achieve the socially desirable level of precaution? From the point of view of ensuring the right amount of risk in society, both rules give the same efficient result. However, distributionally they are different. In the case of negligence, your neighbor may be engaging in dangerous activity that causes you harm. But provided the neighbor was taking the right amount of precaution, you have to bear the costs of your ill fortune, at least under negligence. So although you do not benefit from your neighbor's risky activities, you may have to bear the costs. Some would argue that is not fair.

One striking advantage of negligence, however, is that the courts are much less burdened. And establishing the legal standard of care can be a costly process. Only when an injurer may have been negligent do the courts need be involved. And, arguably, no rational injurer who is aware of the costs and benefits of his or her actions should take precaution that is less than the legal standard. On the other hand, with strict liability, the courts become involved every time an accident occurs, to assess damages.

When does negligence apply and when does strict liability apply? Negligence is the traditional form of liability. In recent years in the United States, more and more types of harm have been legislatively moved to the realm of strict liability. The largest category of harms that falls under strict liability is product liability—when a product injures a customer or user.

C. Joint and Several Liability

Over the past several decades in the United States and Europe, another form of liability has emerged that is particularly important for environmental damage—joint and several liability. Refer back to the example of the tortuous chain of causation connecting hazardous waste in a landfill and contaminated groundwater that is used for drinking. This can present a problem for establishing causation, usually necessary to collect damages under negligence or strict liability. The groundwater becomes contaminated and an individual develops cancer. Whom should the victim sue? Whose pollution caused the cancer? Suppose a landfill is owned by a small company that is paid to dispose of hazardous wastes from several large local chemical companies. The landfill leaks and the landfill company goes bankrupt. Whom do you sue?

These problems are common to environmental hazards and risks. Long chains of causation make it easier to establish that someone caused damage than to establish who caused the damage. This is compounded by the very long time lags involved in environmental damage. During these long lags, ownership of companies change, some firms go bankrupt, records are lost, and memories fade. The end result is that liability is more difficult to establish and thus damages are more difficult to assess and collect. The important role of liability is to encourage potential injurers to take precautions when they engage in risky activities. If one is unlikely to be sued, even if behaving negligently, then the incentive effects of liability are lost and there will be an insufficient amount of precautionary behavior.

One solution to this problem is the concept of *joint and several liability*. If several parties are potentially responsible for causing an accident, then suit may be brought against any one for all of the damages. Thus in the case of the bankrupt landfill, injured parties may choose to sue the richest of the various chemical companies that contributed waste to the landfill, and sue for all damages. The defendant may then choose to try to recover damages from other potentially responsible parties. The idea is that someone has to absorb the costs of the accident and it might as well be one of the parties that contributed to the accident, rather than the victim. If the victim has to recover from each individual that might have contributed to the accident, it is much less likely that suit will be brought and thus it is less likely that the incentive properties of liability will work in the proper way.[20]

IV. LIABILITY VERSUS DIRECT REGULATION

Though liability requires the involvement of government, to promulgate laws and administer courts, liability is much more decentralized than direct regulation of safety or environmental hazards. In direct regulation, the government indicates both the level of safety to be provided and the appropriate precautionary behavior. This requires a great deal of *ex ante* (in advance) information collection and rule construction. Similar information must be collected in the case of liability, but *ex post* (after an accident). If risk is low and accidents infrequent, liability has significant informational and thus efficiency advantages.

A. Disadvantages of Liability

So why isn't liability always preferred to direct regulation? One answer is that for hazards that are common, and risks significant, it may be more efficient for a regulator to define appropriate precautionary behavior than to burden the courts with that task for countless lawsuits. This is a cost argument: regulation in some cases can involve lower costs for information acquisition.[21]

Another problem with liability is that suit is not always brought, even when it should be. This may be for a variety of reasons, not the least of which is the cost (including inconvenience) to the plaintiff of bringing suit. If an injurer is not held responsible for damage when it should be, the incentive properties of liability will be diluted.

Another problem with liability is bankruptcy. A firm cannot be successfully sued for damages that exceed the net assets of the firm; the firm will simply go bankrupt if it must pay damages that exceed its value. This means that a firm will not take the proper precautions to avert an accident with very large damages; at least liability does not provide the proper incentives.[22]

Another problem with liability is that the firm, *ex ante,* is uncertain about how the courts will actually determine the legal standard of care, should an accident occur. If a firm is risk averse, it may provide excessive care because of this uncertainty (hedging its bets). Furthermore, there may be a systematic bias in how a firm perceives the legal standard of care as determined by a court. This may be due to deep pockets of the firm, the reputation of the firm, or many other reasons.

B. Combined Use of Liability and Regulation

Frequently we see the combined use of liability and direct regulation. For instance, with prescription drug safety in many parts of the world, new drugs must pass a rigorous approval process before being marketed to the public. However, drug manufacturers still face liability for any problems the drugs might have. Laws govern the proper transportation and disposal of hazardous wastes, whereas other laws govern liability for hazardous waste spills or accidents.[23]

So why do we have both types of regulation? Is use of both redundant? Or are the two types of regulations somehow complementary? There are two views of this question. Both involve elaborating on the simple view of liability and accidents that we have described above. Both approaches involve defects in liability and direct regulation; thus the use of both approaches achieves a better result than either alone.[24]

Suppose we are concerned with regulating an activity that leads to accidents of various sizes. The activities are not all identical and potential injurers know what the accident size is associated with their activities. For any accident size, D, define the optimal level of precaution as $x^*(D)$. Figure 18.7 illustrates how x^* rises with D, up to the maximum accident size of D_{max}.

Now consider what direct regulation might achieve. Here we will assume that the regulator does not have enough information to distinguish between activities that lead to large accidents versus activities that lead to small accidents. Thus the regulator has to choose one single best level of precaution. That is shown in Figure 12.7 as x_R and it is the same, whatever D is. Note that for small accidents, the regulatory level of precaution is too great; for large accidents it is too small.

Finally, we introduce liability. With liability, the courts are able to determine, after the fact, the level of damage and the amount of precaution that should have been taken. In a perfect world, the amount of precaution associated with liability will be $x^*(D)$, a quantity that varies with D. But suppose that not all suits that should be filed actually are filed. This may happen for a variety of reasons, discussed above. This will tend to lower the level of precaution, since it lowers the expected liability costs for the potential injurer. The level of precaution that will be associated with liability is shown as $x_L(D)$ in Figure 18.7. Note that for any accident size, it is strictly less than x^*. Note also that x_L flattens out for damage in excess of A. This reflects that fact that the firm will not take precautions to avoid accidents that exceed the net assets of the firm, A. If an accident exceeds A, the firm will simply declare bankruptcy. This effectively places an upper limit on precaution.

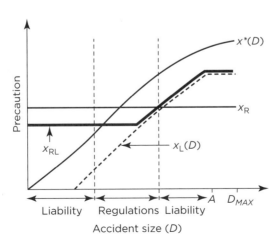

FIGURE 18.7 Illustration of joint use of liability and direct regulation. $x^*(D)$, optimal level of precaution; x_R, optimal level of precaution with direct regulation; $x_L(D)$, precaution provided by liability; $x_{RL}(D)$, precaution with joint use of liability and direct regulation.

Which is best? It depends on the accident size. For any given accident size, we prefer the approach (direct regulation or liability) that gets us closest to x^*.[25] Figure 18.7 shows three regions, with the center region favoring direct regulation and the other two regions favoring liability. Which is best? It really depends on the distribution of damages. If most accidents occur with size that favors direct regulation, direct regulation may be best.

What about using both together? If both are used together, direct regulation effectively provides a lower bound on precaution. For large accident sizes, liability will be the driving force behind precaution; for smaller accidents, direct regulation will apply. However, since regulation applies just to smaller accidents, it should be set at a lower level than when it applied to all accidents. In Figure 18.7, the optimal combination of direction regulation and liability is shown as x_{RL} (D).

Note that the optimal regulation with liability is lower than without liability. This result has significant implications. Suppose, for instance, that hazardous waste storage is being regulated. This means that the regulation governing how wastes are stored should not be designed for infrequent large accidents but rather for smaller accidents; the threat of liability will take care of providing precaution for large accidents.

V. INSURANCE

Environmental risks often involve the slight possibility of very large accidents and damages. Certainly this would characterize the risks associated with nuclear power and hazardous waste disposal. We have seen that both liability and regulation can provide some protection against these risks, though not perfect protection. Many have advocated the use of environmental hazard insurance in conjunction with liability. Insurance has a number of advantages. An obvious one is that there would be some assurance that if an accident were to occur, victims would be compensated; the prospects of a bankrupt injurer would be less onerous. Another advantage would be that insurance companies could provide a level of expert advice to potential injurers intermediate between the centralized regulator and the potential injurer. Insurers that help an insured reduce risks would reward the insured with lower rates. There is an incentive for the two parties to work together. A third advantage to insurance is the standard one: risk exposure is reduced and spread among many. Thus if a firm is risk averse regarding large environmental accidents (and any but the largest firms probably are), insurance provides a way of converting a lottery into a sure payment.

Probably the major question to ask in the environmental context is, will insurance spontaneously emerge from the private sector or are there impediments to the private provision of insurance? If so, can governmental action remove these impediments?

A. Conditions for Insurability

For an insurance market to spontaneously emerge to insure a particular environmental risk, it is necessary that the risk be attractive to insurers and that the premiums be attractive to potential injurers. Generally, for a potential loss to be insurable six basic criteria must be met:[26]

1. The loss must be amenable to risk pooling.
2. There must be a clear loss.

3. The loss must be in a well-defined period of time.
4. The frequency of loss must allow a premium calculation.
5. Moral hazard must not be too severe.
6. Adverse selection must not be significant.

Each of these conditions needs some explanation.

1. Risk Pooling. Because most of us are risk averse, we dislike being exposed to risks that have the potential to create large losses—large with respect to our individual assets. This is why we seek fire insurance on our house or collision insurance on our new car. On the other hand, we bear the risk of small losses without much problem—we typically do not insure small appliances from the risk of breaking. Although it might appear that insurance works by contracting with a less risk-averse large firm to bear a risk, that is not really the case. Insurance works through risk pooling.

Fire insurance is a good example. Suppose the risk of fire causing $10,000 damage to a house is 0.001 in any particular year (one in a thousand). The expected value of this risk is $10,000 X 0.001 = $10. If an individual does not insure the house, in most years there will be no damage; but occasionally, a big loss will occur. Suppose 10 people get together and annually contribute $10 each to a pool to cover their fire losses. The pool will increase by $100 annually and roughly every 100 years an accident will occur. It is still possible that several accidents may occur in a row and bankrupt the group. Now suppose 100,000 people get together and each contributes $10 annually to a fund. The fund can expect approximately 100 fires per year. There may be a few more one year and a few less another year. What happens as we expand the number of houses in the pool is that the variability of the annual loss declines. With the 100,000 houses in the pool, it is almost certain that there will be approximately 100 houses that are damaged each year. We have moved from a situation of no losses most years with a large loss once in a thousand years (on average) to a case in which we have 100 losses every year with much smaller variability. This is risk pooling.

For risk pooling to work, the multiple risks must be uncorrelated as in the above example. Whether a fire happens in one house is unrelated to whether a fire happens in another house. Some risks have a systematic component. Earthquake losses are an example of this. Suppose a company insures 100,000 houses against earthquakes. What will happen is that in most years there will be no claims, but when an earthquake hits many houses will file claims, particularly if there are only a few areas susceptible to severe earthquakes. Thus insuring the 100,000 houses has not smoothed out the losses as in the fire insurance case. An insurer may be subject to wild fluctuations in claims. Nothing may have been solved. The risk has been shifted to a company with more assets, but the company is covering more risks. In situations such as this, effective insurance is unlikely to be provided by the market.

2. Clear Loss. For an insurance market to function, it must be clear when a loss has occurred. For instance, it would be difficult to insure against mental anguish from an accident because it is impossible to determine the severity of mental anguish when a loss has occurred—it is private unverifiable information possessed by the injured party.[27] And most losses that are difficult to verify are equally easy to counterfeit. There are of course losses that are easy to verify and difficult to fake—death for instance.

The loss from an environmental hazard may be difficult to establish. For instance, suppose it is proved that company X has contaminated the groundwater with a known carcinogen, and a city's water supply has been contaminated exposing the citizenry to a risk. Has a loss occurred? Is exposure to the risk a loss or must someone contract cancer? Has anyone who contacts cancer suffered a loss? Keep in mind that cancers are not uncommon and it may be difficult, if not impossible, to establish that a particular cancer is due to the contaminated water.[28]

Another feature associated with environmental losses is defining exactly what is covered. Is it feasible to insure a company against all possible environmental obligations, including those as yet undiscovered? In covering a risk, it is important that the potential losses be clearly delineated as well as verifiable.

3. Loss in Well-Defined Period. Why is it difficult to insure a risk for which the damage may occur at any time in the future, without time limit? The simplest explanation is that eventually nearly everything happens. Any house will eventually burn down (if it is not torn down). Every hazardous waste landfill will eventually leak. Furthermore, as time goes on, information changes. It is difficult to appreciate fully the potential damage from a landfill over the coming year, let alone in the coming 10 or 20 years. In 10 years, the institutional environment, as well as the understanding of the physical environment, may have changed substantially. This is particularly the case with environmental risks. So for an insurer to offer coverage over a very long time period, the premiums will probably be so great as to be unattractive to potential injurers.

Unfortunately, many environmental risks have very long gestation periods. If a chemical company "accidentally" dumps solvents on the ground behind the factory, it may take many years for those solvents to leak into the water table. Furthermore, it may take many years of consumption of contaminated water for people to receive a substantial dose of the carcinogen. Finally, cancers typically have long gestation periods, with decadal delays between exposure to the carcinogen and diagnosis of the cancer. Thus several decades may transpire between the risky activity (dumping the solvent) and the damage (the cancer).

4. Frequency of Loss Allows Premium Calculation. Obviously it is necessary to compute the premium to charge for the insurance. And the premium that is charged is not a minor detail; an incorrect premium can cause the market to fail. If the premium is too large, no insurance will be sold; if it is too small, insurers will lose money or possibly become bankrupt. If we have experience with a loss, it is possible to calculate a premium based on the historic frequency of loss. For instance, we have a great deal of information on house fires and can thus compute the probability that a randomly chosen house will burn down in a year—exactly the information needed to compute a premium.

If we do not have much experience with a loss, it is necessary to speculate on the loss frequency and magnitude. If there is a great deal of uncertainty about the risk (as there often is with environmental risks), it is likely that the insurer will err on the high side in estimating damage or loss frequency. After all, experience tells us that with environmental risks, time has the tendency to generate bad news more frequently than good news.

Reflecting back on the discussion of risk and uncertainty, risk is much more insurable than uncertainty. Risk involves known probabilities of events, which makes calculating a premium feasible. Uncertainty, on the other hand, where there is ambiguity regarding just what the probability is of a loss, as well as the probability of different size losses, is much more difficult for an insurer to deal with.[29]

5. No Moral Hazard. The opportunity for the insured to influence the occurrence of the accident must be minimal. This does not preclude observable actions by the insured, such as using a double instead of a single hull on a tanker for transporting crude oil. The problem is that when there is a risk of loss, people are careful. If the insurer removes the risk of loss, the incentive to be careful is gone. If the insurer can monitor the amount of care, there is no problem. If there are significant activities that are hidden to the insurer, the insurer must assume the worst. This raises premiums, often to the point at which they become unattractive to the injurer.

An example of this would be insuring bicycles on a college campus, where bicycle theft is a popular means of raising revenue. If an insurer noted that approximately 1% of all bicycles on campus are stolen every year, and the average value of those bicycles is $200 (which gives an expected loss of $2 per year), and then offers a theft policy for $5 per year, covering $200 of loss, the insurance company could expect to make money. But what happens is that those with insurance will be much less likely to lock their bike, more likely to leave it unattended overnight, and generally to take less care to prevent it from being stolen. Thus the insurer may be bewildered to find that the loss rate is 5%, for an average loss per policy of $10, twice the premium. The insurer raises its rates to $15 and finds that the loss rate goes up because people are buying insurance instead of locks. Eventually the premiums rise so high that the market collapses. This is an example of how moral hazard can prevent an insurance market for a particular risk from emerging.

Fortunately, many environmental risks are generated by large companies in which it is easier to monitor how much care is being taken to prevent hazards. With a large company it becomes cost effective for the insurer to monitor the activities of the injurer, using audits and inspections as well as involvement in safety procedures. This tends to reduce the significance of moral hazard.

6. No Adverse Selection. Adverse selection is a problem for regulation, as we saw in the previous chapter. It is also a problem for insurance. If there are some injurers that are more likely to have large losses, the insurance company must be aware of that in calculating premiums, since premiums are related to expected loses. If there are characteristics of the injurers that (1) influence the likelihood and magnitude of a loss and (2) are unobservable to the insurer, the insurance company must assume the worst and charge a comparatively high premium. This premium will be unattractive to injurers who are comparatively good risks; thus they will not buy insurance. This means that the only injurers that will be attracted to insurance will be the bad risks; this may further increase rates. The outcome will be either no market at all, or a much thinner market than desired.

An example of adverse selection is private unemployment insurance. Suppose a firm offered a policy that would pay you your wage should you be terminated in your job during the term of the policy. The insurance company has no economical way of determining how likely a person is to lose his or her job. Furthermore, the people most likely to take out such insurance are the people who feel their job is in real danger. Because of this, the insurance company must set rates high, which makes insurance unattractive to all except those in the greatest danger of job loss. In the end, only those people who have a very large chance of losing their job will be interested in insurance; premiums for this will be so high as to be unattractive to nearly everyone. The market collapses.

Adverse selection is probably not a severe problem for environmental risks because the insurance company can determine whether a company is more likely to have an accident based on past performance or facility characteristics (in the case of a landfill).

B. Insurability of Environmental Risks

The next logical question is, how well do particular environmental risks satisfy these conditions of insurability? Take for instance the insurability of a hazardous waste dump. Wastes can leak from the dump into the groundwater, leading to contaminated drinking water and resulting in illnesses and deaths. There are a large number of such dumps in existence now and any leakages should be uncorrelated from one dump to another. So condition (1) would appear to be satisfied.

It is less clear when a loss has occurred. The damage that is being insured against is health effects from contaminated drinking water. It may be very difficult to determine what the effects actually are. There may be elevated cancer rates, but there may be other processes that could have led to these cancers. Mental trauma from consuming contaminated drinking water will be harder to verify than cancer. Thus condition (2) is not well satisfied for our example of a waste dump.

As is well known, a leaking waste site can take many years to manifest itself in adverse health effects. Clearly an insurer can limit the length of time of coverage, but that may leave the risk underinsured. To be fully covered, the length of time must be nearly indefinite. This violates condition (3).

Hazardous waste dumps, at least those built in recent years, are quite reliable and leak very infrequently. Although this is good from an environmental point of view, it is not good from the point of view of being able to calculate insurance premiums. Consequently, condition (4) is not met.

Does moral hazard exist? Here, chemical risks would appear to pass the test. Although a dumpsite can take action to influence the probability of an accident, most of these are verifiable and observable. An insurance company can inspect an operation from time to time and can observe physical precautions that have been installed to reduce the likelihood of an accident. Thus condition (5) is met.

Adverse selection can probably be handled by observing the claims record of an insured. A new policyholder will be charged premiums assuming they are a bad risk. Over time, with a good record, those premiums could drop. Thus adverse selection would not appear to be a serious problem for chemical risks.

In summary, insurance may emerge to cover some environmental risks, but for others the conditions of insurability are not met. This is unfortunate. However, it may be possible to design insurance instruments or adjust liability law so that more risks become insurable.

SUMMARY

1. Objective risk involves direct observation of the probability of risky events occurring (based on historical experience), such as the probability of a randomly chosen airplane flight ending in a crash. A subjective risk is an individual's perception of the

probability of the same event. Subjective risk is often termed uncertainty, whereas objective risk is simply called risk.

2. Risks to which exposure is voluntary are usually valued less than risks that are involuntary.

3. Expected utility is a common way of evaluating the utility of a risk. The certainty equivalence of a risk is the sure quantity of a good, consumption of which gives the same utility as the risk.

4. In considering the value of a risk-reducing investment, the expected surplus is the expected value of the state-dependent surpluses from the risk-reducing investment. State-dependent values are the values after the uncertainty has been resolved and the risky event has occurred. The option price is the maximum sure payment that would be made for the risk-reducing investment prior to uncertainty being resolved. The option value is the difference between option price and expected surplus. It is positive if option price is greater than expected surplus.

5. The expected value of perfect information is the amount that total expected value of a risk will increase if perfect knowledge of the outcome of uncertain events is known in advance.

6. Often environmental damage is irreversible. In such a case, there is an additional value associated with being cautious about causing environmental damage. That is called the quasioption value and is the value of perfect information, conditional on initially preserving the environment.

7. Strict liability involves the injurer always paying damages to the injured in the case of an accident. Negligence involves payment of damage only if the injurer has been negligent, defined as taking less precaution than is socially optimal (the "legal standard of care").

8. When there are several potential parties that could have caused an accident, joint and several liability holds each potentially responsible for all damages.

9. The primary purpose of liability is to induce injurers to take the proper amount of precaution. A secondary purpose is to seek a fair share of the burden of damages in the case of an accident.

10. A major advantage of liability is that the government need acquire detailed information on damages and control costs only when an accident happens that ends up in court. This reduces regulatory costs.

11. Major disadvantages of liability are bankruptcy and factors that discourage valid cases from being brought to court (including the cost of bringing suit). Both tend to dilute the incentives for potential injurers to take the right amount of precaution.

12. Direct regulation (*ex ante* regulation) can be combined with liability (*ex post* regulation) to correct some of the problems of liability. In this case, the level of direct regulation should be set below the appropriate level when liability is not involved.

13. Six basic conditions are needed for insurance markets to spontaneously emerge: (1) risk pooling, (2) clear loss, (3) limited loss period, (4) frequent loss, allowing premium calculation, (5) no moral hazard, and (6) no adverse selection.

1. Assume you are the President of British Petroleum (BP). You note that the Exxon Valdez spill cost Exxon Corp. approximately $8 billion. You are trying to decide on the thickness of the hull of your new supertanker. Your engineers tell you that the probability of an accident ever occurring (p) is inversely proportional to hull thickness: $pt = 0.002$ where t is the hull thickness in centimeters. But the costs of a thicker hull rise rapidly as the thickness rises. Costs (in million $) are given by $C(t) = t^2$ where t is the thickness in centimeters. Assume an accident's damage is the same as with Exxon. What is the socially desirable hull thickness? If there is a probability of 10% that BP will not be found liable in case of an accident, what will BP choose as a hull thickness (ignoring the fact that BP may be socially responsible and take the socially desirable route)? (*Hint:* Use calculus or graphs and pay attention to units.)

2. The local dry cleaner is concerned about the risks from its use of chemicals, which evaporate into the air and occasionally are spilled onto the ground. The cleaner is concerned about liability for environmental damage. How likely is it that insurance will be available to cover the liability exposure of the dry cleaner? Why?

3. Consider Sarah's bright idea to build a dam in the scenic Grand Canyon of the western US to provide electricity to the nearby urban area of Las Vegas. To make things simple, suppose the dam costs $1 billion to build and that it can be entirely built in the first year. A stream of benefits and costs ensue over the following decades. However, there is uncertainty about those costs and benefits. With an 90% probability the net present value of the stream of ensuing benefits is $1.2 billion. With a 10% probability the loss of the natural resource is a real bummer and net present value of the stream of ensuing benefits is 0. The discount rate is 5% per year.

    a. What is the expected value of the ensuing benefits? What is the net benefit of building the dam today (benefits less costs)?

    b. Suppose we could wait a year to build the dam. In a year's time, all the costs and benefits will be the same, except pushed one year into the future. You are told by your environmental advisors that in a year it will be clear if we really need the Grand Canyon. What is the net benefit today of deferring the decision to build the dam until next year?

4. You are in charge of designing a new hazardous waste landfill for Kiev. You are trying to decide whether it is worth spending R 1,000,000 to install a special liner that reduces the probability of a leak from 0.001 to 0.0001. If a leak occurs, the expected number of fatal cancers in Kiev can be expected to rise a total of 100. What value of a fatal cancer (in R) is necessary to justify your installation of the special liner? Assume risk neutrality.

*5. In the context of Figure 18.3, suppose that the risk involved with the hazardous waste landfill is objective. This may be because leaks occur often enough that the probability of a leak can be objectively established. Suppose a bank is willing to loan the municipality money for the water supply with the loan paid off by a payment whose size depends on whether the landfill leaks. The expected value of the payment is equal to the amount loaned. Show on a copy of Figure 18.3, the maximum amount that could be borrowed from the bank to pay for the water supply. Explain.

6. If a potential victim can take precautions to avoid an accident (such as looking both ways before crossing a street), which liability system yields more efficient levels of precaution, strict liability or negligence? Why?

7. One of the arguments for punitive damages (damages paid to the plaintiff in excess of actual damages) is that such damage payments compensate for the fact that lawsuits are not always filed, even if justified. Explain.

8. In Figure 18.3, option value is shown as positive (option price is greater than expected surplus). Using the same locus and the same probabilities of each state occurring, change the state-contingent value of risk reducing investment to show how option value could be negative. Why is this counterintuitive? Discuss.

NOTES

1. Problems arise when the effect of a hazard is very slight. In such cases, it is very difficult to detect adverse effects using epidemiology, i.e., statistics on the general population. An alternate approach involves laboratory studies. However, in these cases the problem of detecting slight effects also exists. It is compounded by the problem of extrapolating from one species (e.g., mice) to another (humans). In the United States, two major food additive issues of this sort were the artificial sweetener sodium saccharin and the apple growth enhancer Alar.

2. See Slovic et al. (1979).

3. See Slovic et al. (1979) for more discussion of this point.

4. U.S. Secretary of Defense, Donald Rumsfeld, from briefing February 12, 2002.

5. See Knight (1921).

6. For the most part, evidence about how we perceive risks comes from the psychological literature. See Slovic et al. (1979) for a discussion of voluntary versus involuntary risks as well as other attributes of risk that shade our perceptions of their seriousness.

7. The key assumption necessary to use expected utility theory to value risks is called the independence axiom. Basically, it states that if we compare two risks, our relative ranking of those risks should be independent of other risks we may be taking. Varian (2005) discusses this at an elementary level. Although expected utility theory is the most common way of evaluating risks, there are other approaches that use different assumptions about how people evaluate risks. For an advanced treatment of this issue, see Mas-Colell et al. (1995).

8. This example is suggested by Smith and Desvousges (1988).

9. This is a stylized example, since there may be many other reasons for preserving an ecosystem.

10. Premultiply Eq. (18.3a) by π_L and premultiply Eq. (18.3b) by $1 - \pi_L$. Then add the two equations together and you have Eq. (18.5).

11. Actually, if there is a risk-neutral agent that will fairly exchange lotteries on the future into sure payments today, then there is a quantity even larger than the option price, called the fair bet point, that is the true maximum value of the water supply (see Graham, 1981).

12. This example is adapted from Pindyck (1991), who provides a thorough, though advanced, survey of some of this literature. Fisher et al. (1972) and Krutilla and Fisher (1985) describe an actual application to putting a dam in Hell's Canyon, a spectacular section of the Snake River in the western United States. Arrow and Fisher (1974) and Henry (1974) first articulated this concept in the context of environmental protection.

13. Note the mathematical formula for an infinite sum, $\sum_{t=0}^{\infty} AF^t = A/(1-F)$. In this case A = 150 and F = 1/1.1 = 0.9091, yielding a sum of 1650 (check it yourself).

14. The term quasioption value originated with Arrow and Fisher (1974), though its precise meaning has been debated for many years. Hanemann (1989) appears to have had the last word on this, defining the quasioption value in a two-period model such as we have described

as the expected value of perfect information conditional on no development occurring initially. Others have defined it as the loss in overall value due to the fact that the environmental destruction is irreversible.

15. See Krutilla and Fisher (1985) for a number of other more in-depth analyses of the importance of quasioption value. For an application to cumulative pollutants such as greenhouse gases, see Kolstad (1996a, 1996b).

16. The model presented here has been simplified somewhat from the model presented in Fisher and Hanemann (1986).

17. The common law tradition is found in England and former colonies, such as the United States. Most of the rest of the world, including most of Western Europe and Asia (and one state of the United States—Louisiana), follow a civil law tradition. Civil law is made by legislatures and courts enforce the written law. Common law is drawn from more diverse sources, particularly past judicial decisions. Refer to Cooter and Ulen (2008) for further discussion of these differences and the apparent convergence of the two approaches in modern times.

18. This assumes that one can establish that what the potential injurer did caused the accident. This may be nontrivial; for instance, consider the difficulty of establishing that a particular chemical "caused" a cancer that the victim developed.

19. We are assuming here, and throughout this section, that the victim is passive and can take no action to avoid an accident. This is obviously not always the case. When the victim can take some action to avoid or reduce the size or probability of an accident (such as looking both ways before crossing a road), we have negligence with a defense of contributory negligence. An analysis of contributory negligence would take us too far afield. See Cooter and Ulen (2008) for a complete treatment of this and other issues associated with liability.

20. Tietenberg (1989) provides a discussion of joint and several liability as well as an economic interpretation of the concept.

21. One could also argue that having multiple firms carry out detailed benefit–cost analyses of the same risky behavior is more costly than doing it centrally, by the regulator.

22. Shipping oil internationally illustrates this point. In recent years, one-ship companies have emerged to transport oil, thus limiting liability to the value of one oil tanker (MacMinn and Brockett, 1995). Beard (1990) investigates the problems of bankruptcy.

23. In the United States, the primary governing statute is the Resource Conservation and Recovery Act (RCRA). In the United States, the primary law is the Comprehensive Environmental Response, Compensation and Liability Act (CERCLA), which includes provision for the "Superfund," a fund financed by chemical producers to clean up waste sites without establishing fault in advance.

24. The two primary results on the simultaneous use of regulations and liability are given by Shavell (1984) and Kolstad et al. (1990). The example here is based on Shavell (1984).

25. The goal is actually to minimize the welfare losses from deviating from x^*. For the discussion here, a reasonable approximation is to try to get as close to x^* as possible.

26. For a discussion of insurability in general, see Mehr (1986). Insurability in the case of catastrophic environmental risks is covered by Katzman (1988) and Jaffe and Russell (1997). Cook and Graham (1977) cover the case of insuring irreplaceable goods. Freeman and Kunreuther (1997) provide an accessible treatment of the insurability of environmental risks.

27. A court may award a victim of an accident, which insurance may then cover. The court's finding is observable.

28. This issue is explored by Harr (1995) in a very readable account of a court case in which an attempt was made to connect leukemias with hazardous waste spills.

29. Freeman and Kunreuther (1997) discuss insurance and environmental risks. Kunreuther and Michel-Kerjan (2007) discuss insurability in the specific case of climate change.

REGULATION WITH MULTIPLE JURISDICTIONS

IN THIS CHAPTER, WE ARE CONCERNED WITH COMPETITION, COORDINATION, AND COLLUSION between jurisdictions in the setting of pollution control policy. Jurisdictions may be states or localities within a country or jurisdictions may be sovereign nations. The basic determining factor is that what goes on in one state influences actions in other states. Thus the first question we ask concerns competition among jurisdictions for capital and the role that environmental regulation may play in that competition. Would we expect states to weaken their environmental regulations to attract capital and thus jobs? A closely related question is the effect differences in environmental regulations among countries have on trade and the location of industry. Will countries with lax environmental regulations end up as "black holes," specializing in dirty industries? The last question we ask concerns the problem of transboundary pollution—pollution generated in one state that causes damage in other states. These transboundary pollutants are becoming more and more important in the world—carbon dioxide leading to climate change and chlorofluorocarbons leading to ozone depletion are only two examples. Control of these pollutants requires coordination among sovereign states. It is not easy to forge a treaty that is effective, enforceable, and to which countries will voluntarily agree.

I. JURISDICTIONAL COMPETITION

Firms compete against one another in market economies to produce a variety of goods of differing quality and price. Governments also compete against one another for economic gain. However, instead of competing in terms of the products they offer, governments compete to attract firms, for the purposes of providing jobs, tax revenue, income, and advantage to existing domestic firms. How do governments compete? The primary tools available to governments are tax policy, including tariffs, and regulatory policy, including environmental regulation. A government may offer low taxes to entice a company to locate in its jurisdiction. A government may subsidize production by a company to enhance the company's competitiveness overseas. A government may erect tariff barriers to protect domestic industries. One worry shared by many environmentalists and nonenvironmentalists is that governments will use environmental regulations to attract business, to the detriment of the environment. They worry that to bring in that new automobile manufacturing facility, the local community may offer to relax environmental regulations.

This governmental competition may go on at various levels. Within the United States, individual states or localities may compete with one another to attract businesses and jobs. Within the European Union, member states may compete with one another for economic activity. And internationally, where income differentials are the greatest, countries may compete with one another to attract industry. From our point of view, the critical issue is the extent to which environmental regulations are used for such competition. We might expect to see jurisdictions loosening environmental regulations to attract business. We might see jurisdictions specializing in waste assimilation, whether generating pollution from their own factories or by storing wastes generated elsewhere. We might see jurisdictions subsidizing pollution control to give their own industries a competitive advantage without sacrificing environmental quality.

Within federations, such as the United States or the European Union, the federal government may restrict competition among jurisdictions, if it is determined that such competition leads to undesirable consequences. Most Federal environmental regulation in the United States is specifically written to minimize the extent to which localities can use environmental regulations as a tool to attract business, despite the fact that marginal damage from a unit of pollution may vary considerably from one location to another as a result of variations in population density and physical characteristics of the locale. An issue is the proper division of responsibility for environmental protection between the Federal government and member states.

At the international level, environmental regulations vary substantially from one country to another. A simple reason for this is that environmental quality is a normal good (as discussed in the previous section): the wealthier people are, the more environmental quality they demand. Thus we would expect the citizens of a rich country to demand more environmental quality than the citizens of a poor country. But the real question is, do these differences among countries make much difference to potential polluters? If they do, we might expect to see the emergence of "pollution havens," countries that specialize in polluting industries. At a less extreme level, we might expect countries with weaker environmental regulations to have a relatively high concentration of "dirty" industries.

A. Pollution Havens

Environmental regulations cost polluters money. Firms subject to tighter environmental regulations will incur higher costs than firms subject to weaker or nonexistent environmental regulations. If we have two countries identical in all respects except for the tightness of environmental regulations, economic theory would indicate that the country with weak environmental regulations would offer a cost advantage to polluting industries and would thus tend to specialize in these industries.[1] The country with the tighter regulations would tend to specialize in cleaner industries and import the output of dirty industries. This is a natural conclusion from standard international trade theory: countries will have a comparative advantage in goods produced with factors that are in relative abundance. In this case the environment as an allowable dumping ground for pollution would be the factor that is scarce or abundant.

Although this theoretical result is not in much dispute, its empirical significance is of great policy interest. If we were to expect a significant amount of such specialization, the establishment of free trade areas may be of concern not only to traditional constituents, such as labor unions, but also to environmental groups. In fact, the environment was a major issue in the debate in the United States over the North American Free Trade Agreement. The issue was whether a free trade zone involving Canada, the United States, and Mexico would result in a significant number of Canadian and U.S. industries moving to Mexico, seeking out weaker environmental regulations. Similarly, should Eastern Europe join the European Union, will firms migrate to the East where environmental regulations may be laxer? Furthermore, if tight environmental regulations tend to drive firms elsewhere, this will be another factor militating against tighter environmental regulations at home.

It turns out to be not very easy to detect an effect of different environmental regulations on international competitiveness and trade, probably because the effect is a weak one at best. There are two basic approaches to examining this question. One is to determine whether countries with lax regulations actually do specialize in exporting goods associated with pollution in their manufacture. A second approach is to examine capital flows in polluting industries and try to determine whether countries with lax regulations tend to attract relatively more of that capital compared to countries with tighter regulations.[2]

One of the primary models explaining international specialization is the Heckscher–Ohlin model of international trade.[3] A basic result of the model is that countries will have a comparative advantage in goods produced with endowed factors that are in relative abundance. A country with plentiful hydroelectric resources will specialize in goods with significant electricity content (such as aluminum); a country with plentiful labor will specialize in labor-intensive goods (such as clothing); a country with a large capital stock will specialize in capital-intensive goods (such as automobiles). The natural extension to the environment is that a country with a large assimilative capacity for pollution should specialize in pollution-intensive goods. However, it is not just assimilative capacity that determines the receptiveness of a country to polluting firms; income is just as important. The citizens of countries with high incomes will demand high levels of environmental quality. The degree of strictness of environmental regulations will thus result from two factors: the endowment of assimilative capacity in a country and the average or median level of per capita income in a country (or some other proxy related to citizen demand for environmental protection).[4]

One way of determining if lax environmental regulations tend to attract dirty industries is to use the Heckscher–Ohlin model to explain trade in goods that are associated with pollution and try to determine if environmental variables are significant. For instance, let X_{ij} be the net exports of industry i from country j. Let E_{jk} be the endowments in country j of basic factor k, such as capital, skilled labor, land, and natural resources (assume there are K different basic factors). Finally, let R_j be the strictness of environmental regulations in country j (a higher R is more strict). The Heckscher–Ohlin model would have X_{ij} explained by E_{jk} and R_j:

$$X_{ij} = \alpha_i + \beta_{i1} E_{j1} + \beta_{i2} E_{j2} + \ldots + \beta_{iK} E_{jK} + \delta_i R_j + u_{ij} \tag{19.1}$$

or some other functional form involving the same basic variables. In Eq. (19.1), u_{ij} is an error term, representing variables that have been omitted, measurement errors, or other factors than may lead to errors in characterizing the relationship between right-hand-side variables in Eq. (19.1) and net exports. If Eq. (19.1) is estimated over a large cross section of countries, an indication of whether the laxity of environmental regulations influences trade is the statistical significance and sign of δ_i, the coefficient on R_j, the strictness of environmental regulation.

James Tobey (1990) has done just such a statistical analysis. He uses observations on 23 countries, about half industrialized and half developing, examining net exports of five particularly dirty industries: mining, paper, chemicals, steel, and other metals. Using 11 different categories of resource endowments (such as capital, different kinds of labor, different kinds of land, and different natural resources), he fails to find any statistical significance in δ_i, the coefficient on the strictness of environmental regulations.[5]

One problem with finding evidence that differential environmental regulations influence international trade is that the effect is probably small. Because of this, some authors have focused on the margin most likely to be sensitive to the effect: international flows of capital. The logic is that the nature of the capital stock in any country and thus the country's specialization in one industry or another is the result of investments made over many decades. Looking for effects in the capital stock of environmental regulations that may have existed for a decade or two at most is likely to be futile. Any effects are far more likely to show up in marginal changes in the capital stock: current investment. Movements of capital from one country to invest in industry in another are called foreign direct investment (*FDI*). If lax environmental regulations tend to attract dirty industries, then we should expect to see *FDI* for dirty industries concentrated in countries with lax environmental regulations, all else being equal. As with explaining trade in the Heckscher–Ohlin model, we start with an equation that attempts to explain *FDI* in industry *i* into county *j*:

$$FDI_{ij} = \alpha_i + \beta_{i1} F_{1j} + \beta_{i2} F_{2j} + \ldots + \beta_{iK} F_{Kj} + \delta_i R_j + u_{ij} \tag{19.2}$$

where F_{kj} is the level of variable *k* influencing *FDI* in country *j* (for instance, tax policy), R_j is the strictness of environmental regulations in country *j*, and u_{ij} represents variables and noise that are unaccounted for. Although Eq. (19.2) is linear, it could take many forms, involving the same basic variables. Unfortunately, there has not been much empirical work in trying to measure δ_i in Eq. (19.2). A number of authors have statistically estimated variants of Eq. (19.2), although few with an explicit variable for environmental regulation.[6] Xing and Kolstad (2002) have examined *FDI* from the United States for several sectors. Although their sample is small, they find δ_i to be significantly negative for the chemical industry, a highly polluting industry, but statistically indistinguishable from zero for the electronics industry, an industry with relatively low levels of pollution.[7] This suggests that lax environmental regulations do attract *FDI* for polluting industries.

Why, when our intuition tells us that polluting firms should be attracted to jurisdictions with lax environmental rules and regulations, is the empirical evidence for this behavior so weak? Ederington et al. (2005) examine three hypotheses for why this effect appears to be so small: (1) most trade in the world is among developed countries, where differences in environmental rules and regulations are likely to be transitory; (2) only industries that are "footloose" and able easily to relocate production are likely to exhibit this behavior; and (3) pollution abatement costs are such a small part of total costs that these cost differences are unlikely to motivate behavior. In an empirical analysis of trade patterns, the authors find support for the first two of these hypotheses but not the third.

The general consensus of the empirical literature on pollution havens and the effect of environmental regulations on trade is that the effect is very weak at best. Some authors find no effect; other authors find an effect, though only a weak one.

B. A Simple Model of Jurisdictional Competition

Would we expect a jurisdiction to weaken environmental regulations to attract business (capital)? The answer to this question is mixed. If the jurisdiction is operating in the best of all possible worlds, it should neither subsidize nor tax capital movements into a jurisdiction. Furthermore, it is not in a jurisdiction's best interest to relax environmental regulations to attract business. However, if we are in a second-best world in which capital is being taxed, it may be efficient to offset that taxation with a reduction in the stringency of environmental regulations. We can see this with a simple model.[8]

Start with a large number of jurisdictions with fixed populations in each. Jurisdictions compete with one another for capital (K), imposing tax rates on capital (which may be negative—subsidies) and regulations on pollution emissions within the jurisdiction (E). Localities need capital to provide jobs which provide income. Local residents also desire environmental quality. Additionally, capital taxation may be necessary to raise money for running the local government and providing local public goods. Industrial activity uses labor and capital and produces goods plus pollution. The production function can be written as $Y(K,L,E)$, where K is inputs of capital, L is inputs of labor, E is allowed emissions of pollution, and Y is goods output. We can assume the units for output are such that its price is one. Figure 19.1 shows how output changes with capital. Also, higher emissions allow higher levels of output. One assumption we will make is that industrial activity exhibits constant returns to scale in labor and capital inputs. In other words, if labor and capital inputs are doubled, both goods and pollution output are doubled.

Finally we need to characterize the preferences of the residents of each jurisdiction. We will assume residents are identical within a community with a utility function that depends on per capita consumption of goods (C) and pollution: $U(C,E)$. Environmental quality (the pollution level) is chosen by the locality. Consumption comes from the

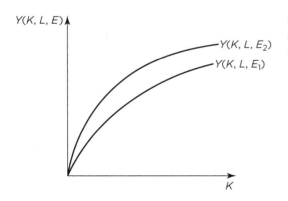

FIGURE 19.1 Output with two emisson levels, $E_2 > E_1$. K, inputs of capital: L, inputs of labor; E, allowed emissions of pollution; Y, goods output.

wage income associated with the firms that are attracted to the jurisdiction plus any tax revenue raised by taxing the firms in the jurisdiction plus any profit generated by local industry after labor and capital have been paid.

We now focus on a single, arbitrarily chosen jurisdiction and ask what level of capital taxation and environmental quality it should choose, considering that it is competing against all of the other jurisdictions. Thus labor is now fixed at $\overline{L}$, since we assumed no mobility among communities.

It takes a bit of development to reach our final result, so a preview may be in order. First we will look at how industry may respond to a capital tax, t, and pollution limit E. How much capital will industry choose to locate in a municipality with a tax of t and pollution limit E? Having established how the firm responds to jurisdictional tax and environmental policies, we then determine what levels of the capital tax and environmental quality will maximize utility for our representative consumer. We do this in two steps: (1) For any level of E, what is the optimal capital tax? (2) What is the optimal E? We are then in a position to develop our results that (1) the optimal capital tax is zero, but (2) a positive capital tax induces a lowering of environmental quality standards.

1. The Optimal Tax on Capital Is Zero Keep in mind that the capital market is competitive; in fact the competitive world price of capital is r. Thus if the market provides the amount of capital K to the community, the owners of capital are paid rK. This leaves $Y(K,L,E) - rK$ for the residents of the community. If capital is taxed at the rate t, the wages and profits drop to $Y(K,L,E) - (r + t) K$ but the total income of the population is supplemented by the tax revenues, tK, to give total consumption (equal to income) of $Y(K,\overline{L},E) - (r + t)K + tK = Y(K,\overline{L},E) - rK$. It might seem that the tax rate has no effect on income; however, the tax rate influences the amount of capital that is attracted and this in turn affects income.

If firms are faced with a capital tax of t and pollution limit E, in a locality with a wage w, the profits are

$$\Pi(K,\overline{L},E) = Y(K,\overline{L},E) - wL - (r+t)K \tag{19.3}$$

As we know, profits are maximized by setting the value of marginal product for each factor (labor and capital) equal to its price:

$$MP_K(K,\overline{L},E) = r + t \tag{19.4a}$$

$$MP_L(K,\overline{L},E) = w \tag{19.4b}$$

Since the labor supply in the municipality is fixed, the wage will adjust to clear the market. Figure 19.2 shows how the value of the marginal product of capital changes with the amount of capital. Also shown in Figure 19.2a is the choice of capital in response to a tax of t and no tax, when the emission level is E_2. Remember that L is fixed. Note that as the tax level increases, the amount of capital decreases. Figure 19.2b shows how the level of capital the firm chooses varies with the tax rate. Note also that just about any level of capital can be attracted to the jurisdiction, simply by choosing the right t.

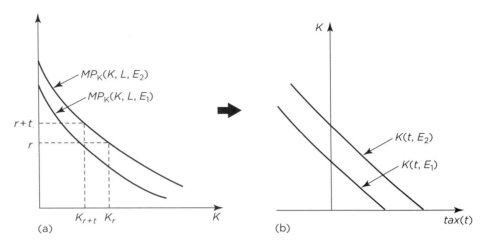

FIGURE 19.2 (a,b) Value marginal product of capital (MP_K), two emisson levels ($E_2 > E_1$) and capital (K) as a function of the capital tax rate (t) and emission levels. K_r, amount of capital demanded with no tax on capital, emissions at E_2; K_{r+t}, amount of capital demanded with tax t on capital, emissions at E_2.

What is the optimal tax on capital? To answer this we first determine the right amount of capital for the community. The consumption level for a tax of t, capital K, and emissions E is simply

$$C\overline{L} = Y(K,\overline{L},E) - (r+t)K + tK \qquad (19.5a)$$

$$= Y(K,\overline{L},E) - rK \qquad (19.5b)$$

In Eq. (19.5b), note that the level of the tax does not appear explicitly, only implicitly in that K is determined by t. A higher t gives a lower K and a lower Y. Now for any particular level of E, what should the community want K to be? That is simple—whatever maximizes per capita consumption, C. That will *give* maximum utility. From Eq. (19.5b), consumption is maximized when K is chosen so that the value of the marginal product of capital is equal to the price of capital services, r:

$$MP_K (K,E) = r \qquad (19.6)$$

But this happens only when $t = 0$ [as can be seen from Eq. (19.4a)]. If t is high, there is too little capital and output suffers; with a large subsidy to capital, the difference between output and capital payments (i.e., consumption) is low. So our first result is that it is always desirable to have no tax on capital (neither a tax nor a subsidy).

2. The Optimal Level of Emissions Now that we have determined the optimal capital tax rate, what should the optimal emission limit be? The representative consumer's utility depends on consumption and emissions: $U(C,E)$. The consumer will maximize this utility subject to the constraint that C and E must be attainable. E is under the control of the municipality but C depends on how much capital is attracted. Since K depends on t and E, we can write it as $K(t,E)$. We can also write the identity for consumption:

$$C = \{Y[K(t,E),\overline{L},E] - rK(t,E)\}/\overline{L} \qquad (19.7)$$

Equation (19.7) defines the feasible consumption levels, given t and E. If we plot the (C,E) combinations that satisfy Eq. (19.3) for $t = 0$ we obtain a positively sloped line as shown in Figure 19.3 (line BD). As allowed emissions rise, output increases (as shown in Figure 19.1), and as a consequence consumption also increases. But in addition, the capital stock rises (see Figure 19.2b), which increases output and surplus available for consumption.

Also shown in Figure 19.3 are indifference curves for the consumer (lines RS, VW). The optimal choice for $t = 0$ is the combination (E_0,C_0). The slope of the indifference curve is the marginal rate of substitution between consumption and pollution for our representative consumer. Furthermore, the slope of the production feasibility line is the marginal rate of transformation between emissions and consumption. They are equal at the optimum. This is the first-best amount of pollution. So our second result, analogous to our first result about the capital tax rate, is that emission regulations should not be relaxed (or tightened) to attract capital.

3. Emissions Levels When the Tax on Capital Is Positive Now suppose that for some reason the tax on capital is positive $(t > 0)$. One understandable reason for this would be that the community has a need for tax revenue and finds it necessary to obtain this revenue, at least in part, from capital taxation. This is very common. A property tax is a tax on capital. Most business income taxes are basically taxes on capital income.

Our question now is, what happens to the limit on pollution when t becomes positive? Figure 19.3. illustrates the result. Shown in Figure 19.3 is the production possibility frontier for a capital tax $t > 0$ (line OA). For any emission level, attainable consumption is less with a positive tax. Note that in Figure 19.3 allowed emissions increase to E_1, largely to compensate for the overly high tax on capital.[9] Even though the indifference curve is tangent to the production function at this point, the tax on capital results in a difference between the marginal value of capital in production $(r + t)$ and its price (r). Thus we do not have efficiency.

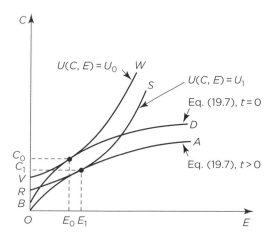

FIGURE 19.3 Optimal levels of emissions (E) and per capita consumption (C) for different capital taxation rates (t). Equation (19.7) is feasible combinations of C and E. BD, feasible combinations of C,E with $t = 0$; OA, feasible combinations of C,E with $t > 0$; VW,RS, indifference curves for typical consumer; (E_0,L_0), efficient levels of E and C, $t = 0$; (E_1,C_1), efficient levels of E and C, $t > 0$.

This is our third result. If for some reason there is a positive tax rate on capital, a jurisdiction may in fact loosen its environmental regulations relative to what we would find in a first-best world.

To summarize: if jurisdictions/countries offer foreign firms tax-free status, it would not be in the best interest of these jurisdictions to loosen environmental regulations to attract capital. If, on the other hand, conditions are such that the jurisdiction must tax capital, we might see the complementary use of weak environmental regulations to make up for the capital taxation. In reality, we might expect positive capital taxation to exist in countries that are not excessively worried about attracting capital. It seems logical that such countries would not feel strongly enough about attracting capital that they would resort to substantial weakening of environmental regulations. This is just speculation, however; what happens in reality is an empirical question.

II. INTERACTING POLICIES: TRADE AND ENVIRONMENT

In the last section we examined the competition among jurisdictions for advantage, and the use of environmental regulations to promote that advantage.

In this section we examine a similar question, though in the context of international trade policies among and between countries. In particular, we are concerned about interactions between a country's policies vis-à-vis international trade and a country's environmental policies. Can advantage in international trade be gained through manipulation of environmental policies?

In the next section we are concerned with the interplay between free trade agreements and environmental policy. Often environmental considerations are major impediments to free trade agreements. Conversely, environmental regulations have sometimes been used as disguised barriers to trade, in violation of agreed free trade agreements.

In the subsequent section we examine two countries involved in strategic trade. This means that the countries are large enough players in the international market for there to be some market power. This allows trade policy to actually be used to advantage. In this context, can environmental policy further enhance a country's advantage?

A. Free Trade Agreements and the Environment

Free trade has been a holy grail for many governments over the past few decades. The European Union started out as the European Iron and Steel Community, in the early 1950s, with a goal of establishing one market for coal, iron, and steel products. The General Agreement on Tariffs and Trade (GATT) also emerged after World War II, with a goal of facilitating world trade. In the 1990s GATT was replaced by the World Trade Organization (WTO), though the goals remained. The North American Free Trade Agreement (NAFTA) emerged in the early 1990s and involved Mexico, the United States, and Canada.

Free trade agreements are concerned with reducing tariffs and other barriers to trade among member countries. Reducing tariffs is relatively easy to stipulate in an agreement; defining and reducing trade barriers is more difficult. Often trade barriers will be erected for reasons that appear to have nothing to do with trade, yet give subtle (or not so subtle) advantage to domestic producers. The boxed example relating to the Danish Bottle Bill is a good example.

The WTO has developed a fairly sophisticated set of rules to deal with disguised trade barriers. Basically, a country may not restrict imports based on the way in which the products were produced—their process and production methods (PPM). Imports can be restricted based on the characteristics of the imported product (provided the same restrictions are applied to domestic products). For instance, a ban may be placed on the import or sale of beef with detectable levels of synthetic hormones. But restricting a product based on its PPM, when there is no detectable impact on product characteristics, is deemed a way of favoring domestic production.

This leads to a problem with some global environmental problems. In several famous cases, the United States attempted to restrict the import of seafood that was not caught in an environmentally friendly fashion. U.S. law required that tuna needed to be caught in a dolphin-safe manner and shrimp needed to be caught in a way that protected sea turtles. Although the United States did not fare well in these cases, the WTO found that provided the United States (or any other country imposing such rules) has imposed its rules to

---

Danish Bottle Bill as a Trade Barrier

In an effort to encourage recycling and refilling of beer and soft drinks containers, in 1978–1981 Denmark passed several laws requiring that those beverages must be sold in "returnable containers." As a matter of definition this required that the government approve containers being used and that in practice a large proportion of containers had to actually be returned and refilled. These seem like practical rules to encourage environmentally friendly practices.

This law was contested to the European Commission (EC), the central administrative unit (in Brussels) of the European Economic Community (EEC), which was to become the European Union (EU). One of the central arguments was that this legislation worked as a trade barrier favoring domestic producers. Foreign producers, particularly those seeking to sell modest quantities in Denmark, faced extra burdens associated with setting up a recycling system and having its containers approved. The EC objected and the Danish law was amended in 1984 to exempt small importers (less than 300,000 liters per annum).

This was not the end of the story, however. The EC felt the law still constituted a barrier to trade in violation of the EEC Treaty and brought the case to the European Court of Justice. Although the Danish rules protected the environment, the EC argued that there were other ways of providing similar levels of environmental protection (such as government-run collection recycling systems) that did not have as strong an effect on protecting domestic beverage producers. Furthermore, the fact that beverages without domestic–foreign competition (milk and wine) were exempt weakened Denmark's claim to be pursuing the rule solely for environmental reasons.

The Court ruled against Denmark. (Source: Barrett and Clark, 1992.)[10]

protect the environment in a fair and nondiscriminatory manner, giving other countries flexibility in how they meet the ultimate environmental goal, then such rules would not be in violation of the WTO.[11]

Other concerns with free trade agreements involve the migration of polluting industries from richer countries to poorer countries within an agreement (such as from the United States to Mexico within NAFTA). This may be a valid concern, and was discussed in the previous section in the context of pollution havens. Another concern with free trade is more fundamental, and that is that environmental degradation accompanies prosperity, and trade tends to make us more prosperous. That is a hard criticism to counter except to note that richer societies tend to be willing to devote more resources to environmental protection

B. Strategic Trade

The next issue we confront is the use of environmental regulations as tools to increase the competitive advantage of domestic firms engaged in international trade.[12] The standard view of international trade is that any barriers to trade that a country may impose, either barriers to protect domestic industries or subsidies to exports, can make the country only worse-off as a whole (though parts of the country may obviously be made better-off). If environmental regulations are weakened, domestic firms benefit via lower costs; however, residents who must put up with the pollution are harmed even more. Overall, it is not welfare improving to weaken environmental regulations to enhance trade. This is essentially the same result we saw earlier in this chapter in the context of interjurisdictional competition.

This result breaks down somewhat if industries within a country have market power in the global market. With market power, the overall welfare of a country can be improved by subsidizing exports, although this result applies to very specific circumstances and thus is not universally true. Since weakening environmental regulations is one way of providing a subsidy, it might be the case that there is a real incentive to relax environmental regulations. Several authors have examined this question in some detail.[13] Their models are quite complex, so we will sketch only a rudimentary analysis of this issue here.

The basic setup of our analysis is a specific industrial sector located in two different countries. Each of these two countries has a firm in this sector that is large in the global market and thus enjoys market power. For simplicity, we will assume these firms sell to a third country. This way, we do not have to worry about the welfare of consumers in the two countries, only the welfare of the firms. We will first show that a subsidy to production can be in the best interest of the country offering the subsidy.[14] The firms are assumed to engage in Cournot competition with each other, meaning that each will maximize profits taking the level of output of the other as fixed. We will then examine the subsidy implications of different environmental regulations.

As is the common approach in examining a problem of this nature, we first fix the subsidies at arbitrary levels and see how the firms will respond. Knowing how firms respond to arbitrary subsidies, we can determine what the optimal subsidies are. Or, in our case, the two countries will be competing against each other so we are interested in the equilibrium subsidy levels that result from the competition.

Let the outputs of the large firm in each of the two countries be denoted by D and F, for domestic and foreign. Assume the inverse demand function for their output is $P(Q) = a - bQ$ where $Q = D + F$. Inverse demand is thus linear, with a and b the two positive parameters of the inverse demand function. To make things even more simple, we assume fixed costs are C_D and C_F while variable costs are zero. This is the simplest possible arrangement we can define. Assume that the domestic firm receives a subsidy s per unit production. Profits for the domestic firm are then given by

$$\Pi_D = [a - b(D + F)]D + sD - C_D \tag{19.8a}$$

$$= (a + s - bF)D - bD^2 - C_D \tag{19.8b}$$

For any particular level of output, F, chosen by the foreign firm, how much should the domestic firm produce? Clearly, the domestic firm should produce so that marginal profits are zero; this will maximize profits. To do so, we use Eq. (19.8b) to generate marginal profits, which we then set to zero:

$$M\Pi_D = (a + s - bF) - 2bD = 0 \tag{19.9}$$

which implies that

$$D = (a + s - bF)/(2b) \tag{19.10}$$

This is shown graphically and generally in Figure 19.4. The figure shows a series of concentric isoprofit lines. These are lines of constant profit, defined by Eq. (19.8). Each of these lines represents (F,D) combinations that yield the same level of profit for the

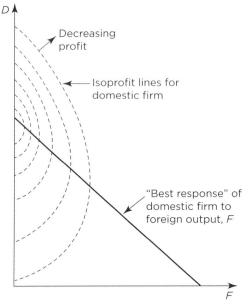

FIGURE 19.4 Best response of domestic firm to foreign output levels.

domestic firm. These isoprofit lines indicate what profit-maximizing level of D should be chosen for any particular level of F. Fix F; the D associated with the highest profit is the D of choice. These Ds are the "best responses" to any given level of F. The solid line in Figure 19.4 shows the best response line—the optimal Ds. This is also Eq. (19.10).

Now we can do the same thing for the foreign firm, deriving its best response to different output levels by the domestic firm. The best response lines for D and F are shown in Figure 19.5. The point at which the two lines intersect is the equilibrium, (D^*,F^*), the D and F levels at which each firm is doing the best it can, given what the other firm is producing. This is what is known as the Cournot equilibrium.[15]

So far, we have ignored the subsidy level implicit in Eqs. (19.8) and (19.10). If we assume the best response lines in Eq. (19.8) are associated with a zero subsidy level, $s = 0$, then what happens if the domestic country increases s to a positive number? From Eq. (19.10) we see that if we increase s, the best response D will increase as well, for any given F. Thus the best response line for D is shifted up as shown in Figure 19.5 for $s >$ 0. Note that this results in a new equilibrium, one with higher D and lower F. As would be expected, a subsidy to firm D results in lower costs for this firm and thus expanded output. It comes at the expense of output from the other firm.

Profits clearly expand for firm D, but to a certain extent these increased profits are due to the subsidy that has to be financed by the general tax revenues of country D. It turns out, however, that the net profits for country D (i.e., taking into account the cost of the subsidy) are actually higher for a positive subsidy than for no subsidy. Thus it is in the best interest of country D to subsidize firm D.[16] In effect the subsidy allows D to take output and profits from F.

Now suppose both countries decide to subsidize exports. This turns out to be a little more complicated. In this case, both countries will try to impose a positive subsidy, but the result will not increase net profits for the countries. In fact, with both countries subsidizing, it turns out that a negative subsidy (an export tax) maximizes net profits if both countries were able to coordinate policies. The reason for this is that the two firms competing against each other produce more output than if they were coordinating output and acting as a cartel. A positive export tax will restrict output and drive the two firms closer to this monopoly cartel level of output and profit. The important point, however, is that two countries competing against each other will subsidize production, and not obtain the point of maximum net profit.

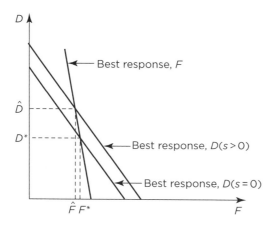

FIGURE 19.5 Effect of a subsidy on Cournot equilibrium output levels. F^*, D^*, foreign and domestic output, no subsidy to D; $\hat{F}$, $\hat{D}$, foreign and domestic output, subsidy to D.

So far, these results are not directly related to environmental matters. However, suppose we have exactly the same situation except that pollution is generated in conjunction with output in each country. Pollution causes damage at home (forget about transboundary pollution). Now assume that it is not possible to directly subsidize a domestic industry involved in an export market of the type described above. An obvious reason for being unable to use direct subsidies is that such subsidies may violate free trade agreements. A natural way of subsidizing the industry is to relax environmental regulations. Instead of directly paying a subsidy to the polluter, the relaxed regulations reduce polluter costs at the expense of the citizens who must endure greater levels of pollution.

Consider a firm that generates pollution in direct proportion to output. We will focus on only one firm, but the setup is as above: there are two firms/countries with market power selling into a third country. If output of our firm is D, then emissions are αD. Suppose the efficient Pigovian fee is t^*. If the firm is subject to the Pigovian fee, its profits are

$$\Pi_t = [a - b(D + F)]D - C_D - t^* \alpha D \tag{19.11}$$

If the country would like to offer a subsidy s^* per unit output but is unable to do so, it can instead lower the Pigovian fee to $(t^* - s^*/\alpha)$ resulting in profits

$$\Pi_s = [a - b(D + F)]D - C_D - (t^* - s^*/\alpha)\,\alpha D$$
$$= [a - b(D + F)]\,D - C_D - t^*\alpha D + s^*D \tag{19.12}$$

Lowering the appropriate pollution tax is a way of granting a subsidy of s^*D. The down side is that there will be more output than desired and more pollution.[17]

What does all of this mean? The basic result is that subsidies can be in the self-interest of a country when its industries enjoy market power internationally (but not always, as we showed). Since direct subsidies may be difficult to pursue, subsidies in the form of lax environmental regulations may be attractive. This is somewhat worrisome in that it may be difficult to determine whether a country is being too lax in protecting the environment.

III. TRANSBOUNDARY POLLUTION

The last issue we will consider is that of transboundary pollution—pollution that migrates beyond the jurisdiction with the power to control that pollution. Greenhouse gas emissions are a classic example. Greenhouse gases emitted in Norway contribute to climate change worldwide. Or consider acid rain pollution from emissions from power plants in the United Kingdom that may be blown across the North Sea to Sweden and Norway. How do you control such pollutants?

There are three basic situations that we will consider. The simplest one is two adjoining countries with pollution and goods produced in one country; the pollution migrates across the international boundary and is consumed in the other country. Goods are also shipped to the victim country. One way of solving this is for the victim to levy a tariff on imports that were produced with pollution. The question is, how well will such a countervailing tariff work if the tariff is related to pollution damage but applied to goods imports?

The second situation is an extension of this two-country model with pollution migrating across borders. But here these two countries are involved in a plethora of international transactions, including but not limited to trade in pollution-intensive goods. Is it possible that sanctions in unrelated markets can be used to drive the polluting country to generate pollution levels that are Pareto optimal?

The third situation involves a group of countries with a common pollution problem. The pollution problem is common in that each country pollutes and each country suffers damage from the aggregate levels of pollution. Carbon dioxide, leading to global warming, is a good example of such a pollutant. Effective control of the externality must involve international agreements. Can such agreements be effective and binding, considering the fact that there is no international supergovernment that can enforce such environmental agreements?

A. Countervailing Tariffs

We first consider a very simple situation involving two countries. One country, the polluter, has an industry that produces a good that is exported to the other country. Unfortunately, the industry also generates pollution that is entirely exported to the other country, which we will call the victim country (for example, the factory is on the border and all the pollution blows into the victim country). To correct the pollution problem, the victim country levies a tariff on imports of the good, with the tariff equal to the total pollution damage divided by the quantity of goods being imported. Thus the tariff revenue the victim country collects will be exactly equal to the damage inflicted on it by the polluter country. Does this correct the problem in an efficient manner? The answer is "no," except in very particular circumstances. Only when all of the goods produced are exported to the victim country and when marginal damage is equal to average damage from pollution could the countervailing tariff be efficient. In such a case, the victim country has complete control over the producer of the good. However, because of this, the victim country is a monopsonist and will likely levy an import tariff, in the absence of pollution. Consequently, efficient pollution control will be difficult to establish.

Consider a simplification of this example. Suppose the marginal and average damages from pollution are the same. Pollution is also produced in direct proportion to the amount of goods produced. This is simpler than the case of allowing abatement technology—in order to reduce pollution, output must be reduced. Also suppose that the good is consumed in the polluter country as well as the victim country. Finally, assume that the victim country does not levy a tariff to exploit its monopsony power but only to correct for the pollution externality. Figure 19.6 shows this situation. Shown are the two markets: the polluter market (19.6a) and the victim market (19.6b). Shown is the marginal private cost of producing the good as well as the demand for the good in each of the two countries. The first-best pollution policy would be a Pigovian fee of t^* on all production of the good, equal to marginal damage from the pollution. This raises the marginal cost of production in both markets, as shown in Figure 19.6. Only those consumers for whom the marginal value of the good exceeds the private marginal costs ($MC_{private}$) plus the marginal pollution damage (t^*) will consume the good. Sales of the goods will be q_p^* and q_V^* in the two countries and this will be efficient. Now suppose that such a first-best correction of the externality does not take place. Instead, there is no emission fee in the polluter country, leading to output of q_p^-. The only recourse the victim country has is to levy a tax per unit of the good imported (t'). Ideally, this tax would be set so as to maximize

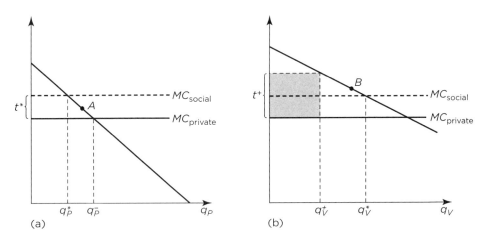

FIGURE 19.6 Countervailing tariff in response to transboundary pollution. (a) Polluter market; (b) victim market. t*, first-best Pigovian fee; t^+, countervailing tariff levied by victims; q_P^*, q_V^*, first-best consumption levels, polluter and victim markets; $q_{\bar{P}}$, consumption in polluter market without emission fee; q_V^+, consumption in victim market with countervailing tariff; shaded area, pollution damage with countervailing tariff t^+.

consumer surplus less environmental damage. As the import duty is increased, pollution will decline (since output in the home country will decline) but surplus from goods consumption will also decline. The tax is shown in Figure 19.6b, as well as the total tax revenue, $(t^+ q_V^+)$. Total damage is $[t^*(q_P^- + q_V^+)]$. This is shown in Figure 19.6.

Why is this not an efficient correction of the externality? In other words, why is this not Pareto efficient? One reason is that there are consumers in the victim market who are precluded from consuming the good but for whom the value of the good exceeds the value of consumers in the polluter market. For instance, the consumer corresponding to point A in the polluter market consumes the good whereas the consumer labeled B in the victim market does not consume the good. Yet, the marginal value of the good for B exceeds the marginal value for A. In fact, with an efficient Pigovian fee, consumer A would not be consuming the good—the consumer's value is less than the marginal social cost of producing the good. So we see that there is room for a Pareto improvement among consumers. What about the quantity of pollution? Is that efficient? Note from Figure 13.9 that the efficient amount of output (which is directly proportional to the amount of pollution) is $q_P^* + q_V^*$ but the quantity that will be produced with a countervailing tariff is $q_P^- + q_V^+$. These two quantities are unlikely to be the same.

Efficiency in pollution generation really requires that all consumers of the dirty good see the total social cost of their consumption. That is the basic problem with the countervailing tariff. And the problem gets worse if more than two countries are involved. If there are multiple consuming countries each country will levy a tariff related to damage in that country only, ignoring damage in other countries. Such an arrangement is unlikely to lead to efficiency.

In summary, a countervailing tariff can help correct a transboundary pollution problem but is unlikely to totally correct the problem.

B. Issue Linkage

The previous section assumed that the victim country would levy countervailing tariffs equal to the pollution damage. Although that is one approach to dealing with transboundary pollution, the fact is that countries deal with each other on a multitude of issues, not only economic but political and cultural as well. It may be that the victim country has little ability to coerce the polluter to reduce emissions; however, the victim country may have a great deal of power on a totally unrelated issue, such as involvement in a joint defense treaty.[18] By withholding agreement on the joint defense treaty, the victim country may be able to force the polluter to reduce pollution levels. In essence, the victim country can threaten sanctions of one sort or another against the polluter country if the polluter country does not adopt pollution regulations to achieve, the efficient amount of pollution. This is termed "issue linkage" and is more of a political than economic question, so it will not be addressed further here.

C. Designing International Environmental Agreements

We now turn to the most general of international pollution problems, one in which there are many countries contributing pollution to a common pool that damages all countries. Only an international agreement among countries can hope to solve the problem. An example is the emission of greenhouse gases such as carbon dioxide. The emission of greenhouse gases may lead to global climate change, such as warming and sea level rise. It makes no difference where the gases are emitted; the effect on the global climate is the same. However, due to climate change some countries may incur greater damage than others. Some arctic countries may benefit from warming whereas some low-lying coastal countries may suffer greatly from sea level rise. The emissions of chlorofluorocarbons (CFCs) to the atmosphere, leading to ozone depletion, is another example of a global pollutant. In this case, a treaty (the Montreal Protocol) has been forged to deal with the problem.[19]

The basic problem in designing an effective international environmental agreement is that there is no supranational organization to enforce such an agreement. In effect, the agreement must not only be self-enforcing but it must be sufficiently appealing to all parties involved for them to agree to it in the first place.

The difficulties in forging an effective international environmental agreement are not unlike the problems faced in constructing effective cartels. A cartel is a group of producers that coordinates its production to increase its market power and thus increase its profits. Such cartels typically cannot rely on enforcement of agreements by third parties. If the cartel consists of a group of domestic firms within a single country, the cartel is usually illegal and thus any agreement is nonenforceable in court. If the cartel is a group of countries (such as OPEC), just as with environmental agreements, there is no supranational enforcement body. Successful cartels must rely on self-enforcement, voluntary participation, and effective restrictions on output. The work that has been done in understanding what makes cartels work can be applied to understand what makes international environmental agreements work (or not work).

Drawing on what has been learned about the operation of cartels,[20] it is straightforward to infer what is needed for an international agreement to operate effectively. For an international environmental agreement to work (i.e., be self-enforcing), it should have three basic characteristics:

1. **Cheating and nonparticipation deterred.** The agreement should be structured so that countries want to belong to the agreement, even if they are free to leave. This means that not-belonging to the agreement must be seen as undesirable; furthermore, cheating while in the agreement must also be deterred.
2. **Individually rational.** Each country should be better off joining the agreement than not joining the agreement.

Ozone vs. Carbon Dioxide

Probably the two most infamous global environmental problems of the last half century are ozone depletion and global warming.

In the 1970s scientists discovered that chlorofluorocarbons (CFCs), in wide use in applications ranging from refrigerants to spray can propellants, were depleting the ozone layer in the stratosphere. This depletion was expected to lead to elevated skin cancers and other consequences of higher levels of ultraviolet radiation making its way to the surface of the earth. In 1987, the Montreal Protocol was negotiated to phase out the production of CFCs. Nearly all countries of the world, including the United States and China, have ratified the Protocol. The Montreal Protocol is widely viewed as successfully solving the global CFC problem.

Global warming from the production of carbon dioxide and other greenhouse gases was recognized as an issue in the nineteenth century, though only in the last two decades has it moved front and center in the global environmental policy debate. In 1997 the Kyoto Protocol was negotiated to reduce greenhouse gas emissions from developed countries. The target, to be achieved by 2012, is approximately 8% below 1990 levels. Although the Protocol has been ratified by enough countries for it to go into effect, the United States is not one of those. Furthermore, major emitters in the developing world (China and India) have no emission reduction obligations under the Protocol. The Kyoto Protocol is widely viewed as a first step, but in the end is an inadequate solution to the climate change problem.

Many papers have been written about why the Montreal Protocol worked so much better than the Kyoto Protocol. One reason for this disparity is simply the nature of the problems. The benefits compared to the costs associated with taking action are so much more favorable in the case of CFCs. Furthermore, the Montreal Protocol achieves near-universal adherence because the industrialized countries pay to make it worthwhile for the developing world to join the protocol. No such provisions exist in the Kyoto Protocol. Furthermore, punishments for violators are stipulated in the Montreal Protocol but not the Kyoto Protocol. In essence, the Montreal Protocol has the three desirable characteristics of an international environmental agreement: it is self-enforcing, it is individually rational for all countries to join, and there are clear environmental gains.[21]

3. **Environmentally improving.** Pollution levels attained by the agreement should be a potential Pareto improvement over the status quo.

The reason for the first of these conditions is that there must be an incentive-based way of keeping the agreement together. Many countries may find it in their own interest to be a free-rider on an agreement, rather than undertake the obligations inherent in reducing emissions. If a set of countries tightens carbon regulations, some industries may move to nonsignatory countries and export their carbon-intensive goods back to the signatory country, not only neutralizing the environmental gain but putting the nonsignatories at an advantage. (This is known as "leakage.") One way of deterring free-riding is for participating countries to levy import duties on goods advantageously produced by nonsignatories. A similar issue pertains to signatory countries that fail to live up to treaty obligations. Cheating on the part of signatories must be deterred with predetermined penalties that countries have an incentive to levy.

The reason for the second condition is that countries that join an agreement out of anything but self-interest may not be reliable members. There may be many reasons why a country joins an agreement, including a sense of obligation or a desire to do good. But if the country is better off in the agreement than not, participation is on a much more solid footing, and much more immune to domestic political pressures to weaken participation.

The third condition is trivial and somewhat redundant with the second point, but some environmental agreements have a great deal of activity but very little ultimate environmental protection.

It is easy to contemplate an international agreement that meets two of these three criteria; it is quite another thing to design an agreement that meets all three conditions.[22]

D. The Size of International Environmental Agreements

To answer the question of how many countries will choose to join an self-enforcing international environmental agreement (IEA), we will construct a very simple model of an IEA.[23] Despite its simplicity, it will help us understand why IEAs work and also what their limitations are. The basic goal is to understand why countries might voluntarily come together to solve an environmental problem, particularly when free-riding can look very attractive.

Start with N identical countries, each of which generates emissions: country i emits e_i. Furthermore, each country can make two choices: to pollute or to abate. Pollution for country i means $e_i = 1$; no pollution (abate) means $e_i = 0$. The payoff to a country will similarly be simple:

$$\Pi_i = e_i - \gamma \left[\Sigma_j e_j \right] \tag{19.13}$$

There are two parts to this payoff. The first part is the private payoff from polluting (e_i) and the second part is the damage from the pollution emitted by all countries ($\gamma \left[\Sigma_j e_j \right]$). For any country, abatement is more costly than polluting. If the country pollutes, the private payoff will be 1; if it does not pollute, the private payoff will be zero. (Units have been normalized so that the private payoff is either 0 or 1.) Thus the first term is e_i, which will be 0 if the country abates and 1 if the country pollutes. The damage from pollution depends on how much is emitted by all countries ($\Sigma_j\, e_j$)—this is, after all, a transbound-ary pollutant.

There is one remaining variable in Eq. (19.13): γ. This variable represents the average damage from a unit of emissions. To obtain the total damage from emission for country i, multiply the total world emissions ($\Sigma_j\, e_j$) by the average damage (γ). We can limit the values of γ to be not too small nor too large. If γ is too small, the environmental problem becomes too small to do anything in the best of times. If γ is too large, then the environ-mental problem is so large that a country will abate, regardless of what other countries do. The intermediate territory for values of γ – where an IEA might be of some use—is $1/N < \gamma < 1$.

Now that we have stipulated both the pluses and the minuses of emissions to indi-vidual countries, we turn to the question of what strategies countries will pursue, act-ing in their own self-interest. There are three cases that are of particular interest: (1) all countries acting together, cooperatively; (2) each country going it alone; and (3) some countries banding together in an IEA with the remaining countries pursuing their own independent strategy.

1. The Cooperative Solution. When countries act together cooperatively, they seek to coordinate their actions to maximize the well-being of individual countries. Since all the countries are the same, there are two possible outcomes: all the countries abate or all the countries pollute. Inspection of Eq. (19.13) tells us that if all abate, the payoff is 0. If all pollute, the payoff is $1-\gamma N$. Because $\gamma > 1/N$, $1-\gamma N < 0$. This means that abatement is best for the world. In other words, the cooperative outcome is everyone abates and the payoff for each country is 0.

2. The Noncooperative Solution. At the other extreme, there is no coordination whatso-ever among countries. Each country is on its own. For instance, if I am country 1, I can write my payoff from Eq. (19.13) as

$$\Pi_1 = e_1 - \gamma\, e_1 - \gamma\, [\Sigma_{j>1}\, e_j] \tag{19.14}$$

My choice is either $e_1 = 0$ or $e_1 = 1$. Because $\gamma < 1$, it is clear from Eq. (19.14) that my payoff is higher with $e_1 = 1$ (pollute). When the other countries go through a similar calculation, they come to the same conclusion: pollute. The payoff for each country is $1-\gamma N$ (which we know is < 0).

Each country is worse off with this noncooperative outcome than with the coop-erative outcome. This is the essence of the environmental problem. We have it because people/firms/countries act in their own self-interest. We would be better off if people cooperated. But cooperation is not easy to achieve.

Note also that a larger γ leads to an even bigger gap in payoffs between the two outcomes. (Conversely, the closer γ gets to zero, the smaller the payoff gap between coop-eration and noncooperation). Recall that a larger γ means the damage from polluting is higher.

3. An International Environmental Agreement (IEA). Now we allow M countries to get together to form an environmental agreement. Think of this as a two-stage process. In the first stage, countries sort into those in the agreement and those who prefer to sit on the sidelines (the "fringe"). Call this the membership stage. In the second stage (the emissions stage), the countries in the agreement act cooperatively and make a decision about whether to abate or not. The countries in the fringe also make a decision in the second stage.

The best way to look at a two-stage problem like this is to work backward. If there *were* M countries in an agreement, what would each country do and what would the payoffs be? Then, moving to the beginning, knowing what the payoff is from different-size IEAs (payoffs for different Ms), we can ask the question of how big the IEA will be.

Starting with the emissions stage, we know that the fringe will always decide to pollute, from the same logic as we saw in the noncooperative discussion above. If the M members of the IEA pollute, the individual payoff to members of the IEA will be $1-\gamma N$. If the M members of the IEA decide to abate, each member's payoff will be $-\gamma(N-M)$. Clearly, whichever payoff is higher determines what the IEA members will do:

$$-\gamma(N-M) \geq 1-\gamma N \Leftrightarrow M \geq 1/\gamma \Leftrightarrow \text{IEA members abate} \qquad (19.15)$$

Equation (19.15) specifies the conditions under which the members of the IEA will abate; if those conditions are not met, the members of the IEA will pollute. Note that when the payoffs in Eq. (19.15) are the same between abating and polluting, we assume that the IEA abates (a "tie" tips in favor of the environment).

What these results mean is that $1/\gamma$ is the critical size for an IEA. For IEAs with size less than $1/\gamma$, polluting will be the action of choice; for IEAs with size greater than or equal to $1/\gamma$, abate is the action of choice.

Figure 19.7 shows the payoff to individual members of the IEA and the fringe, as a function of the size of the IEA (M). Note that for small IEA's ($M < 1/\gamma$), the IEA members decide to pollute, which is the same decision as the fringe. Therefore all countries have a payoff of $1-\gamma N$. For larger M, when $M \geq 1/\gamma$, the members of the IEA change their decision and decide to abate. The fringe remains polluting, which is why each member of the fringe gets a payoff exactly 1 higher than each member of the IEA.

We now turn to the first stage and ask how big the IEA will be. The easiest way to think of this is to suppose the IEA is of some arbitrary size—say. $\hat{M}$ Then ask the questions "Will any country want to leave and join the fringe?" or "Will any member of the

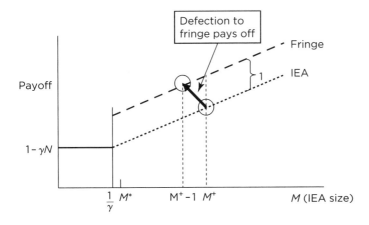

FIGURE 19.7 Payoff to IEA and fringe members as a function of IEA site.

fringe want to join the IEA?" If the answer to either of these question is "yes," then an IEA of size $\hat{M}$ will not work—it will not be "stable." The forces at work will either want to make it smaller (if someone wants to leave) or to make it larger (if someone wants to join). It turns out that there is one and only one stable IEA and the number of countries in it (M^*) will be equal to or just slightly higher than $1/\gamma$.[24]

The reason for this result can be gleaned from Figure 19.7. For IEAs that are too large, IEA members will want to defect to the fringe. This can be seen from the figure for IEA size M^+. If a member of the IEA compares its payoff within the IEA to what the country could obtain if it defected to the fringe (thus making the IEA smaller by 1, to M^+-1), it sees that it is better off joining the fringe. However, at M^*, where one member leaving means the number of members in the IEA drops to less than $1/\gamma$, and thus the IEA begins polluting, belonging to the fringe becomes less attractive than staying in the IEA.

This result, that the size of the IEA is approximately $1/\gamma$, means that the larger γ is, the smaller the IEA. Recall that the larger γ is, the greater the difference between the cooperative and noncooperative solutions—the greater the *need* to cooperate on solving the environmental problem. Putting these two results together, we conclude the greater the need, the smaller the IEA.[25] This is discouraging because it means that for bigger environmental problems, with greater environmental damage, the difficulties will be greater in holding together a group of countries to solve the problem.

SUMMARY

1. Environmental regulations can act as disguised trade barriers in the context of free trade agreements. If the regulations are written in such a way as to treat domestic and foreign producers similarly and to provide flexibility to foreign producers in terms of how environmental goals are achieved, then the regulations may not be in conflict with free trade agreements.

2. For an international environmental agreement to be effective, it must meet three conditions: (a) be self-enforcing, (b) be individually rational for each country, and (c) be environmentally improving overall.

3. Different regions of a country (e.g., states of the United States), different countries of a federation (e.g., countries of the European Union), or independent countries of the world are interested in attracting capital and businesses to provide jobs and income. Countries may use preferential tax rates or concessions on environmental regulations to attract business. In a competitive environment the first-best strategy for a country is to neither subsidize nor tax capital and to grant no concessions on environmental protection. If, however, it is necessary to tax capital, it may be in a country's interest to weaken environmental regulations to make up for the tax on capital.

4. Because of the income effect on demand for environmental quality, we would expect environmental regulations to be more lax in poorer countries. This might result in poor countries attracting and then accumulating the particularly dirty industries of the world. The empirical evidence on this effect is quite weak. Most studies are unable to find evidence of this "pollution haven" effect. A few studies do find some evidence that lax environmental regulations attract dirty industry.

5. When a country has an industry that has market power internationally (for instance, because of its size), there are ways in which the country can help the industry, increasing income for the industry and the country. A subsidy to the industry can be in the best interest of the country. If a subsidy is not possible (for instance, because of free-trade agreements), weakening environmental regulations can be a more subtle way of offering the industry a subsidy.

6. Transboundary pollution is difficult to control because the damage from the pollution occurs in a locality that has no authority over the generator of the pollution. There are three ways of controlling this problem. One involves the victim country levying tariffs on imports from the country generating the pollution. Another approach involves linking international agreements between the two countries on totally unrelated issues to controlling the pollution problem. A third and most common approach is to forge international agreements on pollution control, such as the Montreal Protocol on control of ozone-depleting substances (e.g., chlorofluorocarbons). The problem with international agreements is that participation is of course voluntary, but at the same time sanctions for violating the terms of the agreement must be biting. It is not always possible to forge an effective environmental agreement to control transboundary pollution.

PROBLEMS

1. In the early 1990s, the chief economist of the World Bank came under a great deal of criticism for suggesting that developing countries take advantage of opportunities to import hazardous and nonhazardous wastes for storage and disposal. Why was he making this argument? What are the arguments against his position?

2. In the example (Section II.B) of the two countries with market power, assume that inverse demand is $P(Q) = 10 - Q$ where $Q = D + F$ is measured in tons and P in dollars per ton. Assume fixed costs are equal to one for both firms.

   a. First assume no subsidy ($s = 0$). In a plot of D (vertical axis) vs. F (horizontal axis), plot several isoprofit lines for the domestic firm. Plot the best response for the domestic firm, showing the domestic firm's profit maximizing choice of D as a function of F. (This is similar to Figure 19.7.)

   b. Since the foreign firm has identical costs to the domestic firm, add the foreign firm's best response line to your graph. What is the resulting level of output for the two firms, the resulting profit for each of the firms, and the profits for each of the two countries (where a country's profit is equal to its firm's profit less the cost of the subsidy)?

   c. What happens to output for each firm if the domestic country only institutes a subsidy of $0.50 per ton? Show your answer graphically and calculate it as well.

   d. Calculate the profit for each of the two firms and profits for each of the two countries. Compare your answer with that of part (b). Which country has done better with the subsidy?

   e. What happens to output if both countries institute subsidies of $0.50 per ton? Show this on your graph and calculate the result as well.

    f.   For this case of two subsidies, calculate the profit for each of the two firms and the profit for each of the two countries. Compare your answer with that of part (b). How have the two countries fared in comparison to the case of no subsidies?

*3. In the example (Section II.B) of the two countries with firms with market power, competing internationally, determine the optimal subsidy for country D. Assume only country D uses a subsidy. Do this in two parts. First examine how the firms in each country will produce, given a subsidy level, s, in country D. Then solve these reaction functions for the equilibrium level of output in each of the two countries. These should depend only on a, b, and s. Then, for the second part, write an expression for net profit for country D. The expression should be in terms of a, b, and s only. Next determine the s that maximizes this net profit. Use calculus or show the result graphically for several different values of a and b.

4. In Figure 19.6, the optimum (E_0, C_0) is shown as the point at which the marginal rate of transformation of E for C equals the consumer's marginal rate of substitution of E for C. Yet E is a public bad. Why does this appear to violate the Samuelson conditions for optimal provision of a public bad/good?

5. How does Figure 19.2 support the following statement: "Looking at how countries of different income at any point in time supply environmental quality (the environmental Kuznets curve) does not necessarily indicate how an individual country's environmental quality will change as that country's income rises."

NOTES

1. Professor Michael Porter of Harvard University has advanced the proposition that tight environmental regulations can actually enhance international competitiveness over the long run; tight regulations induce firms to innovate and ultimately lower costs ahead of their competitors (Porter and van der Linde, 1995). This is a controversial proposition not widely accepted within the economics profession (see Palmer et al., 1995).

2. Jaffe et al. (1995) provide a highly readable summary of the evidence on the effect of environmental regulation on international industrial "competitiveness." There have been a number of recent papers that address this issue and review the debate, including Eskeland and Harrison (2003), Levinson and Taylor (2008), and Ederington et al. (2005). See also the compendium of papers on the topic in Fullerton (2006).

3. Refer to any standard textbook on international trade, such as Husted and Melvin (2010).

4. Another factor, other than income and assimilative capacity, that may lead to relaxed environmental regulation is described by Chichilnisky (1994). She argues that poorer countries have less developed institutions for providing public goods and regulating public bads. Thus even if the citizenry demands a certain level of environmental protection, the country will be unable to provide it.

5. There are two obvious explanations for Tobey's results. One is that a sample of 23 countries is too small to find a significant effect unless it is very strong indeed. Alternatively, it may be that total exports are too coarse a measure to pick up subtle effects of environmental regulations. Low and Yeats (1992) look at a slightly more sensitive measure, the *revealed comparative advantage*. This is the ratio of the fraction an industry makes up of a country's exports relative to the world average for the industry. They find only slightly more evidence than Tobey that lax environmental regulations attract industry. Another explanation has to do

with his measure of environmental regulatory strictness. It is based on a subjective assessment of regulations made by other researchers. It is not easy to summarize the degree of strictness of a large body of law and regulation. There may be many regulations, but they may be poorly enforced. There may be few regulations, but they may be very effective and stringently enforced. This problem of measuring the strictness of environmental regulations in the context of finding evidence of pollution havens is considered by Xing and Kolstad (2002).

6. Wheeler and Mody (1992) estimate the determinants of *FDI* using a variety of explanatory variables; however, the closest they get to an environmental regulation variable is one associated with "bureaucracy and red tape" in obtaining approvals and permits generally.

7. The Xing and Kolstad (2002) analysis uses approximately the same size data set as Tobey (1990)—roughly 20 countries. The study also uses a second equation to explain the stringency of environmental regulations, treating the stringency as an unobserved variable. Although this is an innovation in the measurement of stringency, it is not without problems. Basically, it introduces another layer of uncertainty into the problem of determining if regulations affect *FDI*.

8. The model presented here is based loosely on Oates and Schwab (1988). Markusen et al. (1995) provide a different treatment of the use of environmental regulations to attract capital.

9. The graph does not unequivocally show this since perversely shaped indifference curves could conceivably yield the opposite result, much as one can show how quantity demanded of a Giffen good decreases when its price goes up. However, Oates and Schwab (1988) give a mathematical proof of the result stated here.

10. One of a series of cases in the World Resources Institute's Sustainable Enterprise Program, available online at www.bellinnovation.org.

11. Refer to Neumayer (2004) for detail on this issue. See also Esty (1994) and Farber and Hudec (1996).

12. It should be pointed out that this is a different issue than the use of environmental regulations as disguised nontariff barriers to trade. For instance, the Danish requirement of a deposit on beverage bottles was alleged to be a trade barrier, hindering distant beverage suppliers (who must incur large costs to return their bottles for refilling). However, the courts found otherwise (Rehbinder, 1993).

13. Barrett (2003) provides one of the more complete analyses of strategic environmental policy at a theoretical level. See also Copeland (1992), Ulph (1992), and Barrett (1997).

14. This result that export subsidies are desirable is due to Brander and Spencer (1985).

15. The Cournot equilibrium involves several firms choosing quantities to produce, assuming the level of output by the other firms is fixed.

16. This result is relatively easy to show using calculus. Write the net profit for country D and find the s that maximizes that net profit. It will be positive.

17. A Pigovian fee provides an incentive to provide the correct amount of pollution and for the polluter to pay for damage from that pollution. In a more general framework, if the firm is directed to emit a certain amount of pollution and not required to pay damage from that pollution, that can be considered a subsidy without sacrificing quantities of pollution. In this example, a quantity regulation on pollution would be preferred to an emission fee.

18. Folmer (1993) couches this in terms of the two countries playing repeated games on a variety of issues. If a country has no power in one particular game, the country can threaten in another game in which it may have power. Folmer refers to this situation as interrelated games and suggests that transboundary pollution problems can be solved in this context.

19. See Murdoch and Sandler (1997).

20. Osborne (1976) discusses necessary ingredients for a successful cartel.

21. Refer to Barrett (1999, 2003, 2008), among others, for a discussion of these issues.

22. Barrett (1994, 1997) develops a theory of self-enforcing environmental agreements that meets the first two conditions and concludes that the gain resulting from the agreement is very small. Hoel (1992) discusses another approach to international agreements.

23. The first explicit economic model of an international environmental agreement appears to be Barrett (1994). The model presented here is adapted from Ulph (2004). See also Kolstad and Ulph (2008).

24. We are being a little loose here since $1/\gamma$ is likely not an integer and IEAs must have an integer number of members. To be more accurate, the size of the unique stable IEA is the smallest integer that is greater than or equal to $1/\gamma$. Furthermore, even though there is a unique size of a stable IEA, there are many different IEAs of that size, involving different countries (since all the countries are identical).

25. Scott Barrett (1994) was the first to point out this depressing result. Laboratory experiments suggest a more optimistic result, that a larger γ leads to a larger IEA (Burger and Kolstad, 2009), though in a context of individuals making decisions, not countries.

20

DEVELOPMENT AND GROWTH

FOR THE MOST PART WE HAVE BEEN CONCERNED WITH THE BEHAVIOR OF FIRMS SUBJECT to environmental regulations. How do we construct workable regulations for such firms? How will firms react to specific regulations? In this chapter we turn to broader considerations, including treatment of developing economies.

We first examine a basic issue: how does income affect the demand for environmental quality? Specifically, should we expect poorer countries to impose environmental regulations that are similar to rich countries or will income dictate differences? If this is the case, how will regulations tighten as income increases?

A second set of issues concerns the broader consequences of environmental regulations. Another concern is properly accounting for environmental protection in our aggregate measures of economic performance, such as gross national product (GNP) and productivity. It is commonly held that environmental regulations retard growth and "hurt" the economy. But standard measures of growth and economic health omit the benefits of a clean environment.

I. THE INCOME EFFECT AND THE DEMAND FOR ENVIRONMENTAL QUALITY

Why are oil refineries located in poor rather than rich sections of cities? Why do developing countries tend to have more lax environmental regulations than rich countries? Do we expect environmental protection to become more or less important globally as the decades pass? The answers to these questions hinge on how income influences demand for environmental protection. As people become wealthier, they seem to demand more and more environmental protection. Conversely, at any point in time, the poor seem to demand less protection (in terms of being willing to pay less for protection) than the rich.

Consider an individual's demand for any good. As the individual's income increases, we would expect the quantity of the good consumed to change, keeping other factors (such as prices) constant. If the quantity consumed increases, we call the good a *normal good*; if the quantity decreases with increases in income, we call it an *inferior good*. If the quantity demanded of a normal good goes up by a greater percentage than the percentage income increases, we also call the good a *luxury good*; otherwise it is simply a *necessary good*.[1] These terms are not terribly imaginative, but they do offer an important classification scheme that helps explain differences in concern for the environment among countries and people of different income levels.

It is generally accepted that environmental quality is a normal good; indeed, most goods are normal. Whether it is also a luxury good is less clear. As we all know, environmental quality is not a homogeneous good; it encompasses diverse concerns such as drinking water quality, urban air quality, global climate, wilderness access, and species diversity. The question is not whether each of these is desirable, but how demand for these goods increases when income increases. This is a very important empirical question.[2] As the world becomes wealthier, the extent to which environmental protection becomes more or less important depends on the income elasticity of demand for environmental quality. Differences in pollution levels in different countries can be explained by differences in income.

Making the connection between individual demand for environmental quality and societal demand involves a number of steps and assumptions. How income affects individual demand must be translated into aggregate demand. Aggregate demand from the populace must then be translated into demand on the part of government. The government translates consumer demand into binding regulations that apply to polluters. If a government is democratically elected, the actions of legislators will at least approximate the will of the people. If a government is less representative, general demand for environmental quality may fail to be translated into environmental quality.

What makes measuring the effect of income changes difficult is that observed levels of pollution are the result of the interaction of supply of environmental quality and demand for environmental quality. Figure 20.1 illustrates this. Shown in Figure 20.1 is a demand curve for environmental quality for one income level (AB), and two demand curves associated with higher income, one ($A'B'$) corresponding to a modest income effect on demand and one corresponding to a stronger effect ($A''B''$). Also shown in Figure 20.1 is a supply/marginal cost curve for environmental quality (CD), along with a possible alternate supply curve, $C'D'$. The forces that are causing income to increase for the consumer will most likely also change the supply conditions for the polluting firms and in Figure 20.1 we show marginal costs rising from an income increase. This is consistent with the notion that a richer economy will have a larger industrial base, which will increase the marginal cost of providing a given level of environmental quality. (Of course the supply curve could also drop. When incomes rise, institutions may develop that make it easier and cheaper to institute pollution controls.) Note that the original efficient level of environmental quality is point E. With a small upward shift in the demand for environmental quality, the efficient level decreases to F; with a larger shift in the demand curve, the efficient level becomes G, an improvement relative to E.[3]

An income increase, keeping everything else constant has a clear impact on the quantity of environmental quality demanded—increased income increases demand, resulting in a shift from E to H. But if factors that increase income also shift the supply curve for environmental quality, the overall effect is ambiguous. We could have either deterioration or improvement in environmental quality.

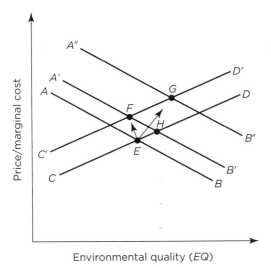

FIGURE 20.1 Effect of a shift in demand and supply/marginal cost for environmental quality. *AB*, base demand for environmental quality; *A'B'*, demand for environmental quality with increased income, modest income effect; *A"B"*, demand for environmental quality with increased income, large income effect; *CD*, base supply of environmental quality; *C'D'*, supply of environmental quality, higher income; *E*, base provision of environmental quality; *F*, environmental quality, modest income effect; *G*, environmental quality, high income effect; *H*, environmental quality, increased income, no supply effect.

Because differences in environmental quality are most pronounced in comparing different countries rather than regions of a single country, a number of researchers have examined different countries around the world, trying to infer the relationship between national income and environmental quality. Figure 20.2 shows the relationship between income and the most basic of environmental goods—access to clean drinking water. There are two graphs in Figure 20.2, one for 1975 and one for 1986. These graphs were estimated by Shafik (1994) using 86 observations from different countries around the world. The data were more scattered than is obvious in Figure 20.2; only 46% of the variability of the variable of interest was explained by the analysis. Nevertheless, Figure 20.2 clearly shows that as incomes increase, this environmental variable improves. As our intuition would suggest, these graphs show that richer countries have higher levels of at least this measure of environmental quality. Figure 20.3 shows a similar curve for smoke (suspended particulates). This is somewhat more complicated to present since the smoke concentration varies widely within a country. What is shown is a modified scatter plot of the median concentration of suspended particulate matter (basically smoke) for assorted cities of the world,[4] as reported by the World Bank. Also shown is a statistical fit to nearly 500 data points, done by researchers at Princeton University (Grossman and Krueger, 1995). The data clearly show that for low incomes, as income levels increase, smoke levels

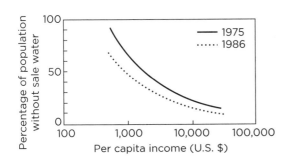

FIGURE 20.2 Relationship between per capita income and access to safe water. (From Shafik, 1994.)

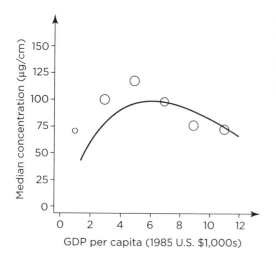

FIGURE 20.3 Relationship between per capita GDP and smoke concentrations in cities. Circles represent the mean value of concentration median over an interval with the diameter proportional to number of data points. Line is the best statistical fit to data. (From Grossman and Krueger, 1995, p. 363.)

increase. But this effect peaks for incomes in the neighborhood of U.S. $6000 per capita, from which point increases in income reduce the concentration of smoke. Some decades ago, Simon Kuznets developed curves showing how income inequality changed as per capita income in a country increases. He found that income inequality initially increased and then decreased. Because of the similarity, curves showing how environmental quality or pollution change with changes in income in a country are known as *environmental Kuznets curves*. Such curves are shown in Figures 20.2 and 20.3.

It is important to be somewhat cautious in interpreting curves such as the ones presented in Figures 20.2 and 20.3. These curves were generated using data for different countries for the same year. However, most people interpret them as showing what will happen to environmental quality as income rises in a specific country over time. This is not the same thing as comparing countries at one point in time. Unfortunately, we do not have a long enough time series of data to examine what happens to individual countries over time. Even if we did, the confounding effects of innovation and technical progress would make interpreting the data difficult. If all countries represented in Figures 20.2 and 20.3 were exactly the same except for income and environmental quality, we might be justified in assuming a country would follow such a curve over time as it develops. However, individual countries are very different from one another and there may be factors that sort countries by income that we are not taking into account. For instance, poor countries may tend to have very high population densities and rich countries may have low population densities and these differences may explain part of the patterns in Figures 20.2 and 19.3. If this were the case, we would not expect a country with high population density to follow the same curve as its income rises. Population density may also play a role in the cost of pollution control. Low population density correlates with a high assimilative capacity of the environment, which is the environment's ability to naturally cleanse itself. At the simplest level, the more pollution is spread out, the easier it is for the environment to deal with it. Thus countries with high population density would have higher costs of providing environmental quality.

The empirical literature on environmental Kuznets curves divides pollutants into three categories, depending on what happens to pollution levels as incomes rise. Figure 20.2 represents the case of environmental quality rising as incomes rises.

Figure 20.3 represents the case of environmental quality first falling and then rising. A third category involves continual deterioration as income rises. Evidence suggests that pollutants falling into this category would include generation of municipal solid waste and emissions of greenhouse gases, leading to global warming.[5]

Why are environmental Kuznets curves interesting and/or useful? The policy question is how to improve the level of environmental quality in poor countries.[6] One approach would be for international organizations to invest heavily in cleaning up the environment and protecting natural resources, while at the same time directing economic growth away from pollution-intensive sectors. However, if one believes a relationship such as is illustrated in Figures 20.2 and 20.3, then a viable policy would be to focus energy on increasing incomes. Once the peak has been reached, environmental quality will start to improve without any extra intervention.

II. PRODUCTIVITY GROWTH AND TECHNOLOGICAL CHANGE

Looking at economic growth through a normative lens, growth has been blamed for many environmental ills. Certainly industrialization (with associated pollution) has accompanied the growth of economies. Furthermore, as we saw in the context of the Kuznets curve, many modern environmental problems get worse as people get richer. On the other hand, economic growth need not mean growth in material consumption. Art appreciation consumes few resources yet is a perfectly legitimate form of consumption. There is no fundamental reason why consumption growth cannot be "green." Furthermore, as long as population is growing, some overall increase in economic wealth is necessary just to keep per capita income constant. These are important normative issues that we will not address in this chapter.

Focusing on the positive issues associated with growth, a fundamental question in economics is, why do personal incomes increase and standards of living improve over time? The three primary reasons are usually thought to be expansion of the workforce, accumulation of capital (including human capital—educated and trained workers), and innovation/invention. Innovation and invention allow an economy to make more with the same sets of inputs. Productivity is the general term for the ability of an industry or an economy to produce goods and services with a given set of inputs. Productivity and the growth in productivity are of fundamental importance to an economy for the simple reason that they are major determinants of the level and growth of per capita income. We are concerned when productivity growth is slow; in such cases we look for reasons for the slow growth. In the past, fingers have been pointed at environmental regulations as a reason for slow productivity growth.

Innovation and invention can have two effects on economic activity. They can quite simply reduce the costs of production, allowing an increase in output over time, keeping inputs of labor and capital constant. Alternatively, they may improve the quality of a product. The electric light bulbs manufactured a century ago burned out more quickly than today's electric lights and were thus inferior. Automobiles continue to become more expensive, yet the quality of automobiles continues to improve.

TABLE 20.1 Total Factor Productivity Growth in Selected Countries (Percentage per Year)

Country	1960–1973	1973–1979	1979–1996	1995–2006
United States	1.9	0.1	0.6	1.4
Japan	5.7	1.1	1.1	1.1
Germany	2.6	1.8	0.6	1.1
France	3.7	1.6	1.3	1.1
Italy	4.4	2.0	1.2	−0.1
United Kingdom	2.7	0.7	1.5	1.2
Sweden	1.9	0.0	1.1	1.4
Australia	2.1	1.1	0.8	1.4

Source: OECD (stats.oecd.org).

Productivity growth is the standard measure used to gauge progress of this sort due to innovation and invention. Suppose we are comparing two time periods, this year and last year. Technology in a particular industry has improved over that period. This technological improvement has lowered the cost of production. This reduction in the cost of production will lower product price, and thus demand will increase as well as output. So how do we measure the growth in productivity? The productivity growth over a year is defined[7] as the rate of growth in quality-adjusted output less the rate of growth of quality-adjusted inputs.[8] The rate of growth would typically be measured in percentage terms per year. As an example, suppose we note that over a year the output of electricity has grown by 2% while the inputs into electricity manufacture (fuel, capital, labor) increased only by 0.5%. We would label this difference as productivity growth: 1.5% per year (2%–0.5%). As a more realistic example, from 1948 to 1979 output in the United States grew by 3.4% per year, on average. But inputs of capital and labor grew by 2.6% per year, leaving 0.8% as a residual, attributable to productivity growth (Jorgenson, 1988). Because the unobservable "productivity growth" is the difference between two measurable quantities (output growth less input growth), we speak of productivity growth as a residual. Table 20.1 presents estimated productivity growth rates economy-wide for a number of industrialized countries over the past half century. Note that the 1960s were a period of rapid productivity growth in many of the countries listed, particularly those that needed the most rebuilding following World War II. Starting in the 1970s there was an across-the-board slowdown in productivity growth. There has been a great deal of speculation and research into the causes of this somewhat mysterious "productivity slowdown" of the 1970s. One possible culprit is the rise in environmental regulation in the 1970s.[9]

A. Measuring Total Factor Productivity Growth

To understand how environmental regulation could have contributed to the productivity slowdown, it is important to first understand how we measure productivity growth. Start with a standard production function of the form

$$Y = A\,f(L,K) \tag{20.1}$$

where Y is output, L is input of labor, K is input of capital, and A is simply a parameter that changes over time as technology changes (the time dependence of the variables is suppressed for clarity). The parameter A allows output to expand without additional inputs. Thus it represents the level of technology.[10] Equation (20.1) typically is for an individual firm, but may represent the aggregate output–input relationship for an industry or even the entire economy. If we move forward one step in time and let all of the variables change a small amount, we obtain[11]

$$Y + \Delta Y = (A + \Delta A) f (L + \Delta L, K + \Delta K) \tag{20.2}$$

Equation (20.2) represents the equilibrium input and output choices of a firm or industry in the second time period. We can subtract Eq. (20.1) from Eq. (20.2), and manipulate the resulting equation a bit to obtain

$$\Delta Y = \Delta A \, f(L,K) + MP_L \, \Delta L + MP_K \, \Delta K \tag{20.3}$$

where MP_L and MP_K are the marginal products of labor and capital, respectively.[12] If we divide Eq. (20.3) by Eq. (20.1) we obtain

$$\Delta Y/Y = \Delta A/A + (L \, MP_L/Y) \, \Delta L/L + (K \, MP_K/Y) \, \Delta K/K \tag{20.4}$$

Note that the terms in parentheses in Eq. (20.4) are the shares of each input (in value terms) in the total value of output. We would expect the price of an input to be set to the value of the marginal product of that input and for total cost to equal the value of output (zero profits). Thus $(p_Y \, MP_L)$ would be the price of labor (with p_Y the price of output) and $p_Y \, Y$ would be the value of output. We can rewrite Eq. (20.4) as

$$\Delta A/A = \Delta Y/Y - s_L \, \Delta L/L - s_K \, \Delta K/K \tag{20.5a}$$

where

$$s_L = p_L L/(p_L L + p_K K) \tag{20.5b}$$

$$s_K = p_K K/(p_L L + p_K K) \tag{20.5c}$$

We can simplify Eq. (20.5a) further by dividing the equation by Δt and substituting A for $\Delta A/\Delta t$, Y for $\Delta Y/\Delta t$, etc.:

$$\frac{\dot{A}}{A} = \frac{\dot{Y}}{Y} - s_L \frac{\dot{L}}{L} - s_K \frac{\dot{K}}{K} \tag{20.6}$$

Note in Eq. (20.6) that s_i is the value share of factor i in cost.[13] Equation (20.6) states that the rate of change of A ($\dot{A}/A$) is equal to the rate of change in output less the rate of change of inputs, weighted by their relative importance (defined by value shares). A is the parameter that stands for the level of technology. Equation (20.6) defines what is known as multifactor or total factor productivity growth, because it recognizes changes in both output and all of the input factors. The productivity growth figures in Table 20.1 are for total factor productivity.

B. Single Factor Productivity

Sometimes it is easier to measure some of the inputs than others. For instance, it is far easier to observe labor inputs than capital inputs, simply because of the difficulty of measuring the quantity and depreciation of capital and the ease of counting hours worked. Consequently, growth in labor productivity is often used as a simple measure of productivity growth. Labor productivity growth is defined as the percentage change in output less the percentage change in labor inputs. As we can see in Eq. (20.6), if labor and capital stay in fixed proportions and grow at the same rate, there is no loss in accuracy. In other words, if we assume $\dot{L}/L = \dot{K}/K$, then Eq. (20.6) reduces to

$$\dot{A}/A = \dot{Y}/Y - s_{L}\, \dot{L}/L - s_{K}\, \dot{K}/K$$
$$= \dot{Y}/Y - (s_{L} + s_{K})\dot{L}/L$$
$$= \dot{Y}/Y - \dot{L}/L \qquad (20.7)$$

Of course, labor and capital may not grow at the same rate. If they do not, labor productivity may be lower or higher than multifactor productivity growth. For instance, suppose from one period to the next, the price of capital increases relative to labor but technology does not change. This is illustrated in Figure 20.4. Shown in the figure 20.4 is a unit isoquant for a firm using labor and capital. The price of capital is initially p_k', which results in labor use L' and capital use K'. Now raise the price of capital to p_k''. We see that capital use declines (to K'') and labor use increases (to L''). We see a substitution into labor, away from capital. There is no change in technology from one period to the next because the unit isoquant in Figure 20.4 remains fixed from one period to the next (instead of moving inward as would occur with gains in productivity). If we were observing only labor productivity, we would see a decline in productivity since more labor is being used to produce the same output. Thus labor productivity growth would give a distorted view of multifactor productivity growth.[14]

To see this more generally, suppose we are comparing two periods in which productivity as well as the relative price of capital and labor (capital has become more expensive)

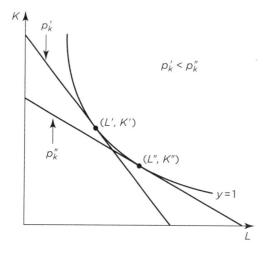

FIGURE 20.4 Change in factor use from a price increase for capital, no change in technology. L', K', base labor and capital use (price of capital = p_k'); L'', K'', labor and capital use after price increase for capital to p_k''; $y = 1$, combination of labor and capital that gives one unit of output.

have changed. Because of the price change, we would expect $\dot{K}/K = \dot{L}/L - B$ where B is some positive number. In other words, capital use will grow more slowly than labor use ($\dot{K}/K < \dot{L}/L$) due to the relative price change. Ignoring the small changes that may occur in factor shares, Eq. (20.6) can be written as

$$\dot{A}/A = \dot{Y}/Y - s_L \ \dot{L}/L - s_K \ \dot{K}/K$$
$$= \frac{\dot{Y}}{Y} - s_L \frac{\dot{L}}{L} - \left(s_K \frac{\dot{L}}{L} - B\right)$$
$$= \frac{\dot{Y}}{Y} - s_L + s_K \frac{\dot{L}}{L} + s_K B$$
$$= \dot{Y}/Y - \dot{L}/L + s_K B \qquad\qquad (20.8)$$

which in words is

$$\text{Total Productivity Growth} = \text{Labor Productivity Growth} + s_K \ B$$

Because both s_K and B are positive, a measure of labor productivity growth will understate the rate of total factor productivity growth.

C. Bias from Omission of Environmental Factors

So how does this all relate to the environment? The environment is an input into the production of many goods. Steel cannot be manufactured without using the environment as a dumping ground for pollution. Let E denote the input of environment into production for a firm. If the firm uses a little E, that is equivalent to disposing of only a small amount of pollution; a large E would correspond to dumping a large amount of pollution. Production of output now involves K, L, and E: capital, labor, and environment. If the environment is cheap to use (no regulation), firms will tend to use a good deal of E. If the environment becomes more expensive to use (tight regulations or a high emission fee), firms would substitute other factors (such as capital), using less of E.

What has happened over the last four decades throughout the world is that the effective price of the environment has gone up dramatically. In the 1960s in many places, the environment could be freely used for pollution disposal. That is typically not the case today. If the environment is neglected as a factor in measures of productivity and the price of the environment increases, measures of productivity growth will understate the extent of real productivity growth. This is analogous to the case we just discussed in which labor productivity growth will understate multifactor productivity growth when there is a simultaneous increase in the price of nonlabor inputs (capital).

How serious is this potential understating of productivity growth? Equation (20.8) indicates the error that occurs when productivity growth ignores one of the inputs. In Eq. (20.8), the distortion was introduced by ignoring capital, focusing on labor productivity. But a version of Eq. (20.8) could be generated with the environment as the missing input. As can be seen from Eq. (20.8), the size of the value share of environmental inputs in total costs is an important determinant of the extent of the understatement of productivity gains. The larger the share, the greater the understatement.[15] Thus industries with significant pollution or pollution control would be expected to show the greatest divergence between true productivity growth and measures that omit the environment.

Several studies have tried to correct productivity measures for environmental regulations. Robert Repetto and colleagues at the World Resources Institute have calculated multifactor productivity growth for several industries, taking into account the use of the environment as an input.[16] Figure 20.5 shows the growth of productivity over the period 1970–1990 for two industries in the United States, electricity generation and agriculture. Electricity generation in particular has moved from a situation of free use of the environment to one of strict regulation of emissions. Shown in Figure 20.5 is the value of A in Eq. (20.1), normalized to a base year. The change in A over time would yield information needed to calculate the rate of productivity growth. Figure 20.5a shows productivity for electricity generation. Note that the conventional measures of productivity in electricity show a decline over the 20-year period. However, when the environment is included, the result is reversed—productivity (negative productivity growth) increases, though modestly. Figure 20.5b presents a similar picture for agriculture in the United States. Conventionally measured multifactor productivity increases significantly over the 20-year period. However, in this sector, correcting for the omission of the environment only modestly increases the estimate of productivity levels. Pollution is less significant to agriculture than to electric power.

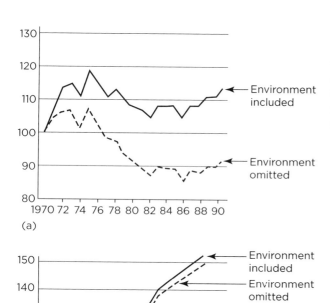

FIGURE 20.5 Sectoral multifactor productivity in United States with and without adjustment for use of environment. (a) Electricity (1970 = 100); (b) agriculture (1977 = 100). Solid line accounts for use of environment; broken line omits use of environment. (From Repetto, 1996, pp. 27, 41.)

Conrad and Morrison (1989), in another interesting study, compare traditional measures of productivity growth with "corrected" measures, taking into account the environment, for the manufacturing sectors of the United States, Canada, and Germany. To compute the corrected measure, they make two assumptions: that pollution regulations are efficient and that only capital expenditures can reduce pollution emissions. The implication of these assumptions is that the marginal cost of pollution abatement capital to the firm must be equal to the marginal damage from the pollution avoided by one more unit of abatement capital. These are strong assumptions, but making them allows the authors to show that for the United States in the period 1960–1967 (a period of weak environmental regulation), conventional and adjusted productivity growth measures are about the same (2.9% per year), whereas in the period 1972–1980 period (a period of tightening environmental regulations), the adjusted measure is 2.4% per year compared to 2.2% for the conventional way of measuring productivity growth. The results for Germany and Canada were less pronounced.

What do we learn from this discussion? Simply that in judging productivity gains, if we give signals to firms to save on the use of one input (the environment), we should count efforts to innovate to reduce the firm's reliance on the environment, even if that comes at the expense of other inputs. Thus if we want a true measure of how much innovation has taken place, we should include all of the relevant factors. Excluding the environment from measures of multifactor productivity growth would be expected to understate productivity growth in a period in which environmental regulations are tightening.[17]

D. Induced Innovation

The main thrust of the discussion of the previous section is that placing a higher "price" on the environment (through tighter regulations) tends to influence factor choice: if the environment–labor price ratio increases, one would expect production to use relatively less of the environment and relatively more labor. We saw how that process tends to bias productivity measures when the environment is ignored.

It is a small additional step to suggest that relative prices will steer innovation and invention toward saving the more expensive factor.[18] This is the "induced innovation hypothesis" put forward by John Hicks in the first half of the last century—a change in relative prices induces innovation to conserve, in production processes, the increasingly expensive input.

This is an important question. If the price of the environment is increased, either directly through emission taxes or marketable permits, or indirectly through prescriptive regulations, what will innovation do to the cost of abatement? Many modern environmental problems are very costly to solve. Climate change is an example. In order to significantly reduce emissions of greenhouse gases, many governments are relying on innovation to lower the cost of abatement, for instance, lowering the cost of high fuel efficiency in automobiles. Because abatement costs are an important input into the environmental policy debate, these are fundamental questions: how effective is tightening environmental regulations in both producing innovation and lowering abatement cost?

From a theoretical point of view, it is clear that innovators will pay attention to relative prices in directing research activities. But we also know that innovators cannot appropriate all the benefits of their innovations—there are intellectual "spillovers." These spillovers are externalities that tend to reduce investment in research because the innovators cannot appropriate all of the gains from that research. Publicly funded research may dilute the private incentives for innovation. The real issues then are empirical. What evidence is there regarding the significance of the induced innovation hypothesis? Can it be quantified? What is the effect of government research on private-sector innovation? Will early introduction of strong environmental regulations pay off in terms of significantly reducing abatement costs in the future?

There is a large literature addressing this question. The general conclusion of this literature is that the induced innovation hypothesis holds, particularly in the case of energy inputs.[19] However, analyses of the effect such innovation will have on reducing the long-term costs of meeting environmental targets has suggested the contribution of innovation will be modest.[20]

Are Energy Efficiency Gains from Innovation or Increases in Energy Prices?

Newell et al. (1999) take an innovative approach to this problem. They look at window air conditioners and other energy using appliances for a multidecadal period from the 1950s to the 1990s, spanning periods of low energy prices (the 1960s) and high energy prices (the 1970s and 1980s). Window air conditioners can use a good deal of electricity. The question the authors asked is whether improvements in efficiency of these appliances tracked increases in the price of energy. For data, they use the Sears catalog from 1958 to 1993. As most North Americans of a certain age know, the Sears catalog was a fixture of rural (and urban) life in the continent for about a century, offering just about anything by mail, including window air conditioners. The catalog contains important information on efficiency and price for a variety of goods.

The authors find that in the low energy price part of their data set (the 1960s), innovation was occurring, improving the quality of the appliances, but that innovation tended to be energy-using (not energy-saving). This is consistent with innovation using more of whichever factor is cheap. However, when energy prices became higher and were increasing, this trend in innovation turned around; innovation became energy-saving. In fact, they find that the energy price increases of 1973 onward were responsible for ¼ to ½ of the efficiency gains they observed. Another interesting finding is that government requirements to affix energy efficiency labels to appliances had a strong positive effect on efficiency.

III. GREEN NATIONAL ACCOUNTING

We have all become accustomed to news reports on the state of our economy. Such reports rely on such basic statistics as the unemployment rate, the rate of growth of gross domestic product (GDP), or the imbalance in foreign trade accounts. Such information on the economy has not always been so readily available. In the early 1930s Simon Kuznets, an economist born in Russia but who had emigrated to the United States, developed the first detailed accounting of the U.S. economy. During the 1930s and 1940s this system of accounts developed, in part, to assist with planning the war effort in World War II. From that point on, the United States has maintained a set of National Income and Product Accounts (NIPA). Other countries have set up similar systems of national accounting. After World War II, the United Nations established a System of National Accounts (SNA), defining standards to use in national accounting that would permit comparisons across countries.

Other than providing news releases for the media, what purposes do the national accounts serve? Although private firms and investors can benefit from knowledge about the condition of the economy, the primary purpose of the national accounts is to assist policy makers in government.[21] Incentives to encourage saving may result from knowledge that the national savings rate is low compared to similar countries. Monetary policy is guided by statistics on the money supply, economic growth and inventory levels, among other things. Nearly all government policies that are designed to intervene in the economy rely substantially on economic data contained in the national accounts. Even ostensibly noneconomic policies such as environmental regulation and funding of scientific research are influenced by data in the national accounts. A major justification for investing in R&D is the demonstrated gains to economic growth that have been contributed by innovation and invention (as discussed in the previous section). Environmental policy can be affected in a negative way. National accounting data can indicate the extent to which environmental protection is retarding conventionally measured economic growth. Or, in many developing countries, significant harvesting of forests or mining of minerals is promoted on the basis of its effect on growth in GNP (it raises the growth rate, some say misleadingly).

National income accounting can be easily illustrated with an example. Suppose we have a very simple economy, consisting of two companies and consumers: the AJAX coal company (a mining company), the Edison Power Company, an electric power producer (who uses coal to generate electricity), and consumers who consume electricity.

AJAX has underground coal reserves and operates an open pit mine. A new law requires that following mining, mined land be returned to its original state, regraded, and vegetated. AJAX has complained bitterly that this new law is costing the company a great deal and, as a result, coal prices have had to be increased. The company also maintains an exploration division that works to add new coal reserves to the company's inventory of reserves. In 2010, AJAX produced 5,000 tons of coal and sold it for £20 per ton. AJAX's exploration department succeeded in finding 2,500 tons of additional reserves on AJAX lands. A summary of AJAX's operations is given in Table 20.2. All of AJAX's coal was sold to the Edison company for the generation of electricity.

Edison produced £300,000 worth of electricity in 2010, along with 100 tons of sulfur dioxide air pollution. These emissions were lower than they used to be, before environmental regulations were enacted. A summary of Edison's income and expenses is also given in Table 20.2.

How might we measure the total output of this little economy? One way would be to add together the value of everything produced from the two firms: £100,000 + £300,000 = £400,000. But this is not quite right because coal is counted twice, both as output of AJAX and as part of the value of Edison's electricity. A more appropriate way would be to look at the *value added* to purchased raw materials by each company (labor and capital are not considered purchased raw materials). AJAX does not buy anything except labor and capital so its value added is £100,000. Edison purchases £100,000 of coal so its value added is £200,000. This makes the total value added by these two firms £100,000 – £200,000 = £300,000.

TABLE 20.2 Sample Accounts

AJAX Mining Company, 2010		
Expenses		
Wages		£50,000
Mining labor	£30,000	
Exploration labor	£10,000	
Land reclamation labor	£10,000	
Depreciation of mining equipment		£10,000
Income		
Sales of 5,000 tons @ £20/ton		£100,000
Edison Power Company, 2010		
Expenses		
Wages		£100,000
Pollution control labor	£10,000	
Production labor	£90,000	
Coal purchases		£100,000
Depreciation of generating equipment		£20,000
Income		
Sales of electricity		£300,000

The goal of National Income and Product Accounting is to summarize the productive activities of the economy. The overall output of a nation's economy is termed the gross domestic product. The term "gross" is used because depreciation is excluded. In the process of producing, equipment gets older, some equipment is retired, and some equipment becomes obsolete. This depreciation of equipment should really be subtracted from the measure of output to obtain a better idea of true output. If depreciation is subtracted from GDP, we obtain NDP—net domestic product. Depreciation is not so easy to calculate. (Think of some capital good you may own—perhaps a radio. How much did it depreciate last year?) Hence the common use of GDP rather than NDP. In our example, there is depreciation of mining equipment and electric power equipment. Deducting depreciation would bring the measure of output down by £30,000 to £270,000.

Although the methods of generating national accounts have evolved over the decades, they are not perfect. Illegal activities are generally excluded, for example. Housekeeping for pay is included whereas housekeeping within the family is excluded. The value of the environment to the economy is also excluded, and this has been the source of significant criticism over the past three decades. For instance, when oil is pumped from the ground, the oil is counted in GDP. But it could be argued that the inventory of oil in the ground is being depleted and that this inventory reduction should be a subtraction from GDP.[22] Using up our oil is making us poorer, not richer. Similarly, pollution is not included in the national accounts. Pollution is a product like any other with two exceptions: it is not marketed and it has a negative value. If a firm produces $100 of goods and $30 of pollution damage, it seems reasonable to value its total output at $70, rather than at $100 as is currently done in most national accounting systems.

Let us examine these resource and environmental issues one at a time. Consider first the case of nonrenewable resources (such as oil). The traditional way of dealing with depletion of nonrenewable resources is to ignore the depletion. The justification is that the value of additions to the reserve stock is ignored so depletion may also be ignored. This is somewhat like saying we ignore inventory additions so we can ignore inventory reductions.[23] But this would only be reasonable if additions balanced subtractions. Reserves are decreased by production and increased by exploration. In our little economy, perhaps we should deduct the value of the net amount of coal reserves that are depleted. The value of these reserves is difficult to determine, but one way of doing this is to estimate the cost of finding new reserves.[24] In the example, £10,000 of exploration effort resulted in 2,500 tons of new coal—a finding cost of £4 per ton. AJAX found 2,500 tons and used 5,000 tons for a net loss of 2,500 tons. Thus the 2,500 tons lost could be viewed as reducing reserves by £4 X 2500 = £10,000. Taking this deduction reduces our measure of output to £270,000 – £10,000 = £260,000. Excluding depletion is somewhat like saying that your income has gone up when you decide to sell all the furniture in your house! Your cash flow may increase but you are no richer for liquidating your assets.

What about pollution? In some sense pollution is conceptually simple. If one of the outputs has negative value then it should reduce the measure of net output. One problem is that there is no market and thus no obvious value to impute to the pollution. However, as we have seen, the nonexistence of a market does not mean the pollution has no value. There are methods for imputing the value of pollution. Take our example of the Edison Power Company. If the damage from sulfur dioxide is £100 per ton, then the 100 tons of emissions are causing £10,000 of damage. This reduces net output to £260,000 – £10,000 = £250,000.

What about expenditures on pollution abatement (Edison) and land reclamation (AJAX)? These are necessary expenses of doing business. Land reclamation expenses are necessary to prevent the land from degrading. The pollution control expenses for Edison are necessary to prevent even more pollution from being emitted. In much the same way that janitorial services for keeping the workplace tidy are legitimate inputs into production, these pollution control expenses are valid expenditures. Thus no further adjustment is needed.

In summary, we have seen that a conventional measure of gross output, GDP, starts at £300,000 in our economy. Depreciation of man-made capital, depletion of natural resources, and damage from pollution reduce this to £250,000. Table 20.3 summarizes this. Although our numbers here are fabricated, these adjustments can be significant in reality. In fact, Repetto et al. (1989) examined GDP numbers for several resource-exporting developing countries.[25] They conclude that on the basis of conventionally measured GDP figures these countries appear to be growing rapidly, but in fact they are growing much more slowly. A significant portion of these economies is based on mining and forestry. When the value of depleted natural resources (such as forests) is included, the rates of growth are significantly reduced. To the extent public policy encourages depletion of natural resources, correcting the accounts (which are using in formulating public policy) can have significant policy implications.

Although our example may make the inclusion of the environment in national accounts appear straightforward, that is not the case. In the case of natural resources, a large issue is determining the value of resources in the ground or standing in forests. For pollution, it is ambient concentrations, which cause damage, and those concentrations are often imperfectly observed. This is compounded by the difficulties in determining damage from ambient pollution.

TABLE 20.3 Different Accounting Measures of Output

	Ajax	Edison	Total
Gross output (£)	100,000	300,000	400,000
Gross domestic product (GDP) (£)	100,000	200,000	300,000
Net domestic product (NDP) (£)	90,000	180,000	270,000
NDP with depletion (£)	80,000	180,000	260,000
NDP with depletion and pollution (£)	80,000	170,000	250,000

Many governments are very interested in extending their national accounts to include the environment, and as a result, have thought through many of the details necessary for the inclusion. The United Nations has proposed a System of Environmental and Economic Accounting (SEEA) as a "satellite system" to the conventional System of National Accounts (SNA). Similarly, the United States has proposed a "satellite system" termed the integrated environmental economic and satellite accounts (IEESA).[26] Undoubtedly, these companion accounting systems will undergo a great deal of maturation in the coming years.

Eco-Domestic Product for Mexico

The World Bank has attempted to adjust the standard GDP for Mexico for a variety of environmental factors, such as depletion of forests, soils, and oil as well as pollution. The result is reported in the following table (Adapted from Table 1 in Hamilton, 1994).

Table 20.4 Eco-domestic Product for Mexico, 1985 (Trillions of Pesos)

Gross domestic product (GDP)	47,392
Depreciation	5,331
Net domestic product (NNP)	42,061
Oil depletion	1,470
Net forest depletion	164
Deforestation losses	763
Eco-domestic product 1 (EDP1)	39,663
Soil erosion	449
Solid waste	197
Groundwater depletion	192
Water pollution	662
Air pollution	1,656
Eco-domestic product 2 (EDP2)	36,507

Note. Environmental and natural resource use lowers GDP very substantially.

SUMMARY

1. Productivity growth is defined as the rate of growth of output less the rate of growth of inputs into production. Both inputs and outputs should be measured in constant quality units. The rate of growth of inputs as a whole is a weighted average of the rates of growth of all inputs, with weights being value shares in cost. This definition of productivity growth corresponds to multifactor or total productivity growth.

2. Single factor productivity growth is defined as the rate of growth in quality-adjusted output less the rate of growth of a single input. The most common measure of single factor productivity growth is labor productivity growth.

3. Single factor productivity growth may be higher or lower than multifactor productivity growth, depending on changes that may occur in relative prices of inputs, or relative intensity of input use, among other things.

4. Standard measures of productivity omit the uses of environmental resources. To the extent that environmental resources have become more costly to use over the past few decades, measures of productivity growth that omit these resources will understate true multifactor productivity growth. This is particularly true for heavily polluting industries.

5. Gross domestic product is a conventional measure of output of an economy and consists of the value added by all of the productive enterprises in an economy. When capital depreciation is subtracted, net domestic product is obtained. The depletion of natural resources and damage to the environment are usually excluded from this measure. "Green" national accounts aim to correct this. With green accounts, net depletion of natural resources would be a deduction from the overall measure of output as would damage to the environment. A major problem with moving to green accounts is valuing resource depletion and environmental damage.

PROBLEMS

1. In the example of the AJAX coal mining company and the Edison Electricity company, suppose there was no law requiring reclamation of the land after coal mining. Thus the coal mining company had no expenditures for land reclamation. The damage to the land is just as serious, and approximately equal to twice what is now spent on land reclamation. What would the net domestic product (NDP) be before the reclamation law, taking into account natural resource depletion and environmental degradation? Explain.

2. How does Figure 20.2 support the following statement: "Looking at how countries of different income at any point in time supply environmental quality (the environmental Kuznets curve) does not necessarily indicate how an individual country's environmental quality will change as that country's income rises."

3. The table below shows the use of labor and capital in the caviar industry of Beluga for two particular years. Also shown is the output of caviar and water pollution. Caviar output is shown in millions of eggs, pollution in tons of biological oxygen demand (BOD), labor in person-years, and capital in Rubles. The price of labor is constant at R 10,000 per person year, and capital services at R0.20 per Ruble of capital stock.

Calculate productivity growth for these 2 years (using value shares for 1997). In particular, calculate labor productivity growth and total factor productivity growth (excluding pollution). Assuming pollution damage is R10,000 per unit, calculate total factor productivity growth, including pollution (considering pollution as an input).

Year	Caviar output	Pollution	Labor	Capital stock
1997	100,000	20	50	1,000,000
1998	103,000	10	51	1,000,000

NOTES

1. The ratio of the percentage change in quantity demanded to the percentage change in income is of course the income elasticity of demand. If the income elasticity is negative, we have an inferior good; otherwise we have a normal good. If the income elasticity is greater than 1, we have a luxury good; if it is between 0 and 1, we have a necessary good.

2. Kriström and Riera (1996) review a number of studies, primarily European, and conclude that the evidence suggests a positive income elasticity of demand less than one, i.e., environmental quality is a normal good but not a luxury good. In an interesting study of voter actions on environmental issues in California, Kahn and Matsusaka (1997) conclude that the environment is a normal good for mean income individuals, but that some environmental goods are inferior for higher income individuals. One explanation for this is that some environmental goods, such as urban parks, are provided privately by higher income people. Thus this result does not necessarily mean that park-like open spaces are inferior, only that *publicly provided* open spaces may be inferior.

3. Kelly (2004) presents a theoretical model of what determines this shifting of supply and demand for environmental quality. See also Carson (2010), Andreoni and Levinson (2001) and Copeland and Taylor (2004). Kolstad (2006) discusses a similar structural relationship in the context of carbon emissions.

4. The data are found in the Global Environmental Monitoring System (GEMS), a joint effort of the United Nations Environment Program and the World Health Organization.

5. The interested reader is referred to Thompson and Strohm (1996) and Dinda (2004) for reviews of this literature and Grossman and Krueger (1995) for a quantitative estimation of a number of Kuznets curves for enviornmental quality. More detail is included in Shafik and Bandyopadhyay (1992) and Shafik (1994). Bohn and Deacon (2000) focus on poorly developed property rights in explaining how environmental quality changes as income changes; Kelly (2004) adapts a simple optimal growth model to show how the environmental Kuznets curve emerges from standard economic theory. See also Carson (2010). See Stern (2004) for a skeptical view of the environmental Kuznets curve.

6. The World Bank's 1992 World Development Report (World Bank, 1992) is devoted to the environment and development; there is considerable discussion in that document of the policy significance of environmental Kuznets curves.

7. Strictly speaking, productivity growth is the percentage increase in output, keeping inputs constant, thus excluding returns to scale in the measure of productivity growth. If the economy exhibits constant returns to scale, which empirical evidence suggests is generally the case, these two definitions are identical.

8. By quality adjusted, we mean taking into account any changes in the quality of inputs and outputs that may have occurred. Alternatively, simply keep quality fixed in making the calculation.

9. Jorgenson (1988) provides a readable overview of the growth evidence in the United States. Repetto et al. (1996) present a very accessible discussion of the role of environmental regulation in the productivity slowdown. Jorgenson and Wilcoxen (1990) estimate that environmental regulations in the United States are responsible for reducing conventionally measured economic growth (not productivity growth) in 1974–1985 from 2.7% per year to 2.5% per year. This estimate does not include the benefits of environmental regulations, only the cost.

10. Technology could make individual factors more productive. The representation of Eq. (20.1) is the most straightforward, where technology affects all factors equally ("neutral" technical change).

11. Using calculus, totally differentiate Eq. (20.1) to obtain Eq. (20.3): $dY = dA f + A f_L dL + A f_K dK = dA f + MP_L dL + MP_K dK$. Equation (20.5a) follows: $dA/A = dY/Y - s_L dL/L - s_K dK/K$.

12. The marginal product of labor is $A[f(L + \Delta L, K) - f(L,K)]/\Delta L$. In deriving Eq. (20.3), we have assumed that $f(L + \Delta L, K + \Delta K)$ is essentially the same as $f(L,K)$, which is true if ΔL and ΔK are very small. Calculus simplifies the derivation considerably.

13. We have condensed several steps into one in moving from Eq. (20.4) to Eq. (20.5). One assumption is that in equilibrium the price of a factor is equal to the value of marginal product. The second assumption is that with a constant cost industry, costs will be equal to the value of output.

14. A change in relative prices for inputs is not the only thing that can introduce a wedge between multifactor and single factor productivity growth. Technical change can be biased towards the use of a particular factor or towards saving the use of another factor.

15. The rate of change of use of environmental inputs relative to other inputs is also important in Eq. (20.8).

16. Refer to Repetto et al. (1996). In their study they impute a value to the emissions of the industry in question based on estimates of damage from pollution. Thus as pollution levels are reduced, the net value of output rises more rapidly than when pollution is neglected. This is not quite the same as changing the price of the environment over time, though conceptually very similar.

17. In a closely related analysis, Squires (1992) estimates productivity in a Pacific fishery, in which the environmental input of the stock of fish is usually excluded from measures of productivity. Although the stock of fish was sometimes growing and sometimes declining in his sample, his results clearly indicate the importance of including the fish stock in a measure of productivity growth.

18. In economics, there is a distinction among invention, innovation, and diffusion, a distinction generally ascribed to Joseph Schumpeter, an economist from the first half of the twentieth century. Invention involves the creation of new technological possibilities; innovation involves the commercialization of new technologies; and diffusion involves the actual adoption and use (by consumers and firms) of commercially available products.

19. Popp (2002) conducts an interesting study of the effect of energy prices on new U.S. private patents in several energy technology sectors. He concludes that patenting responds to relative prices. He also concludes that government funded R&D has a weakly negative to neutral effect on private patents. Newell et al. (1999), discussed in the text, also find evidence of the induced innovation hypothesis.

20. Refer to Nordhaus (2002) and Goulder and Mathai (2000).

21. National accounts are used by a very diverse set of people and institutions. For example, investors use national accounts to gauge profitability of different industries. Demand for output of specific industries (e.g., automobiles) may be highly correlated with the health of the overall economy.

22. When a firm produces goods that go into inventory, the value of those inventory additions increases measures of output. When goods are drawn from inventory and sold, there is no addition to measures of output.

23. The United States Department of Commerce (1994a) points out that in the United States in the early 1940s, depletion was deducted from measures of output. This was dropped in 1947 because of the omission of explicit treatment of additions to reserves.

24. The marginal (not average) cost of finding new reserves is equal to the marginal value of new reserves only if the firm is efficiently exploring.

25. See Crowards (1996) for an example of adjusting for resource depletion in the national accounts of Zimbabwe.

26. Peskin (1976) provides an early discussion of steps needed to extend national accounts to the environment. More recently, the U.S. National Academy of Sciences examined the question (Abraham and Mackie, 2005; Nordhaus and Kokkelenberg, 1999;). For a treatment by government offices responsible for national accounting, see United States Department of Commerce (1994a) and United Nations (2003). See also several chapters on the topic in Jorgenson et al (2006).

REFERENCES

Abraham, Katherine G. and Christopher Mackie (Eds.), *Beyond the Market: Designing Nonmarket Accounts for the United States*, (National Academies Press, Washington, DC, 2005).

Abrams, B. and M. Schmitz, "The 'Crowding-Out' Effect of Government Transfers on Private Charitable Contribution," *Public Choice, 33*:29–41 (1978).

Adar, Zvi and James M. Griffin, "Uncertainty and the Choice of Pollution Control Instruments," *J. Environ. Econ. Mgmt., 3*:178–188 (1976).

Ainslie, George W., *Picoeconomics* (Cambridge University Press, Cambridge, England, 1992).

Aivazian, Vadouj A. and Jeffrey L. Callen, "The Coase Theorem and the Empty Core," *J. Law Econ., 24*:175–181 (1981).

Akerlof, George, "The Market for Lemons: Quality Uncertainty and the Market Mechanism," *Quart. J. Econ., 84*:488–500 (1970).

Alberini, Anna and Alan Krupnick, "Cost of Illness and Willingness to Pay Estimates of Improved Air Quality: Evidence from Taiwan," *Land Econ. 76*:37–53 (2000).

Anderson, J. W., "The Kyoto Protocol on Climate Change: Background, Unresolved Issues and Next Steps," Resources for the Future Discussion Paper (Resources for the Future, Washington, DC, January 1998).

Andreoni, James, "Impure Altruism and Contributions to Public Goods—A Theory of Warm-Glow Giving," *Econ. J., 100*:464–477 (1990).

Angelini, Fabio, "Glossary of Terms and Events Relevant to European Community Environmental Law," *Ecolog. Law Quart., 20*:177–196 (1993).

Arora, Seema and Timothy N. Cason, "An Experiment in Voluntary Environmental Regulation: Participation in EPA's 33/50 Program," *J. Environ. Econ. Mgmt., 28*:271–286 (1995).

Arora, Seema and Shubhashish Gangopadhyay, "Towards a Theoretical Model of Voluntary Overcompliance," *J. Econ. Behav. and Org., 28*:289–309 (1995).

Arrow, Kenneth J., *Social Choice and Individual Values* (Wiley, New York, 1951).

Arrow, Kenneth J., *Social Choice and Individual Values*, 2nd Ed. (Yale University Press, New Haven, CT, 1963).

Arrow, Kenneth J. and Anthony C. Fisher, "Environmental Preservation, Uncertainty, and Irreversibility," *Quart. J. Econ., 88*:312–319 (1974).

Arrow, Kenneth and Robert Lind, "Uncertainty and Evaluation of Public Investment Decisions," *Am. Econ. Rev., 60*:364–378 (1970).

Arrow, K.J., W.R. Cline, K-G Maler, M. Munasinghe, R. Squiteri, and J.E. Stiglitz, "Intertemporal Equity, Discounting and Economic Efficiency," Chapter 4 in *Intergovernmental Panel on Climate Change, Climate Change 1995: Economic and Social Dimensions of Climate Change* (Cambridge University Press, Cambridge, 1996).

Ashby, Eric and Mary Anderson, *The Politics of Clean Air* (Oxford University Press, Oxford, England, 1981).

Atkinson, Scott E., "Marketable Pollution Permits Acid Rain Externalities," *Can. J. Econ., 16*:704–722 (1983).

Atkinson, Scott E. and Donald H. Lewis, "A Cost-Effectiveness Analysis of Alternative Air Quality Control Strategies," *J. Environ. Econ. Mgmt.,* **1**:237–250 (1974).

Atkinson, Scott E. and T. H. Tietenberg, "The Empirical Properties of Two Classes of Designs for Transferable Discharge Permit Markets," *J. Environ. Econ. Mgmt.,* **9**:101–121 (1982).

Averchenkov, Alexander, Alexander Golub, Konstantin Gofman, and Vladimir Groshev, "The System of Environmental Funds in the Russian Federation," in OECD Centre for Co-Operation with the Economies in Transition, *Environmental Funds in Economies in Transition* (OECD, Paris, 1995).

Barnett, A. H., "The Pigouvian Tax Rule under Monopoly," *Am. Econ. Rev.,* **70**:1037–1041 (1980).

Barnett, Harold J. and Chandler Morse, *Scarcity and Growth* (Johns Hopkins University Press, Baltimore, 1963).

Baron, David P., "Design of Regulatory Mechanisms and Institutions," in R. Schmalensee and R. Willig (Eds.), *Handbook of Industrial Organization* (North-Holland, Amsterdam, 1989).

Baron, David P., "A Positive Theory of Moral Management, Social Pressure and Corporate Social Performance," *J. Econ. Mgmt Strategy,* **18**:7–43 (2009).

Baron, David P. and David Besanko, "Regulation, Asymmetric Information and Auditing," *Rand J. Econ.,* **15**:447–470 (1984).

Barrett, Scott, "Self-Enforcing International Environmental Agreements," *Oxford Econ. Papers,* **46**:878–894 (1994).

Barrett, Scott, "The Strategy of Trade Sanctions in International Environmental Agreements," *Res. Energy Econ.,* **19**:345–362 (1997).

Barrett, Scott, "Montreal versus Kyoto," pp. 192–219 in Inge Kaul, Isabelle Grunberg and Marc A. Stern (Eds.), *Global Public Goods* (Oxford University Press, New York, 1999).

Barrett, Scott, *Environment and Statecraft* (Oxford University Press, Oxford, 2003).

Barrett, Scott, "Climate Treaties," *Oxford Rev. Econ. Policy,* **24**:239–258 (2008).

Barrett, Scott and John Clark, "Danish Bottles (A)," [Case Study] (World Resources Institute, Washington, DC, 1992) [Available at www.bellinnovation.org].

Bartik, Timothy J., "The Estimation of Demand Parameters in Hedonic Price Models," *J. Polit. Econ.,* **95**:81–88 (1987).

Bartik, Timothy J., "Evaluating the Benefits of Non-marginal Reductions in Pollution Using Information on Defensive Expenditures," *J. Environ. Econ. Mgmt.,* **15**:111–127 (1988).

Bator, F. M., "The Anatomy of Market Failure," *Quart. J. Econ.,* **72**:351–379 (1958).

Baumol, William J. and David F. Bradford, "Detrimental Externalities and Nonconvexities of the Production Set," *Economica,* **39**:160–176 (1972).

Baumol, William J. and Wallace E. Oates, *The Theory of Environmental Policy,* 2nd Ed. (Cambridge University Press, Cambridge, England, 1988).

Bayless, Mark, "Measuring the Benefits of Air Quality Improvements: A Hedonic Salary Approach," *J. Environ. Econ. Mgmt.,* **9**:81–99 (1982).

Beard, T. Randolph, "Bankruptcy and Care Choice," *Rand J. Econ.,* **21**:626–634 (1990).

Bedell, Christine, "Feedlot Price: $1.82/Month," Santa Maria (California) *Times,* pp. A-l and A-6 (June 28, 1996).

Belton, Valerie and Theodor J. Stewart, *Mulltipe Criteria Decision Analysis* (Kluwer, Boston, 2002).

Bergson, A., "A Reformulation of Certain Aspects of Welfare Economics," *Quart. J. Econ.,* **52**:314–344 (1938).

Bergstrom, T. C., D. L. Rubinfeld, and P. Shapiro, "Micro-based Estimates of Demand Functions for Local School Expenditures," *Econometrica,* **50**:1183–1206 (1982).

Bergstrom, Theodore, Lawrence Blume, and Hal Varian, "On the Private Provision of Public Goods," *J. Public Econ.,* **29**:25–49 (1986).

Bernheim, D. and A. Rangel, "Beyond Revealed Preference: Choice—Theoretic Foundtions for Behavioral Welfare Economics," *Quart. J. Econ.,* **124**:51–104 (2009).

Binkley, Clark S. and W. Michael Hanemann, "The Recreation Benefits of Water Quality Improvement: Analysis of Day Trips in an Urban Setting," U.S. Environmental Protection Agency Report EPA-600/5-78-010, Washington, DC (June 1978).

Bird, Lori, Claire Kreycik, and Barry Friedman, "Green Power Marketing in the United States: A Status Report," 11th Ed. Report NREL/TP-6A2-44094 (National Renewable Energy Laboratory, Golden, CO, October 2008).

Bishop, Richard C., "Endangered Species and Uncertainty: The Economics of the Safe Minimum Standard," *Am. J. Ag. Econ.*, **60**:10–18 (1978).

Bishop, Richard C., Thomas A. Heberlein, and Mary Jo Kealy, "Contingent Valuation of Environmental Assets: Comparisons with a Simulated Market," *Natural Resources J.,* **23**:619–633 (1983).

Boardman, Anthony E., David H. Greenberg, Aidan R. Vining, and David L. Weimer, *Cost–Benefit Analysis: Concepts and Practice* (Prentice-Hall, Upper Saddle River, NJ, 2006).

Bockstael, Nancy E., W. Michael Hanemann, and Cathy L. Kling, "Modeling Recreational Demand in a Multiple Site Framework," *Water Resources Res.,* **23**:951–960 (1987).

Bockstael, Nancy E., Kenneth E. McConnell, and Ivar E. Strand, "Benefits from Improvements in Chesapeake Bay Water Quality," Vol. III of "Benefit Analysis Using Indirect or Imputed Market Methods," U.S. Environmental Protection Agency Report EPA-230-10-89-070 (Washington, DC, October 1989).

Bockstael, Nancy E., Kenneth E. McConnell, and Ivar Strand, "Recreation," in J.B. Braden and C.D. Kolstad (Eds.), *Measuring the Demand for Environmental Quality* (North-Holland, Amsterdam, 1991).

Bohm, Peter, "Estimating Demand for Public Goods: An Experiment," *Eur. Econ. Rev.,* **3**:111–130 (1972).

Bohn, Henning and Robert T. Deacon, "Ownership Risk, Investment, and the Use of Natural Resources," *Am. Econ. Rev.*, **90**:526–549 (2000).

Bovenberg, A. Lans, "Green Tax Reforms and the Double Dividend: An Updated Reader's Guide," *Int. Tax and Public Finance*, **6**:421–443 (1999).

Bovenberg, A. Lans and Ruud A. de Mooij, "Environmental Levies and Distortionary Taxation," *Am. Econ. Rev.,* **84**:1085–1089 (1994).

Bower, Blair T., "Mixed Implementation Incentive Systems for Water Quality Management in France, the Ruhr, and the United States," pp. 212–227 in P.B. Downing and K. Hanf (Eds.), *International Comparisons in Implementing Pollution Laws* (Kluwer-Nijhoff, Boston, 1983).

Boyce, Rebecca R., Thomas C. Brown, Gary H. McClelland, George L. Peterson, and William D. Schulze, "An Experimental Examination of Intrinsic Values as a Source of the WTA-WTP Disparity," *Am. Econ. Rev.,* **82**:1366–1373 (1992).

Boyle, Kevin J., "Contingent Valuation in Practice," Chapter 5 in P.A. Champ, K.J. Boyle, and T.C. Brown, *A Primer on Nonmarket Valuation* (Kluwer, Dordrecht, 2003).

Boyle, Melissa A. and Katherine A. Kiel, "A Survey of House Price Hedonic Studies of the Impact of Environmental Externalities," *J. Real Estate Lit.,* **9**:117 (2001).

Braden, John B. and Charles D. Kolstad, *Measuring the Demand for Environmental Quality* (North-Holland, Amsterdam, 1991).

Braden, John B. and Stef Proost, "Economic Assessment of Policies for Combating Tropospheric Ozone in Europe and the United States," pp. 365–413 in J.B. Braden, H. Folmer, and T.S. Ulen (Eds.), *Environmental Policy with Political and Economic Integration: The European Union and the United States* (Edward Elgar, Cheltenham, England, 1996).

Brander, James A. and Barbara J. Spencer, "Export Subsidies and International Market Share Rivalry," *J. Int. Econ.,* **18**:83–100 (1985).

Bresnahan, B. W., M. Dickie, and S. Gerking, "Averting Behavior and Urban Air Pollution," *Land Econ.,* **73**:340–357 (1997).

Bresnahan, Timothy F. and Dennis A. Yao, "The Nonpecuniary Costs of Automobile Emissions Standards," *Rand J. Econ.,* **16**:437–455 (1985).

Broadway, Robin W. and David E. Wildasin, *Public Sector Economics,* 2nd Ed. (Little, Brown, Boston, 1984).

Brookshire, David S., Mark A. Thayer, William D. Schulze, and Ralph d'Arge, "Valuing Public Goods: A Comparison of Survey and Hedonic Approaches," *Am. Econ. Rev.,* **72**:165–177 (1982).

Brown, Gardner, "Estimating Non-Market Economic Losses from Oil Spills: Amoco Cadiz, Steuart Transportation, Zoe Colocotroni" (unpublished manuscript, Department of Economics, University of Washington, Seattle, undated).

Brown, Gardner M., Jr., Richard Congar, and Elizabeth A. Wilman, "Recreation: Tourists and Residents," Chapter 4 in U.S. National Ocean Service, *Assessing the Social Costs of Oil Spills: The Amoco Cadiz Case Study,* National Oceanic and Atmospheric Administration Report, NTIS PB84-100536, Washington, DC (July 1983).

Brown, James N. and Harvey S. Rosen, "On the Estimation of Structural Hedonic Price Models," *Econometrica,* **50**:765–768 (1982).

Browning, Edgar K., "On the Marginal Welfare Cost of Taxation," *Am. Econ. Rev.,* **77**:11–23 (1987).

Bruzelius, Nils, *The Value of Travel Time: Theory and Measurement* (Croom Helm, London, 1979).

Buchanan, James M., "External Diseconomies, Corrective Taxes, and Market Structure," *Am. Econ. Rev.,* **59**:174–77 (1969).

Buchanan, James M. and William Craig Stubblebine, "Externality," *Economica,* **29**:371–384 (1962).

Buchanan, James M. and Gordon Tullock, "Polluters Profits and Political Response: Direct Controls Versus Taxes," *Am. Econ. Rev.,* **65**:139–147 (1975).

Bulckaen, Fabrizio, "Emissions Charge and Asymmetric Information: Consistently a Problem?," *J. Environ. Econ. Mgmt.,* **34**:100–106 (1997).

Burger, Nicholas and Charles Kolstad, "Voluntary Public Goods Provision, Coalition Formation, and Uncertainty" (National Bureau of Economic Research Working Paper W15543, Cambridge, Mass, 2009).

Burger, Nicholas and John Lynham, "Betting on Weight Loss…and Losing: Personal Gambles as Commitment Mechanisms" (unpublished manuscript, Dept. of Economics, University of California, Santa Barbara, 2008).

Cabe, Richard and Joseph A. Herriges, "The Regulation of Non-Point-Source Pollution Under Imperfect and Asymmetric Information," *J. Environ. Econ. Mgmt.,* **22**:134–146 (1992).

Calabresi, Guido "Transaction Costs, Resource Allocation and Liability Rules—A Comment," *J. Law Econ.,* **11**:67–73 (1968).

Carlton, Dennis W. and Glenn C. Loury, "The Limitations of Pigouvian Taxes as a Long-run Remedy for Externalities," *Quart. J. Econ.,* **95**:559–566 (1980).

Carlton, Dennis W. and Jeffrey M. Perloff, *Modern Industrial Organization,* 4th Ed. (Pearson Addison-Wesley, New York, 2004).

Carson, Richard, "Constructed Markets," in J. B. Braden and C. D. Kolstad (Eds.), *Measuring the Demand for Environmental Quality* (North-Holland, Amsterdam, 1991).

Carson, Richard T. *Contingent Valuation: A Comprehensive Bibliography and History* (Edward Elgar, Northampton, MA, forthcoming, 2010).

Carson, Richard T., "The Environmental Kuznets Curve: Seeking Empirical Regularity and Theoretical Structure," *Rev. Environ. Econ. Policy,* **4**:3–23 (2010).

Carson, Richard T. and W. Michael Hanemann, "Contingent Valuation," Chapter 17 in K.G. Maler and J.R. Vincent (Eds.), *Handbook of Environmental Economics* (North Holland, Amsterdam, 2005).

Carson, Richard T. and Robert C. Mitchell, "The Issue of Scope in Contingent Valuation Studies," *Am. J. Ag. Econ.,* **75**:1263–1267 (1993).

Carson, Richard T., Leanne Wilks, and David Imber, "Valuing the Preservation of Australia's Kakadu Conservation Zone," *Oxford Econ. Papers,* **46**:727–749 (1994).

Champ, Patricia A., R. C. Bishop, T. C. Brown, and D. W. McCollum, "Using Donation Mechanisms to Value Nonuse Benefits from Public Goods," *J. Environ. Econ. Mgmt,* **33**:151–162 (1997).

Champ, Patricia A., Kevin J. Boyle, and Thomas C. Brown, *A Primer on Nonmarket Valuation* (Kluwer, Dordrecht, 2003).

Chattopadhyay, Sudip, "Esimating the Demand for Air Quality: New Evidence Based on the Chicago Housing Market," *Land Econ.*, **75**:22–38 (1999).

Chichilnisky, Graciella, "North-South Trade and the Global Environment," *Am. Econ. Rev.*, **84**:851–874 (1994).

Christensen, Jon, "Unlikely Partners Create Plan to Save Ocean Habitat Along with Fishing," *New York Times* (8 August 2006).

Christiansen, V., "Which Commodity Taxes Should Supplement the Income Tax?," *J. Public Econ.*, **24**:195–220 (1984).

Clark, David E. and Leslie A. Nievers, "An Interregional Hedonic Analysis of Noxious Facility Impacts on Local Wages and Property Values," *J. Environ. Econ. Mgmt.*, **27**:235–253 (1994).

Clawson, Marion and Jack L. Knetsch, *Economics of Outdoor Recreation* (Johns Hopkins University Press, Baltimore, 1966).

Coase, R. H., "The Coase Theorem and the Empty Core: A Comment," *J. Law Econ.*, **24**:183–187 (1981).

Coase, Ronald H. "The Problem of Social Cost," *J. Law Econ.*, **3**:1–44 (1960).

Conrad, Jon M., *Resource Economics* (Cambridge University Press, Cambridge, England, 1999).

Conrad, Klaus and Catherine Morrison, "The Impact of Pollution Abatement Investment on Productivity Change: An Empirical Comparison of the U.S., Germany and Canada," *South. Econ. J.*, **55**:684–697 (1989).

Cook, Phillip J. and Daniel A. Graham, "The Demand for Insurance and Protection: The Case of Irreplaceable Commodities," *Quart. J. Econ.*, **91**:143–156 (1977).

Cooter, Robert D., "How the Law Circumvents Starrett's Nonconvexity," *J. Econ. Theory*, **22**:499–504 (1980).

Cooter, Robert D., "Coase Theorem," in J. Eatwell, M. Milgate, and P. Newman (Eds.), *The New Palgrave: A Dictionary of Economics* (Macmillan, London, 1987).

Cooter, Robert and Thomas Ulen, *Law and Economics*, 5th Ed. (Pearson/Addison-Wesley-Longman, Boston, 2008).

Copeland, Brian R., "Taxes versus Standards to Control Pollution in Imperfectly Competitive Markets," University of British Columbia Department of Economics Discussion Paper 91–03, Vancouver, BC, Canada (1992).

Copeland, Brian and Scott Taylor, "Trade, Growth and the Environment," *J. Econ. Lit.*, **42**:7–71 (2004).

Cornes, Richard and Todd Sandler, *The Theory of Externalities, Public Goods and Club Goods*, 2nd Ed. (Cambridge University Press, Cambridge, England 1996).

Costanza, Robert (Ed.), *Ecological Economics: The Science and Management of Sustainability* (Columbia University Press, New York, 1991).

Costello, Christopher, Steven Gaines, and John Lynham, "Can Catch Shares Prevent Fisheries Collapse?," *Science*, **321**:1678–1681 (2008).

Courant, Paul N. and Richard Porter, "Averting Expenditure and the Cost of Pollution," *J. Environ. Econ. Mgmt.*, **8**:321–329 (1981).

Coursey, Don L., John L. Hovis, and William D. Schulze, "The Disparity Between Willingness to Accept and Willingness to Pay Measures of Value," *Quart. J. Econ.*, **102**:679–690 (1987).

Court, Louis M., "Entrepreneurial and Consumer Demand Theories for Commodity Spectra," *Econometrica*, **9**:135–162 (1941).

Cremer, H. and F. Gahvari, "Second Best Taxation of Emissions and Polluting Goods," *J. Public Econ.*, **80**:169–197 (2001).

Crocker, Thomas, "The Structuring of Atmospheric Pollution Control Systems," pp. 61–86 in H. Wolozing (Ed.), *The Economics of Air Pollution* (Norton, New York, 1966).

Cropper, Maureen L. and Wallace E. Oates, "Environmental Economics: A Survey," *J. Econ. Lit.*, **30**:675–740 (1992).

Cropper, Maureen L., Sema K. Aydede, and Paul R. Portney, "Rates of Time Preference for Saving Lives," *Am. Econ. Rev. Papers Proc.,* **82**(2):469–472 (May 1992).

Cropper, Maureen L., Sema K. Aydede, and Paul R. Portney, "Preferences for Life Saving Programs: How the Public Discounts Time and Age," *J. Risk Uncertainty,* **8**:243–265 (1994).

Crowards, Tom M., "Natural Resource Accounting: A Case Study of Zimbabwe," *Environ. Res. Econ.,* **7**:213–241 (1996).

Cummings, Ronald G., Davis S. Brookshire, and William D. Schulze (Eds.), *Valuing Environmental Goods: An Assessment of the Contingent Valuation Method* (Rowman & Allanheld, NJ, 1986).

d'Arge, Ralph C., William D. Schulze, and David S. Brookshire, "Carbon Dioxide and Intergenerational Choice," *Am. Econ. Rev. Papers Proc.,* **72**(2):251–256 (May 1982).

Dahlman, Carl J., "The Problem of Externality," *J. Law Econ.,* **22**(1):141–162 (1979).

Dales, John, *Pollution, Property and Prices* (University of Toronto Press, Toronto, 1968).

Dasgupta, Partha, Peter Hammond, and Eric Maskin, "On Imperfect Information and Optimal Pollution Control," *Rev. Econ. Studies,* **47**:857–860 (1980).

Davis, R., "Recreation Planning as an Economic Problem," *Natural Resources. J.,* **3**:239–249 (1963).

Deacon, Robert and Charles Kolstad, "Valuing Beach Recreation Lost in Environmental Accidents," *J. Water Resources Planning Mgmt.,* **126**:374–381 (2000).

Deacon, Robert and Perry Shapiro, "Private Preference for Collective Goods Revealed Through Voting on Referenda," *Am. Econ. Rev.,* **65**:943–955 (1975).

Denicolò, Vincenzo, "Pollution-reducing Innovations Under Taxes or Permits," *Oxford Econ. Papers,* **51**:184–199 (1999).

Denicolò, Vincenzo, "A Signaling Model of Environmental Overcompliance," *J. Econ. Behav. Org.,* **68**:293–303 (2008).

Depres, Christophe, Gilles Grolleau, and Naoufel Mzoughi, "Contracting for Environmental Property Rights: The Case of Vittel," *Economica* **75**:412–34 (2008).

Deschenes, Olivier and Michael Greenstone, "The Economic Impacts of Climate Change: Evidence from Agricultural Output and Random Fluctuations in Weather," *Am. Econ. Rev.,* **97**:354–385 (2007).

Des Jardins, Joseph R., *Environmental Ethics: An Introduction to Environmental Philosophy,* 2nd Ed. (Wadsworth, Belmont, CA, 1997).

Desvousges, William H., F. Reed Johnson, Richard W. Dunford, Sara P. Hudson, K. Nicole Wilson, and Kevin J. Boyle, "Measuring Natural Resource Damages with Contingent Valuation: Tests of Validity and Reliability," in J. A. Hausman (Ed.), *Contingent Valuation: An Assessment* (North-Holland, Amsterdam, 1993).

Diamond, Peter A. and Jerry A. Hausman, "Contingent Valuation: Is Some Number Better than No Number?," *J. Econ. Perspect.,* **8**(4):45–64 (1994).

Dickie, Mark and Shelby Gerking, "Willingness to Pay for Ozone Control: Inferences from the Demand for Medical Care," *J. Environ. Econ. Mgmt.,* **21**:1–16 (1991).

Dillman, Don A., Jolene D. Smyth, and Leah Melani Christian, *Internet, Mail and Mixed Mode Surveys,* 3rd Ed. (John Wiley, Hoboken, NJ, 2009).

Dinda, Soumyananda, "Environmental Kuznets Curve Hypothesis: A Survey," *Ecolog. Econ.,* **49**:431–455 (2004).

Downing, Paul and William Watson, "The Economics of Enforcing Air Pollution Controls," *J. Environ. Econ. Mgmt.,* **1**:219–236 (1974).

Dreze, Jean, "Distribution Matters in Cost–Benefit Analysis: A Comment on K.A. Brekke," *J. Public Econ.,* **70**:485–488 (1998).

Driesen, David, "Design, Trading and Innovation," in Jody Freeman and Charles Kolstad (Eds.), *Moving to Markets in Environmental Regulation* (Oxford University Press, New York, 2007).

Duggan, John and Joanne Roberts, "Implementing the Efficient Allocation of Pollution," *Am. Econ. Rev.,* **92**:1070–1078 (2002).

Eckert, H., "Inspections, Warnings and Compliance: The Case of Petroleum Storage Regulation," *J. Environ. Econ. Mgmt.*, **47**:232–259 (2004).

Ederington, Josh, Arik Levinson, and Jenny Minier, "Footloose and Pollution-Free," *Rev. Econ. Stat.*, **87**:92–99 (2005).

Ekeland, Ivar, James J. Heckman, and Lars Nesheim, "Identification and Estimation of Hedonic Models," *J. Polit. Econ.*, **112**:S60–S109 (2004).

Ellerman, A. Denny and Barbara K. Buchner, "The European Union Emissions Trading Scheme: Origins, Allocation, and Early Results," *Rev. Environ. Econ. Policy*, **1**:66–87 (2007).

Epple, Dennis, "Hedonic Prices and Implicit Markets: Estimating Demand and Supply Functions for Differentiated Products," *J. Pol. Econ.*, **95**:59–80 (1987).

Epple, Dennis and Holger Sieg, "Estimating Equilibrium Models of Local Jurisdictions," *J. Pol. Econ.* **107**:645–681 (1999).

Eskeland, Gunnar S., "A Presumptive Pigovian Tax on Gasoline: Complementing Regulation to Mimic an Emission Fee," *World Bank Econ. Rev.*, **8**:373–394 (1994).

Eskeland, Gunnar S. and Ann E. Harrison, "Moving to Greenher Pastures? Multinationals and the Pollution Haven Hypothesis," *J. Dev. Econ.*, **70**:1–23 (2003).

Esty, Daniel C., *Greening the Gatt: Trade, Environment, and the Future* (Institute for International Economics, Washington, DC, 1994).

Faber, Malte, "How To Be an Ecological Economist," *Ecolog. Econ.*, **66**:1–7 (2008).

Farber, Daniel A. and Robert E. Hudec, "GATT Legal Restraints on Domestic Environmental Regulations," in J. Bhagwati and R. Hudec (Eds.), *Fair Trade and Harmonization,* (MIT Press, Cambridge, MA, 1996).

Ferber, R. and W. Z. Hirsch, "Social Experimentation and Economic Policy: A Survey," *J. Econ. Lit.*, **16**:1379–1414 (1979).

Fernandez, L. F., A. A. Keller, "Cost Benefit Analysis of MTBE and Alternative Gasoline Formulations," *Environ. Sci. and Policy*, **3**:173–188 (2000).

Feshbach, Murray and Alfred Friendly, Jr., *Ecocide in the USSR* (Basic Books, New York, 1992).

Fisher, Anthony C. and W. Michael Hanemann, "Option Value and the Extinction of Species," pp. 169–190 in V. Kerry Smith (Ed.), *Advances in Applied Micro-Economics,* Vol. 4 (JAI Press, Greenwich, CT, 1986).

Fisher, Anthony C., John V. Krutilla, and Charles J. Cicchetti, "The Economics of Environmental Preservation: A Theoretical and Empirical Analysis," *Am. Econ. Rev.*, **62**:605–619 (1972).

Folmer, Henk, Pierre van Mouche, and Shannon Ragland, "Interconnected Games and International Environmental Problems," *Environ. Res. Econ.*, **3**:313–335 (1993).

Food and Agriculture Organization of the United Nations, *State of the World's Forests, 2009* (FAO, Rome, 2009).

Foster, Vivien and Robert W. Hahn, "Designing More Efficient Markets: Lessons from Los Angeles Smog Control," *J. Law Econ.*, **38**:19–48 (1995).

Freeman, A. Myrick III, *The Benefits of Environmental Improvement* (Johns Hopkins University Press, Baltimore, 1979).

Freeman, A. Myrick III, "Depletable Externalities and Pigouvian Taxation," *J. Environ. Econ. Mgmt.*, **11**:173–179 (1984).

Freeman, A. Myrick III, *The Measurement of Environmental and Resource Values: Theory and Methods* (Resources for the Future, Washington, DC, 1993).

Freeman, Paul K. and Howard Kunreuther, *Managing Environmental Risk through Insurance* (Kluwer, Boston, 1997).

Freixas, X., R. Guesnerie, and J. Tirole, "Planning Under Incomplete Information and the Ratchet Effect," *Rev. Econ. Studies*, **52**:173–192 (1985).

Friedman, Milton, *Essays in Positive Economics* (University of Chicago Press, Chicago, 1953).

Fullerton, Don (Ed.), *The Economics of Pollution Havens* (Edward Elgar, Cheltenham, England, 2006).

Fullerton, Don and Thomas C. Kinnaman, "Household Responses to Pricing Garbage by the Bag," *Am. Econ. Rev.,* **86**:971–984 (1996).

Gamper-Rabindran, Shanti, "Did the EPA's Voluntary Industrial Toxics Program Reduce Plants' Emissions? A GIS Analysis of Distributional Impacts and a By-Media Analysis of Substitution," *J. Environ. Econ. Mgmt.,* **52**:391–410 (2006).

Geanakoplos, John, "Three Brief Proofs of Arrow's Impossibility Theorem," *Econ. Theory,* **26**:211–215 (2005).

Gerard, David and Lester B. Lave, "Implementing Technology Forcing Policies: The 1970 Clean Air Act Amendments and the Introduction of Advanced Automotive Emissions Controls in the United States," *Technolog. Forecasting Soc. Change,* **72**:761–778 (2005).

Gerking, Shelby and Linda Stanley, "An Economic Analysis of Air Pollution and Health: The Case of St. Louis," *Rev. Econ. Stat.,* **68**:115–121 (1986).

Gersbach, Hans and Amihai Glazer, "Markets and Regulatory Hold-up Problems," *J. Environ. Econ. Mgmt.,* **37**:151–164 (1999).

Gollier, C., B. Jullien, and N. Treich, "Scientific Progress and Irreversibility: An Economic Interpretation of the 'Precautionary Principle,'" *J. Public Econ.,* **75**:229–253 (2000).

Goodman, Allen C., "Andrew Court and the Invention of Hedonic Price Analysis," *J. Urban Econ.,* **44**:291–298 (1998).

Goulder, L. H. and K. Mathai, "Optimal CO_2 Abatement in the Presence of Induced Technical Change," *J. Environ. Econ. Mgmt.,* **39**:1–38 (2000).

Goulder, Lawrence H., "Environmental Taxation and the Double Dividend: A Reader's Guide," *Int. Tax and Public Finance,* **2**:157–183 (1995).

Goulder, Lawrence H., Ian W. H. Parry, and Dallas Burtraw, "Revenue-Raising Versus Other Approaches to Environmental Protection: The Critical Significance of Preexisting Tax Distortions," *Rand J. Econ.,* **28**:708–731 (1997).

Graham, Daniel A., "Cost-Benefit Analysis Under Uncertainty," *Am. Econ. Rev.,* **71**:715–725 (1981).

Gramlich, Edward M., *A Guide to Benefit–Cost Analysis,* 2nd Ed. (Waveland Press, Long Grove, IL, 1990).

Gray, Wayne B. and Mary E. Deily, "Compliance and Enforcement: Air Pollution Regulation in the US Steel Industry," *J. Environ. Econ. Mgmt.,* **31**:96–111 (1996).

Green, Leonard and Joel Myerson, "Exponential versus Hyperbolic Discounting of Delayed Outcomes: Risk and Waiting Time," *Am. Zoologist,* **36**:496–505 (1996).

Greene, William, *Econometric Analysis* (Prentice-Hall, Upper Saddle River, NJ, 2007).

Griliches, Zvi, "Hedonic Price Indexes for Automobiles: An Econometric Analysis of Quality Change," in Zvi Griliches (Ed.), *Price Indexes and Quality Change: Studies in New Methods of Measurement* (Harvard University Press, Cambridge, MA, 1971).

Grossman, Gene M. and Alan B. Krueger, "Economic Growth and the Environment," *Quart. J. Econ.,* **112**:353–377 (1995).

Gupta, Usha, "Valuation of Urban Air Pollution: A Case Study of Kanpur City in India," *Environ. Res. Econ.,* **41**:315–326 (2008).

Hadker, Nandini, Sudhir Sharma, Ashish David, and T. R. Muraleedharan, "Willingness-to-pay for Borivli National Park: Evidence from a Contingent Valuation," *Ecolog. Econ.,* **21**:105–122 (1997).

Hahn, Robert W., "Economic Prescriptions for Environmental Problems: How the Patient Followed the Doctor's Orders," *J. Econ. Perspect.,* **3**:95–114 (1989).

Hahn, Robert W., "Market Power and Transferable Property Rights," *Quart. J. Econ.,* **99**:753–765 (1984).

Hahn, Robert W. and Gordon Hester, "Where Did All the Markets Go?: An Analysis of EPA's Emission Trading Program," *Yale J. Reg.,* **6**:109–153 (1989).

Hahn, Robert W. and Roger G. Noll, "Designing a Market for Tradeable Emissions Permits," Chapter 7 in W. Magat (Ed.), *Reform of Environmental Regulation* (Ballinger, Cambridge, MA, 1982).

Hamilton, Kirk, "Green Adjustments to GDP," *Resources Policy,* **20**:155–168 (1994).

Hammack, J. and G. M. Brown, Jr., *Waterfowl and Wetlands: Towards Bioeconomic Analysis* (Johns Hopkins University Press, Baltimore, 1974).

Hanemann, W. Michael, "Information and the Concept of Option Value," *J. Environ. Econ. Mgmt.,* **16**:23–37 (1989).

Hanemann, W. Michael, "Willingness to Pay and Willingness to Accept: How Much Can They Differ?," *Am. Econ. Rev.,* **81**:635–647 (1991).

Hanemann, W. Michael, "Valuing the Environment through Contingent Valuation," *J. Econ. Perspect.,* **8**(4):19–43 (1994).

Hardin, Garrett, "Tragedy of the Commons," *Sci.,* **162**:1243–1248 (1968).

Harford, Jon, "Averting Behavior and the Benefits of Reduced Soiling," *J. Environ. Econ. Mgmt.,* **11**:296–302 (1984).

Harford, Jon D., "Firm Behavior Under Imperfectly Enforceable Pollution Standards and Taxes," *J. Environ. Econ. Mgmt.,* **5**:26–43 (1978).

Harford, Jon D., "Self-Reporting of Pollution and the Firm's Behavior Under Imperfectly Enforceable Regulations," *J. Environ. Econ. Mgmt.,* **14**:293–303 (1987).

Harford, Jon D. and Winston Harrington, "A Reconsideration of Enforcement Leverage When Penalties Are Restricted," *J. Public Econ.,* **45**:391–395 (1991).

Harr, Jonathan, *A Civil Action* (Random House, New York, 1995).

Harrington, Winston, "Enforcement Leverage When Penalties Are Restricted," *J. Public Econ.,* **37**:29–53 (1988).

Harrison, David Jr. and Daniel L. Rubinfeld, "Hedonic Housing Prices and the Demand for Clean Air," *J. Environ. Econ. Mgmt.,* **5**:81–102 (1978).

Harrison, Glenn W. and John A. List, "Field Experiments," *J. Econ. Lit.,* **42**:1009–1055 (2004).

Harvey, Charles M., "The Reasonableness of Non-Constant Discounting," *J. Public Econ.,* **53**:31–51 (1994).

Hausman, J. A. (Ed.), *Contingent Valuation: An Assessment* (North-Holland, Amsterdam, 1993).

Hausman, Jerry A., Gregory K. Leonard, and Daniel McFadden, "A Utility-Consistent, Combined Discrete Choice and Count Data Model Assessing Recreational Use Loses Due to Natural Resource Damage," *J. Public Econ.,* **56**:1–30 (1995).

Hausman, Jerry A. and David A. Wise (Eds.), *Social Experimentation* (University of Chicago Press, Chicago, 1985).

Hawken, Paul, Amory Lovins, and L. Hunter Lovins, *Natural Capitalism* (Little Brown, Boston, 1999).

Hay, Bruce L., Robert N. Stavins, and Richard H. K. Vietor (Eds.), *Environmental Protection and the Social Responsibility of Firms: Perspectives from Law, Economics, and Business* (Resources for the Future, Washington, DC, 2005).

Head, J. G., "Public Goods and Public Policy," *Public Finance,* **17**:197–219 (1962).

Heal, Geoffrey, *When Principles Pay: Corporate Social Responsibility and the Bottom Line* (Columbia University Press, New York, 2008).

Helland, Eric, "The Enforcement of Pollution Control Laws: Inspections, Violations and Self-Reporting," *Rev. Econ. Stat.,* **80**:141–153 (1998).

Heller, Walter P. and David A. Starrett, "On the Nature of Externalities," in Steven A. Y. Lin (Ed.), *Theory and Measurement of Economic Externalities* (Academic Press, New York, 1976).

Hindricks, Jean and Gareth D. Myles, *Intermediate Public Economics* (MIT Press, Cambridge, MA., 2006).

Henry, Claude, "Investment Decisions under Uncertainty: The 'Irreversibility Effect,'" *Am. Econ. Rev.,* **64**:1006–1012 (1974).

Heyes, A. and N. Rickman, "Regulatory Dealing—Revisiting the Harrington Paradox," *J. Public Econ.,* **72**:361–378 (1999).

Heyes, A. G., "Cutting Environmental Penalties to Protect the Environment," *J. Public Econ.,* **60**:251–265 (1996).

Hicks, John R., "The Valuation of the Social Income," *Economica,* **7**:105–124 (1940).

Hirschleifer, Jack, "From Weakest-Link to Best-Shot: The Voluntary Provision of Public Goods," *Public Choice*, **41**:371–386 (1983).

Hoel, Michael, "International Environment Conventions: The Case of Uniform Reduction of Emissions," *Environ. Res. Econ.,* **2**:141–159 (1992).

Hoffman, Elizabeth and Matthew L. Spitzer, "The Coase Theorem: Some Experimental Tests," *J. Law Econ.,* **25**:73–98 (1982).

Holmström, Bengt, "Moral Hazard in Teams," *Bell J. Econ.,* **13**:324–340 (1982).

Horowitz, John and Kenneth E. McConnell, "A Review of WTA/WTP Studies," *J. Environ. Econ. Mgmt.,* **44**:426–447 (2002).

Hourcade, J. C., R. Richels, J. Robinson, W. Chandler, O. Davidson, J. Edmonds, D. Finon, M. Grubb, K. Halsnaes, K. Hogan, M. Jaccard, F. Krause, E. La Rovere, W. D. Montgomery, P. Nastari, A. Pegov, K. Richards, L. Schrattenholzer, D. Siniscalco, P. R. Shukla, Y. Sokuna, P. Sturm, and A. Tudini "A Review of Mitigation Cost Studies," in J. Bruce, H. Lee, and E. Haites (Eds.), *Climate Change 1995: Economic and Social Dimensions of Climate Change* (Cambridge University Press for the Intergovernmental Panel on Climate Change, Cambridge, England, 1996).

Howe, Charles W., "Taxes versus Tradable Discharge Permits: A Review in the Light of the U.S. and European Experience," *Environ. Res. Econ.,* **4**:151–169 (1994).

Huppes, Gjalt and Robert A. Kagan, "Market-Oriented Regulation of Environmental Problems in the Netherlands," *Law Policy,* **11**:215–239 (1989).

Husted, Steven and Michael Melvin, *International Economics,* 8th Ed. (Prentice Hall, Englewood Cliffs, NJ, 2010).

Intergovernmental Panel on Climate Change, *Climate Change 2007: Synthesis Report: Summary for Policymakers* (IPCC, Geneva, 2007).

Isaac, R. M. and J. M. Walker, "Group Size Effects in Public Goods Provision: The Voluntary Contributions Mechanism." *Quart. J. Econ.,* **103**:179–199 (1988).

Jacoby, Henry D. and A. Denny Ellerman, "The Safety Valve and Climate Policy," *Energy Policy*, **32**:481–491 (2004).

Jaffe, Adam B., Steven R. Peterson, Paul R. Portney, and Robert Stavins, "Environmental Regulation and the Competitiveness of U.S. Manufacturing," *J. Econ. Lit.,* **33**:132–163 (1995).

Jaffe, Adam B. and Robert N. Stavins, "Dynamic Incentives of Environmental Regulations: The Effects of Alternative Policy Instruments on Technology Diffusion," *J. Environ. Econ. Mgmt.,* **29**:S-43–S-63 (1995).

Jaffee, D. M. and T. Russell, "Catastrophe Insurance, Capital Markets and Uninsurable Risks," *J. Risk and Insurance*, **64**:205–230 (1997).

Jaffee, A., R. Newell, and R. Stavins, "Technological Change and the Environment," in K. Maler and J. Vincent (Eds.), *Handbook of Environmental Economics* (North-Holland, Amsterdam, 2003).

Jorgenson, Dale W., "Productivity and Postwar U.S. Economic Growth," *J. Econ. Perspect.,* **2**(4):23–42 (1988).

Jorgenson, Dale W. and Peter J. Wilcoxen, "Environmental Regulation and U.S. Economic Growth," *Rand J. Econ.,* **21**:314–340 (1990).

Jorgenson, Dale W., J. Steven Landefeld and William D. Nordhaus (Eds.), *A New Architecture for the US National Accounts,* National Bureau of Economic Research Studies in Income and Wealth, Vol. 66 (2006).

Just, Richard E., Darrell L. Hueth, and Andrew Schmitz, *Applied Welfare Economics and Public Policy* (Prentice-Hall, Englewood Cliffs, NJ, 1982).

Kahn, Mathew and John G. Matsusaka, "Demand for Environmental Goods: Evidence from Voting Patterns on California Initiatives," *J. Law Econ.,* **40**:137–173 (1997).

Kahneman, Daniel and Jack L. Knetsch, "Valuing Public Goods: The Purchase of Moral Satisfaction," *J. Environ. Econ. Mgmt.,* **22**:57–70 (1992).

Kahnemann, Daniel, Jack Knetsch, and Richard Thaler, "Experimental Tests of the Endowment Effect and the Coase Theorem," *J. Polit. Econ.*, **98**:1325–1348 (1990).

Kaldor, Nicholas, "Welfare Propositions of Economics and Interpersonal Comparisons of Utility," *Econ. J.*, **49**:549–552 (1939).

Kanemoto, Y., "Hedonic Prices and the Benefits of Public Projects," *Econometrica*, **56**:981–989 (1988).

Kaplow, Louis and Steven Shavell, "Law Enforcement with Self-Reporting of Behavior," *J. Polit. Econ.*, **102**:583–606 (1994).

Katzman, Martin, "Pollution Liability Insurance and Catastrophic Environmental Risk," *J. Risk Uncertainty*, **55**:75–100 (1988).

Keeney, Ralph and Howard Raiffa, *Decisions with Multiple Objectives* (Wiley, New York, 1976).

Kelly, David, Charles Kolstad, and Glenn Mitchell, "Adjustment Costs from Environmental Change," *J. Environ. Econ. Mgmt.*, **50**:468–495 (2005).

Kelly, David L., "On Environmental Kuznets Curves Arising from Stock Externalities," *J. Econ. Dyn. Control*, **27**:1367–1390 (2004).

Kelman, Steven, "Cost–Benefit Analysis: An Ethical Critique," *AEI Journal on Government and Society Regulation*, pp. 33–40 (Jan/Feb 1981).

Keohane, Nathaniel O., Erin T. Mansur, and Andrey Voynov, "Averting Regulatory Enforcement: Evidence from New Source Review," *J. Econ. Mgmt. Strategy*, **18**:75–104 (2009).

Khanna, Madhu and L. A. Damon, "EPA's Voluntary 33/50 Program: Impact on Toxic Releases and Economic Performance of Firms," *J. Environ. Econ. Mgmt.*, **37**:1–25 (1999).

King, Andrew A. and Michael J. Lenox, "Industry Self-Regulation without Sanctions: The Chemical Industry's Responsible Care System," *Acad. of Mgmt. J.*, **43**:698–716 (2000).

Klaassen, Ger, "Trade-offs in Sulfur Emission Trading in Europe," *Environ. Res. Econ.*, **5**:191–219 (1995).

Kmenta, Jan, *Elements of Econometrics*, 2nd Ed. (Macmillan, New York, 1986).

Kneese, Alan V., *Water Pollution: Economic Aspects and Research Needs* (Resources for the Future, Washington, DC, 1962).

Kneese, Allen V. and Blair T. Bower, *Managing Water Quality: Economics, Technology, Institutions* (Johns Hopkins University Press, Baltimore, 1968).

Kneese, Allen V. and William D. Schulze, "Ethics and Environmental Economics," Chapter 5 in A. V. Kneese and J. L. Sweeney (Eds.), *Handbook of Natural Resource and Energy Economics*, Vol. I (North-Holland, Amsterdam, 1985).

Knight, Frank H., *Risk, Uncertainty and Profit* (Houghton Mifflin, Boston, 1921).

Kolstad, C. D., "Uniformity vs. Differentiation in Regulating Externalities," *J. Environ. Econ. Mgmt.*, **14**:386–399 (1987).

Kolstad, C. D., T. Ulen, and G. Johnson, "Ex Ante Regulation vs. Ex Post Liability for Harm: Substitutes or Complements?" *Am. Econ. Rev.*, **80**:888–901 (1990).

Kolstad, Charles D., "Empirical Properties of Economic Incentives and Command and Control Regulations for Air Pollution Control," *Land Econ.* **62**:250–268 (1986).

Kolstad, Charles D., "Clean Air and Energy: Reform of the PSD Provisions of the Clean Air Act," *J. Air Waste Manage. Assn.*, **40**:177–184 (1990).

Kolstad, Charles D., "Fundamental Irreversibilities in Stock Externalities," *J. Public Econ.*, **60**:221–233 (1996a).

Kolstad, Charles D., "Learning and Stock Effects in Environmental Regulation: The Case of Greenhouse Gas Emissions," *J. Environ. Econ. Mgmt.*, **31**:1–18 (1996b).

Kolstad, Charles D., "Interpreting Estimated Environmental Kuznets Curves for Greenhouse Gases," *J. Envir. Dev.*, **15**:42–49 (2006).

Kolstad, Charles D. and John B. Braden, "Environmental Demand Theory," in J. B. Braden and C. D. Kolstad (Eds.), *Measuring the Demand for Environmental Quality* (North-Holland, Amsterdam, 1991).

Kolstad, Charles D. and Rolando Guzman, "Information and the Divergence Between Willingness-to-Accept and Willingness-to-Pay," *J. Environ. Econ. Mgmt.* (1999).

Kolstad, Charles D. and Alistair Ulph, "Learning and International Environmental Agreements," *Climatic Change* **89**:125–141 (2008).

Kolstad, Jonathan and Frank Wolak, "Using Environmental Emissions Permit Prices to Raise Electricity Prices: Evidence from the California Electricity Market" (working paper, University of California Energy Institute, Berkeley, CA, 2008).

Kopp, Raymond J. and V. Kerry Smith, "Benefit Estimation Goes to Court: The Case of Natural Resource Damage Assessments," *J. Policy Analysis. Mgmt.*, **8**:593–612 (1989).

Kotchen, Matthew J., "Green Markets and the Private Provision of Public Goods," *J. Polit. Econ.*, **114**:816–834 (2006).

Kotchen, Matthew J. and Michael R. Moore, "Private Provision of Environmental Public Goods: Household Participation in Green Electricity Programs," *J. Environ. Econ. Mgmt.*, **53**:1–16 (2007).

Kotchen, Matthew J. and Klaas van't Veld, "An Economics Perspective of Treating Voluntary Programs as Clubs," pp. 67–68 in M. Potoski and A. Prakash (Eds.), *Voluntary Programs: A Club Theory Perspective* (MIT Press, Cambridge, MA, 2009).

Kozeltsev, Michael and Anil Markandya, "Pollution Charges in Russia: The Experience of 1990–1995," in R. Bluffstone and B. A. Larson (Eds.), *Controlling Pollution in Transition Economies: Theories and Methods* (Edward Elgar, Cheltenham, England, 1997).

Krämer, Ludwig, *Focus on European Environmental Law* (Sweet and Maxwell, London, 1992).

Kriström, Bengt and Pere Riera, "Is the Income Elasticity of Environmental Improvements Less Than One?" *Environ. Res. Econ.*, **7**:45–55 (1996).

Krutilla, John and Anthony Fisher, *The Economics of Natural Environments,* 2nd Ed. (Johns Hopkins University Press, Baltimore, 1985).

Krutilla, John V., "Conservation Reconsidered," *Am. Econ. Rev.*, **57**:777–786 (1967).

Kuminoff, Nikolai, "Recovering Preferences from a Dual Market Locational Equilibrium," (unpublished manuscript, Virginia Tech April 2007).

Kunreuther, Howard and Erwann O. Michel-Kerjan, "Climate Change, Insurability and Liability," University of Pennsylvania Law Review, **155**:1795–1842 (2007).

Kwak, Seung-Jun and Clifford S. Russell, "Contingent Valuation in Korean Environmental Planning: A Pilot Application to the Protection of Drinking Water in Seoul," *Environ. Res. Econ.*, **4**:511–526 (1994).

Kwerel, Evan, "To Tell the Truth: Imperfect Information and Optimal Pollution Control," *Rev. Econ. Studies,* **44**:595–601 (1977).

Laffont, Jean-Jacques, "More on Prices vs. Quantities," *Rev. Econ. Studies,* **44**:177–186 (1977).

Laffont, Jean-Jacques, *Fundamentals of Public Economics* (MIT Press, Cambridge, MA, 1989).

Laffont, Jean-Jacques and Jean Tirole, *A Theory of Incentives in Procurement and Regulation* (MIT Press, Cambridge, MA, 1993).

Laffont, Jean-Jacques and Jean Tirole, "Pollution Permits and Environmental Innovation," *J. Public Econ.*, **62**:127–140 (1996).

Laibson, David, "Golden Eggs and Hyperbolic Discounting," *Quart. J. Econ.*, **112**:443–477 (1997).

Leape, Jonathan, "The London Congestion Charge," *J. Econ. Perspect.*, **20**:157–176 (2006).

Lenaerts, Koen, "The Principle of Subsidiarity and the Environment in the European Union: Keeping the Balance of Federalism," in F. Abraham, K. Deketelaere, and J. Stuyck (Eds.), *Recent Economic and Legal Developments in European Environmental Policy* (Leuven University Press, Leuven, Belgium, 1995).

Leopold, Aldo, *A Sand County Almanac* (Oxford University Press, New York, 1949).

Lerner, Abba, "The 1971 Report of the President's Council of Economic Advisors: Priorities and Efficiency," *Am. Econ. Rev.*, **61**:527–530 (1971).

Levin, S. A., S. Barrett, S. Aniyar, W. Baumol, C. Bliss, B. Bolin, P. Dasgupta, P. Ehrlich, C. Folke, I. Gren, C. S. Holling, A. Jansson, B. Jansson, K. Maler, D. Martin, C. Perrings, and E. Sheshinski, "Resilience in Natural and Socio-economic Systems," *Envir. Dev. Econ.*, **3**:222–254 (1998).

Levinson, Arik and M. Scott Taylor, "Unmasking the Pollution Haven Effect," *Int. Econ. Rev.*, **49**:223–254 (2008).

Lewis, Tracy R., "Protecting the Environment When Costs and Benefits Are Privately Known," *Rand J. Econ.*, **27**:819–847 (1996).

Libecap, Gary D. and Steven N. Wiggins, "Contractual Responses to the Common Pool—Prorationing of Crude Oil Production," *Am. Econ. Rev.*, **74**:87–98 (1984).

Lichtenberg, E. and D. Zilberman, "Efficient Regulation of Environmental Health Risks," *Quart. J. Econ.*, **103**:167–178 (1988).

Lind, R. C., K. J. Arrow, G. R. Corey, P. Dasgupta, A. K. Sen, T. Stauffer, J. E. Stiglitz, J. A. Stockfisch, and R. Wilson, *Discounting for Time and Risk in Energy Policy* (Resources for the Future, Washington, DC, 1982).

Lind, Robert C, "Spatial Equilibrium, the Theory of Rents, and the Measurement of Benefits from Public Programs," *Quart. J. Econ.*, **87**:188–207 (1973).

Linklaters and Paines Solicitors, "United Kingdom," in M. Boes (Ed.), "Environmental Law," in R. Blanpain (Ed.), *International Encyclopaedia of Laws* (Kluwer Law International, Boston, 1992).

List, John, "Neoclassical Theory versus Prospect Theory: Evidence from the Marketplace," *Econometrica,* **72**:615–625 (2004).

List, John (Ed.), Using Experimental Methods in Environmental and Resource Economics (Elgar, Northampton, Mass., 2007).

Low, Patrick and Alexander Yeats, "Do 'Dirty' Industries Migrate?," Chapter 6 in Patrick Low (Ed.), *International Trade and the Environment,* World Bank Discussion Papers #159 (World Bank, Washington, DC, 1992).

Luenberger, David, *Microeconomic Theory* (McGraw-Hill, New York, 1995).

Lyon, Randolph M., "Regulating Bureaucratic Polluters," *Public Finance Rev.*, **18**:198–220 (1990).

Lyon, Thomas P. and John W. Maxwell, *Corporate Environmentalism and Public Policy* (Cambridge University Press, Cambridge, England, 2004).

Lyon, Thomas P. and John W. Maxwell, "Corporate Social Responsibility and the Environment: A Theoretical Perspective," *Rev. Environ. Econ. Policy*, **2**:240–260 (2008).

MacMinn, Richard D. and Patrick L. Brockett, "Corporate Spin-offs as a Value Enhancing Technique When Faced with Legal Liability," *Insurance: Math. Econ.*, **16**:63–68 (1995).

Maddison, David and Andrea Bigano, "The Amenity Value of the Italian Climate," *J. Environ. Econ. Mgmt.*, **45**:319–332 (2003).

Magat, Wes and W. Kip Viscusi, "Effectiveness of the EPA's Regulatory Enforcement: The Case of Industrial Effluent Standards," *J. Law Econ.*, **33**:331–360 (1990).

Magat, Wesley A., Alan J. Krupnick, and Winston Harrington, *Rules in the Making: A Statistical Analysis of Regulatory Agency Behavior* (Resources for the Future, Washington, DC, 1986).

Mäler, Karl-Göran, *Environmental Economics: A Theoretical Inquiry* (Johns Hopkins University Press for Resources for the Future, Baltimore, 1974).

Malik, Arun S., "Markets for Pollution Control When Firms Are Noncompliant," *J. Environ. Econ. Mgmt.,* **18**:97–106 (1990).

Margolis, Joshua D., Hillary Anger Elfenbein, and James P. Walsh, "Does It Pay to Be Good? A Meta-analysis and Redirection of Research on the Relationship between Corporate Social and Financial Performance" (working paper, Harvard Business School, Cambridge, MA, July 26, 2007).

Margulis, Sergio, "The Use of Economic Instruments in Environmental Policies: The Experience of Brazil, Mexico, Chile, and Argentina," in *Applying Economic Instruments to Environmental Policies in the OECD and Dynamic Non-Member Economies* (OECD, Paris, 1994).

Markusen, James R., Edward R. Morey and Nancy Olewiler, "Competition in Regional Environmental Polices with Plan Locations Are Endogenous," *J. Public Econ.*, **56**:55–77 (1995).

Martin, Robert E., "Externality Regulation and the Monopoly Firm," *J. Public Econ.*, **29**:347–362 (1986).

Mas-Colell, Andreu, Michael D. Whinston, and Jerry R. Green, *Microeconomic Theory* (Oxford University Press, New York, 1995).

Maxwell, James and Forrest Briscoe, "There's Money in the Air: The CFC Ban and Dupont's Regulatory Strategy," *Bus. Strat. Environ.*, **6**:276–286 (1997).

Mayeres, I. and S. Proost, "Marginal Tax Reform, Externalities and Income Distribution," *J. Public Econ.*, **79**:343–363 (2001).

McAusland, Carol and Chris Costello, "Avoiding Invasives: Trade-Related Policies for Controlling Unintentional Exotic Species Introductions," *J. Environ. Econ. Mgmt.*, **48**:954–977 (2004).

McConnell, Kenneth E. and T. T. Phipps, "Identification of Preference Parameters in Hedonic Models: Consumer Demands with Nonlinear Budgets," *J. Urban Econ.*, **22**:35–52 (1987).

McFadden, Daniel, "Conditional Logit Analysis of Discrete Choice Behavior," in Paul Zarembka (Ed.), *Frontiers of Econometrics* (Academic Press, New York, 1973).

McGartland, Albert M. and Wallace E. Oates, "Marketable Permits for the Prevention of Environmental Deterioration," *J. Environ. Econ. Mgmt.*, **12**:207–228 (1985).

Meade, James, "External Economies and Diseconomies in a Competitive Situation," *Econ. J.*, **62**:54–67 (1952).

Meade, James E., *The Theory of Externalities* (AW Sijthoff, Leiden, The Netherlands, 1973).

Mehr, Robert I., *Fundamentals of Insurance,* 2nd Ed. (Irwin, Homewood, IL, 1986).

Mendelsohn, Robert, "Measuring Climate Impacts with Cross-Sectional Analysis," *Climatic Change*, **81**:1–7 (2007).

Mendelsohn, Robert, William D. Nordhaus, and Daigee Shaw, "The Impact of Global Warming on Agriculture: A Ricardian Study," *Am. Econ. Rev.*, **84**:753–771 (1994).

Milgrom, Paul and John Roberts, *Economics, Organization and Management* (Prentice-Hall, Englewood Cliffs, NJ, 1992).

Milliman Scott R. and Raymond Prince, "Firm Incentives to Promote Technological-Change in Pollution-Control," *J. Environ. Econ. Mgmt.*, **17**:247–265 (1989).

Mills, Edwin S., "An Aggregative Model of Resource Allocation in a Metropolitan Area," *Am. Econ. Rev. Papers Proc.*, **57**(2): 197–210 (1967).

Mishan, E. J., "The Postwar Literature on Externalities: An Interpretive Essay," *J. Econ. Lit.*, **9**:1–28 (1971).

Mitchell, Robert C. and Richard T. Carson, *Using Surveys to Value Public Goods* (Johns Hopkins University Press, Baltimore, 1989).

Montero, Juan-Pablo, "A Simple Auction Mechanism for the Optimal Allocation of the Commons," *Am. Econ. Rev.*, **98**:496–518 (2008).

Montgomery, W. David, "Markets in Licenses and Efficient Pollution Control Programs," *J. Econ. Theory,* **5**:395–418 (1972).

Mueller, Dennis C., *Public Choice III* (Cambridge University Press, Cambridge, England, 2003).

Murdoch, James C. and Todd Sandler, "The Voluntary Provision of a Pure Public Good: The Case of Reduced CFC Emissions and the Montreal Protocol," *J. Public Econ.*, **63**:331–349 (1997).

Musgrave, Richard A., *The Theory of Public Finance* (McGraw-Hill, New York, 1959).

Myles, Gareth D., *Public Economics* (Cambridge University Press, Cambridge, England, 1995).

Nash, Roderick Frazier, *The Rights of Nature: A History of Environmental Ethics* (University of Wisconsin Press, Madison, 1989).

National Oceanic and Atmospheric Administration, U.S. Department of Commerce, "Natural Resource Damage Assessments Under the Oil Pollution Act of 1990," *Federal Register,* **58**:4601–4614 (January 15, 1993).

National Park Service, Land and Recreational Planning Division, "The Economics of Public Recreation: An Economic Study of The Monetary Evaluation of Recreation in the National Parks," U.S. Department of the Interior (Washington, DC, 1949).

Navrud, Ståle and E. D. Mungatana, "Environmental Valuation in Developing Countries: The Recreational Value of Wildlife Viewing," *Ecolog. Econ.*, **11**:135–151 (1994).

Netusil, N. R., S. Chattopadhyay, and K. Kovacs, "Estimating the Demand for Tree Canopy: A Second-Stage Hedonic Price Analysis," *Land Econ.* (forthcoming, 2009).

Newell, Richard G., Adam B. Jaffe, and Robert N. Stavins, "The Induced Innovation Hypothesis and Energy-Saving Technological Change," *Quart. J. Econ.*, **114**:941–995 (1999).

Newell, Richard G. and William A. Pizer, "Discounting the Distant Future: How Much Do Uncertain Rates Increase Valuation," *J. Environ. Econ. Mgmt.*, **46**:52–71 (2003).

Newell, Richard G., James N. Sanchirico, and Suzi Kerr, "Fishing Quota Markets," *J. Environ. Econ. Mgmt.*, **49**:437–462 (2005).

Neumayer, Eric, *Weak Versus Strong Sustainability: Exploring the Limits of Two Opposing Paradigms*, 2nd Ed. (Edward Elgar, Cheltenham, England, 2003).

Neumayer, Eric, "The WTO and the Environment: Its Past Record is Better than Critics Believe, but the Future Outlook is Bleak," *Global Environ. Politics*, **4**:1–8 (2004).

Newhouse, Joseph P., *Free for All?: Lessons from the Rand Health Insurance Experiment*, (Harvard University Press, Cambridge, MA, 1993).

Nordhaus, William, *A Question of Balance: Weighing the Options on Global Warming Policy* (Yale University Press, New Haven, CT, 2008).

Nordhaus, William D., "Economic Growth and Climate: The Carbon Dioxide Problem," *Am. Econ. Rev.*, **67**:341–346 (1977).

Nordhaus, William D., "To Slow or Not to Slow: The Economics of the Greenhouse Effect," *Econ. J.*, **101**:920–937 (1991).

Nordhaus, William D., *Managing the Global Commons: The Economics of Climate Change* (MIT Press, Cambridge, MA, 1994).

Nordhaus, William D., "Climate Amenities and Global Warming," in N. Nakicenovic, W. D. Nordhaus, R. Richels, and F. C. Toth (Eds.), *Climate Change: Integrating Science, Economics, and Policy,* Proceedings of Conference at International Institute of Applied Systems Analysis (IIASA), Laxenburg, Austria, IIASA Report CP-96-1 (December 1996).

Nordhaus, William D., "Modeling Induced Innovation in Climate Change Policy," Chapter 8 in A. Grubler, N. Nakicenovic, and W. D. Nordhaus (Eds.), *Technological Change and the Environment* (Resources for the Future, Washington, DC, 2002).

Nordhaus, William D., "A Review of the *Stern Review on the Economics of Climate Change*," *J. Econ. Lit.*, **45**:686–702 (2007).

Nordhaus, William D. and Edward C. Kokkelenberg (Eds.), *Nature's Numbers: Expanding the National Economic Accounts to Include the Environment* (National Academies Press, Washington, 1999).

Oates, Wallace and D. Strassmann, "The Use of Effluent Fees to Regulate Public-Sector Sources of Pollution: An Application of the Niskanen Model," *J. Environ. Econ. Mgmt.*, **5**:283–291 (1978).

Oates, Wallace E., Paul R. Portney, and Albert M. McGartland, "The *Net* Benefits of Incentive-Based Regulation: A Case Study of Environmental Standard Setting," *Am. Econ. Rev.*, **79**:1233–1242 (1989).

Oates, Wallace E. and R. M. Schwab, "Economic Competition Among Jurisdictions: Efficiency Enhancing or Distortion Inducing?," *J. Public Econ.*, **35**:333–354 (1988).

Oates, Walace E. and Diana L. Strassmann, "Effluent Fees and Market Structure," *J. Public Econ.*, **24**:29–46 (1984).

OECD, *Economic Instruments for Environmental Protection* (Organization for Economic Cooperation and Development, Paris, 1989).

OECD, *Environment and Taxation: The Cases of the Netherlands, Sweden and the United States,* (Organization for Economic Cooperation and Development, Paris, 1994a).

OECD, *Managing the Environment: The Role of Economic Instruments* (Organization for Economic Cooperation and Development, Paris, 1994b).

OECD, *Environmental Taxes in OECD Countries* (Organization for Economic Cooperation and Development, Paris, 1995).

OECD, *Voluntary Approaches for Environmental Policy: Effectiveness, Efficiency and Usage in Policy Mixes* (Organization for Economic Cooperation and Development, Paris, 2003).

OECD, *Environment at a Glance: OECD Environmental Indicators* (OECD, Paris, 2006).

OECD, "Pollution Abatement and Control Expenditure in OECD Countries," Report ENV/EPOC/ SE(2007)1 (OECD, Paris, 2007).

O'Ryan, Raul E., "Cost-Effective Policies to Improve Urban Air Quality in Santiago, Chile," *J. Environ. Econ. Mgmt.,* **31**:302–313 (1996).

O'Riordan, Timothy and James Cameron (Eds.), *Interpreting the Precautionary Principle* (Earthscan, London, 1994).

Orlitzky, Marc, Frank L. Schmidt, and Sara L. Rynes, "Corporate Social and Financial Performance: A Meta-Analysis," *Org. Studies,* **24**:403–441 (2003).

Osborne, D. K., "Cartel Problems," *Am. Econ. Rev.,* **66**:835–844 (1976).

Ostrom, Elinor, *Governing the Commons: The Evolution of Institutions for Collective Action* (Cambridge University Press, New York, 1990).

Page, Talbot, "Sustainability and the Problem of Valuation," Chapter 5 in Robert Costanza (Ed.), *Ecological Economics: The Science and Management of Sustainability* (Columbia University Press, New York, 1991).

Palmer, Karen, Wallace E. Oates, and Paul R. Portney, "Tightening Environmental Standards: The Benefit-Cost or the No-Cost Paradigm?," *J. Econ. Perspect.,* **9**(4):119–132 (1995).

Palmquist, Raymond B., "Hedonic Methods," in J.B. Braden and C.D. Kolstad (Eds.), *Measuring the Demand for Environmental Quality* (North-Holland, Amsterdam, 1991).

Pargal, Sheoli and David Wheeler, "Informal Regulation of Industrial Pollution in Developing Countries: Evidence from Indonesia," *J. Polit. Econ.,* **104**:1314–1327 (1996).

Parry, Ian W. H., "Pollution Taxes and Revenue Recycling," *J. Environ. Econ. Mgmt.,* **29**(No. 2, Part 2):S-64–S-77 (1995).

Pasurka, Carl, "Perspectives on Pollution Abatement and Competitiveness: Theory, Data, and Analyses," *Rev. Environ. Econ. Policy,* 2:194–218 (2008).

Peltzman, Samuel, "Toward a More General Theory of Regulation," *J. Law Econ.,* **19**:211–240 (1976).

Peskin, Henry M., "National Accounting Framework for Environmental Assets," *J. Environ. Econ. Mgmt.,* **2**:255–262 (1976).

Pfaff, Alexander S. P. and Chris William Sanchirico, "Environmental Self-Auditing: Setting the Proper Incentives for Discovery and Correction of Environmental Harm," *J. Law, Econ. Org.,* **16**:189–208 (2000).

Pfaff, Alexander and Chris William Sanchirico, "Big Field, Small Potatoes: An Empirical Assessment of EPA's Self-Audit Policy," *J. Policy Analysis Mgmt.,* **23**:415–432 (2004).

Phaneuf, Daniel J., "A Random Utility Model for Total Maximum Daily Loads: Estimating the Benefits of Watershed-Based Ambient Water Quality Improvements," *Water Resources Res.,* **38**(11):36-1—36-10 (2002).

Pigou, Arthur C., *The Economics of Welfare,* 4th Ed. (Macmillan, London, 1962).

Pindyck, Robert S., "Irreversibility, Uncertainty and Investment," *J. Econ. Lit.,* **29**:1110–1148 (1991).

Pindyck, Robert S., "Uncertainty, Extreme Outcomes and Climate Change Policy" (working paper, MIT, 2009).

Plott, Charles R., "Externalities and Corrective Policies in Experimental Markets," *Econ. J.,* **93**:106–127 (1983).

Polesetsky, Mathew, "Will a Market in Air Pollution Clean the Nation's Dirtiest Air? A Study of the South Coast Air Quality Management District's Regional Clean Air Incentives Market," *Ecol. Law Quart.*, **22**:359–411 (1995).

Polinsky, A. Mitchell "Notes on the Symmetry of Taxes and Subsidies in Pollution Control," *Can. J. Econ.*, **12**:75–83 (1979).

Polinsky, A. Mitchell and Steven Shavell, "Amenities and Property Values in a Model of an Urban Area," *J. Public Econ.*, **5**:119–129 (1976).

Pommerehne, Werner W., "Measuring Environmental Benefits: A Comparison of Hedonic Technique and Contingent Valuation," in D. Bös, M. Rose, and C. Seidl (Eds.), *Welfare and Efficiency in Public Economics* (Springer-Verlag, Berlin, 1988).

Popp, David, "Induced Innovation and Energy Prices," *Am. Econ. Rev.*, **92**:160–180 (2002).

Porter, Michael E. and Claas van der Linde, "Toward a New Conception of the Environment-Competitiveness Relationship," *J. Econ. Perspect.*, **9**(4):97–118 (1995).

Porter, Richard C., "Michigan's Experience with Mandatory Deposits on Beverage Containers," *Land Econ.*, **59**:177–194 (1983).

Portney, Paul, "Corporate Social Responsibility: An Economic and Public Policy Perspective," pp. 107–31 in Bruce L. Hay, Robert N. Stavins, and Richard H.K. Vietor (Eds.), *Environmental Protection and the Social Responsibility of Firms: Perspectives from Law, Economics and Business* (Resources for the Future, Washington, DC, 2005).

Portney, Paul, "The (Not So) New Corporate Social Responsibility: An Empirical Perspective," *Rev. Environ. Econ. Policy*, **2**:261–275 (2008).

Portney, Paul R., "The Contingent Valuation Debate: Why Economists Should Care," *J. Econ. Perspect.*, **8**(4):3–17 (1994).

Portney, Paul R. and Robert Stavins (Eds.), *Public Policies for Environmental Protection*, 2nd Ed. (Resources for the Future, Washington, DC, 2000).

Prakash, Aseem and Matthew Potoski, *The Voluntary Environmentalists* (Cambridge University Press, Cambridge, England, 2006).

Puller, Steven L., "The Strategic Use of Innovation to Influence Regulatory Standards," *J. Environ. Econ. Mgmt.*, **52**:690–706 (2006).

Quigley, John M., "Nonlinear Budget Constraints and Consumer Demand: An Application to Public Programs for Residential Housing," *J. Urban Econ.*, **12**:177–201 (1982).

Randall, A., B. Ives and C. Eastman, "Bidding Games for Valuation of Aesthetic Environmental Improvements," *J. Environ. Econ. Mgmt.*, **1**:132–149 (1974).

Randall, Alan, "The Problem of Market Failure," *Natural Res. J.*, **23**:131–148 (1983).

Randall, Alan, "A Difficulty with the Travel Cost Method," *Land Econ.*, **70**:88–96 (1994).

Randall, Alan and John Stoll, "Consumer's Surplus in Commodity Space," *Am. Econ. Rev.*, **71**:449–457 (1980).

Regan, Donald H., "The Problem of Social Cost Revisited," *J. Law Econ.*, **15**:427–437 (1972).

Rehbinder, Eckard, "Environmental Regulation Through Fiscal and Economic Incentives in a Federalist System," *Ecol. Law Quart.*, **20**:57–83 (1993).

Reinhardt, Forest L., Robert N. Stavins, and Richard H. K. Vietor, "Corporate Social Responsibility through an Economic Lens," *Rev. Environ. Econ. Policy*, **2**:219–239 (2008).

Reisner, Marc, *Cadillac Desert* (Viking Press, New York, 1986).

Repetto, Robert, William Magrath, Michael Wells, Christine Beer, and Fabrizo Rossini, "Wasting Assets: Natural Resources in the National Income Accounts" (World Resources Institute, Washington, DC, June 1989).

Repetto, Robert, Dale Rothman, Paul Faeth, and Duncan Austin, "Has Environmental Protection Really Reduced Productivity Growth?" (World Resources Institute, Washington, DC, October 1996).

Revkin, Andrew C., "Carbon-Neutral Is Hip, but Is It Green?" *New York Times* (April 29, 2007).

Ridker, Ronald G. and John A. Henning, "The Determinants of Residential Property Values with Special Reference to Air Pollution," *Rev. Econ. Stat.*, **49**:246–257 (1967).

Roback, Jennifer, "Wages, Rents and the Quality of Life," *J. Political Econ.*, **90**:1257–1278 (1982).

Roback, Jennifer, "Wages, Rents and Amenities: Differences among Workers and Regions," *Econ. Inq.*, **26**:23–41 (1988).

Roberts, Marc J. and Michael Spence, "Effluent Charges and Licenses Under Uncertainty," *J. Public Econ.*, **5**:193–208 (1976).

Rosen, Sherwin, "Hedonic Prices and Implicit Markets: Product Differentiation in Perfect Competition," *J. Political Econ.*, **82**:34–55 (1974).

Rosenberger, Randall S. and John B. Loomis, "Benefit Transfer," Chapter 12 in P.A. Champ, K.J. Boyle, and T.C. Brown, *A Primer on Nonmarket Valuation* (Kluwer, Dordrecht, 2003).

Russell, C. S., W. Harrington and W. J. Vaughn, "Enforcing Pollution Control Laws," Chapter 4 in *Economic Models of Monitoring and Enforcement*, (Resources for the Future, Washington, DC, 1986).

Saffran, Bernard, "Recommendations for Further Reading," *J. Econ. Perspect.*, **10**:199–206 (1996).

Sagoff, Mark, "Should Preferences Count?" *Land Econ.*, **70**:127–144 (1994).

Sam, Abdoul G. and Robert Innes, "Voluntary Pollution Reductions and the Enforcement of Environmental Law: An Empirical Study of the 33/50 Program," *J. Law Econ.*, **51**:271–296 (2008).

Samuelson, Paul, "The Pure Theory of Public Expenditure," *Rev. Econ. Stat.*, **36**:387–389 (1954).

Samuelson, Paul, *Foundations of Economic Analysis* (Harvard University Press, Cambridge, MA, 1947).

Sandel, Michael J., "It's Immoral to Buy the Right to Pollute," *New York Times* (Dec. 17, 1997).

Sandmo, Agnar, "Optimal Taxation in the Presence of Externalities," *Swedish J. Econ.*, **77**:86–98 (1975).

Schelling, Thomas C., "Intergenerational Discounting," *Energy Policy,* **23**:395–401 (1995).

Schlenker, Wolfram, W. Michael Hanemann, and Anthony C. Fisher, "Will U.S. Agriculture Really Benefit from Global Warming? Accounting for Irrigation in the Hedonic Approach," *Am. Econ. Rev.*, **95**:395–406 (2005).

Schmalensee, Richard, "Option Demand and Consumer's Surplus: Valuing Price Changes Under Uncertainty," *Am. Econ. Rev.,* **62**:813–824 (1972).

Schmalensee, Richard, Paul Joskow, A. Denny Ellerman, Juan Pablo Montero, and Elizabeth M. Bailey, "An Interim Evaluation of Sulfur Emissions Trading," *J. Econ. Perspect.*, **12**:53–68 (1998).

Schmutzler, Armin and Lawrence H. Goulder, "The Choice Between Emission Taxes and Output Taxes under Imperfect Monitoring," *J. Environ. Econ. Mgmt.*, **32**:51–64 (1997).

Schoenbaum, T. J. and R. H. Rosenberg, *Environmental Policy Law* (Foundation Press, Westbury, NY, 1991).

Schulze, William and Ralph C. d'Arge, "The Coase Proposition, Information Constraints and Long Run Equilibrium," *Am. Econ. Rev.*, **64**:763–772 (1974).

Sedjo, Roger A., "Forest Sustainability Issues and Certification Activities Since UNCED," Issue Brief 02–20 (Resources for the Future, Washington, DC, August 2002).

Sedjo, Roger A. and Stephen K. Swallow, "Voluntary Eco-Labeling and the Price Premium," *Land Econ.*, **78**:272–284 (2002).

Seelye, Katherine Q., "Utility Buys Town It Choked, Lock, Stock and Blue Plume," *New York Times* (May 13, 2002).

Segerson, Kathleen, "Uncertainty and Incentives for Nonpoint Pollution Control," *J. Environ. Econ. Mgmt.*, **15**:87–98 (1988).

Segerson, Kathy and Thomas Miceli, "Voluntary Environmental Agreements: Good or Bad News for Environmental Protection?," *J. Environ. Econ. Mgmt.*, **36**:109–130 (1998).

Seip, Kalle and Jon Strand, "Willingness to Pay for Environmental Goods in Norway: A Contingent Valuation Study with Real Payment," *Environ. Res. Econ.*, **2**:91–106 (1992).

Seskin, Eugene P., Robert J. Anderson, Jr., and Robert O. Reid, "An Empirical Analysis of Economic Strategies for Controlling Air Pollution," *J. Environ. Econ. Mgmt.*, **10**:112–124 (1983).

Shafik, Nemat, "Economic Development and Environmental Quality: An Econometric Analysis," *Oxford Econ. Papers,* **46**:757–773 (1994).

Shafik, Nemat and Sushenjit Bandyopadhyay, "Economic Growth and Environmental Quality: Time-Series and Cross-Country Evidence," Policy Research Working Paper WPS 904 (World Bank, Washington, DC, June 1992).

Shavell, Steven, "A Model of the Optimal Use of Liability and Safety Regulation," *Rand J. Econ.,* **15**:271–280 (1984).

Shogren, Jason F., Seung Y. Shin, Dermot J. Hayes, and James B. Kliebenstein, "Resolving Differences in Willingness to Pay and Willingness to Accept," *Am. Econ. Rev.,* **84**:255–270 (1994).

Shibata, H. and J. S. Winrich, "Control of Pollution When the Offended Defend Themselves," *Economica,* **50**:425–38 (1983).

Sieg, Holger, V. Kerry Smith, H. Spencer Banzhaf, and Randy Walsh, "Estimating the General Equilibrium Benefits of Large Changes in Spatially Delineated Public Goods," *Int. Econ. Rev.,* **45**:1047–1077 (2004).

Sigman, Hilary, "A Comparison of Public Policies for Lead Recycling," *Rand J. Econ.,* **26**:452–478 (1995).

Sigman, Hilary, "Midnight Dumping: Public Policies and Illegal Disposal of Used Oil," *Rand J. Econ.,* **29**:157–178 (1998).

Simpson, R. David, Michael A. Toman, and Robert U. Ayres (Eds.), *Scarcity and Growth Revisited* (Resources for the Future, Washington, DC, 2005).

Slade, Margaret E., "Trends in Natural Resource Commodity Pricing: An Analysis of the Time Domain," *J. Environ. Econ. Mgmt.,* **9**:122–137 (1982).

Slovic, Paul, Baruch Fischoff, and Sarah Lichtenstein, "Rating the Risks," *Environment,* **21**:14–20, 36–39 (April 1979). [Reprinted in T. Glickman and M. Gough (Eds.), *Readings in Risk* (Resources for the Future, Washington, DC, 1990).]

Small, Kenneth A., *Urban Transportation Economics* (Harwood Academic Publishers, Reading, MA, 1992).

Smith, V. Kerry (Ed.), *Scarcity and Growth Reconsidered* (Johns Hopkins University Press, Baltimore, 1979).

Smith, V. K. and W. H. Desvousges, "The Valuation of Environmental Risks and Hazardous Waste Policy," *Land Econ.,* **64**:211–219 (1988).

Smith, V. Kerry and William Desvousges, *Measuring Water Quality Benefits* (Kluwer, Boston, 1986).

Smith, V. Kerry and Ju Chin Huang, "Hedonic Models and Air Pollution: Twenty-Five Years and Counting," *Environ. Res. Econ.,* **3**:381–394 (1993).

Smith, V. Kerry, Holger Sieg, H. Spencer Banzhaf, and Randall P. Walsh, "General Equilibrium Benefits for Environmental Improvements: Projected Ozone Reductions under EPA's Prospective Analysis for the Los Angeles Basin," *J. Environ. Econ. Mgmt.,* **47**:559–584 (2004).

Solow, Robert, "An Almost Practical Step Towards Sustainability," Invited Lecture, Resources for the Future, Washington, DC (October 8, 1992).

Spulber, Daniel F. "Effluent Regulation and Long-Run Optimality," *J. Environ. Econ. Mgmt.,* **12**:103–116 (1985).

Spulber, Daniel F., "Optimal Environmental Regulation under Asymmetric Information," *J. Public Econ.,* **35**:163–181 (1988).

Spulber, Daniel F., *Regulation and Markets* (MIT Press, Cambridge, MA, 1989).

Squires, Dale, "Productivity Measurement in Common Property Resource Industries: An Application to the Pacific Coast Trawl Fishery," *Rand J. Econ.,* **23**:221–236 (1992).

Stafford, S. L., "The Effect of Punishment on Firm Compliance with Hazardous Waste Regulations," *J. Environ. Econ. Mgmt.,* **44**:290–308 (2002).

Stanners, David and Philippe Bourdeau, *Europe's Environment: The Dobřiš Assessment* (European Environment Agency, Copenhagen, 1995).

Starrett, David, *Foundations of Public Economics* (Cambridge University Press, Cambridge, England, 1988).

Starrett, David and Richard Zeckhauser, "Treating External Diseconomies—Markets or Taxes?," in John W. Pratt (Ed.), *Statistical and Mathematical Aspects of Pollution Problems* (Marcel Dekker, New York, 1974).

Statman, Meir, "Socially responsible indexes—Composition, performance, and tracking error," *J. Portfolio Mgmt.*, **32**:100–109 (2006).

Stavins, Robert N., "Transaction Costs and Tradeable Permits," *J. Environ. Econ. Mgmt.,* **29**:133–148 (1995).

Stern, David I., "The Rise and Fall of the Environmental Kuznets Curve," *World Dev.*, **32**:1419–1439 (2004).

Stern, Nicholas, *The Economics of Climate Change: The Stern Review* (Cambridge University Press, Cambridge, England, 2006). [Also available to download at www.hmtreasury.gov.uk/sternreview_index.htm.]

Stevens, William K., "Salvation at Hand for a California Landscape," *New York Times* (Feb. 27, 1996).

Stigler, George, "The Economic Theory of Regulation," *Bell J. Econ.*, **2**:3–21 (1971).

Strotz, R. H., "The Use of Land Rent Changes to Measure the Welfare Benefits of Land Improvement," in J.E. Haring (Ed.), *The New Economics of Regulated Industries: Rate-Making in a Dynamic Economy* (Economics Research Center, Occidental College, Los Angeles, 1968).

Taylor, Laura O., "The Hedonic Method," Chapter 10 in P.A. Champ, K.J. Boyle, and T.C. Brown, *A Primer on Nonmarket Valuation* (Kluwer, Dordrecht, 2003).

Telle, Kjetil, "The Threat of Regulatory Environmental Inspection: Impact on Plant Performance," *J. Reg. Econ.*, **35**:154–178 (2009).

Thaler, Richard and Sherwin Rosen, "The Value of Saving a Life: Evidence from the Labor Market," in Nestor E. Terleckyj (Ed.), *Household Production and Consumption* (National Bureau of Economic Research, New York , 1975).

Thomas, Alban, "Regulating Pollution Under Asymmetric Information: The Case of Industrial Wastewater Treatment," *J. Environ. Econ. Mgmt.,* **28**:357–373 (1995).

Thompson, Peter and Laura A. Strohm, "Trade and Environmental Quality: A Review of the Evidence," *J. Environ. Dev.,* **5**:363–388 (1996).

Tideman, N. and G. Tullock, "A New and Superior Process for Making Social Choices," *J. Polit. Econ.,* **84**:1145–1159 (1976).

Tierney, John, "Betting the Planet," p. 53 *et seq, New York Times Magazine* (December 2, 1990).

Tierney, John, "Where the Tuna Roam," *New York Times* (November 4, 2006).

Tietenberg, Thomas, "Disclosure Strategies for Pollution Control," *Environ. Resource Econ.*, **11**:587–602 (1998).

Tietenberg, Thomas H., "Indivisible Toxic Torts: The Economics of Joint and Several Liability," *Land Econ.,* **65**:305–319 (1989).

Timmins, Christopher, "If You Can't Take the Heat, Get out of the Cerrado…Recovering the Equilibrium Amenity Cost of Nonmarginal Climate Change in Brazil," *J. Reg. Sci.,* **47**:1–25 (2007).

Tinbergen, Jan, "On the Theory of Income Distribution," *Weltwirtschaftliches Archiv*, **77**:155–173 (1956).

Tirole, Jean, *The Theory of Industrial Organization* (MIT Press, Cambridge, MA, 1988).

Tobey, James A., "The Effects of Domestic Environmental Policies on Patterns of World Trade: An Empirical Test," *Kyklos*, **43**:191–209 (1990).

Toman, Michael A., "Economics and 'Sustainability: Balancing Trade-offs and Imperatives," *Land Econ.,* **70**:399–413 (1994).

Ulph, Alastair, "The Choice of Environmental Policy Instruments and Strategic International Trade," in Rudiger Pethig (Ed.), *Conflicts and Cooperation in Managing Environmental Resources* (Springer-Verlag, Berlin, 1992).

Ulph, Alistair, "Stable International Environmental Agreements with a Stock Pollutant, Uncertainty and Learning," *J. Risk Uncertainty*, **29**:53–73 (2004).

Um, Mi-Jung, Seung-Jun Kwak, and Tai-Yoo Kim, "Estimating Willingness to Pay for Improved Drinking Water Quality Using Averting Behavior Method with Perception Measure," *Environ. Resource Econ.*, **21**:287–302 (2002).

United Nations, *Handbook of National Accounting: Integrated Environmental and Economic Accounting 2003* (United Nations, New York, 2003). [Available at www.unstats.un.org/unsd/envaccounting/seea2003.pdf.]

United Nations Environment Programme, *Beijing 2008 Olympic Games: An Environmental Review* (Nairobi, 2008).

United States Bureau of the Census, *Statistical Abstract of the United States: 1988,* 108th Ed., Washington, DC (1987).

United States Bureau of the Census, Pollution Abatement Costs and Expenditures: 2005, Report MA200(5) (U.S. Government Printing Office, Washington, DC, 2008).

United States Council on Environmental Quality, Executive Office of the President, *Environmental Quality: 25th Anniversary Report* (Government Printing Office, Washington, DC, 1997).

United States Department of Commerce, Bureau of Economic Analysis, "Integrated Economic and Environmental Satellite Accounts," *Survey Current Business,* **74**(4):33–49 (1994a).

United States Department of Commerce, Bureau of Economic Analysis, "Accounting for Mineral Resources: Issues and BEA's Initial Estimates," *Survey Current Business,* **74**(4):50–72 (1994b).

United States Environmental Protection Agency, "Guideline Series: Control of Volatile Organic Compound Emissions from Wood Furniture Manufacturing Operations" (EPA Office of Air and Radiation, Office of Air Quality Planning and Standards, Research Triangle Park, NC, April 1996). [Available at www.epa.gov/ttn/atw/wood/finalctg.pdf.]

United States Environmental Protection Agency, *The Benefits and Costs of the Clean Air Act: 1970 to 1990,* Office of Air and Radiation, U.S. Environmental Protection Agency, Washington, DC (October 1997).

United States Environmental Protection Agency, *Acid Rain and Related Programs 2006 Progress Report,* Report Number EPA-430-R-07-011 (Washington, DC, 2007).

United States Environmental Protection Agency, "Valuing the Protection of Ecological Systems and Services," U.S. EPA Report EPA-SAB-09-012 (Washington, DC, 2009).

Varian, Hal, "A Solution to the Problem of Externalities When Agents Are Well-Informed," *Am. Econ. Rev.*, **84**:1278–1293 (1994).

Varian, Hal R., *Intermediate Microeconomics,* 7th Ed. (Norton, New York, 2005).

Viner, Jacob, "Cost Curves and Supply Curves," *Zeitschrift für Nationalökonomie,* **3**:23–46 (1931).

Viscusi, W. Kip, "Economic Foundations of the Current Regulatory Reform Efforts," *J. Econ. Perspect.,* **10**(3): 119–134 (1996).

Viscusi, W. Kip and Joseph E. Aldy, "The Value of a Statistical Life: A Critical Review of Market Estimates throughout the World," *J. Risk Uncertainty,* **27**:5–76 (2003).

Viscusi, W. Kip, John M. Vernon, and Joseph E. Harrington, Jr., *Economics of Regulation and Antitrust* 4th Ed. (MIT Press, Cambridge, 2005).

Vogel, David, *The Market for Virtue,* (Brookings Institution Press, Washington, DC, 2005).

Weart, Spencer R., "The Discovery of the Risk of Global Warming," *Physics Today,* pp. 34–40 (January 1997).

Weimer, David L. and Aidan R. Vining, *Policy Analysis: Concepts and Practice,* 4th Ed. (Pearson Prentice-Hall, Upper Saddle River, NJ, 2005).

Weitzman, Martin L., "Prices vs. Quantities," *Rev. Econ. Studies,* **41**:477–491 (1974).

Weitzman, Martin L., "Optimal Rewards for Economic Regulation," *Am. Econ. Rev.,* **68**:683–691 (1978).

Weitzman, Martin L., "On the Environmental Discount Rate," *J. Env. Econ. Mgmt.*, **26**:200–209 (1994).

Wheeler, David and Ashoka Mody, "International Investment Location Decisions: The Case of US Firms," *J. Int. Econ.*, **33**:57–76 (1992).

Whittington, Dale, Subhrendu K. Pattanayak, Jui-Chen Yang, and K. C. Bal Kumar, "Household Demand for Improved Piped Water Services: Evidence from Kathmandu, Nepal," *Water Policy*, **4**:531–556 (2002).

Wier, M., K. Birr-Pedersen, H.K. Jacobsen, J. Klok, "Are CO_2 Taxes Regressive? Evidence from the Danish Experience," *Ecolog. Econ.*, **52**:239–251 (2005).

Willig, Robert, "Consumer's Surplus Without Apology," *Am. Econ. Rev.*, **69**:469–474 (1979).

Wilson, Richard, "Analyzing the Daily Risks of Life," *Tech. Rev.*, **81**(4):41–46 (1979). [Reprinted in T. Glickman and M. Gough (Eds.), *Readings in Risk* (Resources for the Future, Washington, DC, 1990).]

World Bank, *World Development Report 1992: Development and the Environment* (Oxford University Press, New York, 1992).

World Bank, *2009 World Development Indicators* (World Bank, Washington, DC, 2009).

World Resources Institute, *World Resources 1998–99* (Oxford University Press, New York, 1998).

World Resources Institute, *World Resources 2008: Roots of Resilience: Growing the Wealth of the Poor* (World Resources Institute, Washington, DC, 2008).

Worm, Boris, Edward B. Barbier, Nicola Beaumont, J. Emmett Duffy, Carl Folke, Benjamin S. Halpern, Jeremy B. C. Jackson, Heike K. Lotze, Fiorenza Micheli, Stephen J. Palumbi, Enric Sala, Kimberley A. Selkoe, John J. Stachowicz, and Reg Watson "*Impacts of Biodiversity Loss on Ocean Ecosystem Services*," *Sci.*, **314**:787–790 (2006).

Xepapadeas, A. P., "Environmental Policy under Imperfect Information: Incentives and Moral Hazard," *J. Environ. Econ. Mgmt.*, **20**:113–126 (1991).

Xing, Yuqing and Charles D. Kolstad, "Do Lax Environmental Regulations Attract Foreign Investment?" *Environ. Resource Econ.*, **21**:1–22 (2002).

Yao, Dennis A., "Strategic Responses to Automobile Emissions Control: A Game-Theoretic Analysis," *J. Environ. Econ. Mgmt.*, **15**:419–438 (1988).

Yardley, Jim, "Chinese Dam Projects Criticized for their Human Costs," *New York Times* (November 17, 2007).

AUTHOR INDEX

SUBJECT INDEX